Victoria

Susie Ashworth

Tim Flannery, Jocelyn Harewood, Cathy Lanigan, Campbell Mattinson, Lisa Mitchell, Sally O'Brien, Miriam Raphael, Nina Rousseau

Destination Victoria

The beauty of Victoria is that it manages to pack a huge variety of magnificent beaches, stunning mountains, diverse wildlife, outdoor activities, arts events, festivals, historic townships, and gourmet food and wine regions into a relatively compact corner of Australia.

Melbourne, Australia's cultural capital, is reason enough to head south. Boasting lush gardens, bustling markets, slick city restaurants and cafés, a vibrant social calendar, countless sporting events and the best shopping in Australia, there's always something new and enticing to do in this sophisticated city.

Outside Melbourne, visitors are still spoiled for choice, with stunning national, state and coastal parks and marine reserves. Victoria's most famous stretch of coastline is the Great Ocean Rd, with its distinctive rocky outcrops, wild ocean beaches and sleepy fishing villages, but Wilsons Promontory National Park shouldn't be missed either. Here you'll find glorious beaches with snow-white sands and aquamarine waters (you'll think you're in Queensland until you dip a toe in the chilly water).

In the state's north, the High Country is a magnet for skiers and snowboarders hitting the winter slopes, while spring and summer bring their share of horse riders and bushwalkers treading the wildflower-strewn territory. For a taste of colonial history and bush landscapes, you can't go past the mighty Murray River, with its obligatory paddle-steamer rides and string of riverside townships. Farther south, there's the Goldfields region, with its seductive mix of historic sights and luxurious spas and B&Bs. Victoria is also nirvana for foodies, with top-class wineries and gourmet hotspots dotted throughout the state.

Victoria is more proof, if any is needed, that good things do come in small packages.

CHRISTOPHER GROENHOU

Highlights Victoria

Aussie rules (p139) at the Melbourne Cricket Ground (MCG)

Get the pick of the crop at Melbourne's Queen Victoria Market (p92)

Coffee lovers scratch the caffeine urge at Ici (p130), in Fitzroy

OTHER HIGHLIGHTS

- Find yourself in the thick of the Otways' forest canopy via the the elevated Otway Fly (p211) walkway
- Catch sight of southern rights having a whale of a time from Logans Beach in Warrnambool (p220)
- Get a taste of Aboriginal culture at the excellent Brambuk – The National Park Cultural Centre (p269), in the Grampians

PETER HENE

Rock fans flock to see the Twelve Apostles (p215), at Port Campbell National Park

JOHN BANAGAN

Play peek-a-boo with a joey at Healesville Sanctuary (p171)

Meet the locals at the Royal Botanic Gardens (p97) in Melbourne

JOHN BANAG

JONATHAN CHESTER

A rock climber angles for top position at Mt Arapiles (p274), in the Wimmera

Blow hot air above the vineyards of the Yarra Valley (p172)

JOHN HAY

Make a rush for Sovereign Hill (p239), a re-creation turn-of-the-century gold-mining town, in Ballarat

RICHARD I'ANSON

Froth and bubble at the Hepburn Spa Resort (p246)

GREG ELMS

Tread lightly along the sand dunes at Cape Howe, in the remote Croajingolong National Park (p390)

GRANT DIXON

Make a break: Bells Beach (p199) in Torquay

RODNEY HYETT

CHRIS MELLOR

Families enjoy beachside activities on Raymond Island (p374), in the Gippsland's Lakes District

GREG ELMS

Moor yourself in Mallacoota (p389)

Be charmed by the historic town of Daylesford (p244)

DAWN DELANEY

8

PHIL M WEYMOUTH

Kids hitch a ride on the children's lift
at Mt Buller (p334)

Throw a pink fit at the Pink Lakes (p286) in the
Murray-Sunset National Park

MANFRED GOTTSCHA

Get ready for the Prom (p366): wildlife, beautiful beaches and over 80km of walking tracks

PAUL SINCLAI

Contents

Regional Map Contents

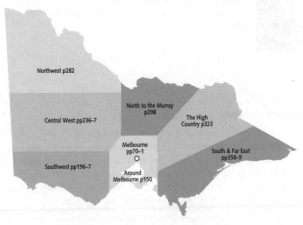

Northwest p282

North to the Murray
p298

Central West pp236–7

The High
Country p323

Melbourne
pp70–1

South & Far East
pp358–9

Southwest pp196–7

Around
Melbourne p150

The Authors

SUSIE ASHWORTH　　　　　　　　Coordinating Author

Susie spent most weekends and holidays in her childhood traipsing around her home state of Victoria with her family. It gave her a love of the southern state that never quite left her, despite a decade of living elsewhere; in the Blue Mountains, Sydney and London. In the late '90s she finally succumbed to the call of the Aussie highway and left Sydney, in an old Holden towing a camper trailer, to explore outback, coast, and country towns in regional New South Wales and Victoria for six months. When the money ran out, she settled in her childhood city of Melbourne, where she now works as a freelance editor and occasional author for Lonely Planet.

My Victoria

The great thing about Melbourne (p66), apart from its parade of festivals and events, is the many wonderful destinations within a couple of hours of the city. Head in any direction, coast or country, and you're bound to stumble across yet another fabulous weekend retreat. In the southwest, a favourite escape of mine is to a self-contained cottage on sprawling farmland backing the wild ocean beaches of Johanna (p214), on the Great Ocean Rd. To the east, a stomping ground for me and thousands of Victorians is the spectacular Wilsons Promontory National Park (p366), with its many bushwalks and resident wombats. On drives up to Sydney, I always try to find time for picture-perfect Marlo (p386), near the NSW border, where the Snowy River meets the sea.

JOCELYN HAREWOOD　　Central West, Northwest, North to the Murray

Jocelyn has lived in Victoria most of her life and loves the place. When she's not working for Lonely Planet, she writes works of fiction, set around Melbourne, the Grampians or Benalla. But researching for this guide was an amazing experience. She was fortunate to cover Victoria's outer regions, where the roads are long, the horizons wide and the people enthusiastic. So many hidden treasures. Enough to inspire lots more novels and travel plans.

LONELY PLANET AUTHORS

Why is our travel information the best in the world? It's simple: our authors are independent, dedicated travellers. They don't research using just the Internet or phone, and they don't take freebies in exchange for positive coverage. They travel widely, to all the popular spots and off the beaten track. They personally visit thousands of hotels, restaurants, cafés, bars, galleries, palaces, museums and more – and they take pride in getting all the details right, and telling it how it is. For more, see the authors section on www.lonelyplanet.com.

CATHY LANIGAN South & Far East

After living in South Gippsland for three years in her late teens, Cathy decided that Gippsland was a gorgeous place to live. More than a decade, and a few stints of living overseas, later she and her partner did the sea-change thing and moved to East Gippsland with their now four-year-old daughter. The family happily joined in researching national parks, beachside towns and cool cafés.

LISA MITCHELL Southwest

Australia may not have the mountain peaks she craves, but freelance writer Lisa Mitchell continues to travel extensively around the country. Childhood holidays spent crammed in a caravan with her family of six has instilled in Lisa an enduring passion for the cosy hinterlands, wild coasts and remote tracts of Oz. In Victoria, she prefers the Great Ocean Rd in winter, beach walks by thrashing surf, the Otways' rolling hinterland and the exuberant, waggy welcomes of accommodation owners' 'guard dogs'.

SALLY O'BRIEN Melbourne

Sally was born in Melbourne, but fled not long after her first winter. She returned about 28 years later to find the city much changed. Life in Victoria's capital includes swimming at the St Kilda Sea Baths, evenings at Federation Square, procrastination at many of Fitzroy's cafés, searching for the perfect little bar in the city lanes, shopping sprees in South Yarra and dance classes at Chunky Move. She doesn't notice the weather anymore and gets very homesick when she's away – a sure sign of love.

MIRIAM RAPHAEL High Country

A keen ski-bunny herself, Miriam jumped at the chance to check out the delights of Victoria's snowfields. Unfortunately she found her road trip way-laid by an obsession with regional produce, and the need to stop at every cheese shop, chutney store, winery and bakery in northeast Victoria. When Miriam's not darting around eastern Australia for Lonely Planet, she works as a freelance journalist and producer, and plans her next adventure.

NINA ROUSSEAU
Around Melbourne

Around Melbourne – what a gig! So much fun, so convenient, and so much to rediscover and explore. There's something truly satisfying about writing up your own backyard. Nina currently works as a Melbourne restaurant reviewer and freelance writer/editor.

CONTRIBUTING AUTHORS

Tim Flannery wrote the Environment chapter (p36). Tim's a naturalist, explorer and writer. He is the author of a number of award-winning books, including *The Future Eaters* and *Throwim Way Leg* (an account of his adventures as a biologist working in New Guinea), and the landmark ecological history of North America, *The Eternal Frontier*. His latest book, about Australia, is *Country*. Tim lives in Adelaide, where he is director of the South Australian Museum and a professor at the University of Adelaide.

Campbell Mattinson wrote the Victorian Wineries chapter (p56). Campbell has worked in journalism since 1987 and has specialised in wine writing for the past five years. He now writes widely on wine in Australia and the UK, is the publisher of *Winefront Monthly*, edits *Australian Sommelier* magazine, is the drinks editor for *Inside Out* magazine, the wine columnist for *Table* and regularly contributes to *Australian Gourmet Traveller – Wine*. In 2003 Campbell was nominated for a World Food Media Award. He thinks that after all that he should be either distressed, tired, drunk or just plain sick of wine, but he still can't get enough and loves every minute of it.

Dr David Millar wrote the Health chapter (p419). Dr Millar is a travel-medicine specialist, diving doctor and lecturer in wilderness medicine, who graduated in Hobart, Tasmania. He has worked all over Australia (except the Northern Territory) and as an expedition doctor with the Maritime Museum of Western Australia, accompanying a variety of expeditions around Australia, including the Pandora wreck in Far North Queensland and Rowley Shoals off the northwest coast. Dr Millar is currently a medical director with Travel Doctor in Auckland.

Getting Started

It may be Australia's smallest mainland state, but Victoria packs an astonishing number of national parks, historic towns and stunning natural landscapes into its relatively small size. Getting around is easy and distances between attractions are manageable, making short breaks from Melbourne and from other states very popular. Indeed, with so much on offer throughout the year, your hardest task will be choosing what to see next.

For an idea of where to start, see p18. Also consider using Tourism Victoria's online Travel Planner (www.visitvictoria.com.au), which offers maps, travel ideas and a route planner that you can tailor to your specific tastes.

WHEN TO GO

The saying goes that if you don't like the weather in Victoria, just wait 10 minutes… Notorious for its unpredictability, the state's famous 'four seasons in one day' climate can occasionally catch travellers unawares. It's a good idea to dress in layers, so you can rug up or strip off as the weather dictates.

See Climate (p396) for more information.

Warm summer days and nights attract the crowds from December to February, Victoria's busiest times for tourism. Average summer highs are around 26°C, but it's not uncommon to find the mercury pushing past 40°C.

Once the six-week school holidays start in mid-December, Victorians take to the roads en masse, heading for beachside holiday houses, camping grounds and resorts. In summer, accommodation prices rise considerably in the popular holiday hotspots (particularly on the coast), and rooms are often booked well in advance (see p392).

Autumn is a blissful time in the southern state, with mild, still days, and an array of warm autumnal foliage splashing the state's gardens and parks with vivid colour. The Easter school holiday period in early April is another busy time on Victoria's roads and in the coastal regions, so planning and booking ahead is advised.

June and July are the coldest months, with average maximum temperatures nudging 14°C and dropping to a minimum of 7°C. It's a great time to do as the locals do, rugging up and heading off to a game of Aussie rules (football), or heading to the slopes. There are good snowfields within three hours' drive of the city, and the season usually runs from mid-June until mid-September.

DON'T LEAVE HOME WITHOUT…

- Clothes for all conditions, even at the height of summer or the depths of winter.
- Sunscreen, sunglasses and a hat to deflect ultra fierce UV rays.
- Wet-weather gear.
- A travel insurance policy (p401).
- Extra-strength insect repellent to fend off merciless flies and mosquitoes.
- Knowing what your embassy/consulate in Australia (p399) can and can't do to help you if you're in trouble.

Though Victoria's spring weather can be wildly unpredictable, it's a great time to take in a string of popular festivals and events, including the Australian Football League (AFL) grand final, the Melbourne Festival and the Spring Racing Carnival (for more information, see p113).

COSTS & MONEY

At the current rate of exchange, Australia is inexpensive if you're from the USA, Britain or continental Europe, making holidays in Victoria economical for international visitors, with reasonably priced accommodation, excellent-value food and average daily costs.

Of course, your holiday can be as cheap or as expensive as your tastes demand. A midrange traveller who plans to hire a car, see the sights, stay in midrange B&Bs or hotels, and indulge in a slap-up restaurant meal in the evening, should expect to spend about $150 to $160 per day (if travelling as part of a couple).

At the low-cost end, if you camp or stay in hostels, cook your own meals, avoid big nights out in the pub and catch buses everywhere, you could probably manage on $45 per day; for a budget that realistically enables you to have a good time, set aside $60. Of course, these low-cost figures don't factor in a tempting splurge in one of Melbourne's fabulous bars and restaurants, which can punish the purse.

Currency exchange rates are on the Quick Reference page (inside front cover). See also Directory, p402.

LONELY PLANET INDEX

1L petrol 90¢-$1.20

1L bottled water $2-3

Pot of beer (VB) $2.80

Souvenir T-shirt $20

Street snack (meat pie) $2.50

TRAVEL LITERATURE

Before heading down to Victoria, find some inspiration in one of these books.

For brutally honest insights about Melbourne, try Tim Flannery's *The Birth of Melbourne* (2002), which includes first-hand accounts of the city from 1802 to 1903, from a mixed bag of pioneers and travellers, such as John Batman, Mathew Flinders, Marcus Clark and Rudyard Kipling.

Bypass: The Story of a Road (2004), by ex-Jesuit priest Michael McGirr, traces his bike ride along the well-trammelled Hume Hwy from Sydney to Melbourne. McGirr entertains with the characters he meets along the way, as well as a host of historical figures, including explorers, bushrangers, athletes and criminals.

The Melbourne Book: A History of Now, by Maree Coote, is a stunning pictorial ode to this superb city, with a mix of dramatic photographs, and contemporary stories and interviews. Other inspirational pictorial books include the *Mornington Peninsula Sea Breeze & Sand* (2003), by Anne Monteith and Bryce Dunkley, and Steve Parish's photographic guides, *Melbourne* and *Victoria*.

INTERNET RESOURCES

Age (www.theage.com.au) For up-to-date local news, features and opinions.

Commonwealth Bureau of Meteorology (www.bom.gov.au/weather/vic) Up-to-the-minute information on Victorian weather and warnings.

Lonely Planet (www.lonelyplanet.com) Succinct summaries, links to other sites and the Thorn Tree bulletin board.

Parks Victoria (www.parkweb.vic.gov.au) Excellent site, with extensive profiles on all of Victoria's national and marine parks.

Tourism Victoria (www.visitvictoria.com) Official state tourism site, with excellent sections on festivals and events, accommodation, restaurants, tours and attractions.

Victorian Government (www.vic.gov.au) Official website of the state government of Victoria, and gateway to information and services in the state.

TOP TENS

Must-See Movies
Essential trip preparation can be done from a comfy lounge with a bowl of popcorn in one hand and a remote in the other. Head down to your local video store to pick up these Aussie flicks, filmed or based in Victoria. For reviews of some of these, see p33.

- *Picnic at Hanging Rock* (1975) directed by Peter Weir
- *The Getting of Wisdom* (1977) directed by Bruce Beresford
- *Mad Max* (1979) directed by George Miller
- *Proof* (1991) directed by Jocelyn Moorhouse
- *Spotswood* (1991) directed by Mark Joffe
- *Romper Stomper* (1992) directed by Geoffrey Wright
- *The Castle* (1997) directed by Rob Sitch
- *Head On* (1998) directed by Geoffrey Wright
- *Chopper* (2000) directed by Andrew Dominik
- *Ned Kelly* (2003) directed by Gregor Jordan

Top Reads
The following page-turners have won critical acclaim in Australia and abroad, and give a strong sense of Victorian history and landscapes.

- *For the Term of His Natural Life* (1874) by Marcus Clarke
- *The Fortunes of Richard Mahony* (1930) by Henry Handel Richardson
- *Power Without Glory* (1950) by Frank Hardy
- *My Brother Jack* (1964) by George Johnston
- *Monkey Grip* (1977) by Helen Garner
- *Oscar & Lucinda* (1988) by Peter Carey
- *Loaded* (1995) by Christos Tsiolkas
- *The Brush-Off* (1998) by Shane Maloney
- *Three Dollars* (1998) by Elliot Perlman
- *True History of the Kelly Gang* (2000) by Peter Carey

Favourite Festivals & Events
Victorians love any excuse for a celebration, and flock to the festivals and big sporting events that seem to cram every weekend of the year. These are our top 10 reasons to get festive – other events are listed on p399 and throughout this book.

- Australian Open Tennis Championships, January (p114)
- Moomba Festival, March (p114)
- Port Fairy Folk Festival, March (p224)
- Melbourne International Comedy Festival, April (p114)
- Rip Curl Pro, late March–early April (p199)
- Stawell Gift, April (p266)
- Royal Melbourne Show, September (p115)
- AFL Grand Final, September (p115)
- Spring Racing Carnival, late September–early November (p115)
- Boxing Day International Test Match Cricket, 26 December (p115)

Itineraries

CLASSIC ROUTES

BEACHES & MOUNTAINS

One Week/Geelong–Great Ocean Rd–
Grampians National Park–Ballarat–Melbourne

First on most travellers' must-see list (and for good reason) is the Great
Ocean Rd, one of the world's most spectacular coastal routes. From Geelong, head south to the surf mecca of **Torquay** (p196), where you can stock
up on wetsuits before starting your scenic drive. Give yourself plenty of
time to stop at the many lookouts along the way. Other popular pitstops
include the family-oriented **Anglesea** (p199), a great spot to learn how to
surf; look-at-me **Lorne** (p203), with its city-style café scene; and the pretty
summer resort of **Apollo Bay** (p208). But the headline act of the coastal route
is **Port Campbell National Park** (p214), with its distinctive limestone outcrops
rising dramatically out of the ocean, drawing hordes of visitors. Continue
on the Great Ocean Rd to **Warrnambool** (p217), where you may spot southern right whales cavorting off the coast. Continue on the coastal Princes
Hwy, stopping off for ice cream at the historic town of **Port Fairy** (p222), or
Victoria's oldest town, **Portland** (p226). Then head north along the Henty
Hwy for the Aboriginal rock art sites, excellent bushwalking and fresh
mountain air of the **Grampians National Park** (p267). Next, make a beeline east
on the Western Hwy for historic **Ballarat** (p237), with its kitschy Sovereign
Hill gold-rush town replica and Eureka Stockade centre. From here you
have a clear run back down the Western Hwy to Melbourne.

This 840km trip
combines sun-
kissed beaches,
picture-postcard
national parks,
sleepy fishing
villages and towns
rich in history. You
could easily see the
major sights in a
week, but to make
the most of the
outdoor activities
on offer along the
way, you'll need
to devote a few
more days.

COASTAL CRUISE   Two weeks/Melbourne–Mallacoota

After a couple of days indulging in the sights, moods and tastes of **Melbourne** (p66), nature lovers may be ready to shrug off their city clobber in favour of casual clothes (don't forget your sun hat, swimsuit and shades in summer). Head east for **Wilsons Promontory National Park** (p366), a mountainous coastal park of squeaky white sands, aquamarine waters and well-trodden bushwalking territory. Continue east along the South Gippsland Hwy, stopping off briefly to see the lush green temperate rainforests of **Tarra Bulga National Park** (p363). Dip your toes in the water at **Seaspray** (p375) at the beginning of the sprawling Ninety Mile Beach, before continuing on to Bairnsdale and **The Lakes National Park** (p376), an enticing region of winding waterways, sand dunes and glorious beaches. After a few days of pure relaxation, head north on the Princes Hwy to the rural service town of Orbost, where you hang a right to follow the final leg of the Snowy River to the sea and **Marlo** (p386), a sleepy fishing village that marks the beginning of **Cape Conran Coastal Park** (p386). Back on the Princes Hwy, whizz through the last little corner of Victoria to **Mallacoota** (p388), a village of hippies, surfers and retirees near the NSW border. The low-key town is completely surrounded by **Croajingolong National Park** (p390), a coastal wilderness park popular with canoeists, bird-lovers and holidaymakers seeking some much-needed rest and recreation.

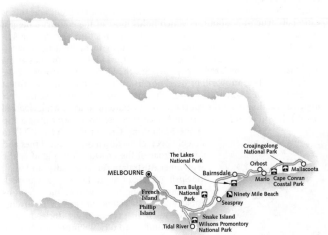

You can complete this 830km trip comfortably in two weeks, but with so many appealing stops en route, why rush? Devote a couple of months to going bush, learning how to surf, catching your own dinner or simply lying on beaches without a care in the world.

TAILORED TRIPS

CHILD'S PLAY

Victoria caters well for kids, with a stack of city-based boredom busters, including the faded but ever-popular **Luna Park** (p104) amusement park; the modern **Melbourne Museum** (p99), with dinosaur skeletons and its very own Children's Museum; **Scienceworks** (p107), with fun interactive games for brainiacs; and the **Aquarium** (p93) and **Melbourne Zoo** (p98) for animal lovers. Get a taste for the country at the **Collingwood Children's Farm** (p112), or bus around the faux savannah **Werribee Open Range Zoo** (p151), spotting giraffes and rhinos. Kids with a head for heights love the **Otway Fly** (p211),

where they can wander among the tree canopy and taunt their acrophobic parents. Or there's the **Phillip Island Penguin Parade** (p188), a fond childhood memory for a large proportion of Victorians. Many a child has come home from Ballarat's **Sovereign Hill** (p239) with a mouthful of humbugs and dreams of striking it lucky; and the littlies won't want to miss a trip on the Dandenongs' very own steam train, **Puffing Billy** (p177). Sporty types can learn to surf at **Anglesea** (p199) or hit the slopes at **Mt Hotham** (p338), depending on the season. If your timing's right, don't miss the sideshow alleys and nightly waterskiing shows of the **Moomba Festival** (p114) in March; or the animal nursery and filled-to-bursting showbags of the **Royal Melbourne Show** (p115) in September.

A GOOD SPORT

For many Aussies their favourite sport is akin to a religion, and this is especially true in Melbourne, which holds most of the country's biggest sporting events. The year's first grand-slam tennis tournament, the **Australian Open** (p114), attracts grunting tennis pros to Melbourne in January, while in March Albert Park echos with the rumble of engines at the **Australian Formula One Grand Prix** (p114). See the world's elite surfers at the **Rip Curl Pro** (p199) in April, or head northwest to see the country's fittest sprinters in the **Stawell Gift** (p266). But for thousands, these events are a mere distraction from the sport that really matters, **Australian rules football** (p139). If you're in the city from March to September, don't miss a trip

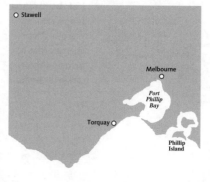

to the Melbourne Cricket Ground (MCG) to sip cold beer, chow down on hot meat pies and join the roar of the crowd. Not long after the September Australian rules football grand final, the Spring Racing Carnival begins: a five-week program featuring the country's most famous horse race, the **Melbourne Cup** (p140), in November. As much an excuse to get dressed up in your best duds as to pick a winner, Melbourne Cup Day is a public holiday for Melburnians, while regional Victorians have a flutter in office sweeps, and head to the pub for a bet and a long lunch. In summer, cricket is the main game, with the traditional favourite being the **Boxing Day test** (p140), played at the MCG.

Snapshot

Premier Steve Bracks and his Australian Labor Party (ALP) government breezed through their second election in 2002 with a landslide victory. The ALP won a huge majority in the Lower House, and seized control of the Upper House for the first time in 146 years. But at the time of writing, the political mood had shifted, with the government under attack for planning to impose tolls on the much-needed Mitcham–Frankston freeway (also known as the Scoresby freeway) in the outer east. In this car-dependent city, it was a risky move to create a tollway and hit the hip pocket of so many drivers. Enormous hikes in land tax were also a contentious issue, with the state government reaping huge financial rewards from the recent property boom. Although landowners and voters in the 'burbs were promising to punish Bracks at the next state election in 2006, the failure of Liberal Party leader Robert Doyle to sell himself as a strong potential alternative premier made the election outcome by no means certain.

On the architectural front, Melbourne's recent flurry of development has its fair share of detractors as well as fans (for more information on the city's modern architecture, see p32). For every local who brands Federation Square and the new-wave Southern Cross station (formerly known as Spencer St Station) as slick, avant garde and edgy, there's another who crinkles the nose and labels them radical, tacky and downright ugly. And as scores of luxury high-rise apartment buildings in the Docklands and inner city continue to multiply and scrape the skies, it beggars the question: who's actually going to live in them?

By the time you read this, the 2006 Commonwealth Games may well be over, but it didn't escape the wrath of some party poopers who saw the international sporting extravaganza as a right royal waste of time and money. Though you'd think that sports-crazed Melbourne would be a perfect fit for the event, some would have preferred to see government dollars flowing into the state's hospitals and schools instead of its sporting ovals and pools. But sport is big business in Oz, and nowhere more so than in Victoria. When the Australian Football League (AFL) season arrives in March, everyone seems to go into a footy feeding frenzy, with newspapers, radio and TV devoting more space and air time to a controversial bit of biffo or a damaged hamstring than just about anything else (for more on AFL and other popular sports, see p31).

Melbourne's recent housing boom has turned some locals into millionaires, but it has also priced many first-home buyers out of the market. After seven years of consistent growth, house prices began to stabilise and even drop in 2004. At the time of writing, there was speculation about rising interest rates and heavily mortgaged owners were becoming nervous – although they still avidly tune in to their favourite auction and home renovation TV shows.

Affectionately ribbed by Aussies from other states for its unpredictable weather, Victoria has been in the grip of a drought for several years. Solid winter and spring rain in 2004 repaired some of the damage from parched years but, at the time of writing, water catchments were still low. On such a big dry continent, one of the biggest issues facing state and federal governments is land and water management. In March 2005, the Victorian Minister for Water announced a new set of permanent water restrictions to try to curb Melburnians' wasteful ways. Locals are finally

FAST FACTS

Population: approximately 5,000,000 (Mar 2005)

Victorians born overseas: about 25%

Head of state: Governor HE Mr John Landy

Victoria's state emblems: Leadbetter's possum (mammal), helmeted honeyeater (bird), common heath (flower)

Gross State Product (GSP) growth: approx 2.6% (2002-03)

Inflation: 2.2% (Dec 2003)

Percentage of Australian exports: 25%

Unemployment rate: 6.4% (Feb 2004)

Average income: $40,650

Number of countries that broadcast Melbourne-made soapie Neighbours: 60

being forced to accept that the splashingly good old rainy days of their youth may be over. For more information, see the boxed text (p39).

Another tricky issue for government that continues to hit the headlines has been the establishment of wind farms in regional Victoria. Critics say they're big, noisy and ugly, destroy beloved pristine landscapes and affect land values. Fans say they're beautiful, efficient and a clean source of energy that lessens the state's dependence on other, non-sustainable (and polluting) energy sources. For more information on Victorian environmental issues, see p36.

History

EARLY ABORIGINAL HISTORY

Exactly when the Aborigines journeyed from Southeast Asia to the Australian mainland is a matter of conjecture. Some say that Australia's earliest inhabitants struck land at least 40,000 years ago; others are convinced it was closer to 50,000 or possibly 70,000 years ago; others simply date Australian Aboriginal culture as the beginning of time in the Dreaming. The Victorian Aboriginal people lived in some 38 different dialect groups that spoke 10 separate languages. These groups were further divided into clans and sub-clans, each with its own customs and laws, and each claiming ownership of a distinct area of land. The Aborigines' complex traditional culture was largely based on a close spiritual bond with that land. Despite this, the British considered the continent to be *terra nullius* – a land belonging to no one. Before British colonisation, the Yarra Valley region was occupied by members of the Woi wurrung–speaking clan of the Kulin Nation, known as the Wurundjeri.

For more information on Victoria's Aboriginal heritage, visit the excellent Bunjilaka indigenous centre at the Melbourne Museum (p99).

For more information on the history of the Victorian indigenous people, visit the Koorie Heritage Trust Cultural Centre (☎ 03-8622 2600; www.koorieheritage trust.com; 295 King St, cnr Little Lonsdale St; ☒ 10am-4pm Mon-Fri).

THE EUROPEANS

Although Captain James Cook still gets the kudos for 'discovering' Australia in 1770, the earliest coastal exploration by Europeans was by Dutch sailors, such as Dirk Hartog and Abel Tasman, in the early to mid-17th century.

In January 1788 Australia's first colony was set up under the command of Captain Arthur Phillip at Sydney Cove in New South Wales (NSW). The first Victorian settlement was established in 1803 when a small party of convicts, soldiers and settlers led by Captain David Collins arrived at Sorrento on Melbourne's Port Phillip Bay. But less than a year later the settlement was abandoned due to the lack of a fresh water supply, and the group sailed to Van Diemen's Land (Tasmania) and founded Hobart.

In 1824 Hamilton Hume and William Hovell made the first overland journey south from Sydney to the shores of Port Phillip Bay. The arrival at Portland of Edward Henty, his family and a flock of sheep from Van Diemen's Land in 1834 marked the first permanent European settlement in the Port Phillip district (now Victoria).

In 1836 the colony's surveyor-general, Major Thomas Mitchell, crossed the Murray River (then called the Hume) near Swan Hill and travelled southwest to find the rich volcanic plains of the Western District. He wrote glowing reports of the fertile country and dubbed the region Australia Felix (Fortunate Australia). Major Mitchell's enthusiasm encouraged pastoralists to rush into Victoria and within 10 years Europeans outnumbered Aborigines.

FOUNDING OF MELBOURNE

Although two Tasmanians, John Batman and John Pascoe Fawkner, are widely recognised as the founders of Melbourne (or Bearbrass as Batman

TIMELINE

60,000–35,000 BC	1803
The first humans colonise Australia from Southeast Asia sometime between 60,000 and 35,000 BC	First European settlement established at Sorrento

originally dubbed the new settlement), recent reports suggest that it was the surveyor John Helder Wedge who chose the site on the banks of the Yarra.

In 1835 a group of businessmen from Van Diemen's Land formed the Port Phillip Association with the intention of establishing a new settlement on Port Phillip Bay. In May of that year their representative, John Batman, purchased about 240,000 hectares of land from the Aborigines of the Dutigalla clan.

The concept of buying or selling land was foreign to the Aborigines, but in return for their land they received an assorted collection of blankets, tomahawks, knives, looking glasses, scissors, handkerchiefs, various items of clothing and 50lb of flour. Once the treaty was signed, other members of the association joined Batman and the settlement of Melbourne was established on the northern side of the Yarra River.

John Pascoe Fawkner and a group of Tasmanian settlers left for Port Phillip six months later and settled the south of the Yarra. Fawkner became a driving force behind the new settlement. By the time of his death in 1869, Melbourne was flourishing and he was known as the 'Grand Old Man of Victoria'. History doesn't remember John Batman as kindly, however. Within four years of his dodgy deal with the Aborigines, he died of syphilis.

ABORIGINAL RESISTANCE

Aboriginal Melbourne – The Lost Land of the Kulin People (re-released 2001), by Gary Presland, gives valuable insights into the culture and life of the region's original inhabitants.

Estimates suggest that before the Europeans arrived, Victoria's Aboriginal population was between 60,000 and 100,000; by the late 1840s it had dropped to 15,000 and by 1860 there were only around 2000 people. It's a sad fact that the only Europeans to gain a detailed understanding of Aboriginal life were the few escaped convicts who lived with the tribes. The white settlers generally regarded the Aborigines as a hindrance to their settlement and 'civilising' of the land. Dispossessed of their lands, Aboriginal culture was disrupted and people were killed in their thousands – initially by introduced diseases, such as smallpox, dysentery and measles, and later by guns and poison.

EARLY SETTLEMENT

In *The Birth of Melbourne* (2002), Tim Flannery brings together a fascinating (often depressing) collection of first-hand accounts of the southern city from 1802 to 1903. Contributors include John Batman, Matthew Flinders, Marcus Clarke and Rudyard Kipling.

The settlement at Melbourne developed with astonishing speed, and became a packing-case village of tents and hovels almost overnight. By 1836 so many people from Britain had moved to the Port Phillip Bay area that the administrators of NSW had to declare the area open to settlement. In 1837 the military surveyor Robert Hoddle drew up plans for the new city, laying out a geometric grid of broad streets in a rectangular pattern on the northern side of the Yarra River. Within three years there were well over 10,000 Europeans in the areas surrounding Melbourne.

The earliest provincial towns were established at places such as Portland and Port Fairy, on the southwestern part of Victoria's coast, and Port Albert on the southeastern part. The earliest inland settlements were sheep stations, typically small and self-sufficient communities. As the new communities grew in size and confidence, they began to agitate for separation from NSW.

1851	1854
Victoria wins separation from the colony of NSW	Gold miners rebel and are brutally attacked by soldiers and police during the Eureka Stockade

BOOM...

In 1851 Victoria separated from NSW, and Melbourne became the capital of the newly proclaimed colony. In the same year gold was discovered at Bathurst in NSW. Fearing that the young city's workers would desert for the northern goldfields, a committee of Melbourne businessmen offered a reward to anyone who found gold in Victoria. Even in their wildest dreams they couldn't have foreseen what followed.

The first gold strike was at Warrandyte in May 1851, and in the next few months massive finds followed at Buninyong and Clunes near Ballarat, Mt Alexander near Castlemaine and Ravenswood near Bendigo. The gold rush brought a huge influx of immigrants from around the world. In particular, Chinese diggers flooded into the state. Within a year there were about 1800 optimists disembarking at Melbourne every week.

The town became a chaotic mess. As soon as ships arrived in the harbour, their crews would desert and follow the passengers to the goldfields. Business in Melbourne ground to a standstill as most of the labour force left to join the search. Shanty towns of bark huts and canvas tents sprang up to house the population, which doubled within a decade.

But a generation later, bolstered by the wealth of the goldfields, ragged Melbourne had matured and refined itself into one of the world's great Victorian-era cities. The gold rush produced enough wealth for Victoria to make the transition from a fledgling colony into a prosperous and independent state, but it also brought with it tensions. In the early days of the rush authorities introduced a compulsory licence fee, but in 1854 a group of miners at the Ballarat diggings rioted and burned their licences in protest at the inequality of the fees. Twenty-five miners were killed during what is known as the Eureka Rebellion, and it changed forever the political landscape in Victoria. (For details, see the boxed text, p241.)

For a sense of what a gold-mining township was like in the 1860s, tourists visit Sovereign Hill (p239). Adults might find the gold-rush re-creation a bit cheesy, but kids love it.

The prosperous gold-rush years inspired a flowering of arts and culture in the city. Melburnians used their new-found wealth to build an extravagant city. The 1850s saw many landmarks established, from the public library and university to the Melbourne Cricket Ground (MCG). Large areas were set aside and planted as public parks and gardens. By the 1880s Melbourne was being referred to as the 'Paris of the Antipodes'.

Although relatively few made their fortunes on the goldfields, many of those who had flocked to Melbourne to get rich (but failed) stayed on as workers, shopkeepers and farmers. In Victoria's growing rural communities, many tried to scratch a living from a small scrap of land granted by the government. Tough times and clashes with oppressive police created a climate of dissent. Ned Kelly (1855–80) was a local outlaw who became famous for protecting himself with a home-made suit of armour. After the bushranger's gang killed three policemen, Ned was captured and brought back to Melbourne Gaol (p92) for execution. Ned was the subject of the first Australian feature film, *The Story of the Kelly Gang* (1906), a 1960s film starring Mick Jagger, and the 2003 *Ned Kelly*, starring Heath Ledger. Despite his crimes, Ned remains one of Australia's most enduring folk heroes. For more information on his rise and fall, see p303.

The 'Welcome Stranger' was a record-breaking 72kg gold nugget, found in 1869 near Moliagul in Victoria, and estimated to be worth $4 million today.

The Eureka flag, featuring the Southern Cross, became a symbol of resistance for Aussies after Ballarat's Eureka Stockade (1854), when authorities shot more than 30 diggers for their rebellion against expensive mining licences.

Melburnians have been meeting in the same familiar place – 'under the clocks' – at Flinders St Station for more than 100 years.

1923	1930
Vegemite, a savoury yeasty breakfast spread, is invented in Melbourne	Phar Lap wins the Melbourne Cup, confirming his status as a hero of the people

...AND BUST

The 1880s were boom times for Melbourne, but there was also an air of recklessness. Money from the goldfields and from overseas was invested in real estate and building works, and speculation led to spiralling land prices that couldn't last. In 1888 Melbourne hosted the Great Exhibition in the opulent Exhibition Buildings (p99). No expense was spared in the construction of the buildings or the exhibition itself, but this flamboyant showing off to the world was Melbourne's swan song.

In 1889 the property market collapsed and the decade that followed was a period of severe economic depression. Victorians left the state in droves, seeking employment and a brighter future elsewhere, and Melbourne didn't really recover until the post-war development boom of the 1920s.

ABORIGINES PROTECTION ACT

Between 1861 and 1863 the Board for the Protection of Aborigines gathered many of the surviving Aborigines and placed them in reserves run by Christian missionaries at Ebenezer, Framlingham, Lake Condah, Lake Tyers, Ramahyuck and Coranderrk. These reserves developed into self-sufficient farming communities and gave their residents a measure of independence, but they also inflicted serious damage on indigenous culture.

The Aborigines Protection Act of 1886 stipulated that only 'full-blooded' Aborigines or 'half-castes' older than 34 years of age could remain in the reserves – others had to leave and 'assimilate into the community'. The effect of the act was to separate families and eventually destroy the reserves themselves. By 1923 the only operating reserves were at Lake Tyers, with just over 200 residents, and Framlingham, with only a handful of people.

By the early 1900s further legislation designed to segregate and 'protect' Aborigines was passed. It restricted their right to own property and seek employment. The Aboriginals' Ordinance of 1918 allowed the removal of children from Aboriginal mothers if it was suspected that the father was non-Aboriginal.

Children were still removed from their families as recently as the mid-1970s and today they are referred to as the Stolen Generations.

FROM FEDERATION

With Federation, on 1 January 1901, Victoria became a state of the new nation of Australia. Melbourne was the country's capital and the seat of federal government until it moved to Canberra in 1927. But Australia's loyalties and many of its legal ties to Britain remained. When WWI broke out, Australian troops went to fight in the trenches of France, Gallipoli and the Middle East.

There was more expansion and construction in Victoria in the 1920s, but all this stopped with the Great Depression, which hit Australia hard. In 1931 almost a third of breadwinners were unemployed and poverty was widespread. During the Depression the government implemented a number of major public works programmes and workers were put on sustenance pay ('susso'). Melbourne's Yarra Boulevard, St Kilda Rd and the Great Ocean Rd were all built by sustenance workers.

1956	1967
Melbourne hosts the Olympic Games	Ronald Joseph Ryan is executed at Pentridge Prison; he is the last man to be hanged in Victoria

One shining light during these gloomy times was a plucky young chestnut gelding called Phar Lap, who won the hearts of the people with an unparalleled winning streak, including the famous Melbourne Cup in 1930. Sadly, the horse died in mysterious circumstances in the USA two years later, and was mourned by a nation. More than 70 years later Phar Lap remains one of the most popular exhibits in the Melbourne Museum.

For the sad story of Australia's most famous racehorse, Phar Lap, grab the 1983 movie from the video store…but don't forget the tissues.

When war broke out once again in 1939, Australian troops fought with the British in Europe and the Middle East, but after the Japanese bombed Pearl Harbor, Australia started to feel threatened. When Britain called for more Australian troops, Prime Minister John Curtin refused; Australian soldiers were needed closer to home.

Ultimately it was the USA that helped protect Australia from the Japanese, defeating them in the Battle of the Coral Sea. This event was to mark the start of a profound shift in Australia's allegiance away from Britain and towards the US. To learn more about the thousands of Victorians who sacrificed their lives in the two world wars, visit the moving Shrine of Remembrance (p96).

POST WWII

WWII also marked the beginnings of a radical shift in Australia's immigration policies. White Australia's overwhelmingly Anglo-Celtic makeup was challenged by the arrival of non-British migrants, fleeing the upheaval of WWII in Europe. The post-war government hoped that the increase in population would strengthen Australia's economy and contribute to its ability to defend itself. 'Populate or Perish' became the catchphrase. Between 1947 and 1968 more than 800,000 non-British European immigrants came to Australia, along with almost a million British immigrants. The majority arrived on ships that docked first at Port Melbourne's Station Pier, where a large percentage of the new arrivals settled. With the demise of the government's insidious White Australia policy in the 1970s, migrants began to arrive from Southeast Asia and the Middle East, adding to the multicultural mix. Melbourne's Immigration Museum (p93) features the stories of migrants to Melbourne from the 1800s to the present day. (See also p32 for further information on Melbourne's multicultural mix.)

The city's Victorian heritage was irrevocably altered by the post-war construction boom. The city hosted the Olympic Games in 1956 and hectares of historic buildings were bulldozed as the city prepared to impress visitors with its modernity. Construction continued in the 1960s under the Liberal premier Henry Bolte, culminating in the boom years of the 1980s.

Land prices rose continuously throughout the '80s. In the competitive atmosphere of the newly deregulated banking industry, banks queued up to lend money to speculators and developers. The city centre and surrounds were transformed as one skyscraper after another sprang up. Even the worldwide stock-market crash in 1987 didn't slow things down, but in 1990 the property market collapsed, just as it had 100 years earlier. By 1991 Australia was in recession once again; unemployment was the highest it had been since the early 1930s and Victoria was the state hardest hit.

1970	1983
The West Gate Bridge, under construction, collapses in October killing 35 people	The Ash Wednesday fires destroy around 2000 homes and take the lives of 47 Victorians

RECENT TIMES

From 1992 to 1999 a Liberal–National party coalition led by Jeff Kennett ruled the state. Its policies improved the economy, but Kennett's perceived arrogance and his government's failure to properly address social-welfare and infrastructure issues alienated large segments of the community.

The state election in 1999 resulted in a minority victory for Labor under the leadership of Steve Bracks. Labor promised to improve services in the country and run a more accountable government, concentrating on health and education. Bracks' continued popularity and 'nice guy' image, and the limited appeal of opposition leader Robert Doyle, helped Labor win a second term in a landslide victory in 2002.

2002	2006
Federation Square opens in October	The Commonwealth Games are brought to Australia's sporting capital in March

The Culture

REGIONAL IDENTITY

Despite the stereotype of tanned, outback-dwelling, muscle-bound croc wrestlers, most Australians are urban and urbane – more comfortable wrangling a bruschetta-and-macchiato brunch than wrestling an oversized reptile. And nowhere in the country is this more obvious than in Victoria's capital, Melbourne, which locals like to brand the cultural centre of the Antipodes. They also like to claim notoriety as Australia's capital of sport, shopping, food and coffee – though Aussies from other states may disagree.

Melbourne has a stylish European flavour that is not found elsewhere in the country. Perhaps it emerged because of the weather that sends black-clad locals scurrying into restaurants and bars for prolonged lunches and philosophical discussions. Perhaps town planning had something to do with it (think stunning Victorian-era architecture, expansive streets, and wide pavements flooded with café tables and chairs). More likely it's the rich multicultural nature of the city. About 40% of Melburnians have come from somewhere else, bringing with them the best food, fashion and culture their countries have to offer.

'Melbourne serves up a lengthy and rich calendar of cultural and sporting events'

Victorians tend to be pretty parochial, loving where they live, defensive and proud of their state, critical of that big flashy city to the north (Sydney) that seems to get all the attention. Like Aussies from other states, they complain that federal politics and the national media are too Sydney-centric. When the national broadcaster (ABC) dared to move its sport coverage from Melbourne to Sydney in 2004, there was a near riot in the streets.

Although almost three-quarters of Victorians like to call Melbourne home, there's an increasing number of 'sea changers', who are choosing the quieter lifestyle, stunning natural beauty and cheaper house prices of regional towns within two hours of the city. Popular areas for alternative living are Daylesford, the Surf Coast towns of Torquay and Anglesea, and Healesville and Yarra Glen in the Yarra Valley.

But life in provincial Victoria is very different from the slick quasi-European Melbourne streets, with families doing it ever tougher, struggling with a decade of drought conditions and a farming population that continues to shrink. Despite state-government promises to better their lot, those who live in rural areas can only look on as the majority of Victorians who live in Melbourne seem to get most of the attention and services.

LIFESTYLE

HM Hyndman, in his *Record of an Adventurous Life*, said of Melbourne in 1870:

I have been a great deal about the world and I have moved freely in many societies, but I have never lived in any city where the people at large, as well as the educated class, took so keen an interest in all the activities of human life, as in Melbourne at the time I visited it. Art, the drama, music, literature, journalism, wit, oratory all found ready appreciation. The life and vivacity of the place were astonishing.

It's nice to see that some things don't change. Melbourne, where the vast majority of Victorians live, still serves up a lengthy and rich calendar of cultural and sporting events for its eager citizens. An active and involved population keep attendance records high at everything from the theatre, opera and ballet to weekend footy matches. Victorians also find time to make the most of the many lush green gardens and parks in the state, some of the best shopping in the country, and a diverse collection of quality cafés and restaurants. They can also boast a high standard of living (indeed, the *Economist* named Melbourne the 'world's most liveable city' in 2002 and 2003).

Victorians love their traditions…and there are many of them. Getting all frocked up to attend the fashion-plate event of Oaks Day at Flemington Racecourse; browsing through the weekend papers at a favourite café; grabbing last-minute tickets for shows at the annual Comedy, Writers' or Arts Festivals or any of the many events that cram each weekend. Active types take to their bikes to cycle along Port Phillip Bay's Beach Rd or one of the state's many rail trails on weekends, while joggers flood the Tan (the track around the Botanical Gardens; p97) and Albert Park Lake (p105). Others spend their weekends fuelled by caffeine and alcohol, hanging out in the city's trendy bars, pubs and clubs, catching their favourite bands, or trawling the main shopping streets in Richmond, Fitzroy or St Kilda for bargains. And then there's sport, a state-wide obsession (see opposite).

Despite famously unpredictable weather, the beach holiday is still the ideal for many Victorian families, who flock to the coastal regions of the state in search of sunny days on the sand and in the surf. Those who don't trust Victoria's fickle climate simply wait until the depths of winter and then wing it to Queensland resorts, such as Noosa and the Sunshine Coast, to shake off the winter blues.

The Australian Dream has long been to own a house on a quarter-acre block and the majority of Victorians still rate home ownership highly on their life 'to do' list. Inside the average middle-class suburban home, you'll probably find a married heterosexual couple, though it's becoming more likely they will be de facto, or in their second marriage. Our 'mum and dad' couple will have an average of 1.4 children, probably called Jessica and Jack, Australia's names of the moment. But the birth rate has been falling over the last few years, as more couples put off having children to focus on higher education, travel and financial security before parenthood. Melbourne's increasingly higher property prices are another factor influencing this procrastination. Politicians from both major parties have scrambled to come up with ideas to encourage more breeding, from family-friendly work policies to 'baby bonuses' worth a few thousand dollars. Despite their efforts, at the time of writing, a quarter of Aussie women of child-bearing age were expected to remain childless.

POPULATION

Victoria has a population of approximately five million people, making up about 25% of the total Australian population. Around 72% of these live in the Melbourne metropolitan area, 18% live in other urban centres and 10% in rural areas.

Of the main regional population centres, Geelong, Ballarat, Bendigo, Shepparton, Warrnambool, Mildura, Wodonga, Morwell and Traralgon all have populations over 20,000. The northwest and the High Country are the most sparsely populated areas in the state.

Estimates suggest there are around 20,000 Koories (Aborigines from southeastern Australia) and Torres Strait Islanders in Victoria, more than half living in Melbourne. Mildura, Robinvale, Swan Hill, Echuca, Shepparton, Bairnsdale, Orbost and Warrnambool all have significant Koorie populations. There are also several independent Koorie communities around the state, including those at Lake Condah, Lake Tyers and Framlingham.

Lonely Planet's *Aboriginal Australia & the Torres Strait Islands* offers fascinating insights on Aboriginal culture and history, and has an extensive section on Victoria.

INDIGENOUS CULTURE

Because of early policies of 'dispersion' and later of assimilation, many Aboriginal languages and cultures have been lost, and no Victorian Aboriginal people live a purely traditional lifestyle.

However, some groups are active in preserving their cultures and there are Aboriginal cultural centres dotted around the state that are worth visiting, including Brambuk – The National Park Cultural Centre (p269), the Krowathunkoolong Keeping Place (p373) and the Dharnya Centre (p311).

When in Melbourne, pop in to the Melbourne Museum (p99) to see the Bunjilaka indigenous centre, visit Federation Square's Ian Potter Centre (p88), which has a fascinating Aboriginal and Torres Strait Islander collection of ancient and contemporary art; or take an Aboriginal Heritage Walk (see p113) in the Royal Botanic Gardens.

SPORT

Victorians just can't get enough of their sport, with a high participation rate, even higher spectator numbers and an enormous range of big-ticket sporting events each year.

Football (AFL)

There's no sport in Victoria that arouses more passion and pride than Australian rules football (Aussie rules). Melbourne is the national (and world) centre for the sport, and the **Australian Football League** (AFL; http://afl.com.au) administers the national competition.

During the footy season (March to September), the vast majority of Victorians become obsessed: entering tipping competitions at work, discussing groin injuries and suspensions over the water cooler, and devouring huge chunks of the daily newspapers devoted to mighty victories, devastating losses and the latest bad-boy behaviour (on and off the field) of the sport's biggest stars. Monday night disciplinary tribunals allocate demerit points for every bit of blood and biffo, and players can then be banned from playing. Fans follow these proceedings with almost as much attention as the games themselves. One thing is certain: footy fans always know better than the umpires, who have been a longstanding target for hecklers. Once disparagingly referred to as 'white maggots' because of their lily-white uniforms, they're now decked out in bright orange livery so players can spot them in the thick of the game. But it doesn't stop the occasional player from knocking one down in the scramble for the ball.

Though the comp developed from the Victorian Football League, it has featured successful teams from other states for several years – much to the dismay of Victorians everywhere. When the Brisbane Lions won three premierships in a row from 2001 to 2003, and Port Adelaide followed up with victory in 2004, grown men cried. Other interstate teams are based in Perth, Fremantle, Sydney and a second from Adelaide.

But the focus of AFL is still squarely in Victoria where it should be, with games regularly pulling monster crowds and enormous TV audiences. For information about venues and going to a game, see p139.

Cricket

In summer, sports fans' focus quickly shifts and the hordes head for the **Melbourne Cricket Ground** (MCG; www.mcg.org.au) to catch the drama of one-day and Test match cricket (the five-day international version of the game). As one of the strongest cricket teams in the world, Australia has enjoyed a decade of success, with records broken and world cups won. But the team has also been criticised for its sledging tactics on the field and its

For an insight into the passion AFL engenders on and off the field, grab a video of David Williamson's Aussie classic, *The Club* (1980; director Bruce Beresford). Though a little dated, it perfectly captures the Aussie fixation with all things sporty.

See www.bushrangers.com.au for more information on the wins and losses of the Victorian cricket team.

win-at-all-costs style. Victoria's most successful cricket player of recent times is Shane Warne, a controversial figure who has copped a lot of flak for his off-field shenanigans, but at the time of writing was Test cricket's greatest wicket taker of all time.

The first day of the traditional Boxing Day Test in Melbourne (on 26 December) is huge, with an average crowd of 70,000. That's a lot of spectators, considering it's the day after Christmas and there's no chance of seeing a result that day! There are regular interstate matches where the Victorian Bushrangers battle against other states for the national championship (formerly known as the Sheffield Shield but now named after a brand of cow juice). For more information on seeing a match, see p139.

Horse Racing

'The Melbourne Cup is Australia's top horse-racing event since 1861'

Melbourne must be one of the only cities in the world to nominate a public holiday for their big annual horse race. The **Melbourne Cup** (www.melbournecup .com), see p140, described as the 'race that stops the nation', is Australia's top horse-racing event and has been attracting crowds of punters since 1861. In 1930 a crowd of over 70,000 flocked to the racecourse to see the beloved champion Phar Lap win the Cup by three lengths – even today Phar Lap is one of the most popular exhibits at the Melbourne Museum. Held on the first Tuesday in November at Flemington Racecourse, the Cup is part of the annual Spring Racing Carnival, a chance for workers everywhere to have a flutter in office sweeps, get all dressed up, drink celebratory champagne or have a traditional Cup barbecue.

Smaller cities and towns also have their own horse-racing tracks and races. The historic Hanging Rock Picnic Races are held each year at Hanging Rock (p169). Another popular event that draws big crowds is Warrnambool's Grand Annual Steeplechase (p220).

MULTICULTURALISM

Multiculturalism has long been embraced by the state of Victoria, with around 25% of the population born overseas. Today there are Victorians from around 233 countries, speaking around 180 different languages and with 116 religions. The top five non-English languages spoken are Italian, Greek, Vietnamese, Cantonese and Arabic.

What was once a microcosm of British society has become a rich patchwork of different cultures, with a large portion of immigrants in the past 60 years arriving in Victoria as refugees. Initially, they tended to be Europeans fleeing the devastation of WWII, then came a wave of Vietnamese escaping the war in their homeland, while more recently, they are families seeking safe harbour from conflicts in the Balkans, Africa, the Middle East and Afghanistan.

Despite the diversity of people coming to Victoria, there are few racial 'ghettos' – most ethnic groups are dispersed fairly evenly throughout the state, and intermarriage is quite common. To learn more about the history of multiculturalism in Victoria and the richness of its cultures, visit Melbourne's Immigration Museum (p93).

ARTS
Architecture

Victoria's earliest buildings were built in the Old Colonial style (1788–1840), a simplified version of Georgian architecture. The earliest settled towns, such as Portland, Port Fairy and Port Albert, provide the best examples of this period.

Appropriately, the most prominent architectural style in the state is Victorian (1840–90), which was an expression of the era's confidence, progress and prosperity. It drew on various sources, including classical, romantic and Gothic, and as the era progressed designs became more elaborate, flamboyant and ornamental. Melbourne is acknowledged as one of the world's great Victorian-era cities. There are many outstanding examples of Victorian architecture in the city centre and inner suburbs, such as Carlton, East Melbourne, Parkville, St Kilda and South Melbourne. The provincial gold-rush centres, such as Bendigo, Ballarat, Castlemaine and Beechworth, are also renowned for their splendid Victorian architecture.

With the collapse of Melbourne's land boom in the early 1890s and the subsequent severe economic depression, a new style of architecture evolved. The Federation style was in many ways a watered-down version of Victorian architecture, featuring simplicity of design and less ornamentation. From around 1910 the most prominent style of residential architecture was a hybrid between the Federation and California Bungalow styles. The Art Deco style was also prominent from the 1920s, but after the Great Depression architecture became increasingly functionalist and devoid of decoration.

'The city is something of a playground for modern architects'

Of course, there's far more to Melbourne than just Victorian and Art Deco architecture. The city is something of a playground for modern architects, and the last few years have seen several notable structures go up. The redesign of Melbourne's major institutions reflects its increasingly outward-looking nature. The prim Victorian architecture for which the city is known has shuffled aside to make way for bold, angular newcomers. The current minimal aesthetic is complicated with exposed concrete, geometric shapes, metallic cladding and curtain walled glass. Recent examples include Federation Square (p87), the Australian Centre for Contemporary Art (p95) and the main railway hub Southern Cross Station (formerly known as Spencer St Station). Another new addition to the Melbourne cityscape is the residential Eureka Tower, which superseded the Rialto as Melbourne's tallest building and will feature an observation deck on the 88th floor. Firmly believing that bigger is better, Grocon (its high-profile developer) proudly touts the apartment building as the tallest in the world, and has even asked government bigwigs to approve a 50m telecommunications tower on top to make sure it stays that way. The Eureka is due to be opened in late 2005.

Cinema

Most people need little introduction to Australia's vibrant film industry, one of the oldest in the world, and a playground for contemporary screen greats Geoffrey Rush, Cate Blanchett, 'our' Nicole (Kidman) and Russell Crowe (born in New Zealand, but we claim him, anyway).

NATIONAL TRUST

The Victoria branch of the **National Trust** (☎ 03-9656 9800; www.nattrust.com.au; Tasma Tce, 4 Parliament Place, East Melbourne; ✆ 9am-5pm) is dedicated to preserving buildings in all parts of the state, and has 23 historic properties open to the public.

Membership of the National Trust entitles visitors to free entry to all historic houses and gardens in Australia, and costs $56/77 for individuals/families per year, plus a $33 joining fee (only payable in the first year). Nonmembers who visit a property pay a day fee.

The Trust also produces some excellent literature, including a fine series of walking-tour guides to Melbourne and some of Victoria's historic towns. These guides are often available from local tourist offices or from National Trust offices and are usually free, whether you're a member of the National Trust or not.

Melbourne is the birth-place of the Australian film industry and cinema historians regard the Salvation Army recruitment film, *Soldiers of the Cross* (1900), as the world's first 'real' movie. It was originally screened at the Melbourne Town Hall and cost £600 to make.

A high number of important films have been made in Victoria, and it is hoped that the recent addition of a world-class film studio at Melbourne's Docklands will help deliver even more of the same.

Recent films made in the state include *Ned Kelly* (2003), yet another tribute to the legendary bushranger; *Crackerjack* (2002), a contemporary comedy set around lawn bowls; and *Chopper* (2000), about the eponymous ex-crim. The quirky-comedy genre is well covered by the Melbourne-based Working Dog production company: *The Dish* (1999) and *The Castle* (1997) are supreme examples, poking fun at Australian stereotypes, but done with respect for their subjects.

Other local films to look out for are *Proof* (1991), a poignant film about a blind photographer set in St Kilda; *Malcolm* (1986), about a simple genius who builds a one-person tram; *Death in Brunswick* (1991), a black comedy about life in Melbourne's seedy underbelly; and *Spotswood* (1991), a nostalgic look at life and industrial relations in 1960s Melbourne. Uncompromising local director Geoffrey Wright's films include the savage *Romper Stomper* (1992), an early Russell Crowe show stopper about a neo-Nazi skinhead gang based in the Melbourne inner suburb of Footscray; and *Head On* (1998), the coming-of-age tale of gay sex, drugs and futility, starring small-screen star Alex Dimitriades.

Benchmark Australian films from the 1970s include the *Picnic at Hanging Rock*, a haunting tale of school girls who mysteriously disappear into the bush; *The Getting of Wisdom* (1977), about a naive country girl admitted to a prestigious boarding school in the 1880s; and *Mad Max*, featuring Mel Gibson before his meteoric rise.

For film venues, see p137.

Literature

Victoria has produced plenty of outstanding writers. Classic works include *The Songs of a Sentimental Bloke* by CJ Dennis, *The Magic Pudding, Red Heap* and *Saturdee* by Norman Lindsay, *For the Term of His Natural Life* by Marcus Clarke, *The Getting of Wisdom* and *The Fortunes of Richard Mahony* by Henry Handel (Florence Ethel) Richardson, *Picnic at Hanging Rock* by Joan Lindsay and *My Brother Jack* by George Johnston. Also, look for the work of Charmian Clift, Frank Hardy, Hal Porter and Alan Marshall.

The annual Victorian Premier's Literary Awards in October are organised by the State Library of Victoria, and recognise the best local literary works in a range of categories. For more information, see www.slv.vic.gov.au/programs/literary/pla.

Among Victoria's contemporary writers, the best known is probably Peter Carey (now living in New York), who won the Booker Prize in 1988 for his novel *Oscar & Lucinda* and in 2002 for his novel based on the letters of Ned Kelly, *True History of the Kelly Gang*.

Helen Garner's works are mostly set in Melbourne, and include *The Children's Bach, Postcards from Surfers, Cosmo Cosmolino* and *Monkey Grip*. More recent novels with a Melbourne bent include Shane Maloney's *Stiff*, Andrew Masterton's *Last Days*, Elliot Perlman's *Three Dollars* and Neal Drinnan's *Pussy Bow*.

Other contemporary Melbourne writers include Kerry Greenwood, Morris Lurie, Carmel Bird, Barry Dickins, Gerald Murnane, Robert Dessaix, Rod Jones, Andrea Goldsmith, Christos Tsiolkas, Sonya Hartnett, Clare Mendes, Fiona Capp and Michelle de Kretser.

Music

Victoria's rich musical heritage covers the spectrum from rock to classics, and Melbourne's dynamic music scene has consistently produced many of Australia's outstanding bands and musicians. Local artists worth seeking out include Paul Kelly for his whimsical lyrics and guitar, Stephen

Cummings for some classy lulling, Tex Perkins for some bad-arse spunk, the Dave Graney Show (self-confessed King of Pop), Kim Salmon for wildly unique rock and Lisa Miller for downright lovely folksy tunes. Melbourne's answer to The Strokes, Jet, are enjoying the 'new rock' revival, winning a Grammy and, the Australian equivalent, a stack of ARIAs in 2004. Other energetic young standouts include Architecture in Helsinki for some cutesy brass-infused pop and Cat Empire for an upbeat fusion of styles. Mainstream mainstays include Kate Ceberano and David Bridie.

While a large proportion of Melburnians avidly support the local music scene, the population itself is not large enough to retain some of the city's most successful acts. So, while she'll always be 'our Kylie', ex-soap star turned pop princess Ms Minogue no longer resides here. And Nick Cave and the Dirty Three use their rock-star passports to live in a host of other cities.

Despite the exodus of such talent, you can head out on any night and be guaranteed to find someone, somewhere, fronting the stage bathed in blue and red spotlights. Mostly, you'll be rewarded with a polished ensemble, confidently delivering its own compositions. For a list of live-music venues, see p133.

In the classical sphere, Melbourne is known for being home to the great idiosyncratic composer Percy Grainger and singer Nellie Melba. The Melbourne Symphony Orchestra performs regularly in Hamer Hall, and is famed for its spirited recitals. Chamber, choral, light opera, new music and opera performances are a feature at the Victorian Arts Centre (p95).

> Victoria produced one of the greatest opera singers of all time, Dame Nellie Melba (1861–1931), whose name lives on in such things as Melba toast and peach Melba. She also gazes out from Australia's $100 bill.

Visual Arts

Although various amateur artists practised their craft in the early days of the colony, the history of Victorian painting begins in earnest in the 1850s. The artists of the time sought to capture scenes of the gold rush, city life of Melbourne and pastoral images of the Victorian bush. Major artists of this time include Samuel Thomas Gill and Thomas Clark.

In the late 1800s the Heidelberg School was born, influenced by French landscape painters of the Barbizon school, who favoured simple, un-adorned renderings of natural scenes and rural life. The group takes its name from the bush camp at Heidelberg where they were based. Major painters of the Heidelberg school include Tom Roberts, Arthur Streeton, Frederick McCubbin and Charles Condor. These artists were the first local artists to paint in a distinctively Australian style rather than in imitation of Europeans.

Following WWI Victorian painters, influenced by such European giants as Gauguin, Cezanne and Van Gogh, started experimenting with modern art styles. Influential artists of the post-WWI period include George Bell and Arnold Shore. These artists were influential in the creation of the Contemporary Art Society in Melbourne, which gave further impetus to the modern-art movement in Victoria.

In the 1940s a revolution in Australian art took place at Heide (p107), the home of John and Sunday Reed in suburban Bulleen. Under their patronage, a new generation of bohemian young artists (including Sir Sidney Nolan, Albert Tucker, Arthur Boyd, Joy Hester and John Perceval) redefined the direction of Australian art.

In the late 1970s, 1980s and 1990s, artists such as Jenny Watson, John Nixon and Howard Arkley, along with the anti-establishment group Roar, were at the forefront of a new wave of local artists challenging the conventions of the art marketplace.

Environment Tim Flannery

Tim Flannery is a naturalist, explorer and writer. His latest book, about Australia, is *Country*. Tim is director of the South Australian Museum and a professor at the University of Adelaide.

Australia's plants and animals are just about the closest things to alien life you are likely to encounter on Earth. That's because Australia has been isolated from the other continents for a very long time – at least 45 million years. The other habitable continents have been able to exchange various species at different times because they've been linked by land bridges. Just 15,000 years ago it was possible to walk from the southern tip of Africa right through Asia and the Americas to Terra del Fuego. Not Australia, however. Its birds, mammals, reptiles and plants have taken their own separate and very different evolutionary journey, and the result today is the world's most distinct – and one of its most diverse – natural realms.

The first naturalists to investigate Australia were astonished by what they found. Here the swans were black – to Europeans this was a metaphor for the impossible – while mammals such as platypuses and echidnas were discovered to lay eggs. It really was an upside-down world, where many of the larger animals hopped, where each year the trees shed their bark rather than their leaves, and where the 'pears' were made of wood (a woody pear is a relative of the waratah).

It's worthwhile understanding the basics about how nature operates in Australia. This is important because there's nowhere like Australia, and once you have an insight into its origins and natural rhythms, you will appreciate the place so much more.

Tim Flannery's *The Future Eaters* is a 'big picture' overview of evolution in Australasia, covering the last 120 million years of history, with thoughts on how the environment has shaped Australasia's human cultures.

THE LAND

There are two big factors that go a long way towards explaining nature in Australia: its soils and its climate. Both are unique. Australian soils are the more subtle and difficult to notice of the two, but they have been fundamental in shaping life here. On the other continents, in recent geological times, processes such as volcanism, mountain building and glacial activity have been busy creating new soil. Just think of the glacial-derived soils of North America, northern Asia and Europe. They feed the world today, and were made by glaciers grinding up rock of differing chemical

---

VICTORIA'S PLANT LIFE *Susie Ashworth*

Unlike the vast flat middle of Australia, Victoria's landscapes are rich with diverse native flora, from the mosses, lichens and tree ferns of the rainforests to the hardy mallee scrub of the semiarid desert areas. More than 35% of the state is covered in forest – some native, and some commercial pine plantations. On the other hand, large areas have been cleared for agriculture.

Most of the state's landscapes now combine native Australian flora, which evolved over thousands of years in isolation from the rest of the world, and exotic species that have been introduced in the 200 years since the arrival of Europeans.

The two most common native plant groups are eucalypts and wattles (acacias), but there are also 2000 species of native wildflowers, which vary from region to region and provide colourful exhibitions, particularly during spring and summer.

Top Five Wildflower Spots

- Lower Glenelg National Park (p231)
- Grampian National Park (p267)
- Little Desert National Park (p276)
- Croajingolong National Park (p390)
- Warrandyte State Park (p172)

composition over the last two million years. The rich soils of India and parts of South America were made by rivers eroding mountains, while Java in Indonesia owes its extraordinary richness to volcanoes.

All of these soil-forming processes have been almost absent from Australia in more recent times. Only volcanoes have made a contribution, and they cover less than 2% of the continent's land area. In fact, for the last 90 million years, beginning deep in the age of dinosaurs, Australia has been geologically comatose. It was too flat, warm and dry to attract glaciers, its crust too ancient and thick to be punctured by volcanoes or folded into mountains. Look at Uluru and Kata Tjuta (the Olgas) in the Northern Territory. They are the stumps of mountains that 350 million years ago were the height of the Andes. Yet for hundreds of millions of years they've been nothing but nubbins.

Under conditions such as these no new soil is created and the old soil is leached of all its goodness, and blown and washed away. The leaching is done by rain. Even if just 30cm of it falls each year, this adds up to a column of water 30 million kilometres high passing through the soil over 100 million years, and that can do a great deal of leaching. Almost all of Australia's mountain ranges are more than 90 million years old, so you will see quite a lot of sand here, and lots of country where the rocky 'bones' of the land are sticking up through the soil. It is an old, infertile landscape, and life in Australia has been adapting to these conditions for aeons.

Australia's misfortune in respect to soils is echoed in its climate. In most parts of the world outside the wet tropics, life responds to the rhythm of the seasons – summer to winter, or wet to dry. Most of Australia experiences seasons – sometimes very severe ones – yet life does not respond solely to them. This can clearly be seen by the fact that although there's plenty of snow and cold country in Australia, there are almost no trees that shed their leaves in winter, and no Australian animals hibernate. Instead there is a far more potent climatic force that Australian life must obey: El Niño.

The cycle of flood and drought that El Niño brings to Australia is profound. The rivers – even the mighty Murray River, the nation's largest, which runs through the southeast and constitutes the majority of the northern border of Victoria – can be miles wide one year, while you can literally step over its flow the next. This is the power of El Niño, and its effect, when combined with Australia's poor soils, manifests itself compellingly. As you might expect from this, relatively few of Australia's birds are seasonal breeders, and few migrate. Instead, they breed when the rain comes, and a large percentage are nomads, following the rain across the breadth of the continent.

So challenging are conditions in Australia that its birds have developed some extraordinary habits. The kookaburras, magpies and blue wrens you are likely to see – to name just a few – have developed a breeding system called 'helpers at the nest'. The helpers are the young adult birds of previous breedings, which stay with their parents to help bring up the new chicks. Just why they do this was a mystery until it was realised that conditions in Australia can be so harsh that more than two adult birds are needed to feed the nestlings. This pattern of breeding is very rare in places like Asia, Europe and North America, but it is common in a wide array of Australian birds.

WILDLIFE

Australia is, of course, famous for being the home of the kangaroo and other marsupials. Unless you visit a wildlife park, such creatures are not easy to see as most are nocturnal, although it is possible

For more information about native flora throughout the state, including a full list of district groups, see the website of the Victorian chapter of the Australian Plants Society (http://home .vicnet.net.au/~sgapvic).

B Beale and P Fray's *The Vanishing Continent* gives an excellent overview of soil erosion across Australia. Fine colour photographs make the issue more graphic.

Pizzey and Knight's *Field Guide to Birds of Australia* is an indispensable guide for bird-watchers and anyone else even peripherally interested in Australia's feathered tribes. Knight's illustrations are both beautiful and helpful in identification.

VICTORIA... BIGGEST, TALLEST, LONGEST Susie Ashworth

- Victoria covers 227,600 sq km – just 3% of the country's land mass. It's the smallest mainland state, roughly equivalent in size to Great Britain.
- Mt Bogong (1986m) and Mt Feathertop (1922m) are the two highest points in the state.
- The Goulburn (566km) is Victoria's longest river.
- Victoria's capital, Melbourne, contains 70% of the state's population.
- Victoria has 184 islands.
- At 209 sq km, Lake Corangamite is Victoria's largest lake.
- The tallest tree ever measured was a *Eucalyptus regnans* at Watts River, Victoria, reported in 1872. It was 132.6m (435ft) tall.
- The longest damper bread ever baked was 100m long, and was the joint effort of 1500 girl guides in Melbourne in 1998.

---

to see a kangaroo in rural areas in the daytime. Their lifestyles, however, are exquisitely attuned to Australia's harsh conditions. Have you ever wondered why kangaroos, alone among the world's larger mammals, hop? It turns out that hopping is the most efficient way of getting about at medium speeds. This is because the energy of the bounce is stored in the tendons of the legs – much like in a pogo stick – while the intestines bounce up and down like a piston, emptying and filling the lungs without needing to activate the chest muscles. When you travel long distances to find meagre feed, such efficiency is a must.

Marsupials are so efficient that they need to eat a fifth less food than equivalent-sized placental mammals (everything from bats to rats, whales and ourselves). But some marsupials have taken energy efficiency much further. If you get to visit a wildlife park or zoo you might notice that far-away look in a koala's eyes. It seems as if nobody is home – and this is near the truth. Several years ago biologists announced that koalas are the only living creatures that have brains that don't fit their skulls. Instead they have a shrivelled walnut of a brain that rattles around in a fluid-filled cranium. Other researchers have contested this finding, however, pointing out that the brains of the koalas examined for the study may have shrunk because these organs are so soft. Whether soft-brained or empty-headed, there is no doubt that the koala is not the Einstein of the animal world, and we now believe that it has sacrificed its brain to energy efficiency. Brains cost a lot to run – our brains typically weigh 2% of our bodyweight, but use 20% of the energy we consume. Koalas eat gum leaves, which are so toxic that they use 20% of their energy just detoxifying this food. This leaves little energy for the brain, and living in the tree tops where there are so few predators means that they can get by with few wits at all.

The peculiar constraints of the Australian environment have not made everything dumb. The koala's nearest relative, the wombat (of which there are three species), have large brains for a marsupial. These creatures live in complex burrows and can weigh up to 35kg, making them the largest herbivorous burrowers on earth. Because their burrows are effectively air-conditioned, they have the neat trick of turning down their metabolic activity when they are in residence. One physiologist who studied their thyroid hormones found that biological activity ceased to such an extent in sleeping wombats that, from a hormonal point of view, they appeared

> Despite anything an Australian tells you about koalas (aka 'drop-bears'), there is no risk of one falling onto your head (deliberately or not) as you walk beneath their trees.

to be dead! Wombats can remain underground for a week at a time, and can get by on just a third of the food needed by an equivalent-sized sheep. One day perhaps, efficiency-minded farmers will keep wombats instead of sheep. At the moment, however, that isn't possible, for the largest of the wombat species, the northern hairy-nose, is one of the world's rarest creatures; with none existing in Victoria and only around 100 surviving in a remote nature reserve in central Queensland.

One of the more common marsupials you might catch a glimpse of in the national parks around Australia's major cities are the species of antechinus, or marsupial mouse. These nocturnal, rat-sized creatures lead an extraordinary life. The males live for just 11 months, the first 10 of which consist of a concentrated burst of eating and growing. And like teenage males, the day comes when their minds turn to sex, which then becomes an obsession. As they embark on their quest for females they forget to eat and sleep. Instead they gather in logs and woo passing females by serenading them with squeaks. By the end of August – just two weeks after they reach 'puberty' – every single male is dead, exhausted by sex and burdened with swollen testes. This extraordinary life history may have evolved in response to Australia's trying environmental conditions. It seems likely that if the males survived mating, they would compete with the females as they tried to find enough food to feed their growing young. Basically, antechinus dads are disposable. They do better for antechinus posterity if they go down in a testosterone-fuelled blaze of glory.

One thing you will see lots of in Australia are reptiles. Snakes are abundant, and they include some of the most venomous species known. Where the opportunities to feed are few and far between, it's best not to give your prey a second chance, hence the potent venom. Snakes will usually leave you alone if you don't fool with them. Observe, back quietly away and don't panic, and most of the time you'll be OK. For information on the treatment of snake bites, see p421.

> Of Australia's 155 species of land snakes, 93 are venomous. Australia is home to something like 10 of the world's 15 most venomous snakes.

THE BIG DRY *Susie Ashworth*

Despite Victoria's reputation for overcast skies and drizzly days, the southern state has been in the grip of a drought since the mid-1990s. Like most parts of Australia, farmers around Victoria have been hit hard by almost a decade of drought and the wait for decent rainfall has been too long for some, who have been forced to sell up and head to the city. Country towns have suffered too, as small businesses have been forced to close and young families have moved to Melbourne in search of work.

Sadly, record levels of rain in early 2005 did little to ease the pain (apparently it will take two years of above-average rainfall to do that), though it did urge the state government to remove the stage two water restrictions that Melbourne had put up with for 18 months. City slickers jumped for joy as the bans on watering lawns and hosing down cars were lifted. However, the temporary restrictions were promptly replaced by Victoria's first permanent water rules in March 2005, aiming to promote the sensible long-term use of the precious drop. Making water saving a life-time habit for Melburnians is the main goal for the powers-that-be, who anticipate that a rising population and future dry conditions will put even more pressure on Melbourne's H_2O stores.

Of course, country folk can only dream of having the water supplies available to them that those in the big smoke moan about. They've been saddled with much stricter restrictions for years; their loss not just a pristine lawn, but their crops, stock and livelihood.

For more information about water saving and the effects of the drought on the state, see the websites of **Melbourne Water** (www.melbournewater.com.au), **Save Water** (www.savewater.com.au) and the Victorian government's **Environment Gateway** (www.environment.vic.gov.au).

ENVIRONMENTAL CHALLENGES

For more on various local environmental issues and campaigns, click onto the websites of the Victorian National Parks Association (VNPA; www.vnpa.org.au) and the Victorian branch of the Wilderness Society (www.wilderness.org .au/regions/vic).

The European colonisation of Australia, commencing in 1788, heralded a period of catastrophic environmental upheaval for the continent, with the result that Australians today struggle with some of the most severe environmental problems to be found anywhere in the world. It may seem strange that a population of just 20 million, living in a continent the size of the USA (minus Alaska), could inflict such damage on its environment, but Australia's long isolation, its fragile soils and difficult climate have made it particularly vulnerable to human-induced change.

Damage to Australia's environment has been inflicted in several ways, the most important being the introduction of pest species, destruction of forests, overstocking of rangelands, inappropriate agriculture and interference with water flows. Beginning with the escape of domestic cats into the Australian bush shortly after 1788, a plethora of vermin, from foxes to wild camels and cane toads, have run wild in Australia, causing extinctions in the native fauna. One out of every 10 native mammals living in Australia prior to European colonisation is now extinct, and many more are highly endangered. Extinctions have also affected native plants, birds and amphibians.

The destruction of forests has also had a profound effect. Most of Australia's rainforests have suffered clearing, while conservationists fight with loggers over the fate of the last unprotected stands of 'old growth'. Many Australian rangelands have been chronically overstocked for more than a century, the result being extreme vulnerability of both soils and rural economies to Australia's drought and flood cycle, as well as extinction of many native species. The development of agriculture has involved

VICTORIA'S PROTECTED AREAS *Susie Ashworth*

Despite its relatively small size (by Australian standards anyway), Victoria has an enormous range of national parks, with vastly different weather and terrain, from the remote red-sandstone ridges and dunes of the Big Desert Wilderness Park (p285) and the frost-bitten peaks of the Alpine National Park (p337) to the distinctive ocean outcrops of Port Campbell National Park (p214) and the spectacular rugged mountains of Wilsons Promontory National Park (p366). Such diversity of landscapes and climates provides outdoor enthusiasts with a broad menu of activities to choose from (for some ideas, see p43).

Victoria has 39 national parks, 30 state parks and three wilderness parks, making up around 17% of the state's total area. In November 2002, the state Labor government proclaimed Victoria's new marine national parks system, which established 13 marine national parks and 11 marine sanctuaries in a bid to protect vulnerable marine plants and animals.

National parks generally have the best facilities, with good picnic and camping areas in most parks. No pets are permitted. A handful of state parks allow horse riding, mountain biking, four-wheel-driving and dog walking, but many don't allow any of these activities. It's a good idea to check the available facilities and rules and restrictions for each park before heading out. The wilderness parks are remote and rugged regions whose appeal lies in their untouched quality; there are no facilities within the parks, pets are not permitted and visitors need to be experienced and very well equipped. Access is by foot only. For tips on responsible bushwalking, see the boxed text on p45.

Victoria's parks are managed by **Parks Victoria** (☎ 13 19 63; www.parkweb.vic.gov.au), which has a useful 24-hour information line. Visit its excellent website for national park profiles and a full list of outdoor activities, the best places to do them, and tour companies who can take you there.

Entrance to most national parks in Victoria is free, with the exception of the big five – Wilsons Promontory National Park (p366), Mount Buffalo National Park (p347), Mornington Peninsula National Park (p184), Baw Baw National Park (p324) and Yarra Ranges National Park (p174). If you plan to spend lots of time in these parks, get an annual national parks pass ($64.90). Camping in many parks is free, though the more popular parks charge up to $11 per site for up to six people.

land clearance and the provision of irrigation, and here again the effect has been profound.

In terms of financial value, just 1.5% of Australia's land surface provides over 95% of agricultural yield, and much of this land lies in the irrigated regions of the Murray–Darling Basin. This is Australia's agricultural heartland, yet it too is under severe threat from the salting of soils and rivers. Irrigation water penetrates into the sediments laid down in an ancient sea, carrying salt into the catchments and fields. If nothing is done, the lower Murray River will become too salty to drink in a decade or two, threatening the water supply of Adelaide, a city of over a million people.

Despite the enormity of the biological crisis engulfing Australia, governments and the community have been slow to respond. It was in the 1980s that coordinated action began to take place, but not until the '90s

---

GREEN MATTERS *Susie Ashworth*

Many Victorians are passionate about preserving Victoria's natural heritage, and environmental issues are often front-page news throughout the state.

One of the biggest issues in recent times has been the state government push to embrace wind farms as a clean alternative source of energy, instead of relying solely on heavily polluting coal-generated electricity from the Latrobe Valley. Some rural property owners have jumped at the chance to cash in, welcoming the towering white turbines on their wind-swept land. But protests abound from the not in my back yard (Nimby) brigade, who say the turbines are noisy, ugly and a menace to property values. Wind farms that have already been established since 2000 include Codrington Wind Farm (2001), near Port Fairy, and Challicum Hills Wind Farm (2003), near Ararat. The enormous Portland Wind Project is expected to be operational by mid-2005. Several more wind farms are still on the drawing board, causing angst to regional Victorians who will have no choice but to live with their constant whoosh, whoosh, whoosh. If you'd like to make up your own mind and see the towers for yourself, you can take a tour of Codrington Wind Farm (p226). For more information on wind energy around Victoria, see the website of the **Australian Wind Energy Association** (www.auswea.com.au).

High on the green agenda is the emotive issue of logging Victoria's old-growth forests. Conservationists despair that majestic ancient trees are being sold off for a few cents as woodchips to Japanese paper companies, while local water catchment areas suffer as surrounding forest is decimated. East Gippsland is Victoria's last and largest area of ancient forest, protecting some 300 rare and threatened plant and animal species. Though 35% of East Gippsland's forests fall within the boundaries of national parks, the remainder of the forests under state government control are being logged at a rapid rate, much to the distress of concerned conservationists who have flocked to the area to protest. The state Labor government's Sustainable Forest (Timber) Bill of 2004 was met with unanimous disapproval from green groups, who said it simply maintained the status quo in favour of business, allowing existing logging and woodchipping deals to go ahead. For more information about the fight to save the forests, see (p385).

Generations of mountain cattlemen have grazed their stock in the High Country's spectacular Alpine National Park. It's tradition, a way of life, and many of them don't see any good reason to change. Hence, the bitter tussle between conservationists and cattlemen over the future of grazing in northeastern Victoria. In May 2005, the state government announced that it was bringing an end to the 170-year tradition of running cattle through the national park, banning the heavy-hoofed creatures from the fragile landscape. Though the government also promised $5 million in compensation to the farming families, the outcry from cattlemen and country folk was immediate and angry. Farmers mourned the loss of their heritage and livelihood, and claimed that the Man from Snowy River would be rolling in his grave. Meanwhile, green groups jumped for joy at the decision. No more damaged creekbeds, fouled waterways, trampled wildflowers and millions of cow pats. For some it's the end of an era. For others, the beginning of a new one. Also see the boxed text, p336, for more information on the cattle grazing debate.

that major steps were taken. The establishment of **Landcare** (www.landcareaustralia.com.au), an organisation enabling people to effectively address local environmental issues, and the expenditure of $2.5 billion through the National Heritage Trust Fund have been important national initiatives. Yet so difficult are some of the issues the nation faces that, as yet, little has been achieved in terms of halting the destructive processes. Individuals are also banding together to help. Groups such as the **Australian Bush Heritage Fund** (www.bushheritage.asn.au) and the **Australian Wildlife Conservancy** (AWC; www.australianwildlife.org) allow people to donate funds and time to the conservation of native species. Some such groups have been spectacularly successful; the AWC, for example, already manages many endangered species over its 1.3 million acre holdings.

So severe are Australia's problems that it will take a revolution before they can be overcome, for sustainable practices need to be implemented in every arena of life – from farms to suburbs and city centres. Renewable energy, sustainable agriculture and water use lie at the heart of these changes, and Australians are only now developing the road-map to sustainability that they so desperately need if they are to have a long-term future on the continent.

Victoria Outdoors

Victoria's excellent network of national parks and state forests makes it a great playground for outdoor enthusiasts, with countless tracks to follow, mountains to climb, waves to surf and hills to ski.

BOATING

Despite its relatively small size, Victoria boasts expansive stretches of coastline and some spectacular inland lake systems, and boating is a popular pastime throughout the state. City-based yachties tend to gravitate to the many sailing clubs around Port Phillip Bay – for details of major clubs, see p109. Other popular boating areas around the state include the sprawling Gippsland Lakes system, the water-sports playground of Lake Eildon (p329) and the low-key cruisey Mallacoota Inlet (p389) near the border. Holidaymakers can get out on the water by hiring yachts and launches, which work out to be quite economical for a group of people.

Hiring a houseboat and cruising off into the sunset with some good friends is a classic way to spend a holiday in Victoria. With mile after mile of pretty, meandering waterway, the Murray River on the Victoria–New South Wales (NSW) border is perfect for peacefully puttering along, enjoying the distinctive Aussie bushland along the river and watching the historic paddle-steamers pass by. For houseboat hire options, see the sections on Mildura (p290), Swan Hill (p294) and Echuca (p314). Closer to the city, visitors can also hire houseboats at Lake Eildon (p329), near Mansfield.

Prices vary wildly for houseboat rentals. In the low season a two-bedroom houseboat might cost $950 per week; come the holidays in late December and January, the same boat might cost $3000. Many houseboats will sleep up to eight people, but there may be charges for additional people after the first two people.

If time is against you, you can still get out on the water and enjoy the Murray river-scapes on a historic paddle-steamer. Cruises ranging from one hour to several days operate out of riverside towns, such as Echuca (p313) and Mildura (p288).

BUSHWALKING

In Victoria's extensive and diverse network of national parks and state forests, walkers enjoy everything from short doddles through rainforest gullies, to more challenging hikes in rugged alpine regions and extended walking trails that trace the coastline. The infrastructure is usually excellent, with marked trails, campgrounds with fireplaces, toilets and fresh water, and park visitors centres.

Though a magnet for skiers and snowboarders in the winter months, the High Country is also one of the most popular areas for bushwalking in the state, particularly for experienced walkers. Springtime blankets of wildflowers, spectacular alpine scenery and a wide range of walks for different fitness and skill levels attracts local and international walkers alike. Favourite stomping grounds include Baw Baw National Park, Cathedral Range State Park, Mt Hotham (p339), Mt Beauty (p343) and Mt Buffalo.

If coastal treks are more your scene, head down to Wilsons Promontory National Park (p368) in Gippsland, with stacks of marked trails from Tidal River and Telegraph Bay that can take anywhere from a few hours to a couple of days to complete. Expect squeaky white sands and

For national park news and updates, and detailed descriptions of national park trails, see the Parks Victoria website (www .parkweb.vic.gov.au), or pick up brochures from park visitors centres.

GOING WALKABOUT

If you've got a few days up your sleeve and want to spend it going bush, consider tackling one of Victoria's longer walks, ranging in length from 250km to over 750km. If you've only got the time and stamina for a few days of trekking, don't fret. Thousands of walkers venture on to these trails each year, and most are only on track for two or three days – usually for the most spectacular bits.

A wide range of information, including books, maps and brochures, is available on the following walks. If you need more specific details, ask a park ranger; they usually know the terrain like the back of their hand.

The Great South West Walk

Tranquil eucalyptus forests, cliff-lined rivers, enticing snow-white beaches and dramatic bays. No wonder bushwalkers get tingles when they talk about their days on this popular coastal trail. At 250km, the **Great South West Walk** (www.greatsouthwestwalk.com) is the longest coastal track in the state. Starting from the visitors information centre in Portland, the walk follows the coastline all the way to the small township of Nelson, then heads inland beside the Glenelg River to the South Australian border before looping back to Portland. To walk the full distance you'll need at least 10 days, although the walk is designed to allow people to walk shorter sections – from a few hours to a couple of days. For more information, see the boxed text on p230.

Australian Alps Walking Track

Cutting right through the Baw Baw Plateau and the Bogong High Plains, this spectacular track treats walkers to a succession of spectacular views and some of the state's finest walks. Running all the way from Walhalla, east of Melbourne, to Mt Pilot on the outskirts of Canberra, the full track demands more than 680km of walking, but only a handful of people cover the full distance and you can easily choose sections of the track that suit you. For ideas on where to pick up the trail, see The High Country chapter (p322). Most parts of the track traverse alpine areas and, as weather conditions can be extreme, walks should only be undertaken by the experienced and adequately prepared. The best times of year are late spring, summer and early autumn (ie November to March), but alpine conditions are variable so be prepared for bad weather at any time of year.

John Siseman's *The Alpine Walking Track* is an excellent source of information.

The Bicentennial National Trail

The brainchild of Aussie horseman and businessman RM Williams, this 5330km trail runs the full length of Australia's east coast from Cooktown in far north Queensland to Healesville on the outskirts of Melbourne. Designed for long-distance walking and horse riding, it includes a mix of roads, fire trails and walking tracks passing through national parks, and the Victorian section traverses the spectacular High Country of the Great Dividing Range.

For more information, contact the **Bicentennial National Trail** (☎ 1300 138 724; http://home.vicnet .net.au/~bnt; PO Box 259, Oberon, NSW 2787), which publishes a general information booklet as well as 12 detailed books covering the entire route. The website gives a good overview of the trail and has an extensive list of resources, including suggested books, videos and website links.

aquamarine waters (they're icier than they look), bushland full of wildlife, distinctive orange rocks and stunning coastal vistas.

Heading 250km inland from Melbourne, there's the Grampians National Park (p269), with more than 150km of well-marked walking tracks past towering waterfalls and sacred Aboriginal rock-art sites, through eucalypt forests, along rocky outcrops and atop mountains with sweeping views of the Wimmera Plains. Back on the coast and almost tipping over into NSW, the Croajingolong National Park (p390), near Mallacoota in East Gippsland, offers rugged inland treks and easier coastal walks past historic lighthouses and over sand dunes. Close to the city, one of the best places for a weekend tramp is Kinglake National Park (p172), with its fern-filled gullies and thick eucalypt forest.

There are more than 70 active bushwalking clubs around the state. Many conduct regular walks and outings, and most welcome newcomers. For a full list of clubs, contact the **Federation of Victorian Walking Clubs** (☎ 03-9455 1876; http://home.vicnet.net.au/~vicwalk).

Responsible Bushwalking

Please consider the following when bushwalking, for your safety and to help preserve the ecology and beauty of Victoria.

- Stay on established trails, avoid cutting corners, and stay on hard ground where possible.
- Before tackling a long or remote walk, tell someone responsible about your plans and contact them when you return.
- Use designated campgrounds where provided. When bush camping, look for a natural clearing and avoid camping under river red gums, which have a tendency to drop their branches.
- Keep your vehicle on existing tracks or roads.
- Don't feed native animals.
- Take all your rubbish out with you – don't burn or bury it.
- Avoid polluting lakes and streams – don't wash yourself or your dishes in them, and keep soap and detergent at least 50m away from waterways.
- Use toilets where provided – otherwise, bury human waste at least 100m away from waterways (taking a hand trowel is a good idea).
- Boil water for 10 minutes (or purify with a filter or tablets) before drinking it.
- Don't bring dogs or other pets into national parks.
- Use a gas or fuel stove for cooking.
- Don't light fires unless necessary– if you do need a fire, keep it small and use only dead fallen wood in an existing fireplace. Make sure the fire is completely extinguished before moving on. On total fire ban days, don't (under any circumstances) light a fire – and that includes fuel stoves.

CANOEING & KAYAKING

Canoeing and kayaking offer travellers the chance to see parts of Victoria they might otherwise miss – river gorges, lake edges and remote sections of wilderness, such as along the Snowy River. Trips can be as short as a couple of hours, or extended adventures.

Melbourne's Yarra River (p108) is popular with paddlers, with its gentle lower reaches suitable for families and more exciting rapids of about grade three up in the Yarra Valley (p172).

Keen canoeists hankering for multiday trips on the water head to the Glenelg River (p231) in the southwest. The river works its way through deep gorges with stunning riverside wildflowers and birdlife. Best of all it has special riverside camp sites en route, many of which are only accessible by canoe.

Canoe hire costs anywhere from $35 to $75 per day, depending on the operator. Extra expenses may include equipment delivery and pickup.

Sea-kayaking has also become popular along Victoria's beaches and bays, with the added bonus of spotting wildlife, such as sea lions, gannets, penguins and dolphins. Apollo Bay (p209) is a good place for short trips.

CYCLING

Those who cycle for fun have come to the right place, with some great cycling routes for day, weekend or even multiweek trips. Melbourne has

Lonely Planet's *Walking in Australia* covers 19 walks in Victoria, ranging from half-day strolls in Melbourne to a five-day coastal walk.

Open Spaces Publishing (www.osp.com.au/index .html) offers a range of local walking guides, including *Daywalks Around Melbourne* and *Weekend Walks Around Melbourne*, both by Glenn Tempest, and *Bushwalks in the Victorian Alps* by Glenn van der Knijff.

A great source of information on canoeing and kayaking in the state is Canoeing Victoria (☎ 03-9459 4251; www.canoevic.org.au), which publicises upcoming events and offers courses for beginners.

RAIL TRAILS

If you're looking for somewhere to cycle that is traffic-free and gives you a taste of the Victorian countryside, one of the state's many rail trails may be just the thing for you.

Victoria boasts 25 rail trails that follow the pathway of old, disused railway tracks, and are shared by walkers, cyclists and horse riders. Much to the delight of amateur cyclists, trails are flat and gentle with no big hills, providing ideal bike-riding conditions for families and for out-of-condition cyclists. There are several short tracks in metropolitan Melbourne and many more dotted around the state, ranging from short 1km pedals to 97km epic journeys.

One of the most popular trails for Melburnians is the **Lilydale to Warburton Trail** (p174), just an hour from the city, which leads cyclists through 38km of picturesque farmland and riverside natural bush. The trail has been a boon for the pretty town of Warburton, which helps cyclists recharge their batteries with home-made pies, and large helpings of scones, jam and cream.

For High Country cycling, there's the **Murray to Mountains Rail Trail** (p344), which starts in Bright, passes through Wangaratta, Beechworth, Myrtleford and Porepunkah, and has popular segments that weave their way through pine forests and original Aussie bushland.

For summaries of each trail, including maps, gradient profiles and historical notes for the region, grab a copy of *Rail Trails of Victoria & South Australia*. Alternatively, get inspired by checking the website of **Rail Trails Australia** (☎ 03-9306 4846; www.railtrails.org.au).

---

an excellent network of long urban bike trails, and in country areas you'll find thousands of kilometres of diverse cycling terrain, much of it readily accessible by public transport. Highlights include the Great Ocean Rd, one of the world's most spectacular coastal roads, and the exhilarating climbs and descents of the High Country. Best of all, the state has a great network of sealed country roads, along which your most common companions are likely to be magpies (beware of the occasional dive-bombing attack in spring).

If your timing's right, you may be able to participate in one of Victoria's big annual cycling events. The **Great Victorian Bike Ride** (www.bv.com.au; adult $630, child under 17/child under 10 $490/120) is a 10-day annual ride attracting thousands of cyclists of all ages and fitness levels. Payment for this fully supported ride includes meals, mechanical support and access to camping grounds. Hosted in different parts of the state each year, cyclists can find themselves pedalling down the scenic Great Ocean Rd, powering along from Swan Hill to Melbourne, or tripping from rugged Mt Hotham to coastal Mornington.

If time is an issue, the 210km **Around the Bay in a Day** (www.bv.com.au; entry fee around $75-90) in mid-October might be more achievable. This annual event attracts thousands of keen cyclists each year, and covers the length of Port Phillip Bay from Melbourne to Sorrento, across on the ferry to Queenscliff and back to Melbourne (or vice versa). For more information on highlights along the route, see the boxed text (p179).

For information on bike hire and everyday city cycling, see p108. For more useful tips and advice on cycling around the state, see p412.

FISHING

Victoria is full of fanatical fisherfolk who rise well before the crack of dawn to head to their favourite fishing hotspot. There are hundreds of places around the state where you can dangle a line or two – whether you want to fly fish for rainbow trout in a mountain stream, lure a yabby out of a dam, catch a deep-river redfin or hook a yellowtail kingfish from a surf beach.

East of Melbourne, the vast Gippsland Lakes system (see p371) around Bairnsdale, Paynesville, Metung and Lakes Entrance has been a mecca for fisherfolk for decades, with large snapper and bream often on the end

---

Excellent sources of information for pedal pushers include Bicycle Victoria (☎ 03-8636 8888; www.bv.com.au) and the Melbourne Bicycle Touring Club (☎ 03-9517 4306; www.mbtc.org.au).

Bike Paths Safe Escapes (www.bikepaths.com.au) is a comprehensive guide to the state's best cycling tracks, both city and country. Features include colour maps, useful cycling tips and a list of the best café pit stops en route. Lonely Planet's *Cycling Australia* guide covers five multiday rides in Victoria, including the Great Ocean Rd and the High Country.

of the line. Right on the NSW border, Mallacoota (p389) is another favourite family fishing spot, with excellent estuary, river and ocean fishing yielding catches of bream, flathead, whiting and mulloway.

Along the Great Ocean Rd, you'll find countless idyllic fishing villages to base yourself, including Apollo Bay and Port Campbell. Warrnambool (p219) is another fave with anglers, offering the chance to hook mullet, bream or garfish in the Merri and Hopkins Rivers, or whiting, Australian salmon and trevally off the wild ocean beaches.

Inland, patient types can learn to cast a fly in search of the elusive trout near Marysville (p326), Alexandra (p328) or Lake Eildon (p329).

Be aware that in November 2002 some 13 marine national parks and 11 marine sanctuaries were established by the state government, and all fishing was banned in these protected areas. For a full list of no-go zones, see the website of **Parks Victoria** (www.parkweb.vic.gov.au). To fish elsewhere in Victoria's marine, estuarine or freshwaters, those between the ages of 18 and 70 need to purchase a Recreational Fishing Licence (RFL), which cost $5.50 for 48 hours, $11 for 28 days or $22 for a year, and are available from most tackle shops and Department of Primary Industries (DPI) offices.

Chum up to the expert behind the counter at your closest fishing tackle shop to score tips on the best fishing hotspots in the area. Size limits and seasons are outlined in the free booklet *Victorian Recreational Fishing Guide,* which is available online at www.dpi.vic.gov.au, along with a stack of other useful fishy info.

> For the latest on fishing news, tips, licences and regulations, see www .fishvictoria.com.

> Keen anglers who plan to spend more than a day or two with a line in the water will appreciate a good guide to identify fishing hotspots around the state. Try *Fishing Around Melbourne* by popular fishing guru Rex Hunt or, if you're heading farther afield, grab a copy of *The Victorian Fishing Atlas* by John Ross.

HORSE RIDING
The sound of thundering hooves, the crackle of undergrowth, the skilful horses and riders weaving through forests and galloping across stunning snow-capped mountains, the swell of the music… It's impossible to watch *The Man from Snowy River,* the film about 19th-century cattlemen in Victoria's High Country, without getting the itch to saddle up and go trailblazing through this stunning horse-riding terrain. Some of the state's best riding is found in these mountains, and a swag of companies offer visitors the chance to find their inner jackaroo, with a choice of one-hour burls to multiday pack trips (some as long as 12 days). For some recommended companies, see the sections on Mansfield (p331), Dinner Plain (p340) and Mt Beauty (p343).

But for those who have dreams of cantering along a lonely windswept beach as the sun sets on the horizon, Victoria's coastline is an enticing alternative. Close to Melbourne, it's possible to ride through bush and beach in the Mornington Peninsula National Park's Cape Schanck (p185), or you can head farther afield to beach locations along the Great Ocean Rd, including Aireys Inlet (p201) and Apollo Bay (p208).

Prices average $30 for a one-hour ride, $70 for a half-day ride and $140 for a full-day ride.

> Largely set in Victoria's High Country, *The Man from Snowy River* (1982, director George Miller) is a rather soppy romance loosely based on an iconic Aussie poem by Banjo Patterson. But it's worth hiring for its spectacular scenes of horses galloping across dramatic alpine landscapes.

SKIING & SNOWBOARDING
Skiing in Victoria has come a long way from its modest beginnings in the 1860s when Norwegian gold miners started sliding around Harrietville in their spare time. Today it's a multimillion-dollar industry with three major and six minor ski resorts.

The snowfields are northeast and east of Melbourne, scattered around the High Country of the Great Dividing Range. The two largest ski resorts are Mt Buller (p334) and Falls Creek (p341). Mt Hotham (p338) is smaller, but has equally good skiing, while Mt Baw Baw (p324) and Mt Buffalo (p347) are smaller resorts, popular with families and less-experienced

---

ADVENTURE SPORTS

Not everyone has a taste for white-knuckle, thrill-seeking sports, but for those who do, Victoria has plenty to keep the adrenalin junkie happy.

The windswept headlands of the Great Ocean Rd and the alpine peaks of the High Country are ideal venues for hang-gliding and paragliding. For more information on schools and sites around the state, contact the **Victorian Hang Gliding and Paragliding Association** (www.vhpa.org.au).

Rafters looking for some white-water action usually find some fun rapids after the snows have melted, from around August to December, in the High Country (p325). Expect to pay around $155/270 for a one-/two-day trip.

Rock climbers have plenty of tantalising cliffs and crags to conquer in Victoria. Mt Arapiles (p275), in the Western District near Horsham, is world famous for its huge variety of climbs for all skill levels, with colourful names such as Violent Crumble, Punks in the Gym and Cruel Britannia. Not far away is the Grampians National Park (p269), where rock climbing and abseiling have become increasingly popular at spots like Mt Stapylton and Black Ian's Rock. At Mt Buffalo (p347), in the Victorian Alps, there is a variety of good granite climbs, including those on the Buffalo Gorge wall. For more information about rock-climbing sites, contact the **Victorian Climbing Club** (www.vicclimb.org.au).

---

skiers. The ski season officially commences on the first weekend of June. 'Ski-able' snow usually arrives later in the month, and there's often enough snow until the end of September. Spring skiing can be idyllic, as the weather may be sunnier and warmer, and the crowds smaller.

If you're thinking about a day trip to the snowfields, Mt Buller and Mt Baw Baw are the closest options to Melbourne for downhill skiers, while cross-country skiers can choose between Lake Mountain (p327), Mt Stirling (p336) or Mt St Gwinear (p326). See the **Official Victorian Snow Report** (www.vicsnowreport.com.au/report.html) or call the **Mountain Information Line** (☎ 1902 240 523, per min 55c) for the latest on snow, weather and road conditions.

Resort entry fees are usually around $26 per car per day in winter; cross-country skiers pay a trail-use fee per adult/child of approximately $10/5, plus a car entry fee of around $10. As a rough guide, you're likely to pay approximately $35 for equipment hire and per adult/child/family around $82/44/225 for daily lift tickets in the high season (late June to mid-September). Note that hire rates are cheaper if you hire for longer periods. For a package deal (which can include meals and/or lessons, lift tickets, ski hire and transport), you can book directly with a lodge, through a travel agent or through an accommodation booking service.

For a listing of on-mountain accommodation, see the relevant Sleeping sections in the High Country chapter (p322). In July and August it is advisable to book your accommodation, especially for weekends. In June or September it's usually possible to find something if you just turn up.

SURFING

With its exposure to the relentless Southern Ocean swell, Victoria's rugged coastline provides plenty of quality surf. But the chilly water (even in summer) has the hardiest surfer reaching for a wetsuit. A full-length 3mm to 4mm thick wetsuit is the standard for winter, and booties, helmets and even wetsuit gloves might make that extra-long session a bit easier.

Local and international surfers gravitate to Torquay (p196), on the Great Ocean Rd, home to legendary brands Quicksilver and Ripcurl, as well as the largest surf lifesaving club in the state. Here you'll find mega surf shops at Surf City Plaza, the Surfworld Museum and plenty of experienced waxheads eager to teach you how to ride a wave. Nearby, Bell's

Beach (p199) plays host to the Rip Curl Pro every Easter, bringing with it an international entourage of pro surfers, sponsors and spectators.

The Shipwreck Coast, west of Cape Otway as far as Peterborough, offers possibly the most powerful waves in Victoria. It faces southwest and is open to the sweeping swells of the Southern Ocean. The swell is consistently up to 1m higher than elsewhere, making it the place to go if you're after big waves. However, extreme care must be taken, as some breaks are isolated, subject to strong rips and undertows, and are generally only for the experienced surfer. It's probably best to surf with someone who knows the area.

For the less experienced, popular places with surf schools include Anglesea (p199) and Lorne (p203), along the Great Ocean Rd, or on Phillip Island (p189) and Lakes Entrance (p379), east of Melbourne.

Telephone **surf reports** (☎ 1900 931 996, 1900 983 268 for the Mornington Peninsula) are updated daily. Other useful resources for surfers include the websites of **Surfing Australia** (www.surfingaustralia.com), with news, events and lots of useful links to surf schools around the state, and **Peninsula Surf** (www.surfshop.com.au), which offers a brief summary of 'today's surf' for places like Warrnambool, Bells Beach, Flinders and Woolamai.

The Atlas of Australian Surfing, Travellers Edition, by legendary Oz surfer Mark Warren, reveals the biggest waves and the best-kept secret surf in Australia. Features include maps and plenty of practical advice, including warnings about monster waves, sharks and unfriendly locals.

Food & Drink

For lots of useful information on local-produce shops, wine and food matches, and seasonal ingredients, see the website of local food writers Allan Campion and Michelle Curtis (www.campionandcurtis.com).

Victorian cuisine has come a long way since its bland colonial British beginnings. Today the gastronomic melting pot is diverse and delicious, a mix of super fresh, high quality ingredients and fantastic culinary influences from all over the world. You'll be surprised by the range and wealth of food available in restaurants, markets, delis and cafés – especially in Australia's culinary capital of Melbourne, where dining out is a lifestyle.

Wine connoisseurs will be in their element, particularly in the Yarra Valley, Mornington Peninsula and Rutherglen wine regions where big-name and small-name vineyards abound, many producing critically acclaimed regional wines (for more information, see p56).

STAPLES & SPECIALITIES

Australia's best food comes from the sea. Nothing compares to this continent's seafood, harnessed from some of the purest waters you'll find anywhere, and usually cooked with great care. Don't miss it.

Don't know what fish that is? *The Australian Seafood Handbook*, edited by GK Yearsley, PR Last and RD Ward, tells you the real name, the local name and plenty more.

Victoria is also renowned for its quality land-based produce, whether it be crisp mouthwatering apples from Shepparton, delicious tangy oranges from Mildura, scrumptious berries from Gippsland or the Mornington Peninsula, gourmet cheeses from Milawa or Timboon, melt-in-your-mouth trout from the High Country, or bush foods and spices grown for a distinctive Aussie flavour.

Thanks to a large migrant population, travellers are also treated to a huge choice of global flavours and cuisines. It doesn't matter where it's from, there's an expat community and interested locals keen to cook and eat it. You can fill up on excellent Greek *moussaka* (baked dish of layered minced lamb, tomatoes and eggplant) or souvlaki (and a bottle of retsina to wash it down), delicious Italian *saltimbocca* (slices of veal and ham, rolled up with sage leaf and braised), focaccia and pasta, or good, heavy German dumplings; you can perfume the air with garlic after stumbling out of a French bistro, or try all sorts of Middle Eastern and Arab treats. The Chinese and their cuisine have been here since the gold-rush days, while more recently Indian, Thai, Japanese, Vietnamese and Malaysian restaurants have become an everyday part of the Aussie food scene.

DRINKS

You're in the right country if you're after a drink. Once a nation of tea and beer swillers, Australia is now turning its attention to coffee and wine. And lucky for you, some of the country's finest wines can be found in Victoria (see p56).

Victorians generally take their coffee drinking very seriously, with Italian-style espresso machines in virtually every café, boutique roasters all the rage and, in urban areas, the qualified *barista* (coffee maker)

VEGEMITE

Open any cupboard in any Melbourne suburb – nay, any Australian suburb – and you'll find a jar of iconic black goop. **Vegemite** (www.vegemite.com.au) was 'discovered' in Melbourne at the Fred Walker Cheese Company in 1922, an accidental by product of the beer-making process, made from leftover brewer's yeast. This distinctive vegetable-extract spread is no longer Australian owned, but no less loved by Australians.

virtually the norm. Expect the best coffee in Melbourne, decent stuff in most large centres and gourmet regions, and a chance of good coffee in many rural areas. Melbourne's café scene rivals the most vibrant in the world – the best way to immerse yourself is by wandering the city centre's café-lined lanes.

There's a bewildering array of beer available in bottle shops, pubs, bars and restaurants. There are local beers, such as Victoria Bitter (VB), Melbourne Bitter, Carlton Draught, Foster's and Crown Lager; interstate beers, such as Cascade Pale Ale, the Cooper's range, XXXX (pronounced 'four-ex') and Toohey's; and international beers like Steinlager and Budweiser, among many others. You won't have to stumble too far to find a pub with Guinness on tap.

Local beers have an alcohol content of around 4.9% (considerably higher than the average UK or US lager), and light beers range from 2.7% to 2.9%. Beer comes in bottles (750mL), stubbies (375mL) and cans (375mL). When ordering beer on tap at the bar you ask for a 'glass' (200mL) or a 'pot' (285mL).

An institution in Victoria and around Australia, Stephanie Alexander's The Cook's Companion *is a best-selling culinary resource that you'll probably spot in Aussie kitchens everywhere.*

CELEBRATIONS

Aussies love a good party – and where better to indulge in food and wine than the great outdoors? Barbecues (barbies) are big, with many celebratory toasts made over a char-grilled sausage or two. Even the traditional Chrissie baked dinner is often dropped in favour of a barbecue, full of seafood and quality steak. At this time prawn prices skyrocket, chicken may be eaten with champagne at breakfast, and the meal is usually in the afternoon, after a swim, and before a good, long siesta. Melbourne Cup Day is another popular day for barbies, though it's also traditional to dress up, and head to the Flemington Racecourse car park to sip champagne and dine on breakfast and lunch from the boot of your car.

As the Aussie palate has become more sophisticated and the food industry more diverse, food and wine festivals have increased in number and popularity. Victoria hosts countless harvest picnics, food festivals and gourmet events. The following are some of our favourites:

Prom Country Slow Food Festivals (www.slowfood.com.au; Aug) South Gippsland winter event celebrating slow food (food that is neither processed nor mass-produced). Features master classes, organic-farm tours and traditional country afternoon teas.

Taste of Victoria (www.tasteofvictoria.com.au; early Feb) A celebration of Victoria's best produce tied in with a picnic-like atmosphere at Melbourne's Flemington Racecourse.

Yarra Valley Grape Grazing Festival (www.grapegrazing.com.au; mid-Feb) Combines tastings of the region's best wines with delicious local food.

Melbourne Food & Wine Festival (www.melbournefoodandwine.com.au; mid-Mar–late Mar) Australia's largest food and wine festival is held at venues across the city, and includes market tours, wine tastings, cooking classes, presentations by celebrity chefs and the World's Longest Lunch (held simultaneously in the city and at dozens of regional centres across the state).

Gourmet Wine & Food Race Meeting (25 Apr) Held in Avoca on Anzac day. Combines horse races with gourmet food and wine.

Grampians Grape Escape Wine & Food Festival (www.grampiansgrapeescape.com.au; early May) Held in Halls Gap. Showcases top local restaurants, produce, wines and entertainment.

Winery Walkabout Weekend (Queen's Birthday weekend, Jun) Longstanding wine and produce festival held at wineries in Rutherglen, Milawa and Glenrowan, and on the streets of Rutherglen.

Elsewhere in the state, most wine regions throw harvest festivals, which combine wine tastings with samples of the region's best local produce (for more on the wine regions, see p56).

Melbourne's coffee connoisseurs continue to squeeze in to the institution that is Pellegrini's Espresso Bar (p124), still going strong after more than five decades in business.

Barbecue lovers will learn many useful recipes and tongue-in-cheek tricks of the trade from Alan Campion's Secret Men's BBQ Business *and his follow-up* King of the Grill*.*

WHERE TO EAT & DRINK

Melbourne is one of the world's great cities for eating out. The city's high food standards have spread to many areas of country Victoria, and most larger towns have an excellent range of eateries for every style and budget. In some smaller places, however, you might only have a choice between a café (sometimes dubious), a Chinese restaurant (usually pretty bland) and the local pub (often excellent – and cheap – if you like steak).

Typically, a restaurant meal in Victoria is a relaxed affair. It may take 15 minutes to order, another 15 before the first course arrives, and maybe half an hour between entrées and mains. The upside of this is that any table you've booked in a restaurant is yours for the night, unless you're told otherwise. So sit, linger and live life in the slow lane.

A competitively priced place to eat is in a club or pub that offers a counter meal. This is where you order at the kitchen, usually staples, such as a fisherman's basket, steak, mixed grills, chicken cordon bleu or Vienna schnitzel, take a number and wait until your meal is called out over the counter or intercom. You pick up the meal yourself, saving the restaurant money on staff and you on your total bill.

Solo diners find that cafés and noodle bars are welcoming, good fine-dining restaurants often treat you like a star, but sadly, some midrange places may still make you feel a little ill at ease.

One of the most interesting features of the dining scene is the Bring Your Own (BYO), a restaurant that allows you to bring your own alcohol. If the restaurant also sells alcohol, the BYO bit is usually limited to bottled wine only (no beer, no casks) and a corkage charge is added to your bill. The cost is either per person, or per bottle, and ranges from nothing to $15 per bottle in fancy places. Be warned, however, that BYO is a dying custom, and many, if not most, licensed restaurants don't like you bringing your own alcohol, so ask when you book.

Most restaurants open at noon for lunch and from 6pm or 7pm for dinner. Australians usually eat lunch shortly after noon, and dinner book-

---

Foodies seeking the latest scoop on where to dine in town should grab a copy of the *Age* on a Wednesday for its culinary section, Epicure.

Every year, Melbourne restaurateurs anticipate their all-important inclusion in the *Age* newspaper's annual restaurant guides, *The Good Food Guide* and *Cheap Eats*, which include ratings for hundreds of restaurants in the city and around the state.

TOP EATS AROUND VICTORIA

Flower Drum (☎ 03-9662 3655; 17 Market Lane) Melbourne's most famous and highly acclaimed Chinese restaurant (p122).

Chocolate Buddha (☎ 03-9654 5688; Federation Square) An excellent central location at Fed Square, relaxed communal dining atmosphere, and huge range of healthy Japanese-style soups and noodles (p124).

Richmond Hill Café & Larder (☎ 03-9421 2808; 48-50 Bridge Rd, Richmond) Established by local culinary legend Stephanie Alexander, Richmond Hill offers fabulous imaginative breakfasts, and a wine and cheese shop at the back (p127).

Milawa Factory Bakery & Restaurant (☎ 03-5727 3589; Factory Rd, Milawa) A cheese lovers' heaven (p349).

Stefano's (☎ 03-5023 0511; The Grand Hotel, Seventh St, Mildura) *The Good Food Guide*'s 'Country Restaurant of the Year' for 2005 is a must for food lovers visiting the top part of the state (p291).

Lake House (☎ 03-5348 3329; King St, Daylesford) Offers a delicious seasonal menu and an enticing dining room with lake views (p248).

Portofino (☎ 03-5568 2251; 28 Bank St, Port Fairy) A fabulous gourmet option right in the middle of quaint Port Fairy (p225).

Healesville Hotel (☎ 03-5962 4002; 256 Maroondah Hwy, Healesville) A grand old hotel converted into a gourmet mecca, with informal front bistro, stunning fine dining room or casual outdoor tables (p173).

Ripe (☎ 03-9755 2100; 376-78 Mt Dandenong Tourist Rd, Sassafras) Cute café-produce store with superb meals, and an extensive range of preserves, handmade chocolates, cheeses and deli items (p178).

Simone's Restaurant (☎ 03-5755 2266; 98 Gavan St, Bright) Outstanding Italian cooking with delicious seasonal produce (p346).

FARMERS' MARKETS

The humble monthly farmers' market is fast becoming a tradition in Melbourne and country Victoria, with 28 separate markets operating at the time of writing. These popular community events give city slickers and townies the chance to buy lovely fresh (often organic) produce direct from farmers, and give small hobby farmers and home gardeners somewhere to sell their lovingly tended fruit and veg.

For an up-to-date list of farmers' markets around the state, see the Australian Farmers' Market Association website (www.farmersmarkets.org.au).

---

ings are usually made for 7.30pm or 8pm, though in major cities some restaurants stay open past 10pm.

Quick Eats

The usual big-name fast-food outlets have infiltrated towns and highways all over the state. Other quick eats come from milk bars, which serve old-fashioned hamburgers (with bacon, egg, pineapple and beetroot if you want). Every town has at least one busy fish 'n' chip shop, particularly in the beachside areas, and it's an Aussie tradition to take your battered flake (shark) and chips down to the beach, where you can enjoy the sea breeze and be harassed by persistent seagulls.

Another Aussie tradition (particularly at the football) is the ubiquitous meat pie – usually steak and gravy in a pastry case, sometimes with vegetables added or with chicken instead of beef. Pizza has been a popular family staple for decades. Most home-delivered pizzas are of the American variety (thick with lots of toppings), but more traditional Italian woodfired options can be found in pizzerias around Victoria, even in country towns.

Keep an eye out for the more exotic (eg Indian, Lebanese, Turkish, Malaysian) takeaways, which are usually very good and offer excellent value for money.

Self-Catering

Throughout Melbourne and Victoria you'll find a superb range of fresh and affordable produce – vegetables, fruit, meat, seafood, bread and much more. Melbourne's wonderful markets are the best showcases for the local produce – for reviews of Melbourne's favourite markets, see the boxed text (p141). But in every suburb and country town you'll find good local stores that can supply your every culinary need. Most major centres also have supermarkets with an extensive range of food and drinks, and smaller towns have milk bars and small grocery stores with a more limited range of food and drinks.

VEGETARIANS & VEGANS

You're in luck. Melbourne is full of cafés and restaurants serving delicious vegetarian fare (see p122), and most regional centres and touristy towns offer plenty of choice as well. Vegans will find the going much tougher, but there are usually dishes that are vegan-adaptable at restaurants. When on the road, beware the meat-obsessed roadhouses, which generally serve traditional and bland meaty meals. It's often better to plan ahead and bring your own healthy snacks along.

EATING WITH KIDS

Dining with children in Australia is relatively easy. Avoid the flashiest places and children are generally welcomed, particularly at Chinese, Greek

'it's an Aussie tradition to take your battered flake (shark) and chips down to the beach'

BILLS & TIPPING

The total at the bottom of a restaurant bill is all you really need to pay. It should include goods and services tax (GST; as should menu prices) and there is no 'optional' service charge added. Waiters are paid a reasonable salary, so they don't rely on tips to survive. Often, though, especially in urban Australia, people tip a few coins in a café, while the tip for excellent service can go as high as 15% in whiz-bang establishments. The incidence of add-ons (bread, water, surcharges on weekends etc) is rising.

---

or Italian restaurants. Kids are usually at home in cafés, and you'll often see families dining early in bistros and clubs. Many fine-dining restaurants don't welcome small children (assuming they're all ill-behaved).

Most places that do welcome children don't have separate kids' menus, and those that do usually offer everything straight from the deep fryer – crumbed chicken and chips, for example. Better to find something on the menu (pasta or salad) and have the kitchen adapt it slightly to your child's tastes.

In Victoria, the opening dish in a three-course meal is called the entrée, the second course (the North American entrée) is called the main course, and the sweet bit at the end is called dessert, sweets, afters or pud.

HABITS & CUSTOMS

Australian table manners are fairly standard – avoid talking with your mouth full, wait until everyone has been served before you eat, and don't use your fingers to pick up food unless it can't be tackled another way.

If you're lucky enough to be invited to dinner at someone's house, always take a gift. You may offer to bring something for the meal, but even if the host downright refuses – insisting you just bring your scintillating conversation – still take a bottle of wine. Flowers or a box of chocolates are also acceptable.

'Shouting' is a revered custom where people in a bar or pub take turns to buy drinks for their group. Just don't leave before it's your turn to buy! At a toast, everyone should touch glasses.

Smoking is banned in eateries throughout Victoria, so sit outside if you love to puff. And never smoke in someone's house unless you ask first. Even then it's customary to smoke outside.

COOKING COURSES

There are several highly regarded cooking classes available in Melbourne and country Victoria for lovers of the culinary arts.

The **Queen Victoria Market Cooking School** (☎ 03-9320 5835; www.qvm.com.au), at Melbourne's historic markets, runs a range of day, evening and weekend classes from its Chef Kitchen. Classes feature a full palette of fresh produce and products from the market, along with a changing programme of local chefs (from $70).

Howqua Dale Gourmet Retreat (☎ 03-5777 3503; www.gtoa.com.au), near Mansfield, runs highly regarded weekend cooking schools ($990 all-inclusive with twin-share accommodation), and food tours run by talented chef Marieke Brugman.

EAT YOUR WORDS

Australians love to shorten everything, including peoples' names, so expect many other words to be abbreviated. Some words you might hear:

barbie – a barbecue, where (traditionally) smoke and meat are matched with lashings of coleslaw, potato salad, beer and raucous conversation

Chiko Roll – a large, spring roll-like pastry for sale in takeaway shops

Esky – an insulated ice chest to hold your *tinnies*, before you put them in your *tinny holder*

DOS & DON'TS

- ▪ Do show up for restaurant dinner reservations on time. Not only may your table be given to someone else if you're late, staggered bookings are designed to make the experience more seamless.
- ▪ Don't expect a date to pay for you. It's quite common among younger people for a woman to pay her own way.
- ▪ Do tip (up to 15%) for good service, when in a big group, or if your kids have gone crazy and trashed the dining room.
- ▪ Don't expect servile or obsequious service. Professional waiters are intelligent, caring equals whose disdain can perfectly match any diner's attempt at contempt.
- ▪ Do offer to take meat and/or a salad to a barbecue.
- ▪ Do shout drinks to a group on arrival at the pub.
- ▪ Don't ever accept a shout unless you intend to make your shout soon after.
- ▪ Do offer to wash up or help clear the table after a meal at a friend's house.
- ▪ Do ring or send a note of thanks (even an email) the day or so after a dinner party.
- ▪ Don't tip for bad service.

Mod Oz – modern Australian cuisine influenced by a wide range of foreign cuisines
pav – pavlova, the meringue dessert topped with cream, and commonly adorned with passionfruit, strawberries and kiwifruit
sanger/sando – a sandwich
snags – sausages
Tim Tam – a commercial chocolate biscuit that lies close to the heart of most Australians
tinny – usually refers to a can of beer, but can also be the small metal boat you go fishing in (and you'd take a few tinnies in your tinny, in that case – though only a few, for safety's sake)
tinny holder – insulating material that you use to keep the tinny ice cold, and nothing to do with a boat
Vegemite – salty, black breakfast spread, popular on toast, adored by the Aussie masses, much maligned by visitors

Victorian Wineries

Open the creaking door and take in the smell. The dry earth. The heady oak. The cake-like sweetness of grapes and wood and pure clean wine. In Victoria you can walk into a winery most days and have the wine's maker smile, open the bottle and pour you a glass. Now let the flavours rocket to the corners of your mouth and suck on the full, ripe deliciousness of fermented grapes. *This* is the real taste of Victoria.

Victoria is the wine capital of Australia, with the most number of wineries (more than 500), wine regions and wine styles to be tasted and slurped and enjoyed – and, remarkably, much of it is freely open to the public. Is there anywhere else in the world so open and generous with its wine? And this wine is so diverse. Hot, warm and flavoursome, or cool, crisp and pure – depending on whether you're in the centre of the state, or in the south, respectively.

You'll learn more about wine in a day of touring than you have in drinking it for years. You'll discover unknown tastes, textures and varieties. You'll fall in love with wine's magic as you explore the region that nurtures it. But don't go touring expecting to find bargains. A winery is rarely the cheapest place to buy wine, but that doesn't mean it isn't often still the best. Wine is a perishable foodstuff. It suffers badly from exposure to heat and light and, in some cases, long-distance travel (it dislikes excessive vibration). Purely from a quality viewpoint then, wine will never be in such tip-top tasting condition as it is straight from the cellar door.

> There are two great Australian wine-buying guides published each year in Australia: *The Penguin Good Australian Wine Guide*, and James Halliday's *Wine Companion*.

YARRA VALLEY

Not too long ago the Yarra Valley's wines were badly overpriced. The valley's a region with a long history of winegrowing, dating back to the 1830s, but it all fell away in the early part of the last century and only started breathing again in the 1960s, with the bulk of the wineries you see today created from 1980 onwards. At its modern heart then the Yarra Valley has had a child-of-the-'80s philosophy that greed is good, made worse by the fact that it's the closest wine region to Melbourne (its land, and therefore wine, prices have reflected that closeness).

Today, the Yarra Valley's wine prices are becoming more competitive because wine competition in Australia is at an historic fierceness. In recent years many Yarra Valley wineries have lowered (or kept static) prices, increased quality, and become better focussed on the wine styles that it does best.

> The website www .yarravalleywine.com is a great source of the latest Yarra Valley news and events – as well as information on its history, wineries, wine styles and opening hours. Worth checking if you're looking for a special event.

The Yarra Valley is a cool-climate area, which means that its wines are cool too. This is generally not a place for hot, thumping, thick shiraz – it's an elegant place where lighter, more food-friendly styles like chardonnay, pinot noir and sparkling wines are born and tended. Drive out to the rudely scenic **TarraWarra Estate** (☎ 03-5962 3311; www.tarrawarra.com.au; 311 Healesville Rd, Yarra Glen; ☺ 10.30am-4.30pm) and see for yourself: its deep, juicy, rollicking chardonnay runs flavours of grapefruit and peach along your tongue before forcing your lips to dive again at the glass.

The real rising star of the Yarra Valley is **Yering Station** (☎ 03-9730 0100; www.yering.com; 38 Melba Hwy, Yering; ☺ 10am-5pm Mon-Fri, to 6pm Sat & Sun). It's a winery of moneyed magnificence, but the quality of the wines is unquestioned. Here's where Victoria's most hedonistic shiraz lives (the shiraz-viognier blend), a wine that is as supple and soft as the inside of

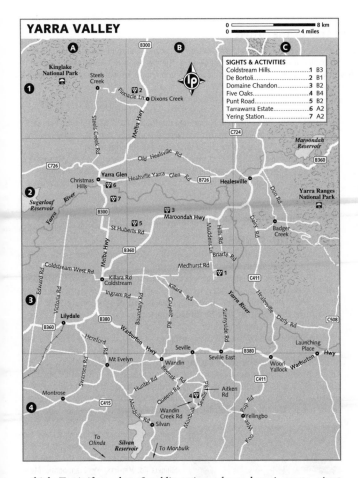

YARRA VALLEY

SIGHTS & ACTIVITIES	
Coldstream Hills	1 B3
De Bortoli	2 B1
Domaine Chandon	3 B2
Five Oaks	4 B4
Punt Road	5 B2
Tarrawarra Estate	6 A2
Yering Station	7 A2

a thigh. Try it if you dare. Sparkling wine – dry and semi-sweet – pinot noir, rosé and chardonnay here are also outstanding. This is the ultimate modern Victorian winery.

Other Yarra Valley wineries are neither less charming, nor less addictive: the cellar door at **Coldstream Hills** (☎ 03-5964 9410, www.coldstreamhills.com.au; 31 Maddens Lane, Coldstream; ☹ 10am-5pm) is a much smaller affair but its view of the valley proper is unrivalled. The green vines stretch up the hill with the dedication of a lycra bodysuit, and the wines produced from them have a blue-sky purity. Dry, tangy chardonnay, pungent pinot noir, and smooth merlot are all good here.

Other top Yarra Valley wineries:

De Bortoli (☎ 03-5965 2271, www.debortoli.com.au; Pinnacle Lane, Dixons Creek; ☹ 10am-5pm) Old-fashioned, in a '70s kind of way, but the wines are well priced and of high quality. Wines to suit all tastes. A good **restaurant** (☹ lunch daily, dinner Sat) too.

Punt Road (☎ 03-9739 0666, www.puntroadwines.com.au; 10 St Huberts Rd, Coldstream; ☹ 10am-5pm) New player. Tiny cellar door. Not a hair out of place. Great-value cabernet, merlot, and pinot gris.

'green vines stretch up the hill with the dedication of a lycra body suit'

THE BIG BRIGHT STAR OF THE FUTURE

The small addition of viognier to shiraz is a craze waiting to happen – and an increasing number of wineries know it. Look out for them as you tour around. The silkiest, most sumptuous, sexiest grand poo-bah of them all is the Yering Station Reserve Shiraz Viognier, made out of the Yarra Valley. Beg, borrow or steal for a glass.

Most wineries provide free tastings, though in the Yarra Valley and on the Mornington Peninsula some charge between $2 and $5 for the privilege – usually refundable if you purchase anything. Small price for the experience.

Five Oaks (☎ 03-5964 3704, www.fiveoaks.com.au; 60 Aitken Rd, Seville; ☺ 10am-5pm Sat & Sun) The Yarra Valley was once renowned for its cabernet sauvignon – rather than today's chardonnay and pinot noir. Five Oaks is of the old, earthy, cabernet school. Great setting.

Domaine Chandon (☎ 03-9739 1110, www.domainechandon.com.au; Green Point, Maroondah Hwy, Coldstream; ☺ 10.30am-4.30pm) The Australian outpost of the famous French champagne house. Sit down, order a glass of sparkling wine and a knob of cheese, and look out over the vineyard.

Be sure to pick up a copy of the *Yarra Valley Wine Touring Guide* from visitors centres in the region. For more on the Yarra Valley, see p169.

MORNINGTON PENINSULA

If anyone tells you that the wines of the Mornington Peninsula aren't much good, tell them they're living in the past. The place has changed. It's a wine region that started as a bit of a lark for bored doctors and soon built a reputation for ordinary, overpriced wine. Now, 25 years after they first started planting vines here, the area is full of passionate folk keen to capture the spirit of this beautiful sparkling sand-and-sea landscape in their fragrant, elegant, wine.

Main Ridge Estate (☎ 03-5989 2686; www.mre.com.au; 80 William Rd, Red Hill; ☺ noon-4pm Mon-Fri, to 5pm Sat & Sun) is the best winery on the peninsula, and while its wines aren't cheap the place captures what wine touring is all about. It's small, passionate, and vital, with the wine made at one end of the tasting room. Ripe, peachy chardonnay and exquisite, cherried pinot noir are the go. Dancing to a similar tune are **Eldridge Estate** (☎ 03-5989 2644; www.eldridge-estate.com.au; 120 Arthurs Seat Rd, Red Hill; ☺ noon-4pm Mon-Fri, 11am-5pm Sat & Sun),

T'Gallant Winery (opposite)

JAMES BRAUND

Paringa Estate (☎ 03-5989 2669; www.paringaestate.com.au; 44 Paringa Rd, Red Hill South; ☺ 11am-5pm), **Stonier** (☎ 03-5989 8300; www.stoniers.com.au; 362 Frankston-Flinders Rd, Merricks; ☺ 11am-5pm), **Merricks Creek Wines** (☎ 03-5989 8868; www.merrickscreek.com; 44 Merricks Rd, Merricks), which is open noon to 5pm on the first weekend of month, with longer hours during summer, and **Willow Creek Vineyard** (☎ 03-5989 7448; www.willow-creek.com.au; 166 Balnarring Rd, Merricks; ☺ 10am-5pm), all of which are leading producers of these varieties. Of these Stonier not only makes fine wine but is very child-friendly – something that Paringa Estate isn't particularly.

Being in cool-climate southern Victoria, the Mornington Peninsula makes largely cool-style wines. A few places do grow shiraz: Paringa

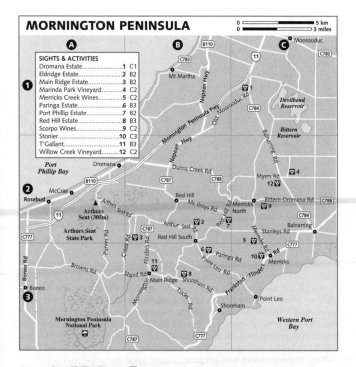

MORNINGTON PENINSULA

SIGHTS & ACTIVITIES
Dromana Estate.....................1	C1
Eldridge Estate.......................2	B2
Main Ridge Estate..................3	B2
Marinda Park Vineyard.........4	C2
Merricks Creek Wines............5	C2
Paringa Estate.......................6	B3
Port Phillip Estate.................7	B2
Red Hill Estate......................8	B3
Scorpo Wines.........................9	C2
Stonier...............................10	C3
T'Gallant.............................11	B3
Willow Creek Vineyard.........12	C2

Estate, **Port Phillip Estate** (☎ 03-5989 2708; www.portphillip.net; 261 Red Hill Rd, Red Hill South; ⏰ 11am-5pm Sat & Sun, daily Dec & Jan) and **Scorpo Wines** (☎ 03-5989 7697; www .scorpowines.com.au; 23 Old Bittern–Dromana Rd, Merricks North; ⏰ daily by appointment); and cabernet sauvignon: **Dromana Estate Limited** (☎ 03-5974 4400; www.dromanaestate .com.au; 555 Old Mooroduc Rd, Tuerong; ⏰ 11am-5pm) and Willow Creek Vineyard. But in the main you'll find that chardonnay, pinot noir, and pinot gris do best, all in a style that goes slashingly well with food.

Other wineries to consider:

T'Gallant (☎ 03-5989 6565; www.tgallant.com.au; cnr Mornington–Flinders & Shands Rds, Main Ridge; ⏰ 10am-5pm) Renowned as the maker of a salty, sexy, luscious pinot gris ripped with tropical fruit fragrance. Try it.

Marinda Park Vineyard (☎ 03-5989 7613; www.marindapark.com; 238 Myers Rd, Balnarring; ⏰ 11am-5pm) Range of wines given the full quality treatment (the best grapes, high-quality oak if necessary, and bottled fresh), and an (alcoholic) apple cider made with superior champagne yeasts.

Red Hill Estate (☎ 03-5989 2838; www.redhillestate.com.au; 53 Shoreham Rd, Red Hill South; ⏰ 11am-5pm) Great view – the best of any winery on the peninsula. Good wines, including some excellent sparkling (champagne-style) wine.

See also the Top 10 Liquid Lunches boxed text on p184. For information on the Mornington Peninsula region, see p179.

RUTHERGLEN

One of the great contradictions of Australian wine is that the Rutherglen region, perhaps Australia's highest regarded wine region on the international stage, is considered one of the dowdiest in its home country. It's

Pinot gris is a white wine, while pinot noir is a red wine. Both are made widely, and well, in southern Victoria.

With 22 Victorian wine regions clamouring for attention, wine or wine-and-food festivals are pretty much a weekly event somewhere in Victoria. A full, updated guide to Victorian wine festivities is included on www.visitvictoria.com (look under Food and Wine).

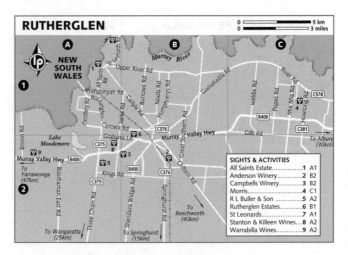

considered too hot, too stodgy, too rustic (if wine can be such a thing) and, oddly enough, too alcoholic.

It's all complete rot of course – a great wine is a great wine and Rutherglen as a region makes more great wines than most. It also makes big, sweet red wines of lacklustre quality, but what it makes spectacularly are treacle-rich, syrupy sweet, profoundly flavoured fortified wines under the names of muscat and tokay. These sell for anywhere between $12 and $350 per bottle, and at all prices they are magnificent. Pour one of these babies in your mouth and prepare to start slobbering for more. They're golden brown, aged for decades in big old wooden barrels, and taste like earth-drilled toffee. Nothing matches chocolate cake better.

Rutherglen also does the rustic, old-fashioned, affordable, great-wine-made-in-an-old-shed look better than anyone. Wine has been made there for more than 150 years and not much has changed in all that time. It's the same families growing grapes and making wine on the same plots out of the same sheds, using the same big oak barrels.

The absolute must-visit though is **All Saints Estate** (☎ 02-6035 2222; www .eldtrain.com.au/allsaints.htm; All Saints Rd, Wahgunyah; 🕑 9am-5.30pm Mon-Sat, 10am-5.30pm Sun), and when you rock up to the winery you'll see why. It's a big old castle-like building that's been beautifully maintained and preserved. Surrounding it are majestic grounds and gardens.

Not that it's Rutherglen's only must-visit winery – so too is **Warrabilla Wines** (☎ 02-6035 7242; www.warrabillawines.com.au; Murray Valley Hwy; 🕑 10am-5pm). Here the appeal's not so much the fortified wines as the table wines, though Warrabilla's shiraz and durif wines are so potent that you wouldn't want to light a match near them. Routinely weighing in at above 16% alcohol, the red wines of Warrabilla are some of the biggest, baddest, strongest red wines known to humankind. The very strange thing is that they are also very good.

The best of Rutherglen are **Morris** (☎ 02-6026 7303; Mia Mia Rd; 🕑 9am-5pm Mon-Sat, 10am-5pm Sun), **RL Buller & Son** (☎ 02-6032 9660; www.buller.com.au; Three Chain Rd, Rutherglen; 🕑 9am-5pm Mon-Sat, 10am-5pm Sun), **Stanton & Killeen Wines** (☎ 02-6032 9457; www .stantonandkilleenwines.com.au; Jacks Rd; 🕑 9am-5pm Mon-Sat, 10am-5pm Sun), and **Campbells** (☎ 02-6032 9458; www.campbellswines.com.au; Murray Valley Hwy; 🕑 9am-5pm Mon-Sat, 10am-5pm Sun). All produce superb fortified wines, while the shiraz and durif

'Warrabilla's shiraz and durif wines are so potent that you wouldn't want to light a match near them'

WINE & FOOD

Food and wine are like Lennon and McCartney – at their best when matched together. Combine them both in a vineyard setting and Hey Jude, you've got yourself a great day out. Fortunately, there's no shortage of food at Victorian wineries, with accompanying restaurants and cafés commonplace. Quality of food, wine and service is generally very good.

Top choices include the following:

Pickled Sisters Café (☎ 03-6033 2377; Distillery Rd, Wahgunyah; ☺ lunch Wed-Mon, dinner Fri & Sat) At Cofield Winery, Rutherglen.

Wine Bar Restaurant (☎ 03-9730 1107; 38 Melba Hwy, Yering; ☺ lunch) At Yering Station, Yarra Valley.

Montalto Wines Restaurant (☎ 03-5989 8412; www.montalto.com.au; 33 Shoreham Road, Red Hill South; ☺ lunch daily, dinner Fri & Sat) Mornington Peninsula.

La Baracca Cafe (☎ 03-5989 6565; cnr Mornington–Flinders & Shands Rds, Main Ridge; ☺ lunch daily, dinner Sep-Feb) T'Gallant winery, Mornington Peninsula.

Mitchelton Restaurant (☎ 03-5736 2222; www.mitchelton.com.au) At Mitchelton Wines, Nagambie (p62).

Provincial Café (☎ 03-5989 7613; www.darlingparkwinery.com; 232 Red Hill Road, Red Hill) At Darling Park winery, Mornington Peninsula.

Joseph's Restaurant (☎ 03-9731 4420; www.shadowfax.com.au; K Road, Werribee) At Shadowfax winery, Werribee.

For even more winery lunch options, see the Top Ten Liquid Lunches boxed text, p184.

---

of Campbells, Buller, **Rutherglen Estates** (☎ 02-6032 8516; www.rutherglenestates.com .au; Tuileries Complex, Drummond St; ☺ 10am-6pm) and Morris can also be good.

Other Rutherglen wineries worth visiting:

Anderson Winery (☎ 02-6032 8111; www.andersonwinery.com.au; Chiltern Rd; ☺ 10am-5pm) Inconsistent, but when they're good they're brilliant. Famed for its frothy, fabulous sparkling shiraz.

St Leonards (☎ 02-6033 1004; www.stleonardswine.com.au; St Leonards Rd, Wahgunyah; ☺ 10am-5pm) Near the banks of the Murray River; charmingly relaxed. Quality has jumped recently.

The handy *Rutherglen Touring Guide* is available from Rutherglen's **visitors centre** (☎ 02-6033 6300, 1800 622 871; info@rutherglenvic.com.au; 57 Main St; ☺ 9am-5pm). For more information on Rutherglen, including wining and dining, see p307.

NAGAMBIE, HEATHCOTE & BENDIGO REGION

The difference between Australian shiraz and the European version is that the Aussie stuff is big and boisterous while European shiraz is renowned for its cool reserve. Australian shiraz wants to shag you on the first date; European shiraz works up to holding your hand by date five. If you're interested in, or can't get enough of, the eager-beaver Australian style, then the band that stretches from Nagambie through Heathcote and on to Bendigo is the place for you. The wines are well priced, rich and bold. And the wide, open, yellow-dry paddocks, where you're highly likely to spot a wild kangaroo, are strewn with sun-bleached gum trees.

Nagambie Lakes Region

Near Seymour, this region is the living, beating heart of traditional Australian red wine. At the historic **Tahbilk winery** (☎ 03-5794 2555; www.tahbilk.com .au; Goulburn Valley Hwy; ☺ 9am-5pm Mon-Sat, 11am-5pm Sun) there's red dirt all over the floor, the big dust-crusted underground cellar is open to the public, there are press and wine-show clippings from decades past still stuck to the walls, and the wines are without fault, and of great diversity. Sweet whites, medium-bodied reds, wines that taste of thick black cherry and

The vine insect *phylloxera* destroyed most Victorian vineyards in the late 1800s, but a small vineyard patch at the Tahbilk winery, first planted in 1860, miraculously survived.

wines that are so leathery and soft you'll want to snog them. If you only go to one Australian winery – Tahbilk should be it.

Then again a visit to Tahbilk's neighbour, the **Mitchelton winery** (☎ 03-5736 2222; www.mitchelton.com.au; Mitchelton-Tabilk Rd, Nagambie; ☺ 10am-5pm), is just as essential although it's the polar opposite of Tahbilk. Mitchelton is modern, grandiose, and carries wines that are bigger and oakier (some of the wines taste like vanilla custard), but its array of reds and whites represents a good range of Australian wine. As well, Mitchelton backs onto the river, has an excellent restaurant, and for pure life-among-the-vines pleasure is difficult to beat.

If you've still got wine-energy after that duo, head up towards Nagambie and take in the **Murchison Winery** (☎ 03-5826 2294; www.murchisonwines.com.au; ☺ 10am-5pm Fri-Mon) – actually, head here first. Run by the desperately keen, desperately talented Sandra (a cheesemaker) and Guido (a winemaker) Vazzoler, you not only get to taste some rich, blackcurranty wines that stain your lips purple, but also float all your cheese and wine queries in one stop.

> Max Allen's classic wine book *Red and White* takes a rollicking ride through Victoria's main wine regions, as well as other regions around Australia. It's a gem.

Heathcote

The future of Australian shiraz lies in the deep, ancient soils of Heathcote, and after a lot of talk the area is now living up to its enormous promise. Expect to find a bevy of long-flavoured, smooth-as-silk, ripe shiraz lovelies here – and if you look hard enough, some damn fine cabernet and merlot too.

A few years ago, if you'd driven to Heathcote to find its wine gems you might have come away disappointed (the two best wineries, Jasper Hill and Wild Duck Creek, are so popular they're now closed to new customers) – but you get a much better run now. For starters, there's a good wine centre in town, the **Emeu Inn** (☎ 03-5433 2668; www.emeuinn.com; 187 High St; ☺ 11am-5pm Thu-Mon), see p321; while the **Heathcote Winery** (☎ 03-5433 2595; 185 High St; ☺ 11am-5pm) is in better wine form than ever – ask for a taste of the red shiraz-viognier blend which is so smooth and juicy it's like sucking on a blood-plum smothered in mango.

The real wine action is north of the town, up along the Northern Hwy. Here look especially for **Munari** (☎ 03-5433 3366; 1129 Northern Hwy, Heathcote; ☺ 10.30am-5.30pm Tue-Sun) and **Barnadown Run** (☎ 03-5433 6376; www.barnadownrun .com.au; 390 Cornella Rd, Toolleen; ☺ 10am-5pm, phone first).

Bendigo

Scattered around Bendigo are a number of wineries slowly-but-steadily creating a wine splash. It's a wine area that often goes unnoticed, but shouldn't. The red wines are sheer marriage material – strong, warm and flavoursome – and great Bendigo wine names like **Water Wheel** (☎ 03-5437 3060; www.water wheelwine.com; Raywood Rd, Bridgewater On Loddon; ☺ 11am-5pm) and **Balgownie Estate** (☎ 03-5449 6222; www.balgownieestate.com.au; Hermitage Rd, Maiden Gully; ☺ 11am-5pm) offer fantastic value for money. Seek them out. If visiting on a weekend, the excellent **Pondalowie** (☎ 03-5437 3332; 6 Main Street, Bridgewater-on-Loddon) is a must.

THE PYRENEES

Rough, rustic, undulating and significantly French-influenced, the compact Pyrenees wine region has over a dozen, good-quality wineries that offer a considerable variety of wine styles: flavoursome, mouth-filling, glossy shiraz is the area's best wine, but everything from good pinot noir (Dalwhinnie) to excellent, harvested-by-moonlight sparkling wine (Taltarni, Blue Pyrenees Estate), to rich cabernet sauvignon (Redbank,

Dalwhinnie) is on offer here. The wineries are also well distributed in the Pyrenees; getting from one winery to another is quick and easy. There is also a good mix of wine personalities at play here: old and new, rustic and modern. Wineries worth visiting include the following:

Dalwhinnie (☎ 03-5467 2388; www.dalwhinnie.com.au; Taltarni Rd, Moonambel; ☺ 10am-5pm) The region's wine star. Expensive, but beautiful – chardonnay, pinot noir, cabernet and shiraz. The cellar door also commands the area's best view.

Summerfield (☎ 03-5467 2264; www.summerfieldwines.com; Main Rd, Moonambel; ☺ 9am-5.30pm Mon-Sat, 10am-5.30pm Sun) Good-value, big-flavoured juicy red wines of great power and substance. Intimate cellar door. Essential stop.

Blue Pyrenees Estate (☎ 03-5465 3202; www.bluepyrenees.com.au; Vinoca Rd, Avoca; ☺ 10am-4.30pm Mon-Fri, to 5pm Sat & Sun) Wide range of styles at a wide range of prices. After having a go at some of the reds here, cleanse your mouth with the excellent sparkling wines.

Taltarni (☎ 03-5459 7900; www.taltarni.com.au; Taltarni Rd, Moonambel; ☺ 10am-5pm) Has had its ups and downs but wine quality is now on a rapid ascent. Lovely wines galore – it's the area's more traditional champion.

Redbank (☎ 03-5467 7255; www.sallyspaddock.com.au; 1 Sally's Lane, Redbank; ☺ 9am-5pm Mon-Sat, 10am-5pm Sun) Taste a bevy of beautifully prepared red wines – and you can get a coffee here. A good, small, family business.

The *Great Grape Road* is a useful wine-touring brochure available from Avoca's **visitors centre** (☎ 03-5465 3767, 1800 206 622; www.pyreneesonline.com.au; 122 High St; ☺ 9am-5pm).

> There's no grape variety called 'sauvignon' – the real names are cabernet sauvignon (red) and sauvignon blanc (white).

GRAMPIANS

Shiraz is the grape that Australia does best. And the Grampians region does shiraz as well as anywhere. Shiraz has been thriving here since the 1850s, and ever since it has made peppery, tarry, European-styled wines of tip-top quality.

The fact that the Grampians wine region was born of a gold rush has a real-life, modern advantage: the miners dug underground cellars that stretch for miles, most notably below the monumental **Seppelt** (☎ 03-5361 2222; www.seppelt.com.au; Moyston Rd, Great Western; ☺ 10am-5pm), and those cellars are still used today. Seppelt is a confusing winery. It produces both the best and the worst of wines, though these days it makes more of the former than the latter – try its excellent, purple, frothy sparkling shiraz on for size. The wines make it a must-visit winery, but the tour of the cellar 'drives' below (kilometres of tunnel dug to store wine at cool, constant temperatures) is a wine experience you will never forget.

Other significant players in the area include **Mount Langi Ghiran** (☎ 03-5354 3207; www.langi.com.au; 80 Vine Rd, Buangor; ☺ 9am-5pm Mon-Fri, noon-5pm Sat & Sun), which was recently fitted with a new, modern tasting room and is sign-posted off the Western Hwy between Beaufort and Ararat, and **Best's** (☎ 03-5356 2250; www.bestswines.com; 111 Bests Rd, Great Western; ☺ 10am-5pm Mon-Sat, 11am-4pm Sun), near the town of Great Western. Both are shiraz producers of the highest standard, and Best's is another winery worth visiting for its history alone. Both wineries have a large range of wines to suit most tastes.

Contact the visitors centres at **Ararat** (☎ 1800 657 158; www.ararat.vic.gov.au; 91 High St, Ararat) or **Halls Gap** (☎ 03-5356 4616, 1800 065 599; Grampians Tourist Rd, Halls Gap) for more details.

ALPINE VALLEYS

Wine has been produced in this northeast part of Victoria continuously for more than 100 years (particularly in the Glenrowan area) but it's only in the past 20 years that it has become a widespread winemaking force. It is now Australia's fastest growing wine region.

The area can be broken into small, distinct areas which share a common trait: they wrap closely to the foothills of the Great Dividing mountain range, some more closely than others (Glenrowan and Milawa reach out into the drier flatlands), which adds a drift of mountain cool to their generally warm, stable, summer climate.

This alpine aspect makes the region arguably Australia's most beautiful wine area from a scenic touring perspective. The valleys are green and narrow, the mountains blue and imposing, the vineyards often driven up sheer slopes. This is also the only Australian wine region where it's possible to look out at snow-topped mountains while you drink a glass of bright, mountain-pure, sunny wine. Chardonnay, pinot noir, shiraz, cabernet sauvignon, merlot, sangiovese, sparkling wine and dessert wine all grow well in this area.

For more information see www.northeastvalleys.info.

King Valley

This is a breathtakingly beautiful area and, as yet, it is unspoiled by excessive tourist traffic. The star performer is undoubtedly **Pizzini** (☎ 03-5729 8278; www.pizzini.com.au; 175 King Valley Road, Whitfield; ☽ 10am-5pm), whose (Italian grape varietal) sangiovese is fruity, fleshy, savoury and fine – as indeed are all the wines here. The other stand-out winery is **Dal Zotto Estate** (☎ 03-5729 8321; Estate Edi Rd, Cheshunt; ☽ 10am-5pm), totally focussed on quality and making riesling and cabernet of special note.

Glenrowan

Just off the Hume Hwy this is a tiny, but significant, wine-growing region. **Baileys of Glenrowan** (☎ 03-5766 2392; www.baileysofglenrowan.com.au; Taminick Gap Rd, Glenrowan; ☽ 9am-5pm Mon-Fri, 10am-5pm Sat & Sun) winery is a terrific display of historic, traditional winemaking, and includes an excellent winemaking museum. Dark-coloured, chocolatey shiraz is the star, at a range of prices, all presented in the cosiest cellar door imaginable.

The other winery of note here is **Booth's** (☎ 03-5766 2282; Booths Rd; ☽ 10am-5pm) of Taminick. You will not find a more idiosyncratic winery in all Australia. The wines are blood-rich and, for their style, dirt cheap.

For more Glenrowan wineries information see p302.

Milawa & Ovens Valley

A famous wine region dominated by a single winery: **Brown Brothers** (☎ 03-5720 5500; www.brown-brothers.com.au; Milawa; ☽ 9am-5pm). More of an institution than a winery, this is Australia's most popular cellar door, despite being ostensibly stuck in the middle of nowhere. They do things right though, and although the wines themselves are not exceptional the range is enormous and there is almost zero chance that you won't find something that you like. The tasting area is large, and the service friendly and informative. A key part of its enormous success is that visitors to the winery never feel intimidated – it's an easy, enjoyable place to spend time. You haven't really visited an Australian winery until you've been to Brown Brothers.

Although there are other wineries in the Milawa area – and the **Wood Park** (☎ 03-5727 3367) winery, based at the premises of the Milawa Cheese Factory, can be excellent – for a long time Brown Brothers has been the reign supreme. But from a pure wine-quality viewpoint though the newish **Gapsted** (☎ 03-5751 1383; www.gapstedwines.com.au; Great Alpine Rd, Gapsted; ☽ 10am-5pm), on the road to Myrtleford, now betters Tahbilk. Here everything from

Many tobacco farmers in Victoria's King and Ovens Valleys now also grow grapes and make wine. Not the first time cigarettes and wine have gone together.

an easy sweet-ish white (petit manseng) to robust, silken, voluptuous cabernet sauvignon is produced, and it's all served in a tastefully elegant setting – they even have toys and books for the kids.

For more on the Milawa Gourmet region see p348.

Beechworth

The wineries of Beechworth produce the area's best wines – but the area's best wines are difficult to come by. This area is famous for producers that go by the names of Giaconda, Savaterre, Castagna, and Battely, but none of these wineries have cellar doors. If you're in the area and you've got something big to celebrate (these wines are expensive), pick wines from these producers off a restaurant wine list or from the **Beechworth Wine Centre** (Ford St, Beechworth). Prepare to be impressed by the ultimate Victorian wines.

Of the wineries that are accessible to the public, the best is **Pennyweight** (☎ 03-5728 1747; Pennyweight Lane, Beechworth; ☽ 10am-5pm).

> For the best selection of wines from Victoria's smallest wineries, try the Cloudwine store (☎ 03-9699 6700; www.cloudwine.com.au; 317 Clarendon Street, South Melbourne).

Kiewa Valley

A new wine region and, due to its remoteness, unlikely to ever be a significant one – which is just fine by those who take the time to visit it. Near the Mt Beauty township, it's a seriously beautiful part of the world, and when you sit on the outside deck of the **Annapurna Winery** (☎ 03-9739 1184; www.annapurnawines.com.au; Simmonds Creek Rd, Tawonga South, ☽ 10am-5pm Fri-Sun) and look up at Mt Bogong (Victoria's highest mountain), it's extraordinarily easy to be charmed as you sip excellent, dry, zippy sparkling white.

OTHER REGIONS

Victoria is aflood with wine regions. Just because a region is not yet considered major does not mean it doesn't make stellar wines.

Craiglee (☎ 03-9744 4489; www.craiglee.com.au; Sunbury Rd, Sunbury; ☽ 11am-5pm Sun), just 15 minutes from Melbourne Airport, is just such a star, producing incredibly spicy, cherried, juicy shiraz of high style. West of Melbourne, in the Geelong wine region, there is increasing wine activity. The seaside **Spray Farm** (☎ 03-5251 3176; www.sprayfarm.com.au; 2275 Portarlington Rd), on the Bellarine side of Geelong, is postcard-beautiful, while the lavish new **Pettavel** (☎ 03-5266 1120; www.pettavel.com; 65 Pettavel Rd, Waurn Ponds; ☽ 10am-5pm), on the west side of Geelong, is the perfect place for a long lunch.

A short drive north of Melbourne is the Macedon region – it's one of Victoria's coolest areas and produces crisp, clear, almost sharp sparkling wines, fragrant whites and increasingly impressive pinot noir. There is also fine wine touring to be enjoyed in the Henty wine region in western Victoria – inland from the coast at Portland, on the road to Hamilton. Wine regions also thrive around Mildura, Ballarat, and parts of Gippsland.

> Wine for sale from Spray Farm winery
>
> PHIL M WEYMOUTH

Melbourne

Melbourne is Australia's most thrilling city. In recent times she has well and truly shucked off her 'always the bridesmaid' tag and come into her own as Australia's most innovative, interesting and admirable capital. Melbourne is a fabulous melange of the old and new, the bold and the subtle, the indoors and the outdoors, the planned and the impromptu. Tree-lined boulevards and stencil-covered alleys hold countless treasures and commercial endeavours to feed, clothe, shelter and entertain you; character-filled neighbourhoods and precincts hum with life; low-key stretches of sand and verdant gardens offer both escape and social outlets. It may not be as spectacularly located as other cities or have the sunniest climate, but you'll find that the locals, who come from every corner of the globe, have made an art form of cultivating what's good about the city, and that they're often of a sunnier disposition than their northern neighbours. Melbourne inspires steadfast devotion from her citizens and repeat visits from others, and attracts newcomers seeking the latest and greatest – she punches well above her weight for a city of her size. That said, don't expect brash boasts or pompous bluff, Melbourne is a gentle, beguiling, well-mannered, cardigan-clad place that just happens to produce some of the most innovative art, music, cuisine, fashion, performance art, architecture, design and ideas in the country – and don't forget sport, which shares top billing in many residents' affections. Or the coffee, which can inspire religious devotion. In Melbourne, you can feed your tummy, your imagination and your soul – and all in style.

HIGHLIGHTS

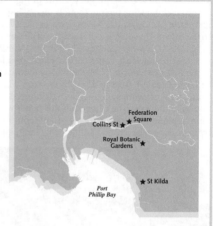

- Enjoying a truly great meal at one of the city's excellent **eateries** (p122)
- Scaling the heights for a bird's-eye view of the city at the **Melbourne Observation Deck** (p91) on Collins St
- Getting moved at the **Australian Centre for the Moving Image** (p89) at Federation Square
- Filling your lungs with sea air in sunny **St Kilda** (p103)
- Discovering your favourite new **drinking den** (p130) in one of the city centre's lanes
- Enjoying a morning shop at one of Melbourne's famous **food markets** (p141)
- Going green in the **Royal Botanic Gardens** (p97)
- Catching the next big thing in rock'n'roll at a sweaty inner-city **live-music venue** (p133)

■ TELEPHONE CODE: 03 ■ www.thatsmelbourne.com.au ■ www.melbourne.citysearch.com.au

HISTORY

Melbourne was founded and experienced its greatest period of development during the reign of Queen Victoria (1837–1901), and the city is in many ways a product of its formative era, both architecturally and socially. It's a traditionally conservative city of elaborate Victorian-era buildings, gracious parks and gardens, and tree-lined boulevards.

The first European settlers arrived in 1835, but within just 50 years Melbourne was transformed from a small village into a major city, and remains the youngest city of its size in the world. The first European settlement was established on Port Phillip Bay at Sorrento in 1803, although within a year it was abandoned and the settlers moved south to Tasmania. In 1835 a group of Tasmanian entrepreneurs returned and established a permanent settlement near the site of today's city centre. In 1837 the city was laid out in a geometric grid, one mile (1.61km) long and half a mile (805m) wide, that came to be known as the Golden Mile and is now referred to as 'the Block'.

In 1851 the colony of Victoria became independent from New South Wales (NSW), and almost immediately the small town of Melbourne became the centre for Australia's biggest gold rush. The immense wealth from the goldfields was used to build the city, and this period of great prosperity lasted until the end of the 1880s, when the collapse of the property market led to a severe depression.

Post-WWII Melbourne's social fabric has been greatly enriched by an influx of people and cultures from around the world. Several building booms, most notably that of the 1980s and late 1990s, have altered the city physically so that it is now a striking blend of past and present, with ornate 19th-century buildings sitting alongside towering skyscrapers and what seems like a million modern apartment complexes (many of them empty).

ORIENTATION

Melbourne hugs the shores of Port Phillip Bay, with the city centre on the north bank of the Yarra River, about 5km inland from the bay. Since its founding, the Central Business District (CBD) has been bordered by the Yarra River to the south, the Fitzroy Gardens to the east, Victoria St to the north and Spencer St to the west. However, the huge Docklands project has extended the western border, and Federation Square has changed the southern border, physically and psychologically connecting the city to the Yarra River, while the Southgate complex at Southbank has finally helped the city cross the river. Most of the places and attractions covered in this chapter are within the city and inner-suburban areas, and many are easily accessible by public transport. One of the easiest ways to explore the city is to take a tram ride – a quintessential Melbourne experience. The main streets running east–west in the city's block-shaped grid are Collins and Bourke Sts, crossed by Swanston and Elizabeth Sts.

The heart of the CBD is the Bourke St Mall, between Swanston and Elizabeth Sts. Swanston St, running north–south through the city, can't seem to make up its mind as to whether it's a pedestrian mall or an ordinary street, but it's a busy thoroughfare regardless. After crossing the Yarra River, Swanston St becomes St Kilda Rd, a tree-lined boulevard running all the way south to St Kilda and beyond.

Beside the Yarra River, on the corner of Swanston and Flinders Sts, is Flinders St station, the main station for suburban trains. 'Under the clocks' at the station is a popular meeting place. The other major station, for country and interstate services, is Southern Cross station (until recently named Spencer St station), at the western end of Bourke St.

The inner suburbs that surround the city centre are often likened to a ring of 'villages', each with its own particular character.

If you arrive in Melbourne by long-distance bus or on the airport bus, you'll arrive in the city at Southern Cross station coach terminal on the western side of the city centre. See p145 for more details about travel between the city centre and the city's airports.

See p149 for attractions beyond the urban area.

Maps

You can pick up a free copy of the *Melbourne Visitors Map*, which is sufficient for a cursory exploration of the city, at the **Melbourne Visitor Information Centre** (Map pp72-4; Federation Square, Melbourne) or at the **information booth** (Map pp72-4; Bourke St Mall).

The excellent *Mobility Map* of Melbourne, catering to disabled travellers, is also available

MELBOURNE

MELBOURNE IN...

One Day

Get your bearings by ascending to the **Melbourne Observation Deck** (p91) in Rialto Towers. Come back down to earth and follow our walking tour (p110) through the centre of the city, starting at **Federation Square** (p87) and ending with lunch in **Chinatown** (p92). In the afternoon, a **Melbourne River Cruise** (p113) will allow you to see the city from the Yarra, and you'll dock at **Southgate** (p94) when it's over, allowing you to catch a performance at the **Victorian Arts Centre** (p95) before having dinner and drinks at some great spot, such as **Movida** (p123).

Two Days

Art beckons, so head for the **National Gallery of Victoria (NGV) International** (p94) to see not only the art on the walls but also the stained-glass ceiling in the Great Hall. After that, visit the wonderful **Queen Victoria Market** (p92), and get consumed by the atmosphere as you consume deli goods, fruits and snacks. Unwind in one of the city's parks, preferably the **Royal Botanic Gardens** (p97), before spending time partying in **St Kilda** (p103) and dining out at one of its restaurants.

One Week

A full week will allow you to squeeze in the **Ian Potter Centre** (p88), the **Melbourne Museum** (p99) and the **Immigration Museum** (p93), plus a film or two at **ACMI** (p89). You'll also have time to indulge in a monster shop along **Chapel St** (p102), a trip to the **Melbourne Zoo** (p98) and a sojourn to **Williamstown** (p106). See Around Melbourne (p149) for jaunts outside the city's perimeters if you feel like beating the city buzz.

---

from the Melbourne Visitor Information Centre and the Bourke St Mall information booth, and can be viewed online at the **Access Melbourne** (www.accessmelbourne.vic.gov.au) website.

Street directories published by companies such as Gregory's, Melway and UBD are detailed and extremely handy if you're driving. They can be purchased from newsagents and bookshops for around $50. The *Greater Melbourne Street Directory* (by Melway) serves as the common reference point for all Melburnians, and many businesses often list their relevant grid details for the directory in their contact information. **Map Land** (Map pp72–4; ☎ 9670 4383; 372 Little Bourke St, Melbourne) in the CBD has a great selection of mapping materials.

INFORMATION
Bookshops

Books for Cooks (Map pp76–8; ☎ 8415 1415; 233–235 Gertrude St, Fitzroy) If you've run out of recipes, look no further than this fine foodies' shop, which can also help track down hard-to-find and out-of-print cookbooks, in addition to stocking all the current favourites, both local and overseas.

Borders (Map p82; ☎ 9824 2299; Jam Factory, 500 Chapel St, South Yarra) This vast store has a huge selection and late opening hours – although it lacks warmth and any sense of true bibliophilia.

Brunswick St Bookstore (Map pp76–8; ☎ 9416 1030; 305 Brunswick St, Fitzroy) A wonderful Fitzroy fixture, this bookshop has an excellent selection of fiction and nonfiction, and some of the most drool-worthy art and design tomes (upstairs).

Cosmos Books & Music (Map p83; ☎ 9525 3852; 112 Acland St, St Kilda) This stylish St Kilda shop has a good selection of books and music, and helpful staff.

Foreign Language Bookshop (Map pp72–4; ☎ 9654 2883; 259 Collins St, Melbourne) This basement bookshop is *the* place for foreign-language books, dictionaries, magazines and even board games. Staff are multilingual and very knowledgable.

Hares & Hyenas (Map p82; ☎ 9824 0110; 135 Commercial Rd, Prahran) This is the place for gay and lesbian titles.

Hill of Content (Map pp72–4; ☎ 9662 9472; 86 Bourke St, Melbourne) An intimate shop with a range of well-selected titles, Hill of Content exudes a classic bookshop atmosphere and is hard to leave once you've settled in for a browse.

Kill City (Map p82; ☎ 9510 6661; 226 Chapel St, Prahran) Not many cities can claim a bookshop entirely devoted to crime and detective novels – the books here cover everything from classic crime capers to bloodthirsty gore fests.

Little Bookroom (Map pp72–4; ☎ 9670 1612; 185 Elizabeth St, Melbourne) Your kids (and no doubt you) will love this long-established children's book specialist.

Reader's Feast (Map pp72–4; ☎ 9662 4699; Midtown Plaza, cnr Bourke & Swanston Sts, Melbourne) This is a good general bookshop in the city, with a solid range of all types of books, including travel guides and travel literature.

Readings (Map pp76–8; ☎ 9347 6633; www.readings
.com.au; 309 Lygon St, Carlton) This Carlton institution is a
godsend for anyone wanting to peruse shelves packed with
the best books, DVDs and CDs that you can think of. The
bargain table is deservedly popular. In-store appearances by
well-known local and international authors take place on a
regular basis – check the website for details.
Travellers Bookstore (Map pp76–8; ☎ 9417 4179; 294
Smith St, Collingwood) The name is a dead giveaway, and
there's even a travel agent on the premises.

Emergency

In case of emergency, dial ☎ 000; a free call
from any phone. You will be connected to
an operator who will divert your call to the
police, ambulance service or fire brigade.
See also Emergency Rooms, right.
Lifeline Counselling (☎ 13 11 14; ☾ 24hr) Available
in six languages.
Poisons Information Centre (☎ 13 11 26; ☾ 24hr)
Police station (Map pp72–4; ☎ 9247 5347; 228-232
Flinders Lane, Melbourne; ☾ 24hr)
RACV Emergency Roadside Service (☎ 13 11 11;
☾ 24hr)
**Royal Women's Hospital Centre Against Sexual
Assault** (Map pp76–8; ☎ 9344 2201; Royal Women's
Hospital, 132 Grattan St, Carlton; ☾ 24hr)

Internet Access

You'll find Internet services almost anywhere. Most youth hostels and guesthouses
have portals, many of which are free. Almost
every hotel has phone jacks in the room, and
many now have broadband access. Internet
cafés are very common in touristed parts of
the city. Access is $2 to $10 per hour, depending on the time of day you wish to log on.
E:fiftyfive (Map pp72–4; ☎ 9620 3899; 55 Elizabeth
St, Melbourne; per hr from $2; ☾ 9am-1am Mon & Tue,
9am-2am Wed & Thu, 9am-3am Fri, noon-3am Sat, noon-
11pm Sun) Recently voted the most stylish Internet café by
Yahoo Mail Internet Awards, this buzzing place has coffee,
beer and snacks available, and DJs playing nightly.
Net City (Map p83; ☎ 9525 3411; 7/63 Fitzroy St,
St Kilda; per hr from $4.50; ☾ 9.30am-11pm) Reliable
provider in this popular beachside suburb.
World Wide Wash (Map pp76–8; ☎ 9419 8214; 361
Brunswick St, Fitzroy; per hr $6; ☾ 9.30am-10pm) Cover
all the necessary bases – wash your clothes, drink your
coffee and check your emails.

Internet Resources

www.melbourne.citysearch.com.au Will tell you
where to eat, drink and be merry, wherever you find
yourself in Melbourne.

www.melbourne.vic.gov.au The official website of
the city.
www.thatsmelbourne.com.au Reams of information
about things to see and do around town.
www.theage.com.au The home page of Melbourne's
quality broadsheet newspaper.
www.visitmelbourne.com The official tourism website
for the city.

Medical Services

Travellers' Medical & Vaccination Centre (Map
pp72–4; ☎ 9602 5788; www.traveldoctor.com.au;
Level 2, 393 Little Bourke St, Melbourne) This service
dispenses excellent information about the latest vaccinations needed for travel to most countries. Appointments
are necessary.

CHEMIST
Mulqueeny Midnight Pharmacy (Map p82; ☎ 9510
3977; cnr Williams Rd & High St, Prahran; ☾ 9am-mid-
night)

DENTIST
Dental Emergency Service (Map pp76–8; ☎ 9341
1040; Royal Dental Hospital of Melbourne, 720 Swanston
St, Carlton; ☾ 8.30am-9.15pm)

EMERGENCY ROOMS
Major public hospitals with 24-hour accident
and emergency wards that are close to the
city centre include:
Alfred Hospital (Map pp84–5; ☎ 9276 2000;
Commercial Rd, Prahran)
Royal Melbourne Hospital (Map p79; ☎ 9342 7000;
Grattan St, Parkville)
St Vincent's Hospital (Map pp76–8; ☎ 9288 2211;
41 Victoria Pde, Fitzroy)

Money

Exchanging foreign currency or travellers
cheques is no problem at most banks (although they will charge you a transaction
fee). There are foreign-exchange booths
located at Melbourne airport's international terminal; these are open to meet all
arriving flights. Most of the large hotels
will also exchange currency or travellers
cheques for their guests, but the rate they
offer might not be so good. Your best bet is
probably **American Express** (Map pp72–4; ☎ 1300
139 060; 233 Collins St, Melbourne), which offers
a commission-free service if you use its
travellers cheques.

(Continued on page 87)

A

B

C

D

Medway Golf Club

1

BRAYBROOK

Western Hwy

10

Hampstead Rd

MAIDSTONE

Highpoint Shopping Centre

Fairbairn Park

Rosamond Rd

Raleighs Rd

Ballarat Rd

South Rd

MARIBYRNONG

Pipemakers Park

Riverside Golf Course

Epson Rd

ASCOT VALE

Maribyrnong Rd

Ascot Vale

Mt Alexander Rd

CityLink

See Parkville & North Melbourne Map (p79)

Brunswick Rd

Showgrounds

8

Flemington Racecourse

Smithfield Rd

Newmarket

Racecourse Rd

Flemington Bridge

Flemington Rd

Royal Park

Footscray Park

Maribyrnong River

3

FOOTSCRAY

Ballarat Rd

Kensington Rd

Kensington

KENSINGTON

South Kensington

Macaulay

Macaulay Rd

2

TOTTENHAM

Tottenham

Sunshine Rd

Geelong Rd

Barkly St

Williamstown Rd

West Footscray

Middle Footscray

Footscray

Hyde St

Whitehall St

5

Dynon Rd

Footscray Rd

NORTH MELBOURNE

North Melbourne

To Princes Fwy

Somerville Rd

Anderson St

Seddon

Yarraville

Hyde St

Ballarat St

COODE ISLAND

WEST MELBOURNE

Dudley St

New Quay Prm

Telstra Dome

3

BROOKLYN

Francis St

McIvor Reserve

YARRAVILLE

Westgate Golf Course

Stony Creek

Yarra River

Lorimer St

Victoria Harbour

DOCKLANDS

ALTONA NORTH

West Gate Fwy

YARRAVILLE

Hudsons Rd

FISHERMANS BEND

Salmon St

Todd Rd

CityLink

Blackshaws Rd

Spotswood

West Gate Bridge

Westgate Park

West Gate Fwy

Brooker St

7

Hall St

SPOTSWOOD

4

Newport Lakes Park

Mason St

NEWPORT

Newport

Maddox Rd

Challis St

See Williamstown Map (p86)

Newport Park

North Rd

Webb Dock

Williamstown Rd

PORT MELBOURNE

Sandridge Beach

Bay St

ALBERT PARK

Beacon Cove

Princes Pier

Beaconsfield Pde

Victoria Ave

Altona Lakes Public Golf Course

WILLIAMSTOWN NORTH

Champion Rd

Williamstown Cemetery

Kororoit Creek Rd

Melbourne Rd

Victoria St

Douglas Pde

Greenwich Bay

The Strand

Lagoon Pier

Station Pier

Pier

North Williamstown

Ferguson St

Jawbone Conservation Reserve

Williamstown Beach

Osborne St

WILLIAMSTOWN

Williamstown

Bay Cruises

Hobsons Bay

5

Altona Coastal Park

Williamstown Beach

Esplanade

Altona Bay

Ferries to Tasmania

6

Port Phillip Bay

See South Melbourne & Albert Park Map (pp84–5)

0 — 2 km
0 — 1 mile

SIGHTS & ACTIVITIES
Fairfield Amphitheatre.....................**1** G2
Fairfield Boathouse & Tea Gardens....**2** G2
Flemington Racecourse....................**3** C2
Harold Holt Swim Centre..................**4** H5
Maribyrnong River Cruises................**5** C2
Melbourne Planetarium................(see **7**)
RPS – the Board Store.......................**6** F6
Scienceworks.....................................**7** B4
Showgrounds.....................................**8** C1
Yoga Tree...**9** F6

SLEEPING
Asley Gardens Big 4 Holiday Village.**10** A1

DRINKING
Wall Two 80......................................**11** F6

ENTERTAINMENT
Red Stitch...**12** F5

Eades
Park

See p76

Roden St

Stanley St

Rosslyn St

King St

Walsh St

Milton St

Queen Victoria
Market

Franklin St

1

Railway Pl

Rosslyn St

Dudley St

City
Bowling
Club

54

**Flagstaff
Gardens**

•31

Singers La

Wills St

Dudley St

Batman St

Spencer St

WEST MELBOURNE

King St

Australian Federal
Police Headquarters

2

Jeffcott St

Adderley St

Latrobe St

Flagstaff

•46

Commonwealth
Law Courts

Little Lonsdale St

William Angliss
Institute
of TAFE

61

Magistrates
Court

Lonsdale St

Supreme
Court

48.30

24,30,70,CityCircle

Melbourne
City Mail
Centre

72,86

Crombie La

Gresham St

Church St

Garden
Plaza

55

3

Harbour Esp

57•

Wurundjeri Way

City
Power
Station

94

72

66

86,35,96

70

Australian
Stock Exchange

•47

4

Southern
Cross
(Spencer St)

Godfrey St

Francis St

31,109,112

King St

71

Le Meridien

51•

Flinders La

48,CityCircle

DOCKLANDS

62

69

Collins St

Downie St

Flinders St

Queens W

39

5

Car
Park

Batman
Park

Kings
Bridge

North Wharf Rd

Charles
Grimes
Bridge

Wurundjeri Way

World
Trade
Centre

Melbourne
Convention
Centre

World
Trade
Centre

86,109,112

Clarendon St

6

Charles
Grimes Bridge

Spencer St
Bridge

29•

Yarra River

41•

South Wharf Rd

49

See p84

0 _____ 200 m
0 _____ 0.1 miles

See p77

SIGHTS & ACTIVITIES
Conservatory	**1** B3
Cooks' Cottage	**2** B3
East Melbourne Tennis Centre	**3** D2
Eastern Hill Fire Museum	**4** A1
Fairies Tree	**5** C2
Fitzroy Gardens	**6** B2
Melbourne Cricket Ground (MCG)	**7** C5
Old Treasury Building	**8** A2
St Patricks Cathedral	**9** A1
Tasma Terrace	**10** A2
Treasury Gardens	**11** A3
Tudor Village	**12** B2

SLEEPING
Albert Heights	**13** D1
Eastern Town House	**14** D1
George Powlett Motel/Apartments	**15** D3
Georgian Court	**16** C3
Hotel Lindrum	**17** A3
Knightsbridge Apartments	**18** C3
Magnolia Court	**19** D2
Mercure Hotel Melbourne	**20** A3
Park Hyatt	**21** A2

ENTERTAINMENT
Melbourne Park	**22** B5
Olympic Park	**23** C6
Open Air Cinema	(see 25)
Rod Laver Arena	**24** B5
Sidney Myer Music Bowl	**25** A6
Ticketek	(see 24)

SHOPPING
Aveda Retreat on Spring	**26** A3
Counter	**27** A3

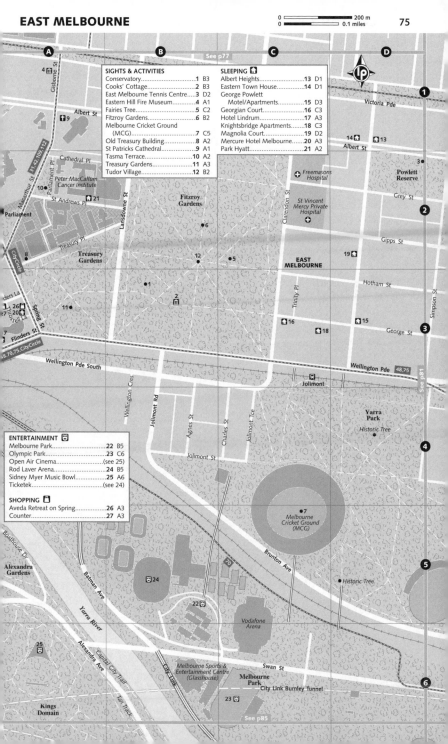

A **B** **C** **D**

1

Davis St

Melbourne
Cemetery

Princes St

Cemetery Rd East

Victoria Pl

47

College Cres

Lytton St

Lygon St

1,22,25

Neill St

See p80

Keppel St

Kay St

2

PARKVILLE

Palmerston St

Swanston St

Cardigan St

Rathdowne St

Pitt St

Canning St

Station St

Tin Alley

Palmerston St

Union Rd

Spencer Rd

See p79

University
of
Melbourne

14

62

29

Elgin St

Drummond St

24

Macarthur Pl North

**Macarthur
Square**

3

Monash Rd

3
34

46

27

MacArthur Pl South

Wilson Ave

Dorrit St

51

Faraday St

Faraday St

University St

Murchison St

Royal
Womens
Hospital

5

Bardy St

**Murchison
Square**

Carlton St

Owen St

Grattan St

4

Leicester St

Lincoln Sq
North

Argyle Pl North

**Lincoln
Square**

Pelham St

**Argyle
Square**

Pelham St

CARLTON

Carlton St

Carlton
Gardens
North

16

Lincoln Sq South

Argyle Pl South

50

5

Bouverie St

4

Swanston St

Cardigan St

Lygon St

Rathdowne St

18

Nicholson St

19

Queensberry St

22

20

1,3,5,6,8,16,22,64,67,72

Earl St

Drummond St

11

96

6

Victoria St

MELBOURNE

15

Trades
Hall

Carlton
Gardens
South

Franklin St

Bowen St

17

Mackenzie St

Victoria St

23,24,34,CityCircle

86,95,96

RMIT

See p73

La Trobe St

Spring St

0 — 200 m
0 — 0.1 miles

E **F** **G** **H**

Council St
Reeves St
Hilton St

Queens Pde

Alexandra Pde
Eastern Hwy
Cecil St
□ 12
Eastern Hwy

Brunswick St

Nicholson St

See p80

Westgarth St

Leicester St
112
Fitzroy St
Rose St
49 □
41 □
Kerr St
48 □ □ 25
35
Spring St

George St
Napier St
Emma St
Mater St
Blanche St
Budd St
Wellington St

Hotham St
Keele St

28 □

8
@
□ 64
36
2 ● □ 33
32
Johnston St
52 □
53 □
10
Argyle St

Easey St

Sackville St
39 □

Victoria St

Mahoney St

61 □

Young St
Chapel St

Johnston St
57 □

Smith St
Bedford St
Perry St

Bell St
60 □

Greeves St
Exhibition St
55 □
St David St
31 □

FITZROY
John St
42 □

Kent St

38 □

59 □ □ 26
King William St

Hanover St

40 □
Moor St

63 □

Hodgson St

9 ●● 7

Otter St

Emerald St

See p81

Stanley St

John St

Condell St

Charles St

Atherton
Reserve

Webb St

Palmer St

Fitzroy St

Brunswick St

Napier St

Gore St

Little Gore St

Little Smith St

Oxford St

Cambridge St

Wellington St

Gipps St
54 □
Glasshouse Rd

Peel St

56 □
86
21 □

Gertrude St
43 □
13 ●
37
58 44 45
□ □ □ □
1
30 □

Little Napier St

Young St

George St

Gore St

Smith St

Little Oxford St

Derby St

Langridge St

COLLINGWOOD

Little Victoria St
Mason St

St
Vincents
Hospital

See p75

24,109

0 ————— 500 m
0 ————— 0.3 miles

INFORMATION
Royal Melbourne Hospital........**1** D5

SIGHTS & ACTIVITIES
Grainger Museum.....................**2** D5
Queen Victoria Market..............**3** D6
Royal Melbourne Zoo...............**4** C3
Royal Park.............................**5** C4
Royal Park Golf Course............**6** D2

SLEEPING
Chapman Gardens....................**7** C4
Hotel Y.................................**8** D6
Melbourne Metro.....................**9** C6

EATING
Akita....................................**10** C5
Courthouse Dining Room........**11** C6
Don Camillo's........................**12** D6

ENTERTAINMENT
Arthouse..............................**13** D6
Comic's Lounge.....................**14** C6

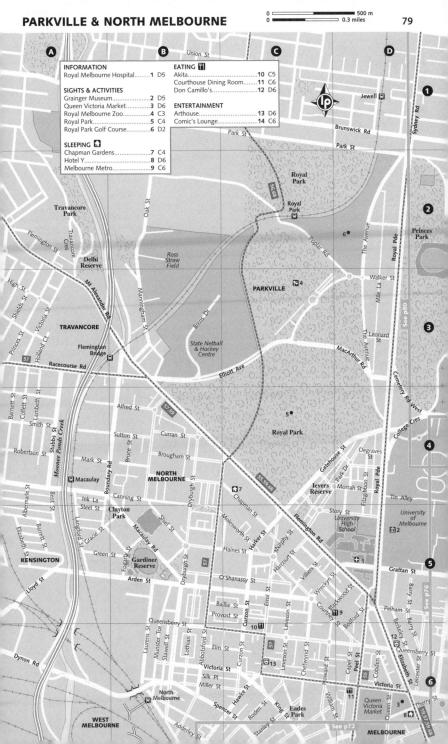

0 — 500 m
0 — 0.3 miles

SIGHTS & ACTIVITIES
Edinburgh Gardens.........................1 D5
Melbourne General Cemetery..........2 A6
North Fitzroy Bowls.......................3 C5
Princes Park.................................4 A4

SLEEPING 🏠
Quest on Lygon............................5 B6

EATING 🍴
Moroccan Soup Bar........................6 C5
Rathdowne Street Foodstore............7 B6
Tin Pot..8 D5
Zum Sum.....................................9 B6

ENTERTAINMENT 🎭
Empress Hotel.............................10 C4
Storeroom..................................11 D4

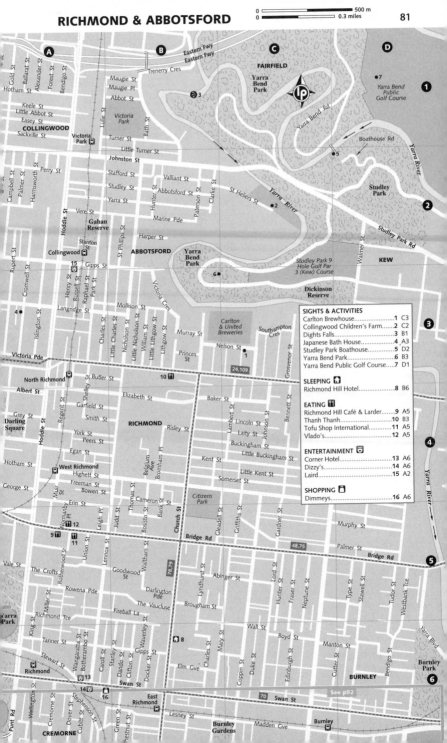

| 0 | 500 m |
| 0 | 0.3 miles |

SIGHTS & ACTIVITIES

Carlton Brewhouse	1 C3
Collingwood Children's Farm	2 C2
Dights Falls	3 B1
Japanese Bath House	4 A3
Studley Park Boathouse	5 D2
Yarra Bend Park	6 B3
Yarra Bend Public Golf Course	7 D1

SLEEPING

Richmond Hill Hotel	8 B6

EATING

Richmond Hill Café & Larder	9 A5
Thanh Thanh	10 B3
Tofu Shop International	11 A5
Vlado's	12 A5

ENTERTAINMENT

Corner Hotel	13 A6
Dizzy's	14 A6
Laird	15 A2

SHOPPING

Dimmeys	16 A6

0 _____ 500 m
0 _____ 0.3 miles

INFORMATION
Borders.......................................(see 20)
Hares & Hyenas Bookshop........**1** A5
Kill City.......................................**2** A5
Mulqueeny Midnight Pharmacy...**3** C6

SIGHTS & ACTIVITIES
Como House.................................**4** C3
Prahran Aquatic Centre...............**5** B5
Toorak Villageland......................**6** D3

SLEEPING 🛏
Como...**7** B3
Hotel Claremont.........................**8** A3
Toorak Manor..............................**9** C4

EATING 🍴
Borsch, Vodka & Tears................**10** A6
Da Noi...**11** A3
David's...**12** A5
Jacques Reymond.......................**13** C6
Orange...**14** A6
Pearl..**15** B2

DRINKING 🍷
Back Bar......................................**16** A6
Candy Bar...................................**17** A5
Pound...**18** B3

ENTERTAINMENT 🎭
Boutique.....................................**19** A5
Cinema Europa...........................**20** B4
Market Hotel...............................**21** A5
OneSixOne..................................**22** A6
Revolver......................................**23** A5
Xchange Hotel............................**24** A5

SHOPPING 🛍
Como Centre...............................**25** B3
Country Road..............................**26** B3
Dinosaur Designs.......................**27** B3
Greville Records.........................**28** A5
Mecca Cosmetica........................**29** A3
Prahran Market...........................**30** A5
RM Williams................................**31** A5
Scanlan & Theodore...................**32** B3

See p85

INFORMATION

Carlisle Contemporary Health Practice..**1**	C3
Cosmos Book & Music....................**2**	B3
Net City....................................**3**	B2

SIGHTS & ACTIVITIES

Esplanade Sunday Market................**4**	A3
Historic Corroboree Tree.................**5**	C1
Jewish Museum of Australia..............**6**	C2
Linden Art Centre & Gallery.............**7**	B3
Luna Park................................**8**	B3
Neighbours Ramsay St Tour.............**9**	B2
Rock 'n' Roll Skate Hire.................**10**	B2
Royal Melbourne Yacht Squadron...**11**	A2
St Kilda Botanical Gardens.............**12**	C4
St Kilda Bowling Club....................**13**	B1
St Kilda Cycles...........................**14**	B3
St Kilda Pier.............................**15**	A3
St Kilda Sea Baths......................**16**	A3
St Kilda Town Hall.......................**17**	D3

SLEEPING ⬆

Base......................................**18**	C3
Cabana Court Motel.....................**19**	A1
Hotel Tolarno...........................**20**	B2
Marque..................................**21**	B2
Medina Executive St Kilda..............**22**	B1
Olembia Guesthouse....................**23**	C2
Prince...................................(see 43)

EATING ⬆

Azalea...................................**24**	A2
Baker D Chirico.........................**25**	B1
Bedouin Kitchen........................**26**	C3
Cafe a Taglio............................**27**	B1
Cafe di Stasio...........................**28**	B2
Cicciolina...............................**29**	C4
Claypots................................**30**	C4
Galleon.................................**31**	B3
Il Fornaio...............................**32**	A2
Soul Mama..............................**33**	A3
Stokehouse.............................**34**	B3

DRINKING ⬇

Doulton Bar.............................**35**	C4
George Public Bar.......................**36**	B2
Greyhound Hotel........................**37**	D3
Mink Bar................................**38**	A2
Racer...................................**39**	B4

ENTERTAINMENT 🎭

Esplanade Hotel........................**40**	A3
George Cinemas.........................**41**	B1
Girl Bar................................(see 43)
Palais Theatre..........................**42**	B3
Prince Bandroom.......................(see 43)
Prince of Wales.........................**43**	A2
Theatreworks...........................**44**	B3

SHOPPING 🛍

Aesop..................................(see 43)
Dot & Herbey...........................**45**	C4
Honeyweather & Speight...............**46**	C3
Raoul Records..........................(see 30)

INFORMATION
Alfred Hospital	**1** G5
German Consulate	**2** H2
Indonesian Consulate	**3** G6
Malaysian Embassy	**4** G4
US Embassy	**5** G4

SIGHTS & ACTIVITIES
Aboriginal Heritage Walk	(see 17)
Albert Park Golf Course	**6** F4
Albert Park In-Line Skates	**7** B5
Australian Centre for Contemporary Art (ACCA)	**8** E1
Bike Now	**9** E2
Fawkner Park	**10** G4
Government House	**11** G1
Governor La Trobe's Cottage	**12** F2
Jolly Roger School of Sailing	**13** E3
Melbourne Sports & Aquatic Centre	**14** D4
Old Melbourne Observatory & Visitor Centre	**15** F1
Portable Iron Houses	**16** C2
Royal Botanic Gardens	**17** G2
Shrine of Remembrance	**18** F2
South Melbourne Town Hall	**19** D2
St Vincent Gardens	**20** C3
Sze Yup Temple	**21** E3
Victorian Tapestry Workshop	**22** D3

SLEEPING
Albany South Yarra	**23** G3
City Park Hotel	**24** E2
Nomads Market Inn	**25** D2
Tilba	**26** G3

EATING
Graham	**27** A4
Isthmus of Kra	**28** E2
Misuzu	**29** C4
Montague Food Store	**30** D2
O'Connell's	**31** C2

ENTERTAINMENT
Butterfly Club Art Bar	**32** D2
Chunky Move	**33** E1
CUB Malthouse	**34** E1
Moonlight Cinema	(see 17)

SHOPPING
South Melbourne Market	**35** D2

0 — 500 m
0 — 0.3 miles

E 🚇 33
Grant St

F
Lithingstow Ave
See p75

G
Olympic Park

H
Gosch's Paddock

🏛 8
🚇 34

Miles St
Doddis St
Wells St
St Kilda Rd
Middleton La

Govement House Dr
Kings Domain

City Link
Yarra River
Capital City Track

City Link (Monash Fwy)
Alexandra Ave

1

Sturt St
Wells Pl

🏛 11

Ornamental Lake

Anderson St
Clowes St
Punt Rd

2

15
Ian Potter Foundation Children's Garden
Birdwood Ave
National Herbarium
18 ℹ
12 🏛

17

Nymphea Lily Lake

Little Bank St
28 🍴

3.5.6.16.25.64.67.72
Melbourne Grammar School

Domain Rd
🅿 2

Park St
24 🏠
Kings Way
Albert Rd
Bowen La
Bromby St

Arnold St
Adams St
Domain St
Hope St
Millswyn St
Park St
Leopold St
Marne St
Walsh St

3

Cobden St
21 🏨
Eastern Rd
Palmerston Cres
Thomson St

26 🏠
23

Toorak Rd
8

SOUTH YARRA

Albert Rd
Albert Rd Dr
Lakeside Dr

Arthur St
Queens La

Fawkner Park

Ralston St

Aquatic Dr
13

10

Pasley St
Nicholson St
Albion St

4

Gunn Island

Albert Park Lake

6

Louise St
4
Hanna St
Albert Cricket Ground

Argo St
Margaret St
Hyland St

Punt Rd

Commercial Rd
72

PRAHRAN

5
Alfred La
🏢 1

Roy St

Baker La
Athol St

Moubray St
Wesley College

Alfred St
Donald St
Perth St

Greville St

5

ALBERT PARK

Aughtie Dr

Beatrice St
Queens La

Victorian School for Deaf Children

3.5.6.16.64.67

6 High St

Canterbury Rd

Lorne St

Andrew St
Raleigh St
Gladstone St

6

Neville St
McGregor St
Park Rd
Canterbury Pl
Langridge St

3
3.67

WINDSOR

Upton Rd

Henry St

ST KILDA WEST

Patterson St
Park St
Longmore St
York St
Village Green Dr

Union St
Queens Rd
Lakeside Dr

See p83

Queens Way
Peel St
Punt Rd

5.64

Nelson St

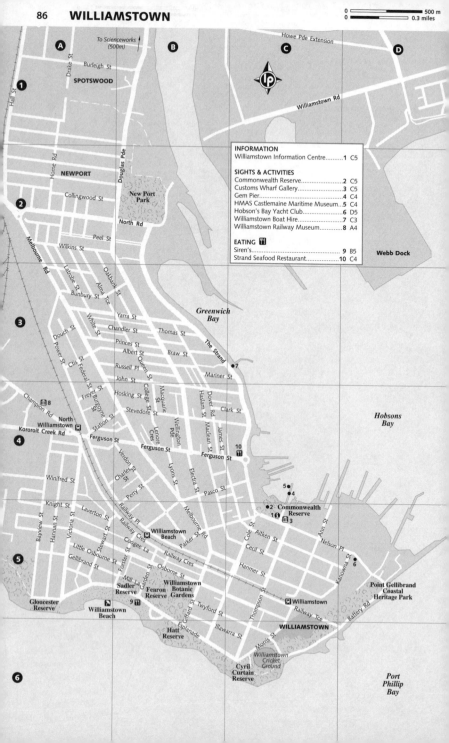

0 _____ 500 m
0 _____ 0.3 miles

A   **B**   **C**   **D**

To Scienceworks
(500m)

Howe Pde Extension

Burleigh St

Drake St

Hall St

1

SPOTSWOOD

Williamstown Rd

Home Rd

Douglas Pde

NEWPORT

Collingwood St

New Port
Park

2

North Rd

Peel St

Wilkins St

Melbourne Rd

Latrobe St

Oakbank St

Alma Tce

Bunbury St

Yarra St

White St

Chandler St

Thomas St

Douch St

Princes St

Braw St

Albert St

Queen St

Russell Pl

John St

Clis St

Federal St

Power St

Freyer St

Hosking St

College St

Macquarie St

Dover Rd

Haslam St

Clark St

Champion Rd

North
Williamstown

Burgoyne St

Stevedore St

Wellington
Pde

Maclean St

James St

Kororoit Creek Rd

Station St

Lenore
Cres

Ferguson St

Ferguson St

Ferguson St

Verdon St

Lyons St

Electra St

Winifred St

Charles St

Perry St

Pasco St

Knight St

Laverton St

Railway Pl

Railway Cres

Melbourne Rd

Parker St

Cole St

Aitken St

Cecil St

Bayview St

Hannah St

Victoria St

Stewart St

Little Osbourne St

Forster St

Coogee La

Railway Cres

Williamstown
Beach

Hanmer St

Gellibrand St

Mill La

Garden St

Osborne St

Sadler
Reserve

Fearon
Reserve

Williamstown
Botanic
Gardens

Twyford St

Thompson St

Gloucester
Reserve

Williamstown
Beach

Esplanade

Illawarra St

Morris St

WILLIAMSTOWN

Hatt
Reserve

Cyril
Curtain
Reserve

Williamstown
Cricket
Ground

Williamstown

Railway Tce

Battery Rd

Point Gellibrand
Coastal
Heritage Park

Nelson Pl

Ann St

Kanowna St

Commonwealth
Reserve

**Greenwich
Bay**

The Strand

Mariner St

**Hobsons
Bay**

Webb Dock

**Port
Phillip
Bay**

1   **2**   **3**   **4**   **5**   **6**

(Continued from page 69)

Post

Suburban branches of Australia Post are everywhere and keep general business hours.
Melbourne GPO (General Post Office; Map pp72-4; ☎ 13 13 18; cnr Little Bourke & Elizabeth Sts, Melbourne; ☼ 8.30am-5.30pm Mon-Fri, 9am-4pm Sat, 10am-4pm Sun) Poste restante services are available here, in addition to regular mail services. You'll need to bring identification.

Tourist Information
TOURIST OFFICES

Melbourne City Ambassadors can be found in the core of the CBD between 10am and 5pm Monday to Saturday. These volunteers can help with information, directions and advice about what to see, but they're not free guides. Look for them in their distinctive red outfits.

Melbourne Visitor Information Centre (Map pp72-4; ☎ 9658 9658; Federation Square, Melbourne; ☼ 9am-6pm) An excellent source of information about Melbourne events and attractions. Multilingual assistance is available for booking tours and accommodation, and plenty of printed material is on offer. It's also home to the Melbourne Greeter Service, which pairs visitors with volunteer 'greeters' based on language, age and interests for a half-day walking orientation of the city. The service is available daily, but must be booked a minimum of three working days in advance.

Information Booth (Map pp72-4; Bourke St Mall, Melbourne; ☼ 9am-5pm Mon-Fri, 10am-5pm Sat & Sun) A small information booth that has most of the same materials and helpful staff as the Melbourne Visitor Information Centre.

Information Victoria (Map pp72-4; ☎ 1300 366 356; 356 Collins St, Melbourne) Another useful source of information. This government-run bookshop stocks a wide variety of publications about Melbourne and Victoria.

Melbourne airport An information counter in the arrivals hall of the international terminal that opens to meet all incoming flights. The staff can help with ground transport into the city, as well as giving general advice about the city.

Met Shop (Map pp72-4; ☎ 13 16 38; Town Hall, cnr Swanston & Little Collins Sts, Melbourne; ☼ 8.30am-5.30pm Mon-Fri, 9am-1pm Sat) For information about Melbourne's public transport.

OTHER SERVICES

Translating and Interpreting Service (☎ 13 14 50; ☼ 24hr)

Travellers' Aid Society of Victoria (Map pp72-4; ☎ 9654 2600; Level 2, 169 Swanston St, Melbourne; ☼ 8am-5pm Mon-Fri) Offers free assistance for stranded travellers, information, advice, showers and wheelchair-accessible toilets. There are also support services for disabled, mobility impaired and aged people.

Travel Agencies

The following are some reliable Melbourne travel agencies:

Flight Centre (☎ 13 13 13, 9670 0477; www.flightcentre .com.au) You'll find these all over the CBD and in most inner suburbs.

STA Travel (☎ 9349 2411; www.statravel.com.au) This is another nationwide discount travel agency with branches across Melbourne.

YHA Australia (Map pp72-4; ☎ 9670 9611; www.yha .com.au; 83 Hardware Lane, Melbourne) This is a good budget place to look for Australian travel deals, as well as YHA membership etc.

SIGHTS

Central Melbourne (the CBD), has the greatest concentration of attractions in the Melbourne area. While it's compact enough to cover on foot, it's also possible to navigate it on the many trams that crisscross the area (see p147 for details). Other neighbourhoods that tend to attract large numbers of visitors include the burgeoning riverfront 'precincts' of Docklands and Southgate, while north of town you'll find Carlton, Fitzroy, North Melbourne and Parkville. South-of-the-city attractions can be found in South Yarra, Prahran, South Melbourne, Albert Park and St Kilda. Southwest of the CBD, at the mouth of the Yarra River, you'll find picturesque Williamstown.

Central Melbourne
FEDERATION SQUARE

The empty rail yards that once stretched along the Yarra River east of the station have now been replaced by a riotous explosion of steel, glass and abstract geometry known as **Federation Square** (Map pp72-4; www.fedsq.com; cnr Flinders St & St Kilda Rd, Melbourne), an ambitious move by city planners to create a focal point for all of Melbourne and to connect the city centre with the Yarra River. Since it opened in 2002, Federation Square has become the city's new hub, where visitors and locals gather, and cultural events take place.

To bridge the gap between the city and the river, engineers built a 3.8-hectare deck over the rail yards on the eastern side of Flinders St station. Over this, they constructed one of the most daring architectural experiments that this city has ever seen – for a long time

MELBOURNE

TOP FIVE FREE MELBOURNE

Many of Melbourne's attractions are available to all and sundry without the need to open your wallet. Here are our five faves:

- Most of Melbourne's parks and gardens are free to visit, including the **Royal Botanic Gardens** (p97), **St Kilda Botanical Gardens** (p103), **Birrarung Marr** (opposite), **Flagstaff Gardens** (p94) and **Fitzroy Gardens** (p93).

- There are a number of opportunities to visit art galleries for nix, including the permanent collections at the **Ian Potter Centre: NGV Australia** (below) and the **NGV International** (p94), and the commercial galleries on Flinders Lane.

- The beautifully situated **Shrine of Remembrance** (p96) is free, offers good views of the city, and is an oasis of solemnity and calm.

- Any of Melbourne's markets are worth a visit, to see what's on offer or just to people-watch – our personal picks are the **Queen Victoria Market** (p92) and **South Melbourne Market** (p141).

- The **City Circle Tram** (p113) is a free ride around town for when you simply can't put your legs under any more strain – and all to the accompaniment of informative recorded commentary.

---

residents debated whether it was shaping up to be a success or failure, but it looks as though the city is unanimous – it's a winner.

The design for the main buildings of Federation Square was the product of an international competition won by the Lab architecture studio of London, in association with the firm of Bates Smart of Melbourne. The futuristic design takes the triangle as one of its central decorative motifs, the permutations of which are endlessly played out in the steel, glass and sandstone faces of the buildings.

Federation Square is centred on its **plaza**, a spacious open courtyard that extends from Princes Bridge deep into the complex. Sadly, disabled access for the plaza is not what it could be, although the interiors of the complex are good in this respect. The new **Melbourne Visitor Information Centre** (p87) is in the Shard Building at the northwestern corner of the plaza. Opposite the visitors centre is a commercial building that houses a flashy **pub** and a variety of **eateries** that overlook the Yarra River.

Next along is the dramatic glass and steel **atrium**, and the adjoining **amphitheatre**. The atrium functions as an undercover walkway between Flinders St and the Yarra side of the complex, along which visitors can stop for coffee at the cafés and restaurants lining the promenade. The 450-seat amphitheatre serves as a venue for musical, stage and public events.

The complex is also home to the Ian Potter Centre: NGV Australia (below) and ACMI (opposite).

IAN POTTER CENTRE: NGV AUSTRALIA

This rather awkwardly named **gallery** (Map pp72-4; ☎ 8662 1553; www.ngv.vic.gov.au/ngvaustralia; Federation Square; admission free; 10am-5pm Mon-Thu, 10am-9pm Fri, 10am-6pm Sat & Sun) is housed in a dramatic building at the eastern end of Federation Square. The centre houses the NGV's impressive collection (over 20,000 pieces) of Australian art from the colonial to the modern periods, freeing the old St Kilda Rd premises of the gallery to concentrate on its international collection and international exhibitions.

The fine collection of well-known Australian painters includes the work of modernists Sir Sidney Nolan, Arthur Boyd, Fred Williams, Albert Tucker and John Perceval, and Australian impressionists, including the Heidelberg school's Tom Roberts, Frederick McCubbin, Charles Condor and Arthur Streeton (for more information see p35). Female Australian artists represented at the gallery include the impressionists Jane Sutherland and Clara Southern, as well as Margaret Preston and, in contemporary art, Rosalie Gascoigne, Bea Maddock and Janet Davison. Newer works include sculptor Ricky Swallow's *iMan* skulls, Howard Arkley's airbrushed renditions of Melbourne suburbia and various photographic works.

The ground floor of the gallery features the popular Aboriginal and Torres Strait Islander collection. Temporary exhibitions (you often need to pay for these) can be found on other floors throughout the year.

AUSTRALIAN CENTRE FOR THE MOVING IMAGE

On the northern side of Federation Square's plaza stands **ACMI** (Map pp72-4; ☎ 9663 2583; www .acmi.net.au; Federation Square; ☟ 10am-6pm), a museum dedicated to film, TV and digital media. The centre's facilities include the Screen Gallery, a state-of-the-art digital gallery; cinemas; a studio; a lending library; and research facilities. The Screen Gallery is the centre's main showcase and hosts a variety of image-based exhibitions, both domestic and international. The building is also the new headquarters of SBS (the Special Broadcasting Services of Australia), Australia's multicultural broadcaster.

An intriguing addition to Melbourne's cultural landscape, ACMI has been beset by infighting and funding problems since it opened, but is easily one of the more rewarding sights in town – especially if you can catch a screening (times vary) of a cinematic gem or a script reading at the regular **Popcorn Taxi** (www.popcorntaxi.com.au) events.

BIRRARUNG MARR

Melbourne's first major park in over 100 years, **Birrarung Marr** (Map pp72-4; ☎ 9658 9955; Batman Ave) lies between Federation Square, Batman Ave and the Yarra River. The 8.3-hectare park, comprising undulating hillocks, native plants, barbecues and bike paths was built in conjunction with Federation Square and makes use of land that had formerly been sitting empty or occupied by the Flinders St rail yards.

The park is divided into three terraces of varying levels, all of which are connected by elevated footbridges. In the centre of the park, the **Federation Bells** are a collection of specially commissioned bells that play a variety of compositions between 8am and 9am, 12.30pm and 1.30pm, and 5pm and 6pm.

The park can be reached from the Federation Square car park, Batman Ave or by walking along the river. **ArtPlay** (☎ 9664 7900; www.artplay.com.au) is housed in one of the old railway buildings on-site and offers creative

weekend and holiday workshops for children between five and 12 years of age.

SWANSTON ST

Running through the heart of the city, Swanston St passes City Square and the Westin Melbourne (p118) as it makes its way from the Yarra River up to the State Library of Victoria. City decision makers have decided in the past to turn it into a pedestrian mall, but at present it's open to vehicular traffic after 7pm. Unfortunately, much of the lower stretch of the street is still decidedly low-rent in tone – a mix of souvenir stores, fast-food outlets and people who look as though they'd rather be elsewhere. Attempts to elevate the mood of the street are travelling at a pace commensurate with the many trams that travel the strip.

At street level, the **Manchester Unity Building** (Map pp72-4; cnr Swanston & Collins Sts) is easily missed, but if you raise your eyes you'll see a marvellous example of a 1930s Art Deco building. It had the city's first escalators, and the original ventilation system was cooled in summer by tons of ice!

The **Melbourne Town Hall** (Map pp72-4; tour bookings ☎ 9658 9658; townhalltour@melbourne.vic.gov .au; cnr Swanston & Collins Sts), built between 1870 and 1880, is another fine civic building (don't miss the beautiful wood-panelled Council Chamber). Until the Melbourne Concert Hall was built across the river in the arts precinct (p94), this was Melbourne's main concert venue; one of the most memorable 'performances' given here was the balcony appearance by the Beatles in front of thousands of hysterical fans during their 1964 tour of Australia. Free guided tours of the building are held at 11am and 1pm from Monday to Friday, and on the first Saturday of each month at 11am, noon and 1pm. The tour includes a wander round the back to view the magnificent 10,000-pipe organ. This instrument was of international significance as the largest entirely new organ built within the British Empire during the interwar period, and was widely recognised for its symphonic qualities and extraordinary solidity of construction.

The current **Melbourne City Baths** (Map pp76-8; ☎ 9663 5888; www.melbournecitybaths.com.au; cnr Swanston & Victoria Sts; ☟ 6am-10pm Mon-Thu, 6am-8.30pm Fri, 8am-6pm Sat & Sun) were built in 1903 in the Edwardian baroque style (colloquially nicknamed 'blood and bandages' – you'll see why) and originally served as the public baths in a bid to stop locals from washing themselves in the grotty Yarra River. With the addition of a gymnasium and squash courts (see p110) in 1980, the City Baths are a great place for a dip (see p110) and a workout.

State Library of Victoria

Between Little Lonsdale and Latrobe Sts, the **State Library** (Map pp72-4; ☎ 8664 7000; www .slv.vic.gov.au; 328 Swanston St; admission free; ☒ 10am-9pm Mon-Thu, 10am-6pm Fri-Sun) was built in various stages from 1854 and boasts a Classical Revival façade. When it was completed in 1913, the reinforced concrete dome over the octagonal **La Trobe Reading Room** was the largest of its kind in the world. After 1959 the copper sheeting installed over the skylights maintained a scholarly gloom over the space, but this was removed in 2002 and light now illuminates the period features, oak desks and heavy chairs, not to mention any reading material you may have once strained your eyes over.

The library's collection is notable for its coverage of the humanities and social sciences, as well as art, music, performing arts, Australiana and rare books dating back to a 4000-year-old Mesopotamian tablet. The collection also includes the records from the ill-fated Burke and Wills expedition to be the first Europeans to cross Australia from south to north in 1860-61, and various interesting items are on display.

COLLINS ST

Melbourne's most elegant streetscape, Collins St has both a fashionable end and a financial end: the western end (from Elizabeth St to Spencer St) is home to bankers and stockbrokers, while the eastern or top end is mostly five-star hotels and exclusive boutiques. The top end is generally known as the 'Paris end' because it is lined with plane trees (beautifully fairy-lit at night), grand buildings, upmarket European boutiques (Chanel, Hermès and the like) and street cafés, and exudes a certain stately, gracious charm.

Facing each other on the northwestern and northeastern corners of Russell and Collins Sts are two of Melbourne's most historic churches: the 1873 **Scots Church** (Map pp72-4; 140 Collins St), built in the decorative Gothic style, and the 1866 **St Michael's Church** (Map pp72-4; 120 Collins St), the first church in

Victoria to be built in the Lombardic Romanesque style. The **Athenaeum Theatre** (Map pp72-4; ☎ 188 Collins St) dates back to 1886 and is topped by a statue of Athena, the Greek goddess of wisdom. Across the road is the magnificent **Regent Theatre** (Map pp72-4; 191 Collins), which underwent a major restoration and reopened in the mid-1990s after being saved from demolition. It now hosts mostly mainstream blockbuster theatrical fare.

The section of Collins St between Swanston and Elizabeth Sts contains some interesting examples for students of 1930s architecture, a period in which the emphasis lay more on façades and external ornamentation than on integrated design. Some of the better buildings are the former **Wertheim's Lyric House** (248 Collins St) and the Art Deco **Kodak House** (252 Collins St), with its lovely stainless-steel façade.

Block Arcade (Map pp72–4), which runs between Collins and Elizabeth Sts, was built in 1891 and is a beautifully intact 19th-century shopping arcade. Its design was inspired by the Galleria Vittorio Emanuele II in Milan, and features intricate mosaic-tiled floors, marble columns, Victorian window surrounds and the magnificently detailed plasterwork of the upper walls. The arcade has been fully restored, and houses some specialist shops. Connecting Block Arcade with Little Collins St, **Block Place** is a bustling lane filled with cafés, outdoor tables, an endless stream of caffeine fiends and a few clothes shops.

The financial sector also has some of Melbourne's best-preserved old buildings. The original façade of the **CBA Bank** (333 Collins St) building was one of the most extreme examples of classicism of its time, but unfortunately the bank decided to 'update' its image in 1939 and the new façade represents the austerity of between-the-wars architecture. The interior is another matter, however, and you should wander inside to enjoy the restored magnificence of the domed foyer.

The block between William and King Sts provides a striking contrast between the old and the new. The Gothic façade of the three **Olderfleet Buildings** (471-477 Collins St) has been well preserved, and **Le Meridien at Rialto** (495 Collins St) is an imaginative five-star hotel behind the façades of two marvellous old Venetian Gothic buildings, with the original cobbled lane between them covered as an internal atrium. These older buildings are dwarfed by the soaring **Rialto Towers** (Map pp72-4; 525 Collins St), one of Melbourne's tallest buildings. See below for details on the Rialto's observation deck.

At the **Stock Exchange Building** (Map pp72-4; 530 Collins St) you can wander through the impressive central foyer and check out the glass-fronted lifts running up the outside of the atrium. Since the computerisation of the exchange, there's not much to see in the public gallery apart from a big screen and some public terminals.

Melbourne Observation Deck

On the 55th floor of what was until recently Melbourne's tallest building, the Rialto Towers, is the justifiably popular **Melbourne Observation Deck** (Map pp72-4; ☎ 9629 8222; www.melbournedeck.com.au; 525 Collins St; adult/concession/child $12.50/9/7; ☽ 10am-10pm), which offers spectacular 360-degree views of Melbourne's surrounds. You can get to the top by stairs (over 1250 of them) or by ear-popping lift (elevator). It's a great way to orientate yourself (thanks to the free binoculars), and the admission price includes a screening of a short video about Melbourne. For wheelchair access, use the Collins St entrance to the building.

At the time of writing, **Eureka Tower** (Southbank), a modern apartment complex due to be completed in late 2005, had just become the tallest building in Melbourne. When completed, it will be 300m high, and it too will have an observation deck.

BOURKE ST

The area in and around the centre of Bourke St is home to the city's main department stores and some high-street vendors. The mall section between Swanston and Elizabeth Sts is closed to traffic, and pedestrians share the **Bourke St Mall** with an assortment of buskers and trams (beware the latter!).

On the corner of Bourke and Elizabeth Sts you'll find the **GPO building** (Map pp72-4) which suffered a fire in September 2001 and has risen from the ashes in its new incarnation of (what else?) an agglomeration of speciality stores and natty boutiques.

On the other side of the mall, the **Royal Arcade** (Map pp72-4; www.royalarcade.com.au) built from 1869 to 1870 is Melbourne's oldest arcade. It's lined with souvenir, travel, food and jewellery shops, and if you look up you'll see the fine detail of the original 19th-century arcade. At the Little Collins

St end of the arcade, the tall figures of **Gog** and **Magog** stand guard. These mythological giants were modelled on the original figures in London's Guildhall University and have been striking the hour (with their hammers) on the clock since 1892.

SPRING ST

Standing at the eastern end of Collins St beside the Treasury Gardens, the **Old Treasury Building** (Map p75; ☎ 9651 2233; www.oldtreasurymuseum.org.au; Spring St; adult/concession $8.50/5; ☽ 9am-5pm Mon-Fri, 10am-4pm Sat & Sun) is considered Melbourne's most elegant 19th-century building. Built in 1862 with huge basement vaults to store much of the $200 million worth of gold that came from the Victorian goldfields, it was designed by the 19-year-old government draftsman JJ Clark, who went on to become one of the city's finest architects. It now houses three permanent exhibitions ('Built on Gold', 'Making Melbourne', and 'Growing up in the Old Treasury') in the **Gold Treasury Museum**.

Between Bourke and Little Collins Sts, the **Windsor Hotel** (Map pp72-4; ☎ 9633 6000; www.thewindsor.com.au; 103 Spring St) is a marvellous reminder of the 19th century and a time when things were built not only to last but to impress. Constructed in 1883 and designed by Charles Webb, the hotel was extensively refurbished in the 1980s, allowing it to retain the title of the city's grandest hotel. If you're not staying here, it's still well worth a look (see p115).

Opposite the Windsor Hotel, the **Parliament House of Victoria** (Map pp72-4; ☎ 9651 8568; www.parliament.vic.gov.au; Spring St) building was started in 1856, when the two main chambers, the Lower House (Legislative Assembly) and the Upper House (Legislative Council), were built. The library was built in 1860, Queen's Hall in 1879, and the original plans also included a dome over the entrance. The dome is still on the drawing board (and no doubt always will be), and the side façades were never completed to plan. Despite being incomplete, this structure is still the city's most impressive public building. Australia's first federal parliament sat here from 1901, before moving to Canberra in 1927.

The interiors are superb and well worth seeing. There are free half-hour tours at 10am, 11am, noon, 2pm, 3pm and 3.45pm from Monday to Friday on days when parliament isn't in session. Ask about the story behind the second ceremonial mace that went missing from the Lower House in 1891 – rumour has it that it ended up in a brothel of a different sort. The tour guide points out some fascinating design aspects and explains the symbolism underlying much of the ornamentation. Another way to see the houses is to visit when parliament is in session, and these tours can be arranged by phoning or visiting the website.

The small and pretty **gardens** behind Parliament House are open to the public, as are the **Parliament Gardens** (Map pp72–4) to the north. The steps of Parliament House give great views of Bourke St, the Windsor Hotel and the elaborate façade of the restored **Princess Theatre** (Map pp72–4).

At the top of Spring St, the building of the **Royal Australasian College of Surgeons** (Map pp72–4) stands alone, a marvellous and restrained example of 1930s architecture, which is unfortunately not open to the public.

CHINATOWN
Little Bourke St has been the centre for the Chinese community in Melbourne since the days of the gold rush, and it's a fascinating walk along the section from Spring St to Swanston St.

Chinatown is the only area of continuous Chinese settlement in the country, as well as being one of Melbourne's most intact 19th-century streetscapes. In the 1850s the Chinese set up their shops alongside brothels, opium dens, boarding houses and herbalists; these days, the area is much more salubrious and is dominated by restaurants and discount traders. It still retains its industrious, entrepreneurial air though, and is a sensory delight.

Check out the former **Chinese Mission Hall**, built in 1894 by a Chinese evangelist. The interesting **Museum of Chinese Australian History** (Map pp72–4; ☎ 9662 2888; 22 Cohen Pl; adult/concession $6.50/4.50; ☒ 10am-5pm) documents the long history of Chinese people in Australia. The museum's entrance used to be guarded by Dai Loong, a huge Chinese dragon that has since been replaced by the 218kg Millennium Dragon, which snakes its way through the city streets during Chinese New Year (see p114). The museum also conducts walking tours around Chinatown for $15/12 adult/concession. The tours last two hours and commence at 11am Monday to Friday.

There are many well-preserved old buildings and warehouses in Little Bourke St and in the narrow cobbled lanes that run off it, and it can be fun just to wander around, especially if you're hungry. Sunday morning yum cha is very popular with Australians of Chinese descent and everyone else in Melbourne, and this is the busiest and liveliest time to visit. For eating reviews of the area, see under Central Melbourne, p122.

QUEEN VICTORIA MARKET
Bounded by Elizabeth, Victoria, Franklin and Peel Sts, the **Queen Victoria Market** (Map p79; ☎ 9320 5822; www.qvm.com.au; 513 Elizabeth St; ☒ 6am-2pm Tue & Thu, 6am-6pm Fri, 6am-3pm Sat, 9am-4pm Sun) is the mother of all Melbourne markets. A lively mix of Melburnians and visitors flock here to shop for a wide variety of produce and goods: fresh fruit and vegetables, meat, fish, seafood, poultry, deli and baked goods, clothing and general wares. Saved from demolition in the 1970s, the market has been on the site for more than 130 years, and many of the sheds and buildings are registered by the National Trust.

If you want an up-close look at the market, why not consider taking a tour? There are a couple of options to choose from and they are a great way to feel at home in the chaotic atmosphere. For more information, visit the website.

OLD MELBOURNE GAOL
This gruesome old jail, now a **penal museum** (Map pp76–8; ☎ 9663 7228; Russell St; adult/child $12.50/7.50; ☒ 9.30am-5pm), is at the northern end of Russell St. It was built, with bluestone, in 1851–53 and used until 1929. In all, 135 prisoners were hanged here. It's a dark, dank and spooky place, and its displays include death masks and histories of noted bushrangers and convicts, Ned Kelly's iconic armour, the very gallows from which Ned was hanged and some fascinating records of early 'transported' convicts, indicating just what flimsy excuses could be used to pack people off to Australia's unwelcoming shores. There are some rather camp candlelight tours (not suitable for children under 12) of the jail at 7.30pm on Wednesday, Friday, Saturday and Sunday that cost $57.60/20/13 per family/adult/child – book through **Ticketek** (☎ 13 28 49).

IMMIGRATION MUSEUM

The inspiring **Immigration Museum** (Map pp72-4; ☎ 9927 2700; 400 Flinders St; adult/concession & child $6/free; ☺ 10am-5pm) uses multimedia displays to give a moving account of the lives of Melbourne's immigrants from the early 19th century to the present day. The museum is housed in the beautifully restored Old Customs House (1858–76), which dates back to the days when ships sailed up the Yarra as far as the former Queen's Wharf, at the end of Queen St. Make sure you catch sight of the Long Room, an extraordinary example of Renaissance Revival architecture, and then visit any of the worthy temporary exhibitions that are held on the museum's 2nd floor, often focusing on immigration-related topics, such as death, cooking and transport.

MELBOURNE AQUARIUM

On the river's edge, opposite the imposing Crown Casino, you'll find the **Melbourne Aquarium** (Map pp72-4; ☎ 9620 0999; www.melbourneaquarium .com.au; cnr Queens Wharf Rd & King St; adult/concession/child $22/14/12; ☺ 9.30am-6pm Feb-Dec). The highlights of the aquarium are its floor-to-ceiling coral tank, the 360-degree fishbowl viewing area and the 2.2-million-litre oceanarium. Catching sight of various creatures of the deep has proved popular with many of the city's visitors, and it's a good place to bring the kids, especially if you catch one of the feeding sessions. If you've the time, money and inclination, it's hard to beat a dive with the sharks ($124 to $264 depending on your experience and equipment needs). The aquarium is open until 9pm in January.

OTHER NOTABLE BUILDINGS

Melbourne is an intriguing blend of the soaring new and the stately old, and a few places manage to combine the two sympathetically. The **Melbourne Central** (Map pp72-4; www.melbournecentral.com.au; Latrobe St; ☺ 10am-6pm Mon-Thu, 10am-9pm Fri, 10am-6pm Sat, 11am-6pm Sun) complex, between Elizabeth and Swanston Sts, swallowed a number of Melbourne's smaller streets and alleys when it was first constructed as a monolithic shopping and office complex in the 1990s. Since its recent redevelopment (2004), many of these alleyways have been reinserted into the structure, to give it a more 'authentic' feel. The centrepiece of the building is still the old **shot tower**, which was built on the site in 1889.

Some other notable city buildings include the simple 1848 Georgian **John Smith's House** (Map pp72-4; 300 Queen St); the massive structure of the 1874–84 **Law Courts (now Supreme Court) building** (Map pp72-4; William St), between Little Bourke and Lonsdale Sts; the 1872 **Old Royal Mint** (Map pp72-4; 280-318 William St), adjacent to the Flagstaff Gardens; and the 1842 **St James Cathedral** (Map pp72-4; 419 King St), which was moved to its present site in 1913 and is Melbourne's oldest surviving building.

Victoriana enthusiasts may also find some very small Melbourne buildings of interest – scattered around the city are a number of very fine cast-iron men's urinals. They mainly date from 1903 to 1914, and the **pissoir** on the corner of Exhibition and Lonsdale Sts is classified by the National Trust.

FITZROY & TREASURY GARDENS

The leafy **Fitzroy Gardens** (Map p75; www.fitzroygardens.com; btwn Wellington Pde, Clarendon, Lansdowne & Albert Sts, East Melbourne) divide the city centre from East Melbourne and serve as a verdant retreat from city life. With their stately avenues lined with English elms, these gardens are a popular spot for wedding photographers – on weekend afternoons there's a procession of wedding cars waiting for sundry brides, grooms and attendants to be immortalised on their big day.

Governor La Trobe's nephew designed the original layout in 1857, which featured paths in the form of the Union Jack. James Sinclair, the first curator, was landscape gardener to the Russian tsar Nicholas I until the Crimean War (1853–56) cut short his sojourn. Sinclair amended and softened the original design, and the gardens are now a rambling blend of elm and cedar avenues, fern gullies, flowerbeds and lawns.

In the centre of the gardens are ferneries, fountains and a café. By the kiosk is a miniature **Tudor village** and the **Fairies' Tree**, carved in 1932 by the writer Ola Cohn. The painted carvings around the base of the tree depict fairies, pixies, kangaroos, possums and emus.

In the northwestern corner of the gardens is the **People's Path**, a circular path paved with 10,000 individually engraved bricks that is the nicest bit of whimsy in any park in Melbourne.

Captain Cook's Cottage (Map p75; ☎ 9419 4677; www.cookscottage.com.au; adult/child $4/2; ☺ 9am-5pm)

MELBOURNE

is actually the former Yorkshire home of the distinguished English navigator's parents. It was dismantled, shipped to Melbourne and reconstructed stone by stone in 1934. The cottage is furnished and decorated as it would have been around 1750, complete with handmade furniture and period fittings. There is an interesting exhibit on Cook's life and achievements during his great exploratory voyages of the southern hemisphere.

Nearby, the **Conservatory** (Map p75; admission free; ☼ 9am-5pm), built in 1928, is looking a little dated from the outside, but the glorious floral displays and tropical-rainforest atmosphere inside are well worth a look.

The smaller **Treasury Gardens** (Map p75), a popular lunch-time spot, contain a **memorial to John F Kennedy**, who may not seem the most obvious candidate for a Melbourne memorial, but it's a soothing place to unwind regardless.

FLAGSTAFF GARDENS

The **Flagstaff Gardens** (Map pp72-4; btwn Latrobe, William, Dudley & King Sts), near the Queen Victoria Market, were first known as Burial Hill, as this is where most of the early settlers ended up. As the hill provided one of the best views of the bay, a signalling station was set up here; when a ship was sighted arriving from Britain, a flag was raised on the flagstaff to notify the settlers. Later, a cannon was added and fired when the more important ships arrived, but once newspapers started publishing regular information about shipping, the signalling service became redundant. The gardens are a popular alfresco lunch spot with nearby office workers, and there are regular lunch-time concerts in summer.

Docklands

Near the rear of Southern Cross station, the **Docklands** (Map pp72-4; ☎ 1300 663 008; www.docklands.vic.gov.au) was originally a wetland and lagoon area used by Koories as a hunting ground. Until the mid-1960s it was the city's main industrial and docking district. Demand for larger berths to accommodate modern cargo vessels necessitated a move, leaving the Docklands a virtual wasteland.

Its close proximity to the city centre means the area has become the focus of Melbourne's next big development boom and the city's seemingly unquenchable thirst for yet another 'precinct'. The 52,000-seat **Telstra**

Dome (Map pp72-4; ☎ 8625 7700; www.telstradome.com.au), a sporting and entertainment venue, is the city's alternative footy arena, with a state-of-the-art sliding roof and not one iota of soul. **Tours** (☎ 8625 7277; adult/child $13/5) of the stadium are conducted on weekdays.

The remaining areas of the Docklands, which comprise about 200 hectares of land and water, are being developed into residential, entertainment, dining and business zones that resemble a carefully cultivated city-state of slick amenities. One interesting landmark to note on your visit here is the **Webb Bridge** (Map pp72–4), a sinuous structure reminiscent of a Koorie eel trap.

Southbank

On the southern bank of the Yarra River, across from the CBD, the area known as Southbank is a former industrial wasteland that was transformed in the early 1990s by the **Southgate** (Map pp72–4) development. An arched footbridge crosses the Yarra River from behind Flinders St station, linking the city centre to the Victorian Arts Centre, the National Gallery of Victoria and Southgate itself. Riverside walks, which are reminiscent of Paris to some, flank the river on both sides, and where you once would have seen sawtoothed roofs and smoke billowing from chimney stacks, you'll now see people promenading along the riverside.

The Southgate complex houses three levels of restaurants, cafés and bars, all of which enjoy a unique outlook over the city skyline and the river. There's also an international food hall, a shopping gallery with recognisably upmarket boutiques, and a collection of specially commissioned sculptures and other artworks. For more on the dining possibilities here, see p124.

ARTS PRECINCT

This small area on St Kilda Rd, adjoining the Southgate complex, is the high-culture heart of Melbourne. It contains the National Gallery of Victoria, Melbourne Concert Hall and the theatres of the Victorian Arts Centre, the Victorian College of the Arts, the Australian Centre for Contemporary Art (ACCA) and the Malthouse Theatres.

National Gallery of Victoria: International

The first part of the arts complex to be completed, back in 1968, **NGV International**

(Map pp72-4; ☎ 8620 2222; www.ngv.vic.gov.au/ngv international; 180 St Kilda Rd, Melbourne; admission free; ☺ 10am-5pm) underwent a thorough refurbishment over the new millennium. While 1960s architecture wasn't too many people's favourite, the gallery is one of its better examples. Designed by Sir Roy Grounds, the building is constructed from bluestone and concrete – fitting materials for Melbourne.

The internationally renowned European section has an impressive collection of works by European masters, including Rembrandt, Picasso, Turner, Monet, Titian, Pissarro and Van Dyck. The sculpture courtyard and gallery has some fine works, including sculptures by Auguste Rodin and Henry Moore. The gallery's full collection is too large for permanent display, so many temporary exhibits are featured. Fabulous international blockbusters are also staged here – recent crowd-pleasers include highlights from the Musée d'Orsay, some of Man Ray's finest works and an exposition of Edvard Munch's work.

The **Great Hall** is a highlight, and the best way to see its best feature is to lie on your back on the floor. Melbourne artist Leonard French spent five years creating the amazing stained-glass ceiling. The Gallery Shop is a good place to buy souvenirs, posters, books and postcards.

Victorian Arts Centre

The **Victorian Arts Centre** (VAC; Map pp72-4; ☎ 9281 8000; www.vicartscentre.com.au; 100 St Kilda Rd, Melbourne) is made up of two separate buildings – the Melbourne Concert Hall (aka Hamer Hall) and the Theatres Building – which are linked to each other and the NGV International by a series of landscaped walkways.

Hamer Hall, the circular building closest to the Yarra River, is the main performance venue for major artists and companies, and the base for the Melbourne Symphony Orchestra (MSO). Most of it is below ground, resting in Yarra mud so corrosive that a system of electrified cables is needed to prevent it deteriorating. The **Theatres Building** (foyer ☺ 9am-11pm) is topped by its distinctive Eiffel-inspired spire (illuminated at night), underneath which are housed the State Theatre, the Playhouse and the George Fairfax Studio. The stylish interiors of both

buildings are quite stunning and well worth visiting in their own right, although you should also try to see a performance.

Both buildings feature the works of prominent Australian artists, and in the Theatres Building the **George Adams** and the **Vic Walk Gallery** are free gallery spaces with changing exhibitions of contemporary works.

One-hour tours ($10) of the centre are offered at noon and 2.30pm Monday to Saturday, and a special backstage tour for adults only ($13.50) is offered at 12.15pm Sunday. Call for bookings.

On Sunday, between 10am and 5pm, there's an arts and crafts market in the Arts Centre undercroft, with a variety of goods on offer, many with an Australian bent.

The **Performing Arts Museum** (admission free) in the Theatres Building has changing exhibitions on all aspects of the performing arts – it might be a display of performers' outfits (our Kylie has handed over more than her own weight in sequinned stunners recently) or an exhibit on horror in the theatre.

Australian Centre for Contemporary Art

The resolutely modern **ACCA** (Map pp84-5; ☎ 9654 6422; www.accaonline.org.au; 111 Sturt St, Southbank; admission free; ☺ 11am-6pm Tue-Sun) often resembles a rusting hulk that has run aground, and it holds a variety of differently sized and shaped spaces for various artistic forms. You can find cutting-edge art, and attend regular lectures, screenings and dance performances here (it's the home of the state's dance company, Chunky Move). On the same site is the controversial public sculpture nicknamed the *Yellow Peril*.

CROWN CASINO & ENTERTAINMENT COMPLEX

The 24-hour, nonstop cavalcade of illuminated excess that is the **Crown Casino & Entertainment Complex** (Map pp72-4; ☎ 9292 8888; www.crowncasino.com.au; 8 Whiteman St, Southbank; ☺ 24hr) was fleetingly the world's largest casino (it's still the biggest in the southern hemisphere) and has had an enormous effect on Melbourne. Blamed for numerous urban crises over the years (from kids left in locked cars to underworld money laundering), the casino still manages to attract plenty of customers prepared to part with their hard-earned cash in pursuit of a quick thrill. That said, the sprawling complex also holds an enormous luxury hotel, a variety of nightclubs, a cinema chain, a 900-seat showroom, speciality and luxury stores, plus dozens of cafés and restaurants, should gambling not appeal. It radiates a glitzy international energy that encapsulates the 'could be anywhere' rush of capitalism at its most exaggerated – like everyone else in Melbourne, you'll either love it or hate it.

MELBOURNE EXHIBITION & CONVENTION CENTRE

The unmistakably slick-looking building across the street from the casino is the **Melbourne Exhibition Centre** (Map pp72-4; ☎ 9205 6401; www.mecc.com.au; 2 Clarendon St, Southbank). It hosts trade exhibitions and fairs (from Sexpo to Santa's Kingdom, and the logical marriage of both – the Parents, Babies & Children's Expo) and was designed by Melbourne firm Denton Corker Marshall. It's architecturally interesting, not least for its angled, thrusting 'blade', which is a feature of several building projects around the city and would appear to be Melbourne's contribution to the world of architecture (see also the Melbourne Museum, p99). You may hear this building referred to as 'Jeff's Shed' by locals – a reference to former Victorian premier Jeff Kennett, who ruled the roost when the exhibition centre was constructed. See its website for details of upcoming events.

POLLY WOODSIDE MARITIME MUSEUM

On the Yarra River, in front of the Melbourne Exhibition Centre, is the **Polly Woodside Maritime Museum** (Map pp72-4; ☎ 9699 9760; South Wharf Rd, Southbank; adult/concession/child $10/8/6; ⏱ 10am-4pm). The *Polly Woodside* is an old iron-hulled three-masted sailing ship. Built in Belfast in 1885, she spent the first part of her working life carrying coal and nitrate between Europe and South America. She made the rounding of Cape Horn 16 times and ended her career as a coal hulk, but was bought by the National Trust in the 1970s and restored by volunteers.

The *Polly Woodside* is now the centrepiece of a maritime museum, and rests proudly in a dry dock. Other attractions are the historically listed **cargo sheds**, which house relics, displays and film footage relating to the history of Melbourne's port.

Kings Domain

The area of parkland across from the Melbourne arts precinct is known as **Kings Domain** (Map pp72-4; btwn St Kilda Rd, Domain Rd, Anderson St & Alexandra Ave) and contains the wonderful Royal Botanic Gardens, as well as the Shrine of Remembrance, Governor La Trobe's Cottage and the Sidney Myer Music Bowl.

The whole park is encircled by a former horse-exercising track known as the **Tan**, now a 4km running track that is Melbourne's favourite venue for joggers.

Beside St Kilda Rd stands the massive **Shrine of Remembrance** (Map pp84-5; ☎ 9654 8415; ⏱ 10am-5pm), built as a memorial to Victorians killed in WWI. Its design is partly based on the Mausoleum of Halicarnassus, one of the seven ancient wonders of the world, and it wasn't completed until 1934. The inner crypt is inscribed with the words: 'This holy place commemorates Victoria's glorious dead. They gave their all, even life itself, that others may live in freedom and peace. Forget them not.' These words are heeded every Anzac Day (25 April), when a dawn service at the shrine is attended by thousands, and also on Remembrance Day at the 11th hour of the 11th day of the 11th month – the time at which the Armistice of 1918 was declared. At this moment, a shaft of light shines through an opening in the ceiling to illuminate the Stone of Remembrance. The forecourt, with its cenotaph and eternal flame, was built as a memorial to those who died in WWII. Several other war memorials surround the shrine.

It's worth climbing to the top as there are fine views from the balcony to the city along St Kilda Rd and towards the bay.

Near the shrine is **Governor La Trobe's Cottage** (Map pp84-5; ☎ 9654 4711; cnr Birdwood Ave & Dallas Brooks Dr, Melbourne; admission $2; ⏱ 11am-4pm Mon, Wed, Sat & Sun), the original Victorian government house sent out from the mother country in prefabricated form in 1839. Many of the original furnishings are still on display inside.

The cottage provides a dramatic contrast with the more imposing **Government House** (Map pp84-5; ☎ 9656 9800; Government House Dr, Melbourne; adult/child $11/5.50) where Victoria's governor resides. Built in 1872, it's a copy of Queen Victoria's palace on England's Isle of Wight, and is one of the best examples of the Italianate style in the country. Guided tours are held on Monday, Wednesday and Saturday. The tour price includes entry to La Trobe's Cottage. Bookings are essential.

On the other side of the road from La Trobe's humble cottage are the **Old Melbourne Observatory** (Map pp84-5; Birdwood Ave, Melbourne) and the **National Herbarium** (Map pp84-5) at the main entrance to the Royal Botanic Gardens. The herbarium was established by Baron von Mueller in 1853 as a centre for identifying plant specimens. The Old Observatory houses the **visitors centre** (☎ 9252 2429; ⏲ 9am-5pm Mon-Fri, 9.30am-5.30pm Sat & Sun) for the Royal Botanic Gardens (below).

At the city end of the park is the **Sidney Myer Music Bowl** (Map p75), a functional outdoor performance area in a natural amphitheatre. It's used for all manner of concerts in the summer months, as well as outdoor cinema screenings (see p137).

The small section of park across St Kilda Rd from the Victorian Arts Centre is the **Queen Victoria Gardens** (Map pp72-4), containing a memorial statue of the good Queen herself, a statue of Edward VII astride his horse, and a huge **floral clock**, as well as several more contemporary works of sculpture.

ROYAL BOTANIC GARDENS

Certainly the finest botanic gardens in Australia and arguably among the finest in the world, the **Royal Botanic Gardens** (Map pp84-5; ☎ 9252 2300; www.rbg.vic.gov.au; Birdwood Ave; admission free; ⏲ 7.30am-5.30pm Apr-Oct) are a majestic must see. With a prime location beside the Yarra River (indeed, the river once ran right through the gardens) the beautifully laid-out gardens feature plants from around the world, lakes and a surprising amount of wildlife, including water fowl, ducks, swans, cockatoos, rabbits and possums. Peer over one of the small bridges that are scattered about the gardens and you'll probably see some eels, which have lived here since the Ornamental Lake was a bend of the Yarra. A large (and damaging) colony of fruit bats was resident until recently – they added a huge, noisy and uniquely Gothic image to the park but were 'moved on' thanks to a cacophonous series of alarms (rubbish-bin lids banged both morning and night).

Pick up self-guiding leaflets at the park entrances; these are changed with the seasons and tell you what to look out for at different times of year. There are various entrance gates around the gardens, but the visitors centre is in the Old Melbourne Observatory inside Gate F on Birdwood Ave (see Map pp84-5). The gardens offer a variety of tours, including an **Aboriginal Heritage Walk** (p113). For the delightful **Ian Potter Foundation Children's Garden**, see p112.

During the summer months the gardens are open until 8.30pm and play host to **Moonlight Cinema** (p137) and **theatre performances**.

Along the Yarra River

Melbourne's premier natural feature, the 'mighty' **Yarra River**, is the butt of countless jokes but is actually a surprisingly pleasant river. It is slowly but surely becoming more of an attraction as new parks, walks and buildings appear along its banks. It's rather muddy and periodic reports about its dirtiness mean that swimming in it is not a great idea.

When rowing boats are gliding down it on a sunny day, or you're driving towards the city on a clear night, the Yarra can look quite magical. There are some beautiful old bridges across the river, and the riverside boulevards provide delightful views of Melbourne by day or night.

As it winds its way into the city, the Yarra River is flanked by tree-lined avenues – Batman Ave along the northern bank, Alexandra Ave along the southern. Farther east, the Yarra Blvd follows the river in several sections from Richmond to Kew – like the Great Ocean Rd, the Yarra Blvd was a relief-work project of the Great Depression (p26).

Boat cruises along the river depart from **Princes Walk** (Map pp72-4), just east of Princes Bridge, and from **Southgate** (p113). A series of bike paths start from the city and follow the Yarra River; bikes can be hired from various places in town (see p108 for details). Studley Park Boathouse and Fairfield Park Boathouse are both popular spots where you can hire a canoe and paddle around, enjoy a leisurely Devonshire tea or walk beside the river. (See below for details.)

YARRA BEND PARK

Northeast of the city centre, the Yarra River is bordered by **Yarra Bend Park** (Map p81; www .parkweb.vic.gov.au), much loved by runners, rowers, cyclists, picnickers and strollers.

The park has large areas of natural bushlands (not to mention golf courses and numerous sports grounds) and there are some

MELBOURNE

great walks. In parts of Studley Park (part of Yarra Bend Park), with the song of bellbirds ringing through the trees and cockatoos screeching on the banks, it's hard to believe the city's all around you. The timber buildings of the **Studley Park Boathouse** (Map p81; ☎ 9853 1972; Boathouse Rd, Studley Park; ۞ 9am-5pm) on the riverbank date back to the 1860s, and now house a restaurant, kiosk and café; there are also boats, canoes and kayaks available for hire (see p108). Kanes suspension bridge takes you across to the other side of the river, and it's about a 20-minute walk from here to **Dights Falls** (Map p81), the confluence of the Yarra River and Merri Creek (in Abbotsford), with some great views along the way. You can also walk to the falls along the southern riverbank. On the way is the **Pioneer Memorial Cairn**, which commemorates Charles Grimes (the first European to see the Yarra River, in 1803) and the first settlers to bring cattle from Sydney to Melbourne (in 1836).

Farther upriver, Fairfield Park is the site of the **Fairfield Amphitheatre** (Map pp70–1), a great open-air venue used for concerts and film screenings, among other things.

The **Fairfield Park Boathouse & Tea Gardens** (Map pp70-1; ☎ 9486 1501; www.fairfieldboathouse .com; Fairfield Park Dr, Fairfield; ۞ 11am-4pm Mon-Fri winter, 8.30am-late Sat & Sun year-round) is a restored 19th-century boathouse with broad verandas and a garden restaurant. In summer it's open longer hours on weekdays.

To get to Yarra Bend Park by car, follow Johnston St through Collingwood and turn onto the scenic drive of Yarra Blvd. Better still, hire a bike and cycle around the riverside bike paths – a leisurely 40-minute cruise.

Yarra Park & Melbourne Park

Southeast of the city centre is the sports-centric expanse of parkland known as Yarra Park. It contains the Melbourne Cricket Ground (MCG) and the Richmond Cricket Ground. The adjoining Melbourne Park contains the Melbourne Park National Tennis Centre, Olympic Park, the Vodafone Arena, and several other sports ovals.

MELBOURNE CRICKET GROUND

The **MCG** (Map p75; ☎ 9657 8888; www.mcg.org.au; Brunton Ave, Jolimont), or just 'the G', is the temple in which sports-mad Melburnians worship their heroes. One of the world's great sporting venues, it's imbued with an indefinable

combination of tradition and atmosphere. The first game of Australian rules football was played in 1858, where the MCG and its car parks now stand, and in 1877 the first Test cricket match between Australia and England was played here. The MCG was also the central stadium for the 1956 Melbourne Olympics, and in 2006 the opening and closing ceremonies of the Commonwealth Games will take place here. During 2004 the three grandstands on the northern side of the ground (Ponsford, Olympic and MCC Members Pavilion) were in the throes of being redeveloped into one new stand matching the Great Southern Stand. This should be completed in time for the 2006 Commonwealth Games.

If you fancy getting really close to this hallowed hall of recreation, take a **tour** (☎ 9657 8879; adult/concession $10/6), which depart every half-hour (on non-match days) from 10am to 3pm, and last for 1¼ hours.

Parkville & Carlton

Up this end of town you'll find a cosmopolitan area that blends the intellectual with the recreational, the multicultural with the mainstream.

These two suburbs are divided by the tree-lined Royal Pde. In Parkville there's the University of Melbourne and the Royal Melbourne Zoo; in Carlton there's the Melbourne General Cemetery, and some bustling restaurants in the Italian quarter around Lygon, Drummond and Rathdowne Sts.

ROYAL PARK

This large expanse of open **parkland** contains a number of sports ovals and open spaces, large netball and hockey stadiums, a public golf course, the Royal Melbourne Zoo and the Games Village for the 2006 Commonwealth Games. In the corner closest to the University of Melbourne you'll find a garden of Australian native plants; a little farther north, just south of MacArthur Rd, a **memorial cairn** marks the spot from where the Burke and Wills expedition set off in 1860 on its fateful crossing of the interior.

ROYAL MELBOURNE ZOO

Melbourne's **zoo** (Map p79; ☎ 9285 9300; www .zoo.org.au; Elliot Ave, Parkville; adult/concession/child $20/14.50/9.50; ۞ 9am-5pm) is one of the city's most popular attractions, and deservedly so. Established in 1861, this is the oldest zoo in Australia and the third oldest in the world. In the 1850s, when Australia was regarded as a foreign place full of strange trees and animals, the Acclimatisation Society was formed for 'the introduction, acclimatisation and domestication of all innoxious animals, birds, fishes, insects and vegetables'. The society merged with the Zoological Society in 1861, and together they established the zoo on its present site.

Set in spacious and attractively landscaped gardens with broad strolling paths, the zoo's enclosures are simulations of the animals' natural habitats. The walkways pass through the enclosures – you walk through the bird aviary, cross a bridge over the lions' park, enter a tropical hothouse full of colourful butterflies and walk around the gorillas' very own rainforest. There's also a large collection of native animals in a native-bush setting, a platypus aquarium, an elephant village, fur seals and tigers, plenty of reptiles and lots more to see. You should allow at least half a day for your visit.

In the summer months the zoo hosts **twilight concerts** (see p135 for details). The Roar 'n' Snore programme allows you to camp at the zoo and join the keepers on their morning rounds of the animal enclosures.

CARLTON GARDENS

On the border of Carlton and Fitzroy, just north of Victoria St, are the Carlton Gardens, a pleasant area of open parkland. The gardens are home to the historic **Royal Exhibition Building** (Map pp76-8; ☎ 9270 5000; www.museum.vic.gov.au/reb; Nicholson St, Carlton), a wonder of the southern hemisphere when it was built for the Great Exhibition of 1880. Later it was used by the Victorian Parliament for 27 years, while the Victorian parliament building was used by the National Legislature until Canberra's parliament building was finally completed. It is still used as a major exhibition centre (the oldest surviving example in the world). In 2004 this glorious pile became Australia's first building to earn Unesco World Heritage status. **Tours** (☎ 1300 130 152; adult/concession $4/2) happen daily at 2pm – phone for bookings.

MELBOURNE MUSEUM

In the Carlton Gardens, opposite the Royal Exhibition Building, is the newish **Melbourne Museum** (Map pp76-8; ☎ 13 11 02; www.melbourne .museum.vic.gov.au; 11 Nicholson St, Carlton; adult/concession & child $6/free; ☒ 10am-5pm). Billed as 'the southern hemisphere's largest and most innovative museum', the architecturally imposing building resembles an international air terminal with its open-plan design and modern approach to the use of space. The emphasis is on education and interaction, and the main attractions include Bunjilaka, the Aboriginal Centre; a living forest gallery; and the Australia gallery, with exhibits dedicated to that great Aussie icon Phar Lap (the legendary racehorse), and another dedicated to the TV show *Neighbours* (filmed in Melbourne). The Children's Museum is a great way to keep the kids entertained while here, although we can't help but notice that the video of a woman giving birth (part of the Mind & Body gallery) seems to be the best way to get them to keep quiet. Disabled access is very good.

Beside the museum is Melbourne's IMAX theatre, which screens super-wide format films (see p137).

UNIVERSITY OF MELBOURNE

Established in 1853, the **University of Melbourne** (Map pp76-8; ☎ 8344 4000; www.unimelb.edu.au; Grattan St, Parkville) is well worth a visit. A wander around the campus, on the edge of the CBD, will reveal an intriguing blend of original Gothic-style stone buildings, some incredibly unattractive brick blocks from the less noteworthy 'functionalist' period and a smattering of recent architectural statements. The college buildings, to the north of the campus, are particularly noteworthy for their fine architecture.

The grounds are sprinkled with open lawns and garden areas, and during semester, there's always something going on. The **Ian Potter Museum of Art** (Map pp76-8) is housed in a Nonda Katsalidis–designed building located on Swanston St. The museum is home to the university's large collection of 19th- and 20th-century art, and it features regular exhibitions of contemporary art as well as lectures. On the Royal Pde side of the campus (next to the Conservatory of Music), the **Grainger Museum** (Map p79) – closed for renovations at the time of writing – is dedicated to the life and times of Percy Grainger (1882–1961), an eccentric composer who lived an extraordinary life, and travelled the world collecting and recording folk music on an old Edison recording machine. Grainger set up the museum before his death, and it contains his collections, instruments, photos, costumes and other interesting personal effects.

LYGON ST

Carlton is Melbourne's Italian quarter, and Lygon St is its backbone. Many of the thousands of Italian immigrants who came to Melbourne after WWII settled in Carlton, and Lygon St became the focal point of their community.

Lygon St is the most highly 'developed' example of the multicultural evolution of Melbourne's inner-suburban streets. A fondness lingers for the older, less glamorous version, but those days are well and truly over. The developers moved in and, with their out-with-the-old and in-with-the-new philosophy, they gave Lygon St a face-lift. Lygon St lost its quirky beauty and offbeat appeal, and the bohemian element moved on to Fitzroy and Collingwood. That said, there's still a strong Italian feel to the street and not all the magic has been lost, with plenty of coffee and *gelato* reminding you that the simple pleasures are what make Italian life tick – not touts outside ordinary eateries (and there are a fair few of them).

In among the tourist restaurants and exclusive fashion boutiques, you'll still find a few of the oldies: Readings bookshop (p69) is still here, places like Tiamo (p125) and Jimmy Watson's (p125) have resisted the winds of change; and La Mama, the tiny experimental theatre started by Betty Burstall in 1967, is still going strong in Faraday St (for details see p137).

Lygon St is one of Melbourne's liveliest streets. Day and night it is always filled with people promenading, dining, sipping cappuccinos, shopping and generally soaking up the atmosphere. Each year in late October Lygon St hosts the lively Lygon St Festa (p115), a weekend food-and-fun street party.

OTHER SIGHTS

Two attractive and broad tree-lined avenues, **Drummond St** (Map p79) and **Royal Pde** (Map pp76–8), Carlton, contain outstanding examples of 19th-century residential architecture. Drummond St in particular, from Victoria St to Palmerston St, is one of the most impressive and intact Victorian streetscapes

in the city. **Rathdowne St**, north of Victoria St in Carlton, has a sweet little shopping area, and some great cafés and restaurants. North Carlton and Brunswick (Sydney Rd and the northern ends of Lygon and Nicholson Sts; Map p80) present the less-commercial face of this cosmopolitan area.

Princes Park (Map p80; Princes Park Dr, North Carlton), to the north of the University of Melbourne, has a number of sports grounds, including the Carlton Football and Cricket Clubs' former main ground (known as Optus Oval), as well as a 3.2km fun-and-fitness exercise circuit. A visit to the **Melbourne General Cemetery** (Map p80), next to Princes Park, is a sombre reminder that no matter how many laps of the fun-and-fitness circuit you do, you can't avoid the inevitable. The earliest gravestones date back to the 1850s, and the cemetery is a graphic and historic portrait of the wide diversity of countries from which people have come to settle in Australia.

Fitzroy & Collingwood

Fitzroy is where Melbourne's bohemian subculture moved when the lights got too bright in Carlton. It's a great mixture of artistic, seedy, alternative and trendy elements, and one of Melbourne's most interesting suburbs to live in or to visit, with a vibrant community feel.

In Melbourne's early years Fitzroy was a prime residential area, and the suburb contains some fine terrace houses from the mid-Victorian era, the most notable of which is the 1854 **Royal Terrace** (Map pp76-8; Nicholson St), opposite the Royal Exhibition Building. Later on, the suburb became a densely populated working-class stronghold with a large migrant population. The inner-city location and cosmopolitan atmosphere have attracted students, artists and urbanites, creating the lively blend that now exists.

Brunswick St (Map pp76–8) is Fitzroy's, and probably Melbourne's, liveliest street, and you shouldn't visit the city without coming here. This is where you'll find some of the best food, the weirdest shops, the most interesting people and the coolest clothes. In particular, the blocks on either side of the Johnston St intersection have a fascinating collection of young designer and retro clothes shops, bookshops, galleries, antique dealers, pubs (the highest per capita in Victoria) and, of course, more cafés and restaurants than you can poke a fork at (see p125). There are those who argue that Brunswick St is well past its heyday and is now a yuppie playground – which is true to an extent, but only in parts.

Smith St (Map pp76–8) forms the border between Fitzroy and Collingwood, and this is where the bohemians who think that Brunswick St is going the way of Lygon St have moved, and it's a good reminder of how Brunswick St used to be. It has a great assortment of food stores, bookshops, pubs and restaurants, including some good vegie restaurants and some Vietnamese bakeries thrown in for good measure. The whole area has a slightly down-at-heel look that is sure to appeal after the polished bohemian façades of Brunswick St. It's also something of an artists' colony – many of the city's most interesting emerging talents have studio spaces on Smith St, or close by.

Along Brunswick St north of Alexandra Pde in **North Fitzroy**, there are a few interesting, quirky shops to explore, more historic buildings, the **Edinburgh Gardens** (Map p80; btwn Alfred Cres, St Georges Rd, Brunswick & Curtain Sts), and one or two good pubs in which to enjoy an ale.

Going strong for over 20 years, **Gertrude Contemporary Art Spaces** (Map pp76-8; ☎ 9419 3406; www.gertrude.org.au; 200 Gertrude St, Fitzroy; ☧ 11am-5.30pm Tue-Fri, 1-5.30pm Sat) is a nonprofit art space that holds galleries and studios, and promotes emerging artists, with some excellent exhibitions taking place throughout the year.

East Melbourne

Elegant Victorian townhouses, mansions and tree-lined avenues make up the small residential pocket that is East Melbourne. Streets off Clarendon, Hotham and Powlett Sts are all worth a wander if you're interested in seeing some of Melbourne's most impressive early residential architecture.

Tasma Terrace (Map p75; Parliament Pl), behind Parliament House, is a magnificent row of six attached Victorian terraces. The three-storey terraces were built in 1879 for a grain merchant, a Mr Nipper, and are decorated with enough cast-iron lace to sink a small ship. They also house the offices of **National Trust** (☎ 9656 9800; www.nattrust.com.au; 4 Parliament Pl; ☧ 9am-5pm Mon-Fri), an organisation dedicated to preserving Australia's heritage. It's worth visiting the office – it has

a range of information on National Trust properties, and the interior of the reception office is a great example of over-the-top Victoriana. The terrace next door has also been restored, and you can see the parlour and sitting room with its original Victorian furniture and artworks.

St Patrick's Cathedral (Map p75; ☎ 9662 2233; www.melbourne.catholic.org.au; Cathedral Pl; ☧ 8am-6pm), behind Parliament House, is one of the world's finest examples of Gothic Revival architecture. It was designed by William Wardell, begun in 1863, and built in stages until the spires and west portal were added in 1939. The imposing bluestone exterior is floodlit to great effect by night, and is spectacular when viewed from Brunswick St to the north. The interior is suffused with a golden light, ensuring that every surface gleams – a nice addition to the auditory pleasures of chiming bells and clanging trams. Music recitals are held here on a regular basis, and there's also an annual AFL Grand Final Mass for those who like to combine the sacred and the profane.

Diagonally across Gisborne St from the cathedral is the Eastern Hill Fire Station. The Old Fire Station building was built in 1891. Its ground floor now houses the **Eastern Hill Fire Museum** (Map p75; ☎ 9662 2907; cnr Gisborne St & Victoria Pde; adult/child $5/2; ☧ 9am-3pm Fri, 10am-4pm Sun), which has a historic collection of fire-fighting equipment – fire engines, helmets, uniforms, medals and photos. Facing Albert St, the unattractive façade of the newer building has been brightened up with an eye-catching five-storey mural designed by Harold Freedman, the same mosaicist responsible for the murals at Southern Cross station and the Australian Gallery of Sport & Olympic Museum. The mosaic mural depicts the history and mythology of fire.

Richmond & Abbotsford

As Carlton is to Italy so Richmond is to Vietnam, although there are still many Greek-Australians living here, hangers-on from the previous wave of immigrants to adopt the suburb. You might even find an Irish-Australian from an earlier wave.

The suburb is another centre for Victorian architecture, much of it restored or in the process of restoration. Given Richmond's working-class roots, many of the houses are small workers' cottages and terraces, although the Richmond Hill area (between Lennox, Church and Swan Sts and Bridge Rd) has some impressive old mansions.

Bridge Rd and **Swan St** (both Map p81) form something of a discount fashion centre, with shops where many Australian fashion designers sell their seconds and rejects alongside the outlets of some of Melbourne's popular young designers.

A little north of Richmond in Abbotsford, the **Carlton Brewhouse** (Map p81; ☎ 9420 6800; www.fosters.com.au; cnr Nelson & Thompson Sts, Abbotsford; adult/concession $15/10; ☼ 10am & 2pm Mon-Fri) offers tours of the brewery that makes popular drops, such as Carlton Draught and Melbourne Bitter. Beers lovers are rewarded for their patience in listening to tales of how the 1.5 million bottles produced here come into existence with a free tasting at the end. Bookings are essential.

South Yarra & Toorak

These two inner-city suburbs are on what's referred to as the 'right' side of the river – the high-society side of town. South Yarra is a bustling, trendy and style-conscious suburb – the kind of place where avid readers of *Vogue Living* will feel very at home. Farther east, Toorak is the ritziest suburb in Melbourne and home to some of Melbourne's wealthiest (or at least the most ostentatious) homeowners.

While in the area, visit gracious **Como House** (Map p82; ☎ 9827 2500; www.nattrust.com .au; cnr Williams Rd & Lechdale Ave, South Yarra; adult/child $11/6.50; ☼ 10am-5pm), one of Australia's finest colonial mansions. Overlooking the Yarra River, the house was built between 1847 and 1859 for the wealthy Armytage family. Aboriginal rites and feasts were still held on the banks of the Yarra when the house was first built, and an early occupant wrote of seeing a cannibal rite from her bedroom window (she was undoubtedly mistaken). The verdant grounds (complete with croquet lawn) are filled with flower gardens that are a horticulturalist's dream. Tours of the house take place at 10.30am and then half-hourly until 4pm, and last about half an hour.

TOORAK RD

Forming the main artery through South Yarra and Toorak, Toorak Rd is one of Australia's ritziest shopping streets, frequented by well-known Toorak denizens in their Porsches, Mercedes Benzes and Range Rovers (disparagingly referred to as 'Toorak Tractors'). It's the sort of street where the hairdressers specialise in flippy blonde hairdos and little else.

The main shopping area in South Yarra is along Toorak Rd, between Punt Rd and Chapel St. Along here you'll find dozens of exclusive boutiques, and specialist shops, cafés and restaurants. It's also home to the huge **Como Centre** (Map p82; cnr Toorak Rd & Chapel St, South Yarra), a sleek commercial development that houses upmarket boutiques and shops, offices, cafés and a cinema.

On the southern side of Toorak Rd, between Punt and St Kilda Rds, is **Fawkner Park** (Map pp84–5), an attractive and spacious park with large expanses of grass, tree-lined paths, tennis courts and various sports ovals.

At the Toorak end of Toorak Rd is the smaller and more exclusive group of shops and arcades known as **Toorak Village** (Map p82; btwn Wallace Ave & Grange Rd). This is the local convenience shopping area for some of Melbourne's wealthiest citizens. If you want to see how and where Melbourne's moneyed classes live, go for a drive through streets like St Georges and Grange Rds – you'll see some of the biggest mansions in the country, hedges and walls permitting.

CHAPEL ST

One of Melbourne's major and most diverse retail centres, Chapel St, particularly the South Yarra end (between Toorak and Commercial Rds), is probably Melbourne's busiest and most stylish centre for retail fashion. It's basically wall-to-wall clothing boutiques (with a sprinkling of hip bars and cafés). If you want to see fashion, this is where you'll see it – in the shop windows, sitting outside the cafés and walking along the street.

Prahran

Fun-filled Prahran, surrounded by its more affluent neighbouring suburbs of South Yarra, Toorak and Armadale, is a blend of small Victorian workers' cottages; narrow, leafy streets; and high-rise, government-subsidised flats for low-income earners. The Prahran area is populated by people from a broad range of ethnic backgrounds, and is enlivened and enriched by a wide variety of cultural influences. Despite its upwardly mobile trajectory over the years, it remains unpretentious and easy-going.

Prahran has some lively streets, the most notable being **Chapel St** (Map p82; see also opposite). Prahran's sector of Chapel St stretches from Malvern Rd down to Dandenong Rd, and is more diverse and a little less fashionable than the South Yarra sector. The highlight of the area is the excellent **Prahran Market** (p141), which is on Commercial Rd, just around the corner from Chapel St (and is technically in South Yarra). It was established in 1881 and is still packing in the city's gourmands today.

Commercial Rd (Map p82) is something of a focal centre for Melbourne's gay and lesbian communities, and has a small collection of nightclubs, bars, pubs, bookshops and cafés.

Running west off Chapel St beside the Prahran Town Hall, **Greville St** has a quirky collection of offbeat retro/grunge clothing shops, record shops, bookshops, and some good bars and cafés. It's well worth checking out.

St Kilda

A seaside location and chequered history have made St Kilda one of Melbourne's liveliest and most cosmopolitan areas.

In Melbourne's early days St Kilda was a seaside resort, the fashionable spot for those wanting to escape the increasingly grimy and crowded city. Horse trams, and later cable trams, ran along St Kilda Rd carrying day-trippers, and by 1857 the railway line to St Kilda was completed. During the gold-rush period, many of the wealthier citizens built mansions in St Kilda, and Fitzroy St became one of the city's most gracious boulevards. Hotels were built, dance halls opened, sea baths and fun parks catered for the crowds, and St Kilda was *the* place to go in search of fun and entertainment.

As things became more hectic the wealthy folk moved on to more exclusive areas, like Toorak and Brighton. With the economic collapse of the 1890s, St Kilda's status began to decline. Flats were built and the mansions were demolished or divided up, and by the 1960s and '70s, St Kilda had a reputation as a seedy centre for drugs and prostitution. Its decadent image of faded glories (and cheap rent) attracted a diverse mixture of Jewish immigrants and Eastern European refugees, all sorts of bohemians and plenty of down-and-outers.

In recent years St Kilda has undergone an image upgrade. It has returned to the forefront of Melbourne's fashionable suburbs, but with a few characteristic differences. Its appeal is now a mix of the old and the rejuvenated, the ethnic and the artistic, the stylish and the casual. St Kilda is a place of extremes – backpacker hostels and upmarket restaurants, classy cafés and cheap takeaways, seaside strolls and Sunday traffic jams. Despite its improved image, however, some elements of its seedy past remain, and its carnivalesque vibe has never surrendered to economic or cultural influence. If you're there on a sunny day, prepare to be swept along in a tide of humanity seeking fun, food, cakes, ale, exercise, sex, drugs, rock'n'roll and sea views.

Of interest is a **historic Corroboree Tree** (Map p83), a 350-year-old Aboriginal ceremonial tree between Junction Oval and the intersection of Queens and St Kilda Rds. The **St Kilda Botanical Gardens** (Map p83; ☎ 9209 6666; cnr Blessington & Herbert Sts) were first planted in 1859, and feature a garden conservatory, the Alister Clarke Memorial Garden (a bed of roses), a children's playground, a giant chessboard and a community eco-house. It's one of the area's most delightful spots – there's no better place to stretch out in the sun with a newspaper, a loved one and a piece of cake from Acland St.

The *St Kilda Heritage Walk* brochure, with 22 historic points of interest, is available from the town hall, during normal business hours, on the corner of St Kilda Rd and Carlisle St. The walk concentrates on the foreshore and the Esplanade area, although another interesting walk is to explore the St Kilda Hill area where some of the oldest and grandest buildings remain on the Esplanade, Grey St and the Fitzroy St end of Acland St.

If you follow **Carlisle St** across St Kilda Rd and into Balaclava, you'll find some great Jewish food shops, bakeries, European delicatessens and fruit shops – Carlisle St is much less trendy than the bayside areas, although the gentrification has well and truly begun, with a couple of natty boutiques, bars and cafés wedging in.

The **Jewish Museum of Australia** (Map p83; ☎ 9534 0083; 26 Alma Rd; adult/child $7/4; ☒ 10am-4pm Tue-Thu, 11am-5pm Sun) houses displays relating to Jewish history and culture, the annual cycle of festivals and the origins of Jewish life, as well as hosting regular exhibitions.

See p114 for details on the St Kilda Festival, which sees the suburb overrun with locals and day-trippers alike.

FITZROY ST

Originally a proud and stylish boulevard, Fitzroy St (Map p83) followed St Kilda's decline at the end of the 19th century and became a seedy strip of ill repute. Today Fitzroy St is at the leading edge of St Kilda's revival, and has been given new life by the opening of a growing number of stylish bars, restaurants and cafés. It's one of Melbourne's most interesting eating and drinking precincts, and day and night the street is crowded with a fascinating blend of people.

ACLAND ST

Farther south, the section of Acland St (Map p83) between Carlisle and Barkly Sts was famed for its Continental cake shops, delicatessens, and Central European cafés and restaurants. This part of Acland St became the focal centre for the wave of Jewish and other European refugees who settled in this area during Hitler's rise to power and after WWII, and their influence and presence remain strong. However, the older places are being swamped by stylish bars and eateries, making Acland St another of Melbourne's favourite food strips. The street also has good shops, and on weekends Acland St is bustling with people who come from everywhere to enjoy the atmosphere.

North of Carlisle St it's mostly residential all the way to Fitzroy St – with a few exceptions. A grand old two-storey mansion has been converted into the **Linden Art Centre & Gallery** (Map p83; ☎ 9209 6794; www.lindenarts.org; 26 Acland St; admission free; ☺ 1-6pm Tue-Sun). Registered by the National Trust, this historic building houses a contemporary art gallery, artists' studios, workshops and performance spaces. Plus, there's a children's sculpture garden to distract the youngsters.

SEASIDE ST KILDA

St Kilda's foreshore has undergone the same rejuvenation as the rest of the suburb. The beaches have been cleaned up, the foreshore parks landscaped and bike paths built. The boats and yachts moored in the lee of the breakwater, the Canary Island palm trees planted along the foreshore and people promenading along the pier all add to the ambience.

St Kilda Pier (Map p83) and breakwater is a favourite spot for strollers, who used to reward themselves with a coffee or a snack at **St Kilda Pier Pavillion**, a 19th-century tearoom at the junction of the pier, which burnt down in 2003. In September 2004, a year to the day that it went up in smoke, plans were announced for its reconstruction, in much the same style. You can still head out along the pier.

On weekends and public holidays a **ferry** (☎ 9682 9555; adult/child $6.50/3.25) runs from the pier across the bay to Williamstown, departing hourly from St Kilda between 11.30am and 4.30pm, and from Williamstown between 11am and 4pm.

On the foreshore south of the pier, the Moorish-inspired former St Kilda Baths have been transformed into the **St Kilda Sea Baths** (Map p83), which hold an indoor pool and gym (see p110).

The entrance of **Luna Park** (Map p83; ☎ 9525 5033; www.lunapark.com.au; Lower Esplanade; unlimited ride ticket adult/child $33.95/23.95; ☺ 11am-6pm Sat & Sun), with its famous laughing face, has been a symbol of St Kilda since 1912, and it has been restored to an artistic approximation of its first incarnation. Luna Park is a somewhat dated and old-fashioned amusement park, but that's a big part of the seaside charm. It has some great rides, including the great, old wooden rollercoaster, a beautifully crafted carousel (built by the Philadelphia Toboggan Company and the only one of its kind to leave American shores). There are also dodgems, a Ferris wheel and a ghost train. Luna Park is open daily (and till 11pm Friday and Saturday) during school holidays.

The **Palais Theatre** (Map p83; Lower Esplanade), across the road from Luna Park, was built in 1927. At the time it was one of the largest and one of the best picture palaces in Australia, seating over 3000, and it's still a great venue for a wide variety of live performances (see p138).

Built in 1880, the marvellous **Esplanade Hotel** (Map p83; ☎ 9534 0211; 11 Upper Esplanade) is the musical and artistic heart and soul of St Kilda, and perhaps the best-known pub in Melbourne. The actress Sarah Bernhardt stayed here back in 1891. Today the 'Espy' is much loved by St Kilda's locals, with its live bands (often free), comedy nights, great pub grub and a uniquely grungy atmosphere (the carpet is probably the city's stickiest and the chairs seem to be more gaffer tape than stuffing). Due to its prime location and run-down state, its future is constantly being threatened by developers. See p135 for more details on the Espy.

The **Esplanade Sunday Market** (Map p83; Upper Esplanade; 10am-5pm Sun) features a huge range of open-air stalls selling a variety of arts, crafts, gifts and souvenirs – often with a New Age or Australiana slant.

South Melbourne

As a shanty town of canvas and bark huts on the swampy lands south of the Yarra, South Melbourne had humble beginnings. The area was originally called Emerald Hill, after the grassy knoll of high ground that stood above the muddy flatlands. Now South Melbourne is an interesting inner-city suburb with a rich architectural and cultural heritage, and a few sights worth seeing.

Clarendon St (Map pp84–5) is the main street. It runs through the heart of South Melbourne from Spencer St in the city to Albert Park Lake. In the central shopping section, many of the original Victorian shopfronts have been restored and refitted with their verandas, and you'll find all sorts of shops and quite a few pubs (the survivors from the days when the area boasted a pub on every corner).

Emerald Hill (Map pp84–5), between Clarendon, Park, Cecil and Dorcas Sts, was the first area to be built on and is now a heritage conservation area, with some fine old mansions and terrace houses, and the impressive **South Melbourne Town Hall** (Map pp84-5; 208 Bank St), which has been restored.

The excellent **South Melbourne Market** (p141) dates back to 1867 and is a highlight of the neighbourhood – try to arrange your visit to coincide with a market day, and make sure you scoff a dim sim while you peruse the stalls.

The **Victorian Tapestry Workshop** (Map pp84-5; ☎ 9699 7885; 260 Park St; admission $4; 10am-3pm Mon-Fri) produces large-scale tapestries, which are the collaborative work of weavers and contemporary artists. At the workshop you'll be able to see the creation of 'one of Western civilisation's oldest and richest art forms'. Some pieces are available for sale and tours

($6) take place at 2pm Wednesday and 11am Thursday – call to make a booking.

The 1856 **Sze Yup Temple** (Map pp84-5; 76 Raglan St; admission by donation; 9am-4pm) is said to be one of the finest Chinese temples outside China. It was built by the Sze Yup Society as a place of worship for the Chinese who came during the gold rush.

A set of three **portable iron houses** (Map pp84-5; www.nattrust.com.au; 399 Coventry St; 1-4pm 1st Sun each month), which were prefabricated in England and erected here during the heady gold-rush days of 1853, have been preserved by the National Trust. Many early colonial dwellings were prefabs, and these are some of the few remaining examples. It's tricky to time a visit to these places (and you'll need to book), but check out the exterior at least.

Albert Park

Wedged between South Melbourne and the bay, Albert Park is a small 'village' suburb, populated by an interesting blend of migrants, young families and upwardly mobile types. A large percentage of its Victorian terrace houses and cottages have been renovated, and the suburb is a popular spot with beach-goers in summer and café lovers at any time of the year.

On **Bridport St** (Map pp84–5), between Montague and Merton Sts, is a small but lively shopping area. Here you'll find some excellent and stylish cafés and delicatessens, and a few exclusive speciality shops and boutiques. Just north of the shopping centre are lovely **St Vincent's Gardens** (Map pp84–5), a formal Victorian garden surrounded by sumptuous terrace houses.

In summer crowds of sun lovers flock to Albert Park's beaches, especially those around the Kerferd Rd Pier – it's a great spot to observe Aussie beach culture in action, albeit on flat-as-a-tack waters. The bike path along the foreshore is also excellent for cycling, jogging or in-line skating – don't wander into it by accident unless you like the idea of getting collected at high speed!

Albert Park Lake (Map pp84–5) is a 2.5km-long artificial lake surrounded by parklands, sports ovals, a golf course and other recreation facilities. The lake circuit is popular with strollers, runners and cyclists, and the sight of dozens of dinghies sailing across the lake on a sunny Saturday is one of Melbourne's trademark images. There are several restaurants and bars where you can sit and enjoy the views.

The **Melbourne Sports & Aquatic Centre** (Map pp84–5) on the southwestern corner of Albert Park is a great attraction within the park. It houses an enormous swimming pool, squash courts, a gym, a spa, a giant water slide and much more. For details, see p110.

The road around the lake was used as an international motor-racing circuit in the 1950s, and since 1996 the revamped track has been the venue for the **Australian Formula One Grand Prix** race. (For more details on this race, see p140.)

Port Melbourne

Often simply called Port, Port Melbourne is feeling the gentrification that has swept the inner suburbs, but has kept a few more of its working-class roots than other areas close to the city and still has more than a few connections to Melbourne's criminal underworld. It has retained a few factories and semi-industrial areas, but many of its small Victorian workers' cottages have been restored by the new breed of inner-city dwellers. The areas closest to the bay have undergone a major transformation, with old factory sites being converted into residential developments and a string of apartment buildings near Station Pier.

Bay St (Map pp84–5), the continuation of City Rd, is Port's main street, and runs down to the bay. Many of its historic veranda-fronted terrace buildings have been restored and revamped. Bay St is full of heritage character with a 'village' feel about it – there's a good range of shops and some popular pubs that can slake a thirst if a tour is proving tiring.

Station Pier (Map pp70–1) is Melbourne's major passenger shipping terminal and the departure point for ferries to Tasmania. It also has good views of the city, and a few eateries, plus it holds a lot of memories for much of Melbourne's immigrant population, who arrived here. If you're lucky, the impressive *Spirit of Tasmania* (the ferry to Tasmania) will be in port when you visit.

Williamstown

Back in 1837, two new townships were laid out simultaneously at the top of Port Phillip Bay – Melbourne as the main settlement, and Williamstown as the seaport. With the advantage of the natural harbour of Hobsons Bay, Williamstown thrived, and government services, such as customs and immigration, were based here. Many of the early buildings were built from locally quarried bluestone, and the township quickly took on an air of solidity and permanence.

Then, when the Yarra River was deepened and the Port of Melbourne developed in the 1880s, Williamstown became a secondary port. Tucked away in a corner of the bay, it was bypassed and forgotten for years.

In the last decade or so Williamstown, or Willy as it's often called, has been rediscovered and is experiencing a renaissance. Come on a summer's night and the roar of souped-up drag-racing cars will make those quiet days of the early 19th century seem like a *very* long time ago indeed. Keep an eye out for some of the most obnoxious numberplates in the city, too. It may be the home of state premier Steve Bracks and a lot of the city's most upwardly mobile types, but this raucous street ritual is hogging all the attention at night.

Nelson Pl (Map p86), which follows the foreshore and winds around the docklands and shipyards, was patriotically named after the British Navy's Admiral Horatio Nelson, famous for his victory in 1805 over the combined French and Spanish fleets in the Battle of Trafalgar. Nelson Pl is lined with historic buildings, many of them registered by the National Trust, while the yacht clubs, marinas, boat builders and chandleries along the waterfront all add to the maritime flavour. Williamstown's other attractions include restaurants and cafés, some pubs and bars, art and craft galleries, and speciality shops.

The **Williamstown information centre** (Map p86; ☎ 9397 3791; www.williamstowninfo.com.au; Nelson Pl; ☼ 9am-5pm) is independently operated and can load you up with info. Between Nelson Pl and the waterfront is **Commonwealth Reserve**, a small, leafy park where a **craft market** (☼ 10am-4pm) is held on the first and third Sunday of each month.

Moored at Gem Pier is the **HMAS Castlemaine** (Map p86; www.hmascastlemaine.com; adult/child $5/2.50; ☼ noon-5pm Sat & Sun), a WWII minesweeper that was built in Williamstown in 1941 and has been converted into a maritime museum. It is staffed by volunteers from the Maritime Trust of Australia, and contains interesting nautical exhibits and memorabilia.

Williamstown Railway Museum (Map p86; ☎ 9397 7412; Champion Rd; adult/child $5/2; ☒ noon-5pm Sat, Sun & public holidays, noon-5pm Wed & school holidays), operated by the Australian Railway Historical Society, is a good spot for kids and train spotters. It has a fine collection of old steam locomotives, wagons, carriages and old photos, and mini-steam-train rides for kids. It's part of the Newport Railway Workshops in north Williamstown, and is close to North Williamstown train station.

The **Customs Wharf Gallery** (Map p86; ☎ 9399 9726; cnr Nelson Pl & Syme St; adult/concession $2/1; ☒ 11am-5pm) has 13 rooms of excellent arts and crafts, including oils, watercolours, glassware, jewellery and ceramics. The small but lovely **Williamstown Botanic Gardens** (Map p86; cnr Osborne & Giffard Sts) are also worth a visit.

Scienceworks Museum & Melbourne Planetarium (Map pp70-1; ☎ 9392 4800; www.scienceworks .museum.vic.gov.au; 2 Booker St, Spotswood; adult/concession $6/free, incl Planetarium show adult/concession $12.50/5; ☒ 10am-4.30pm) is under the shadow of the West Gate Bridge. The Scienceworks Museum was built on the site of the Spotswood pumping station, Melbourne's first sewage works, and incorporates the historic old buildings. You can spend hours wandering around inspecting old machines, poking buttons and pulling levers, and learning all sorts of weird facts and figures. The planetarium section usually holds shows daily. The museum is a 10-minute signposted walk from Spotswood train station down Hudsons Rd.

Williamstown Beach, on the southern side of the peninsula, is a really pleasant place for a swim. From Nelson Pl walk down Cole St, or get off the train at the Williamstown Beach station and walk down Forster St.

A good **bicycle path** follows the foreshore reserve and runs all the way to the West Gate Bridge, passing the Scienceworks Museum & Melbourne Planetarium.

Williamstown Ferries (☎ 9506 4144; www.williams townferries.com.au) runs ferries between Gem Pier in Williamstown and Southgate. Ferries travel daily on a regular basis (there may be more departures in good weather and during summer). The ferry stops at Scienceworks Museum & Melbourne Planetarium, *Polly Woodside* and the Melbourne Exhibition Centre/Crown Casino en route.

On weekends and public holidays the same company runs ferries to/from St Kilda Pier (see p104), with hourly departures from Williamstown from 11am to 4pm, and from St Kilda from 11.30am to 4.30pm.

Other Bayside Suburbs

Starting from the city end, Albert Park, Middle Park and St Kilda are the most popular city beaches. Farther around the bay there's **Elwood**, **Brighton** and **Sandringham**, which are quite pleasant. Next comes **Half Moon Bay**, which is pretty good for a city beach, as is **Black Rock** nearby. Beyond here you have to get right around to the Mornington Peninsula before you find some more good bay beaches, including those around **Mt Eliza** and **Mt Martha**. The northern end of Sunnyside Beach at Mt Eliza is a designated nudist area.

If you want to go surfing or see spectacular and remote ocean beaches, head for the **Mornington Peninsula** (p179), southeast of the city, or the **Bellarine Peninsula** (p159), to the southwest; both are a little over an hour's drive away.

HEIDE & SEEK

In the outer suburb of Bulleen is the **Heide Museum of Modern Art** (☎ 9850 1500; www.heide .com.au; 7 Templestowe Rd, Bulleen; admission adult/child $12/8, more for exhibitions; ☒ 10am-5pm Tue-Fri, noon-5pm Sat & Sun). Known as Heide, the museum is on the site of the former home of John and Sunday Reed, under whose patronage the likes of Sir Sidney Nolan, John Perceval, Albert Tucker, Joy Hester and Arthur Boyd created a new movement in the Australian art world. The gallery has an impressive collection of 20th-century Australian art. It is set in a sprawling park with an informal combination of deciduous and native trees, a carefully tended kitchen garden and scattered sculpture gardens running right down to the banks of the Yarra. The Heide Museum is signposted off the Eastern Fwy. Otherwise, take an Eltham-line train to Heidelberg station, from where you can catch National Bus No 291 to the corner of Manningham and Templestowe Rds and walk from there. Heide is closed for refurbishment until 2006, but Heide 1 (the heritage-listed farmhouse) and the gardens are still open.

MELBOURNE

ACTIVITIES

This section covers a range of activities in and around Melbourne – for more details and information on activities around the state, see p43.

Canoeing

Yarra Bend Park (p97) stretches for 12km north of Richmond and offers canoeing at the **Studley Park Boathouse** (Map p81; ☎ 9853 1972; www.studleyparkboathouse.com.au) for $22 per hour (per two-person canoe). A little farther along, the **Fairfield Boathouse** (Map pp70-1; ☎ 9486 1501; www.fairfieldboathouse.com) rents a range of watercraft (including Gentlemen's Rowing Skiffs) from $12 to $26 per hour. You'll need a $10 deposit and photo ID.

Cycling

You're cycling beside the river through a grove of trees, bellbirds are chiming, colourful rosellas are swooping low over the path, and the tangy aroma of hops from the brewery is mingling with the chocolate smell from the biscuit factory. You're somewhere in the country, miles from Melbourne, right? Wrong – you're on the Main Yarra Trail, one of Melbourne's many inner-city bike paths constructed along the riverside green belts. Used by commuters and tourists alike, this 38km-long cycling and walking trail winds along the Yarra River, past historic homes, natural bushland and sports fields, often far from roads.

At least 20 other long, urban cycle paths exist, including one that runs around the shores of Port Phillip Bay from Port Melbourne to Brighton, and those along the Maribyrnong River and Merri Creek; all are marked in the Melway *Greater Melbourne Street Directory*. Melbourne also has a growing network of on-road bike lanes, making this a relatively easy and safe way to explore the city via pedal power. You can get maps from the **Melbourne Visitor Information Centre** (Map pp72-4; ☎ 9658 9658; Federation Square; ☻ 9am-6pm) and **Bicycle Victoria** (☎ 8636 8888; www.bv.com .au). In addition, **VicRoads** (www.vicroads.vic.gov.au) has printable maps of Melbourne's cycle paths on its website.

One note of caution: tram tracks are a major hazard for cyclists in Melbourne. Many cyclists have their own 'wheel-in-a-track' horror story. Cross them on a sufficient angle to prevent your tyre falling into the track.

TREAT YOURSELF

Getting pampered has become something of an art form in Melbourne (not to mention a bit of an obsession), with plenty of places willing to shower you with the attention you deserve. Pick of the bunch is the **Japanese Bath House** (Map p81; ☎ 9419 0268; 59 Cromwell St, Collingwood; ☻ noon-11pm Tue-Fri, noon-8pm Sat & Sun). There's nothing like relaxing in a good hot bath after a day of sightseeing, and this is an authentic Japanese-style bath house with segregated areas for men and women. Each area includes a deep bath and a sauna, and you can also get scrubbed to within an inch of your circulation's life. Bookings are essential.

Wearing a helmet while cycling is compulsory. Places to hire bikes (which generally include a helmet and lock) in Melbourne include the following, all of which are open daily; bring along a credit card or photo ID:

Bike Now (Map pp84-5; ☎ 9696 8588; 100 Park St, South Melbourne) Good-quality bikes for $60 per day.

Hire a Bike (Map pp72-4; ☎ 0412 616 633; near Princes Bridge, Southbank) Close to the city centre and offering bikes for $35 a day.

St Kilda Cycles (Map p83; ☎ 9534 3074; www.stkilda cycles.com.au; 11 Carlisle St, St Kilda) You'll get a helmet and a lock with your bike – for $20 a day (add $5 for overnight hire).

Fishing & Boating

You *can* fish in the Yarra and Maribyrnong Rivers, but you're better off heading down to the bay and hooking a few snapper. Try the Port Melbourne, Albert Park and St Kilda Piers. Tackle shops, such as the **Compleat Angler** (Map pp72-4; ☎ 9620 3320; www.compleatangler .com.au; 387 Flinders Lane, Melbourne) are good places for advice and tips straight from the school of 'Wishin' I was Fishin'.

Boats can be hired for fishing on the bay, but the conditions can be deceptively treacherous – don't go out unless you're sure of the weather (www.bom.gov.au/weather/vic /forecasts.shtml). Try **Williamstown Boat Hire** (Map p86; ☎ 9397 7312; 34 The Strand, Williamstown).

Golf

Melbourne's sand-belt golf courses, such as Royal Melbourne, Victoria, Huntingdale and Kingston Heath, are world famous. It is tough to get a round at these members' courses, but there are also plenty of public courses where anyone can play. You will need to book on weekends. Green fees are around $20 for 18 holes, and most courses have clubs and buggies for hire. There are some good public courses close to town:

Albert Park Golf Course (Map pp84-5; ☎ 9510 5588; www.golfvictoria.com.au; Queens Rd, Albert Park) Next to Albert Park Lake and only 2km from the city.

Royal Park Golf Course (Map p79; ☎ 9387 3585; The Avenue) In Parkville near the zoo – bookings are always a good idea.

Yarra Bend Public Golf Course (Map p81; ☎ 9481 3729; Yarra Bend Rd, Fairfield) Yarra Bend is the pick of the bunch and has 27 holes. Bookings are essential.

In-line Skating

In-line skating is a popular summer activity, and the best tracks are those found around Port Phillip Bay from Port Melbourne to Brighton, especially around St Kilda. You can hire skates from the following places:

Albert Park In-Line Skates (Map pp84-5; ☎ 9645 9099; 179 Victoria Ave, Albert Park; ☺ 10am-7pm Mon-Fri, 9am-7pm Sat & Sun) This place also rents bicycles, but for a mere $7 per hour you can be blading to your hearts' content (padding included). Bring photo ID.

Rock 'n' Roll Skate Hire (Map p83; ☎ 9525 3434; 22 Fitzroy St, St Kilda; ☺ 10am-7pm Mon-Fri, 9am-7pm Sat & Sun) Rates start at $8 per hour or $25 per day, and the equipment is in pretty good condition at this well-patronised business.

Jogging

Melbourne has some great routes for runners. One of the favourites is the Tan track (Map p75) around the Royal Botanic Gardens (p97). The bicycle tracks beside the Yarra and around the bay are also good runs, but watch out for bike riders. Albert Park Lake (p105) is another favourite, and there's always the St Kilda foreshore (p104) area, too.

Lawn Bowls

Experiencing a revival in recent years, lawn bowls are attracting large numbers of young and old folk who appreciate this affordable (games cost $5 to $10), sociable activity that tolerates all levels of fitness and allows you to drink, smoke and be active all at the same time. Try the following greens:

North Fitzroy Bowls (Map p80; ☎ 9481 3137; www.fv bowls.com.au; 578 Brunswick St, North Fitzroy; ☺ daily) This easy-going place has barbecue facilities, night lights and attracts the odd party on weekends. Phone to make a booking and for opening times, which can vary.

St Kilda Bowling Club (Map p83; ☎ 9537 0370; 66 Fitzroy St, St Kilda; ☺ Tue-Sun) Barefoot bowls and a delightfully down-at-heel clubhouse that has the excellent Mountain Goat beer on tap.

Sailboarding & Kitesurfing

Close to the city, Elwood is a very popular sailboarding and kitesurfing area. **RPS – the Board Store** (Map pp70-1; ☎ 9525 6475; www.rpsthe boardstore.com; 87 Ormond Rd, Elwood) can teach you the basics of either sport for $129/75 respectively per introductory outing. All gear is included in the price.

Sailing

With about 20 yacht clubs around the shores of Port Phillip, yachting is one of Melbourne's most popular passions. Races and regattas are held on most weekends, and the bay is a memorable sight when it's sprinkled with hundreds of colourful sails. Conditions can change radically and without warning, making sailing on the bay a challenging, and sometimes dangerous, pursuit. Melbourne's two main ocean races are the Melbourne to Devonport and Melbourne to Hobart, held annually between Christmas and New Year. The Melbourne to Hobart goes around Tasmania's wild west coast, unlike the more famous Sydney to Hobart, which runs down the east coast.

Many yacht clubs welcome visitors who volunteer to crew on racing boats. Phone the race secretary at one of the major clubs if you're keen. Try:

Hobsons Bay Yacht Club (Map p86; ☎ 9397 6393; 268 Nelson Pl, Williamstown) Volunteers get a go on weekends here.

Royal Melbourne Yacht Squadron (Map p83; ☎ 9534 0227; Pier Rd, St Kilda) Postcard-perfect location and crewing opportunities from Wednesday to Sunday.

For more leisurely sailing, dinghies can be hired from the **Jolly Roger School of Sailing** (Map pp84-5; ☎ 9690 5862; www.jollyrogersailing.com .au; Aquatic Dr, Albert Park Lake). Rates for 12-/16-foot sailing boats are $40/50 per hour. You must know how to sail to rent the dinghies (if you don't, you can always take a one-hour lesson for about $55).

Surfing

The closest surf beaches to Melbourne are on the Mornington and Bellarine Peninsulas. Bells Beach on the Great Ocean Rd near Torquay is recognised as a world-class surfing beach. For more on surfing near Melbourne, see p48.

Swimming

Despite Melbourne's reputation for fickle weather, swimming is a popular form of exercise, and thanks to some of the city's indoor (and outdoor) pools, it can be done year-round. The following pools are all worth trying if you feel the need to lap things up.

The **Melbourne Sports & Aquatic Centre** (Map pp84-5; ☎ 9926 1555; www.msac.com.au; Aughtie Dr, Albert Park; admission adult/child $5.70/4.20; ⊙ 6am-10pm year-round) has a fantastic indoor 75m 10-lane pool, several smaller pools, water slides, spa/sauna/steam room and spacious common areas. A visit here can easily double as the day's entertainment, plus you can play squash and use the gym. Childcare is also available.

The stately **Melbourne City Baths** (Map pp76-8; ☎ 9663 5888; cnr Swanston & Victoria Sts; adult/concession $4/3.20; ⊙ year-round) has a 30m indoor pool, as well as a gym, spas, saunas and squash courts.

There are other good pools in Melbourne: **Fitzroy Swimming Pool** (Map pp76-8; ☎ 9417 6493; Alexandra Pde, Fitzroy; adult/concession $3.80/2.20; ⊙ Nov-Mar) This is a nice outdoor local pool (50m) that's popular with locals and host to some cool summer-afternoon entertainment programmes. Call for details.
Harold Holt Swim Centre (Map pp70-1; ☎ 8290 1678; cnr Edgar & High Sts, Glen Iris; adult/concession $4.20/3.40; ⊙ year-round) A swimming pool named after a prime minister who drowned? Hmmmm… Still, there's an indoor pool and a heated 50m outdoor pool.
Prahran Aquatic Centre (Map p82; ☎ 8290 7140; 41 Essex St, Prahran; adult/child $3.80/2; ⊙ Oct-Apr) Good outdoor pool that's very popular with gay men come summer.
St Kilda Sea Baths (Map p83; ☎ 9525 4888; 10-18 Jacka Blvd, St Kilda; adult/child $12/6; ⊙ year-round) Not the cheapest swim in town, but the indoor 25m sea-water pool here is a miracle worker. We can't function unless we start the day with 40 laps and a session in the hydrotherapy spa.

Lastly, don't forget the bay – you can choose from many beaches and the water temperature is tolerable from mid-November to late March, although the water isn't much to look

at. The bay is reasonably clean, although the water tends to look a little murky, especially after high winds and rain.

Tennis & Squash

Tennis-court hire generally costs from $20 to $26 per hour, and costs on weekends or after 4pm.

Except in January, during the Australian Open, you can hire one of the 23 outdoor and five indoor courts of the **Melbourne Park** (Map p75; ☎ 9286 1244; Batman Ave, Melbourne; per hr $20). You can also have a hit-up in leafy surrounds at the **East Melbourne Tennis Centre** (Map p75; ☎ 9417 6511; cnr Simpson & Albert Sts, East Melbourne; $18-26 per hour; ⊙ year-round), where you can also get coached for $66 per hour. For other public courts, see the Yellow Pages.

There are squash courts in the city at the **Melbourne City Baths** (Map pp72-4; ☎ 9663 5888; cnr Swanston & Victoria Sts, Melbourne) and the **Melbourne Sports & Aquatic Centre** (Map pp84-5; ☎ 9926 1555; www.msac.com.au; Aughtie Dr, Albert Park). For courts in other areas, check the Yellow Pages.

Yoga

Melburnians like to iron out the kinks with a variety of yoga styles and asanas. The following places all offer drop-in classes. Check the websites for class timetables:
Action School of Yoga (Map pp76-8; ☎ 9415 9798; www.actionyoga.com; Level 1, 275 Smith St, Collingwood) Teaches Iyengar yoga and has a solid reputation.
Ashtanga Yoga Centre of Melbourne (Map pp76-8; ☎ 9419 1598; www.ashtangamelbourne.com.au; Level 1, 110 Argyle St, Fitzroy) Rigorous Mysore-style classes, and courses for kids and teens, too.
Yoga Tree (Map pp70-1; ☎ 9532 7418; www.yogatree.com.au; 5 Horne St, Elsternwick) Adherents of the Bikram method will be able to sweat it out in style here.

WALKING TOUR

Melbourne's network of alleys, lanes and arcades, plus some of its most interesting buildings, form the basis for this classic city saunter.

Start at **Federation Square** (1; p87) and then head west along Flinders St past magnificent **Flinders St station** (2). From here, cross over to **Young & Jackson's** (3), one of the city's oldest hotels and home to the late-19th-century nude portrait known as Chloe – a Melbourne icon. Head west along Flinders St and turn right (north) into Degraves St, with its quaint cafes, and continue towards Centre Pl, where

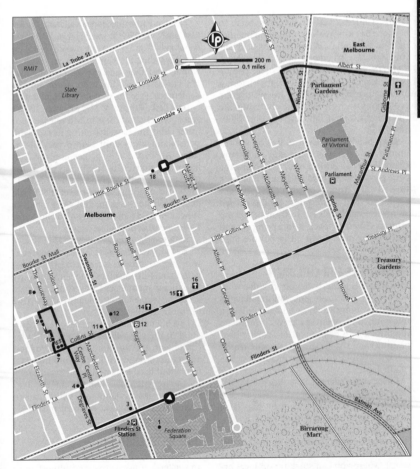

Distance: 2.4km
Duration: 2 hours

you'll spy the fabulous **Majorca Building** (**4**), one of the city's most sought-after slices of real estate. Follow Centre Pl, with its uniquely European feel (it's very reminiscent of Barcelona), through the arcade to lovely, leafy Collins St, where you'll find great architecture at **Lyric House** (**5**; No 248), **Kodak House** (**6**; No 252) and **Newspaper House** (**7**; No 247), with its stunning glass mosaic on the façade.

Cross the street and cut through the Australia on Collins shopping arcade, emerging at Little Collins St. From here, enter delightful **Royal Arcade** (**8**; p91). Start threading your way back to Collins St by taking **Block Pl** (**9**; p90), which is crammed with bustling cafes (making this an ideal pit stop) to **Block Arcade** (**10**; p90). When you emerge on Collins St, head east to its corner with Swanston St and the glorious **Manchester Unity Building** (**11**; p89), which is probably the best example of 1930s' Art Deco architecture in the city. Opposite, the gold-boom wedding cake of **Melbourne Town Hall** (**12**; p89) beckons.

Keep striding east up Collins St, where you'll pass the lovely **Regent Theatre** (**13**; p90). Opposite the theatre and hidden behind a white classical façade is the **Baptist Church** (**14**) at No 170. It was built in 1861–62 on top of an older building (1845), and is the oldest

Baptist Church in Australia (there seem to be more Baptists in Melbourne than in other parts of Australia). Where Collins St meets Russell St is watched over by two churches – **Scots (15**; p90) and **St Michael's (16**; p90) – both excellent examples of High Victorian architecture as espoused by Joseph Reed, a prodigious and prolific contributor to the city's architectural landscape in the 1860s and 1870s.

Keep heading up Collins St. You're now unmistakably at the 'Paris end' of things. Cross Spring St to Macarthur St, passing the back garden of Parliament House and walk towards **St Patrick's Cathedral (17**; p101), a Gothic Revival masterpiece. You've earned yourself a snack at least, so from here, loop around Albert St back into Spring St and follow your nose down Little Bourke St to **Chinatown (18**; p92).

MELBOURNE FOR CHILDREN

Melbourne is a child-friendly city that goes out of its way to make sure children have as many fun things to do as adults. Galleries, museums and open spaces accommodate the littlies with equipment or specific programmes, and some attractions are geared solely for children. We've included a few of our faves.

Collingwood Children's Farm (Map p81; ☎ 9417 5806; St Heliers St, Abbotsford; adult/concession $8/4; ☻ 9am-5.30pm), a bucolic spot by the Yarra River, is festooned with grazing farm animals, such as goats, cows, lambs and ponies, plus there's a delightful **Farmers' Market** (☎ 5657 2337; admission $2; ☻ 8am-1pm 2nd Sat of month), where you can stock up on local or organic produce. A treat for the young and the young at heart.

The northern side of the Bourke St Mall is dominated by the frontages of the Myer and David Jones department stores. During the Christmas season, from mid-November to 7 January, don't miss the famous **Myer Christmas Windows** (Map pp72-4; ☎ 9661 1111; 314 Bourke St, Melbourne). Each year, the department store chooses a different theme and talented artists transform the windows along the mall into a magical world that seems to fascinate adults as much as it does children. If you're in town then, we highly recommend making the annual pilgrimage to the mall to walk the length of the storefront with the legions of children and their minders.

The **Ian Potter Foundation Children's Garden** (Map pp84-5; ☎ 9252 2300; www.rbg.vic.gov.au; Birdwood Ave; admission free; ☻ 10am-4pm Wed-Sun Apr-Oct), at the Royal Botanic Gardens, is an outdoor wonderland that kids can't get enough of. It's closed for a 'big sleep' from July to September – see the website for exact dates.

Luna Park (Map p83; ☎ 9525 5033; www.lunapark .com.au; Lower Esplanade, St Kilda) will release your inner child and have it stuffing its face with sweets and other stuff before you hit the rides. All in the aim of keeping the kids happy, of course. Its Scenic Railway is the oldest continually operating rollercoaster in the world, enabling you to travel at 50km/h, deliver a history lesson, and get a fantastic view of St Kilda and the bay all at the same time. See p104 for more details.

Scienceworks (Map pp70-1; ☎ 9392 4800; www .scienceworks.museum.vic.gov.au; 2 Booker St, Spotswood) will inspire kids to get all scientific, what with hands-on displays and enough ways to expend mental and physical energy to leave the whole family galvanised. See p107 for more details.

Last but not least, almost every neighbourhood in the city will have a park with play equipment, and therefore other kids to meet and muck around with. For more information about local attractions and events, look for the free monthly publication **Melbourne's Child** (www.melbourneschild.com.au), which can be found in cafés and kid-oriented businesses all over town.

QUIRKY MELBOURNE

Hampered by a past reputation for being an austere, conservative and almost dour city, Melbourne may well surprise you with some of its rather endearing quirks.

Wrapture – the Melbourne Scarf Festival (www .craftvic.asn.au/project/scarf/index.htm) celebrates the quintessential Melbourne fashion accessory (and often necessity), with a festival all to itself in the cold winter month of June. Staged by Craft Victoria, it's a great chance to pick up a unique neck-warming work of art and be inspired by local artisans.

If you visit the State Library of Victoria (p90) between 2.30pm and 6pm on a Sunday afternoon, be sure to check out the **Speakers' Forum**, held on the lawn in front of the library. Here, a ragtag group of malcontents hold forth on a variety of issues, while enduring withering heckling from the assembled onlookers. It's a real 'only in Melbourne' event.

If that sounds a little too political for you, perhaps the **Neighbours Ramsay St Tour** (Map p83; ☎ 9534 4755; www.neighbourstour.com.au; 121 Fitzroy St, St Kilda; adult/concession $30/25) is more up your street. A pilgrimage of sorts for many British backpackers, this tribute to the residents of the long-running soap *Neighbours* is a must-do for any devotee of Aussie kitsch. You'll depart from St Kilda and find yourself in the thick of suburbia for a good three hours – more than enough for anyone really.

If you had a local boy make good and become prime minister, you'd probably name something important after him, to ensure his posterity. Maybe a bridge, a building or a road. But a swimming pool? When he drowned? Check out the **Harold Holt Swim Centre** (p110) if you don't believe us.

If you have a despondent-looking 1980s-era computer in your garage at home, Melbourne is the place where it can be given a second life, thanks to **micromusic** – the musical manipulation of 'old' technology. Hear it at Bar Open in Fitzroy (p132).

If you want to see a local dance move, keep an eye out for the **Melbourne Shuffle** in the city's various clubs. You'll recognise it by shuffling foot movements and energetic upper body contortions. Apparently, Melburnians have been identified overseas when a fellow shuffler stumbles upon them miles from home, but still unwilling to relinquish the shuffle.

And, let's not forget the **hook turn**, the wrongest right-hand turn you'll ever make. See p145 for more information.

TOURS

There's a huge array of tours on offer in and around Melbourne. The free *Me!bourne Events* guide, which is updated monthly, is available at visitors centres, hotels and newsagents, and has an extensive section on tours. Ask at the visitors centre in Federation Square if you've got something particular in mind. The National Trust (see p101) publishes the *Walking Melbourne* ($20) booklet, which is particularly useful if you're interested in Melbourne's architectural heritage.

Aboriginal Heritage Walk (Map pp84-5; ☎ 9252 2300; www.rbg.vic.gov.au; Royal Botanic Gardens; adult/ child $15.50/6.60; ☺ 11am Thu & Fri, 10.30am alternate Sun) The Royal Botanic Gardens are on the ancestral lands of the Boonwurrung and Woi wurrung people, and this tour takes you through their story – from song lines to dietary staples, all in 90 fascinating minutes. The tour departs from the visitors centre.

Chinatown Heritage Walk (Map pp72-4; ☎ 9662 2888; www.melbournechinatown.com.au/attractions_walk .html; 22 Cohen Pl; adult/concession $15/12) Get guided through historic Chinatown, with its atmospheric alleys and bustling vibe. You can even get fed on this tour, for a little bit extra and one hour more.

City Circle trams (www.metlinkmelbourne.com.au/city _circle/routes.html) A free service operating from 10am to 6pm daily. This tram travels around the city centre, along Flinders, Spring and Latrobe Sts, and then back along Harbour Esplanade (there are also trams running in the opposite direction). Designed primarily for tourists, and passing many city sights along the way, the trams run every 10 minutes or so. Eight refurbished W-class trams operate on this route. Built in Melbourne between 1936 and 1956, they have all been painted a distinctive deep burgundy and gold. You can even dine on board a tram (www.tramrestaurant.com.au) while taking a scenic night cruise around Melbourne's streets.

City Explorer (Map pp72-4; ☎ 1800 858 687; tickets from 180 Swanston St; adult/child $33/16.50) This service offers double-decker bus tours of Melbourne, with about 20 stops en route. Stops include the Melbourne Museum and the Royal Botanic Gardens.

Maribyrnong River Cruises (Map pp70-1; ☎ 9689 6431; www.blackbirdcruises.com.au; Wingfield St, Footscray; adult/child from $7/4) One- or two-hour cruises are available. The longer cruise goes up the Maribyrnong River (past the Lonely Planet office!) to Avondale Heights. The one-hour cruise heads down to the West Gate Bridge and the docklands. Departures are from the end of Wingfield St in Footscray. Cruises run on Tuesday, Thursday, Saturday, Sunday and public holidays.

Melbourne River Cruises (Map pp72-4; ☎ 9681 3284; www.melbcruises.com.au; Berth 5 & 6, Southbank Lower Promenade, Southgate; adult/child from $14/7.50) Take a one-hour cruise upstream or downstream, or a 2½-hour return cruise. Regular cruises along the Yarra River depart from a couple of locations – check with the company for details. It also operates a ferry between Southgate and Gem Pier in Williamstown. There are three to six sailings daily, depending on the season.

FESTIVALS & EVENTS

Melbourne has festivals year-round, and many of these are thematic, with film, comedy, theatre, sport, food and wine, bringing out locals and visitors alike to revel in Melbourne life.

The free *Me!bourne Events* guide, available at visitor centres, has listings of all

MELBOURNE

GAY & LESBIAN MELBOURNE

Melbourne may not be as well known as Sydney in terms of gaydar quiverings, but it's a relaxed, friendly town, and has an out-enough scene to attract plenty of gay and lesbian visitors. Various free street publications are good sources of information about what's on in Melbourne. Try: the *Melbourne Star*, **MCV** (www.mcv.net.au), **Bnews** (www.bnews.net.au) and **Lesbiana**, which you can find in various bars, clubs and cafés. Hares & Hyenas (p68) is a gay-and-lesbian-centric bookshop with a great range of titles and lots of information.

The **ALSO Foundation** (☎ 9827 4999; www.also.org.au) is a helpful community-based organisation whose website boasts a great services directory. If it's gay sounds that you're after, tune in to **Joy FM** (www.joy.org.au), Melbourne's gay radio station (and sadly enough, Australia's only gay radio station) – you'll find it at 94.9 on the FM dial.

We've listed various entertainment options on p136.

major events going on while you're in town. You can also check it out online at www .melbourne.vic.gov.au/events.

Tickets to most major events can be booked through Ticketmaster7 (p133).

January

Australian Open (www.australianopen.com) One of the four Grand Slam tennis events, held at the Melbourne Park Tennis Centre. The perfect place to swivel your head as you watch the world's best players sweat it out.

Chinese New Year (www.melbournechinatown.com .au; late Jan/early Feb) Enter the dragon, rabbit or some other animal at this bold, bright and quintessentially noisy celebration.

Midsumma Festival (www.midsumma.org.au; mid-Jan– early Feb) Melbourne's annual gay-and-lesbian arts festival comprises over 100 events spread across the city, some political, some frivolous – and seven shades of artistic.

February

St Kilda Festival (www.stkildafestival.com.au) A weekend-long celebration of local arts and culture – food, art, music and writing – and always at its best when the sun is out.

March

Antipodes Festival (www.antipodesfestival.com.au) Held in Melbourne's small Greek quarter on Lonsdale St, between Swanston and Russell Sts, the festival celebrates Greek art, food, culture and music.

Australian Formula One Grand Prix (www.grandprix .com.au) Albert Park gets invaded by the thoroughbreds of the automotive world, and their party-loving hangers-on. Ferrari colours predominate in this Italophile city.

Irish Festival (17 March) Held at venues all over the city, this pissed-up appropriation of all things emerald green reaches a climax on St Patrick's Day.

Melbourne Fashion Festival (www.mff.com.au) A week of ready-to-wear hedonism and fab frocks, with all sorts of artfully accessorised functions, showings and parades.

Melbourne Food & Wine Festival (www.melbournefood andwine.com.au; mid-Mar–early Apr) The main gastronomic event of the year is highly regarded in Australia and overseas.

Melbourne Moomba Waterfest (www.melbourne.vic .gov.au) Ten days of carnivals, fireworks and an outdoor art show, as well as water-skiing and a Dragon Boat Festival, all on the Yarra River. Tries hard to shake its daggy image (the Birdman Rally is unmissable), and, thankfully, usually fails, as do attempts to relegate the whole thing to the scrapheap.

April

Anzac Day (25 Apr) The day begins with a dawn service at the Shrine of Remembrance (p96), followed by a march for returned servicemen along St Kilda Rd into the city.

International Comedy Festival (www.comedyfestival .com.au; Mar) Locals are joined by a wealth of international acts performing at venues all over the city.

International Flower & Garden Show (www.melb flowershow.com.au) Held annually in the Carlton Gardens and bloomin' delightful.

May

Next Wave Festival (www.nextwave.org.au) Held at various city venues, Next Wave presents over two weeks of visual and performing arts from a new generation of artists.

St Kilda Film Festival (www.stkildafilmfestival.com.au; late May) This festival showcases a selection of contemporary Australian short films and videos.

July

Melbourne International Film Festival (www.mel bournefilmfestival.com.au) Two weeks of the newest and the best in local and international films. An excellent exposition, with screenings, talks, forums and a lot of drinking.

August

Melbourne Writers' Festival (www.mwf.com.au; Aug/ Sep) Held annually at various venues throughout this most book-loving of Australia's cities, this 10-day festival covers a wide range of literary genres and issues, with local and international authors speaking, reading, quaffing and writing.

September

AFL Grand Final (www.afl.com.au; Sep) Join in with the spirit of the Australian Football League (AFL) final and pray that it's not contested by two out-of-town teams. Played on the last Saturday of the month.
Melbourne Fringe Festival (www.melbournefringe.com.au; late Sep–Oct) This festival starts with a parade and street party on Brunswick St, and has events to suit a range of tastes and interests.
Royal Melbourne Show (www.royalshow.com.au) The country comes to town for this large-scale agricultural fair at the Royal Melbourne Showgrounds (Map pp70–1) in Flemington. Showbags, baby animals and plenty of rides.

October

Lygon St Festa (www.lygonst.com) Italian culture is celebrated with food stalls, bands and dancers on Lygon St.
Melbourne International Arts Festival (www.melbournefestival.com.au) The city's major arts event has a programme that covers theatre, opera, dance and music, and revolves around an annual theme – the 2004 theme was voice and it covered everything from modern opera to karaoke.
Oktoberfest (www.melboctfest.com) A three-day festival styled on the Bavarian festival of the same name, held at the Royal Melbourne Showgrounds, Flemington. Think beer, drink beer.

November

Hispanic Community Festival Melbourne's small Spanish and Latin American communities take over Johnston St, Fitzroy, for a sometimes lively celebration of Latin culture, and lots of *churros* (Spanish-style sticks of fried batter).
Spring Racing Carnival (www.racingvictoria.net.au; late Oct–Nov) There are two feature races: Caulfield Cup (Caulfield Racecourse) and the Melbourne Cup (Flemington Racecourse). See p140 for details.

December

Carols by Candlelight (www.rvibcarolsbycandlelight.com.au) Christmas carols under the stars at the Sidney Myer Music Bowl, to support the Royal Victorian Institute for the Blind.
International Test Match Cricket (www.mcg.org.au; starts Boxing Day) Held at the MCG.

SLEEPING

Melbourne's sleeping options are broad and generally of a high standard – you can pick from a number of categories in the midrange to top-end scale, with serviced apartments, motels, boutique guesthouses, B&Bs and five-star hotels concentrated in the city centre, East Melbourne and suburbs, such as

---

THE AUTHOR'S CHOICE

Windsor (Map pp72-4; ☎ 9633 6000; www.thewindsor.com.au; 103 Spring St; r from $500; P ☒ ☐) The queen of the scene is still (and probably always will be) the Windsor, Melbourne's 'Grand Lady' and one of our favourite hotels in the world. If the devil is in the detail, then the old-fashioned, haut-luxe embellishments that grace this stately pile are downright satanic. Fabulous rooms, a great sense of history and wonderful service (that has accommodated the whims of such luminaries as Sir Laurence Olivier – with Vivien Leigh, the Duke of Windsor, Gregory Peck and even Metallica) make this more than just a hotel – it's on every local's wish list for a romantic weekend. High tea here is justifiably famous, so if you can't get a room, at least get a scone.

St Kilda and South Yarra. The city centre is convenient and close to theatres, museums and transport terminals, and is also within walking (or should that be staggering?) distance of the city's wonderful nightlife. The alternative is to stay in one of the inner suburbs, such as Carlton or Fitzroy, that surround the city and offer good-quality sleeping, particularly if you're on a budget. There are also good budget options in the pleasant southeastern suburbs near the city centre, including St Kilda and South Yarra.

There are backpacker hostels in the city centre and most of the inner suburbs. It's usually easy to find rooms in winter, but space gets tight in summer – book well in advance if possible. Several of the larger hostels have courtesy buses that pick up from the bus and train terminals. Most offer discounts for weekly and monthly stays.

Most midrange hotels and motels are rated three stars, and they're comfortable but sometimes a little cramped; doubles usually cost the same as singles. There are some excellent B&Bs in Melbourne, many of which are at least as comfortable as a four-star hotel, but charge much less. Boutique hotels are often more like large B&Bs or upmarket guesthouses, sometimes occupying lovely old buildings.

Melbourne's top-end hotels and serviced apartments combine excellent location, attractive décor and attentive service. Generally,

MELBOURNE

CAMPING OPTIONS

Only 9km northwest of the city centre, **Ashley Gardens Big 4 Holiday Village** (Map pp70-1; ☎ 9318 6866; www.ashleygardens.com.au; cnr Ashley St & Ballarat Rd, Braybrook; powered & unpowered sites per 2 people $27-33, d cabins from $70; Ⓟ Ⓢ) is a well-run, spacious park. It's a good option for those who want to stay in camping grounds, especially if you're travelling with children. Also available are well-appointed units that sleep up to six people. You can access the city centre via bus No 220, which departs from Flinders St station.

There are caravan parks along the train links to the city. Other good caravan parks can be found in the Yarra Valley, which offers uncrowded scenery within striking distance of the city. For more on these, see p169.

---

you'll find a range of packages and deals on offer via the Internet. Parking is often of the 'valet' variety and can incur a charge $12 to $25 per day. The prices listed here for top-end places are only rough guidelines; you can usually get lower rates via a wide variety of accommodation packages (which often include meals, massages and access to fitness facilities).

Be aware that during major festivals and events, accommodation in Melbourne is very scarce, so you'll need to make reservations well in advance. This is especially the case during the Australian Formula One Grand Prix, the Melbourne Cup and the Australian Open (see Festivals & Events, p113), at which time you can also expect prices to rise substantially, even for some of the backpacker hostels.

Price categories for this chapter are a little different than for the rest of this book – a reflection of Melbourne's popularity as a tourist destination and also its status as the state's capital. Midrange listings cost $80 to $165 for a double room with bathroom. Anything more than that is regarded as a top-end option and anything less than $80 is classified as budget accommodation, including dorm rooms in hostels. Prices listed here generally apply for most of the year, except for hostels, which have fluctuating prices - you can expect to pay a little more in the high season.

APARTMENT HOTELS & SERVICED APARTMENTS

Melbourne has an ever-expanding range of apartment-style hotels and serviced apartments. More spacious than regular hotels, and with their own kitchen and laundry facilities, this style of accommodation can be better value and more comfortable than

an equivalently priced hotel, especially for people travelling in a group.

Several companies manage many blocks of apartments, and you're likely to be offered a better deal if you speak to headquarters rather than the individual apartment managers. Try:

Oakford (☎ 1800 642 188; www.oakford.com)
Punt Hill (☎ 1800 331 529; www.punthill-apartments .com.au)
Quest (☎ 1800 334 033; www.questapartments.com.au)

Central Melbourne

It's hard to beat the city centre in terms of easy access to shopping, nightlife and cultural attractions. The city centre has some good hostels, which have the advantage of being central and close to the train stations and bus depots, as well as some of the city's most luxurious and elegant accommodation options.

BUDGET

Greenhouse Backpacker (Map pp72-4; ☎ 9639 6400; www.friendlygroup.com.au; 228 Flinders Lane; s/d & tw $55/68; Ⓠ) A short walk from Flinders St station, this large, well-maintained hostel has very clean rooms, pleasant common areas and staff who are happy to help you make the most of its excellent location. Security is solid.

Friendly Backpacker (Map pp72-4; ☎ 9670 1111; www.friendlygroup.com.au; 197 King St; dm $24, d & tw $68; Ⓠ) This is a popular choice with travellers, as it manages to hum with a social vibe yet still maintains efficient, safe standards for its guests (the hostel is open and staffed 24 hours a day). Facilities are good, and there's a choice between mixed and single-sex dorms.

Melbourne Connection Travellers Hostel (Map pp72-4; ☎ 9642 4464; www.melbourneconnection.com;

205 King St; dm $22-26, d & tw $70, tr $81; (🖥) Less chaotic than some of the city's larger hostels, this place has a low-key, easy-going appeal that encourages light-hearted chatter. Common areas are in good nick and 24-hour access is available.

Hotel Bakpak (Map pp72-4; ☎ 9329 7525; www .bakpakgroup.com; 167 Franklin St; dm $23-26, s/d $55/65; 🖥) This backpackers' behemoth offers just about everything the budget traveller could ask for. Its functional, straightforward rooms are sandwiched between the basement bar and rooftop entertainment area, which has great views over the city. There's also a resource centre, which assists in job hunting, although if you're staying here longer than a few nights you may find it all a tad shambolic if you need to get up early for work. Reception is open 24 hours.

MIDRANGE

Duxton Hotel (Map pp72-4; ☎ 9250 1888; www .duxton.com; 328 Flinders St; r from $125; P 🍴 🖥) This heritage-listed hotel is another classic example of Melbourne's architectural history. Built in 1913 as the Commercial Travellers Club, much of the hotel has been restored to its original splendour. Rich, dark-timber panelling and ornate touches are a feature throughout the public areas, while modern touches bring it well into the 21st century for guests wanting right-this-minute amenities. Service is ever-helpful and keen to find the best deal possible.

Atlantis Hotel (Map pp72-4; ☎ 9600 2900; www .atlantishotel.com.au; 300 Spencer St; r from $135; P) A recent addition to the city's sleeping options at this busy end of town. There's good access to transport and city-centre sights, and rooms are pretty damn smart, with no chintz or froufrou anywhere.

Mercure Hotel Melbourne (Map p75; ☎ 9205 9999; www.mercure.com.au; 13 Spring St; r from $132; 🍴) The Mercure maintains a certain 'could be anywhere' sensibility in its décor and standards, but its Spring St location is a gem, with both the Paris end of town and the sporting side of things at your tiptoes. Popular with business types and those who hit town for big weekends at Jolimont.

Hotel Y (Map p79; ☎ 9329 5188; www.hotely.com .au; 489 Elizabeth St; r $80-150) This is an award-winning budget hotel run by the YWCA. The 'Y' has great facilities, including a café

on the premises, and a communal kitchen and laundry. You're also within easy reach of the Queen Vic Market, should you get in the mood to mooch and munch. You don't need to be young, Christian or a woman to stay here either.

Victoria Hotel (Map pp72-4; ☎ 9653 0441; www .victoriahotel.com.au; 215 Little Collins St; s $56-92, d $80-155) The Vic is a Melbourne institution – it's brilliantly located, surrounded by good shops, some great restaurants and cool bars. It's a flexible sort of place too, with the option of having a room with shared or private bathroom.

Astoria City Travel Inn (Map pp72-4; ☎ 9670 6801; www.astoriainternational.com; 288 Spencer St; r $100-130; P 🍴) Swathed in those matching pastel bedspread-and-curtain combos that afflict so many midrange hotels, the Astoria manages to rise above the identikit doldrums by offering evidence of an admirable love of cleanliness, handy access to the western end of town and car parking – a rare thing at this price range (although it'll cost $10 per night). Laundry facilities are also available.

City Square Motel (Map pp72-4; ☎ 9654 7011; www.citysquaremotel.com.au; 67 Swanston St; s/d $85/105) This hotel/motel has fairly basic rooms, but is right in the centre of town. You're not going to find it in the pages of *Condé Naste Traveller*, but you will find it quite easily, as it's in the thick of things. You get all the standard facilities, but no luxuries. Triples ($115) and family rooms ($125) are also available.

Hotel Enterprize (Map pp72-4; ☎ 9629 6991; www .hotelenterprize.com.au; 44 Spencer St; r $90-180; P) The Enterprize is a small and reasonably priced hotel, with good facilities for the business traveller (there are separate areas reserved for this). Amenities are strong, and the range of options should suit most travellers.

Batman's Hill (Map pp72-4; ☎ 9614 6344; www .batmanshill.com.au; 66 Spencer St; r from $155) This is a step up in standards from the budget hotels in this area, and it's in a heritage-listed building to boot. While the rooms are diminutive in dimensions, they're solid on standards, and service is very helpful.

City Limits (Map pp72-4; ☎ 9662 2544; www.city limits.com.au; 20-22 Little Bourke St; r $160; P 🍴) In the heart of the theatre district and close to Chinatown, the City Limits has attractively kitted-out rooms that take full advantage of their petite dimensions. Room rates include a light breakfast and self-catering facilities, although with Chinatown's lights winking so close you'll probably want to dine down the road.

Kingsgate Hotel (Map pp72-4; ☎ 9629 4171; www.kingsgatehotel.com.au; 131 King St; r $100-170) *Lifestyles of the Rich & Famous* it ain't, but well located and perfectly serviceable in a plain way it is. That said, don't tar it with a grotty old brush – it was renovated in 2002, and facilities are in good nick throughout.

Quest Fairfax House Serviced Apartments (Map pp72-4; ☎ 9642 1333; www.questapartments.com.au; 392 Little Collins St; apt from $165; P 𝕏) These apartments are centrally located, but this end of Little Collins St is relatively quiet. Apartments, with all the usual amenities, are comfortable and the complex is well run, with baby-sitting, secretarial services and even Melbourne City Baths memberships on offer.

Pacific International Apartments (Map pp72-4; ☎ 1800 682 003; www.pacificinthotels.com.au; 318 Little Bourke St; apt from $145) These apartments occupy a lovely old heritage building right in the heart of the city, but the interior is resolutely up-to-the-minute and very comfortable. These four-star serviced apartments are well managed and well equipped for both business and leisure travellers.

TOP END

Hotel Lindrum (Map p75; ☎ 9668 1111; www.hotel lindrum.com.au; 26 Flinders St; d from $300) Every inch of this hotel is divine, and it exudes an elegant luxury that never wanders off into overdrive. A former pool hall (hence Felt restaurant), the hotel's details and features emphasise quality and individual style. A close runner-up to the Windsor.

Adelphi Hotel (Map pp72-4; ☎ 9650 7555; www .adelphi.com.au; 187 Flinders Lane; r from $300; 𝕏) It's true, the Adelphi is showing not so much its age, but its era (the early 1990s). That said, no other hotel makes us so nostalgic for the heady days of conspicuous consumption, sharp angles and acidic colour accents. Service is slicker than grease, with exclusive attractions, such as the members-only rooftop bar, one of the best restaurants in town (Ezard, p123), and a cantilevered lap pool that allows you to swim right past the

edge of the building and suspend yourself over Little Collins St. Magnificent.

Park Hyatt (Map p75; ☎ 9224 1234; www.melbourne .park.hyatt.com; 1 Parliament Sq; r from $250; P 𝕏 □ 𝕏) This lavish hotel goes out of its way to remind its guests that they are likely to suffer if they choose to stay anywhere else – after all, even the cushions here are plumped to perfection. There's plenty of wood panelling, marble bathrooms, shiny surfaces and silky service, plus every amenity you can think of and some you may never know you need (Vichy shower anyone?). Business and health facilities are excellent and can even be combined – the hotel has a great tennis court. Those who are mobility impaired or travelling with children are looked after royally.

Westin Melbourne (Map pp72-4; ☎ 9635 2222; www.westin.com.au; 205 Collins St; r from $299; P 𝕏 □ 𝕏) This five-star monolith dominates City Square and has a fabulous lobby that recalls the golden era of travel via ocean liner. Rooms are well appointed and many, especially the ones overlooking Swanston St, will have you feeling that you couldn't possibly be closer to the centre of things, in the best possible way. Themed packages ('Chic Retreat' etc) will make you determined to stay for the rest of your life, but then again, we never met an indoor lap pool that we didn't like.

Punt Hill Manhattan (Map pp72-4; ☎ 1300 731 299; www.punthill.com.au; 57 Flinders Lane; apt from $221; 𝕏 □) The Manhattan lives up to its name, with Soho-style loft spaces filled with super-sized sofas and beds, big windows, high ceilings and good gadgetry, such as DVD players. There are a few parking spaces on offer, but they can get booked out quickly. Fitness fanatics will appreciate the gym and spa. Service is super-friendly and well suited to, well, suits – especially those who like their details to be remembered.

Quest on Bourke (Map pp72-4; ☎ 9631 0400; www .questapartments.com.au; 155 Bourke St; apt from $195; 𝕏 □) This is one of the better apartment options in the CBD. The apartments are stylish, and each has a separate kitchen and living area, business facilities (including voice mail, fax and modem) and bathrooms with a spa. An added bonus is that you can open the windows and get some genuine fresh(ish) air. Not a bad place to stay with children either, as baby-sitting can be arranged.

North Melbourne

BUDGET

Melbourne's YHA hostels are both in North Melbourne, northwest of the city centre.

Melbourne Metro (Map p79; ☎ 9329 8599; www .yha.com.au; 78 Howard St; dm $20-28, s/d $64/74; P 🖳) The YHA showpiece, this huge 348-bed place is well kitted out and managed, and has excellent facilities, including modern bathrooms, a good kitchen, a rooftop patio with barbecues, and a security car park. You can score singles/doubles with bathroom for $76/86, and family rooms and self-contained apartments are also available.

Chapman Gardens (Map p79; ☎ 9328 3595; www .yha.com.au; 76 Chapman St; dm $20-28, s/d $62/60; 🖳) This is smaller and older than the Melbourne Metro, but it can be a bit more intimate and personal in its scope. Most rooms are doubles, although there are also dorms of various configurations. There's a barbecue on the premises, and bikes are available for hire.

Carlton

BUDGET

Carlton does budget well – after all, it is a student enclave. It's a good compromise in terms of location – you're out of the city centre, there are good dining options nearby, and it's an easy walk or tram ride downtown.

Carlton College (Map pp76-8; ☎ 9664 0664; www .carltoncollege.com.au; 95 Drummond St; dm $15-21, s/d $42/50; P) Fabulous old Victorian terrace houses, so typical of the area, have been transformed into small, serviceable rooms with few frills. Kitchen and bathroom facilities are shared, as are recreational areas, which always means that you're at the mercy of others' tidiness habits.

MIDRANGE

Quest on Lygon (Map p80; ☎ 9345 3888; www.quest apartments.com.au; 700 Lygon St; apt from $154; P) These former one- and two-bedroom flats, opposite the Melbourne General Cemetery, have been refurbished to a good standard (with fully equipped kitchen and laundries) and are the sort of rooms that tend to fill quickly with visitors to the nearby university.

Downtowner on Lygon (Map pp76-8; ☎ 9663 5555; www.downtowner.com.au; 66 Lygon St; r from $149; P 🏃 🖳) With a central courtyard for parking, this is a good option for those with cars, and we love the fact that its rates haven't shifted in years. Business facilities are good,

if not quite in mogul league, and some rooms have modest self-catering options – although you won't be stumped for places to eat in this location.

Fitzroy

Fitzroy is one of the better areas of the city in which to be based – you're close to all the restaurants of Brunswick St and you can walk or catch a tram into the CBD.

BUDGET

Nunnery (Map pp76-8; ☎ 9419 8637; www.nunnery .com.au; 116 Nicholson St; dm $23-27, s $75, d & tw $100-110) This is an attractive option, particularly if you're a fan of Victorian-era architecture. Well located on the fringe of the city, opposite the Carlton Gardens and in a converted nunnery, this grand pile has comfortable furniture, a friendly atmosphere and excellent budget dorms if you're travelling in groups. The guesthouse and townhouse accommodation is great for those wanting a strong sense of space and freedom to move about under their own steam – both options are well kitted out and commodious. Budget singles/doubles cost $60/80, but are quite simple.

TOP END

Chifley at Metropole (Map pp76-8; ☎ 9411 8100; www .chifleyhotels.com; 44 Brunswick St; studio/apt from $195/225; P 🏃 🖳) This friendly block of serviced apartments is constructed around a handy courtyard area complete with Tuscan-style pool. Rooms are in excellent shape, with kitchens, and you needn't worry about the noise – it's at the quiet end of Brunswick St.

East Melbourne

MIDRANGE

On the fringe of the CBD, East Melbourne has a pleasant residential feel with its tree-lined streets and grand old Victorian terrace houses. This high-toned neighbourhood flaunts some of the city's most expensive real estate – and some of its best accommodation options – particularly if you want to stay in an apartment. It's also a good spot to be based for sporting events at the MCG.

Knightsbridge Apartments (Map p75; ☎ 9419 1333; www.knightsbridgeapartments.com.au; 101 George St; apt from $139; 🏃) This is an excellent choice for those looking for comfortable, well-furnished accommodation, complete with thick carpets and four-poster beds, that allows you to self-cater but also puts you close to the city's dining options. You're also within walking distance of the city's main sporting arenas. Facilities are spotless, modern and stylish, and great value for the price.

Albert Heights (Map p75; ☎ 9419 0955; www.albert heights.com.au; 83 Albert St; apt from $136; P ☑) The charmingly managed Albert Heights has been getting a spruce-up and its newer 2004-style rooms are excellent. The older rooms are showing their age a tad, but still represent decent value for this location. The small plunge pool, surrounded by greenery, is a cute way to cool off. Remember to ask for relevant discounts if you're an automobile club member – or even if you're not.

Eastern Town House (Map p75; ☎ 9418 6666; 90 Albert St; apt from $125; P ☒) This is a refurbished complex offering good-quality (albeit uninspiring) units. There's a café/bar on the ground floor, and you can walk to the city or the eateries of Victoria St, Richmond, quite easily.

George Powlett Motel/Apartments (Map p75; ☎ 9419 9488; www.georgepowlett.com.au; cnr George & Powlett Sts; s/d/tr $103/110/127; P) These older motel-style rooms with modest kitchenettes and small balconies allow you to hear (and sometimes smell) the crowds at the MCG. The décor is nothing to write home about, but rooms are kept clean and the rates are very low for this neck of the woods.

Georgian Court (Map p75; ☎ 9419 6353; www.geor giancourt.com.au; 21 George St; s/d $105/119; P ☒ ▦) The elegant façade of this friendly B&B augurs well. The interior, a little scuffed but exuding a relaxed appeal, shines in the communal areas, where the living room and breakfast room have so much 'drawing room comedy of manners' charm that you'll forgive your bedroom's tight corners. Cheaper rooms with spotless shared bathrooms are also available.

Magnolia Court (Map p75; ☎ 9419 4222; www .magnolia-court.com.au; 101 Powlett St; r from $140) This bright and friendly boutique hotel has an abundance of lavender bushes, and consists of an older wing (formerly a ladies' finishing college) that dates back to 1862 and a new wing. Rooms in the older section have high ceilings and traditional-style furnishings. The rooms in the new wing are of a good standard, but don't have quite the same charm or proportions. The best option is the self-

contained Victorian cottage (approximately $300), which is ideal for those travelling with children (no under-threes though).

Richmond
MIDRANGE
Richmond boasts few sightseeing landmarks, but has plenty of shops, eateries and pubs, and is so close to the city centre you may as well walk into town. That said, it's also a very short tram trip to the action.

Richmond Hill Hotel (Map p81; ☎ 9428 6501; www.richmondhillhotel.com.au; 353 Church St; s/d $106/123) This big Victorian building has spacious living areas and clean three-star rooms, with hydronic heating in winter and ceiling fans in summer. There are some cheaper 'economy' rooms available, with shared bathrooms (single/double $75/88).

South Melbourne
BUDGET
South Melbourne isn't as good a location as the CBD or Carlton, but it's close to the beach and has easy tram access to both the CBD and St Kilda.

Nomads Market Inn (Map pp84-5; ☎ 9690 2220; www.marketinn.com.au; 143 York St; dm $20-24, d $58) This pleasant hostel in a converted pub is right beside South Melbourne Market, within walking distance of Southgate and close to tram lines. It's not really in the centre of things but is still very well located, particularly if you're into self-catering. Breakfast is included in the price (as is a free beer on arrival), and there are free bicycle rentals.

MIDRANGE
City Park Hotel (Map pp84-5; ☎ 9686 0000; www .cityparkhotel.com.au; 308 Kings Way; r from $125) This hotel doesn't have the most prepossessing location, but the prices are competitive for this bracket and the rooms are in good condition, with all the usual three-star amenities, plus there's a helpful front desk. Larger apartments and spa suites (per night from $180) are also available.

St Kilda
St Kilda is one of Melbourne's most interesting and cosmopolitan suburbs and has a range of budget accommodation, as well as plenty of restaurants and entertainment possibilities. It allows visitors to remain

within easy distance (via the tram) of the city centre, while enjoying the playground aspect of the foreshore area.

BUDGET

Base (Map p83; ☎ 9536 6109; www.basebackpackers .com; 17 Carlisle St; dm $23-29; d from $75; 🖳) Easily the flashest hostel in St Kilda, this well-run place fronts Carlisle St with a bold red feature wall, and shows off inside with sparkling facilities, natty communal areas and enough activities to keep the most revved-up backpackers happy.

Olembia Guesthouse (Map p83; ☎ 9537 1412; www .olembia.com.au; 96 Barkly St; dm/s/d $24/46/78) More like a boutique hotel than a hostel, the facilities at this excellent place are very good, and include a cosy guest lounge, dining room, courtyard and off-street parking (plus a bike shed for bike tourers). The rooms are quite small but all are clean and comfortable, and have washbasins and central heating (shared bathroom, though). It's deservedly popular, so book ahead.

MIDRANGE

Despite its increasingly modish disposition, you can still find a 'motel' in St Kilda.

Cabana Court Motel (Map p83; ☎ 9534 0771; www.cabanacourtapartments.com; 46 Park St; apt from $90; 🅿 🐾) These decent motel-style apartments on pretty, tree-lined Mary St are only a short stroll from the beach and the myriad dining options of busy Fitzroy St. Apartments feature kitchen facilities, TV and that rarest of midrange aquatic delights, bathtubs. Even if it didn't have the tubs, you'd have to love it for the kitsch name alone.

Hotel Tolarno (Map p83; ☎ 9537 0200; www.hotel tolarno.com.au; 42 Fitzroy St; d from $115; 🐾) The rooms have some of the highest ceilings we've ever seen, and while some may not match those dimensions in terms of width, they're all pretty comfy and have sparkling, recently renovated bathrooms. Added flourishes come courtesy of original and colourful artworks on the walls. Choose a room at the back if you're a light sleeper.

Marque (Map p83; ☎ 8530 8888; www.rendezvous hotels.com; 35 Fitzroy St; d from $160; 🅿 🐾 🖳) The Marque is a mid-sized boutique property that offers a range of themed packages catering to the 'I'm worth it' demographic. Rooms are stylish and well appointed, and the location hard to beat, especially if you

plan on spending the bulk of your time playing in St Kilda.

TOP END

Medina Executive St Kilda (Map p83; ☎ 9536 0000; www.medinaapartments.com.au; 157 Fitzroy St; apt from $330; 🅿 🐾) This relatively new branch of the reliable Medina chain has nattily appointed apartments that can sleep up to six people. Various specials are also available at certain times of the year, making them good value for groups, and you're a stone's throw from some of Melbourne's best eating and drinking options, plus the famous foreshore (without the seaweed smell!).

Prince (Map p83; ☎ 9536 1111; www.theprince.com .au; 2 Acland St; r from $200; 🅿 🐾 🖳) Minimalist luxury seeps from every surface, crevice and cranny of this beautifully furnished boutique hotel – the fabulous location only adds to its appeal. Service is discreet, smart and considerate, and you'll find that both business travellers and weekend escape artists are catered to admirably. Eating and entertainment options on the premises mean you need never leave its environs, which is more probable than you may first think.

South Yarra

With a variety of restaurants and shops nearby, this is a good location for those who want to be based outside the CBD and like the attractions of nearby Chapel St and Toorak Rd.

BUDGET

Hotel Claremont (Map p82; ☎ 9826 8000; www .hotelclaremont.com; 189 Toorak Rd; dm/s/d $30/66/76; 🖳) The Claremont, a once-grand home, is now a budget hotel, but that doesn't mean you should picture a grand dame fallen on hard times. Rooms, while simple and a little spartan, are spotless and freshly painted, and the communal bathrooms are in excellent condition. Lavish touches, such as a grand central staircase and oriental rugs, belie the bargain rates.

MIDRANGE

Tilba (Map pp84-5; ☎ 9867 8844; www.thetilba.com .au; cnr Toorak Rd West & Domain St; r from $154) This small and elegant hotel has been lovingly restored in gracious Victorian style. Stepping inside is like taking a trip back in time, and the 15 suites all feature old iron bedsteads,

MELBOURNE

antique lamps, decorative plasterwork and period-style bathrooms. It's highly recommended, with a homey, welcoming feel, although the less expensive rooms are quite small.

Toorak Manor (Map p82; ☎ 9827 2689; www.toorak manor.citysearch.com.au; 220 Williams Rd; d from $145) An excellent boutique hotel, this historic mansion has been impressively converted (every inch seems covered in chintz) and is set in lovely gardens. It has comfortable period-style rooms, cosy lounges and sitting rooms. It's across the street from Hawksburn train station.

Albany South Yarra (Map pp84-5; ☎ 9866 4485; www.thealbany.com.au; cnr Toorak Rd & Millswyn St; r from $110; P) Sleeping configurations abound at the Albury, and range from old-world mansion-wing glamour to more functional rooms suited to less fussy travellers. There are shared kitchen and laundry facilities, and the hotel is close to good parks.

TOP END

Como (Map p82; ☎ 9825 2222; www.mirvachotels.com .au; 630 Chapel St; r from $229; P) The Como specialises in buffing everything to a glossy shine – from the apples in a bowl at reception to your shoes. Service is just as polished, with all manner of dilemmas dispelled for high-maintenance guests at Grand Prix or Melbourne Cup time. Rooms are plush and come in a number of configurations to suit a variety of needs.

EATING

One of the hardest parts of putting a travel guide together is eating all over town and trying to be impartial about it – and Melbourne is the city that may well make or break you as a food lover. Everywhere you go, there are restaurants, cafés, delicatessens, markets, bistros, brasseries and takeaways. And a whole lot of food-literate locals who hold passionate opinions on the best place to get a curry, a roast, a pizza, Peking duck or *panna cotta* (literally, cooked cream), and the best service, the best décor, the best view or the best-kept secret.

Melbourne's ethnic diversity is reflected in the exhaustive variety of its cuisines and restaurants. Food is a local obsession, and people eat out a lot because Melburnians consider their city to be the country's eating capital (Sydneysiders will disagree just as

passionately). Indeed, there are those who believe that Melbourne is one of the world's great eating cities – and they're right. Just don't try to exercise restraint and you'll be fine.

While it's possible to spend well over $100 per person on a meal, you can also eat very well for less than $10, especially at lunch or brunch. In fact, compared with many other world cities, you'll find that food and wine in Melbourne are great value.

Many restaurants are either licensed to sell alcohol or BYO, meaning you can 'Bring Your Own' booze (and usually pay a small – although sometimes large in top-end restaurants – corkage fee), although sadly, this practice is not as widespread as it once was. Smoking is banned in all places where food is consumed (unless you're having a counter meal at a pub, though that will change in 2007). Most restaurants will have a vegetarian dish or two available on their menu.

Central Melbourne

The CBD has some of Melbourne's best and worst restaurants. The bad ones are the most obvious, clogging up the main shopping thoroughfares of the area; the good ones may take a little more effort to find, often hidden down tiny alleyways.

A little like a fin-sized version of New York's Soho, Flinders Lane is gallery central for the contemporary art scene. Plenty of cafés and wonderful little bars in the adjacent laneways meet the demands of a crowd waiting for the happening to happen. Centre Pl (the classic Melbourne alleyway) is on the opposite side of Flinders Lane from Degraves St and becomes a covered arcade as it runs through to Collins St. Take note of the fantastic Art Nouveau-style, wrought-iron lighting overhead as you debate which eatery to frequent.

The area in and around Chinatown, which follows Little Bourke St from Spring St to Swanston St, continues to be one of the city's most popular places to eat. As you would expect, Chinese restaurants predominate here, but delve a little deeper and you can also choose from Greek, Indian, Japanese and modern Australian. Part of the fun is just wandering around and soaking up the atmosphere, and there's always somewhere new to be found in the narrow cobbled lanes that run off Little Bourke St.

Becco (Map pp72-4; ☎ 9663 3000; 11 Crossley St; mains $23-30; ✌ lunch & dinner Mon-Sat) Part restaurant, part bar, part produce store, Becco isn't only big on style, but has the substance to keep people coming back time and time again. Meat and fish dishes are superbly prepared, service is uniformly excellent, the atmosphere comfortably sexy. Book ahead – it's worth it.

Ezard at Adelphi (Map pp72-4; ☎ 9639 6811; 187 Flinders Lane; mains $35-39; ✌ lunch Mon-Fri, dinner Mon-Sat) Teague Ezard's flawless takes on Asian-inspired cuisine keep this basement restaurant buzzing. It's smartly designed and staffed too, making reservations advisable, particularly if you're one of the many who'd like access to the rooftop bar before or after dining. The Balinese-style caramelised eggplant, with tomato, snake beans, lime and chilli sambal dressing transported us to a far balmier climate than the day outside suggested. The tasting menu (with wine, $190) is a great way to experience the whole shebang – and request for vegetarian options are easily dealt with.

Movida (Map pp72-4; ☎ 9663 3038; 1 Hosier Lane; raciones $8.50-15; ✌ lunch Mon-Fri, dinner daily) Nab a table here and then nibble as many tapas as

your heart desires – the *callos a la madrileña* (tripe) will make you swear you're in Madrid. Smart décor, smooth service and a fine opportunity for a little people watching – Spanish style.

Yu-u (Map pp72-4; ☎ 9639 7073; 137 Flinders Lane; lunch set menu $15; ✌ lunch & dinner Mon-Fri) A certain amount of four-course set lunches are made here each weekday, and if you miss out you'll kick yourself. And it's easy to miss out, not least of all because if you blink you'll miss this place as you stroll down Flinders Lane. Inside, you'll find a rarefied world of communal seating, subdued lighting and diplomatic service. Bookings recommended.

Mo Mo (Map pp72-4; ☎ 9650 0660; Basement, 115 Collins St, mains $ 27-39; ✌ lunch Mon-Fri, dinner Mon-Sat) You know a place is popular when it produces its own CD. We're not sure why this is a recent trend among restaurateurs, but we are sure of the fact that the portobello mushroom risotto with Jerusalem artichokes and Egyptian spices is one of the best dishes we've eaten in ages. Middle Eastern flavours and Australian sunniness combine to form a great experience.

Supper Inn (Map pp72-4; ☎ 9663 4759; 15 Celestial Ave; mains $15-30; ✌ dinner) If you're one of those types who likes to find out where the chefs eat when they finish a shift then look no further. Open till very late (2.30am) and serving some of the best late-night *congee*, noodles, dumplings and other yummies to a mixed crowd, this place will either set you up or finish you off depending on whether you're at the beginning or end of your night.

Langton's (Map pp72-4; ☎ 9663 0222; 61 Flinders Lane; mains $35-36; ✌ breakfast, lunch & dinner Mon-Fri, dinner Sat) Langton's cellar location keeps it feeling almost secretive, despite the fact that everyone seems to know that chef Walter Trupp's kitchen produces some of central Melbourne's best dishes. It's a cavernous, industrious space – perfect for a business breakfast or lunch, and service is excellent. There are decent vegetarian options in the lunch and dinner entrées (appetisers), but the mains tend to be carnivorous.

Italy I (Map pp72-4; ☎ 9654 4430; 27 George Pde; mains $28.50-32; ✌ lunch & dinner) Intimate and warm, Italy I is the perfect spot to shuck off a raincoat and get comfortable while well-executed Italian comfort comes out to warm your very soul. We tried a superb *ravioli di pesce con brodo* (ravioli filled with fish and served in a broth; $23) to start and things only got better from there. Service is attentive.

Kuni's (Map pp72-4; ☎ 9663 7243; 56 Little Bourke St; mains $13-27; ⏲ lunch & dinner Mon-Fri) This spare, clean-looking space produces some of the best Japanese in town, and even when it gets packed, there's something serene about the whole experience of dining here. For lunch, grab a bento box (available in vegetarian and non-veg versions) and forget about the outside world.

Chocolate Buddha (Map pp72-4; ☎ 9654 5688; Federation Square; meals $13-21; ⏲ lunch & dinner) Organic noodles and plenty of vegetarian options keep the healthy types flocking to this thriving eatery, where kids will love the chatter, clatter and splatter of Asian treats. Service is aided by a high-tech system that works so well we think there's mind-reading involved.

Degraves Espresso Bar (Map pp72-4; ☎ 9654 1245; 23 Degraves St; dishes around $8-14; ⏲ breakfast & lunch) The perfect antidote to coffee-chain stores, Degraves has oodles of character, spilling out onto atmospheric Degraves St. This is a good place for a morning fry-up, a quick sandwich or an eponymous espresso. Sit on bum-numbing chairs indoors or better ones outdoors, which can be fiercely contested.

Pellegrini's Espresso Bar (Map pp72-4; ☎ 9662 1885; 66 Bourke St; mains $12-14; ⏲ lunch & dinner) This is the classic Melbourne espresso bar, with a reputation built over decades. It's uncomfortable, the food's as rudimentary Italian as you can get and the coffee's only OK. So who's complaining? No one really – this place oozes character, history and charm that other Italo-wannabes can only dream about. Pull up an uncomfy stool, order some fruit cup and eavesdrop on the regulars.

Il Solito Posto (Map pp72-4; ☎ 9654 4466; 113 Collins St; mains $24-35; ⏲ breakfast, lunch & dinner) This excellent basement place is great for Italian staples and has an ambience that's tough to beat. Good wines, available by the glass, keep you company if you're solo at 'the usual place' – if only every little Italian place had this good a formula.

Sud (Map pp72-4; ☎ 9670 8451; 219 King St; mains $23-29; ⏲ breakfast Mon-Fri, lunch & dinner Mon-Sat) A little out of the way but worth the trip, Sud makes elegance and style look easy in both its setting and market-fresh food. Try the whole sardines or the rosemary-and-garlic

roasted potatoes and be transported to the sun-drenched dining tables of your pretend Italian villa. It's popular with business types, so a decent spot for a networking lunch.

Don Don (Map pp72-4; ☎ 9670 7073; 321 Swanston St; mains $5-7.50; ⏲ lunch Mon-Fri) A student stronghold, Don Don dishes out discount Japanese eats to hordes of city workers and students. Sometimes the meat cuts are a little ropey, but generally this place does an admirable job of keeping good food coming quickly and cheaply.

Southbank

The Southgate development at Southbank, on the southern side of the Yarra River, is a popular Melbourne eating spot. The views over the river and city skyline can't be beat, and it's a short walk from here to the galleries, theatres and the gardens of Kings Domain. There're plenty of bars, cafés and restaurants to choose from, and most have outdoor terraces and balconies suitable for alfresco dining in warmer weather. Next door, the Crown Casino & Entertainment Complex is also chock-a-block with restaurants and cafés.

Walter's Wine Bar (Map pp72-4; ☎ 9690 9211; Upper Level, Southgate; mains $25-35; ⏲ lunch & dinner) Walter's blends culinary flair, professional service and a justifiably famous wine list – the name is a dead giveaway. In fact, you'll get the distinct feeling that the food is secondary to the wine here – and that would be a real shame, as the food, Italian in style, is undeniably good.

Mecca (Map pp72-4; ☎ 9682 2999; mid-level, Southgate; mains $26-32; ⏲ lunch & dinner) Mecca matches an elegant style to a creative North African menu. Try anything that features the words 'spiced lamb' and be prepared to follow the spice trail. It's an excellent place to get right into Melbourne's love of taking overseas flavours and techniques and injecting a uniquely Australian sensibility into the experience.

Blue Train (Map pp72-4; ☎ 9696 0111; mid-level, Southgate; mains $6-15; ⏲ breakfast, lunch & dinner) This loud and hugely popular place serves all the mainstream staples in a humming environment that satisfies all sorts. It's a good casual spot to take the kids, as there's bound to be something that appeals to even the fussiest eaters.

Cecconi's (Map pp72-4; ☎ 9292 6887; ground level, Crown Entertainment Complex; mains $29-36; ⏲ lunch

Sun-Fri, dinner daily) Catering to those who espouse the 'bigger is better' philosophy, the man-style serves at Cecconi's seem designed to please types who've come off a day-long winning streak at the Black Jack table and want a steak, pronto. Like a high-roller's room with food.

North Melbourne

North Melbourne doesn't have the glamour or the range of some other inner suburbs, but there are great places to eat if you're prepared to hunt. Victoria St is the place to start your search.

Akita (Map p79; ☎ 9326 5766; cnr Courtney & Blackwood Sts; mains $12-24; ☽ lunch & dinner Mon-Fri) If you find yourself in this part of town, you could do worse than try some of the city's best Japanese food at this most succinct of Japanese delights. Small menu, small wine list, smiles all round – a winning formula.

Courthouse Dining Room (Map p79; ☎ 9329 5394; 86 Errol St; mains $22-27; ☽ lunch Mon-Fri, dinner Mon-Sat) Fans of nouveau pub grub will be in heaven here – it's a stylish place with good-looking décor and international menu items that get it right. Service is helpful should you have trouble making a decision and drink prices are good, as befits a pub.

Don Camillo (Map p79; ☎ 9329 8883; 215 Victoria St; dishes $5-14; ☽ breakfast & lunch daily, dinner Thu & Fri) This is a little Italian place that's been here for yonks (ie the 1950s), and it serves the basics in large, tasty portions. Popular with the true superstars of Melbourne, too – footy players. See how many carbs can fit into a large man around breakfast time.

Carlton

Lygon St is no longer considered much of a trendsetter in Melbourne's restaurant scene, although some of the long-running places are very much worth a visit, and you can still hear Italian being spoken in some of the cafes if you're missing rolled Rs and much gesticulation. Running parallel to Lygon St, Rathdowne St has some good alternatives to its more crowded commercial cousin.

Abla's (Map pp76-8; ☎ 9347 0006; 109 Elgin St; mains $12-17; ☽ lunch Thu & Fri, dinner Mon-Sat) We think this is Melbourne's best Lebanese restaurant, and so do a hell of a lot of other people, meaning that you'll want to book a table as the weekend draws near. On Friday and Saturday nights the compulsory 13-

course banquet gets wolfed down by appreciative crowds, so put on your elasticised pants and tuck in.

Brunetti (Map pp76-8; ☎ 9347 2801; 198 Faraday St; café dishes $3-7, restaurant mains $12-23; ☽ breakfast, lunch & dinner) Behold the mother lode – or should that be mama lode? A stalwart of Italian culinary obsessions, Brunetti is a large haven for those who want excellent coffee, exquisite *dolci* and mouthwatering Roman-influenced dishes. Despite recent renovations and extensions, this place *still* gets absolutely packed – enjoy. After all, when in Rome, or Carlton…

Jimmy Watson's (Map pp76-8; ☎ 9347 3985; 333 Lygon St; mains $19-28; ☽ lunch Mon-Sat, dinner Tue-Sat) Wine and talk are the order of the day at this long-running wine bar/restaurant. It's great for leisurely lunches and excellent dinners. The fare is European with a nod to special Australian ingredients, such as kangaroo. A sterling wine list, as you'd expect, and a fabulous garden area for summer days.

Tiamo (Map pp76-8; ☎ 9347 0911; 303 Lygon St; mains $11-16; ☽ breakfast, lunch & dinner) This historic Lygon St campaigner is an old-fashioned Italian bistro that's popular with students, and has tasty pasta dishes and great breakfasts just like mama couldn't be bothered cooking. It's dark, the playbills on the walls are ancient, service is scatty and you may have to wait for a table, but that's all part of the charm.

Rathdowne Street Foodstore (Map p80; ☎ 9347 4064; 617 Rathdowne St; mains $18-25; ☽ breakfast, lunch & dinner) This high-toned eatery in a terrace house has heavenly breakfast offerings, and a strong lunch and dinner menu – the crispy-skinned salmon is a winner. Coffee is a unique speciality, and it's a charming place to unwind.

Zum Zum (Map p80; ☎ 9348 0455; 645 Rathdowne St; mains $16-19.50; ☽ dinner Tue, lunch & dinner Wed-Sun) This stylish little Middle Eastern café, replete with external mosaic flourishes on its entrance, hits the right notes in the kitchen, with lovingly prepared dips and lamb dishes. We can't fault the *kibbee* – a dish of minced lamb with crushed wheat, filled with onions, pine nuts and yoghurt.

Fitzroy

You haven't really eaten out in Melbourne until you've been to Brunswick St. For many, it's the most fascinating street in town, and for a couple of blocks north and south of Johnston St it's lined with dozens of great cafés, bars, pubs and restaurants offering a surprisingly wide range of cuisines. The prevailing mood is alternative, fashionable, studenty and arty all at the same time – a far cry from the relatively recent past when this area was as rough as guts.

Gertrude St, which runs between Smith and Nicholson Sts, has an interesting collection of galleries, art suppliers and shops, as well as a few eateries.

With so many places to choose from, perhaps the thing to do is to stroll along the street and consider your options. Have a beer here, a glass of wine there, and study the menus and the crowds.

If you venture across Alexandra Pde to North Fitzroy where Brunswick St joins St Georges Rd, you'll find another pocket of interesting cafés and restaurants about 1km north of Alexandra Pde.

Moroccan Soup Bar (Map p80; ☎ 9482 4240; 183 St Georges Rd, North Fitzroy; mains $10-15; ☺ dinner Tue-Sun) Nab a table and prick up your ears as the chatelaine of this fab soup kitchen hardly draws breath as she rattles off a list of soups, entrées and heavenly North African tagines before telling you what you're getting. Wash it all down with mint tea.

Ladro (Map pp76-8; ☎ 9415 7575; 224 Gertrude St; mains $22-27; ☺ dinner Wed-Sun) Winner of the *Age Good Food Guide*'s Best New Restaurant prize in 2005, getting a table in Ladro seems to require begging, borrowing, stealing and selling your first-born. Expect to be served very good pizza (such as the Verde, with green-olive paste, mozzarella, capers and rocket) and then be on the receiving end of the bum's rush if it looks like you'll spend more say, oh, 45 minutes eating. A tad overrated on the whole, but a quintessential Melbourne pizza experience. If you want to feel happy, stick with the roast of the day.

Madame Sousou (Map pp76-8; ☎ 9417 0400; 231 Brunswick St; mains $18-28; ☺ breakfast, lunch & dinner) This is the sort of place that Melbourne excels at – a nod to Europe, a wink at Australia and a firm grasp on all the things that a beautiful space should provide for its diners. Any of the rice dishes are worth choosing – and desserts are always special.

Mario's (Map pp76-8; ☎ 9417 3343; 303 Brunswick St; mains $17-20; ☺ breakfast, lunch & dinner) Melbourne has a surfeit of cocky waiters mov-

ing at lightning speed between tables and bestowing a heavily accented *'prego bella'* on their female prey – sorry, customers. This is where they learnt it. The pasta dishes are uniformly commendable (we can honestly say we've sampled every single one of them), the atmosphere casual enough for you to drop your guard and your baggage, and the coffee kicks like a mule.

Blue Chillies (Map pp76-8; ☎ 9417 0071; 182 Brunswick St; mains $18.90-25; ☺ lunch & dinner) Stylishly kitted out with colourful tins and sundry grocery items arranged in knife-sharp formation, Blue Chillies ties its colours to the mast of 'new Asian' cuisine and features nothing too unknown on the menu, but nothing so daggy as to bring back memories of eating Asian in the 1970s. This place seems to be a popular spot for dates, if that's any help.

Piraeus Blues (Map pp76-8; ☎ 9417 0222; 310 Brunswick St; mains $10-20; ☺ lunch Wed-Fri & Sun, dinner daily) Brunswick St may be a long way from Athens, but the excellent food here will transport you to Greece, and the good folk at Piraeus Blues haven't let the numerous 'Best Greek Restaurant' awards go to their heads. It's a nice, unpretentious place to order a variety of home-cooked dishes and share them with friends.

Vegie Bar (Map pp76-8; ☎ 9417 6935; 380 Brunswick St; mains under $10; ☺ lunch & dinner) The Vegie Bar exudes delicious aromas, and has a great range of vegetarian meals and snacks – it's so popular that you'll wonder if everyone in Fitzroy is a tofu addict. Come early or wait in line.

Babka Bakery Café (Map pp76-8; ☎ 9416 0091; 358 Brunswick St; dishes $5-15; ☺ breakfast & lunch Tue-Sun) Famous for its breads, pastries and the eternally wholesome-looking Babka waitresses, this is also a great place for breakfast, with fabulous dishes like Georgian baked beans with fetta, or buckwheat blinis with kippers, rocket and horseradish butter. For lunch try the heavenly pies. Expect a bit of a wait on weekends.

Tin Pot (Map p80; ☎ 9481 5312; 284 St Georges Rd, North Fitzroy; mains $9-12; ☺ breakfast & lunch) Sometimes the shambolic service threatens to override the experience of hoeing into the wonderful scram *prosciutto* brekkie (scrambled eggs with crispy *prosciutto* and tomato – $11.50), but it never quite happens, so we'll keep coming here and sharing communal tables with the rest of North Fitzroy. It's the kind of café that always smells good – the best advertisement we can think of.

Richmond

Walk down Victoria St and you'll soon realise why this area has become known as Little Saigon. Here, Melbourne's growing Vietnamese community has transformed what was once a dull and colourless traffic route into a fascinating, bustling commercial centre. The stretch of Victoria St between Hoddle and Church Sts is lined with Asian supermarkets and groceries, the footpaths are piled with boxes of exotic fruits and vegetables, and filling the street are discount shops, butchers, fishmongers, and dozens of bargain-priced Vietnamese eateries and restaurants. Along Swan St you'll also find plenty of eateries, some with a Greek flavour. Bridge Rd, which runs parallel to and between Swan and Victoria Sts, also has some great food possibilities but it lacks the atmosphere of some of Melbourne's other great eating streets.

Pearl (Map p82; ☎ 9421 4599; 631 Church St; mains $21-27; ☯ lunch & dinner) Aptly named, this creative temple offers slick, modern dining within a stone's throw of the Yarra. Dishes like watermelon salad with tomato jelly and feta will have you gushing superlatives, and you'll think the world is your oyster. Creative, professional and welcoming. Reservations advised.

Richmond Hill Café & Larder (Map p81; ☎ 9421 2808; 48 Bridge Rd; mains $11-28; ☯ breakfast & lunch daily, dinner Tue-Sat) We love the carefully prepared bistro fare at this popular bar/restaurant, owned by local food icon Stephanie Alexander. Dishes include sumptuous veal shanks, comforting puddings and the best damn cheese on toast we've ever had. There's a *fromagerie* on the premises, too.

Tofu Shop International (Map p81; ☎ 9429 6204; 78 Bridge Rd; dishes $3.50-11; ☯ lunch & dinner Mon-Fri, lunch Sat) Extremely popular with the vegetarian and health-kick crowds, it can be a squeeze finding a stool at the counter come lunch time, but the salads, vegetables, filled filo pastries and 'soyalaki' are tasty, filling and cruelty-free.

Vlado's (Map p81; ☎ 9428 5833; 61 Bridge Rd; set menu $68; ☯ lunch Mon-Fri, dinner Mon-Sat) This place is famous for one thing and one thing only: steak. It serves some of the best in town, and has been known to inspire people to order chops for dessert. Vegetarians will

simply have to go elsewhere for sustenance. A proud and reassuringly unchanged slice of meaty history – get your iron levels sorted out in style.

Thanh Thanh (Map p81; ☎ 9428 5633; 246a Victoria St; mains $6-10.50; ☯ lunch & dinner) Lightning-fast service and our favourite rice paper rolls in the city. Thanh Thanh is a spotless, cheery place and gets packed with fans of its easy Vietnamese treats at budget prices.

South Yarra, Toorak & Prahran

Commercial Rd is the border between South Yarra and Prahran, and features plenty of gay eateries. Prahran Market (p141) is a terrific place to shop, with some of the best fresh fruit and vegetables, seafood and deli items this side of the city. Within the market complex there's a food court with several good places to eat.

Greville St, which runs off Chapel St beside the Prahran Town Hall, has a few good cafés and eateries. The main thoroughfare of Chapel St has places to suit a range of budgets and tastebud preferences. Most of South Yarra's eateries are along Toorak Rd and Chapel St. If you love to shop and eat, you'll be right at home here. There are some stylish cafés and restaurants, from the extravagant to the simple, but this is one of Melbourne's more affluent areas, so there aren't too many cheapies.

Jacques Reymond (Map p82; ☎ 9525 2178; 78 Williams Rd, Prahran; 2-course menu $68, degustation menu $120; ☯ lunch Thu & Fri, dinner Tue-Sat) Easily one of Melbourne's greatest restaurants, Jacques Reymond's kitchen presents artful, imaginative cuisine to dressed-up patrons who are celebrating anniversaries, birthdays and engagements. Service is superb but never haughty – and if you're vegetarian you're about to see that it is perfectly possible to dine out in lavish style without meat. And did we mention that this is all taking place in a mansion? Book well ahead.

Da Noi (Map p82; ☎ 9866 5975; 95 Toorak Rd; mains $25-35; ☯ lunch Fri-Sun, dinner daily) The seasonal menu specialises in Sardinian cuisine, which means you'll find plenty of brilliantly prepared seafood and dishes that seem to have been hunted that very day. The chefs work with what they've got, so things are created and become unavailable throughout the evening, but with enough Italian wine you won't notice that you've no idea what you're going to get. Simple, elegant décor, waiters you can banter with – heaven.

David's (Map p82; ☎ 9529 5199; 4 Cecil Pl; Prahran; mains $17-24; ◯ lunch daily, dinner Fri & Sat) David's does a roaring trade thanks to its imaginative, healthy spin on yum cha with a Shanghainese influence. Brisk, good value and possessed of a strong wine list, this is a great spot to refuel while on a shopping spree.

Borsch, Vodka & Tears (Map p82; ☎ 9530 2694; 173 Chapel St; mains $15-19; ◯ breakfast, lunch & dinner Thu-Sun, dinner only Mon-Wed) Borsch and vodka? Get crying pink tears at this most Polish of Melbourne's eating and drinking dens. This interesting little place is worth a stop for its pleasant, hip atmosphere and modern Polish food. And, yes, there are about 100 types of vodka on offer.

Orange (Map p82; ☎ 9529 1644; 126 Chapel St; breakfast $8.50-15, mains $23-27; ◯ breakfast, lunch & dinner) With a 1970s retro feel, unfailingly chipper service and tasty cross-cultural dishes, this café attracts an interesting, alternative crowd who appreciate the fact that you can get a mean Bloody Mary with your breakfast, no questions asked. There's often very good grooves played at night on the turntables, too, plus a decent little wine list.

St Kilda

In the 1990s St Kilda was discovered by the macchiato crowd, with wood-fired pizza becoming more popular than matzo-ball soup. Fitzroy and Acland Sts are where the majority of cafés and restaurants are to be found, and there are also good places down by the sea.

Baker D Chirico (Map p83; ☎ 9534 3777; Shop 3/4, 149 Fitzroy St; mains $5-8.50; ◯ breakfast & lunch) With sacks of organic flour piled high, and almost toppled by both the heavenly aromas and hungry hordes, carb lovers should make this excellent bakery their first port of call on this strip. Expect miracles from the loaves and rapture from the pastries – and the lunch dishes are damn good, too.

Café di Stasio (Map p83; ☎ 9525 3999; 31 Fitzroy St; mains $29-35; ◯ lunch & dinner) With door handles in the shape of the naughty *cornuto* (cuckold) sign, an interior that suggests the '90s power lunch never died for some and the smoothest white-jacketed service we've come across in ages, Café di Stasio thoroughly deserves its reputation as the best Italian restaurant in Melbourne. Its two-course lunch (which in-

cludes a glass of wine or coffee – $25) allows local semi-starving artists to mix it with corporate types and admire the Bill Henson original on the back wall. And the food? Sublime.

Azalea (Map p83; ☎ 8598 9880; 4 Acland St; mains $22-35; ◯ closed Mon, lunch Tue-Fri & Sun, dinner Tue-Sun) With lots of dark wood, silk cushions, bamboo and considerate service in evidence, Azalea makes for a good business-lunch choice before turning on the romance (albeit communal) in the evening. We plumped for the crispy-skin chicken with five-spice and never looked back, and the *panna cotta* put a smile on everyone's face. The wine list is very good – and well suited to the modern Asian cuisine.

Café a Taglio (Map p83; ☎ 9534 1344; 157A Fitzroy St; mains $15-18, pizza slice around $6; ◯ lunch & dinner) At the city end of Fitzroy St, this is the best place in this neck of the woods for pizza served by the slice, Roman style. A tempting array of Italian staples competes for your attention (the *spaghetti alle vongole*, spaghetti with clams, is a winner), but Melbourne's raging addiction to this pizza will probably have you sticking with the pack and picking a few nicely topped squares.

Il Fornaio (Map p83; ☎ 9534 2922; 2 Acland St; breakfast $2.20-12.50, dinner mains $17-23; ◯ breakfast, lunch & dinner) Breakfast here is among the best in Melbourne, with an on-site bakery concocting some of the most melt-in-the-mouth pastries we've ever surrendered to and scrambled eggs so fluffy they could fly off your fork. Lunch and dinner are also great, with a risotto of braised rabbit, leeks and bacon (complemented by a judicious wine list), the perfect rejoinder to a brutish day outside. Despite all the concrete, this place feels surprisingly cosy.

Galleon (Map p83; ☎ 9534 8934; 9 Carlisle St; meals $5-14.50; ◯ breakfast, lunch & dinner) Just off Acland St, the Galleon has fuelled the creative juices of St Kilda's arts community for years with simple and inexpensive café-style food and fantastic hot breakfasts.

Cicciolina (Map p83; ☎ 9525 3333; 130 Acland St; mains $19-32; ◯ lunch & dinner) To put it bluntly, if this place ever closes down, we're leaving town. A perfect marriage of style and substance (the lamb's brains are fantastic), this intimate yet bustling restaurant is on the small side and doesn't take reservations, which means that if you're not looking lively you're going to be looking at some other menu – make it the bar menu for the snug little bolthole out of the back, where many a best-laid plan to dine gets waylaid.

Claypots (Map p83; ☎ 9534 1282; 213 Barkly St; mains $10-25; ☘ lunch & dinner) It might not look like much from the outside, but the spicy seafood claypots here are delicious, and are influenced by international kitchens, meaning that you could share treats from Malaysia and Morocco. No bookings are taken, so you may have to cross the road to the Doulton Bar (p132) and wait until you're called to dinner – this place is packed by about 6.30pm. Thank your lucky stars if an outdoor table is free in the shabby-chic backyard.

Bedouin Kitchen (Map p83; ☎ 9534 0888; 103 Grey St; mains $15-25; breakfast, lunch & dinner) The blood-red walls and Moroccan light fittings set the scene for sharing excellent *mezze* dishes with friends who can't resist trying just one more dish, just in case you haven't ordered enough. Ask the staff what's special if you simply can't decide. The vegetarian options are excellent – in fact, they lord it over the meat dishes.

Stokehouse (Map p83; ☎ 9525 5555; 30 Jacka Blvd; mains $29.50-39.50; ☘ lunch & dinner) Right on the foreshore, the Stokehouse has the location that everyone else dreams about, with wide windows allowing every ray of light to permeate the charmingly decorated space. The upstairs restaurant menu features classic Mod Oz interpretations of Asian and European themes (try the crispy-skinned snapper with new-season vegetable pithivier, black olives and tomato dressing), making it perennially and justifiably popular. Downstairs, the atmosphere is somewhat loud and the menu is a lot simpler (and cheaper). Reservations are advised for the upstairs dining room.

Soul Mama (Map p83; ☎ 9525 3338; 10 Jacka Blvd; mains $12.50-15.50; ☘ lunch & dinner) In the same building as the St Kilda Sea Baths, Soul Mama isn't afraid to mix things up – the food is presented cafeteria style (you line up and pick what you like for your tray), the service is bright-eyed and bushy-tailed, and you can spend a large part of your time horizontal on a saffron-hued day bed. The sea views are the sort of extra that you would pay an arm and a leg for (but don't). Plus it's vegetarian.

South Melbourne, Port Melbourne & Albert Park

Home to the South Melbourne Market, advertising agencies and video production houses, the historic suburb of South Melbourne has some good cafés and restaurants. Park and Clarendon Sts are the most popular areas for a meal or a coffee. Albert Park has a thriving and trendy café scene, and there are some good daytime eateries around Bridport St and Victoria Ave (this shopping strip is called Dundas Pl).

Montague Food Store (Map pp84-5; ☎ 9682 9680; 406 Park St, South Melbourne; mains $5-15; ☘ breakfast & lunch) This quaint little sun-drenched café serves sandwiches and salads that are a cut above the usual café fare, meaning that you can expect to find plenty to plonk in your bag if you're planning a good stride round the area. Friendly service might tempt you to sit down and take the wait off those feet, though.

O'Connells (Map pp84-5; ☎ 9699 9600; 193 Montague St, South Melbourne; mains $16-32; ☘ lunch & dinner) Dishes here show Mediterranean and pan-Asian influences, and are available throughout this gentrified pub that's at the forefront of the gastro-boozer movement in town. Great for a Sunday lunch with good mates.

Isthmus of Kra (Map pp84-5; ☎ 9690 3688; 50 Park St, South Melbourne; mains $16.50-28.50; ☘ lunch Mon-Fri, dinner) This is one of Melbourne's best and most elegant Asian restaurants. It has delicious southern Thai dishes with a Malaysian influence, and banquets for four or more people – you'll need to book for these, and especially on weekends. In summer there's a delightful courtyard open for dining – you can't beat the red curry with duck on a hot night.

Misuzu (Map pp84-5; ☎ 9699 9022; 7 Victoria Ave, Albert Park; mains $11-30; ☘ lunch & dinner) Small and extremely popular, this 'village-style' Japanese café is worth a special trip to find. The food is outstanding and quite different from the standard fare in most other Japanese restaurants, plus the lantern-bedecked tree outside is a sight to behold. Grab a friend and share a sushi and sashimi platter, plus a bottle of warm or chilled sake, depending on the weather. Reservations are advised on weekends.

Graham (Map pp84-5; ☎ 9676 2566; 97 Graham St, Port Melbourne; ☘ lunch & dinner) This former wharfies' pub keeps the crowds coming

MELBOURNE

TOP FIVE SPOTS FOR A CAFFEINE FIX

Wall Two 80 (Map pp70-1; ☎ 9593 8280, Rear, 280 Carlisle St, Balaclava; ☉ breakfast & lunch) Every man and his wife (and their dog) comes here to soak up the social atmosphere and the best coffee this side of the river.

Pound (Map p82; ☎ 9826 1114; Shop 5, 566 Chapel St, South Yarra; ☉ breakfast, lunch & dinner) Fuel your Chapel St shopping spree with a hit of this strip's finest.

Racer (Map p83; ☎ 9534 9988; 15A Marine Pde, St Kilda; ☉ breakfast & lunch) You'll feel more comfortable here if you pull up to this popular pit stop on your bike. Great coffee, every time, and once the staff gets to know you they'll start bringing it to you unbidden.

Newtown SC (Map pp76-8; ☎ 9415 7337; 180 Brunswick St, Fitzroy; ☉ breakfast & lunch) Fabulously done coffee and a *crema* you'll want to bathe in – such are its restorative properties.

Ici (Map pp76-8; ☎ 9417 2274; 359 Napier St, Fitzroy; ☉ breakfast & lunch) Getting a smile from the staff may take some time, but getting wonderful coffee is easy. Great breakfast eggs, too.

---

thanks to a combination of inventive pub-menu choices, savvy staff, a covered courtyard, friendly and unpretentious service, and a cheery vibe from fellow diners. Grab a perfect porterhouse steak and make like a starving man on it.

Williamstown

Willy has a fine assortment of cafés and restaurants along Nelson Pl, catering to the hordes of day-trippers.

Strand Seafood Restaurant (Map p86; ☎ 9397 7474; cnr The Strand & Ferguson St; mains $25-30; ☉ breakfast, lunch & dinner) The Strand is stylish, simple and ultramodern, with a small bar, an open-air courtyard and good views over the bay. The menu is predominantly seafood (as it should be), most of it very well prepared. Take the ferry over from Southgate for the full nautical experience.

Siren's (Map p86; ☎ 9397 7811; Esplanade; mains $23; ☉ lunch & dinner) Right on Williamstown beach, this converted Art Deco bathing pavilion incorporates a bistro, and a more formal restaurant that leans towards Mediterranean flavours. If you're only after some snacking options, choose from the tapas menu.

Self-Catering

It's only natural that a food-obsessed city like Melbourne would have plenty of good food shops. Supermarkets, often open 24 hours or until midnight, are found in most suburbs – Coles and Safeway are the names to look out for.

Victoria St in Richmond is the place to go for cheap produce and Asian ingredients. With a little imagination, you can believe you've been transported to Saigon.

Lastly, don't forget the city's fabulous food markets (see p141), which can stock a picnic hamper in record time, and also make for some of the most entertaining wandering in Melbourne. Still hungry? Continue down to the Bourke St Mall, where you'll find food courts in both Myer and David Jones (p144) department stores. The one in David Jones is particularly worth a trip. See also p144 for places to buy things to drink.

DRINKING

Melbourne has a famously lively bar scene, thanks to liquor-licensing laws that treat its citizens like adults. You'll find bars hidden down tiny alleys, at the top of darkened staircases and perched atop most of the city's luxury hotels. While the CBD boasts the greatest concentration of (and the greatest) bars, you may find some of the offbeat bars in the nearby suburbs to your liking. Whatever the case, we're sure you'll soon find one to call your own. We've also included some of our fave pubs in this mix, especially if they offer that most heavenly attraction – the beer garden. For pubs that offer live music, see p133.

One other little quirk of Melbourne's imbibing life is the devotion locals apply to getting their fix of leafy greens and fruity roughage via juice. Every shopping or eating strip worth its weight in vegetables will have a juice bar or two, often part of a chain.

Central Melbourne

The following all offer something special, whether it be décor, drinks lists or the 'it' factor.

Gin Palace (Map pp72-4; ☎ 9654 0553; 190 Little Collins St) Gin Palace is the transmutation of a side-alley basement into a sophisticated, dimly lit and beautifully furnished New York–meets–Mittel Europa cocktail bar. One killer martini and you're away and prepared to make this palace your home, brocade, velvet, leopard print and all. It's best on weeknights, when a conversation can be conducted without resorting to sign language. The gin is only a small part of the fun.

Double Happiness (Map pp72-4; ☎ 9650 4488; 21 Liverpool St) An intimate, red-hued space, this Chinese socialist-inspired drinking den will inspire you to grab your own Gang of Four and debate the merits of Maoist sophistry until the ceramic Chairman Mao statue over the fireplace begins to look spookily real. Excellent cocktails, plus Tsing Tao beer.

Cherry (Map pp72-4; ☎ 9639 8122; AC/DC Lane) If you can find it, you're guaranteed to like this bar hidden down a tiny rock'n'roller of an alley off Flinders Lane. It's got rock chops galore (Noel Gallagher wanted to buy it, but was knocked back) and a killer soundtrack, courtesy of the Rolling Stones, the Velvet Underground, the Stooges and – who else? – AC/DC (see p134).

Meyers Place (Map pp72-4; ☎ 9650 8609; 20 Meyers Pl) This enchantingly small, dark bar is popular with students, office workers, artists and everyone in between. Designed by renowned local architecture firm Six Degrees as a low-key drinking spot this place can be credited with starting a revolution of sorts in the city in the 1990s. The drinks list is small, so don't expect to be spoilt for choice.

Troika (Map pp72-4; ☎ 9663 5461; 106 Little Lonsdale St) Troika takes its aesthetic cues from Meyers Place and inspires its devotees by never being too cool, too hot or too anything in particular, except open and ready to give you a drink, and let you get on with your conversation. Don't get us wrong, though – it *is* stylish, it's just that it gives the impression of never trying too hard. A gem.

Misty (Map pp72-4; ☎ 9663 9202; 3-5 Hosier Lane) You wanna play Misty for me? Then you'll need the killer *wasabi*-spiked Bloody Mary that's something of a house speciality at this place. You'll get the feeling that this is how a bar in the 21st century might have been visualised in the eyes of an early 1970s movie-set designer – with a dollop of Kubrick thrown in, as opposed to Eastwood.

St Jerome's (Map pp72-4; no phone; 7 Caledonian Lane) Coming here on a Friday or Saturday night is an exercise in frustration, but stumbling upon this back-alley hidey-hole (with a great backyard) on a weeknight or afternoon is sure to put a smile on your face. DJs specialise in the more out-there end of things at times, the toasties are divine and the crowd friendly.

Rue Bebelons (Map pp72-4; ☎ 9663 1700; 267 Little Lonsdale St) We love this hanky-sized bar, where eavesdropping on creatively dressed patrons reveals such gems as 'I just love shoplifting at Target – I was there when you texted me'. Drinks are affordable, the atmosphere humming and the décor cluttered but cool.

Melbourne Supper Club (Map pp72-4; ☎ 9654 6300; Level 1, 161 Spring St) Reminiscent of a slightly shabby English gentlemen's club, you can throw yourself onto a leather lounge or armchair, and wait for the table service to arrive while scoping the queue that snakes down the stairs and onto the street after 10pm. A frequent inspiration for out-of-towner compliments like 'That's my favourite bar in Melbourne', this is a sophisticated, but unstuffy delight for those in the mood for adult entertainment of the most stylish order. An excellent wine list too.

Fitzroy

Brunswick St in Fitzroy, north of Johnston St, has a variety of approachable and sometimes interesting bars and pubs. Those seeking to escape the crowds might do better by perusing the options on nearby Gertrude St, which has some eclectic choices, or in some of the smaller side streets in the area, where low-key dens and cosy pubs abound. Often pubs and bars in this neck of the woods will throw a DJ, film screening or art exhibition into the mix.

Ume Nomiya (Map pp76-8; ☎ 9415 6101; 197 Gertrude St) This little charmer's nomenclature translates as 'drinking house', and stays true to its name by offering a range of sake, *shochu*, plum wine and Japanese beer, plus some excellent nibbles to assuage hunger pangs. If it's feasting your eyes that matters, art exhibitions take place on a three-week roster.

Standard (Map pp76-8; ☎ 9419 4793; 293 Fitzroy St, Fitzroy) With a great, no, make that *the* great, beer garden and lots of comfy places to sit, the relaxed Standard Hotel is always worth a look.

Yelza (Map pp76-8; ☎ 9416 2689; 245 Gertrude St) Stepping through the door at Yelza is like entering another world, with its dim (lugubrious even) lighting, ornate furniture and gold-and-vermilion–flocked wallpaper. The back garden has a completely different feel and is a good escape from the crowded interior. You can also dine here, but it seems like more fun to make eye contact with other patrons and pretend you're in some updated Poe short story.

Napier Hotel (Map pp76-8 ☎ 9419 4240; 210 Napier St, Fitzroy) A bit of a walk from the madness of Brunswick St, the Napier is a great local. The food's pretty good, it's laid-back and there's a nice little outdoor seating area, plus pool tables.

Polly (Map pp76-8; ☎ 9417 0880; 401 Brunswick St) Polly melds a luxe sensibility with the sort of furniture last seen in a Franco Cozzo commercial – lots of ornate carved wood, lots of velvet, a bit of a fish tank. Ease yourself into a lounge, peruse the drinks list and get set to have trouble getting back up.

Bar Open (Map pp76-8; ☎ 9415 9601; 317 Brunswick St) This is the favourite bar of many a local. Downstairs is a cosy bar/café, with a few couches plus a small courtyard, while upstairs is a wide-open space, which occasionally hosts live acts, including the odd micro-music gig or spoken-word performance.

Monties (Map pp76-8; ☎ 9419 3344; 347 Smith St) A big round bar, an open space and plenty of comfy places to chill out make Monties a local favourite. It's a casual spot for a drink, a chat and a game of stick.

Labour in Vain Hotel (Map pp76-8; ☎ 9417 5955; 197 Brunswick St, Fitzroy) This small pub has a lot of character, a tiny rooftop beer garden and some dedicated locals who appreciate the wide, old-fashioned windows that allow you to watch the world go by, and occasionally beckon for it to come in when a recognisable face appears.

Builder's Arms Hotel (Map pp76-8; ☎ 9419 0818; 211 Gertrude St, Fitzroy) This is a great little local pub, with a variety of options going on – there's a gay night Thursday, intermittent film screenings, pool and live music on occasion. Laid-back and lovely.

Prahran

Prahran vies with Fitzroy as one of the coolest suburbs for a night out in Melbourne. While Fitzroy tends towards the bohemian (or, sometimes, fauxhemian), Prahran is more about attitude and slick style, with a lively gay scene centred on Commercial Rd. Prahran's Greville St is one of the city's favourite areas for a crawl, with bars and cafés popping up all the time.

Candy Bar (Map p82; ☎ 9529 6566; 162 Greville St) The Candy Bar is a grinding Greville St fixture. By day it's a café, by night it's more of a small club where gay-flavoured patrons drink and dance to DJ-played music. If the transvestite-hosted bingo night is still happening, add that to your itinerary pronto.

Back Bar (Map p82; ☎ 9529 7899; 67 Green St) Resembling a funeral parlour from an episode of *The Sopranos*, this bar's friendly welcome will make you feel as though you're part of 'the family' in the best possible way. Take up residence on a well-stuffed couch and enjoy the easy-going atmosphere.

St Kilda

St Kilda is another happening area for a night out in the city, especially on a warm summer evening, when the footpaths are crowded with revellers. Venues range from the huge, historic and grungy Espy to achingly fashionable haunts of the tanned, toothy and tousled.

Mink Bar (Map p83; ☎ 9536 1199; 2 Acland St) Hidden beneath the Prince of Wales Hotel, this lounge-cum-bunker feels worlds away from the chaos up on Fitzroy St. As its name suggests, this plush place has plenty of dark bordello-esque corners for an intimate rendezvous, and a Soviet aesthetic for those into communal consumption of the fabulous vodka menu. For more on the Prince of Wales Hotel, see p135.

Greyhound Hotel (Map p83; ☎ 9534 4189; 1 Brighton Rd) On Saturday night this grotty local boozer with tonnes of rough-round-the-edges charm has drag shows. On other nights you can expect live music and cheap, unpretentious drinks.

George Public Bar (Map p83; ☎ 9534 8822; 127 Fitzroy St) The narrow basement bar of the George is an unpretentious bar that attracts locals and backpackers alike. There's a pool table, a 'thought of the day' (usually beer related) and the thrill of watching other people tread the street upstairs.

Doulton Bar (Map p83; ☎ 9534 2200; Village Belle Hotel, 202 Barkly St) Slipping somewhat in its reputation as an old-school, unfussy local boozer, the Doulton has recently become quite the pick-up joint, with local pretty boys and girls studiously trying to avoid looking like they're on the make when that's the only thing on their minds. That and getting drunk.

ENTERTAINMENT

Melbourne has a thriving nightlife, a lively cultural scene, some great bars and nightclubs, and a population that gives the distinct impression that if they're not watching sport they're getting into some sort of cultural event. The city offers everything from stand-up comedy and live music in a crowded pub, to opera at the Melbourne Concert Hall or a play at one of its numerous theatres – plus a calendar so full of festivals that you'll wonder if there's any art form that doesn't have a week or two devoted to it.

The best source of 'what's on' information is the *Entertainment Guide (EG)*, which is published every Friday in the *Age* newspaper. It lists every event for the coming week, whether it be an edgy installation piece or yet another farewell concert from John Farnham. Another good source of information is via the Internet (www.melbourne.vic.gov.au /events/). Check also **Citysearch** (www.melbourne .citysearch.com.au) for current listings and recent reviews of venues and performances. *Beat* and *Inpress* are free music and entertainment publications that can be found in cafés, pubs, bars and other venues throughout the city.

Tickets & Reservations

Various agencies sell tickets to performances and events around town. Try the following:

Ticketmaster7 (Map pp72–4; ☎ 1300 136 166; www .ticketmaster7.com; Theatres Bldg, Victorian Arts Centre, 100 St Kilda Rd, Melbourne; ☺ 9am-9pm Mon-Sat) The main booking agency for theatre, concerts, sports and other events. Besides taking bookings by phone, Ticketmaster has outlets in places like Myer, Telstra Dome, major theatres and shopping centres.

Ticketek (Map pp72–4; ☎ 13 28 49; www.ticketek .com.au; 225 Exhibition St, Melbourne; ☺ 9am-5pm Mon-Fri, 9am-1pm Sat) Also a branch in the Princess Theatre. Covers large sporting and mainstream entertainment events. You can make bookings by phone or via the Internet.

Half Tix (Map pp72–4; ☎ 9650 9420; Melbourne Town Hall, cnr Little Collins & Swanston Sts, Melbourne; ☺ 10am-2pm Mon & Sat, 11am-6pm Tue-Thu, 11am-6.30pm Fri) Sells half-price tickets to shows and concerts on the day of the performance. Cash payments only.

THE AUTHOR'S CHOICE

Butterfly Club Art Bar (Map pp84–5; ☎ 9690 2000; 204 Bank St, South Melbourne) This adorable terrace house holds a small theatre that hosts regular cabaret performances. Show over, head out the back or upstairs to a uniquely decorated bar, where surfaces are bedecked with the kitsch, the cool and the cute. It's a crazy little place – you may find yourself having to tell a childlike barman what Shiraz is, on the receiving end of a spookily accurate tarot reading or just in the garden getting giggly on cocktails. Magic stuff – the Butterfly Club is the best cocoon in town.

Live Music

Melbourne is widely acknowledged as the country's rock capital, and has enjoyed a thriving pub-rock scene where internationally successful bands, such as AC/DC, Nick Cave & the Bad Seeds and Jet, took their first tentative steps towards becoming part of rock's rollercoaster ride. There are other venues in the city that cover jazz and blues, which we've listed here. Expect to part with between zilch and $30 for live performances, but generally you'll get away with about $10 to $15 for a respected local act.

To find out what's on, check out the *EG* section of the *Age*, or alternatively, tune into FM radio stations, such as 3RRR (102.7; www.rrr.org.au) and 3PBS (106.7), both excellent independent radio stations.

ROCK, POP & ACOUSTIC
Central Melbourne

The city is more of a bar kind of place, but there are a few pubs and rock lounges scattered about.

Ding Dong (Map pp72–4; ☎ 9662 1020; 18 Market Lane, Melbourne) Smoky, raucous, grotty and everything a classic rock'n'roll bar should be – great local and international bands play here, and the crowd is usually up for anything.

Pony (Map pp72–4; ☎ 9654 5917; 68 Little Collins St, Melbourne) If too much rock'n'roll is barely enough, you can party hearty till the very wee hours at this bar on weekends. Shout to hear yourself speak – even after you've long since gone home.

Green Room (Map pp72–4; ☎ 9620 5100; Basement, 33 Elizabeth St, Melbourne) A curiously shaped

HIGHWAY TO HELL

Melbourne has long enjoyed its reputation as the epicentre of Australia's live-music scene – no other city in the country has such a proliferation of venues, artists and keen audiences. So it's only fitting that in early 2004, one of Melbourne's most widely read music journalists, Patrick Donovan from the *Age*, began a campaign to turn one of Melbourne's many 'Corporation Lanes' into something a little more suited to the city's rock'n'roll image. After all, if a city like Madrid has a street named after Australia's greatest rock export, then why not Melbourne, the city that features so prominently in one of the band's more memorable videos? In 'Long Way to the Top' the band were filmed travelling down Swanston St on a flat-bed truck and putting on a show for the locals. This led some council members to suggest that the rather anodyne move of a plaque on the aforementioned street, featuring an 'honour roll' of local musos, would suffice, but this didn't wash with passionate Acca Dacca fans, who maintained the rage and made it clear that only AC/DC Lane, where local bar Cherry (p131) stands, would suffice.

In true council style, there were meetings, comings and goings, toings and froings, and even rumours of a surprise appearance by the band themselves should the name change become a reality. They professed themselves flattered at the idea of a little part of the town they once called home being named after them, but it still looked as though it wouldn't happen. Then, with hardly any warning, it became a reality, and in October 2004 dozens of AC/DC fans gathered in AC/DC Lane (see Map pp72–4) and Lord Mayor John So declared 'Let us Rock'. In true rock'n'roll style, extra street signs have been made to deal with the inevitable theft that will take place, as rock fans souvenir a unique slice of Melbourne memorabilia. And yes, fans will notice that AC/DC should be spelt with a lightning bolt, but it seems Melbourne's makers of street signs can't cope with the rock & roll...

space in the basement of the Flinders Station Hotel, this is a good spot to hear live bands from Thursday to Saturday. A little bit grungy, but very relaxed.

Arthouse (Map p79; ☎ 9347 3917; cnr Queensberry & Elizabeth Sts, North Melbourne) At the Royal Artillery Hotel, this place hosts a wide range of acts, mostly at the heavy or punk end of the spectrum.

Carlton, Fitzroy & Collingwood

In terms of sheer choice, Fitzroy is *the* place for a pub-and-pop crawl in Melbourne. Most venues are along Brunswick St, but there are some gems hidden away from the action on other streets.

Tote (Map pp76–8; ☎ 9419 5320; 71 Johnston St, Collingwood) Where the mosh pit is just that – a pit, and the carpet is as sticky as the tar that must line the lungs of the bands, punters and staff at this stalwart of Melbourne's live music scene. A breath of fresh air, in a strange, smoky way. Live music nightly, except Monday.

Evelyn Hotel (Map pp76–8; ☎ 9419 5500; cnr Brunswick & Kerr Sts, Fitzroy) The Evelyn attracts a mixed bag of local and (occasionally) international acts, and the feel is always warm and welcoming.

Rob Roy (Map pp76–8; ☎ 9419 7180; 51 Brunswick St, Fitzroy) On the corner of Gertrude St, this funky local has a good roster of live pop and rock bands – some for free. We give them credit for bringing back '90s funsters Smudge to Melbourne.

Rainbow Hotel (Map pp76–8; ☎ 9419 4193; 27 St David St, Fitzroy) This old backstreet pub has live bands nightly, ranging from jazz and blues to funk and soul. It's a small, low-key place, and worth sussing out.

Empress Hotel (Map p80; ☎ 9489 8605; cnr Scotchmer & Nicholson Sts, North Fitzroy) This empress likes to rock'n'roll, with live music most nights, despite the valiant efforts of 'new Fitzroy' types who think that buying inner-city properties near pubs gives them the right to change the neighbourhood for the worse. Hmph.

Dan O'Connell Hotel (Map pp76–8; ☎ 9347 1502; 225 Canning St, Carlton) This long-running pub is *the* place in town for acoustic music. There are live acts most nights and, yes, you can get a pint of Guinness to go with it.

Richmond

There are plenty of pubs in this suburb, including a great live-music venue.

Corner Hotel (Map p81; ☎ 9427 7300; 57 Swan St) The Corner Hotel is a major player in the

Melbourne music scene and a good pub in its own right. It has a pleasant feel, and the front bar has some good couches. In summer, don't miss the beer garden; in winter, avoid it like the plague or you'll freeze.

St Kilda

Seaside (or close) music venues include the following:

Esplanade Hotel (Map p83; ☎ 9534 0211; 11 Upper Esplanade) A true Melbourne institution for as long as anyone can remember, the Espy has free live bands almost nightly and on Sunday afternoon. It's also a place to sit back with a beer and watch the sun set over the pier, or have a meal in the Espy Kitchen out the back. Make a pilgrimage at least once!

Prince Bandroom (Map p83; ☎ 9536 1111; 2 Acland St) The Art Deco Prince has been a fixture of the St Kilda scene for years. The downstairs bar is a good spot for shooting pool and for people watching, and the crowd spills onto the street during the warmer months. Upstairs, the band room plays host to local and international acts and popular DJ events.

JAZZ & BLUES

There are a few great jazz joints in Melbourne, and the scene is the best in the country. *EG* has jazz and blues listings.

Bennetts Lane (Map pp72-4; ☎ 9663 2856; www.bennettslane.com; 25 Bennetts Lane, Melbourne) Hidden down a narrow lane off Little Lonsdale St (between Exhibition and Russell Sts), this quintessential dim jazz venue is well worth searching out. It's *the* jazz joint in Melbourne and most big acts who come to town perform here (even Prince played a secret gig when last in town). Another bonus? It's nonsmoking.

Manchester Lane (Map pp72-4; ☎ 9663 0630; www.manchesterlane.com.au; 234 Flinders Lane, Melbourne) This beautifully sleek space hosts a range of jazz gigs – you may even stumble upon some experimental electronic sounds. If only all venues were this gorgeous…

Tony Starr's Kitten Club (Map pp72-4; ☎ 9650 2448; Level 1, 267 Little Collins St) This upstairs bar mixes 1950s and new millennium style as successfully as it does its cocktails. It's got terrific atmosphere and a good menu. Tony must be one smooth chap – he even has a lingerie store downstairs and round the back. Pick up a little something from it before coming here to pick up a little something (no doubt from

the Lovers' Lounge) – or just listen to some great live jazz.

Dizzy's (Map p81; ☎ 9428 1233; 90 Swan St, Richmond) Dizzy's offers smoke-free jazz most nights of the week and attracts some pretty big names. The décor is simple, which allows you to concentrate on the music at hand. There are even 'cry-baby' sessions for those with young families on the first Saturday of the month.

Night Cat (Map pp76-8; ☎ 9417 0090; 141 Johnston St, Fitzroy) The Cat is a large, comfortable space with a great atmosphere, skewwhiff 1950s décor (a Melbourne trademark), and jazz and other contemporary bands.

Melbourne Zoo (Map p79; ☎ 9285 9300; www.zoo.org.au; Elliot Ave, Parkville; adult/concession/child $18/13.50/9; ⏰ 9am-5pm) During January, February and March, the zoo hosts the extremely popular 'Twilights' season of open-air sessions, with jazz or big bands (and some rock'n'roll) performing on Friday, Saturday and Sunday evenings – check website for details.

Nightclubs

Melbourne's club scene is a mixed bag, and what's here today might be gone tomorrow. Clubs range from barn-sized discos, where anyone is welcome, to the smaller and more-exclusive places, where you stand a good chance of a knock-back at the door. Cover charges cost $5 to $20, although some places don't charge at all. Most places have certain dress standards, but it's generally at the discretion of the door staff to decide whether or not you are dressed for the occasion.

The best way to keep up with what's happening is to check the alternative club pages in the entertainment papers or in the *EG* in Friday's *Age* newspaper.

CENTRAL MELBOURNE

The CBD has the largest concentration of clubs. It's a good place for a club crawl, particularly if you like dancing until dawn. One area we'd recommend avoiding is the concentration of clubs on King St, which tends to attract a yobbish element.

Honkytonks (Map pp72-4; ☎ 9662 4555; Duckboard Pl; ⏰ Wed-Sun) Sooner or later, someone's going to tell you that you have to see this place – and you do. The bar is like a shrine to booze, the décor like an acid trip, the music (the turntables are embedded in a white grand piano) sublime and the crowd secretly relieved they got past

MELBOURNE

the door, no matter how nonchalant they play it.

Croft Institute (Map pp72-4; ☎ 9671 4399; 21-25 Croft Alley) Inspiring both devotion and disgust, depending on who you're talking to, the Croft is a hard-to-find laboratory of boozing and schmoozing. We quite like it, mainly because we have a thing for lab equipment and love the perilous climb to the dance floor upstairs. Plus, any bar that puts a first-aid trolley in the ladies' loos makes us laugh.

Ffour (Map pp72-4 ☎ 9650 4494; Level 2, 322 Little Collins St; ☾ Thu-Sat) Where Honkytonks is baroque excess, this is Bauhaus iciness. Great drinks, though (perhaps the best in town), and a refreshing antidote to that Melbourne design ethos of 'bung another second-hand couch in the corner'.

Lounge (Map pp72-4; ☎ 9663 2916; 243 Swanston St; ☾ Wed-Sat) Café by day, club by night, this is a good place for a night out in central Melbourne. The crowd is an up-for-it mix of young studenty types and the gainfully employed, and music crosses the genres from electro to hip-hop. Grab a possie on the balcony on a hot summer's night if you can.

OTHER AREAS

Outside the CBD you'll find many of Melbourne's alternative clubs. Check the street press to see which nights suit your tastes.

Revolver (Map p82; ☎ 9521 5985; 229 Chapel St, Prahran; ☾ nightly) Revolver is a popular venue with Prahran's young, arty crowd. With art- and stencil-covered surfaces, and a packed programme featuring DJs, bands, film nights and spoken word, there's a lot to like here. The cavernous space includes a lounge area and an inexpensive Thai restaurant.

Alia (Map pp76-8; ☎ 9486 0999; 83 Smith St, Fitzroy; ☾ Thu-Sun) Alia is ostensibly a club, but you'll never really feel as though you're in one. It's a mixed, easy-going spot, which has proved popular with lesbians. Decent music may well get you on the smallish dance floor.

First Floor (Map pp76-8; ☎ 9419 6380; Level 1, 393 Brunswick St, Fitzroy; ☾ Tue-Sun) A cavernous space in which to dance, drink and devote yourself to having a good time. It's a smart-looking spot, but not at all precious about it, making it an excellent choice for this neck of the woods if you don't feel like pubbing it.

Boutique (Map p82; ☎ 9525 2322; 132A Greville St, Prahran; ☾ Thu-Sun) Ah, the VIP entrance – how else would celebs know whether they're

coming or going? An upmarket, funky little bastion of fashionable types, and a fun spot to people-watch, as everyone here is very comfortable with the idea of being seen.

OneSixOne (Map p82; ☎ 9533 8433; 161 High St, Prahran; ☾ Wed-Sat) Notorious for having the strictest door policy in the city (you are scrutinised from the street via a letter-box window in the door), but we think you'll find that the bark is worse than the bite. After all, we get in here without any fuss. Shake Some Action, the regular Thursday night get-together, is rockin', stellar fun, with live music and a DJ.

Laundry (Map pp76-8; ☎ 9419 6115; 50 Johnston St; Fitzroy ☾ nightly) Slightly grungy and shambolic, the Laundry attracts all types and does a good job of keeping the entertainment options on a roll – from DJs, pool tables, karaoke and live music.

Gay & Lesbian Venues

Most of the newer generation of bars and clubs in Melbourne are gay- and lesbian-friendly. St Kilda, South Yarra and Prahran are the city's main 'gay precincts', with Prahran's Commercial Rd being the traditional centre of Melbourne's gay culture. Wags joke that it's not the 'gay mile', but the 'gay metre', as Melbourne certainly doesn't rival Sydney when it comes to gay nightlife. That said, it's a lot more relaxed than its northern sister. Other gay-friendly neighbourhoods include Collingwood and Abbotsford, with Northcote being a popular spot for lesbians.

Girl Bar (Map p83; ☎ 9536 1177; www.theprince.com .au; 29 Fitzroy St, St Kilda; admission $15; ☾ one Fri a month) This popular ladies night (in the best sense of the phrase) will have you partying with the cliterati till the sun comes up. The Prince also has a ground-level gay bar that dates back to the 1940s and is a great spot to start the night – it's open daily and is free.

Laird (Map p81; ☎ 9417 2832; 149 Gipps St, Abbotsford; admission free) Men only. Lots of leather, moustaches, beer and brawn. Who's yer daddy?

Peel Hotel (Map pp76-8; ☎ 9419 4762; cnr Peel & Wellington Sts, Collingwood; admission free) The Peel is one of the best-known and most popular gay venues in Melbourne, but it also attracts a lesbian crowd at times. We tend to find ourselves here at the tail end of a big night.

Xchange Hotel (Map p82; ☎ 9867 5144; 119 Commercial Rd, Prahran; admission free-$10) A long-standing fixture on the Prahran scene, the

MELBOURNE TRAIN NETWORK

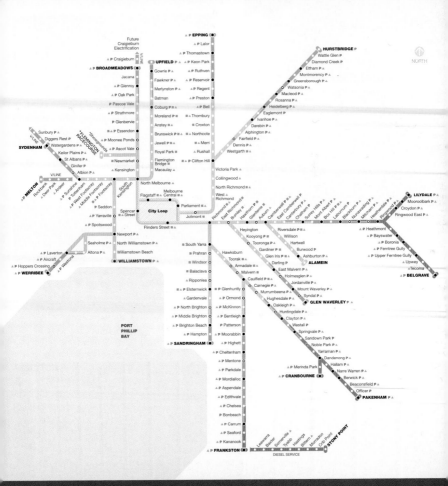

connex

Melbourne Train Network

metlink

Information

Premium Station: Customer service centre staffed from first train to last, seven days a week.
Host Station: Customer service staff at station during morning peak.
*Line to Showgrounds and Flemington Racecourse, only open for special events.

Ticketing Zones

City Saver	Zone 1	Zone 2	Zone 3	Connecting Tram	Connecting Bus	Premium Station	Host Station	Parking

For train, tram and bus information, call **131 638 / (TTY) 9617 2727** or visit **www.metlinkmelbourne.com.au**
Metcard Helpline **(TTY) 1800 652 313**

JAMES BRAUND

Reading the *Entertainment Guide* (EG), Brunswick Street (p100), Fitzroy

Façade of the Australian Centre of the Moving Image (p89), Federation Square

KRZYSZTOF DYDYNSKI

View from the Melbourne Observation Deck (p90), Rialto Towers

JAMES BR

Xchange plays host to a variety of customers and covers all the gay bases. A good, fail-safe meeting spot.

Market Hotel (Map p82; ☎ 9826 0933; 143 Commercial Rd, South Yarra; admission $10-20) A perennially popular nightclub with good house music keeping things going till the sun comes up, and then some.

See also our reviews for the Greyhound Hotel (p132) and the Builder's Arms Hotel (p132).

Cinemas

Melbourne has plenty of mainstream cinemas playing latest releases, although if you've come from the USA or Europe they might be last season's latest. The main chains are Village, Hoyts and Greater Union, and the main group of city cinemas can be found around the intersection of Bourke and Russell Sts. Tickets cost around $15. Check the *EG* in Friday's *Age* or other newspapers for screenings and times.

ACMI (Map pp72-4; ☎ 9663 2583; www.acmi.net.au; Federation Square, Melbourne) The fabulously high-tech cinemas here are our fave place to see a mind-blowing range of films, documentaries and animated features – often geared to a central theme. See p89 for more details.

Astor Theatre (Map p83; ☎ 9510 1414; cnr Chapel St & Dandenong Rd, Prahran) This place holds not-to-be-missed Art Deco nostalgia, with double features nightly of old and recent classics (plus great ice cream).

Cinema Europa (Map p82; ☎ 9827 2440; Level 1, Jam Factory, 500 Chapel St, South Yarra) Good café and bar on the premises, very comfy seats and art-house films.

Cinema Nova (Map pp76-8; ☎ 9347 5331; 380 Lygon St, Carlton) Inside Lygon Court. Great current film releases spread over a number of screening rooms, and bargains to be had on Monday.

George Cinemas (Map p83; ☎ 9534 6922; 133 Fitzroy St, St Kilda) Small cinema space, but handy if you're staying in the area. Licensed.

IMAX (Map pp76-8; ☎ 9663 5454; www.imax.com.au; Rathdowne St, Carlton Gardens, Carlton) Next to Melbourne Museum, this theatre screens films in super-wide 70mm format. Features are listed in the *EG* and on the IMAX website.

Kino (Map pp72-4; ☎ 9650 2100; 45 Collins St, Collins Pl, Melbourne) Recently refurbished and hosting good art-house releases – close to great bars for after-flick drinks.

Lumiere Cinema (Map pp72-4; ☎ 9639 1055; 108 Lonsdale St, Melbourne) Everything here seems almost entirely worn-out, from the chairs to the candy bar, but that really sets the scene for a rainy-day viewing of whatever's just been banned (and is usually French) by the censor.

MOVIES BY MOONLIGHT

If you're in Melbourne between December and March, you can sample one of the city's most popular summertime activities: outdoor cinema. **Moonlight Cinema** (Map pp84–5; www.moonlight.com.au) has almost nightly screenings of newish and classic films in the Royal Botanic Gardens (enter via Gate F on Birdwood Ave in South Yarra). **Open Air Cinema** (Map p75) is similar, with screenings in the Sidney Myer Music Bowl in Kings Domain (enter via Gate 1, Kings Domain, Linlithgow Ave). Prices are about the same as for standard cinemas. Bring along a rug to sit on and a picnic supper, or buy food and drinks. Tickets can also be purchased through **Ticketmaster7** (☎ 1300 136 166; www.ticketmaster7.com).

See also the Movies by Moonlight boxed text, above, for information on summertime outdoor movie screenings.

Theatre

Major theatre performances are always listed in the *EG* in Friday's *Age*. There's no theatre district as such, but the scene is a healthy one, from edgy independent productions to the city's fringe to the biggest, glitziest musicals in the city's ritziest theatrical premises.

THEATRE COMPANIES

Melbourne has a number of well-regarded theatre companies, and the scene is probably the healthiest in the country, with excellent performers, a responsive public and a supportive atmosphere.

La Mama (Map pp76-8; ☎ 9347 6948; 205 Faraday St, Carlton) This place is historically significant to Melbourne's theatre scene. The tiny, intimate forum produces new Australian works and experimental theatre, and has a reputation for developing emerging playwrights.

CUB Malthouse Theatre (Map pp84-5; ☎ 9685 5111; www.playbox.com.au; 113 Sturt St, South Melbourne) At the CUB Malthouse Theatre, this is an outstanding company that stages predominantly Australian works by established and new playwrights. It was previously known as Playbox Theatre.

Melbourne Theatre Company (MTC; Map pp72-4; ☎ 9684 4500; www.mtc.com.au) This is Melbourne's major theatrical company, with performances

PERFORMING-ARTS VENUES

The following venues are used for a variety of artistic endeavours – from theatre to comedy, opera to modern dance.

Athenaeum Theatre (Map pp72-4; ☎ 9650 1500; 188 Collins St, Melbourne) Excellent acoustics and a great venue for the annual Comedy Festival.

Comedy Theatre (Map pp72-4; ☎ 9242 1000; 240 Exhibition St, Melbourne) Bum-numbing seats, but a regular venue for mainstream comedy plays and performances.

Forum Theatre (Map pp72-4; 150 Flinders St, Melbourne) A glorious venue for live music, film-festival events and even raves – with a swirling, inspiring interior that features a night-sky ceiling.

National Theatre (Map p83; ☎ 9534 0221; cnr Barkly & Carlisle Sts, St Kilda) Once the home of Melbourne opera, now a popular community venue, and a good place to see drama and dance.

Palais Theatre (Map p83; ☎ 9537 2444; Lower Esplanade, St Kilda) A great venue that hosts local and international acts, such as Franz Ferdinand and Beck in superb style.

Princess Theatre (Map pp72-4; ☎ 9299 9800; 163 Spring St, Melbourne) A lavish old lady who often stages musicals.

Regent Theatre (Map pp72-4; ☎ 9299 9500; 191 Collins St, Melbourne) A good, grand old venue for musicals. See p90 for more details.

Rod Laver Arena (Map p75; www.mopt.com.au; Batman Ave, Melbourne) An enormous arena that hosts both the Australian Open tennis and populist concert tours for the likes of Sir Elton John and David Bowie. Features a retractable roof, so weather is not an issue.

Sidney Myer Music Bowl (Map p75; www.vicartscentre.com.au/sidneymyermusicbowl/index.htm; Kings Domain) This lush amphitheatre is the perfect place for a performance and a picnic – whether it be Carols by Candlelight or Nick Cave and the Bad Seeds.

Victorian Arts Centre (Map pp72-4; ☎ 9281 8000; www.vicartscentre.com.au; 100 St Kilda Rd, Melbourne) Melbourne's major venue for the performing arts. Flanked by the Yarra River on one side and the National Gallery of Victoria on the other, the complex houses the Melbourne Concert Hall (also called Hamer Hall) and three theatres – the State Theatre, the Playhouse and the George Fairfax Studio. See p95 for more details.

at the Victorian Arts Centre. The MTC stages around 15 productions each year, ranging from contemporary and modern (including many new Australian works) to Shakespearean and other classics. Bums are attracted to seats thanks to a recent policy of getting big-name Australian stars (Rachel Griffiths, Geoffrey Rush et al) to tread the boards.

Red Stitch (Map pp70-1; ☎ 9533 8083; 2 Chapel St, St Kilda) This is a praiseworthy ensemble of local actors, who stage new and interesting works that you can't get to see anywhere else in the city. It's a small space at the rear of 2 Chapel St – opposite the Astor Theatre (p137).

Storeroom (Map p80; ☎ 9486 5651; www.thestoreroom.com.au; cnr St Georges Rd & Scotchmer St, North Fitzroy) Good fringe pickings from overseas and Australia feature on the playbills of this great little space at the rear of the Parkview Hotel.

Theatreworks (Map p83; ☎ 9534 4879; www.theatreworks.org.au; 14 Acland St, St Kilda) This company combines community theatre and storytelling with diverse and innovative productions.

CLASSICAL MUSIC, OPERA & BALLET

Melbourne prides itself on being Australia's most 'highbrow' city, so it should come as no surprise that the more traditional musical and dance artforms attract enthusiastic patronage.

In 1996 Victoria's state opera company was subsumed by Opera Australia, leading to regular howls of protests about the paucity of opera performances in the state. As this book went to press there were hints that the VSO would rise again – watch this space. That said, **Opera Australia** (www.opera-australia.org.au) performs on a regular basis in Melbourne; visit its website for more details.

Classical music buffs will have the **Melbourne Chorale** (www.melbournechorale.com.au), a combination of two choirs that perform a variety of classical and modern works for voice. The **Melbourne Symphony Orchestra** (www.mso.com.au) performs regularly throughout the year and has both a strong reputation and a keen fan base.

The **Australian Ballet** (www.australianballet.com.au) boasts a healthy repertoire and some sterling performers, and it is based in Melbourne.

All of the above can be seen in performance at the Victorian Arts Centre (p95), with tickets available via phone, ticket offices and the Internet.

Comedy

Melbourne prides itself on being the home of Australian comedy, and with its weather, you can see why people like escaping indoors to laugh at life's, and their own, absurdities.

Barry Humphries is without doubt Melbourne's most famous and most brilliant comedian. His sardonic wit and derisive jibes at his homeland are not always played just for laughs. For a fascinating and hilarious insight into growing up in mid-20th-century Melbourne, Humphries' autobiography *More Please* is a must.

A *very* healthy stand-up comedy circuit has developed over the last couple of decades in Melbourne, and since 1987 the International Comedy Festival has been held annually in the city from late March to April. During the festival the city becomes a giant venue, with local comedians joining forces with international acts (including many from the famous Edinburgh Festival) to perform in many pubs, clubs and theatres around town, and on Melbourne's city streets.

Melbourne has a few regular comedy venues and nightspots where stand-up comics stand or fall. Look in the *EG* in the *Age* for weekly gigs.

Comic's Lounge (Map p79; ☎ 9348 9488; www.the comicslounge.com.au; 26 Errol St, North Melbourne) This is the only place in town with daily comedy performances, with acts ranging across the comedy spectrum, from wonderful to woeful – and all for around $10.

Last Laugh Comedy Club (Map pp72-4; ☎ 9650 1977; www.comedyclub.com.au; Athenaeum Theatre, 188 Collins St, Melbourne) Professional stand-up on Friday and Saturday nights, with dinner-and-a-show packages available if you want to try choking on laughter. A great venue for the Comedy Festival, too.

Sport

Australians in general, and Melburnians in particular, are fanatical supporters of sport, especially when it comes to watching it. The two biggest events on the sporting calendar (actually, make that the entire city calendar)

are a horse race and a game of Australian rules football!

You can book tickets for various sporting events through Ticketek or Ticketmaster7 (see p133). A booking fee is charged by both services.

FOOTBALL
Australian Rules Football

Without a doubt, Australian rules football – otherwise known as 'the footy' – is the city's sporting obsession, with games at the **Melbourne Cricket Ground** (MCG; Map p75; ☎ 9657 8888; www.mcg.org.au; Brunton Ave, Jolimont) regularly pulling crowds of 50,000 to 80,000 people. If you're here between April and September you should try to see a match, as much for the crowds as for the game. The sheer energy of the barracking at a big game is exhilarating. Despite the fervour, crowd violence is almost unknown.

The **Australian Football League** (AFL; www.afl.com .au) runs the nationwide competition, and while there are teams based in Perth, Adelaide, Sydney and Brisbane, Melbourne is still considered the game's stronghold, despite the big one (ie the Grand Final) being won by interstate teams for the last few years.

Being the shrine of Aussie rules, the MCG is still widely regarded as the best place to see a match, although the newer but smaller **Telstra Dome** (Map pp72-4; ☎ 8625 7700; www.telstra dome.com.au; Docklands) is a whizz-bang stadium (though many players dislike its playing surface).

Tickets can be bought at the ground for most games, and admission costs about $15 to $20 (and you'll need another few dollars for the obligatory meat pie and beer). Seats can be booked (this might be necessary at big games).

Rugby

Rugby Union has been slow to catch on in Melbourne, but despite this the MCG and Telstra Dome attract enormous crowds to international matches. In 2003 Melbourne played host to the Rugby World Cup, which has boosted the sport's profile and popularity in the city.

Rugby League has made a reasonable impact on Melbourne's sports-mad public with the introduction of Melbourne Storm – the only Melbourne side in the National Rugby League. The Storm won the Grand Final in

1999 after competing in the league for only a couple of years, albeit with players imported mostly from the northern rugby playing states. With this success, the game looked to be gaining a foothold in the heartland of Australian rules football, but recent performances have been lacklustre.

Melbourne Storm's home matches are played at **Olympic Park** (Map p75; ☎ 9286 1600; www.mopt.com.au; Batman Ave). Both codes play between April and September.

Soccer

Soccer has always had a strong fan base in Melbourne, with the Italian, Greek and Croatian communities being particularly avid followers of the game. Interest has been strengthened in recent years with the overseas success of home-grown players and the continued improvement of the national side. The national soccer-league season, which includes four Melbourne teams, commences in October and finishes in May. Contact the **Victorian Soccer Federation** (☎ 9682 9666; www .soccervictoria.org.au) for details on home matches and venues.

CRICKET

The MCG is one of the world's great sports stadiums. For any cricket fan, or general sports fanatic, a visit to the MCG (p98) is not only compulsory but something of a pilgrimage. During summer international test matches, one-day internationals and the Pura Milk Cup (formerly the Sheffield Shield, the national cricket competition) are all played here. The cricket season in Australia is from October to March. General admission to international matches is around $30 and reserved seats start at around $40, with finals costing more (and generally requiring a booking). The cricket event *par excellence* is the traditional Boxing Day Test (held on 26 December), which sells out fast.

HORSE RACING

Horse racing takes place in Melbourne throughout the year – at Flemington, Caulfield, Moonee Valley and Sandown Racecourses – but spring is when the culture of racing is at its most colourful and frenetic.

The **Melbourne Cup** (www.melbournecup.com.au), on the first Tuesday in November, is one of the world's greatest horse races. It's the feature event of Melbourne's Spring Racing

Carnival, which runs through October and finishes with the Emirates Stakes Day on the Saturday following the Melbourne Cup. The carnival's major races are the Cox Plate, the Caulfield Cup, the Dalgety, the Mackinnon Stakes and the holy grail itself, the Melbourne Cup. Apart from these races, Derby Day and Oaks Day feature prominently on the spring-racing calendar.

The two-mile (3.2km) Melbourne Cup, which is always run at Flemington Racecourse, was first run in 1861. The Cup brings the whole of Australia to a standstill for the three-or-so minutes during which the race is run. Cup day is a public holiday in the Melbourne metropolitan area, but people all over the country are affected by Melbourne's spring-racing fever. Serious punters and fashion-conscious race-goers pack the grandstand and lawns of the Victoria Racing Club's beautiful Flemington Racecourse. The city's once-a-year betters make their choice or organise Cup syndicates with friends, and the race is watched or listened to on TVs and radios in pubs, clubs, TAB betting shops and houses right across the land.

If you fancy catching some racing, even outside Cup time, head to **Flemington Racecourse** (Map pp70-1; ☎ 1300 727 575; www.vrc.net .au; 400 Epsom Rd, Flemington), which has regular race meets and is easily accessed by public transport.

MOTOR SPORTS

Melbourne hosts both the **Australian Formula One Grand Prix** (☎ 9258 7100; www.grandprix.com.au /cars) and the Australian round of the World 500cc **Motorcycle Grand Prix** (www.grandprix.com.au /bikes). The Formula One takes place in Albert Park (see p105) in March, and the motorbikes race at Phillip Island (see p189) in October. Tickets for the Formula One Grand Prix start at $39 for a one-day general admission ticket and $599 for a four-day reserved ticket. Tickets can be bought through Ticketmaster7 (see p133) or check the Grand Prix website.

TENNIS

For two weeks each January **Melbourne Park** (Map p75; ☎ 9286 1244; www.mopt.com.au; Batman Ave) hosts the **Australian Open** (www.ausopen.org) tennis championships. Top players from around the world come to compete in the year's first of the big four Grand Slam tournaments. Tickets are available through Ticketek (p133) and range from about $25 for early rounds to over $100 for finals.

SHOPPING

Melbourne offers not only the best shopping in Victoria, but also in Australia. You'll find everything you could possibly want and more than a few goodies you didn't know you wanted until you arrived. The widest array of shops can naturally be found in the CBD, where you can find international heavy-hitters from Paris, London, Tokyo and New York, plus department stores, exclusive shopping centres in renovated buildings, and quirky little boutiques lurking in lanes and alleys. The suburbs are home to a growing legion of factory outlets (try Bridge Rd and Swan St in Richmond) and shopping malls, as well as offbeat boutiques and stores that specialise in particular items. We've included a range of Melbourne-centric shops plus a few other well-known purveyors that can be found elsewhere. Get set to spend and mingle with Melburnians – they love shopping almost as much as they love sport!

Australian Souvenirs

Crumpler (Map pp76-8; ☎ 9417 5338; cnr Gertrude & Smith Sts, Fitzroy) A local company that started out a few years ago making tough-as-nails bags for cycle couriers. Only trouble was, they looked so good they became a fashion accessory. A great local souvenir you won't be ashamed to drag around the world.

Dinosaur Designs (Map p82; ☎ 9827 2600; 562 Chapel St, South Yarra) Fabulous resin *objets d'art* and jewellery moulded in organic shapes and vivid colours – an excellent way to brighten up your home or your body.

RM Williams (Map p82; ☎ 9510 2413; 204 Commercial Rd, Prahran) Bill Clinton doesn't consider a trip to Australia complete till he's snaffled a pair of these famously long-lasting boots. An Aussie icon, even for city slickers.

Bookshops

See Information (p68) for details on Melbourne's many excellent bookshops.

Children's Shops

Bernard's Magic Shop (Map pp72-4; ☎ 9670 9270; 211 Elizabeth St, Melbourne) This magical place

---

TO MARKET TO MARKET

Melbourne's famous markets allow you to experience the city in all its multicultural glory, as locals shop, socialise, and converse in an array of tongues. Not only are the people diverse, the range of goods on display is truly amazing. At a market like the Queen Victoria Market or the Prahran Market, you can choose from at least 10 types of pesto, mountains of mangoes, barrels of olives, walls of cheese, sacks of coffee and more spices than you ever knew existed. Without a doubt, a visit to one of Melbourne's big markets is a great way, perhaps the best way, to spend half a day in the city.

The following are some of Melbourne's best-loved markets:

Camberwell Sunday Market (Station St, Camberwell; ☽ 6am-2.30pm Sun) One of the most popular 'trash and treasure' markets, this has hundreds of stalls piled with everything, including the kitchen sink. Get there early to fight with the fashionistas for the best retro gear, though. The market is behind the Burke Rd shopping strip, close to the Burke Rd–Riversdale Rd corner. It runs nearly up to Prospect Rd.

Prahran Market (Map p82; ☎ 8290 8220; www.prahranmarket.com.au; 163-185 Commercial Rd, Prahran; ☽ dawn-5pm Tue & Sat, dawn-6pm Thu & Fri, 10am-3pm Sun) This may be the best food market in the city, with several organic-produce stores, a fresh-pasta store, flower stalls, great delis, a whole wing devoted to meat (including an organic butcher), a good food court and plenty of sample trays.

Queen Victoria Market (Map p79; ☎ 9320 5822; www.qvm.com.au; cnr Victoria & Elizabeth Sts, City; ☽ 6am-2pm Tue & Thu, 6am-6pm Fri, 6am-3pm Sat, 9am-4pm Sun) The mother of all Melbourne markets, with over 500 stalls selling everything under the sun, including fruit and vegetables (and organic produce), meat and fish, jeans, furniture, budgies and sheepskin products. On Sunday many of the fruit, vegetable, meat and fish stalls are closed (the delicatessens and bakeries stay open, though), and there are dozens more stalls selling jewellery, clothes, souvenirs, antiques and bric-a-brac.

South Melbourne Market (Map pp84-5; ☎ 9209 6295; cnr Cecil & Coventry Sts, South Melbourne; ☽ 8am-4pm Wed, Sat & Sun, 8am-6pm Fri) This general market covers most bases, with excellent delis, foodstuffs, flower stalls, cheap clothes and the addiction-inspiring dim-sim stall that has a permanent queue.

will conjure the inner child right out of you, and impress any littlies that you may have in tow. There are practical jokes galore, plus items that will help the more serious magician with the art of illusion.

Gerlinki Junior (Map pp76-8; ☎ 9419 9169; 217 Brunswick St, Fitzroy) Stocking the funkiest kids' clothes in Melbourne, Gerlinki Junior is the pint-size branch of this hip budget fashion retailer. Lots of hilarious little T-shirts will have you asking if there's any chance that some of them might stretch to fit adults.

Honeyweather & Speight (Map p83; ☎ 9534 3380; 113 Barkly St, St Kilda) This kooky little gem has wonderfully old-fashioned and unusual toys for children who don't need a Playstation to have a good time. Pick up a pint-size ukulele and make some music.

Clothing & Accessories

Alice Euphemia (Map pp72-4; ☎ 9650 4300; Shop 6/37 Swanston St, cnr Flinders Lane, Melbourne) The more experimental end of Melbourne fashion gets a showing here, with inventive fabrics, cuts and finishes that aim to make you look more interesting than you might actually be. A great range of rings, brooches and earrings is displayed, too.

Calibre (Map pp72-4; ☎ 9663 8001; 45 Collins St, Melbourne) Calibre specialises in the sort of suits that make a man look a million bucks. They're classic, yet exude a contemporary sensibility, and can be downplayed or updated with the great range of interesting shirts.

Chiodo (Map pp72-4; ☎ 9663 0044; Basement, 114 Russell St, Melbourne) Chiodo's menswear range features excellent basics that always have an artful (yet still wearable) twist. Fabrics are excellent, workmanship solid and the sales staff know how to get you in order.

Christine (Map pp72-4; ☎ 9654 2011; 181 Flinders Lane, Melbourne) What did the women of Melbourne do before Christine? This treasure-trove of shoes, bags, beads and baubles will update any outfit in record time, and prices range from low to 'if you have to ask, you can't afford it'. The stellar sales staff really know their stuff, too.

City Hatters (Map pp72-4; ☎ 9614 3294; 211 Flinders St) Beside the main entrance to Flinders St station, this is the most convenient place to purchase an Aussie icon, such as an Akubra hat, a trilby or a little something in astrakhan. This place is easily head and shoulders above the rest. Sorry.

Country Road (Map p82; ☎ 9824 0133; 252 Toorak Rd, South Yarra) It seems that every Australian, at some point, has had a bit of Country Road in their wardrobe, whether it be that first suit, those smart leather thongs (flip-flops) or their favourite old study jumper. Not the most adventurous local label, but contemporary enough to be wearable across a range of ages, and sturdily constructed.

Dot & Herbey (Map p83; ☎ 9593 6309; 229 Barkly St, St Kilda) Using vintage fabrics to re-create some of today's coolest looks, this is a great little shop for sourcing the unexpected, as it doesn't slavishly follow female fashion.

Douglas & Hope (Map pp76-8; ☎ 9650 0585; 181 Brunswick St, Fitzroy) This pretty space stocks innovative local and New Zealand fashion designers, but has really earned its stripes by producing some of the most beautiful handmade quilts and cushions, all in eye-catching vintage fabrics. A 50cm x 50cm cushion will set you back about $100, and quilts start at around $900, but they're worth it. There's another branch in the Block Arcade in the city.

Le Louvre (Map pp72-4; ☎ 9650 1300; 74 Collins St, Melbourne) Firmly entrenched in the hearts and minds of Melbourne's society ladies, Le Louvre is the sort of shop where entire season's wardrobes are purchased and price tags aren't acknowledged. There are no racks as such – owner Georgina Weir will simply sort you out with the latest from Paris and other fashion capitals.

Scanlan & Theodore (Map p82; ☎ 9824 1800; 566 Chapel St, South Yarra) Scanlan & Theodore enjoys one of the best reputations in local fashion thanks to its peerless ability to combine flattering, imaginative design and the best fabrics (often from France and Italy) in the business. Whisper-fine evening dresses rub coat-hanger shoulders with luxe suiting, and gorgeous bags and shoes loiter in the hope of attracting your attention. Magic stuff. There's another branch on Little Collins St in the city.

Commercial Art Galleries

Melbourne has dozens of private, commercial art galleries. Check the magazine **Art Almanac** (www.art-almanac.com.au), a monthly guide to all city and regional galleries, which is available from the shops at the National Gallery of Victoria and other galleries. The best place to start your art-gallery tour is in Flinders

SHOPPING STRIPS & SPECIALIST SPOTS

Chapel St in South Yarra is the most commercially fashionable and popular of Melbourne's fashion zones. The section between Toorak and Commercial Rds is lined with up-to-the-minute boutiques, and it's a fascinating area to visit, whether you come to shop or just to check out all the beautiful people (and those who pay their bills). The Prahran and Windsor end of the street is packed with regular local vendors (such as hardware stores and cake shops) and a good selection of interesting boutiques and traders.

Greville St in Prahran is probably *the* most recognised address for retro-style shops and fashion-forward apparel for young party-goers. **Toorak Rd** in South Yarra is the ultimate in expensive, visibly labelled style. This street is home to exclusive designers, specialist shops and galleries that specialise in big-name Australian art – even if you can't afford to buy anything, it's a decent street to wander along. You never know who or what you might see.

High St in Armadale is a curious (and popular) blend of bridal boutiques, antique dealers and Persian-rug shops, plus a lot of homewares shops selling what must be a million scented candles, cushions and 'throws' (pronounced 'thrers' in these parts).

In the city centre, there's a cluster of camera shops along **Elizabeth St**, between Bourke and Lonsdale Sts. **Little Bourke St** is another good area to look for some camera gear, including used equipment. The same street, between Elizabeth and Queen Sts, is Melbourne's outdoor-goods mecca. Gear-heads be warned: if you so much as walk down this street, you won't come away without a new piece of expensive gear, or at least a few urgent cravings. Try also **Hardware Lane** for outdoorsy stuff. If you're looking for imaginative fashions in the city centre, linger longer in lanes like **Flinders Lane**, and **Centre Pl** and **Centre Way** (which connect Flinders Lane to Collins St).

Most of the cheap souvenir stores in the city sell poor-quality knock-offs of Aboriginal art. If you want pieces that have a well-established provenance, you'll have to visit an established gallery and pay accordingly. There are several good galleries in the city centre, and Flinders Lane is an excellent place to start your search (see opposite).

Lane in the city, which includes the following galleries:

Anna Schwartz Gallery (Map pp72-4; ☎ 9654 6131; www.annaschwartzgallery.com.au; 185 Flinders Lane) Leader of the pack when it comes to high-profile modern-art exhibitions in a blindingly white, sometimes chilly space.

Counter (Map pp72-4; ☎ 9650 7775; www.craftvic.asn.au; 31 Flinders Lane) The retail wing of Craft Victoria. Stocks wonderful handmade pieces that aren't in the least bit fusty – they're more like wearable works of art.

Flinders Lane Gallery (Map pp72-4; ☎ 9654 3332; www.flg.com.au; 137 Flinders Lane) Specialising in contemporary Australian (including indigenous) artists since 1990.

Forty Five Downstairs (Map pp72-4; ☎ 9662 9233; www.fortyfivedownstairs.com; Basement, 45 Flinders Lane) Huge space with plenty of room for large-scale modern artworks. Happy to explain anything, too.

Gallery Gabrielle Pizzi (Map pp72-4; ☎ 9654 2944; www.gabriellepizzi.com.au; 141 Flinders Lane) Ground-breaking local exhibitions, including artists such as Christian Thompson and a host of other indigenous talent.

You'll also find good galleries outside the city centre, especially in the suburbs of Fitzroy (Gertrude St is an edgy delight), South Yarra and Prahran.

Cosmetics & Skin Care

Aesop (Map p83; ☎ 9534 9433; 2 Acland St, St Kilda) This starkly chic space is reminiscent of an art gallery, and even if you don't walk into it looking like an oil painting, the heavenly scents and luxurious unguents will soon have you at your best. A world-famous skin-care brand, and avowedly local – our fave product is the Geranium Leaf Body Cleanser.

Aveda Retreat on Spring (Map p75; ☎ 9654 2217; 49 Spring St, Melbourne) This Aveda day spa stocks all the hair- and skin-care preparations you could hope for, plus it offers some excellent pampering treatments – Foot Relief ($65) will ease any sightseeing pains that have hit your tootsies.

Kleins (Map pp76-8; ☎ 9416 1221; 313 Brunswick St, Fitzroy) Stocked floor-to-ceiling with soaps, perfumes, ointments, candles and sundry pampering accessories, Klein's is the sort of outrageously girlie shop that men just don't understand (as they wait, and wait, for decisions to be made).

Mecca Cosmetica (Map p82; ☎ 9827 8711; 166 Toorak Rd, South Yarra) The best place to (air) kiss and make-up in the entire city. Hip lines like Stila, Nars and Prescriptives, cool scents like Fracas and other hard-to-finds, plus a great home-brand nail-polish range. Sales staff are more than happy to play with your face if they're not too busy.

Department Stores & Shopping Malls

The Bourke St Mall has the densest concentration of shops. It's home to the city's two main department stores and scores of other smaller shops. This is probably the best place to start a shopping trip in Melbourne if you're after recognisable brands and basics.

David Jones (Map pp72-4; ☎ 9643 2222; 310 Bourke St, Melbourne) With shops on both sides of the mall, this store is slightly more upmarket than Myer and a good place to look for top-quality goods. There's also the recently reopened Food Hall, which stocks some of the most luscious culinary treats you'll find in the city.

Dimmey's (Map p81; ☎ 9427 0442; 140 Swan St, Richmond) One of the cheapest and most bizarre places to buy just about anything. It's an old-fashioned and chaotic wonderland of junk and bargains, and a visual feast – treat it as a sight rather than a shopping excursion.

GPO Building (Map pp72-4; ☎ 9663 0066; 350 Bourke St, Melbourne) After the GPO burnt down in September 2001, the city's burghers decided that the grand old lady of Bourke St needed a full face-lift and makeover – and *voilà!* Packed with fab boutiques, including Leona Edmiston, Belinda, La Perla and Georg Jensen, this is one of the city's classiest shopping spots.

Melbourne Central (Map pp72-4; ☎ 9922 1100; cnr Elizabeth & Latrobe Sts, Melbourne) This busy shopping centre reopened in 2004 after a few years of snoozing. Lots of fairly mainstream shops, in an interesting building (see p93).

Myer (Map pp72-4; ☎ 9661 1111; 314 Bourke St, Melbourne) There are 12 floors of different departments in two buildings, connected by an elevated skywalk. There's also the famous Myer Christmas window displays during the holiday season (for more details see p112).

QV (Map pp72-4; ☎ 9658 0100; cnr Swanston & Lonsdale Sts, Melbourne) In an imposing modern skyscraper, this shopping centre features all sorts of populist commercial options, and a few cool international options. In the Red Coates Lane area you'll find surf- and skatewear. It's a monster – taking up the whole block between Russell and Swanston Sts.

Food & Wine

Jasper (Map pp76-8; ☎ 9416 0921; 267 Brunswick St, Fitzroy) If trawling back and forth along the caffeinated causeway that is Brunswick St has made you start to think you could do it all yourself, this is the store for you. All manner of coffee paraphernalia and beans abounds – they don't call themselves 'caffeine dealers' for nothing.

Melbourne Cleanskin Company (Map pp76-8; ☎ 9347 9233; 350 Drummond St, Carlton) Australian wine is sought-after the world over, and at this temple of unlabelled (ie cleanskin) wine you'll be able to indulge yourself in local and New Zealand varieties at extremely reasonable prices. There are regular tastings on Saturdays.

Peter Watson (Map pp76-8; ☎ 9417 0209; 113 St David St, Fitzroy) Peter Watson's dressings, marinades, sauces and other condiments are, quite simply, the best barbecue accompaniments we've ever found. Pop in and stock up on premium oils or simply breathe in – this shop smells splendid.

T2 (Map pp76-8; ☎ 9417 3722; 340 Brunswick St, Fitzroy) This stylish tea specialist in Fitzroy is a must for the tea lover. The wonderful aroma wafting out the door draws us in every time, and there's a fabulous range of tea cups, pots and strainers to accompany that perfect blend.

For self-caterers seeking a supermarket, see p130.

Music

Melbourne, as the home of Australia's live music scene, has a great range of music stores, although sadly their number has declined in recent years with the advent of online music and the iPod. For mainstream music in the city, try one of the chains in Bourke St.

Gaslight Music (Map pp72-4; ☎ 9650 9009; 85 Bourke St, Melbourne) Gaslight has one of the most interesting collections of CDs and DVDs in the city. Staff will happily order things in for you, too.

Greville Records (Map p82; ☎ 9510 3012; 152 Greville St) One of the last bastions of the 'old' Greville St, this fabulous music shop has such a loyal following that the great Neil Young invited the owners onstage during his last Melbourne concert. Friendly, knowledgable and so damn cool.

Raoul Records (Map p83; ☎ 9525 5066; 221 Barkly St, St Kilda) Excellent for the latest electronica

CARS & TRAMS

Car drivers should treat trams with caution – trams are about half the weight of an ocean liner and seldom come off second-best in accidents. You can only overtake a tram on the left and you must *always* stop behind a tram when it halts to drop off or collect passengers (except where there are central 'islands' for passengers).

Melbourne has a notoriously confusing road rule, known as the hook turn, for getting trams through the city centre without being blocked by cars turning right. To turn right at many major intersections in the city, you have to pull to the left of the intersection, wait until the light of the street you're turning into changes from red to green, then complete the turn. These intersections are identified by a black-and-white hook sign that reads 'Right Turn from Left Only' and hangs from the overhead cables. This manoeuvre can be disconcerting for first-timers; the trick is to stay calm, observe a few locals doing it, and never start the right turn until you're sure that the light has fully changed and no one is still coming straight through the intersection (along your original line of travel). Once you get the first one down, you'll see there really wasn't anything to worry about!

and lo-fi releases and some of the best vintage vinyl in town, Raoul Records protests the gentrification of St Kilda by naming its Best Record of the Year awards the Slack trophy, after HW Slack, a second-hand shop from the olden days. Sigh.

GETTING THERE & AWAY

International and interstate flights operate out of **Melbourne airport** (☎ 9297 1600; www.mel air.com.au; Tullamarine) and some interstate flights operate from **Avalon airport** (www.avalonairport .com.au). Long-distance trains run from Southern Cross station. The long-distance bus terminal in the city centre is the Southern Cross coach terminal, on Spencer St, and the Skybus airport buses operate from here.

For details of travel to/from Melbourne and places interstate and overseas, see p407. For details of travel between Melbourne and places within Victoria, see p412.

GETTING AROUND
To/From the Airports

Melbourne airport is at Tullamarine (above), 22km northwest of the city centre. It's a modern airport with a single terminal. There are two information desks at the airport: one on the ground floor in the international departure area and another upstairs next to the duty-free shops.

If you're driving, take the Tullamarine Fwy from the airport to the CityLink toll road, which will take you into town. A 24-hour Tulla Pass costs $3.40, and can be purchased from post offices, any Shell petrol station and CityLink offices en route (for details on City-Link see p146).

A taxi between the airport and the city centre costs around $40 (including the cost of the tollway). **Skybus** (☎ 9335 2811; www.skybus .com.au; $13, 20 minutes) operates a 24-hour shuttle-bus service between the airport and the city. In either direction, Skybus has departures approximately every 30 minutes between 6am and midnight, and every hour between midnight and 6am. Buy your ticket from the driver or online; bookings are not usually necessary. You can take your bicycle on the Skybus, but the front wheel must be removed. The service is also wheelchair accessible.

To get to Avalon Airport, you can take a taxi (over $100), or drive (it's about 55km from Melbourne), or take the Avalon Airport Shuttle. See www.avalonairportshuttle .com.au for details.

Car & Motorcycle

If you're lucky enough to find an on-street parking space in the city centre you'll pay from $2 an hour. Check parking signs for restrictions and times, and watch out for clearway zones that operate during peak hour (cars left in this zone at the wrong time will get towed and fined heftily).

There are over 70 car parks in the city, and the Melbourne City Council produces a map-and-brochure guide to city parking – it's available from the Melbourne Visitor Information Centre (p87). Hourly rates vary depending on the location of the car park – $3 to $6 per hour or $12 to $25 per day on weekdays, less on weekends.

CAR HIRE

All the big firms are represented in Melbourne. **Avis** (☎ 13 63 33; www.avis.com.au), **Budget** (☎ 1300 362 848; www.budgetaustralia.com), **Delta Europcar** (☎ 1300 131 390; www.deltaeuropcar.com.au), **Hertz** (☎ 133039;www.hertz.com) and **Thrifty** (☎ 1300 367 227; www.thrifty.com.au) have desks at the airport, and you can find plenty of others in the city. The offices tend to be at the northern end of the city, or in Carlton or North Melbourne. For disabled travellers, Avis rents hand-controlled vehicles.

The *Yellow Pages* lists lots of other firms, including some reputable local operators who rent newer cars but don't have the nationwide network (and overheads) of the big operators.

A number of rent-a-wreck-style operators rent older vehicles at lower rates. Their costs and conditions vary widely, so it's worth making a few inquiries. Beware of distance restrictions: some companies only allow you to travel within a certain distance of the city, typically 100km. And keep in mind, when these companies describe their cars as wrecks, they're not joking. You could try **Rent-a-Bomb** (☎ 9428 0088; www.rentabomb.com.au); expect rates to start at around $35 per day.

TOLL ROADS

CityLink (☎ 13 26 29; www.transurban.com.au) consists of two main sections: the western link that runs from the Calder Hwy intersection of the Tullamarine Fwy down the western side of the city to join with the Westgate Fwy; and the southern link that runs from Kings Way, on the southern edge of the CBD, to the Malvern section of the Monash Fwy. Both sections are tollways.

Tolls are 'collected' electronically by overhead readers from a transponder card displayed in the car (an e-Tag). If you want to use any section of CityLink and don't have an e-Tag, you can purchase a day pass, which is valid for 24 hours from your first trip on any CityLink section, or a weekend pass, which is valid from noon Friday to midnight Sunday. Either pass costs $10.05. If you only intend to use the western link to go from the airport to Flemington Rd, you can purchase a Tulla pass for $3.60. Day and weekend passes can be purchased at any Australian post office, Shell petrol stations, CityLink customer service centres, via the Internet or over the phone.

If you've been naughty and used CityLink without a pass, or, as is more frequently the case, if you simply blunder onto CityLink, you have until midnight the following day to call CityLink and arrange payment for your sins. The penalty for travelling without payment is $100.

If you're hiring a car for your stay in Melbourne, your car-hire company will be able to make arrangements for your day pass should you need one. Lastly, note that motorcycles can use CityLink for free.

Public Transport

Melbourne's public transport system, known as the Met, incorporates buses, trains and the famous trams. There are about 750 trams and they operate as far as 20km out from the city centre. Buses take routes where the trams do not go, and replace them at quiet weekend periods. Trains radiate out from the city centre to the outer suburbs. Services cease around midnight.

For information on public transport, including maps, timetables, fares and zones, contact the **Met Information Centre** (☎ 13 16 38; www.metlinkmelbourne.com.au). **Met Shop** (Map pp72-4; ☎ 13 16 38; Town Hall, cnr Swanston & Little Collins Sts; ⏰ 8.30am-5.30pm Mon-Fri, 9am-1pm Sat) in the city has transport information and sells tickets. If you intend to do any serious exploration of Melbourne, it's a good idea to pick up a copy of its excellent *Melbourne's Public Transport Map* for $2.20. Train stations also have some information.

Prams and strollers are allowed on all transport free of charge.

On Friday and Saturday night (ie early Saturday and Sunday morning), after the trams, buses and trains stop running (around midnight for most services), NightRider buses depart from City Square on Swanston St hourly from 12.30am to dawn for many suburban destinations. The NightRider fare is a flat $6.

TICKETING

Travelling on Melbourne public transport is a breeze with the integrated Metcard ticketing system. Metcards allow you to travel on any and all Melbourne bus, train and tram services, even if you transfer from one to another.

Metcards are available from Metcard vending machines and service counters at train stations, on board trams (tram vending machines only take coins and only dispense two-hour and one-day or 'daily' tickets), from retailers displaying the Met flag (usually newsagents and milk bars, and these may not sell two-hour tickets) and from the Met Shop (opposite). You can purchase tickets directly from the driver on bus services.

The metropolitan area is divided into three zones, and the price of the ticket depends on which zone(s) you will be travelling in and across. Zone 1 covers the city and inner-suburban area (including St Kilda), and most travellers won't venture beyond that unless they're going right out of town.

The adult fares are as follows:

Zones	Two hours ($)	All day ($)	Weekly ($)
1	$3.10	$5.90	$25.90
2 or 3	$2.30	$4.10	$17.80
1 & 2	$5.10	$9.50	$43.70
1, 2 & 3	$7.10	$12.40	$54

City Saver tickets ($2.20) allow you to travel two sections (usually five to nine stops, check the maps on each tram giving this information) on buses or trams in Zone 1, or you can buy a City Saver x 10 card ($19), which gives you 10 short trips. If you plan to use a block of tickets, buy a City Saver 10 two-hour trips ticket or a five daily trips ticket for $25.90.

BUS

Melbourne's privatised bus network is supplemental to the trains and trams – that is to say, it fills the gaps. Generally, buses continue on from where the trains finish, or go to places, such as hospitals, universities, suburban shopping centres and outer suburbs, not reached by other services. If you find you can't get somewhere by train or tram, ring the Met – chances are they will have a bus going that way.

TRAIN

An extensive train network covers the city centre and suburban areas (see the train system map, pp136–7). Trains are generally faster than trams or buses, but they don't go to many inner suburbs, eg Fitzroy, Carlton, St Kilda, South Melbourne or Port Melbourne.

Flinders St station is the main suburban terminal, and each suburban line has a separate platform here. The famous row of clocks above the entrance on the corner of Swanston and Flinders Sts indicates when the next train will be departing from each line.

During the week trains on most lines start at 5am and finish at midnight, and should run every 10 minutes during peak hour, every 15 to 20 minutes at other times, and every 30 minutes after 7pm on weekdays. On Saturday they run every half-hour from 5am to midnight, while on Sunday it's every 40 minutes from 7am to 11.30pm. Of course, these are just rule-of-thumb times.

The city service includes an underground City Loop, which is a quick way to get from one side of the city centre to the other. The stations on the loop are Parliament, Melbourne Central, Flagstaff, Southern Cross (formerly Spencer St) and Flinders St.

Bicycles can be carried free on trains during off-peak times and on weekends. During peak hour you'll need to buy a concession ticket for your bike.

TRAM

Melbourne's trundling trams are one of the city's most distinctive features, but you might have to exercise a little patience as they aren't particularly speedy. Tram routes cover the city and inner suburbs quite extensively. The majority of routes operate as back-and-forwards shuttle services, with the city centre acting as the hub of the wheel and the tram routes as the spokes. This makes it a good system if you want to get to somewhere from the city centre, or vice-versa, but not so good if you want to travel across from one suburb to another. Tram stops are numbered out from the city centre.

There are also 'light-rail' services to some suburbs. These are basically express trams running along disused rail lines.

In theory, trams run along most routes about every six to eight minutes during peak hour and every 12 minutes at other times. Unfortunately, trams have to share the roads with cars and trucks, so they are often delayed. Services are less frequent on weekends and late at night.

Be extremely careful when getting on and off a tram; by law, cars are supposed to stop when a tram stops to pick up and drop off passengers, but that doesn't always happen.

See p113 for details on the free City Circle tram service.

Taxi

There are plenty of taxi ranks in and around the city and you will spot them quite easily, as they are all yellow. The main ones in the town centre are found outside the major hotels, outside Flinders St and Southern Cross stations, near the corner of William and Bourke Sts, on the corner of Elizabeth and Bourke Sts, on Lonsdale St outside Myer, and near the corner of Swanston and Franklin Sts.

Finding an empty taxi in the city on Friday or Saturday night can be difficult, particularly at 'changeover' time – generally around 3am.

Flagfall is $2.80, and the rate is $1.33 per kilometre thereafter. There is a $1 surcharge for rides between midnight and 6am, if you place any luggage in the boot and for telephone bookings. All companies charge the same fares and all taxis are bound by the same regulations.

Yellow Cabs and Silver Top taxis have cars with wheelchair access, or phone ☎ 1300 364 050 to arrange this service. To book a taxi, phone any of the following companies:

Black Cabs Combined (☎ 13 22 27)
Embassy Taxis (☎ 13 17 55)
Silver Top Taxis (☎ 13 10 08)
Yellow Cabs (☎ 13 19 24)

Around Melbourne

The country regions that ring Melbourne are within perfect day-trip distance, easily accessed by car or public transport. Consequently they're popular spots for Melburnians on mini-breaks. Digs are mainly B&Bs and self-contained apartments, many with tension-releasing spas, crackling open fires in winter, and a 'romantic hideaway' ambience.

Wannabe sommeliers in search of top pinot noir and chardonnay should head to the vine-strewn hills and valleys around Healesville, or to the boutique wineries on the Mornington or Bellarine Peninsulas. Walkers and cyclists can explore the myriad trails criss-crossing the national parks. Kinglake and the You Yangs (also popular with rock climbers) are the most accessible from Melbourne, but the historic Mornington Peninsula National Park has bracing coastal walks. Towering mountain-ash forests are found in the Dandenong Ranges. Surfers will find challenging breaks at the choppy (and freezing!) ocean beaches of Phillip Island and the Bellarine and Mornington Peninsulas; learners find their balance at the more sheltered bay beaches. Divers and snorkellers can explore shipwrecks off the coast, while other watery pursuits include swimming with dolphins and seals.

Whatever your bent – spotting penguins or motor-racing legends at Phillip Island, or lunching with llamas on the remote French Island – you'll find something that will suit your style.

AROUND MELBOURNE

HIGHLIGHTS

- Tramping around **Cape Woolamai** (p189) and spotting colonies of shearwaters

- Choo-chooing from Belgrave to Emerald on the **Puffing Billy steam train** (p177)

- Eating lunch with llamas on the isolated and remote **French Island** (p187)

- Clambering up spooky **Hanging Rock** (p169), and back down without getting lost

- Strolling along **Geelong's waterfront** (p154) on a sunny day

- Cycling the **Lilydale to Warburton Rail Trail** (p174)

- Surfing the frothy waves of **Smiths Beach** (p189) on Phillip Island

- Reading the papers over a leisurely break-fast in a **Barwon Heads** café (p166)

- Following the gourmet trail around the **Yarra Valley** and the **Mornington Peninsula** (p184)

★ Hanging Rock

Yarra Valley ★

Lilydale-Warburton ★
Rail Trail

Belgrave ★

Geelong ★

Barwon
Heads ★

Mornington ★   ★ French Island
Peninsula

Smiths ★
Beach   ★
          Cape
          Woolamai

Climate

Towns and regions around Melbourne are subject to climatic winter (June to August) and summer (December to February) extremes; and towns are nearly unrecognisable from their summer tourist peak to the cold, rainy troughs they become in winter. Daily summer temperatures aver-age 25°C in the Geelong region and are a couple of degrees cooler further south, but can peak at around 35°C. Daily winter temperatures average 14°C around Geelong and a chillier 12°C in Phillip Island; the months between June and September experience the most rainfall. It snows in the alpine region during winter and the

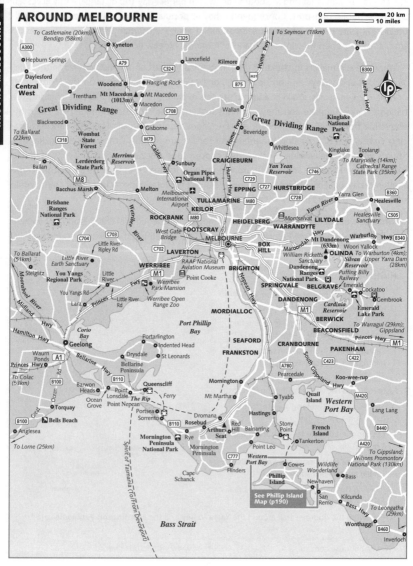

AROUND MELBOURNE

closest snow to Melbourne is on Mt Donna Buang (p174).

MELBOURNE TO GEELONG

It's a one-hour drive southwest down the Princes Fwy (M1) to Geelong. Leave Melbourne via the soaring West Gate Bridge, which offers absolutely superb city and bay views.

OUTER WEST
RAAF National Aviation Museum

Over 100,000 visitors swarm through the wheelchair-accessible **National Aviation Museum** (☎ 03-9256 1300; www.raafmuseum.com.au; Point Cook Rd, Point Cook; admission by donation; ⊗ 10am-3pm Tue-Fri, 10am-5pm Sat & Sun) every year. To the sounds of ambient plane noise and SOS Morse code, wander through the comprehensive museum which has memorabilia about Australia's military history.

Here you will also find over 20 vintage aircraft – including a Tiger Moth and an Avro 504K – on display in the showroom. See some of them fly in the fiendishly popular biennial air pageant (February/ March).

Werribee Park

About 30 minutes southwest of Melbourne, by car or train, is **Werribee Park** (K Rd, Werribee).

The famous **Werribee Open Range Zoo** (☎ 03-9731 9600; www.zoo.org.au; adult/child/family $19/9.50/48, combined zoo & mansion $28/14/70; ⊗ 9am-5pm, last entry 3.30pm) is a definite highlight, especially if you've got kids. Admission includes the safari tour – with educational gems like 'roos can't sweat' and 'hippos can hold their breath underwater for five minutes'. From the bus you'll spot herbivores – emus, bison, Mongolian wild horses, rhinos, zebras and giraffes grazing on the savannah. Specialist tours include a slumber or canoe safari and the extremely popular 'Lion Behind the Scenes', where you can watch hungry lions devour hunks of meat.

The flamboyant Italianate **Werribee Park Mansion** (☎ 03-9741 2444; www.werribeepark.com.au; adult/child/family $12/6/29; mansion ⊗ 10am-3.45pm Mon-Fri & 10am-4.45pm Sat & Sun May-Oct, till 4.45pm daily Nov-Apr), built between 1874 and 1877, is surrounded by beautiful formal gardens, with picnic and barbecue areas. Audio headphones attempt to re-create the sounds of life in the 1880s, and be sure to check out the tiny hologram in the laundry. Dariwill Farm, at the Mansion, is a gourmet café-produce store and the best spot to eat in the park (avoid the zoo's cafeteria).

AROUND MELBOURNE

DETOUR: YOU YANGS REGIONAL PARK & BRISBANE RANGES NATIONAL PARK

From the Princes Freeway (M1), take the signposted exit to You Yangs Forest Reserve. You'll pop out on Old Melbourne Rd. Make a right-hand turn onto Little River Rd, which turns into You Yangs Rd. At the T-intersection of Little River–Ripley and Farrars Rd, turn left onto Farrars Rd then right onto Branch Rd.

This will bring you to the entrance of the **You Yangs Regional Park** (admission per car $3; ⊗ 8.30am-4pm), a fist of granite peaks popular with rock climbers and walkers because of the superb views. It's a scenic drive up Flinders Peak (352m), climbed by explorer Matthew Flinders in 1802. It's a 3.2km walk to the summit. You can't drive to the top but lazier souls can explore by driving the Great Circle Dr, a 12km unsealed road around the park.

The **Brisbane Ranges** are a low range of hills running between the gold-mining towns of Steiglitz and Bacchus Marsh. From the You Yangs, head back to the Little River–Ripley and Farrars Rds intersection and turn left onto Little River–Ripley Rd. Drop into the **Little River Earth Sanctuary** (☎ 03-5283 1602; www.littleriverearthsanctuary.com.au; Little River-Ripley Rd) where you can take guided nature walks and see native Australian fauna. To get to the walking trail from the sanctuary follow the Little River–Ripley Rd until you hit Geelong–Bacchus Marsh Rd (C704) and turn left. Turn right onto Granite Rd and then right onto Staughton Vale Rd, which takes you to the start of the 3km self-guided **Anakie Gorge walking trail** and picnic ground – a particularly picturesque spot for a barbecue. The park has the highest density of koalas in Victoria and you might spot some in the trees around the picnic area. There are several short walks and longer two- and three-day treks throughout the park and, in spring, blooming wildflowers.

Adjacent to the mansion is the **Victoria State Rose Garden** (admission free; ☉ 9am-5pm), with over 5500 bushes arranged in the shape of a giant Tudor rose. Roses bloom from October to May but are at their fragrant peak from November to April.

GETTING THERE & AWAY

Several Met trains run daily from the city to Werribee train station (Zone 2 Met ticket $9.50). From here catch bus No 439, which runs the 5km to the zoo and mansion turn-off Monday to Saturday.

Otherwise take the **Werribee Park Shuttle** (☎ 9748 5094; adult/child return zoo & mansion $20/10, National Aviation Museum & either zoo or mansion adult/child $25/15; ☉ departs 9.30am & 11am, returns 3.30pm),

which leaves from the Victorian Arts Centre and goes to the zoo, mansion and National Aviation Museum – book ahead.

GEELONG

☎ 03 / pop 234,000

Mention Geelong to Melburnians and they'll scoff before launching into a superior diatribe that lists its pitfalls, but if you ask them when they last visited Geelong, it'll be years and years ago. With a $150 million injection of funds, Geelong has finally cleared the junk from its spare room and uncovered a stunning waterfront, replete with beaches, restaurants and bars, on the shores of Corio Bay. Add to that the thriving student population from Deakin University and a recent

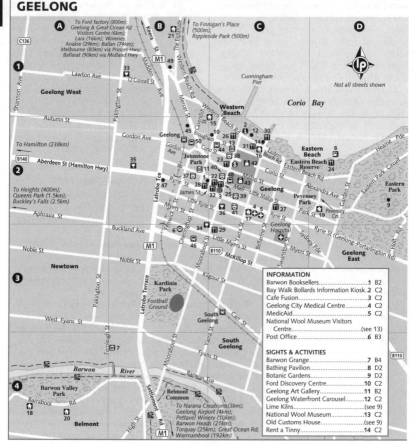

GEELONG

Not all streets shown

INFORMATION
Barwon Booksellers	**1** B2
Bay Walk Bollards Information Kiosk	**2** C2
Cafe Fusion	**3** C2
Geelong City Medical Centre	**4** C2
MedicAid	**5** C2
National Wool Museum Visitors Centre	(see 13)
Post Office	**6** B3

SIGHTS & ACTIVITIES
Barwon Grange	**7** B4
Bathing Pavilion	**8** D2
Botanic Gardens	**9** D2
Ford Discovery Centre	**10** C2
Geelong Art Gallery	**11** B2
Geelong Waterfront Carousel	**12** C2
Lime Kilns	(see 9)
National Wool Museum	**13** C2
Old Customs House	(see 9)
Rent a Tinny	**14** C2

population boom, brought about by rising prices in Melbourne's housing market, and you'll find an edgy, bohemian and contemporary enclave at Geelong's heart. Sure, it's industrial. Major car manufacturers base their companies here and petrochemical and aluminium refineries are as much a part of the city as its lounge bars, boutique shops, galleries, parklands and hardcore nightlife. Home of AFL football team the Cats, Geelong is also renowned for die-hard fanatics who'll turn out en masse in blue and white to rally support for their team.

History
The Wathaurong people were the original inhabitants of Geelong and had lived in the area for more than 25,000 years before white settlers arrived. In 1824 explorers Hume and Hovell made the overland journey from Sydney, finishing their expedition on the northern shores of Corio Bay. John Batman 'purchased' 40,000 hectares of land from local Aborigines in 1835, including a large area around Corio Bay that the Aborigines called Jillong. Like Melbourne, Geelong boomed during the gold rush, as it was one of the main gateways to the goldfields. During the 19th century it was one of Victoria's major wine-growing areas, and by 1877 there were over 100 wineries in the region. Tragedy struck in the 1880s when phylloxera (which causes a vine-root disease) was discovered in the region and the government ordered that all the vines be pulled out. Today Geelong is Victoria's largest regional city, though many see it as an extension of Melbourne and many people commute to work.

Orientation
Geelong is on the western shores of Corio Bay. The Barwon River wends through the city and the Princes Hwy (M1) is the main entry and exit point. To reach Geelong's waterfront, take Bell Pde (about 2km after the Ford factory if you're coming from the north) and follow the Esplanade along the bay. The train station is at the northern end of Fenwick St; Malop, Moorabool and Ryrie are Geelong's main streets.

Information
BOOKSHOPS
Barwon Booksellers (☎ 5221 8388; 2 James St) Specialises in used and antiquarian books.

INTERNET ACCESS
Cafe Fusion (☎ 5221 8586; 138 Moorabool St; per 15min/hr $2/4.50; ☉ noon-9.30 Tue-Sat) Cheaper rates if you have a bite to eat. In summer the café is also open on Sundays.

MEDICAL SERVICES
Geelong City Medical Centre (☎ 5222 1666; 255 Ryrie St; ☉ 8am-8pm)
MedicAid (☎ 5222 6200; 265 Ryrie St; ☉ 8am-10pm) MedicAid also has an after-hours pharmacy, open the same hours as the medical centre.

MONEY
Geelong's banks are near the intersection of Malop and Moorabool Sts.

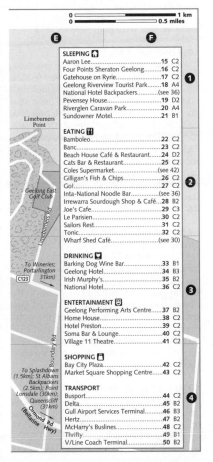

Map labels: Limeburners Point; Geelong East Golf Club; Limeburners Rd; To Wineries; Portarlington (31km); Backpackers; To Splashdown (1.5km); St Albans Backpackers (2.5km); Point Lonsdale (30km); Queenscliff (31km); Boundary Rd; Ormond Rd; (Bellarine Hwy)

Scale: 0 — 1 km; 0 — 0.5 miles

POST

Post office (☎ 13 13 18; 108 Gheringhap St)

TOURIST INFORMATION

Pick up a copy of the *Geelong Visitors' Map* and *What's On* at the visitors centres. The *Mobility Map of Geelong* lists accessible parking, toilets and telephones, as well as the grades of streets in the city centre.

Geelong & Great Ocean Road Visitors Centre (☎ 5275 5797; www.greatoceanrd.org.au/geelong; cnr Princes Hwy & St Georges Rd; ⏰ 9am-5pm) About 7km north of Geelong's centre, it's on the on the eastern (left) side of the road as you come in from Melbourne.

National Wool Museum visitors centre (☎ 5222 2900; 26 Moorabool St; ⏰ 9.30am-5pm)

Sights & Activities

WATERFRONT GEELONG

Wander Geelong's glittering, revamped waterfront, where you can swim, picnic at a foreshore reserve, take a carousel ride or just gaze at yachts bobbing on Corio Bay. On the other side of the road, check out the grand historic homes.

Walking trails extend from **Rippleside Park** (Bell Pde) – which has a children's playground, rock pool and jetty, and barbecues and picnic tables – right up the hill to Limeburners Point.

Pick up a **Bay-Walk Bollards** brochure from the information kiosk at **Cunningham Pier** so you can more formally acquaint yourself with Jan Mitchell's 104 famous painted bollards that give the waterfront its unique character.

Those with kids in tow should stop at the gaudy, hand-carved **Geelong Waterfront Carousel** (☎ 5224 1547; Steampacket Place; adult/child $3/2.50; ⏰ 10.30am-5pm Mon-Fri, to 8pm Sat, to 6pm Sun), a completely refurbished 1898 steam-driven carousel built in New York.

At **Eastern Beach**, stop for a splash about at the Art Deco **bathing pavilion**, opposite the promenade. Boats, rods and tackle can be hired from **Rent a Tinny** (☎ 5222 3222; end of Yarra St; boat hire 1st hr $30, additional hr $15, per day $130, rod & tackle hire $5; ⏰ Nov-Apr).

GEELONG BOTANIC GARDENS & EASTERN PARK

A charming bollard couple greets you at the gates of the beautifully kept **Botanic Gardens** (☎ 5227 0387; www.geelongaustralia.com.au; Eastern Park Circuit, Eastern Park; admission free; ⏰ 7.30am-5pm), a peaceful place for a stroll or picnic. The gar-

dens celebrated their 150th year in 2001. A tree canopy shades the paths, garden beds and fern glades and the '21st century' garden at the entrance features the region's indigenous plants. Also check out the **Old Customs House**, a tiny cottage reputed to be the oldest timber building in Victoria. It was built in Sydney in 1838 and transported here in sections.

Eastern Park surrounds the gardens and is Geelong's largest foreshore reserve, with many trees planted as early as 1859, including some rare species. You'll have to dodge the joggers and power walkers, especially at lunch time, and look out for golf balls flying overhead from the **Geelong East Golf Club** (nine-hole course). On the eastern side of the park, at the end of Limeburners Rd, are the remains of three historic brick and stone **lime kilns** that were built here in 1852.

GEELONG ART GALLERY

The **Geelong Art Gallery** (☎ 5229 3645; www.geelong gallery.org.au; Little Malop St; admission free; ⏰ 10am-5pm Mon-Fri, 1-5pm Sat & Sun), in a gracious neoclassical building, is a thought-provoking and inspiring regional gallery with over 4000 collected works of predominantly Australian art. Purchased in 1900, Frederick McCubbin's *A Bush Burial* is still the gallery's most famous star. Changing contemporary exhibitions have a more international flair and might show works from Croatian or Italian artists, or showcase sculpture and the decorative arts.

NATIONAL WOOL MUSEUM

Housed in a historic bluestone building (1872), the **National Wool Museum** (☎ 5227 0701; www.geelongcity.vic.gov.au/visiting_geelong; 26 Moorabool St; adult/child/family $7.30/3.65/20; ⏰ 9.30am-5pm) has three separate galleries focusing on the history, politics and heritage of one of Australia's founding industries. See the sock-making machine and the massive 1910 Axminster carpet loom that still pumps out carpets, as well as re-creations of shearing sheds and shearers' quarters.

FORD DISCOVERY CENTRE

The **Ford Discovery Centre** (☎ 5227 8700; www.ford .com.au/inside_ford/discovery/Ford_Discovery_Centre.asp; cnr Gheringhap & Brougham Sts; adult/child/family $6/3/15; ⏰ 10am-5pm Wed-Mon) takes both a historical and contemporary look at the Ford motor industry, using interactive displays and exhibits. Rev heads love the 'cars of the future' display and Bathurst-winning Falcons, whereas nannas and grandads reminisce about a bygone era at the heritage exhibits.

HISTORIC HOUSES
More than 100 of Geelong's historic buildings are classified by the National Trust. Several are open to the public, including the **Heights** (☎ 5221 3510; 140 Aphrasia St, Newtown; adult/child/family $6/3/14; ☻ 11am-4pm Wed & Sun), an 1855 weatherboard house prefabricated in Germany and shipped to Australia; and **Barwon Grange** (☎ 5221 3906; Fernleigh St, Newtown; adult/child/family $5/3/12; ☻ 11am-4pm Wed & Sun), an impressive 1856 neo-Gothic brick homestead that's surrounded by 19th-century gardens and overlooks the Barwon River.

Tours
Gallivantours (☎ 5244 0908; www.gallivantours.com.au; 244 Roslyn Rd, Highton; 2-hr Geelong tour $25, winery tours $60-95) Runs tours around Geelong city, the Bellarine Peninsula and surrounding wineries, and along the Great Ocean Rd. Door-to-door pickup from accommodation in Geelong and the Bellarine Peninsula. For more information on wineries in the area, see p65.

Festivals & Events
Skandia Geelong Week (☎ 5229 1418; www.geelongweek.com.au; 22-27 Jan) Held on the Eastern Beach foreshore, Skandia is Australia's largest keel-boat regatta and is a sister event to Skandia Cowes Week in the UK. Around 400 yachts compete and there's a heap of entertainment.
Toast to the Coast (☎ 5225 1200; www.gpac.org.au; Oct) Swirl, sniff and raise your glass at this festival that showcases regional wine and produce. Chefs also run cooking demonstrations.

Sleeping
Geelong's accommodation prices fluctuate from low to high season, and weekend rates, especially Friday and Saturday nights, are more expensive.

BUDGET
National Hotel Backpackers (☎ 5229 1211; www.nationalhotel.com.au; 191 Moorabool St; dm $19, d $40) Upstairs at 'the Nash' (p157) is central Geelong's only backpacker accommodation, and the lack of competition shows. Dorms are cosy, sinks of the 'ye olde' variety, and there's a general lack of maintenance. Good news is that lockers, linen, tea and coffee are free, mattresses

are inner-spring, and staff can offer advice about work in the area. There's also a kitchen, laundry and small sitting room.

The pick of Geelong's caravan parks, and those closest to the centre, all cluster along Barrabool Rd on the south side of the Barwon River. They all have similar amenities such as shady sites, air-con cabins with en suites or spas, playgrounds and camp kitchens.
Geelong Riverview Tourist Park (☎ 5243 6225; 59 Barrabool Rd; powered sites per 2 people from $18, d cabins from $55 ☒) The ritziest, with fairly spacious grounds and lots of greenery – the kiosk and pool are clinchers.
Riverglen Caravan Park (☎ 5243 5505; 75 Barrabool Rd; powered sites per 2 people from $17, d cabins from $50; ☒) Has cedar cottages, shady sites and cabins.

MIDRANGE
Gatehouse on Ryrie (☎ 0417-545 196; www.bol.com.au/gatehouse/g.html; 83 Yarra St; s $80, d $95-110; ☐) Right in the thick of it, this rambling guesthouse is a top midrange option. Room and bed configurations vary, but all are toasty warm in winter and furnished in a slightly Victorian style – windows are double-glazed, which keeps the rooms quiet. One room has an en suite, but bathrooms are only ever shared between two or three rooms. A free continental breakfast is served in the dining room and there's a communal kitchen, sitting room with videos and an 'honesty bar'. The owner doesn't live on site, so definitely call beforehand.
Pevensey House (☎ 5224 2810; www.pevensey-house.com.au; 17 Pevensey Cres; r $110-175; ☒) This beautifully restored B&B is furnished with an eclectic mix of English and French antiques, with a dash of Turkish-Moroccan inspiration thrown in. Each of the immaculate four rooms is themed and might include an 18th-century writing desk, double spa or a heritage four-poster bed draped romantically with all the manchester trimmings. Pevensey's position, near Eastern Beach and the Botanic Gardens, is another strength, as is its 'tower room' panoramas and Jacuzzi in the grounds. As expected, breakfast here is an elegant and delectable feast.
AaronLee (☎ 5222 7733; www.aaronlee.com.au; 30 Western Beach Rd; studio apts $135-150, main house apts $250-335; ☒) The main house apartment are incredibly sumptuous and lavish, but more for honeymooners than midrangers. However the self-contained studios at the rear of the heritage property are equally clean and

modern. They all have DVDs and CD players and either a spa or double shower so you can lather in utmost comfort. Though there is a double sofa bed, the studios are compact and more suitable for couples than families.

Sundowner Motel (☎ 5222 3499; www.sundowner motorinns.com.au; 13 Esplanade; r $110-195; ☒) Part of the Sundowner chain, this standard motel's rooms are small and showing their age, but they're cheap and some come with a balcony and Corio Bay views. There's a heated swimming pool and sauna and each room has a bathroom, TV, telephone and tea- and coffee-making facilities. At the time of research the Sundowner was to be given a face-lift.

TOP END

Four Points Sheraton Geelong (☎ 5223 1377; www .fourpoints.com/geelong; 10-14 Eastern Beach Rd; r from $165; ☒ ☒) If you're after a five-star sleep, check in to Four Points. The beds are wide, sheets soft, doonas white and pillows filled with down. Be dazzled by the sun setting over Corio Bay or watch in-house movies – they're on a pay-per-view basis but some cable channels are free. Business travellers love the full-size keyboards and in-room Net jacks, and everyone loves the buffet hotel breakfast. Four Points often has package deals and reasonable promotion rates.

Eating

Around Little Malop St is where you'll find a clutch of restaurants, cafés and bars filled with Geelong's resident funksters. For food with a view, head to one of the many family-friendly restaurants that line Corio Bay, or grab some fish and chips and chow down on the foreshore. A couple of fine-dining restaurants score highly with the harshest of food critics. In Geelong West, Pakington St is the major café strip. For pubs serving meals, see Drinking (opposite).

RESTAURANTS

Finnigans Place (☎ 5277 9266; Rippleside Park, Bell Pde; mains $20-30; ⏲ lunch & dinner Wed-Sat, breakfast, lunch & dinner Sun) With dreamy views of Corio Bay, Finnigans is a busy and elegant fine-dining restaurant. Touches of Asiana contrast with the modern fit-out. Mains might include saffron linguine with banana prawns, or house-made artichoke ravioli – both wash down well with a bottle of local wine. For breakfast try thyme-infused mushrooms.

Le Parisien (☎ 5229 3110; 15 Eastern Beach Rd; entrees $4-30, mains $30-45; ⏲ lunch Sat & Sun, dinner Thu-Mon) Location, location, location! Right on the water, feast on classic French cuisine *à l'Australienne* (try twist of kangaroo fillet with bush-tomato chutney). All the favourites on the meat-heavy menu are done extremely well. Just convert the bill to euros and you'll pay with a clear conscience.

Banc (☎ 5222 3155; 53 Malop St; lunch $7.50-16, dinner mains $20-30; ⏲ lunch & dinner, closed Sun) With the ethos that we're all individuals, Banc provides different 'zones' and menus to 'recharge' our souls. In the spacious heritage building, form meets function with crisp white tablecloths and white contoured chairs, creating a sophisticated, modernist interior. The food is equally stylish and clean, say a citrus salad for brunch, and chilli-and-lime-crusted fish or potato-and-pea curry with pickled bean shoots for dinner. Look to plasma screens for the daily specials.

Bamboleo (☎ 5229 2458; 86 Little Malop St; lunch $6.50-13, dinner mains $18-28) The self-confessed 'gypsy' owner is from Cadiz, and with Bamboleo's whitewashed walls and traditional Andalusian cooking, it's like a slice of Spain transplanted to central Geelong. Dinner features favourites such as paella and tapas – save room for the chocolate fondue. For lunch there are salads, open sourdough sandwiches and pasta and risotto dishes.

Sailors Rest (☎ 5224 2241; cnr Moorabool St & Esplanade; light meals $16-22, mains $24-31; ⏲ breakfast, lunch & dinner) A breezy café by day and more glamorous fine-diner by night, this popular restaurant serves a varied menu. Dinner offerings include handmade gnocchi, grilled market-fresh fish, risotto and steak. Local wines are available, the coffee is strong, and the staff smooth.

Beach House Cafe & Restaurant (☎ 5221 8322; Eastern Beach Reserve; café $8-18, restaurant mains $24-30; ⏲ café breakfast & lunch daily, restaurant lunch Wed-Sun, dinner Fri-Sun) Right on the bay, overlooking Eastern Beach's promenade and bathing pavilion, Beach House has a casual café where you can grab a cuppa and light meal. Upstairs is the more formal fine-dining restaurant.

CAFES

Go! (☎ 5229 4752; 37 Bellarine St; breakfasts $3.50-7, lunch $4-8, dinner $7-12; ⏲ breakfast & lunch Mon-Sat, dinner Mon-Fri) Go! is a rollicking ride of colour and amusement. The humorous menu has gems such as 'froot loops, most of the staff really' and the popular 'gor mett steak sanga'. Other lunch-time faves include Go!'s sausage roll and straight-up sangas, such as the 'melbourne cricket club (MCC)', which is interpreted with meatloaf, cheddar and chutney in seeded wholemeal bread.

Tonic (☎ 5229 8899; 5 James St; entrees from $10, mains $14-20; ☽ lunch & dinner Mon-Sat) Arrive frayed at the edges and leave relaxed and fed. With its professional service and hearty meals, Tonic really is a tonic. It's a retro café-bar with vinyl chairs and club lounges, and a dedicated commitment to cocktails – the list numbers around 460 and if your cocktail idea is truly original and not on the list, you can achieve immortality and have it named after you.

Cats Bar & Restaurant (☎ 5229 3077; 90 Little Malop St; all-day menu $6-28; ☽ lunch & dinner Tue-Sun) Cats is a large, stylish and laid-back café. Midweek, it's popular with a suity lunch crowd who come for warm chicken salad with fried camembert and a citrus aioli (garlic mayonnaise) dressing. Families come for the dinner menu, which offers an interesting range of curries, pastas and vegetarian dishes. After the dishes are washed, Cats is more a bar for 20-somethings.

Wharf Shed Cafe (☎ 5221 6645; 15 Eastern Beach Rd; pizzas $13-17, mains $12-22; ☽ lunch Mon-Sun, breakfast Sat & Sun) Below Le Parisien (opposite) is this spacious family-friendly café serving thumpin' Mod Oz meals such as chicken souvlaki, gourmet pizzas, beef burgers and filo parcels. More substantial lunch mains include roo fillet and rump steak (not together). But really, it's all about the view.

QUICK EATS
Gilligan's Fish & Chips (☎ 5222 3200; 100 Western Beach Rd; meals from $4-17; ☽ lunch daily, dinner Thu-Sun) Gilligan's has been frying fritters and grilling flathead for the last 10 years. It's a colourful, licensed place with jaunty sea creatures painted on the walls and a slightly deranged shark out front.

Irrewarra Sourdough Shop & Cafe (☎ 5221 3909; 10 James St; lunch $10-18; ☽ breakfast & lunch Mon-Fri) Authentic, handmade bread is what you'll find at this cosy bakery-café. Breakfast on Granola or an almond croissant, or grab an energy shake to go. At lunch Irrewarra's fat sourdough sandwiches – try the chicken caesar – are the stuff of legend.

Joe's Cafe (☎ 5229 3437; 247 Moorabool St; snacks $2.50-8.50 ☽ breakfast, lunch & dinner) Students flock to this lively jukebox joint that pumps out burgers, toasted sandwiches and chicken parmas. It's also the place you come for that all important end-of-night souvlaki – Joe's is open until 4am Friday and Saturday.

SELF-CATERING
There's a **Coles supermarket** (☎ 5221 2677) in Bay City Plaza.

Drinking
Wednesday night is 'industry night' in Geelong, when hospitality workers hit the nightspots and drink with abandon. If you're up for a big one, Wednesday is nearly as big as a Friday or Saturday. There are plenty of pubs and a number of them have live gigs. Check the Friday or Saturday *Geelong Advertiser* or get a copy of *Forte*, a weekly what's-on street-press paper.

National Hotel (☎ 5229 1211; 191 Moorabool St) Never are Geelong's student roots more apparent than at 'the Nash'. Grungy op-shop décor, quirky screen projections and art installations set the scene. Students feast on affordable and generous wok-tossed noodles and Asian soups at the **Inta-National Noodle Bar** (mains $8-11; ☽ lunch Tue-Fri, dinner Tue-Sun) or play Frogger while listening to DJs spin anything from '50s rockabilly to funk. Dance classes are held in the 'groove room' out back and live bands play regularly.

Geelong Hotel (☎ 5221 5699; 214 Moorabool St) There's usually something happening at this barn-sized place, although that something might be guest appearances by members of the Geelong football team. Popular with a sports-oriented crowd.

Irish Murphy's (☎ 5221 4335; 30 Aberdeen St) Just out of the main drag, this is a locally owned Irish pub that's popular with backpackers and lager-loving lads. All the favourite Irish drops are on tap and live bands play most nights, usually from Thursday to Friday, but sometimes Wednesday and Sunday too.

Barking Dog Wine Bar (☎ 5229 2889; 126 Pakington St; mains $12-25; ☽ 9am-late) Classier than your classic pub, the Barking Dog is popular with a 30-something set who drink imported beers and wines by the glass. Meals are served all day and include noodle, pasta and risotto dishes. There's live music Friday to Sunday in the back lounge, ranging from

DJs playing cheesy retro hits to solo cover artists.

Entertainment

Geelong's large student population translates into a lively and reasonably varied bar and club scene, with most of the action in the city centre.

NIGHTCLUBS

Hotel Preston (☎ 5223 2366; 177 Ryrie St; lunch $8-10, dinner $10-18, cover $5; ⦿ lunch & dinner Tue-Sat, Rebar until midnight Wed, 3am Thu, 5am Fri & 6am Sat) Downstairs is a slick pub serving meals, upstairs is Rebar, a cruisey, chilled lounge bar with upside-down lamps, retro décor and a dress code that bans 'suits' and 'bogans'. Thursday nights, original bands play; Friday is hip-hop and funk and soul; and Saturday covers electronic music and DJs. It's as close to a Melbourne mindset as you'll get in Geelong.

Home House (☎ 5222 7333; 40-42 Mooorabool St) This is Geelong's biggest nightspot. It's a multilevel techno and dance venue, with an outdoor chill-out area where you go to party hard and dance until the birds start chirping. There's free entry after midnight and a variety of nights, such as Uni night when uni students come here for cheap drinks. This club has a rough reputation, so take care when going home and try not to leave on your own.

Soma Bar & Lounge (☎ 5223 2235; 114-122 Mooorabool St; Sat cover $10; ⦿ until 3am Mon-Sat) You'll hear Soma before you see it. DJs play lounge and dance music to a multicultural crowd and in the second room there's R&B on Saturday. Head downstairs and score a drink at the white circular bar or rack up a game of pool.

CINEMAS

Village 11 Theatre (☎ 5229 3006; 194 Ryrie St) Geelong's main cinema screens the latest Hollywood blockbusters.

THEATRE

Geelong Performing Arts Centre (GPAC; ☎ 5225 1200; www.gpac.org.au; 50 Little Malop St) Geelong's major arts venue has two theatres – an 800-seat and a 300-seat. Local amateur productions are performed here, as well as touring professional dance, musicals and theatre shows. GPAC also sells tickets to Melbourne shows and other regional theatres.

SPORT

On winter Saturdays check to see if the mighty Cats are playing a home game at **Kardinia Park** (Moorabool St). It's a fervent, family occasion and you'll understand why the whole city's mental health improves when the team is doing well. Cricket is played here in summer.

Shopping

Geelong is the area's major shopping centre. The biggest selection of stores and eateries can be found in the two downtown shopping malls: Bay City Plaza and Market Square shopping centres. For boutique speciality shops with designer clothing and gifts head to the Little Malop St precinct.

Getting There & Away

AIR

For Jetstar air services flying from Avalon Airport, see p410.

BUS

V/Line (☎ 13 61 96; www.vline.com.au) buses arrive and depart from the coach terminal at Geelong train station. The Great Ocean Rd bus runs as far south as Apollo Bay ($22, 2½ hours) via Torquay ($5.30, 30 minutes) and Lorne ($14, one hour and 20 minutes), with services four times daily on weekdays and twice daily on weekends.

On Friday (and on Monday in December and January), a V/Line bus continues around the coast from Apollo Bay to Warrnambool ($47, seven hours), via Port Campbell and the Twelve Apostles.

V/Line buses also run to Ballarat ($12, 1½ hours; three a day Monday to Thursday and Saturday, four Friday, two Sunday).

Other long-distance buses depart from the **Busport terminal** (cnr Gheringhap & Brougham Sts). **McHarry's Buslines** (☎ 5223 2111) operates the Bellarine Transit service, with frequent buses to Torquay (p199) and the Bellarine Peninsula (opposite).

CAR

All the major rental companies have offices in Geelong:
Avis (☎ 5521 1332)
Delta (☎ 5229 8188; www.europecar.com.au; 48 Mercer St)
Hertz (☎ 5229 1100; www.hertz.com.au; 323 Latrobe Tce)
Thrifty (☎ 5222 5888; www.thrifty.com.au; 15 York St)

TRAIN

V/Line (☎ 13 61 96; www.vline.com.au) runs numerous trains from **Geelong train station** (☎ 5226 6525; Gordon Ave), via Werribee, to Melbourne's Southern Cross station (formerly Spencer St station; $10.20, one hour). Trains depart roughly every hour from 5.25am to 9.15pm Monday to Friday, 5.30am to 8.30pm Saturday, and every 1½ hours from 8.30am to 8.30pm Sunday. At peak hour, trains depart every 20 to 30 minutes.

From Geelong, a rail service continues on to Warrnambool ($30; 2½ hours; three a day Monday to Friday and Sunday, two on Saturday).

Getting Around

TO/FROM THE AIRPORT

Gull Airport Service (☎ 5222 4966; www.gull.com.au; 45 McKillop St) runs buses between Geelong and Melbourne airport (one way/return $25/45, one hour and 20 minutes, 13 daily). Pick-up and drop-off points are from Geelong train station and the McKillop St depot.

BUS

Geelong has an extensive city bus network. Most buses operate from Geelong train station and/or Moorabool St. Timetables and route maps are available from major V/Line stations and visitors centres.

TAXI

For a taxi call **Geelong Radio Cabs** (☎ 1800 636 088, 13 10 08).

BELLARINE PENINSULA

The laid-back Bellarine Peninsula forms the northern side of the entrance to Port Phillip Bay. Its surf beaches, wineries, mellow seaside towns, and cafés and restaurants make it a worthy stopover en route to the more high-profile Great Ocean Rd. The peninsula also has accessible diving and snorkelling sites.

Upmarket Queenscliff is a fashionable resort with a swag of fine-dining restaurants, historic hotels and the widest range of accommodation on the peninsula; it's also the transit point for the ferry to Sorrento on the Mornington Peninsula. Port Phillip Bay reputedly has the best water in the world for growing mussels, a crustacean that's made Portarlington famous. Ocean Grove is where

you'll find the most banks and biggest supermarkets – stock up on supplies here, but stay elsewhere. Barwon Heads, with its slice of café culture, and Point Lonsdale, which has the best surf, make relaxed alternatives.

Accommodation prices soar from Christmas to the end of January and many caravan parks have a minimum-stay requirement at this time. Many places also charge more at weekends, even in the depths of winter.

Information

Geelong & Great Ocean Rd Visitor Information Centre (p154) is the Bellarine Peninsula's main information source.

Getting There & Around

McHarry's Buslines (☎ 5223 2111; www.mcharrys.com.au) operates the Bellarine Transit service with buses (around 12 a day Monday to Friday, seven on Saturday and four on Sunday) running to/from Geelong train station and most peninsula towns. One-way fares include Barwon Heads ($4.20, 30 minutes), Ocean Grove ($4.20, 45 minutes), Portarlington ($5.30, 45 minutes), Queenscliff ($6.60, one hour) and Point Lonsdale ($6.60, around 55 minutes).

Queenscliff–Sorrento Car & Passenger Ferries (☎ 5258 3244; www.searoad.com.au; one-way foot passenger/2 adults & car $9/48) run daily services to/from Queenscliff to Portsea and Sorrento on the Mornington Peninsula. In Queenscliff ferries depart hourly from the ferry terminal on Larkin Pde from 7am to 6pm (reduced sailings in winter).

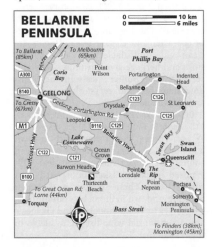

BELLARINE PENINSULA

AROUND MELBOURNE

Geelong & Bellarine Mopeds (☎ 5258 4796; gb mopeds@pipeline.com.au; Johnstone St, Point Lonsdale; per day $50; ◑ 8am-8pm) hire mopeds – perfect for cruising between towns with the wind ruffling your hair. You don't need a licence.

PORTARLINGTON, INDENTED HEAD & ST LEONARDS
☎ 03

These quiet, residential towns are on the north and east coasts of the peninsula. They're low-key resorts that are popular fishing and summer holiday destinations, particularly with families – but leave your surfboard in the car as all three towns face the bay.

During the 19th century, a string of bay steamers called regularly at Portarlington's jetty to take farm produce to Melbourne. The **Portarlington Mill** (☎ 5259 2804; Turner Court; adult/child $2.50/1.50; ◑ noon-4pm Sat & Sun Sep-May), built in 1856, has historical memorabilia about itself and monthly art exhibitions that showcase local artists.

Indented Head is where Matthew Flinders landed in 1802, one of the first visits to the area by a European. In 1835 John Batman landed at this same point, on his way to 'buy' the land that was to become Melbourne. The **Batman Memorial** on the foreshore marks the spot. Nearby, **Taylor Reserve** is a beachfront park with views of the steamer *Ozone* which was sunk in 1925.

Sleeping & Eating

Grand Hotel (☎ 5259 2260; www.portarlingtongrandhotel.com.au; 76 Newcombe St, Portarlington; s/d $40/80, mains $16-27) This big rambling pub has loads of character and elegant grace. Rooms are clean and comfortable with old-fashioned sinks and heritage-style furniture. They also serve classic counter meals in the bistro downstairs: beef and reef (steak and seafood), and chicken parmigiana.

Ol'Duke (☎ 5259 1250; www.theolduke.com.au; 40 Newcombe St, Portarlington; r $130-210, meals $23-28; ◑ lunch & dinner) The poshest place in town and not a doily in sight. Slightly overpriced rooms are compact, modern and clean with exposed bricks, polished floorboards and rustic charm. There are four in the main building, and two in the stables out the back (no horses or views though). Mod Oz meals and a substantial wine list are available in the restaurant.

BENITO BONITO'S TREASURE

Local legend has it that the pirate Benito Bonito, who made a career out of plundering Spanish ships, was sailing the local seas in 1798 when he was spotted and chased by a British ship. Bonito is said to have come ashore near Queenscliff, buried his booty in a cave and fled, never to return. The rumours inspired generations of treasure hunters, one lot even going so far as to form a mining syndicate – they spent two years digging but found nothing. Most of the locals have their own theories about the treasure and who knows, maybe one day it might turn up.

Seaside Resort (☎ 5259 2764; www.portarlingtonresort.com.au; Sproat St, Portarlington; unpowered sites per 2 people low/high season $22/36, d cabins $75-100/$130-170) This well-organised resort has beachfront camping, modern toilet blocks and luxury villas. It also oversees **camping** (unpowered sites per 2 people $32) on the Indented Head, St Leonards and Portarlington foreshores.

Portarlington Bakehouse (☎ 5259 2274; 48 Newcombe St, Portarlington; meals $4.50-11; ◑ breakfast & lunch) A fantastic, home-style bakery-café that cooks sourdough bread in its wood-fired oven. Grab a pie or stop in for poached eggs and mushrooms for breakfast. At lunch pick up a *frittata* (Italian omelette), quiche or filled baguette and definitely leave room for a sweet treat.

Boatmans (☎ 5259 2986; 56 Newcombe St, Portarlington; meals $3.70-11; ◑ lunch & dinner) For a more grease-inspired option, locals rave about the hot roast chickens (seasoned with Boatman's special ingredients), burgers and fish and chips. Boatmans also sells fresh mussels and fish.

Other places that sell fresh mussels:
Aussie Blue Mussels & Shellfish Company (☎ 5259 3088; 42 Geelong Rd)
Mister Mussel (Portarlington Pier) Sells directly from the boat.

QUEENSCLIFF
☎ 03 / pop 3900

Queenscliff's a popular spot with semi-retirees splurging on fine food and wine, and fashionable Melburnians escaping the big smoke for a seaside minibreak, snuggling by open fires in winter, or picnicking on the grassy foreshore in summer.

The town was established for the pilots who steered ships through the treacherous Port Phillip Heads. Known as 'the Rip', this is one of the most dangerous seaways in the world – and the coast is littered with over 200 shipwrecks. In the 1850s Queenscliff was a favoured settlement for diggers who'd struck it rich on the goldfields, and wealthy Melburnians and the Western District's squattocracy flocked to the town. Extravagant hotels and guesthouses built then are operational today, giving Queenscliff a historic charm and grandness.

Orientation & Information
Hesse St is the main drag, running parallel to Gellibrand St. King St takes you to Point

Lonsdale and the ferry terminal is at Larkin Pde. There is limited Internet access (per 30 minutes $3) at the Queenscliffe Visitor Information Centre, and next door at the library.
Point Lonsdale Community Centre (☎ 5258 0888; Nelson Rd) For medical emergencies.
Queenscliffe Visitor Information Centre (☎ 5258 4843; www.queenscliffe.vic.gov.au; 55 Hesse St; ⏰ 9am-5pm)

Sights & Activities
Queenscliff's most impressive historic buildings line Gellibrand St. Take a look at the **Ozone Hotel** (p163), **Lathamstowe** (44 Gellibrand St), **Queenscliff Hotel** (p163) and a row of old **pilots' cottages** (66-68 Gellibrand St) dating back to 1853.

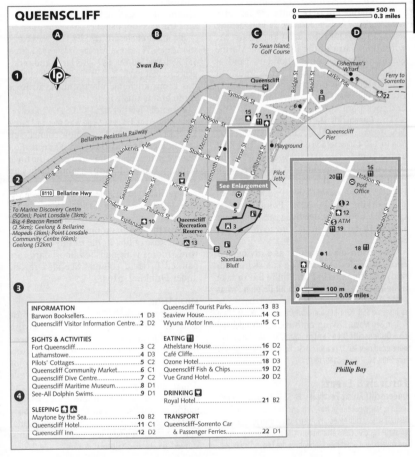

Fort Queenscliff (☎ 5258 1488; cnr Gellibrand & King Sts; tours adult/child $6/4; ☑ 1pm & 3pm Sat & Sun) was built during the 19th century to protect Melbourne from a feared Russian invasion. One-hour and 20 minute guided tours (the only way to see the fort) take in the military museum, magazine, cells and Black Lighthouse.

Run by a group of rail enthusiasts, the **Bellarine Peninsula Railway** (☎ 5258 2069; www.bpr.org .au; return adult/child/family $16/8/50; ☑ 11.15am & 2.30pm Sun year-round) has an immaculate collection of steam-hauled trains that puff and whistle their way along the restored Queenscliff–Drysdale track. The return trip to Drysdale takes 1¾ hours. The railway is open longer hours during school holidays and from 26 December to 26 January.

The **Marine Discovery Centre** (☎ 5258 3344; www.nre.vic.gov.au/mafri/discovery; 2a Bellarine Hwy; trips $20-30; ☑ 10am-4pm school holidays) is the educational arm of the Institute of Marine Sciences. During school holidays (and at other times for groups of six or more) it runs interactive programmes and jaunty excursions, such as snorkelling, canoeing and rock-pool rambles.

The **Queenscliff Maritime Museum** (☎ 5258 3440; Weeroona Pde; adult/child $5/2; ☑ 10.30am-4.30pm Mon-Fri, 1.30-4.30pm Sat & Sun) is an interesting spot as the home of the last lifeboat to serve the Rip; out back is a quaint boat shed lined with paintings. They also run 30-minute **tours** (☎ 0419-513 007; adult/child $6/4; ☑ 9.30am-1pm) of the working lighthouse at Point Lonsdale (p164). Children under five years of age are unable to take the tour due to insurance reasons.

The peninsula is popular as a diving and snorkelling destination. You can swim with seals and dolphins in Port Phillip Bay or take a sightseeing tour with **Sea-All Dolphin Swims** (☎ 5258 3889; www.dolphinswims.com.au; Larkin Pde; sightseeing $50/40, 4-hr swim adult/child $100/90; ☑ 8am & 1pm Sep-May). Diving enthusiasts should try the **Queenscliff Dive Centre** (☎ 5258 1188; http://dive queenscliff.com.au; 37 Learmonth St; 1 dive with/without gear hire $100/50, 2 dives $160/100).

Festivals & Events

Queenscliff Music Festival (☎ 5258 4816; www.qmf .net.au; last weekend in Nov) A major Victorian music festival where contemporary Australian musicians perform on stages and at cafés around town. Most musical genres are covered but a definite highlight is the Legendary Blues

Train. Top blues and roots musicians play in different carriages as the train steams its way around Swan Bay. Get your festival tickets early!

Queenscliff Community Market (☎ 0408-340 932; Lower Princes Park; ☑ 9am-2pm; Sep-May) Held on the last Sunday of the month, this is a fun weekend market with jams and relishes, bric-a-brac and work by local artists.

Sleeping

Accommodation choices consist of intimate B&Bs and guesthouses, opulent historic hotels, a backpackers' hostel and camping grounds. As with other places on the peninsula, rates increase on weekends and during holidays, and nearly triple during the Queenscliff Music Festival (left).

BUDGET

Queenscliff's excellent YHA is part of Queenscliff Inn (see opposite).

Big 4 Beacon Resort (☎ 5258 1133; www.beacon resort.com.au; 78 Bellarine Hwy; powered sites per 2 people $33-50, d cabins $80-190; ☑) This large and modern caravan park, 3.5km west of the centre, has camp kitchens, playgrounds, a movie room and tennis courts.

Queenscliff Tourist Parks (☎ 5258 1765; queenscliff tourist@telstra.com; 134 Hesse St; powered sites per 2 people $25-31, unpowered $19-23) This simple council-run camping ground on Queenscliff's recreation reserve is the closest caravan park to the town centre; it's right on the beach but shady sites are scarce.

Royal Hotel (☎ 5258 1669; 34 King St; s $35, d $70-80, tr $105) The Royal is a top budget accommodation option. Recent renovations in some of the upstairs rooms have given them a fresh lease of life. In the freshly revamped wing, rooms with polished floorboards are painted in vivid colours. See also review under Drinking, p164.

MIDRANGE

Seaview House (☎ 5258 1763; www.seaviewhouse.com .au; 86 Hesse St; s $85-145, d $95-180) Fourteen stylish rooms with bathrooms are furnished in a heritage style (without being over-the-top Victorian) in this cosy guesthouse. Cheaper rooms are compact and come with a shower, while deluxe suites come with a claw-foot bath and bath oils, but all have homely touches and handmade quilts. Two sitting rooms are cosy spots to read the papers, and the continental buffet breakfast includes home-made jams, stewed fruits and filtered coffee.

Queenscliff Inn (☎ 5258 4600; queenscliffinn@big pond.com; 59 Hesse St; YHA dm/d/f $32/75/110, inn d/family $110/170) In the centre of town, this two-storey Edwardian inn has genial hosts and a relaxing, old-world ambience. Downstairs there's a cosy drawing room with open fires and a large dining room. The guest rooms upstairs are decorated in period style and have doonas and electric blankets; bathroom facilities are shared. Rates include breakfast. In the same building as the inn, the YHA rooms are of a high standard and some overlook the bay. Dorms have four single beds (no bunks).

Maytone by the Sea (☎ 5258 4059; www.maytone .com; cnr Esplanade & Stevens St; s $85, d $110-135) Maytone guesthouse makes up for being slightly away from the action with its bay views from the veranda and guest lounge where you can watch the ships chugging in and out of the heads. Each room has its own quirks and configurations – working open fire, en suite, spa etc. Ground-floor rooms are a bit dark (spa rooms are the pick) and an overabundance of the floral pattern in the décor might worry the more aesthetically minded, but the rooms are cosy and comfortable.

Wyuna Motor Inn (☎ 5258 4540; www.wyunamotor inn.com.au; 32 Hesse St; s & d $100-135, f $160, apt $200) Right in the centre of town, Wyuna has spacious but dark motel rooms with heavy furnishings and an '80s-style ambience – some rooms have spas. Wyuna could certainly do with a spruce-up but overall it's a comfortable option.

TOP END

Queenscliff Hotel (☎ 5258 1066; www.queenscliffhotel .com.au; 16 Gellibrand St; B&Bs $125-190, d $150-300) Classified by the National Trust, this hotel has been restored rather than modernised, and is a jewel of old-world splendour. The accommodation is just as it was 100 years ago: small rooms, furnished in the Victorian-style, and no telephones, TVs or radios; bathrooms are shared. You can relax in the comfortable guest lounges or dine in at the wonderful restaurant and bar (see right).

Athelstane House (☎ 5258 1024; www.athelstane .com.au; 4 Hobson St; r from $150) Athelstane looks different for a start – its blonde-wood interior and contemporary décor make no concession to Queenscliff's historic roots. It has beautifully kept, modern top-end accommodation (two-night minimum-stay on weekends). See also review under Eating, right.

Eating

Athelstane House (☎ 5258 1024; www.athelstane.com .au; 4 Hobson St; lunch $9-20, dinner mains $24-30; ⊙ lunch & dinner) The food and wine is as stylish as Athelstane looks – feast on a ploughman's lunch in the all-day café or take your blueberry and white-chocolate cheesecake to the courtyard or deck. At dinner superb Mod Oz mains grace the menu, served with utmost professionalism. See also review under Sleeping, left.

Queenscliff Hotel (☎ 5252 1066; 16 Gellibrand St; set menu $80; ⊙ lunch daily, dinner Wed-Sat) If you want to indulge yourself, or someone else, head to this grand old dame of culinary excellence. It's easy to pretend you've slipped back to the 19th century when you're dining in the formal surrounds of the restored Victorian-era hotel, with its sophisticated ambience. The set-menu offers three courses of superb Mod Oz cuisine.

Vue Grand Hotel (☎ 5258 1544; 46 Hesse St; dinner mains $30, lunch $27) Few dining rooms could beat the ostentatious hoo-ha of this hotel's Grand Dining Room. Walk through the stunning tiled entrance to the striking conservatory and courtyard. Florid menus, written in curly script offer traditional French meals.

Café Cliffe (☎ 5258 1066; 25 Hesse St; all-day menu $8-20; ⊙ lunch) An offshoot of the Queenscliff Hotel, Café Cliffe follows suit with simple but superb food served in a relaxed courtyard herb garden. Salads (such as tender roast-beef salad with crunchy cornichons) are crisp and fresh, cakes sweet and house-made, and wine and produce is for sale in the café.

Ozone Hotel (☎ 5258 1011; 42 Gellibrand St; mains $20-27; ⊙ breakfast, lunch & dinner) The public bar here serves simple meals and there's also a bistro serving upmarket pub food. You can either eat in the Boat Bar, which is hung with a fascinating collection of photos of ships that have been wrecked along this coastline, or in the beer garden out the back.

Couta Boat Café (☎ 5258 4600; 59 Hesse St; focaccias $11, mains $16-23; ⊙ lunch & dinner daily in summer, closed Mon & Tue winter) In clement weather the Couta spills over with holiday-makers, backpackers and weekending Melburnians drinking and eating alfresco. Lunch is classic focaccias – ham, cheese, tomato and pesto; dinner offers heftier modern-European mains.

Queenscliff Fish & Chips (☎ 5258 1312; 77 Hesse St; ⊙ dinner Mon-Fri, lunch & dinner Sat & Sun) Get your freshly grilled fish and chips (from $5.50)

YA GOT BUCKLEY'S

In 1803 William Buckley (1780–1856), a strapping 6ft 7in and a dab hand at building, was transported to Victoria's first settlement (now Sorrento) as a convict – his claim that he had been framed for receiving stolen goods in London refuted.

Managing to steal a gun, Buckley and three other convicts escaped the settlement, though one was shot dead during the escape. The remaining three set off around the bay, thinking they were heading to Sydney, but two turned back, perishing in the process from lack of food and water.

For Buckley, his freedom was too precious to relinquish, and he wandered for weeks, surviving on shellfish and berries. Two Wathaurong (the traditional owners of the area) women eventually found him and, recognising the spear that Buckley had unwittingly plucked from the grave of a Wathaurong warrior, they believed him to be the reincarnation of their kinsman and took him back to his 'family'. Buckley spent the next 32 years with the clan, who taught him their local customs and language as they moved across their country, the Bellarine Peninsula, in search of water, food and trade.

In 1835 another ship sailed into the bay. Not sure how he, a convict, would be received, and barely able to speak his native tongue, Buckley tentatively approached them. The white settlers were startled and even more surprised to discover he was an Englishman. They dubbed him the 'wild white man'.

Apart from the remarkable feat of surviving in the Australian bush, his 1852 book, *The Life & Adventures of William Buckley* (by John Morgan; reissued with an introduction by Tim Flannery 2002), provides a genuine insight into Aboriginal life before white settlement. His role in the mediation between white settlers and the Wathaurong, which prevented unnecessary bloodshed, assured his place in Australian history.

The colloquialisms 'You've got Buckley's mate' and 'Buckley's chance' are based on the story of this 'wild white man' – it means that your plan has little chance of success. For example, to the claim 'I'm going to swim across Bass Strait to Tasmania', the correct response would be 'Ya got Buckley's mate'.

---

wrapped in paper – the old-fashioned way – and eat it by the water. Naturally, you'll have to share the alfresco experience with a host of gulls.

Drinking

Royal Hotel (☎ 5258 1669; 34 King St; mains $8.50-15; ✤ lunch & dinner) For a brew and a pub meal, locals head to the Royal. Food strays into gourmet territory with Mediterranean pizza toppings or a tapas plate, but the old favourites are here too. Beers are crisp and fresh and the pub obviously cleans its lines. You can also stay at the Royal (see p162).

POINT LONSDALE

☎ 03 / pop 1700

Five kilometres southwest of Queenscliff is Point Lonsdale, a laid-back town with a tiny cluster of cafés and still-operational **lighthouse**, built in 1902 (see Queenscliff's Maritime Museum entry p162 for tour information). It's an invigorating walk from the car park at **Rip View lookout**, where you can

watch ships negotiating the treacherous Rip, to **Point Lonsdale Pier** and the lighthouse – just follow the track.

Below the lighthouse is **Buckley's Cave**, where 'wild white man' William Buckley lived with Aborigines for 32 years after he escaped from the convict settlement at Sorrento (see the boxed text Ya Got Buckley's, above).

Point Lonsdale has two **beaches**: the calmer bay beach and the rocky surf beach, which is patrolled by life savers during summer. Don't miss the foreshore around the headland at low tide, when an array of rock pools and caverns become natural aquariums – BYO mask or goggles.

Festivals & Events

Point Lonsdale Market (☎ 0417-037 970; Point Lonsdale Primary School, Bowen Rd; ✤ 9am-2pm), held on the second Sunday of the month year round, is a low-key community market with everything from arts and crafts, plants, flowers, clothing and sculpture. There's also fresh produce, a sausage sizzle, doughnuts and paella.

Sleeping & Eating

Check with the Queenscliffe visitors centre (p161) for details about holiday-house rentals for groups.

Point Lonsdale Guest House (☎ 5258 1142; www .pointlonsdaleguesthouse.com.au; 31 Point Lonsdale Rd; r $95-230; ☒) In Terminus House (1884), new owners are on a doily-eradication programme, giving the decent-sized, nautical-inspired rooms in the sprawling guesthouse a much-needed revamp. A communal kitchen is available to guests and there's a tennis court, games room and barbecue facilities. B&B rooms come with a cooked breakfast, and rooms are available in all sorts of single, double and family spa-suite configurations.

Royal Park Caravan Park (☎ 5258 1765; Point Lonsdale Rd; powered sites per 2 people $25-31, unpowered $19-23; ☽ 1 Dec-1 May) Run by Queenscliff Tourist Parks (p162), this council-run park has lush green sites and is just a dune-hop to the bay. There's a walking track into Point Lonsdale.

Kelp Café (☎ 5258 4797; 67-69 Point Lonsdale Rd; lunch $9-14, dinner mains $24-29; ☽ breakfast, lunch & dinner) Kelp is a welcome addition, its minimalist seaweed-green and silver interior giving Point Lonsdale's strip a contemporary edge and extra pizzazz. Asian and Middle-Eastern inspired dishes might be pan-seared scallops or prawns with chilli and coriander. Lunch offerings include filled pita bread. For breakfast, the coffee is strong and the eggs soft and runny.

This'n'That (☎ 5258 2508; 59 Point Lonsdale Rd; lunch $10-15; ☽ breakfast & lunch, closed Mon & Tue) As the name suggests, this relaxed, small café serves this and that. It's a juice bar and gelati shop and where you come for *involtini* (a type of pastry roulade), quiches, sandwiches and *frittatas* at lunch. Carefully made brekkies make this a firm local favourite.

OCEAN GROVE

☎ 03 / pop 11,300

Ocean Grove is a large town with a surf **beach** – the best waves don't start until further round the coast but ever-hopeful wetsuit-clad surfers bob for hours on the water, while families and canoodling couples watch from the bluff. Ocean Grove is 3km northeast of Barwon Heads and 12km west of Queenscliff.

There are **walking** and **cycling** paths along the beachfront and **scuba diving** and **snorkelling** spots beyond the rocky ledges of the

bluff – further out are wrecked ships that failed to navigate the tricky entrance to Port Phillip Bay.

The **Ocean Grove Nature Reserve** (Grubb Rd), to the north of town, is a large area of natural bushland with 11km of marked walking tracks and lots of native flora, fauna and birdlife.

Sleeping & Eating

Ti-Tree Village (☎ 5255 4433; www.ti-treevillage.com .au; 34 Orton St; cottages $145-230; ☒) Like a glamorous retirement home, Ti-Tree has a range of cosy self-contained garden and spa cottages. Some are grouped close together but they're private enough, and are well maintained with open fires in winter. The playground and communal barbecue areas make it a popular spot with families grilling their day's catch of fish.

Rathlin by the Sea (☎ 5256 1401; 120 Dare St; d $110-130, f $160-170) Two charming apartments are on offer at Rathlin: an en-suite double with ocean views, and a family apartment with a leafy garden aspect. Old-fashioned poster beds and Victorian-era furniture complete the picture. Breakfast is served with a view.

Riverview Family Caravan Park (☎ 5256 1600; www.barwoncoast.com.au; Barwon Heads Rd; powered sites per 2 people $24-40, unpowered $18-32, d cabins $70-145) Sites at this well-run place on the west side of town sit between the Barwon River and the foreshore – make sure you book in summer.

Stock up on supplies at the **Coles supermarket** (☎ 5255 5100; 75 The Terrace; ☽ 6am-midnight).

BARWON HEADS

☎ 03 / pop 1900

The backstreet of the Bellarine Peninsula is about 3km west of Ocean Grove, where the Barwon River meets Bass Strait. Barwon Heads is a peaceful town, made famous by *Sea Change* – a popular TV series – and a beautiful spot with sheltered river beaches and **Thirteenth Beach**, where sirens call to surfers. Standing at the **bluff** gives you panoramas of the ocean and river.

The magnificent **Barwon Heads Golf Club** (☎ 5254 2302; www.bhgc.com.au; Golf Links Rd; green fees guest/nonguest $35/55), set among rolling coastal hills and sand dunes with inspirational ocean views, is one of Victoria's best courses. It's open to the public most days, and also offers accommodation (see p166).

Sleeping

Prices increase on weekends and you'll need to book during school holidays and around Christmas.

Seahaven Village (☎ 5254 1066; www.seahaven village.com.au; 3 Geelong Rd; $160-225; 🔀) Opposite Village Park, Seahaven has a cluster of self-contained studios and cottages decked out in individual nautical themes. Though the close arrangement means that some lack a little privacy, each room is spotlessly clean. Extras include electric blankets, open fires, a full kitchen and CD and video players. Plans are afoot to build attic and tower cottages. Prices are cheaper in the low season, particularly from Sunday to Thursday.

Barwon Heads Caravan Park (☎ 5254 1115; www .barwoncoast.com.au; Ewing Blyth Dr; powered sites per 2 people $32-40, unpowered $18-24, d cabins $70-80, f cabins $120-145, d beach houses $160-210, f beach houses $195-230) Milking *Sea Change* for all it's worth, you can actually stay in the water-frontage beach houses, with bridge and bay views, where the characters lived in the show. Right on the Barwon River, this caravan park has tea tree–shaded sites in summer, and tennis courts and playgrounds where the young tackers can burn some energy.

Barwon Heads Golf Club (☎ 5254 2302; www.bhgc .com.au; Golf Links Rd; d incl meals $380; 🔀) Older-style rooms with an en suite and TV have views of the ocean and golf course – essential for a visual postmortem of the game. Alternatively, click off your spikes and gaze out at the ocean views or revive in the formal restaurant (for members and guests only). Room rates include green fees, breakfast, lunch and a three-course dinner.

Eating & Drinking

Barwon Heads is blessed with some of the best eateries on the Bellarine, nearly all of them on Hitchcock St.

Barwon Orange (☎ 5254 1090; 60 Hitchcock Ave; breakfast & lunch $3.80-15, pizzas $7.80-16, mains $18-20; 🕑 breakfast, lunch & dinner) Low-hanging raffia lamps highlight well-placed splashes of purple and orange, and a chattering crowd creates a warm convivial ambience. Big Bertha – the orange wood-fired oven that cooks up Barwon Orange's thick-crust and crazily topped pizzas, helps the mood along. Innovative menus and quality food earn this café-restaurant a high distinction; breakfast is served until a civilised 3pm.

Starfish Bakery (☎ 5254 2772; 78 Hitchcock St; lunch $5-9; 🕑 breakfast & lunch) This relaxed, colourful bakery-café has leafy views from its big windows. Vibrant pastels and artistic tile trim brighten the interior, along with marine-creature bread sculptures and kids' artwork. Come here for strong coffee, fresh sourdough bread, chunky muffins, *panini* (rolls) and toasties or grab a fat, filled sandwich to go. Breakfasts here are fantastic but late-risers note: lunch starts at 11.30am.

Beachnik Café & Wine Bar (☎ 5254 3376; 48 Hitchcock Ave; lunch $7-14, dinner $7-22; 🕑 breakfast, lunch & dinner) Beachnik is a salvation for Barwon Heads' young surfer crowd. By day it's a chilled café, by night its decking with op-shop furniture makes for a mellow bar. Come here for *mee goreng*, pad Thai and other Asian-inspired meals. Saturday's happy hour from 4pm to 6pm is superb value – sip a cold beer and watch Bellarine musicians play acoustic sets (be sure to check out local heart-throb MJ Taylor if he's strumming).

Phil's Pizza & Pasta (☎ 5254 1477; 49 Hitchcock Ave; pizzas $12-18; 🕑 5.30pm-late) Head here with a rabble of noisy kids and a large appetite. Phil's makes the best pizzas in town and has a tasty gourmet line as well as traditional toppings. In winter Phil's is closed Monday and Tuesday.

At the Heads (☎ 5254 1277; Jetty Rd; meals $17-32; 🕑 lunch & dinner daily, breakfast Sat & Sun) It's all about the view really. Built on stilts over the mouth of the river, this light, airy café-restaurant has huge breakfasts and Italian fare. Its bustling family ambience makes it a fun daytime locale. After dark try the seafood bouillabaisse – fresh seafood cooked in a tomato-Pernod broth.

Wine Pit (☎ 5254 1693; 1/44 Hitchcock Ave; all-day menu $6-15; 🕑 breakfast, lunch & dinner) Swizzle and swirl glasses of regional plonk at the Wine Pit, sectioned off from the road with nautical ropes and bollards. This wholesale winery offers free tastings, especially showcasing the Geelong and Bellarine wineries. Salads, such as roasted lamb or warm chicken, go well with a Kilgour Estate chardonnay, as does a modern interpretation of a caesar with mussels and scallops. Or sample a drop of pinot with a cheese platter.

Barwon Heads Hotel (☎ 5254 2201; www.barwon headshotel.com.au 1 Bridge Rd; mains $18-24; 🕑 lunch &

dinner) Serving slap-up counter meals from its massive bistro to a crowd of die-hard locals, this is where you come to do some serious drinking and place a few bets on greyhound racing. Accommodation is available, but it's noisy on the weekends.

NORTHWEST FROM MELBOURNE

If you're after a day trip from Melbourne, this area of central Victoria, encompassing Mt Macedon, Hanging Rock, Woodend and the tiny towns of Trentham and Blackwood, is perfect for a scenic drive through hilly eucalypt-filled countryside, a gourmet lunch, and wine tasting at a Mt Macedon vineyard. The Lerderderg State Park offers peaceful walks among rolling hills, or clamber up the infamous Hanging Rock (p169).

This area makes a great detour en route to the goldfield towns of Daylesford, Castlemaine and Ballarat. To fully appreciate it, get off the two main roads (the Western and Calder Fwys) and travel the quiet back roads.

Getting There & Away

V/Line (☎ 13 61 96; www.vline.com.au) trains travelling from Melbourne to Bendigo (12 a day Monday to Friday, seven on Saturday and five on Sunday) stop at various destinations. Return fares include Sunbury ($10.20, 40 minutes), Riddells Creek ($15, 50 minutes), Gisborne ($18, 55 minutes), Macedon ($18, one hour) and Woodend ($20, one hour and 10 minutes).

From Woodend, V/Line buses go to/from Daylesford (two daily Monday to Saturday and one on Sunday), also stopping at Trentham (return $8, 20 minutes).

BACCHUS MARSH

☎ 03 / pop 11,300

Bacchus Marsh, 49km from Melbourne, is just off the Western Hwy (M8). It has some fine old **National Trust-classified buildings** as well as a noteworthy **Avenue of Honour**, and is a good base for walks and picnics in the vicinity. The area is noted for its apple orchards and market gardens, and there are roadside fruit and vegie stalls along the roads leading into town.

TRENTHAM & BLACKWOOD

☎ 03 / pop 650 & 300

These two charming towns are on the edge of the Wombat State Forest and Blackwood Ranges.

Gold was first discovered in the area in 1854 by Harry Athorn and Harry Hider. When their discovery became public knowledge, thousands of miners flooded into the densely forested area and searched the gullies and hills for gold. The miners built complex systems of water races to carry river water to their mining sites, and many of these races have now been turned into **walking tracks**. After the gold rush, the forests were heavily harvested for timber.

Two kilometres west of Blackwood, the bountiful **Garden of St Erth** (☎ 5368 6514; www .diggers.com.au/st_erth.htm; Simmons Reef Rd; admission $7, mains $8.50-19; ☺ 9am-5pm Fri-Tue, closed Jun & Jul) is a beautiful four-hectare garden run by the Digger's Club, a well-known gardening club that maintains gardens at historic properties. Built around an 1860s stone cottage, the garden has shaded lawns and stone paths, fragrant flowerbeds, dappled pools and formal gardens. Lunch (or even just cake) at the excellent Café at the Garden of St Erth makes for a thoroughly enjoyable day out.

Blackwood also has its own **mineral-springs reserve** (Golden Point Rd; parking $3) with walking trails (about 1.6km) to pretty **Shaw's Lake**, which is a peaceful swimming spot in summer. Simple hiking maps are available at the Mineral Springs Caravan Park (p168).

AROUND MELBOURNE

DETOUR: LERDERDERG STATE PARK

Lerderderg State Park is in rugged and scenic escarpment country. Its dominant feature is the spectacular gorge of the Lerderderg River. Numerous steep, long **bushwalks** follow the river or old water races cut by gold miners. Overnight walkers can **bush camp** anywhere in the park. **Swimming** holes and sandy beaches along the river make it especially popular in summer. The park lies between the Calder and Western Fwys. The main access road for the northern sector is O'Briens Rd, signposted 3km south of Blackwood. Roads through the park are rough and may be closed after rain; call **Parks Victoria** (☎ 13 19 63) to check.

Sleeping & Eating

Cosmopolitan Hotel & Dining Room (☎ 5424 1616; cnr Cosmo Rd & High St, Trentham; r with/without bathroom $130/100, mains $12-23; ☯ dinner Thu & Fri, lunch & dinner Sat & Sun) The Cosmo, a rustically restored 1860s gold-rush–era coach house, is the pick of the area's accommodation. Six comfy B&B rooms, most with bathroom, are furnished in a romantic heritage style (it's best to book). Definitely stop in for a clean, crisp microbrew at the historic bar, or adjourn to the beer garden – mobile reception is patchy at best in Trentham so calls won't distract you from the pressing matter of which beer to choose next. The spacious dining room offers gourmet pub fare, served with professional flair. Cosmo burgers are a benchmark, but carnivores who like well-cooked meat beware: these patties are rare.

Mineral Springs Caravan Park (☎ /fax 5368 6539; Golden Point Rd, Blackwood; powered/unpowered sites per 2 people $18/15, d caravans $35) A short walk from the Lerderderg River, Mineral Springs is a smallish park with limited shady sites. There's a communal hut with a big fireplace and barbecues.

Issan Trentham (☎ 5424 1811; 42 High St, Trentham; mains $16-30; ☯ dinner Fri-Sun, lunch Sat & Sun) With coloured fairy lights twinkling in the old shopfront window, Issan Trentham continues to cook up fragrantly delicious curries, based on the chef's homeland in northeastern Thailand. It's a romantic spot with Thai decorations among the rural, rustic wooden furniture. Stir-fries are fresh and crisp and there's plenty of vego options.

For a classic pub feed – lamb shanks, parmas, rib-eye steaks etc – where locals don't get any more local than these characters, try the following:

Blackwood Hotel (☎ 5368 6501; Martin St, Blackwood; mains $15-25; ☯ lunch & dinner)

Pig & Whistle (☎ 5424 1213; cnr James Lane & Pearson Rd, Blackwood; mains $14-19; ☯ lunch daily, dinner Mon-Sat)

ALONG THE CALDER HIGHWAY

Northwest from Melbourne to Bendigo are a handful of sites for which it's worth taking the exit off the Calder Hwy.

Check out the **Organ Pipes National Park**, which has some fascinating geological structures – hexagonal basalt columns look like giant organ pipes and form a natural outdoor amphitheatre.

Five kilometres east of the highway, **Sunbury** was the site of a number of large Australian Woodstock-style rock festivals in the early 1970s. It's also the home of Craiglee (p65), established in the 1860s and one of Victoria's most historic wineries.

Cricket enthusiasts will beg for a detour to grand old **Rupertswood** (☎ 03-9740 5020; www .rupertswood.com; Sunbury; house admission by donation, r $160-500; ☯ 9am-5pm), birthplace of the **Ashes**, the Holy Grail of English and Australian cricket. Self-guided tours are available, provided there isn't a wedding in play – it's best to call ahead. Honeymooners staying in the opulent rooms will feel like they've just scored the winning wicket.

Dromkeen Homestead Children's Literature Museum (☎ 03-5428 6701; Kilmore Rd, Dromkeen; admission by donation; ☯ 9am-5pm Tue-Fri, noon-4pm Sun) has an extensive library, a gallery of works-in-progress, and a historical room with original sketches and prints from well-loved Australian works, including *The Magic Pudding* and *Blinky Bill*. Barbecue and picnic in the extensive gardens.

Just north of Gisborne it's worth exiting the Calder Hwy for **Mt Macedon**, a 1013m-high extinct volcano, which has several walking tracks. The scenic route up Mt Macedon Rd takes you past mansions with beautiful gardens and there's a café and picnic grounds near the summit. At the top of the mountain take the summit road to a memorial cross via the **Camel's Hump** (a 10-minute walk each way) for sweeping views. Beyond the summit turn-off, the road heads to quaint Woodend, or you can take the signed road on the right to Hanging Rock.

WOODEND

☎ 03 / pop 3000

Woodend is a small, attractive town nestled on the northern fringe of the Black Forest. In the gold-rush days, bushrangers roamed the forest, robbing travellers en route to the goldfields. These days, it serves as the base for visiting nearby Hanging Rock.

Woodend Visitor Information Centre (☎ 5427 2033; www.macedon-ranges.vic.gov.au; High St; ☯ 9am-5pm) is the information centre for the entire Macedon Ranges area.

Macedon Region Wineries

The Woodend/Mt Macedon area produces a solid range of cool-climate tipples, the soil

In-line skating (p109), St Kilda foreshore

PHIL M WEYMOUTH

Murray cod, Flower Drum restaurant (p122), city centre

GREG ELMS

Night Cat (p135), Fitzroy

JAMES BRAUND

Deli at Prahran Market (p141), South Yarra

CHRIS MELLOR

Puffing Billy steam train (p177)

GREG ELMS

View through the rocks,
Hanging Rock (p169)

GLENN BEANLAND

Wines from Coldstream Hills (p57), Yarra Valley

JOHN HAY

Lifeguard bollards, waterfront Geelong (p154)

CHRISTOPHER GROEN

and climate especially suited to crisp sparkling wines, fragrant whites and impressive pinot noirs. It's the most accessible of the wine regions to Melbourne – only a short 40 minute hop up the Calder Hwy – and has over 30 vineyards. Pick up a *Macedon Ranges & Sunbury Wine Tour* map available at the information centre.

Some goodies to visit include the following:

Knight's Granite Hills (☎ 5423 7264; Burke and Wills Track; knights@granitehills.com.au; ☻ 9am-6pm Mon-Sat, 1pm-6pm Sun) Northwest of Lancefield.

Cope-Williams Winery (☎ 5429 5428; www.cope-williams.com.au; Glenfern Rd, Romsey; ☻ 11am-5pm)

Portree Winery (☎ 5429 1422; www.portreevineyard.com.au; 72 Powells Track, Lancefield; ☻ 11am-5pm Sat & Sun & public holidays)

Sleeping, Eating & Drinking

Bentinck Country House (☎ 5427 2944; www.bentinck.com.au; 1 Carlisle St; s/d $140/190) This English-style B&B guesthouse is set in landscaped gardens on the north side of town. It has period-style guest rooms with en suites, cosy lounges and a restaurant. Dinner and room packages are also available.

Bites Deli & Larder (☎ 5427 4808; 112 High St; mains $7-18; ☻ breakfast & lunch) At this sunny yellow café and produce store you can pick up sandwiches made with thick slabs of bread and deli-style fillings. It's also a top spot for gourmet provisions, including cheeses, sliced meats and an array of pâtés, preserves, olive oils and artisan Fruition breads, for a picnic at Hanging Rock or Mt Macedon.

Maloa House Gourmet Delights (☎ 5427 1608; 97 High St; mains $7-9; ☻ breakfast & lunch Tue-Sun) Maloa House is another Woodend favourite, crammed with local gourmet produce. At lunch pop in for a *frittata* and salad or a posh beef-and-burgundy pie. The coffee is strong, made by boutique Melbourne brewer Jasper – soak it up with a slice of chocolate cake.

Holgates Bar & Restaurant (☎ 5427 2510; www.holgatebrewhouse.com; 79 High St; mains $15-24; ☻ lunch & dinner) Beers lovers have found their spiritual home at this premium microbrewery, where European-style beers are carefully brewed. There are tastings of the various ales, pilsner and an experimental ginger beer – they even have tasting notes. Holgate's restaurant, with polished floorboards and professional staff, serves superb Mod Oz cuisine, matched with beer, and there's live music Friday and Saturday night and Sunday afternoon. At the time of writing en-suite B&B accommodation was being renovated; prices are expected to range from $100 to $150.

HANGING ROCK

A pretty 6km drive northeast of Woodend, **Hanging Rock** is the sacred site of the Wurrendjeri people, the traditional owners of the land. It was made famous by Joan Lindsay's novel and Peter Weir's subsequent film of the same name. *Picnic at Hanging Rock,* about the disappearance of a group of schoolgirls. The rock is a volcanic 'plug' that last erupted seven million years ago and has eroded to its present form. It was a refuge for bushrangers, including the notorious outlaw Dan 'Mad Dog' Morgan.

Clambering up the top is an easy 15-minute walk, thoroughly recommended on a clear day. Along the way, you'll pass the **Pinnacles**, a series of exposed rocks oddly reminiscent of the stone heads of Easter Island. Crimson rosellas dart between ferns and lichen-covered boulders (you might even spot a groggy koala) and the summit views of surrounding farmland and Mt Macedon are travel-mag spreads. Even if you haven't seen the film, it's hard to miss the spooky feeling that hangs over the Rock.

Below is the grassy expanse of **Hanging Rock Reserve** (☎ 1800 244 711; www.hangingrock.info; South Rock Rd, Woodend; admission per car $8; ☻ 8am-5pm), dotted with picnickers. **Picnic race meetings** at the adjacent horse-racing track are held throughout the year, and there's a small **museum** (admission free) and **café** (mains $13-25; ☻ lunch Tue-Sun) at the reserve.

Woodend Taxi (☎ 03-5427 2641) can take you from Woodend to the Rock for about $15.

YARRA VALLEY

☎ 03

The Yarra Valley is an extremely popular day trip or overnighter. Just one hour from Melbourne, it's packed with boutique vineyards producing top wines and serving delicious lunches from their cellar-door restaurants. You can go gourmet ballooning with a glass of champers in hand, cycle along old rail trails, walk through national parks, and see a massive wedge-tailed eagle fly over your head at Healesville Sanctuary wildlife park.

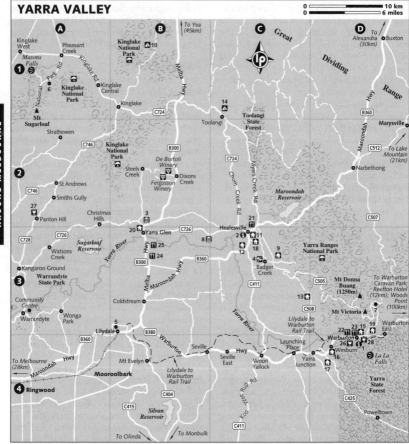

YARRA VALLEY

Gourmet produce stores keep foodies well fed (ask at the visitors centre for a *Yarra Valley Regional Food Trail* brochure). And the views dahling! The views! The Yarra River wends its way through the valley, leaving gorgeous landscapes in its wake.

Orientation & Information

The Maroondah Hwy (B360) runs east from Melbourne to Lilydale, the 'gateway' to the Yarra Valley, continuing northeast through Coldstream to Healesville and Alexandra. Just past Lilydale, the Warburton Hwy (B380) branches off and continues eastward through Woori Yallock, Yarra Junction and Warburton – this area is known as the Upper Yarra Valley. At Coldstream, the Melba Hwy

(B300) branches off the Maroondah Hwy and takes you north to Yarra Glen and the Kinglake Ranges.

Yarra Valley Visitor Information Centre (☎ 5962 2600; www.yarravalleytourism.asn.au; Harker St, Healesville; ☺ 9am to 5pm) is the main visitors centre for the Lower Yarra Valley.

Festivals & Events

Yarra Valley Farmers' Market (☎ 9513 0677; www.yarravalleyfood.com.au; Yering Station vineyard, 38 Melba Hwy, Yering) A sensational produce market, held on the third Sunday of the month, showcasing the finest foods (pasta, cheeses, local wines) the Yarra Valley has to offer.

Shedfest Wine Festival (www.shedfest.com.au; Oct) A chance to sample wine by some of the smaller cold-climate wineries.

Pioneer & Working Horse Festival (Australia Day weekend) Held at Gulf Station; a top family event with working horses, sheepdog trials and farm animals, and stallholders who demonstrate pioneering skills. You can also try your luck in the horseshoe-throwing championship.

Getting There & Around

Car and motorbike are the most convenient forms of transport for touring the Yarra Valley as there are lots of off-road wineries to explore. Cycling is also an option, but it's a hilly area and the highways can be busy (see also the Lilydale to Warburton Rail Trail, p174).

The Met's suburban trains go as far as Lilydale (Zone 3 Met ticket, $12.40).

From Lilydale train station, **McKenzie's Bus Lines** (☎ 5962 5088; www.mckenzies.com.au) runs to/from Healesville (some services continue on to Healesville Sanctuary) and Yarra Glen, while **Martyrs** (☎ 5966 2035; www.martyrs.com.au) buses run to Yarra Junction and Warburton.

LOWER YARRA VALLEY
Sights & Activities

Roughly an hour's drive from Melbourne, the valley is one of Victoria's most accessible wine regions and a popular day trip from the city.

HEALESVILLE SANCTUARY

One of the best places to see Australian native fauna is the **Healesville Sanctuary** (☎ 5957 2800; www.zoo.org.au; Badger Creek Rd, Healesville; adult/child/family $19/9.50/50; 9am-5pm), a wildlife park set in native bushland. Birds flap and peck in the aviaries and wetlands, and other residents include wallabies, kangaroos, dingoes, lyrebirds, Tasmanian devils,

bats, koalas, eagles, snakes and lizards. The Platypus House is a top spot to see these shy creatures underwater, but the real star is the exciting **Birds of Prey** (noon & 2pm) presentation where raptors, including a huge wedge-tailed eagle, dive and swoop above your head, and owls catch a mouse midair.

Martyrs (☎ 5966 2035; www.martyrs.com.au) runs frequent buses to/from Southern Cross station and from Lilydale train station to Healesville Sanctuary.

TARRAWARRA MUSEUM OF ART

Architect Allan Powell won the competition to design the **TarraWarra Museum of Art** (☎ 5957 3100; www.twma.com.au; 311 Healesville-Yarra Glen Rd, Healesville; admission $5; 11am-5pm Tue-Sun) and the space is an architectural triumph. The museum itself displays a collection of modern Australian art dating from the 1950s, from the private collection of the Besen family. Contemporary exhibitions change regularly. You can have lunch or buy some wine at the Tin Cows winery next door.

GULF STATION

A couple of kilometres north of Yarra Glen is **Gulf Station** (☎ 9730 1286; Melba Hwy, Yarra Glen; adult/child/family $8/5/25; 10am-4pm Wed-Sun), a National Trust–classified farm dating back to the 1850s. With the old slab-timber farmhouse, barns, stables and slaughterhouse, original implements and replanted sustenance gardens and orchards, Gulf Station gives an interesting insight into farm life in the 19th century. Kids will enjoy the ducks and geese that wander round the property. There's a big bonfire night on the first Saturday of November.

YARRA VALLEY WINERIES

For comprehensive information about the Yarra Valley wineries and wine touring in the Yarra Valley see p56; and for a potential lunch stop see p184. Pick up a copy of the excellent *Yarra Valley Wine Touring Guide* or the *Yarra Valley Regional Food Trail* brochure from the visitors centres in Healesville (p170) and Warburton (p174), to see you on your way.

KINGLAKE NATIONAL PARK

The largest national park near Melbourne (about 50km away), Kinglake National Park is a huge eucalypt forest on the slopes of the Great Dividing Range. A scenic way to get there from Melbourne is to drive up through Eltham, then up through Kangaroo Ground, Panton Hill and St Andrews.

In the centre of the park, **Kinglake** is a small township with a pub and a few shops and galleries (but no lake!). Eighteen kilometres east, **Toolangi** was the home of the poet and writer CJ Dennis from 1915 to 1935. He wrote many of his famous works here, including the *Sentimental Bloke*.

There are dozens of walking tracks, topnotch picnic spots and scenic lookout points throughout the park. Near the **park office** (☎ 5786 5351; National Park Rd, Pheasant Creek; ☽ 8.30am-5pm Mon-Fri, later in summer) is the popular **Masons Falls Track**, an easy 15-minute walk to a waterfall. Other popular walks include the four-hour return **Mt Sugarloaf Track**, which also leaves from near the park office, and the three-hour return **Andrew Hill Track**, which leaves from the Gums.

Camping areas in Kinglake National Park include the **Gums** (☎ 5786 5351; Eucalyptus-Glenburn Rd; unpowered site per 2 people $22). It's a pretty area with a small stream nearby, but book with the park office as there are only 10 sites and they fill up quickly. It's about 10km northeast of Kinglake off the Melba Hwy.

Murrindindi Scenic Reserve Camping (☎ 5962 9203; Murrindindi; per vehicle $5) is north of Toolangi on the Murrindindi River and contains some great walks to the **Cascades** and **Wilhelmina Falls** – spectacular when the snow melts in spring.

WARRANDYTE STATE PARK

One of the few remaining areas of natural bush in the metropolitan area, **Warrandyte**

State Park (www.parkweb.vic.gov.au) is 24km northeast of central Melbourne. The park is made up of several sections, including Pound Bend, Jumping Creek, Whipstick Gully and Black Flat. Walking and cycling tracks are well marked, there are picnic and barbecue areas, native animals and birds, and an abundance of native wildflowers in the springtime. Although it's a suburb of Melbourne, Warrandyte has, to a degree, managed to retain the feel of a country village. Artists and craftspeople have always been attracted to the area, and there are quite a few galleries and potteries dotted throughout the hills.

One of the best ways to explore the river and park is in a canoe. **Adventure Canoeing** (☎ 9844 3323; www.adventurecanoeing.com.au/yarra_river.asp; self-guided 2-hr/full-day tour per person $40/75, guided tour $110) hires out canoes/kayaks and runs tours.

BALLOONING

Ballooning over the Yarra Valley is a peaceful way to view the hills and vineyards. Flights with the following operators average $280.

Balloon Aloft (☎ 1800 028 568; www.balloonaloft.com)
Global Ballooning (☎ 9428 5703; www.globalballooning.com.au)
Go Wild Ballooning (☎ 9890 0339; www.gowildballooning.com.au)
Peregrine Ballooning (☎ 9662 2800; www.hotairballooning.com.au)

Tours

Eco Adventure Tours (☎ 5962 5115; www.hotkey.net.au/~ecoadven/aboutus.htm) Offers nocturnal spotlighting walks in the Healesville and Marysville area – a good chance to see some of the valley's distinctive plant and animal life.
Yarra Valley Winery Tours (☎ 5962 3870; www.yarravalleywinerytours.com.au; tours $80-180) Winery tours around the Yarra Valley. Tours depart from Lilydale station.

Sleeping

Healesville Motor Inn (☎ 5962 5188; www.healesville-motor-inn.com.au; 45 Maroondah Hwy; s $70-130, d $90-145, f $120-160) This clean and comfortable motel offers all the standard features and, as one guest quoted, 'the best shower in Australia'. The hosts are friendly and helpful and it's one of the better motel choices in the Healesville area.

Badger Creek Caravan & Holiday Park (☎ 5962 4328; www.badgercreekholidays.com.au; 419 Don Rd, Badger Creek; powered sites per 2 people $25-27, unpowered $22-24, d caravans $70, d cabins $76-95; 🅿🅢) With a host of different accommodation options, this camping ground is on the banks of the Badger Creek, close to Healesville Sanctuary (p171) and Puffing Billy (p177). There's oodles of room and a toddler's pool.

Healesville Hotel (☎ 5962 4002; www.healesville hotel.com.au; 256 Maroondah Hwy, Healesville; d Sun-Thu $80, Fri/Sat $105/120) An iconic Healesville landmark, this hotel offers classic upstairs pub rooms with quality linen and TVs; the seven rooms share three spick-and-span bathrooms. Saturday night accommodation can be booked up two months in advance, so get in early if you're after a room. See also below.

Tuck Inn (☎ 5962 3600; www.tuckinn.com.au; 2 Church St, Healesville; r Sun-Thu $135-150, Fri & Sat $150-165) Decked out in a contemporary style, this is a beautiful and stylish guesthouse with friendly hosts. Five immaculate rooms – three queen and two king, which can be turned into twins – have plush mattresses with quality linen and luxury woollen quilts. Each has its own clean-as-a-whistle bathroom, but with showers only, so you can't have a soak. It's a top spot.

Yarra Glen Grand Hotel (☎ 9730 1230; www.yarra glengrand.com.au; 19 Bell St, Yarra Glen; r $140-200) Built in 1888, this hotel in the centre of town is classified by the National Trust. It has been wonderfully restored in period detail and is one of the best country hotels in Victoria. In the magnificent, formal, Victorian dining room you can have two-or three-course meals, and there's a more casual bistro. On Saturday, room and meal packages only are available.

Eating & Drinking

Healesville Hotel (☎ 5962 4002; www.healesvillehotel .com.au; 256 Maroondah Hwy, Healesville; café mains $8-16, dinner mains $24-30; ☽ breakfast, lunch & dinner) The hotel has three separate eating areas: the relaxed produce café, Healesville Harvest; a bistro; and a fine-dining restaurant. Local beers are on tap and it's a cruisey Sunday arvo listening to country music played on vinyl in the leafy garden. See also Sleeping review, above.

Bodhi Tree Café (☎ 5962 4407; 317 Maroondah Hwy, Healesville; mains $9-16; ☽ dinner Wed-Fri, lunch & dinner Sat & Sun) Friendly eco vibes flow from the earth-conscious hippies chilling on salvaged wooden furniture, the pot-belly stove and

the heart-warming pizza smells. There's vego options aplenty and pizzas come in kid-size portions – try a tofu topping, or the more traditional cheesy margherita. There's mellow live music on Friday and Saturdays (cover charge $3).

Yarra Valley Dairy (☎ 9739 0023; McMeikans Rd, Yering; 2-course meals $25, degustation platters from $19.50; ☽ 10.30am-5pm) These renowned cheesemakers sell cheese, produce and wine from their picturesque farm gate. Eat platters of fresh and semi-matured cheeses in the dairy's old milking shed, while feasting on the valley views.

Panton Hill Hotel (☎ 9719 7270; 633 Main Rd, Panton Hill; mains $14-24; ☽ lunch & dinner) A classic country boozer serving slap-up pub grub. Sitting on the back veranda, beer in hand, looking out over the surrounding hills is a peaceful way to recharge. There's live music Thursday and Friday nights, and on Wednesday night, meals are $11.

Grand Hotel (☎ 5962 4003; 270 Maroondah Hwy, Healesville; s/d $30/50, mains $8-20; lunch & dinner, closed Tue for meals) Along the same lines as Panton, the Grand is a local place for a lengthy and raucous drinking session. Meals are served in the bistro or bar and might be a rib-eye steak or alcohol-soaker chicken parma and chips. There are simple pub rooms upstairs, with shared bath.

UPPER YARRA VALLEY

As you follow the Yarra River east towards Warburton, the valley narrows and the Yarra Ranges start to dominate the scenery. Much of the valley's early history relates to the timber industry – more timber has passed through Yarra Junction than any town in the world except for Seattle, Washington, USA. Evidence of the old mills, timber tramlines and charcoal plants can still be found throughout the forests.

Going through mountainous terrain, a scenic drive loops through Healesville, up to Marysville and down to Warburton. There are two ways to go from Marysville down to Warburton. The first is via the Acheron Way (C507), a dirt road through the Yarra Ranges National Park; the second is along Woods Point Rd (C511), east of Warburton, which is popular with motorcyclists from all over Victoria. It's a winding, twisting extravaganza – you'll be happy when the road finally straightens out. Of course, the drive up Mt Donna Buang is nothing to sneeze at.

Warburton & Surrounds

The centre of the Upper Yarra Valley is Warburton, a relaxed, picturesque town set in a lush, green valley by the banks of the Yarra River. In the 19th century it was popular as a health retreat and droves of city slickers came to Warby for lungfuls of fresh mountain air. The township has a sleepy charm and a walk along the river, or up one of the steep hills, restores the spirit and takes care of your daily exercise.

Warburton Water Wheel Visitor Information Centre (☎ 5966 9600; 3400 Warburton Hwy, Warburton; ⏰ 11am-3pm Mon-Fri, 10am-5pm Sat, Sun & holidays) is the main information centre for the Upper Yarra Valley.

SIGHTS & ACTIVITIES
Lilydale to Warburton Rail Trail

Following the 1901 railway line, the 38km **Lilydale to Warburton Rail Trail** (☎ 1300 368 333) is a recreational trail that wends its way from Lilydale, through the beautiful Yarra River valley, to Warburton. It's a hugely popular ride for cyclists (and horse riders). It takes roughly three hours one way, depending on your pedal power, but it's also suitable for the less fit. Call for details, or check out 'Where to Ride' on the Bicycle Victoria website: www.bv.com.au.

The trail starts on the south side of the Maroondah Hwy, roughly 1km from the Lilydale train station (serviced by Met trains). There's parking at Lilydale and Mt Evelyn stations. You can hire bikes from **Lilydale Cycles** (☎ 9735 5077; 6-8 William St East; per half-/full-day $30/20), right next to Lilydale station.

Yarra Ranges National Park

Towering above Warburton is the ruggedly beautiful **Yarra Ranges National Park** (www.park web.vic.gov.au), with forests of mountain ash and cool-climate rainforest. It's home to the endangered Leadbeater's possum.

Mt Donna Buang (1250m) is the highlight of the park, capped with winter snow – the closest snow to Melbourne. 'Donna' was where generations of Melbourne kids got their first look at snow, rode their first toboggan and cried as their first-ever Mr Snowman melted and slid off the bonnet of the family Holden as it descended the mountain. For those who want to recapture the thrill, toboggans can be rented at the toboggan run. Before the summit, the **Rain-**forest Gallery (☎ 5966 5996; Acheron Way) is a fantastic treetop walk along a 40m observation platform through the rainforest canopy.

Keen walkers can take the 6km trail to the summit of **Mt Victoria** from near the Warburton golf course, or the **Cement Creek track**, which leaves from Mt Donna Buang Rd just above the Rainforest Gallery.

Other Sights & Activities

On the way to Warburton, the **Sam Knott Hotel** (Wesburn, Warburton Hwy) is named after an old 19th-century prospector. Sam was immortalised by a Carlton & United Breweries poster, which depicts him standing at a bar, beer in hand, saying 'I allus has wan at eleven'. Sam died before the poster was published, but he lives on in (what's left of) the memories of all Australian beer drinkers. There's a woodcarving of him on top of a huge log in front of the pub's bottle shop.

Powelltown, 16km southeast of Yarra Junction, was a busy timber town during the 19th century, and tramlines and tunnels were built to transport the timber to the railway line. A collection of excellent **forest walks** follow old tram routes. Shorter walks near Powelltown include the **Reid's Tramline Walk**, **Ada Tree Walk** (past a 300-year-old, 76m-high mountain ash) and **Seven Acre Rock Walk**. The two-day, 36km **Walk into History** track takes you all the way from Powelltown to Warburton.

Sleeping

Warburton Motel (☎ 5966 2059; www.countryhaven .com.au/wm.html; Donna Buang Rd, Warburton; s $75-85, d $85-125, f $105) Nestled on a hill overlooking Warburton, this clean motel is surrounded by leafy, colourful gardens. Downstairs rooms have a courtyard, upstairs rooms have verandas. The luxury spa rooms are good value and the owners are knowledgeable about local activities and attractions.

Alpine Retreat Hotel (☎ 5966 2411; www.alpinere treat.com.au; 12 Main St, Warburton; s/d/f $105/145/165; ⏰ lunch & dinner) Upmarket rooms include a buffet breakfast with the works, and there's a TV in each room. See also opposite.

St Lawrence B&B (☎ 5966 5649; www.stlawrence .qsau.com; 13 Richards Rd, Warburton; r with/without spa $160/155) Sited in a beautiful 1860s home surrounded by established gardens, St Lawrence offers three en-suite rooms (one with a spa) decorated in period-style furnishings. Guests share a lounge and dining room. It's a three-minute stroll to the centre of Warburton.

Tarrango Farm B&B (☎ 5967 2123; www.tarrangofarm.com.au; Tarrango Rd, Yarra Junction; s $90-130, d $110-160) This relaxing B&B on an 8-hectare property has guest rooms in the main house and a self-contained cottage. It's a bucolic setting and there's plenty of room for kids to run around and make noise.

Hill'n' Dale Farm Cottages (☎ 5967 3361; www.users.bigpond.com/hillndale; 1284 Don Rd, Launching Place; cottages from $160) Four self-contained cottages, furnished in old-fashioned country stylings, are on a forested property north of Launching Place. Kids love the sheep and alpacas and collecting freshly laid eggs from the hen house. Well-behaved pets are welcome.

Warburton Caravan Park (☎ 5966 2277; www.warburtoncaravanpark.com.au; 30 Woods Rd, Warburton; powered/unpowered sites per 2 people $20/16, d cabins $45-80, d lodge $120; 🔊) At this well-organised caravan park, sites and basic cabins have prime water positions on the banks of the Yarra River and the cedar lodge accommodates up to 13 people. Dog-owners love the fact that their pooch is allowed to stay too (but only on a lead and not in the cabins).

Eating, Drinking & Entertainment

Wild Thyme Cafe (☎ 5966 5050; 3391 Warburton Hwy; meals $14-22; 🕐 lunch & dinner Wed-Sun, breakfast Sat & Sun) Breakfast is hearty portions of eggs and extras – preferably eaten around chunky log tables in the courtyard. The dinner menu has no fear of cream and might involve fresh trout from the local trout farm. Cakes are divine – try the sour-cherry shortcake. There's occasional live entertainment – maybe a drum circle or band – in the courtyard.

Three Sugars (☎ 5966 9521; 3389 Warburton Hwy; mains $10-16; 🕐 breakfast & lunch) Head here to read the papers over a breakfast of soft poached eggs with all the trimmings or pick up a freshly made sandwich for lunch. There's also plenty of sweet goodies and quiche and *frittatas* on display.

Thoroughbred Bakery (☎ 5966 9857; 3400 Warburton Hwy; pies & snacks $4-7) A bakery selling bread, pies, vanilla slices and flaky pastries.

Alpine Retreat Hotel (☎ 5966 2411; www.alpineretreat.com.au; 12 Main St, Warburton; mains $14-22; 🕐 lunch & dinner) Drink in old-fashioned ambience at this rambling, Tudor-style hotel renovated in an Art Deco style. Fancy meals are served in the bistro and atrium, cheaper

meals in the bar, and Wednesday night is pizza night. Upmarket rooms include a buffet breakfast with the works and there's a TV in each room.

Reefton Hotel (☎ 5966 8555; 1600 Woods Point Rd, McMahons Creek; meals $7-15; 🕐 lunch & dinner) A slice of colonial Australia, the Reefton is as authentically local as it gets. Eat your fish and chips or burger out back near the kiln, rusty bikes and enormous bellows, or in the fancier restaurant. The beautiful winding drive is well frequented by motorcyclists who hang out on the timber veranda. There's live music on weekends. Just follow Warburton's Main Rd east – if you hit the Yarra Dam, you've gone too far.

Polish Jester (☎ 5966 9602; Warburton Hwy) It's probably best to give the food here a miss, but the bright-orange Jester, run by a Polish family, is a ripper spot to fuel up on some Polish lagers and have a chinwag with the chatty owners. It was formerly a swagman café, as the Aussie bush mural depicts.

THE DANDENONGS

☎ 03

On a clear day, the Dandenong Ranges can be seen from Melbourne. The 633m-high summit of Mt Dandenong is the highest peak – watch the sun set over the city from the lookout.

Within perfect day-trip distance, the hills are 35km east of the city. Stop for lunch at Olinda (the main town), Sassafras, Ferntree Gully or Emerald, and take a stroll through Dandenong Ranges National Park.

The area was intensively logged, and by the end of the 19th century most of the natural forests of majestic mountain ash had been cleared. In an attempt to mimic the European landscapes, the pioneering settlers planted deciduous trees – oaks, elms, poplars – and the landscape is now a patchwork of exotic and native plants with a lush understorey of tree ferns.

Information

Dandenong Ranges & Knox Visitor Information Centre (☎ 9758 7522; www.yarrarangestourism.com; 1211 Burwood Hwy, Upper Ferntree Gully; 🕐 9am-5pm) Outside the Upper Ferntree Gully train station.

Parks Victoria (☎ 13 19 63; www.parkweb.vic.gov.au; Ferntree Gully Picnic Ground, Mt Dandenong Tourist Rd;

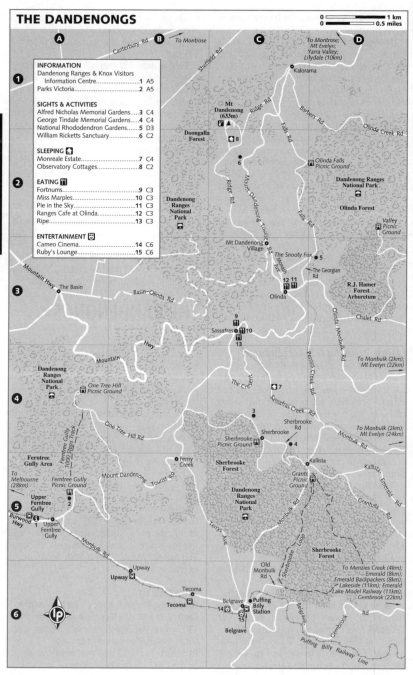

THE DANDENONGS

0 _____ 1 km
0 _____ 0.5 miles

INFORMATION
Dandenong Ranges & Knox Visitors
  Information Centre.........................**1** A5
Parks Victoria.....................................**2** A5

SIGHTS & ACTIVITIES
Alfred Nicholas Memorial Gardens.....**3** C4
George Tindale Memorial Gardens.....**4** C4
National Rhododendron Gardens.....**5** D3
William Ricketts Sanctuary................**6** C2

SLEEPING
Monreale Estate..................................**7** C4
Observatory Cottages.........................**8** C2

EATING
Fortnums...**9** C3
Miss Marples.....................................**10** C3
Pie in the Sky....................................**11** C3
Ranges Cafe at Olinda.......................**12** C3
Ripe..**13** C3

ENTERTAINMENT
Cameo Cinema..................................**14** C6
Ruby's Lounge...................................**15** C6

⏰ 8am-4.30pm Mon-Fri) Maps and advice on walking routes.

Sights & Activities
PUFFING BILLY
Usually full of excited kids, **Puffing Billy** (☎ 9754 6800; www.puffingbilly.com.au; Old Monbulk Rd, Belgrave; Belgrave-Gembrook return adult/child/family $40/20/81) is a restored steam train that toots and puffs its way through the picturesque hills and fern gullies of the Dandenongs. There are lots of different lunch and dinner packages (plus Santa specials around Christmas), but a picnic is also a top option. Timetables vary but generally there are up to six departures on holidays, three or four on other days (on days declared a total fire ban, Puffing Billy doesn't run). The Puffing Billy train station is a short stroll from Belgrave train station, the last stop on the Belgrave suburban line.

Near the pretty town of Emerald, about 15km east of Belgrave, **Emerald Lake Park** (www .emeraldlakepark.com.au; admission free, full-day parking $6), has picnic areas, a water slide and swimming pool, paddle boats for hire and the **Emerald Lake Model Railway** (☎ 5968 3455; 19 Edith Crt, Mount Dandenong; adult/child/family $5.50/3.50/15; ⏰ 11.30am-3pm Tue-Sun winter, till 4.30pm or 5.30pm summer). It's the largest model railway in Australia, with over 2km of tracks and miniature hills, tunnels, towns, shops and people.

DANDENONG RANGES NATIONAL PARK
Dandenong Ranges National Park is made up of the four largest areas of remaining forest in the Dandenongs. There are five sections of the park, all with walking tracks.

The **Ferntree Gully area**, named for its abundance of tree ferns, has several short walks, including the popular **1000 Steps Track** up to One Tree Hill picnic ground (about two hours return). This route is part of the **Kokoda Memorial Track**, which memorialises Australian servicemen who fought and died along New Guinea's Kokoda Trail in WWII.

Sherbrooke Forest has a towering cover of mountain ash trees and a lower level of silver wattles, blackwoods, sassafras and springy tree ferns. The trees are home to a large number of birds, including kookaburras, robins, currawongs and honeyeaters. You can reach the start of the **eastern loop walk** (three hours), roughly 1km from Belgrave station, by walking to the end of Old Monbulk Rd past the Puffing Billy station. Com-

bining this walk with a ride on Puffing Billy makes a great day out. Opposite the Alfred Nicholas Memorial Gardens is the **Sherbrooke Forest picnic ground** where crimson rosellas will peck birdseed from your hand (kids love it). Starting from **Grants picnic ground** near Kallista is the paved **Margaret Lester Forest Walk**, a short walk with wheelchair access (30 minutes), as well as the excellent **Sherbrooke Forest Loop** (about 2½ hours).

Doongalla Forest, on the western slopes of Mt Dandenong, is a mixture of dry forest and exotic plants. **Olinda Forest** has the most undisturbed habitat in the park, and the **Mt Evelyn area** has pockets of rare plant species as well as some strenuous walks.

If you just fancy a drive through the mountain ash, you'll find the roads in Sherbrooke Forest are among the most scenic. Try Monbulk Rd from Belgrave to Kallista, then Sherbrooke Rd from Kallista to the Mt Dandenong Tourist Rd.

WILLIAM RICKETTS SANCTUARY
The leafy **William Ricketts Sanctuary** (☎ 13 19 63; www.parkweb.vic.gov.au; Mt Dandenong Tourist Rd, Mt Dandenong; adult/child/family $6/2.50/14; ⏰ 10am-4.30pm) features Ricketts' kiln-fired clay and ceramic sculptures, inspired by years spent living with Aboriginal people. His personal philosophies shaped the sanctuary, which is set in damp fern gardens with trickling waterfalls, and features sculptures rising out of moss-covered rocks like spirits from the ground. Bus No 688 runs here from Croydon train station. The sanctuary is closed on total fire ban days.

GARDENS
The high rainfall and deep volcanic soils of the Dandenongs are perfect for agriculture, and the area has always provided Melbourne's markets with much of their produce. In spring, gardens and nurseries overflow with visitors who come to see the colourful displays of tulips, daffodils, azaleas and rhododendrons. The gardens are best visited in spring and autumn. All the gardens are closed on total fire ban days.

Giant eucalypts tower over shady lawns and brilliant flowerbeds at the **National Rhododendron Gardens** (☎ 9751 1980; The Georgian Rd, Olinda; adult/child/family $7.50/2.50/17 Sep-Nov, $6/2.50/15 Dec-Aug; ⏰ 10am-5pm). Apart from superb views and chirruping birds, there are groves of cherry blossoms, oaks, maples and beeches, and over 15,000 rhododendrons and 12,000 azaleas.

The **Alfred Nicholas Memorial Gardens** (☎ 9755 2912; Sherbrooke Rd, Sherbrooke; adult/child/family $6/2.50/15; ☺ 10am-5pm) were originally the grounds of the country mansion of Alfred Nicholas, co-founder of Aspro (the water-soluble, headache-relief pill) and the Nicholas pharmaceutical company. At their peak in the late 1930s these were the best private gardens in the country. A downhill walk leads to the very pretty ornamental lake.

Around a couple of bends to the east from the Alfred Nicholas Gardens, the **George Tindale Memorial Gardens** (☎ 9755 2912; 33 Sherbrooke Rd, Sherbrooke; adult/child/family $6/2.50/15; ☺ 10am-4.30pm) are worth a visit. These gardens are smaller and more intimate than the other gardens in the area.

Festivals & Events

The **Dandenong Ranges Folk Festival** (☎ 9729 1723; www.drfolk.com.au), in early March, attracts an excellent line-up of folk, blues and roots, and world-music performers.

Sleeping

A host of B&Bs are dotted throughout the hills. Check with the visitors centre (p175) for a comprehensive listing.

Emerald Backpackers (☎ 5968 4086; www.emerald backpackers.com.au; 2 Lakeview Ct, Emerald; dm/week $20/110; ☐) This basic hostel is geared towards travellers working in the area's plant nurseries, and there's work available year-round so book well ahead. It's an extremely laid-back place in a tranquil setting. It gets busy around 4pm when workers return from the nurseries.

Observatory Cottages (☎ 9751 2436; www.obser vatorycottages.com.au; 10 Observatory Rd, Mt Dandenong; r $150-270) Right near the peak of Mt Dandenong, these sumptuous cottages are among the best-value accommodation options in the area. They're beautifully maintained and furnished in a heritage style. There's a two-night minimum stay on weekends.

Monreale Estate (☎ 9755 1773; www.monreale -estate.com.au; 81 The Crescent, Sassafras; cottages $190-320; ☒) Monreale Estate is a beautifully restored 1920s country house with four luxurious cottages in its idyllic grounds. You will feel like you're hidden away from the world. In winter, the fireside spa is a

> ### THE AUTHOR'S CHOICE
> **Ripe** (☎ 03-9755 2100; 376-378 Mt Dandenong Tourist Rd, Sassafras; mains $8-16; ☺ breakfast & lunch) Lovers of gourmet produce should make a beeline for Ripe, a café-produce store in a cute weatherboard cottage with an outdoor deck. Local produce is found in all manner of jars and bottles, and there's hand-made chocolates, cheeses and deli items. The food is superb – well crafted, innovative and made with quality ingredients.

dream come true – you'll wonder why you don't live like this all the time.

Eating

Ranges at Olinda (☎ 9751 2133; 5 Olinda-Monbulk Rd, Olinda; meals $5-20; ☺ breakfast & lunch daily, dinner Tue-Sat) This stylish eatery serves up contemporary Mod Oz food with flair. Breakfasts (available until noon) are notably delicious. Lunch offerings include pasta and risotto dishes, and pita wraps filled with tandoori chicken or Mexican beef. You can eat alfresco on the deck overlooking the nursery.

Pie in the Sky (☎ 9751 2128; 43 Olinda-Monbulk Rd, Olinda; pies $3.50-5.50, lunch $8-12; ☺ 9.30am-5pm) Pies ahoy! Stop in for traditional favourites and more adventurous combos such as tomato and basil, korma chicken, *rendang* (coconut-based curry), and spinach, rice and feta. They also do sandwiches and have house-made cakes.

Old-fashioned tearooms include **Miss Marples** (☎ 9755 1610; mains $10-14; Sassafras; 382 Mt Dandenong Tourist Rd; ☺ lunch & afternoon tea), inspired by Agatha Christie novels, and the bright and airy **Fortnums** (☎ 9755 1200; 395 Mt Dandenong Tourist Rd, Sassafras; mains $8-17; ☺ lunch & afternoon tea).

Entertainment

Ruby's Lounge (☎ 9754 7445; 1648 Burwood Hwy, Belgrave; ☺ Tue-Sun) Head to Ruby's for a night out in the Dandenongs. By day, it's a café-restaurant. At night it transforms into a kick-ass music venue with live gigs from Thursday to Sunday and a capacity of 330. There are DJs, major touring acts and indie bands. Buy tickets over the phone or at the door.

Cameo Cinema (☎ 9754 7844; www.cameocinemas .com.au; 1628 Burwood Hwy, Belgrave; tickets adult/child $13/9) The cameo is a beautifully restored cinema that has kept its old-fashioned grace. See arthouse and new-release flicks on one of its four screens.

Getting There & Around

You really need your own transport to explore the Dandenongs properly. Cyclists should note that a lot of traffic travels along its otherwise pleasantly narrow, winding roads, especially on weekends. The Met's suburban trains run on the Belgrave line to the foothills of the Dandenongs (Zone 3 Met ticket, $12.40). From Upper Ferntree Gully train station it's a 10-minute walk to the start of the Ferntree Gully section of the national park.

MORNINGTON PENINSULA

Mornington Peninsula is a boot-shaped peninsula between Port Phillip and Western Port Bays. Its been a favourite summer destination since the 1870s, when paddle-steamers carried droves of holidaying Melburnians to Portsea and Sorrento.

The peninsula's ocean beaches, national parks, and wineries make it an action-packed day trip or weekend. Shop at craft and produce markets, pick your own fruit in orchards and berry farms, bushwalk, or snorkel and swim. Sorrento has the biggest range of accommodation and the best eating and drinking spots.

The calm 'front beaches' are on the Port Phillip side. The rugged ocean 'back beaches' face Bass Strait – there are stunning walks along this coastal strip, which is protected as part of Mornington Peninsula National Park.

Foodies and wine snobs will be in their element on the peninsula, which has blossomed into one of Victoria's prime wine-producing regions. There are dozens of wineries, mostly located in the elevated interior around Red Hill and Main Ridge, and a winery lunch is a definite highlight (p184). For a full briefing on wineries in the area, see p56.

Orientation

The Moorooduc Hwy becomes the Mornington Peninsula Fwy, which is the main entry point to the peninsula. Point Nepean

---

ROUND THE BAY IN A DAY

One of the best ways to appreciate Melbourne's bayside location is to circumnavigate Port Phillip Bay, making use of the ferry services between Queenscliff and Sorrento. It's an easy day trip by car (about 200km of driving), but you could make it a two-day trip, staying overnight on either the Bellarine or Mornington Peninsula. You could also do it by public transport or even by bicycle, as do 9000 cyclists each year in a charity fundraiser run by Bicycle Victoria (www.bv.com.au).

Going anticlockwise from Melbourne, the first highlight is the view from the West Gate Bridge, with the city skyscrapers behind you, the industrial areas to the west and the bay stretching south to the horizon. It's a quick 70km down the freeway to Geelong (p152), a city built on the wealth of Western District wool. Look carefully for the road that takes you the 30km to Queenscliff: although it's signposted, it's easy to miss. Ferry services run between Queenscliff and Sorrento (see p181). Book your ticket then look around Queenscliff, particularly the old fort and the grand old hotels.

You can see Port Phillip Heads from the ferry, but it gives them a fairly wide berth to avoid the dangerous current known as the Rip. You might see dolphins frolicking around the bow of the boat, as well as lots of sea birds around Mud Island and the unfinished island fortress called Pope's Eye (see also p181). The ferry runs parallel to the coast past Portsea, and you'll have a good view of the luxury cliff-top houses that overlook the bay. As you come in, the Sorrento beachfront is particularly attractive with its tall pine trees and old-style bandstand rotunda.

There's wonderful coastal scenery on the southern tip of the Mornington Peninsula, on both the Bass Strait side and the bay side, and especially in Mornington Peninsula National Park. Heading back towards the bright lights, you can take the Nepean Hwy, which follows the coast, or the freeway, which runs further inland. Take the more leisurely coastal route if you want to find out about urban sprawl. From Frankston to the city is over 40km of nonstop suburbia, although there are pretty little beaches along the way.

MORNINGTON PENINSULA

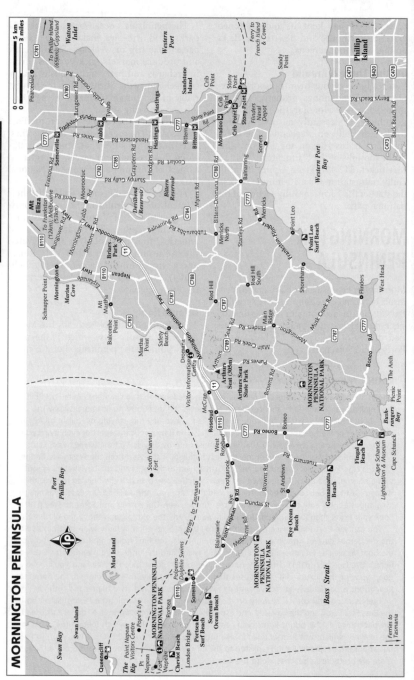

| 0 | 5 km |
| 0 | 3 miles |

Watson Inlet

To Phillip Island (65km); Gippsland

C781

Pearcedale

A780

Tyabb-Tooradin Rd

Western Port

Sandstone Island

Ferry to French Island & Cowes

Phillip Island

C473 B420 C478

Berrys Beach Rd

Ventnor Rd

Back Beach Rd

Hastings

Tyabb

Frankston-Flinders Rd

Tyabb

C777

Someville

Eramosa Rd

Jones Rd

Henderson Rd

Crib Point

Stony Point

Crib Point

Bittern

Stony Point

Morradoo

C777

Stony Point Rd

Flinders Naval Depot

Sandy Point

Western Port Bay

Mt Eliza

To Frankston (12km); Melbourne (53km)

B110

Mornington-Tyabb Rd

Moorooduc

Devilbend Reservoir

Bittern Reservoir

Craydens Rd

Hodgins Rd

Coolart Rd

C782

C785

Stumpy Gully Rd

Myers Rd

C788

Balnarring

Somers

Bungower Rd

Denil Rd

Bentons Rd

Briars Park

11

Balnarring Rd

Tubbarubba Rd

C784

Merricks North

Bittern-Dromana Rd

Merricks

Stanleys Rd

C777

Point Leo

Point Leo Surf Beach

Frankston-Flinders Rd

Schnapper Point

Mornington

Marina Cove

Esplanade

Nepean Hwy

B110

Mt Martha

C783

Balcombe Point

Martha Point

Safety Beach

Dromana

Visitor Information Centre

McCrae

Moorooduc Hwy

Peninsula Link Fwy

Red Hill

C788

C787

Red Hill South

Main Ridge

Main Creek Rd

C789

Seal Rd

Arthurs Seat

Arthurs Seat (305m)

Arthurs Seat State Park

Puvres Rd

Browns Rd

Red Hill

C787

Mornington-Flinders Rd

Musk Creek Rd

Shoreham

C777

Flinders

West Head

Boneo Rd

The Arch

Port Phillip Bay

Mud Island

South Channel Fort

Swan Island

Swan Bay

Queenscliff

The Point Nepean Rip Visitors Centre

Pt Nepean

Fort Nepean

Cheviot Beach

London Bridge

Portsea Surf Beach

Portsea

Sorrento

Sorrento Ocean Beach

B110

Polperro Dolphin Swims

Pope's Eye

MORNINGTON PENINSULA NATIONAL PARK

Ferries to Tasmania

Blairgowrie

Point Nepean Rd

Rosebud

West Rosebud

B110

Boneo Rd

C777

Boneo

MORNINGTON PENINSULA NATIONAL PARK

Rye

Tootgarook

Rye Rd

Dundas St

Browns Rd

St Andrews

Truemans Rd

Gunnamatta Beach

MORNINGTON PENINSULA NATIONAL PARK

Rye Ocean Beach

Melbourne Rd

Cape Schanck Lightstation & Museum

Cape Schanck

Bushrangers Bay

Finsal Beach

Picnic Point

Bass Strait

Ferries to Tasmania

Rd joins the Mornington Peninsula Fwy – alternately, exit around Mornington and take the coast roads, which run along Port Phillip Bay, via Dromana, Rosebud, Blairgowrie and Sorrento to Portsea. The back beaches between Rye, Cape Schanck and Flinders are mostly national park and largely undeveloped. There's a string of small townships along Western Port Bay, including Flinders, Shoreham, Point Leo, Somers and Hastings.

Information

Antipodes Bookshop Gallery (☎ 03-5984 4217; 138 Ocean Beach Rd, Sorrento)
Burnt Toast Cybercafé (☎ 03-5976 5540; Vale St Arcade, Mornington; per 30 min $3; ⏰ 9am-5pm Mon-Fri)
National Australia Bank (☎ 13 22 65; 67 Ocean Beach Rd, Sorrento)
Peninsula Visitor Information Centre (☎ 03-5987 3078, 1800 804 009; www.visitmorningtonpeninsula.org; Nepean Hwy, Dromana; ⏰ 9am-5pm)
Post office (☎ 03-5984 2200; 10 Ocean Beach Rd, Sorrento)
South Coast Medical (☎ 03-5984 5955; 133 Ocean Beach Rd, Sorrento) For 24-hour medical emergency service.

Festivals & Events

Red Hill Community Market (☎ 03-5974 4710; Red Hill Recreation Reserve; ⏰ 8am-1pm 1st Sat of month Sep-May) Held around the football/cricket oval, this old-timer has been running since 1975. Stock up on fresh produce and crafts and snack on grilled corncobs and home-made lemonade.
Sorrento Street Festival (☎ 03-5984 1762; Ocean Beach Rd; Oct) A community festival with a parade down the blocked-off main street, face painting, music and a petting zoo.

Getting There & Around

BUS & TRAIN

Met trains (Zone 3 Met ticket, $12.40; one hour; at least one hourly) run from Flinders St Station to Frankston. From Frankston train station, **Portsea Passenger Service** (☎ 03-5986 5666; www.buslines.com.au/portsea) bus No 788 runs to/from Portsea (one way $8.20; 90 minutes; every half-hour Monday to Friday, hourly on Saturday, every two hours on Sunday), via Mornington, Dromana and Sorrento.
Peninsula Bus Lines (☎ 03-9786 7088; www.buslines.com.au/peninsula) bus Nos 782 and 783 run to/from Frankston train station, via Hastings, to Flinders (one way $4.60, 90 minutes, four daily Monday to Friday).

> **OUT IN THE BAY**
>
> Apart from the seals, dolphins and sea birds, you'll see some unusual and interesting sights when you take one of the cruises from Sorrento Pier out into the bay. The **South Channel Fort** is a small artificial island near the entrance to the bay. It was built in the 1880s to protect Melbourne against a perceived threat of Russian invasion. Many of the 19th-century fortifications and underground passages remain intact, and the island is also a protected haven for birdlife. **Pope's Eye** is the foundation ring of another (unfinished) fort that is now home to a seal colony, and the **Mud Island Wildlife Reserve** is a bird haven.

CAR & MOTORCYCLE

If you're after a more scenic drive than the freeways, take Point Nepean Rd, exit around Mornington and drive the scenic, sedate coast roads (see p179). Via the freeway, the trip from Melbourne takes just over an hour; via the scenic route, around 1½ to 1¾ hours.

FERRY

Car & Passenger Ferries (☎ 03-5258 3244; www.searoad.com.au; one-way foot passenger/2 adults & car $9/48) runs a daily service to/from Sorrento to Queenscliff. From the Sorrento ferry terminal ferries depart hourly from 7am to 6pm (reduced sailings in winter).

Inter Island Ferries (☎ 9585 5730; www.interisland ferries.com.au; return adult/child/bike $18/8/8; ⏰ every 30min 8.30am-5pm, plus 7pm Friday) runs daily to/from Stony Point to Cowes (in Phillip Island) via French Island. There are at least two trips daily year-round.

SORRENTO

☎ 03 / pop 1200

Seaside Sorrento was the site of Victoria's first official European settlement. It was established by an expedition of convicts, marines, civil officers and free settlers that arrived from England in 1803. In summer the town's empty beach houses fill with stressed-out Melburnians in need of R&R, and it heaves with an influx of tourists. In winter, it reverts to a sleepy village and die-hard surfers don wetsuits to tackle the frothy breaks of Sorrento's windswept beaches.

AROUND MELBOURNE

Sorrento has the biggest range of accommodation, cafés and restaurants on the peninsula. Dolphin swims and cruises are incredibly popular, and a trip to Queenscliff on the ferry is a fun outing.

Sights & Activities

There are some grand **19th-century buildings** built from locally quarried limestone around town, including the Sorrento Hotel (1871), Continental Hotel (1875) and Koonya (1878).

There are plenty of **swimming** and **walking** opportunities at Sorrento's wide, sandy beaches and bluffs. At low tide, the **rock pool** at the back beach is a safe spot for adults and children to swim and **snorkel**. The 10-minute climb up to **Coppins Lookout** for peninsula and bay views is worthwhile.

Apart from four **graves** that are believed to hold the remains of 30 original settlers, there's little evidence of Sorrento's original settlement. The **Collins Settlement Historic Site** (Leggett Way), midway between Sorrento and Blairgowrie, marks the settlement site at Sullivan Bay, and a display centre tells its story.

Several operators offer sightseeing and dolphin-watching cruises. The following tours both depart from Sorrento Pier, bookings are essential (you can book online) and cruises run for three to four hours. See also Cape Schanck (p185) for horse riding.

Moonraker Charters (☎ 5984 4211; www.moonraker charters.com.au; adult/child sightseeing $40/35, swimming $80/65; 🕗 8am, noon & 4pm Oct-May, 9am & 1pm Jun-Sep) Offers dolphin swims and sightseeing cruises.

Polperro Dolphin Swims (☎ 5988 8437; www.polperro .com.au; adult/child observers $40/30, swimmers $100; 🕗 8.30am & 1.30pm Oct-Apr) Offers swims with bottlenose dolphins in Port Phillip Bay, and sightseeing tours. Departs from Sorrento Pier; bookings essential.

Sleeping

Prices rise with the temperature, and during mid-December to the end of January, Easter and school holidays, you should definitely book. Although there's a big range of accommodation in Sorrento, it tends to be overpriced.

Sorrento Backpackers Hostel YHA (☎ 5984 4323; www.yha.com.au/hostels/details.cfm?hostelid=105; 3 Miranda St; dm $29; 🖳) An easy-to-miss and architecturally uninspiring building from the outside, the Sorrento YHA receives rave reviews for its cosy ambience. It's a purpose-built hostel

and facilities are of a high standard. The staff organise horse riding, snorkelling and diving trips. Take bus No 788 to stop 18.

Oceanic Whitehall Guesthouse (☎ 5984 4166; www.virtualsorrento.com.au/whitehall.htm; 231 Ocean Beach Rd; r $100-200) This historic, limestone two-storey guesthouse near the back beach offers pristine views from its timber veranda. The majority of rooms share a bathroom but some have en suites and spas; all are clean, with plenty of natural light. At the time of writing, rooms were in the process of being renovated.

Hotel Sorrento (☎ 5984 2206; www.hotelsorrento .com.au; 5-15 Hotham Rd; motel r $140-275, apts $220-340) The legendary Hotel Sorrento has a swag of accommodation. 'Sorrento on the Park' offers standard and overpriced motel rooms in need of a revamp, but the 'On the Hill' double and family apartments are fab. Airy living spaces have modern appliances, spacious bathrooms and glorious views from private balconies. At the time of writing the Heritage suites were closed for renovations.

Sorrento Beach Motel (☎ 5984 1356; www.sorrento beachmotel.com.au; 780 Melbourne Rd; r $140-190; 🐾) Away from Sorrento's main drag, a bright, multicoloured paint job has given this motel's exterior a jaunty lift. Inside, the rooms are a standard motel set-up. The cheaper rooms are fairly underwhelming – dark and lacking in views – but the fancier spa rooms are better value.

Carmel of Sorrento (☎ 5984 3512; www.carmelof sorrento.com.au; 142 Ocean Beach Rd; s $150, d $175-200, self-contained unit $200) This historic limestone cottage in the centre of Sorrento has been tastefully restored in period style. It has a cosy lounge, four Edwardian-style B&B guest rooms with private bathrooms, and two self-contained units out the back. If you love breakfast in bed, a cooked breakfast can be delivered to your door.

Ocean Beach Sorrento (☎ 5984 0094; www.ocean beachsorrento.com.au; self-contained cottage $200) Run by the same owners as Carmel of Sorrento, Ocean Beach is ideal for two couples travelling together (but each en-suite room can be rented individually too). It's a traditionally restored 1896 cottage with immaculate and tasteful period-style rooms. A delicious cooked breakfast is included in the rates.

Oceanic Sorrento (☎ 5984 4166; www.oceanicgroup .com.au; 234 Ocean Beach Rd; apts $200-300; 🐾) Across the road from Whitehall Guesthouse are Oceanic's architecturally designed two-storey apartments with a fresh white interior and private courtyards. In the loft bedrooms, super–king-size beds have an abundance of plump pillows, feather-down doonas and quality linen. The kitchen has modern stainless-steel appliances and there's an in-house movie channel.

Eating

Sorrento's many eateries consist mainly of relaxed cafés and delis. You'll find most of them on Ocean Beach Rd and by the water.

Stringer's (☎ 5984 2010; 2 Ocean Beach Rd; sandwiches & snacks $4-8; ☺ breakfast & lunch) Long-running Stringer's is a Sorrento staple. All the food is home-made and Mornington Peninsula wines are for sale. Grab a smoked-chicken roti wrap or a crusty filled roll for lunch. Regulars love the mini egg-and-bacon pies for breakfast and rich brownies for that post-surf pick-me-up.

Baths (☎ 5984 1500; 3278 Point Nepean Rd; mains $17-30; ☺ breakfast, lunch & dinner) Occupying the site that used to be the sea baths, this sunny café-restaurant offers big breakfasts and premium waterfront views. At lunch and dinner the menu edges into more sophisticated fare, and it's very civilised sitting on the deck with a marlin steak and glass of sauvignon blanc.

Green Olive Gourmet (☎ 5984 5800; 119-125 Ocean Beach Rd; meals $5-18; ☺ breakfast & lunch) This licensed, casual café and produce store serves quality food simply and stylishly. Lounge at the communal table reading the papers over breakfast, or grab a ready-made meal to heat up at home. Lunch-time baguettes filled with deli items are delicious.

Shell's (☎ 5984 5133; 85 Ocean Beach Rd; mains $11-18; ☺ breakfast, lunch & dinner) Slap-bang on Sorrento's main drag, Shell's is an easy-pleaser that attracts starving locals from miles around, especially for breakfast. Big plates arrive laden with thumping portions – if it's too much you can always feed some to the curious sparrows hopping about.

Sunnyside Up (☎ 5984 4255; 3293 Point Nepean Rd; meals $10-17; ☺ breakfast & lunch Thu-Mon, breakfast, lunch & dinner daily in summer) A popular breakfast spot with sea views and a sun-drenched outdoor deck where dogs look longingly at their owners for a bit of bacon. Chilled waiters run mounds of scramblers or soft poached eggs to regulars and weekenders.

Just Fine Food (☎ 5984 4666; 23 Ocean Beach Rd; meals $4-14; ☺ breakfast & lunch) A gourmet deli that gets crammed with hungry customers clamouring for handmade chocolates, flaky pastries and top-notch cakes. Savouries and smallgoods are also on offer, either to eat in or take away.

Smokehouse (☎ 5984 1246; 182 Ocean Beach Rd; pizzas $11-20, mains $24-27; ☺ dinner Thu-Sun, daily summer & school holidays) Head to family-friendly Smokehouse for steaming crispy-thin pizzas, lifted by oar-shaped paddles from the bulbous wood-fired oven. You can choose your own pizza toppings or opt for heftier mains such as pastas, risottos and grills.

Continental Cafe (☎ 5984 2201; 1 Ocean Beach Rd; mains $17-26; ☺ breakfast, lunch & dinner) At the Continental Hotel, this is where you head for fish and chips and stylish Mod Oz grub; eat at weathered picnic tables overlooking the bay or inside the funky and cosy café.

Hotel Sorrento (☎ 5984 2206; www.hotelsorrento .com.au; 5-15 Hotham Rd; mains $18-26; ☺ breakfast, lunch & dinner) Has quality, Mod Oz food including wood-fired pizzas – and terrific views.

Drinking & Entertainment

Like most seasonal resorts, the peninsula comes alive in summer and buzzes for three months before going into hibernation for the rest of the year. However, the peninsula's pub scene is always lively.

Start with a few beers and game of pool while watching a live band at the rowdy Hotel Sorrento (opposite), or Portsea Hotel (p184). Then, kick on at the **Continental Hotel** (☎ 5984 2201; 1 Ocean Beach Rd; ☺ nightclub 9pm-3am Sat), which has a bar (open on weekends and public holidays) and nightclub. **McCrae bus lines** (☎ 5986 2471, 0427-301 868) performs an admirable service of transporting revellers to/from Sorrento to the Portsea Hotel.

Movie buffs will love **Sorrento Atheneum** (☎ 5984 2903; www.sorrentocinemas.com.au; Ocean Beach Rd), which screens all the latest releases.

PORTSEA

☎ 03 / pop 800

At the western tip of the peninsula, Portsea is where many of Melbourne's wealthiest families have built their seaside mansions. It's the starting point of the **Melbourne to Hobart Yacht Race** and there are some fantastic beaches. Head to the **back beach** to see **London Bridge**, an impressive natural rock formation, and hang-gliders leaping off the

TOP TEN LIQUID LUNCHES

We all know food enhances the flavours and complexities of wine, but for many gourmets drinking wine is merely an excuse to bring out the flavours of food. In winery kitchens in the regions around Melbourne, some of the region's top chefs are carving a name for themselves, and a gourmet lunch overlooking vineyards, mountains or the Bass Strait is always cause for celebration. Restaurants range from fine-dining affairs to casual cafés with menus offering Mod Oz cuisine made from fresh, local ingredients and produce. If lunch is over, most places have superb cheese or *charcuterie* (cured or smoked meats) platters with ripe local cheeses, smallgoods and sweet muscatels.

The heading for this boxed text could easily be Top 30 Liquid Lunches and the following suggestions are just a smattering. Don't try to tackle them all on the same day! If you're also after wineries, see p56.

Spuntino (☎ 5989 6565; www.tgallant.com.au; T'Gallant Winery, cnr Mornington-Flinders & Shands Rds, Main Ridge; pizzas $14-26; ☺ lunch)

Main Ridge Estate (☎ 5989 2686; www.mre.com.au; 80 William Rd, Red Hill; mains $12-20; ☺ lunch Sun)

Paringa Estate (☎ 5989 2669; www.paringaestate.com.au; 44 Paringa Rd, Red Hill South; mains $15-26; ☺ lunch Wed-Sun, dinner Fri & Sat)

Max's at Red Hill Estate (☎ 5931 0177; www.maxsatredhillestate.com.au; 53 Red Hill Rd, Red Hill South; mains $16-24; ☺ lunch daily, dinner Fri & Sat)

Oakridge Cafe (☎ 9739 1920; 864 Maroondah Highway, Coldstream; mains $15-25; ☺ lunch)

Rochford's Eyton (☎ 5962 2119; www.rochfordwines.com; cnr Maroondah Hwy & Hill Rd, Coldstream; mains $21-30; ☺ lunch)

Yering Station (☎ 9730 2188; www.yering.com; 38 Melba Hwy, Yering; mains $27-30; ☺ lunch) There's also a produce store, café & farmers' market (p170).

La Campagna (☎ /fax 5964 3704; 176 Rogers Rd, Cape Schanck; mains $11-17; ☺ lunch Sat & Sun)

Pettavel Winery (☎ 5266 1120; www.pettavel.com; 65 Pettavel Rd, Waurn Ponds; mains $26; ☺ lunch)

Kilgour Estate (☎ /fax 5251 2223; 85 McAdams Lane, Bellarine; mains $17-35; ☺ lunch daily, dinner Fri & Sat)

cliff-face. This ocean beach has wild surf and can be dangerous for swimming, so keep between the flags. The **front beaches** offer more sheltered swimming spots.

Dive Victoria (☎ 5984 3155; www.divevictoria .com.au; 3752 Point Nepean Rd; snorkelling with gear $65, 1-/2-dives without gear $50/100) runs diving and snorkelling trips and hires equipment; there are a couple of other dive companies near the Portsea Hotel that also operate trips.

Portsea's beating heart is the sprawling and iconic Tudor-style **Portsea Hotel** (☎ 5984 2213; www.portseahotel.com.au; Point Nepean Rd; s $50-175, d $90-200, lunch & dinner mains $17-30; ☺ breakfast, lunch & dinner). In the restaurant, massive Mod Oz portions are on offer alongside a solid wine list, and the open-air deck overlooks Portsea Pier and the bay. Clean and comfortable rooms provide pub accommodation – room 1 has a corner aspect, open fire, kitchen and TV; room 32 has bay views from its balcony. Be warned though, it's noisy on Friday and Saturday nights when live bands play downstairs.

MORNINGTON PENINSULA NATIONAL PARK

Originally a quarantine station and army base, **Mornington Peninsula National Park office** (☎ 13 19 63; www.parkweb.vic.gov.au; Point Nepean Rd, Portsea; ☺ 9am-5pm, until dusk Jan) opened in 1988 as Point Nepean National Park but was subsequently renamed. Most of the park's attractions are around Point Nepean, but the park also includes the ocean beaches up to and including Cape Schanck and a section of land in the peninsula's interior.

Point Nepean

Land rights have been raging for years on Point Nepean as it was originally suggested that the defence land on the point was going to be sold to property developers, angering the locals. But, after years of highly contentious debate, the UXO (unexploded ordinates) land on Point Nepean has been handed over to Parks Victoria, and the quarantine land will be handed over in the next five years. Parks Victoria are in the process of writing a management plan that will incorporate all three areas of Point Nepean (Mornington Peninsula National Park, the UXO land and the quarantine land), and will eventually change the name to Point Nepean National Park.

Full of super-helpful staff, the well-run **visitors centre** (☎ 03-5984 4276; Point Nepean; ⏰ 10am-5pm) is your first port of call. From here, you can walk or cycle to the point, 12km return (walk or bicycle admission adult/child/family $7.20/3.20/18, bike hire per three hours $15); or take the Point Explorer, a hop-on, hop-off bus service that stops at walks along the way (one-way transport including admission $11/6/26, return $13/8/34). There are plenty of **trails** throughout the park – the visitors centre has all the maps you'll need. From October to April the park is open from 9am to 5pm (6pm in January).

Observatory Point is a sheltered picnic spot with wheelchair access from Gunners car park – en route, take a look at the **graves** of Victoria's first settlers and shipwreck victims.

Cheviot Beach is famous as the spot where former prime minister Harold Holt supposedly drowned in 1967. There's a memorial stone and original, slightly decayed chairs overlooking the wild surf. You may hear the expression 'Do the Harold Holt', which is rhyming slang for 'Do the bolt'.

At the tip is **Fort Nepean**, which played an important role in Australian defence from the 1880s to 1945. On the parade ground are two historic **gun barrels** that fired the first Allied shots in WWI and WWII (see below).

Ocean Beaches

The southwestern coastline of the peninsula faces Bass Strait. Along here are the beautiful and rugged **ocean beaches** of Blairgowrie, Rye, St Andrews, Gunnamatta and Cape Schanck. There are a series of points and bays backdropped by cliffs, sand dunes,

---

THE FIRST SHOT

In August 1914 a German ship was on its way out from Melbourne to the Heads when news of the declaration of war came through on the telegraph. A shot across its bows at Portsea resulted in the ship's capture. The first shot in WWII turned out to be at an unidentified Tasmanian freighter!

---

spectacular scenery and tidal rock pools – this is the fragile natural habitat of coastal birdlife, surfers and rock-fishing people.

It's possible to walk all the way from Portsea to Cape Schanck (26km) along the ocean beaches. It's a fairly easy hike, but it takes around eight hours to walk.

Swimming or surfing is dangerous at these beaches: the undertow and rips can be severe and drownings have occurred. You should only swim in the lifeguard-patrolled areas at Gunnamatta and Portsea during summer.

Cape Schanck
☎ 03

Built in 1859 **Cape Schanck Lightstation** (☎ 5988 6184, 0500 527 891; adult/child/family museum only $8/6/22, museum & lighthouse $10/8/28, daily adult/child $50/25, parking $4; ⏰ 10am-4pm) is a spick-and-span operational lighthouse, which has a kiosk, museum and information centre. Guided tours are held half-hourly in summer, less often at other times. You can stay at **Cape Schanck B&B** (☎ 5988 6184; www.austpacinns.com.au; d $150) in the limestone Keeper's Cottage.

From the lightstation, wander along the **boardwalk** that leads to the cape – the views are phenomenal.

Longer **walks** include tracks around **Bushrangers Bay**, which starts at the Bushrangers Bay car park and winds down to Cape Schanck (return two hours); and **Fingal Beach** (return one hour), which has a picnic area and is 2km north of the Cape.

Ace-Hi Ranch (☎ 5988 6262; www.ace-hi.com.au; 810 Boneo Rd, Cape Schanck; cabins d $80-90, 1-/2-/3-hr rides $28/50/65) is a family-friendly horse-riding ranch and wildlife park with basic cabins. Their bush and beach ride is a fun way to explore – but you'll have sore legs the next day!

PENINSULA INTERIOR & AROUND

Melbourne's urban sprawl extends beyond Frankston to Mornington, Mt Martha and Dromana. The bay **beaches** along this strip are popular with weekenders escaping a Melbourne heatwave, but are largely the domain of residential families.

Briars Park (☎ 03-5974 3686; www.mornpen.vic.gov.au; Nepean Hwy, Mt Martha; admission free, homestead tours adult/child/family $4.50/2/10; ⏰ 10am-4pm), centred around an 1851 homestead, is a gorgeous spot for picnics and walks to bird hides, and eucalypt woodland where you

---

MORNINGTON PENINSULA WINERIES

For comprehensive information on wineries and wine-touring, see p56, and for winery lunches, p184. The *Mornington Peninsula Wine Touring Map* is available from the Peninsula Visitor Information Centre (p181), as well as many of the wineries.

---

might spot koalas, echidnas or kangaroos. The homestead houses the Dame Melba books and Napoleonic collection, which includes political comic strips of the era, locks of Napoleon's hair and his death mask.

Green thumbs will love **Heronswood** (☎ 03-5987 1877; 105 La Trobe Pde, Dromana; adult/child $7/free; ☯ 9.30am-4.30pm Mon-Fri), an 1864 stone building surrounded by established gardens. Coming from Melbourne, the turn-off is just past the visitors centre in Dromana.

Around **Red Hill** and **Main Ridge** you'll enter the rolling hills of the peninsula's wine country. Most of the **wineries** dotted throughout the countryside are small-scale producers, and many are individually run. It's a beautiful drive, marred only by the discussion of 'Who's driving?'. For a more casual bite, make a pit stop at the licensed **Red Hill Bakery** (☎ 03-5989 2733; Shop 5, Point Leo-Shoreham Rd; meals $3-13; ☯ 6am-6pm) for a posh pie (rabbit and Pinot?) and flaky sweet pastry; there's jazz on Sunday afternoons in summer.

Sunny Ridge Strawberry Farm (☎ 03-5989 6273; cnr Mornington-Flinders & Shands Rd, Main Ridge; strawberries/kg $10-12; ☯ Sat & Sun 11am-4pm, tasting tours 11am & 2pm), Australia's largest individual strawberry producer, has dedicated pick-your-own strawberry (November to April) and raspberry (December to March) patches. Berry hankerings are satiated with majestic ice-cream sundaes or the bizarre strawberry wines. From November to April the farm is open daily from 9am to 5pm.

Arthurs Seat State Park

A top spot for a barbecue and bushwalk, **Arthurs Seat State Park** (☎ 03-8627 4699; Arthurs Seat Rd, Dromana) includes several tourist attractions. It's a scenic drive to the summit (305m), and the winding road is a motorcyclist's dream. Stop off at **Murray's Lookout** (247m) and **Seawinds** (Purves Rd; admission free; ☯ 10am-5pm), a public sculpture garden near the summit, for panoramas of the bay, pen-

insula and distant Melbourne skyline. You can also get to the summit via **Arthurs Seat Chairlift** (☎ 03-5987 2565; www.arthursseatchairlift .com.au; Arthur's Seat Rd, Dromana; adult return/single $12/8, child $8/6; ☯ 11am-5pm Mon-Fri, 11am-5.30pm Sat, 11am-6pm Sun), which reopened in October 2004 with watertight safety and a sabotage-proof system. In summer the chairlift opens at 10am.

Kids continue to be bamboozled in the three formal mazes at **Arthur's Seat Maze** (☎ 03-5981 8449; www.arthursseatmaze.com.au; 55 Purves Rd; adult/child $12/8; ☯ 10am-6pm), set among sculpture gardens. The **Maize Maze** (☯ Feb-Apr) is a seasonal maze that changes its design each year.

McCrae Homestead (☎ 03-5981 2866; 11 Beverly Rd, McCrae; adult/child $5/4; ☯ noon-4.30pm Wed, Sat & Sun) is an 1846 timber-slab cottage classified by the National Trust. It houses a collection of colonial furniture and the paintings and writings of pioneer Georgina McCrae.

On top of Arthurs Seat, **Arthurs Hotel** (☎ 03-5981 4444; 790 Arthurs Seat Rd, Arthurs Seat; mains $18-26; ☯ breakfast, lunch & dinner) is a family-friendly hotel, restaurant and café with eagle-eye views and quality food such as duck, calamari and pasta dishes.

WESTERN PORT

Western Port Bay's mainly residential towns are less developed and crowded than their Port Phillip Bay contemporaries, though populations gently swell at weekends and in summer when Melburnians escape to their beach-houses. From Flinders to Hastings, the tiny towns – including **Shoreham**, **Point Leo**, **Merricks**, **Balnarring** and **Somers** – are strung along the low-key coastal strip. The **beaches** are slightly less glamorous than 'the other side', as the shores are often cluttered with clumps of seaweed, but they're still beautiful and mellow places to play, collect shells and swim. The natural environment on this part of the peninsula is also more fertile, with its pine trees and green hills starkly contrasting with the sand dunes and coastal scrub of the Port Phillip side.

Flinders has a busy fishing fleet, rugged beaches with rocky point breaks for surfers and oceanside **golf courses**. From the point at West Head there are views to Phillip Island and, on one side, a sheltered harbour with a jetty. If the wind is southeasterly, you'll often see hang-gliders launching off the cliff-tops here. **Flinders Village Cafe** (☎ 03-5989 0700; 49 Cook St; dinner mains $10-25; ⌚ breakfast & lunch daily, dinner Sat & Sun) is a serene and popular spot for quality food.

Coolart Wetlands & Homestead (☎ 03-5931 4000; www.visitor.com.au/coolart.html; Lord Somers Rd, Somers; adult/child $7/3.50; ⌚ 10am-5pm) is a historic mansion with some interesting old photos, landscaped gardens, nature displays and a great wetlands sanctuary with a wide variety of birdlife – it has seven distinct habitats and 150 bird species.

Mulberry Hill (☎ 03-5971 4138; Golf Links Rd, Baxter; admission by donation; ⌚ tours 1.30pm, 2.15pm & 3pm Sun), is the former home of Joan and Sir Daryl Lindsay. Joan wrote *Picnic at Hanging Rock*, published in 1967, while Sir Daryl was a noted Australian painter.

FRENCH ISLAND

☎ 03 / pop 65

Exposed and windswept, French Island, in Western Port, is two-thirds national park and Victoria's largest island. It retains a wonderful sense of remoteness and tranquillity. Using alternative energy sources, its handful of environmentally aware residents live ecologically, organically and sustainably. The coastline is mainly salt marsh and mangroves, there's farmland in the south, and the gently undulating interior has open woodland with blooming wildflowers in spring.

Tankerton is the main settlement and where the ferry docks. There's little more than the licensed **French Island General Store** (☎ 5980 1209; Lot 1, Tankerton Rd, Tankerton), which sells everything from bait, ice, organic cappuccinos, fresh produce, souvenirs and hardware. It's also the post office and has Eftpos. The **French Island Tourist Information Centre** (☎ 5980 1241; www.frenchisland.org; Lot 4, Bayview Rd) has sporadic opening hours.

Six settlements were established on the island in the 1890s. Growing and drying chicory, the coffee substitute, developed into a thriving industry, and the remains of **kilns** and original **homesteads** are dotted around the island. From 1916 to 1975 it was home to McLeod Prison, a prison farm that's now a guesthouse.

The main attractions are **bushwalks**, **bicycle rides**, a huge variety of bird species, including **mutton-bird rookeries**, and one of Australia's largest **koala colonies**.

Tours

French Island Eco Tours (☎ 1300 307 054; www.frenchislandecotours.com.au; half-/full day tour $65/85; ⌚ Thu & Sun) Runs tours around the island and explores McLeod Eco farm. Stories focus on the island's heritage, wildlife and unique perspective of living sustainably with nature. Tours depart from Stony Point (on the peninsula) and Cowes (on Phillip Island). Price includes ferry transfers and lunch.

French Island Llama Expeditions (☎ 5980 1287; www.fillamas.com.au; tour $75) Hang out with llamas on this quirky and relaxed day-long tour, which includes a walk through the island's first olive grove and a gourmet picnic lunch.

Sleeping & Eating

McLeod Eco Farm (☎ 5678 0155; www.mcleodecofarm.com; McLeod Rd; s/d bunkrooms $35/60, d guesthouse $65/130) A historic property (formerly the island's prison), with kitchen facilities, lounge, organic farm and beautiful gardens. It's 21km from the ferry, but pick-ups are included in the price. Rooms are very basic, but guesthouse rooms are more upmarket.

French Island B&B (☎ 5980 1209; www.frenchislandbandb.com.au; Lot 1, Tankerton Rd; s/d $55/110, fully catered $90/180) Next door to the French Island General Store is this simple, comfortable two-bedroom cottage that's suitable for families or two couples travelling together. It's fully self-contained and includes a breakfast basket and transport to/from the island.

Tortoise Head Guest House (☎ 5980 1234; www.tortoisehead.net; 10 Tankerton Rd, Tankerton; s/d $70/140) A short walk from the ferry, this place has knockout water views, but is a little worn in parts for the price. The cabins are the best value. Breakfast is included.

French Island Farm (☎ 5980 1278; www.frenchisland.org/business.html; 4 The Anchorage, Tankerton; s $80-90, d $140-160) This spotless option offers 360° views from a sunny hilltop, kitchen, lounge, en-suite bathrooms and free pickups. Rates include a cooked breakfast with the works.

There are two camping grounds on the island. One is the privately run **Bayview Camping Ground** (☎ 5980 1241; unpowered sites per 2 people $10) at the back of the tourist information centre. It has a toilet, shower and washbasin. The other is the beachside **Fairhaven camping ground** (☎ 5980 1294; www.parkweb.vic.gov.au; unpowered sites free) on the western shore in French Island National Park. It has a compost toilet, fires aren't permitted and you must carry everything in and out. Bookings are essential.

Getting There & Around

Inter Island Ferries (☎ 9585 5730; www.interisland ferries.com.au) runs a service to/from Tankerton to Stony Point (adult/child/bike $9/4/4, 10 minutes, at least two daily).

Met trains run from Melbourne to Stony Point (Zone 3 Met ticket, $12.40; one hour 50 minutes, six daily) – you change to a diesel train at Frankston.

There are no sealed roads so riding can be tough going, but you can hire **bikes** (per day $11) from the kiosk at the jetty on summer weekends and public holidays, and from the general store (p187).

PHILLIP ISLAND

☎ 03

Phillip Island is a penguin parade of subcultures. Shops sell petrol-head paraphernalia for the Motorcycle Grand Prix or penguin-related tourist tack, while next door you'll find hippies sniffing essential oils. Alongside holidaying Melburnians, sun-bronzed surfers mingle with sheep and cattle farmers in Cowes' cafés and restaurants, while Japanese tourists feed hot chips to squawking gulls.

The island's 6700-strong winter population swells to 40,000 in summer when it's packed with holidaying families and tourists. So what's there to do? Phillip Island has a selection of excellent beaches, from the wild surf at Woolamai and the other south coast beaches, to sheltered bay beaches on the north side. There are also chances to see some of Australia's native fauna at the insanely popular Penguin Parade, and Koala Conservation Centre.

Orientation

Phillip Island – about 100 sq km in area – is at the entrance to Western Port Bay, 125km southeast of Melbourne. It's connected to the mainland by a bridge across the Narrows from San Remo to Newhaven. Cowes, on the north coast, is the main town, with sheltered beaches, pubs and the most accommodation; nearly everything is along Thompson Ave or the Esplanade. South is where you'll find the surf beaches. On the east coast is Rhyll, a small fishing village with the island's main boat ramp. Ventnor is another small settlement on the west.

Information

Cowes Medical Centre (☎ 5952 2072; 14 Warley Ave, Cowes)

National Australia Bank (☎ 5952 3613; 50 Thompson Ave)

Post office (☎ 13 13 18; 73-79 Thompson Ave)

Visitors centre (☎ 5956 7447, 1300 366 422; www .phillipisland.net.au; Phillip Island Rd, Newhaven; ☼ 9am-5pm, to 6pm Jan) The centre sells the 3 Parks Pass (adult/child/family $28/14/72), which covers admission to the Penguin Parade, Koala Conservation Centre and Churchill Island. Tickets are also available at the individual attractions.

Waterfront Internet Service (☎ 5952 3312; Shop 1/30 Thompson Ave, Cowes; per hr $6)

Sights & Activities

PHILLIP ISLAND NATURE PARK
Penguin Parade

Who would have thought that little penguins could be such money-spinners? The complex at **Phillip Island Nature Park** (☎ 5951 2800; www.penguins.org.au; Summerland Beach; penguin parade adult/child/family $16/8/40; ☼ 10am-last penguin show) comprises a gift shop (penguin snow-dome collectors will be pleased), café and purpose-built concrete amphitheatres that hold up to 3800 oohing and aahing spectators. Seagulls are the support act, then after sunset the little penguins emerge from the sea, waddling resolutely up the beach to their nests. Penguin numbers are at their highest in summer when they're rearing their young, but they parade year-round. You'll need good eyesight as they are the world's smallest penguins, but, recognising a way to make even more money, the nature park runs specialised **tours** (adult $25-75) so you can get even closer to the little fellas. The visitors centre (above) has a board with the day's predicted penguin arrival time; book ahead in summer.

KOALA CONSERVATION CENTRE

With elevated boardwalks at treetop level, the **Koala Conservation Centre** (☎ 5952 1307; off Phillip Island Rd; adult/child/family $8.50/4.25/23; ☼ 10am-5pm) lets you peer at koalas munching on eucalyptus leaves; there's also an interpretive visitors area. Note that they sleep 20 hours a day, so it's probable they'll be dozing, but sightings are guaranteed. **Eco tours** (adult $6; ☼ 11.30am year-round) are on offer. The centre has extended opening hours in summer.

CHURCHILL ISLAND
Small **Churchill Island** (☎ 5956 7214; off Phillip Island Rd; adult/child/family $8.50/4.25/23; ☻ 10am-4.30pm) is a working farm, and where Victoria's first crops were planted. There's a historic homestead and established gardens. Easy tracks loop round the island and there are farming demonstrations. Churchill Island is connected to Phillip Island by a narrow bridge – the turn-off is signposted about 1km west of Newhaven. The island is open longer hours in summer.

MOTOR RACING CIRCUIT
See the major role that motor racing has played on Phillip Island at the **Motor Racing Circuit** (☎ 5952 2710; www.phillipislandcircuit.com.au; Back Beach Rd; ☻ 8.30am-5.30pm Mon-Fri), which was revamped to stage the Australian Motorcycle Grand Prix in 1989. The **visitors centre** (☎ 5952 9400; ☻ 9am-5pm) at the motor racing circuit runs one-hour **walking tours** (adult/child/family $12/6/28, museum & tour $16/8/38; ☻ 11am) of the track, and you can have your photo on the winner's podium.

BEACHES
Ocean beaches on the south side of the island include **Woolamai beach**, a surf beach with dangerous rips and currents, and breaks that are best for advanced surfers. More predictable surf and conditions are found at **Smiths Beach**, which caters to all levels of competence and is popular with families. Both beaches are patrolled in summer.

If you're not a strong swimmer or you worry about your kids in the surf, head to the quieter, sheltered northern beaches.

Island Surfboards (☎ 5952 3443; www.islandsurfboards.com.au; 65 Smiths Beach & 147 Thompson Ave, Cowes; surfing lesson $40, surfboard hire per hr/day $10/35) gives surfing lessons and hires out boards and wetsuits.

SEAL ROCKS & THE NOBBIES
Off Point Grant, the extreme southwestern tip of the island, a group of rocks called the Nobbies rise from the sea. Beyond these are Seal Rocks, inhabited by Australia's largest colony of fur seals. The rocks are most crowded during the October–December breeding season, when up to 6000 seals laze on the rocks. You can view the seals from boardwalks or from a boat cruise (see Tours, right).

BIRDS & WILDLIFE
Mutton birds, also known as shearwaters, colonise in the sand dunes around Cape Woolamai. They migrate from Japan and Alaska, resting at Phillip Island every year from around 24 September to April. Your best chance of seeing them is at the penguin parade as they fly in at dusk, or at the shearwater rookeries at Woolamai Beach.

You'll also find a wide variety of water birds, including **pelicans** (which are fed at Newhaven at 11.30am daily), ibis and swans in the swampland at the **Rhyll Inlet and Wetland**. There's a boardwalk and lookout here, and the **Oswin Roberts Walking Track** (two hours) takes you through the most important birdwatching areas.

At **Phillip Island Wildlife Park** (☎ 5952 2038; Thompson Ave; adult/child/family $11/5.50/30; ☻ 10am-5pm), about 2km south of Cowes, there's over 100 different species of Australian native wildlife. The broad cross-section includes koalas, cassowaries, quolls and Tassie devils, and you can handfeed wallabies and roos. Kids love it. The park is open longer hours in summer.

WALKING & CYCLING
There are plenty of interesting **walking** and **cycling tracks** on the island. Rugged Cape Woolamai has three beautiful walking tracks that start and finish at the Woolamai car park; you can do a circuit of the cape in about three hours. Keen hikers should pick up the *Suggested Walks on Phillip Island* brochure from the visitors centre.

Tours
For penguin-related eco tours see Phillip Island Nature Park (opposite).

Aviation Centre (☎ 5956 7316; www.phillipislandaviationcentre.com; Phillip Island Airport, Newhaven; 15-/25-/35-/45-min flights per person $45/65/85/105; ☻ daily year-round) Scenic flights ranging from a 15-minute zip around Cape Woolamai to a 45-minute loop around Western Port Bay. Minimum of two people.

Duck Truck Penguins Plus! (☎ 5952 2548; www.yha.com.au/hostels/print.cfm?hostelid=102; tours $145) Run by Amaroo Park YHA, the Penguins Plus package includes three nights' dorm accommodation, a picnic lunch, penguin-parade admission, an island tour, bike hire and transport to/from Melbourne.

Wildlife Coast Cruises (☎ 5952 3501; www.bayconnections.com.au; Rotunda Bldg, Jetty Car park, The Esplanade, Cowes; tours $25-135; ☻ Nov-May) Runs a cruise around Seal Rocks and trips to French Island and Wilsons Promontory. Tours depart from Cowes jetty.

Festivals & Events

In addition to the following events, V8 Supercars race at various times throughout the year – contact the Motor Racing Circuit (p189) for more information.

Superbike World Championship (www.superbike .it; Mar) A classier crowd revs up at this three-day world championship event to see big production bikes tackle the circuit.

Australian Motorcycle Grand Prix (http://bikes .grandprix.com.au; Oct) Now this one's a massive three-day event that's held annually. Turn up to see Phillip Island go off!

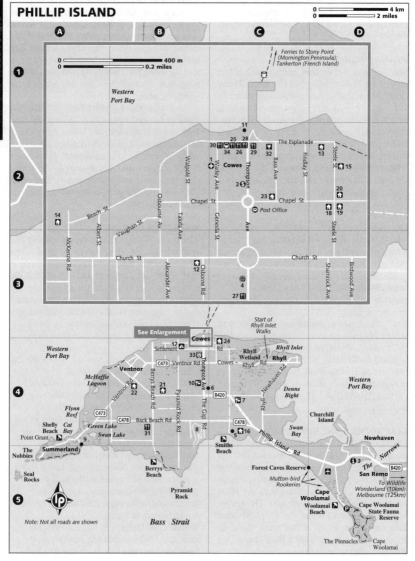

PHILLIP ISLAND

Sleeping

Phillip Island accommodation prices have distinct Himalayan-style peaks and below-sea-level troughs. During motor-racing events, Christmas, Easter and school holidays, book as far in advance as possible; during winter you'll score rock-bottom bargains. The visitors centre (p188) has an accommodation booking service or book online at www.phillipisland.net.au.

BUDGET

Amaroo Park YHA (☎ 5952 2548; www.yha.com.au /hostels/print.cfm?hostelid=102; 97 Church St; powered sites per 2 people $30, 10-/4-share $23/25, 4-share with bath $30, f cabins $135-145; 💻 🐾) This well-run hostel has leafy grounds, a pool and a charming old homestead. The 10-bed dorms are clean, if a little cramped. There's a communal kitchen and barbecue areas, bar, lounge with a fireplace and TV room. Ring the hostel about the shuttle service to/from Melbourne or check if the V/Line bus drivers will drop you near the door.

There are a dozen or so caravan parks; most of them are in Cowes (pick up a *Caravan Parks on Phillip Island* brochure from the visitors centre). Sites range from $25 to $38. You aren't allowed to camp or even sleep in your car in any public area on the island.

Cowes Caravan Park (☎ 5952 2211; www.cowescaravan park.com.au; 164 Church St; powered sites per 2 people $27-37, unpowered $25-37, d cabins $70-105) Well run and near a sheltered beach – it has spacious grounds, shady sites, a kiosk, barbecue and camp kitchen, and a playground.

Beach Park (☎ 5952 2113; 2 McKenzie Rd; powered/ unpowered sites per 2 people $25-50/23, d cabins $65-140; 🐾) Has beach frontage, leafy sites, heated swimming pool, kiosk, camp kitchen and TV room.

MIDRANGE

Midrange accommodation on Phillip Island is largely depressing – most places need a revamp or cater to conference groups so they don't need to try. B&Bs are a better option and, if you can afford it, upgrading to a top-end option is worthwhile.

Holmwood (☎ 5952 3082; www.holmwoodguesthouse .com.au; 37 Chapel St, Cowes; B&B s/d $140/170, townhouse $215, 3-course dinner $50; 🐾) This delightful and well-kept boutique guesthouse, with a leafy, colourful garden, offers cosy B&B rooms; self-contained modern cottages with wood fires, spas and private courtyards; and a two-bedroom family townhouse. Extra pillows sit plump in quality linen, and bathrobes wait in the cupboards. Breakfast offers that little bit extra with freshly squeezed juice, garden-fresh tomatoes and herbs, and home-made jam. Afternoon tea is also included and they even have an espresso machine.

Genesta House B&B (☎ 5952 3616; www.genesta.com .au; 18 Steele St, Cowes; B&B $120-150) This cosy and luxurious B&B with four guest rooms is in a beautiful old house surrounded by leafy garden. The peaceful garden has a barbecue area and a heated saltwater spa to soak away those walking kinks. Leave the kids at home.

Otira Homestead (☎ 5956 8294; www.otira.com.au; Ventnor Beach Rd, Needle's Eye; d B&B $140-150, cottages $200) In a bucolic setting, with sheep dotting the paddocks surrounding the 1920s homestead, Otira offers reasonably priced and private rooms (furnished in farmhouse chic) in the main house and two- and three-bedroom cottages. In-house guests receive breakfast in the dining room, while freshly laid eggs and bacon are delivered to the cottages.

Penguin Hill Country House B&B (☎ 5956 8777; www.phillipisland.net.au/trip; cnr Backbeach & Ventnor Rds, Ventnor; B&B d $130) Close to the Nobbies and Penguin Parade, this B&B has beach views from its serene, rural location. Three en-suite rooms – made cosy with antique furniture and books – are available; guests share a sitting room and eat a cooked breakfast in the dining room.

Anchor Inn & Waves Apartments (☎ 5952 1351; www.thewaves.com.au; 1 The Esplanade; Anchor Inn r $115-170, Waves apts $160-250; ⊠) The Anchor Inn offers beachside, standard three-star motel accommodation popular with families. The beachside, four-star apartments offer generic but snazzy self-contained accommodation, with a balcony (many overlook the beach), spa and kitchenette. Rates include breakfast.

Kaloha Holiday Resort (☎ 5952 2179; www.kaloha .com.au; cnr Steele & Chapel Sts, Cowes; r $70-240; ⊠) A motel and caravan park right in Cowes. There's variety of generic and slightly dark, motel rooms (some with spas) with simple cooking facilities, and a range of cabins. Kids love the solar-heated saltwater pool.

TOP END

Castle Villa by the Sea (☎ 5952 1228; www.thecastle .com.au; 7 Steele St, Cowes; apts $225-330, ste $125-165) If you're after a romantic getaway with healthy doses of splurging and pampering, lay your hat at the immaculate, Mediterranean-style Castle Villa. Boutique self-contained apartments and suites are furnished individually with modern, artistic opulence – you feel like you're renting a house rather than a room. Artworks by Jeni Doyle grace the walls and the outdoor Jacuzzi in the Castle suite is a winner. Downstairs, Boyle's restaurant is available exclusively to guests.

Cliff Top (☎ 5952 1033; www.clifftop.com.au; 1 Marlin St, Smiths Beach; r $210-240) Cliff Top is on a private estate right on Smiths Beach with views of Bass Strait and Pyramid Rock. There are seven stylish and luxurious rooms with an airy, modern ambience and private balcony or patio. Special touches – such as a continental breakfast basket brought to your room – make this a memorable stay. Truly, you'll be so relaxed you'll never want to leave!

Also recommended:

Rothsaye on Lovers Walk (☎ 5952 2057; www.roth saye.com.au; 2 Roy Crt, Cowes; B&B d from $140, cottages $150-180) Beautiful self-contained cottages close to the beach.

Quest Phillip Island (☎ 5952 2644; www.questapart ments.com.au; cnr Bass Ave & Chapel St, Cowes; apts $170-325)

Eating

Cowes is the best place on the island to satiate hunger cravings. There's the standard collection of greasy-spoon takeaways and pizza places, plus a couple of upmarket restaurants.

Madcowes (☎ 5952 2560; 17 The Esplanade; meals $4-12; ☯ breakfast & lunch) A stylish, breezy café-foodstore cooking big brekkies and quality lunches. Health it up with some Bircher muesli or go for thick and fluffy ricotta hotcakes with caramelised banana, yoghurt and maple syrup. At lunch wash down a roast beef and brie sandwich with some Victorian wine – all by the glass.

Fortuna Noodles Express (☎ 5952 3888; Shop 1, 15-16 The Esplanade; mains $9-12; ☯ lunch & dinner) A noodle bar with spicy wok-fried Hokkien noodles, coconut laksa and red and green Thai-style curries. Fortuna bridges the gap between the budget fish and chipper and expensive café and restaurant meals.

Jetty (☎ 5952 2060; cnr The Esplanade & Thompson Ave; mains $18-25; ☯ dinner, closed Tue & Wed Apr-Sep) Spacious and modern, this restaurant has a big open kitchen, lots of tables inside and out, and a long wall banquette. Busy chefs barbecue kangaroo fillet and whip up nasi goreng. Meals are hearty and draw on European and Asian cuisines for inspiration. From 26 December to 26 January Jetty is open for lunch and dinner.

Fisherman's Wharf (☎ 5952 6077; Shop 4, 15-16 The Esplanade; meals $2-10; ☯ lunch & dinner) Head here for fish and chips, burgers and souvlakis. Depending on the season, you can feast on fresh sea perch, barramundi and flounder, calamari, scallops and NZ mussels. As written in the fish-and-chip shop handbook, décor is a nautical theme.

Isola de Capri (☎ 5952 2435; cnr The Esplanade & Thompson Ave; mains $17-23; ☯ dinner Mon-Fri, lunch & dinner Sat & Sun) This bustling Italian bistro, overlooking Western Port Bay, has a variety of stock-standard favourites such as margherita and capricciosa pizzas, pasta carbonara

BUSH DOOF *David Burnett*

Warbling magpies, crusty camper vans pottering down dusty bush tracks, blue Australian skies arching overhead…and 120 decibels of thumping electronic bass, throbbing through the gum trees.

This superficially odd amalgamation of urban music and rural escape is at the heart of every 'bush doof' – Melbourne's particular contribution to the world of electronic dance music.

In recent years Melbourne has become the centre of Australia's thriving electronic music scene, with most of the action focused on the city's many techno bars and mainstream dance clubs. But, largely unnoticed by the sweaty hordes doing the Melbourne stomp in giant downtown city venues, a parallel scene with a world audience has emerged to make southeastern Australia one of a handful of 'must visit' destinations for underground DJs from Goa to Tel Aviv.

The bush doof evolved from the outdoor 'raves' of the early '90s – the key ingredients being dance music, a huge sound system, a few hundred 'ferals' stomping away on a dusty dirt dance floor, trippy lighting (and, as one might expect, the appropriate recreational chemicals). Small hit-and-run dance parties, intended to slip under the radar of the local constabulary, have lately become large, well-organised, multistage festivals, often featuring major international acts and two or three days of round-the-clock beats.

Hundreds of visitors from dance-crazy countries like Israel, Japan, Sweden and the UK descend on the doofs of southeastern Australia during the warmer months, and it can be hard at times to find an Aussie accent among the punters, each sporting an unnaturally wide grin. The summer of 2004–05 alone saw major international psy-trance acts such as GMS and Protoculture play to dance floors perhaps a tenth the size of their typical European audiences, in beautiful bush settings a few hours' drive from Melbourne.

Earthcore (www.earthcore.com.au) the largest regular outdoor event near Melbourne, which attracts as many as 10,000 people each November, held its 10th anniversary party in 2003. The **Rainbow Serpent Festival** (www.rainbowserpent.net), usually held on the Australia Day long weekend in January, is another very popular shindig. They tend to take place at different locations around Melbourne each time.

If you're in Melbourne between November and April, keep an eye on the street press for details of upcoming doofs – event organisers often arrange buses or car pools for those without transport. Tickets range from $15 for a small party to $100 or more for the larger, multiday festivals.

Oh, and why 'doof'? 'Cause that's what it sounds like (doof, doof, doof, doof…).

and veal schnitzel. It's very old-school and popular with families.

Phillip Island Vineyard & Winery (☎ 5956 8465; Berrys Beach Rd; platters $14-17; ☺ 11am-5pm Apr-Oct) Sample the velvety wines made by renowned Diamond Valley wine makers and share platters full of delectable morsels such as cheeses, terrine, smoked salmon, trout fillets and pâté. With views of Bass Strait and Western Port Bay from the cellar door, this is a worthy stopover. The winery closes at 6pm from November to March.

For self-catering, head to the **IGA minimart** (☎ 5952 1363; cnr Settlement St & Thompson Ave; ☺ 7am-10pm) and bottle shop.

Drinking & Entertainment

During the high season the island is festive and full, with live bands playing at several of the pubs; in winter it's as quiet as a retirement home after 9pm. During racing events, the island's nightspots heave with a drunken mass of excited flag-waving revellers – either join 'em or stay at home, as you're certainly not going to beat 'em.

Isle of Wight Hotel (☎ 5952 2301; The Esplanade, Cowes; covers $5-8, mains $16-24; ☺ lunch & dinner, Splash 10pm-2am) Isle of Wight is a rambling pub with a front bar, TAB, bottle shop, fantastic beer garden and Splash – the upstairs cocktail bar, which has live bands, jam sessions and DJs spinning commercial dance and hip-hop. Meals are stock standard: veal parmigiana, and cuts of meat cooked to your taste. Average motel rooms are on offer out back (single/double/triple $65/85/105).

Star Bar (☎ 5952 2060; cnr The Esplanade & Thompson Ave; cover $10; ☺ 7pm-2am Fri & Sat) At the back of the Jetty restaurant, Star Bar is Phillip Island's nightclub. It's a mixed clientele, which the music reflects with DJs spinning up a grab bag of commercial techno, dance, hip-hop and R&B.

Banfields Cinema (☎ 5952 2088; 192 Thompson Ave, Cowes; adult/child $12/9; ☺ Fri, Sat & Tue, daily school holidays; ⚐) This 200-seat cinema screens the latest releases. There's also standard motel accommodation available, some rooms with spas ($80 to $150), and a restaurant, barbecue area and children's playground.

Getting There & Around

Travelling by car from Melbourne, take the Monash Fwy (M1) and get off at the Phillip Island exit onto the South Gippsland Hwy (M420) near Cranbourne. The alternative to the M1 is a slow trip through St Kilda and Dandenong on the Princes Hwy.

The only direct service from Melbourne to Cowes is a **V/Line** (☎ 13 61 96; www.vline.com

.au) bus (one way $17, three hours and 20 minutes) departing at 3.50pm from Southern Cross station Monday to Friday. Other services run daily but require taking a Met train to Dandenong station and then two different coaches. Another option is to take a Met train from Melbourne to Stony Point ($7, one hour 50 minutes, six daily), then catch the ferry.

Inter Island Ferries (☎ 9585 5730; www.interisland ferries.com.au; return adult/child/bike $18/8/8; ☺ every 30min 9.10am-5.25pm, plus 7.45pm Fri) runs to/from Cowes to Stony Point (on the Mornington Peninsula) via French Island. There are at least two trips daily year-round.

There's no public transport around Phillip Island. You can hire bicycles from **Ride On Bikes** (☎ 5952 2533; info@rideonbikes.com.au; 2-17 The Esplanade, Cowes; bike hire per half-/full-day $15/25) and Amaroo Park YHA (p191).

Cowes/San Remo taxis (☎ 5952 2200) also service Phillip Island.

Southwest

The southwest crams loads into its string-bean stretch; strap on your jet pack. The amazing Great Ocean Rd (B100) winds its way from Torquay to Warrnambool and attracts seven million snap-happy visitors annually. Beyond, the thrashing Shipwreck Coast is all spooky stories and dramatic beachscapes. If these don't appeal, surely the enchanted Otway Ranges hinterland will, with its (literally) breathtaking walks, waterfalls and hillside townships.

The urge to embrace a seaside or rural idyll obsesses many travellers along this route, thanks to its dangerously scenic drives and top-notch lodgings. It might be the stormy backdrop of heaving swells and sunlit sea spray by those ragged rock sculptures, the Twelve Apostles, that snag your senses. Or the storybook wonderland of Apollo Bay's roly-poly hills that prompts your urge to nest. Otways walks reveal eucalypts and myrtle beech of unhuggable girth, while Warrnambool delivers whale babies each spring. Emus, wallabies and koalas are easily spotted in the early morning, and you'll wonder how you ever lived without bird song.

There are family beaches, surf beaches, don't-dare-swim beaches and endless arcs of sandy white to amble on from Princetown to Cape Bridgewater. In stark contrast is the ancient volcanic beauty of the Western district's gargantuan crater lakes by the Princes Hwy.

All this, and you're rarely more than 30 minutes from a decent latte and avocado-chicken wrap. One thing: serious road accidents occur, so stop and swap – it's only fair to share this scenic spectacular with the mug behind the wheel, stuck peering around corners for road hogs and occasionally wayward international drivers.

SOUTHWEST

HIGHLIGHTS

- Photographing the **Great Ocean Road** in all its moods – like you need telling
- Snuggling by a log fire in an **Otways' bush retreat** (p207)
- Trundling the Otways' back roads in a horse-drawn **gypsy wagon** (p232) to camp lakeside
- Going **café crawling** in Lorne (p205) or Apollo Bay (p210)
- Paying homage to bizarre rock formations at **Port Campbell National Park** (p214) at dawn or dusk
- Supervising the annual **whale convention** (p219) from Warrnambool's shores
- Feeling humbled by the raw beauty of wild beach walks along the **Shipwreck Trail** (p213)
- Canoeing through the chalky gorge of the **Glenelg River** (p231)

- www.greatoceanroad.org
- www.visitotways.com

Getting There & Around

AIR

Interstate visitors can fly into Avalon airport, 22km from Geelong, with **Jetstar** (☎ 13 15 38; www.jetstar.com) and take the door-to-door **Avalon Airport Shuttle** (☎ 5278 8788; www .avalonairportshuttle.com.au) along the Great Ocean Rd as far as Lorne.

BUS & TRAIN

Trains from Melbourne's Southern Cross station (formerly Spencer St station) travel to Geelong and then connect with **V/Line** (☎ 13 61 96; www.vline.com.au) buses that cruise along the Great Ocean Rd as far as Apollo Bay ($32.30), via Torquay ($15.50), Anglesea ($18.20) and Lorne ($26.20) four times daily Monday to Friday, and twice daily on Saturday and Sunday. At 1.40pm Friday (and Monday during the Christmas holidays), a V/Line bus continues around the coast from Apollo Bay to Port Campbell and Warrnambool, which is a transport hub for the coast and for the Western District.

V/Line trains from Melbourne to Warrnambool ($83.80) via Geelong, Colac, Camperdown and Terang depart from Southern Cross station three times daily Monday to Saturday, with two trains on Sunday that swap to a bus service from Geelong to Warrnambool.

Wayward Bus (☎ 1300 653 510; www.waywardbus .com.au) follows the southwest coast to South Australia as part of its Melbourne to Adelaide trip; you can do stopovers too. For more information, see p411.

CAR

There's no public transport to the Otway Ranges. Access is by your own vroom-vroom or hire one through **Avis** (☎ 5521 1332) in Geelong. You can also hire cars through Lorne Automotive Services (see p206). Or check out Melbourne car hire (p146).

SURF COAST

TORQUAY

☎ 03 / pop 8000

Torquay is the capital of Australia's booming surfing industry and an OK spot to kick

SOUTHWEST

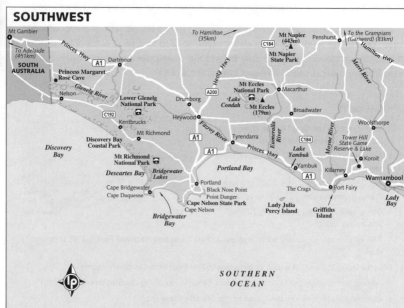

back if your goal is a beach 'n' book break, a surf lesson or serious shopping for surf wear or gear. Otherwise, attractions and diverse activities are light on in this beachside suburban sprawl.

Orientation & Information
The two main streets for shopping and eating, Gilbert St and Bell St, run perpendicular to the Esplanade.

Geelong and Great Ocean Road Visitors Centre (☎ 5275 5797; Stead Park, Princes Hwy, Corio) This huge centre is 72km from Melbourne, and shares a prominent roadside stop with McDonalds and KFC.

Visitors centre (☎ 5261 4219; www.greatoceanroad.org /surfcoast; Surf City Plaza, Beach Rd) Otherwise, Torquay has a small office in the same building as the Surfworld Australia Surfing Museum.

Sights & Activities
Torquay's action revolves around gorgeous local beaches that satisfy everyone from kids in floaties to world-champion surfers. **Fisherman's Beach**, protected from ocean swells, is the family fave. The **Front Beach**, ringed by shady pines and sloping lawns beckons

lazy bums, while surf life-savers patrol the frothing **Back Beach** during summer.

The **Surfworld Australia Surfing Museum** (☎ 5261 4606; adult/child/family $8/5.50/18; ⏲ 9am-5pm), at the rear of the Surf City Plaza, pays stylish tribute to the nation's champs.

For the when-in-Rome types, you can test your balance on the beach breaks with the places listed below. Two-hour surf lessons cost about $50; you can hire surfing gear at Go Ride a Wave's store in Torquay, or buy your own at the second-hand surf shops next to the Plaza in Baines Cres. Call to find out operating hours in the low season.

Go Ride a Wave (☎ 1300 132 441; http://graw.com.au; ⏲ 9am-5pm daily in summer) Anglesea (143b Great Ocean Rd, Anglesea); Torquay (1/15 Bell St, Torquay)

Gally's Surf Coaching (☎ 5261 3542; www.gallyssurf coaching.com.au; 27 Nicholson Cres, Jan Juc; ⏲ 8am-6pm daily in summer)

Westcoast Surf School (☎ 5261 2241; ⏲ 9am-5pm daily in summer)

Southern Exposure (☎ 5261 2170; www.southern exposure.com.au; 55b Surfcoast Hwy, Torquay; ⏲ 10am-5pm daily in summer)

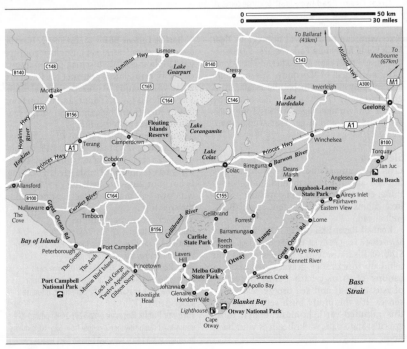

SOUTHWEST

AVOIDING BED BUGS

So you're travelling alone. Along the southwest coast, operators of B&Bs and self-contained accommodation like to confirm that: 'You're on your own? Really? Just you? Right, well, um...' To many, you're an anomaly, but prices for singles are usually more negotiable. As a rule of thumb, count on the cost being about $20 less than the doubles prices quoted in this chapter. Genuinely charming singles can do even better.

The biggest bed bug is the lack of budget options. There's a good range of caravan parks along the coast, but cabins have taken over much of the camping space. Still, the newer cabins are much better than dreary motel rooms, so do consider them.

Unless you book months in advance, beds are scarce along this coast over Easter and late December/January. During this time, prices skyrocket greedily and most places have a minimum one-week stay.

In winter, you have loads more bargaining power. Rates and availability during mid-year school holidays are less crazy, and the more nights you stay, the cheaper it gets.

Good-weather weekends are usually busy, and minimum two-night stays often apply at top spots like Lorne or Port Fairy on weekends throughout the year, but these are noted in reviews.

Yawn, then there are the 101 pesky rate variations. The range of prices quoted in this chapter are for double rooms in low/high season: low season being February to November, excluding school holidays, which attract a shoulder season rate (not listed), and Easter, which attracts a high-season rate, as does late December through January and public holidays (for information on holidays, see p400). Note that price categories are a little different in this chapter to the rest of the book. Budget is anything up to $90 for a double, midrange from $90 to $160 for a double, and top end is anything beyond that.

For longer stays in self-contained digs, check out these websites:

Great Ocean Properties (www.greatoceanproperties.com.au)
Great Ocean Road (www.greatoceanroad.com.au)

Kids who can't swim will appreciate **Tiger Moth World Adventure Park** (☎ 5261 5100; Blackgate Rd; adult/child under 4 $9.50/free; ⏰ 10am-5pm), 5km northeast of Torquay. It's basically a giant play park with paddle boats, mini golf and daily air shows. It also offers joy flights on vintage Tiger Moths (one passenger, $130) and Tiger Cats (takes two, $95 each).

Sleeping

Over the summer and Easter, Torquay gets flooded and it's hard to find budget anything, especially in caravan parks big on deluxe cabins and small on tent space. Book well ahead.

Ironbark Haven B&B (☎ 5263 2224; www.ironbarkhaven.com; 3 Point Addis Rd, Pt Addis; d low/high season $120/140) It's halfway to Anglesea, but as you wind up this orange-gravel drive under a canopy of stringy-bark gums, the scent of Aussie bush and sea breeze relax your senses. It's the pretty bush setting around this rammed-earth homestead that most appeals. State park walks begin at your back door.

Norfolk Cottage B&B (☎ 5264 8182; 22 Island Dr; d low/high season $90/130; ✖) English country garden, home-made biscuits, plump doona of pretty print, and a gourmet breakfast are what you'll enjoy at this traditional B&B. The design is mock-Tudor, and its top floor is all yours, from the gargantuan beige spa-room to the vaulted ceiling.

Wattle Court Retreat (☎ 5261 9354; wattlecourt@myaccess.com.au; 12 Wattle Crt, Jan Juc; d $150) In suburban Jan Juc, this bright, two-storey apartment has a wonderful bush-garden decking. From your king-size bed, the view from the windows will make you feel nestled among the tree tops.

Other recommendations:

Sea-Enna Cottage (☎ 5261 4667; signific@pipeline.com.au; 21 Zeally Bay Rd; d low/high season $120/140) Vividly decorated, and close to shops.

Bells Beach Lodge (☎ 5261 7070; www.bellsbeachlodge.com.au; 51-53 Surfcoast Hwy; dm from $20, d low/high season $45/60; 🖳) Neat, intimate backpackers.

Torquay Public Reserve (☎ 5261 2496; powered/unpowered camp sites per 2 people from $25/10, d cabins low/high season $65/100) Just behind Back Beach.

Torquay Holiday Resort (☎ 5261 2493; 55 Surfcoast Hwy; enquiries@torquayholidayresort.com.au; camp sites per 2 people from $23, d cabins low/high season $49/79; 🖭) Tidy and kid-friendly.

Eating
Outside holiday seasons, the tourist trickle dictates opening hours.

Growlers (☎ 5264 8455; 23 The Esplanade; mains $15-26; 🕑 breakfast, lunch & dinner) From the shaded veranda or dark-wood interior you have peek-a-boo views through pines to the front beach. The menu is inventive, and you want the coconut-and-banana pancake with mango marmalade.

Imperial Rhino (☎ 5261 6780; 3 Bell St; mains $15-17; 🕑 breakfast, lunch & dinner) Match your noodle fetish – vermicelli, Hokkien, rice stick or just plain flat – with tossed Asian vegies, tofu or Thai red curry. It feels very Zen: long wooden tables and loads of natural light.

Seaweed Sushi (☎ 5264 8899; 22 Pearl St; mains $4-15; 🕑 lunch) Fresh Tokyo rolls and all the side dishes you expect for a satisfying, healthy snack. Perch at the street-facing bar and watch folk cruise by.

Rose (☎ 5261 2038; 220 Great Ocean Rd, Torquay; mains $18-26; 🕑 lunch & dinner Thu-Mon, breakfast Sun) The Rose doubles as a function centre but its rich plum hues set a romantic, fine-dining mood. The menu offers satisfying Mod Oz cuisine, from lamb shanks and duck to risotto and cheesy soufflé. On summer days, enjoy veranda views across the valley.

Getting There & Away
McHarry's Buslines (☎ 5223 2111; www.mcharrys.com.au) has frequent services from Geelong to Torquay ($5.30). In Torquay, buses arrive and depart from the corner of Pearl and Boston Sts, behind the Gilbert St shopping centre.

V/Line (☎ 136196) buses, which run from Geelong to Apollo Bay, also stop here ($15.50).

TORQUAY TO ANGLESEA
The Great Ocean Rd between Torquay and Anglesea heads slightly inland, with a turn-off about 7km from Torquay to **Bells Beach**. The powerful point break at Bells is part of international surfing folklore and it's the site of a world-championship surfing contest every Easter. Since 1964, Victoria's **Rip Curl Pro** has drawn thousands of skeg heads and grommets to watch autumn's biggest swells shimmy with the world's best surfers –

waves have reached up to 6m during the contest! General admission tickets cost $11 per day, or you can buy a cheaper four-day pass. Contact **Surfing Victoria** (☎ 03-5261 2907) for more details.

Nine kilometres southwest of Torquay is a turn-off to windy **Point Addis** – it's 3km down to the car parks and beach-walking trails that are popular with surfers, hang-gliders and swimmers. Also here is the sign-posted **Koori Cultural Walk**, a 1km circuit trail to the beach through the **Ironbark Basin**, a nature reserve with birdies galore.

If you're feeling peppy, you might enjoy tackling the **Surf Coast Walk** that follows the coastline from Torquay to Moggs Creek, south of Aireys Inlet. The full distance takes about 11 hours, but the walk can be done in stages. The *Surf Coast Touring Map*, available from tourist offices in Geelong and along the coast, has this walk marked on it.

ANGLESEA
☎ 03 / pop 2200
Shuffling around sipping good coffee, roo watching and bodyboarding are your chores here. Anglesea is a cosy seaside village, popular with families for its terrific beaches and camping. The town winds around the gum-green Anglesea River, and its accommodation makes the most of tranquil bush settings.

Infromation
There's no visitors centre – just a lonely information booth with brochures, across from the main shopping centre. It's not staffed outside summer, or outside school and public holidays.

Off Shore Cafe (Anglesea Shopping Complex; ☎ 5263 3644) in the mini mall has Internet access.

Sights & Activities
During school holidays and summer, customers rule seven days a week. Otherwise, business hours ebb and flow with the tourists.

Roo Watch: **Anglesea Golf Club** (☎ 5263 1582; Noble St) has a resident kangaroo population that grazes blithely on the fairways as golfers fire off golf balls around them. You can always see a posse or two along the Golf Links Rd boundary, or else check the view from the club's bistro.

The front beach is good for a tumble and rinse cycle, while sheltered **Point Roadknight** is gentler for kiddies. Hire surf or beach-play equipment from the **Anglesea Surf Centre** (☎ 5263 1530; cnr Great Ocean Rd & McMillan St) or **Go Ride A Wave** (☎ 1300 132 441; 143b Great Ocean Rd), which also gives surfing lessons, as does **Southern Exposure** (☎ 5261 2170). Lessons cost about $50 for two hours. Approximate hire costs: bodyboards/surfboards with wet-suits per two hours $20/25; kayaks per two hours $40.

Little kids love this stuff: **Eco Logic Education & Environment Services** (☎ 5263 1133; www.ecologic .net.au) guides 'marine rock-pool rambles' and night time 'possum prowls'. A good back up is **Anglesea Paddleboats** (☎ 0408-599 942) by the river. It hires out canoes and paddleboats (one adult and two children per 15 minutes $10) every good-weather day during sum-mer, school holidays and most Sundays.

Otherwise, let them loose in **Coogoorah Park**, a small bushland nature reserve beside the river, with a playground, picnic facilities and walking paths.

Sea-Mist Holiday Farm (☎ 5288 7255; horse rides 1/2hr $25/40), 17km northwest of town at Wens-leydale farm, leads horse rides several times a day through state forest.

If you're up for a wander, there's always the **Surf Coast Walk** (see p199).

Sleeping

Rivergums B&B (☎ 5263 3066; 10 Bingley Pde; d low/ high season $92/160; ☒) Tucked by the river with wonderfully tranquil views, this luxuriant, spacious and tastefully furnished room has a cloud-soft bed and enough extra touches to make you feel lusciously pampered. It's excellent value, within walking distance to shops, and cheaper without breakfast.

Roadknight Cottages (☎ 5263 1820; 26 Great Ocean Rd; cottages for 4 people from $155) Heading towards Lorne, these two-storey cottages sit among a pretty native-garden setting, each with private decking. They're comfy and self-contained, sleeping up to six. Prices based on two-night minimum stay; bookings must be week-long in January.

Surf Coast Spa Resort (☎ 5263 3363; www.surf coastspa.com.au; 105 Great Ocean Rd; d low/high season $95/145) Ask for the doubles with decks and garden settings, up the back. These motel units with soft furnishings inspired by Monet's pastel-splotched pallet are either pretty, or a little dated, depending on your mood.

Point Luxury B&B (☎ 5263 3738; www.thepoint anglesea.com.au; d low/high season from $185/200; ☒) Heaven sits high on this hillside overlook-ing Point Roadknight and the Bass Strait. The style is modern Mediterranean, crisp and fresh with dramatic ocean views and pretty bush settings able to be seen from the balconies and common lounge. The king-size beds, gourmet breads at break-fast and complimentary port are welcome extras.

Some other options:

Anglesea Family Caravan Park (☎ 5263 1583; www .angleseafcp.com.au; Cameron Rd; camp sites per 2 people low/high season $25/31, d cabins from $65) River and beach access.

Anglesea Backpackers (☎ 5263 2664; 40 Noble St; dm low/high season $20/25, d with bathroom $60/80) Spotless, if a tad strict.

Eating

Residents aren't exactly burdened with choice but Anglesea has the basics – takeaways, pub, bakery.

Cafe Jetty (☎ 5263 1420; 119 Great Ocean Rd; mains $8.50-$15; ☽ breakfast & lunch) It feels like you're in someone's beachside backyard, with rough-hewn wooden tables atop and white pebbles underfoot. It's crazy-busy, and does excellent coffee, slices and smoothies, good focaccias and the never-say-die sandwich.

Shelles By the River (☎ 5263 2500; 113 Great Ocean Rd; mains $20-29; ☽ breakfast, lunch & dinner) The menu reads like a classy affair but the ambience on the outside decking, and the crumpled-linen clad tables within, say kick back and enjoy. Shelles is fully licensed with a good selection of well-prepared seafood and meat dishes.

Albatross Cafe and Bar (☎ 5263 1010; 89 Great Ocean Rd; mains $18-24; ☽ breakfast, lunch & dinner) It's the token groovy café and bar, splashed in outback-Oz tones and well positioned for world-watching inside or out. The menu is limited, with a surprise local special-ity: 'Kangaroo Wrap'. Fresh from the golf course?

Furios Restaurant and Cafe (☎ 5263 3216; 95 Great Ocean Rd; mains $15-25; ☽ breakfast & lunch daily, dinner Sat) For an Italian restaurant, this broad, inventive menu of pumpkin-and-leek lasagne and crab cakes venture to go way beyond Nonna's secret recipes. Fantastic home-baked muffins too. Open for dinner nightly in summer.

Getting There & Away
V/Line (☎ 13 61 96) buses link Anglesea with Geelong ($7.30) and Apollo Bay ($13.30).

AIREYS INLET
☎ 03 / pop 1000

South of Anglesea, the Great Ocean Rd finally meets the coast and starts its spectacular coastal run. Aireys Inlet has a cruisy vibe with a hint of sophistication and a seaside-village attitude. It's mostly popular with those who find Lorne too edgy. Midway between Anglesea and Lorne, it is next door to some of the southwest's prettiest beaches. It was originally established as a terminus for the Cobb & Co coach service from Geelong.

You can access the Internet at Aireys Inlet Caravan Park (see right).

Sights & Activities
There are some great **beaches** in Aireys, backed by tall, volcanic cliffs with tidal rock pools along the foreshore just below the lighthouse. Ragged rock stacks such as **Eagle Rock** and **Table Rock** jut from the ocean. These are easily accessed from car parks that lead down to walking tracks. A few kilometres toward Lorne, you'll find two particularly glorious stretches at **Fairhaven** and **Moggs Creek**. A surf life-saving club patrols the beach at Fairhaven during summer, and at Moggs Creek, hang-gliders launch themselves from the cliff-tops to land on the sands below.

Roo Watch: go past the General Store, heading towards Lorne. At the bottom of the hill, just before the bridge, is an expanse of uninspired, grassy-looking wetland that attracts a brood of **kangaroos**, especially in the early morning.

Great Ocean Road Adventure Tours (☎ 5289 6841; ⏰ 9am-5pm) has half-day hire of surf-boards ($25), mountain bikes ($25), and canoes ($25) for paddling on Painkalac Creek. It also creates self-guided bicycle tours (from $25 to $45).

Split Point Lighthouse and its keepers' cottages were built in 1891 to prevent ships from becoming too familiar with this piece of Australia's 36,000km coastline. The walking tracks and lookout have top views.

Signposted off the main road is a replica of an 1852 **settler's hut**, made from bark, which was destroyed by the 1983 Ash Wednesday bush fires that devastated this area.

The **Surf Coast Walk** continues along the coast here, or pick up copy of *A Guide to Walks in the Angahook-Lorne State Park* (about $5), available from visitor information centres, or visit the Aireys Inlet Caravan Park (see below) which has a free guide to local walks. Signposted trails start from Distillery Creek picnic ground, 2.5km north of Aireys, and the Moggs Creek picnic ground, 3km west of Aireys Inlet.

Blazing Saddles (☎ 5289 7322; 1¼-/2¼-hr rides $35/55), about 2km inland, has horse rides in the bush and along the beach.

Sleeping
Aireys lacks budget accommodation but is well endowed with sumptuous B&Bs.

BUDGET
Ocean Inlet at Fairhaven (☎ 5289 7313; oceaninlet@bigpond.com; 34 Wybellenna Dve, Fairhaven; d $90) How cute is this? A gazebo-style bedsit with sofa bed and floor-to-ceiling windows overlooking native gardens. Next door is a teensy cabin containing your kitchenette and bathroom, with breakfast bar. Or, there's the sleek, indulgent Shorehouse from $200 a night! And a room with disabled facilities.

Aireys Inlet Caravan Park (☎ 5289 6230; www.aicp.com.au; 19-25 Great Ocean Rd; powered/unpowered sites per 2 people from $22/20, d cabins with bathroom low/high season $65/105; 🖳 🐾) A neat little park lacking shady trees but close to the township's few stores.

MIDRANGE & TOP END
Cimarron B&B (☎ 5289 7044; www.cimarron.com.au; 105 Gilbert St; d low/high season $125/175) Time to cocoon and rejuvenate your spirits in this superb, rustic, yet sophisticated, homestead with its book-lined walls and veranda views across Bass Strait. Two unique, loft-style doubles have vaulted ceilings and treetop or sea views, or there's a den-like apartment. Out back, it's all state park and wildlife. Gay friendly, too.

Inlet Hideaway B&B (☎ 5289 7471; inlethideaway@bigpond.com; 34 Hopkins St; d low/high season $120/140, cabin $140/160) Musky, sweet-scented bush engulfs your senses in this wintry A-frame retreat tucked away down an unsealed road. Upstairs are two rooms with triangular windows looking out onto treetops or there's a separate, much larger, loft-style cabin. Rowan, the host, is easy going.

Aireys Overboard (☎ 5289 7424; www.aireysoverboard.com.au; Barton Crt; d low/high season $150/250; 🐾)

SOUTHWEST

Wave-like radial-sawn weatherboards give this contemporary beach house a unique exterior. The elegant interior with warm, wood floors and wattle and storm-blue hues, combined with a log fire and double spa, urge you to burrow in for days. Love the outdoor shower!

Seahaven B&B (☎ 5289 6408; seahavenbandb@iprimus.com.au; 62 Wybellenna Dve; d $100; ❄) It's bright and basic with terrific views of the inlet. Fix your own breakfast and catch the morning sun on your balcony while spotting kangaroos in the wetlands below. Private, with convenient access to town.

LorneView B&B (☎ 5289 6430; www.lorneview.com.au; 677 Great Ocean Rd, Eastern View; d low/high season $120/160; ❄) Six kilometres west of Aireys Inlet or 14km east of Lorne, these light, spacious, tastefully styled rooms (one with ace views) are directly across from the beach. You'll feel carefree.

Eating

Diversity is about to knock on Aireys' door, but it ain't here yet. Apart from the quaint general store, a gourmet seafood deli, and a handful of ordinary cafés, fine fare is limited. At the time of writing, a relaxed Mediterranean restaurant was also expected to open.

Truffles Cafe Restaurant (☎ 5289 7402; 34 Great Ocean Rd; mains $15-$25; ❄ breakfast, lunch & dinner) House wine, coffee and cakes – tick. Big tick for service and ambience. The meals are presented well, although the dinner menu is rather limited. Happy days – lentil burgers are available at lunch.

Aireys Inlet Hotel (☎ 5289 6260; 45 Great Ocean Rd; mains $15-22; ❄ lunch & dinner) Beside the usual pub grub, this menu pays attention to vegetarians via stir-fries, risottos and pasta. The fish and chips are fantastic, as are the beer garden's views towards Lorne. You'll need a hat and sunscreen.

Lightkeeper's Stables Tea Room and Gallery (☎ 5289 7148; Federal St; sandwiches $5-8; ❄ breakfast & lunch) If you're up for a light lunch, there's an OK toasted sandwich or Devonshire tea to be had here, and a decent cuppa. Walls are lined with fading photos of local historic events.

Getting There & Away

V/Line (☎ 13 61 96) buses link Aireys Inlet with Geelong ($10.20) and Apollo Bay ($10.20).

OTWAY RANGES

It's the contrast between this woolly coastal mountain range and the crashing surf it rolls towards that makes the Great Ocean Rd such a spectacular route. The Otway Ranges stretch from Aireys Inlet to Cape Otway past Apollo Bay, and for folks with a little time to spare it's definitely worth exploring this storybook hinterland (See also p211).

Within the Otway Ranges is the Angahook-Lorne State Park and the Otway National Park but, at the time of writing, the state government was considering bringing both under the Otway Ranges National Park moniker and expanding the park's area. Fret not, visitors centres won't forget the many walks contained within the **Angahook-Lorne State Park** in a hurry.

Eucalypts dressed in raggy bark and older, gnarly cousins create haunting corridors in the mists. Offshoot trails reveal dozens of small streams and cascades in this high rainfall area, where each winding road, in rain and sun, stirs a new mood. More than 100 species of birds live here, as well as many cute Australian critters from echidnas and bats to possums and swamp wallabies. The park covers 22,000 hectares of coast and hinterland between Anglesea and Kennett River. There are heaps of well-signposted walking tracks. Several follow the old tramlines used to cart timber out of the forests (see p232).

Much of this area was devastated by the 1983 Ash Wednesday bushfires. Thankfully, speedy recovery after fire is a natural trait of eucalypt forests. The main access roads into the park and walks are via the sealed Deans Marsh–Lorne road, which heads north out of Lorne, and the sealed Erskine Falls Rd, which runs from Lorne to Erskine Falls. This last road continues on to the more rugged scenery of the Mt Sabine–Benwerrin road, which runs along the spine of the Otway Ranges.

Most of the **walks** near Lorne start from either the Blanket Leaf or Sheoak Creek picnic areas, or the Erskine Falls car park. You can drive to these areas to walk, or simply to picnic. There's a terrific walking guide called *A Guide to Walks in Angahook-Lorne State Park* (about $5) available from Lorne's visitors centre or Parks Victoria (see opposite).

Here are three of the most popular walks:

Erskine Falls Walk Starting at the car park, this 7.5km, one-way trail descends steeply down steps to a lookout, and then to the base of the falls. It follows the Erskine River past Straw Falls and Splitter's Falls to a natural amphitheatre used for church services prior to 1875. It's moderate to difficult and takes about three hours, but don't attempt it in wet weather; the walk includes river crossings.

Kalimna Falls Walk Starting from the Sheoak Creek picnic area, this easy 9km circuit (three hours) along an old timber tramway passes both the upper and lower Kalimna Falls and takes you into fern gullies. The Falls aren't particularly large though.

Sheoak Falls Walk Also starting from the Sheoak Creek picnic area, this moderate-to-difficult 9km return walk (3½ hours) takes you to the 15m drop and deep pool of the falls and brings you back via the Castle Rock lookout. You'll come across regrowth forest, bridges, the Cumberland River panorama and, hopefully, some koalas.

There are designated camping areas within the park but it's cold, wet, serious camping most of the year and no fires are allowed. If you're still interested, contact Parks Victoria in Lorne.

LORNE

☎ 03 / pop 1200

Observing Lorne's Saturday-swamped main street, you wonder if this coastal town has bitten off more citysiders than it can chew. During peak seasons, car parks and accommodation are scarce, otherwise life here is fairly peaceful. Has Lorne retained its charm despite slick development? As Aussies like to say: 'Yeah-no, yeah-no', which means 'sort of'.

Built around the Erskine River and the shores of Loutit Bay, Lorne and its significant natural assets even enchanted Rudyard Kipling who, after visiting in 1891, wrote the poem *Flowers*, which includes the lines: 'Gathered where the Erskine leaps, Down the road to Lorne…'

Information

Parks Victoria (☎ 13 19 63; www.parkweb.vic.gov.au; 86 Polwarth Rd) If you're interested in camping, come here for more details.

Visitors centre (☎ 5289 1152; 144 Mountjoy Pde) This office is often crammed with folks, but staff are very helpful.

Sights & Activities

There are more than 50km of **walking tracks** through the Otway Ranges behind Lorne (see opposite) and the visitors centre has good maps and guides to the walks. Other-

wise, **EcoLogic Education and Environment Services** (☎ 5263 1133; www.ecologic.net.au), based in Anglesea, organises guided walks for a minimum of two people.

If nature irks you, at least drive to **Teddy's Lookout** and inland along the scenic Erskine Falls Rd. At **Erskine Falls**, it's an easy walk to the waterfalls' viewing platform, but the cardio-fit can attempt the 250 steps down to the base, and 250 back up! The visitors centre can also suggest lovely loop drives through the Otway Ranges (see also the detour inland from Apollo Bay, p211).

Even if contemporary art doesn't grab you, visit **Qdos Arts** (☎ 5289 1989; www.qdosarts.com; Allenvale Rd; ☀ 10am-late; closed Wed Apr-Nov). Apart from stunning exhibitions, the building's striking architecture and sculpture garden enhance this magical bush setting, and the licensed café is excellent.

Ambling is essential along Lorne's white-sand **beaches** in the north and its reef and rock pools in the south. A surf life-saving club patrols the main beach in summer, and you can hire bodyboards and wetsuits from the **Lorne Surf Shop** (☎ 5289 1673; 130 Mountjoy Pde; ☀ 9am-5.30pm), or catch a surfing lesson with **Go Ride A Wave** (☎ 1300 132 441) or **Southern Exposure** (☎ 5261 2170); about $50 for two hours.

Festivals & Events

Falls Festival (www.fallsfestival.com) Lorne's New Year's Eve celebration is a two-day shindig that contains the merrymaking of thousands of partygoers on a farm not too far from town, while families and fireworks occupy the foreshore. Falls assembles a top line-up of rock groups, and the $100 ticket price includes camping.

Pier to Pub Swim (www.lornesurfclub.com.au; early Jan) This popular event sees up to 4500 swimmers splashing their way 1.2km across Loutit Bay to the Lorne Hotel. Registration fills up fast: apply online.

Sleeping

Lorne has loads of accommodation for bush and beach lovers but it is incredibly hilly. BYO donkey. You'll find there is often a minimum two-night stay on weekends and prices nearly double over summer, but in winter rates are sometimes negotiable.

For other options, ask the visitors centre or try the **Great Ocean Road Accommodation Centre** (☎ 5289 1800; www.gorac.com.au; 136 Mountjoy Pde; ☀ 9am-5.30pm), located next door to the pharmacy.

SOUTHWEST

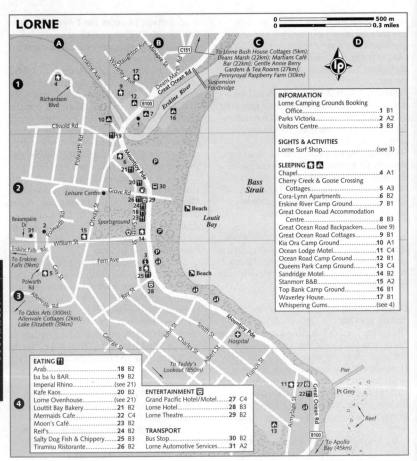

BUDGET

Great Ocean Road Backpackers (☎ 5289 1070; www.yha.org.au; 10 Erskine Ave; dm low/high season $24/30, d $60/70) This is a country-cosy, two-storey timber lodge nestled among the gum trees, with companionable cockatoos and magpies. An excellent place to chill. Dorms are spacious, and doubles are excellent value.

Lorne Camping Grounds Booking Office (☎ 5289 1382; www.lorneforeshore.asn.au; 2 Great Ocean Rd; powered/unpowered sites per 2 people from $22/18, d cabins with bathroom low/high season $80/122) manages bookings for five good caravan parks. Book well ahead for peak-season stays.

Erskine River Park The prettiest; on the left-hand side of the Great Ocean Rd as you enter Lorne, just before you

cross the bridge. It's positioned on the northern bank of Erskine River.

Top Bank Park Nestles along the southern bank of the river.

Ocean Rd Park On the right-hand side of the Great Ocean Rd as you enter Lorne, opposite Erskine River Park.

Kia Ora Park Also on the right, tucked beside the bridge.

Queens Park Two and a half kilometres further, at the southern end of town, on a hillside.

MIDRANGE & TOP END

There are several motels in town and both the town's pubs have rooms.

Chapel (☎ 5289 2622; thechapellorne@bigpond.com; 45 Richardson Blvd; d low/high season $150/180) Outstanding. This contemporary two-level A-frame retreat is glossy-mag material, with choice Indonesian furnishings, happy

DETOUR: DEANS MARSH

Deans Marsh Rd, signposted as you enter Lorne, heads into the hills for 22km to a two-store township. This winding, sun-dappled road is a mesmerising drive. In spring, the forested corridor explodes with vibrant wildflowers. About 14km in, the road unfolds in long sweeping curves with undulating pastoral views to your right. At Deans Marsh, you can relax with a coffee at kooky **Martians Cafe Bar** (☎ 5236 3350; 12 Lorne Rd; light meals $6-13; 9am-9pm daily in summer, Wed-Sun in winter). It's an airy shed with blue corrugated-iron walls, '70s-style 'chandeliers' and mishmash furniture. Outside is a woodchip playground. Heading back the way you came, after 12km take the unsealed Mt Sabine Rd on your right; it's a narrower corridor of rugged bush beauty (not advisable in wet weather, when it's potholed and boggy). After 8.5km, turn left onto Erskine Falls Rd with its more varied foliage, and stop at **Erskine Falls lookout**, before cruising 8km into Lorne. The loop is 54km.

From December to April, it's berry-picking season around Deans Marsh. To reach **Gentle Annie Berry Gardens and Tea Rooms** (☎ 5236 3391; 520 Pennyroyal Valley Rd, Deans Marsh; 9am-5pm, closed May-Nov), turn left at the primary school, which is on Deans Marsh Rd, into Pennyroyal Valley Rd and travel 4km to sample terrific Devonshire teas, preserves and chutneys. Or visit **Pennyroyal Raspberry Farm** (☎ 5236 3238; Division Rd, Murroon; 10am-5pm Dec-Jan) which grows organic produce. From the general store, take a right-hand turn along the Deans Marsh/Birregurra Rd and travel 4km to turn left into Bush's Rd. It's another 6km to Division Rd, where you turn left, and travel 1km to the farm gates. Both farms are well signposted from Deans Marsh.

splashes of colour and bay windows that seem to tumble into the forest below. It's a snuggle-your-love-bug getaway, with double shower and complimentary robes.

Stanmorr B&B (☎ 5289 1530; www.stanmorr.com; cnr William & Otway Sts; d low/high season $140/225) Genteel Stanmorr does a modern rendition of 1920s charm, with elegantly furnished, timber-panelled rooms of lemon cream and tulip green. Birds (fed daily) keep a close eye on guests, and there are sea or garden views. For indulgence, book the studio.

Cherry Creek and Goose Crossing Cottages (☎ 5289 2107; 93-99 Polwarth Rd; cottages $100-150) These two homey cottages with eclectic furnishings are set in a lovely, rambling 2-acre garden with dogs and squawking geese for company: imagine you are staying with eccentric grandparents. Cherry Creek sleeps five; Goose Crossings sleeps two. Kids and pets welcome.

Allenvale Cottages (☎ 5289 1450; Allenvale Rd; d low/high season $135/220) Home comforts aren't lost in these early-century-style timber cottages. They're 2km northwest of Lorne, dotted among shady trees and plush grass, complete with bridge and babbling brook. It's a storybook setting, ideal for families.

Lorne Bush House Cottages (☎ 5289 2477; www.lornebushcottages.com.au; 1860 Deans Marsh Rd; d low/high season $140/160) Set high on a hill, these cottages have cute loft bedrooms with superb bush, valley or ocean views. Hopefully you're

a fan of golden pine, no-fuss furniture. Great for families. A minimum two-night stay applies on weekends.

Waverley House (☎ 5289 2044; waverleyhouse@iprimus.com.au; cnr Great Ocean Rd & Waverley Ave; d low/high season $155/210) There's a hint of aristocracy in these spacious rooms with high ceilings, wide windows and balconies looking onto a manicured front garden. All have kitchenettes. Room 5 is the pick.

Great Ocean Road Cottages (☎ 5289 1070; www.greatoceanroadcottages.com; 10 Erskine Ave; d low/high season $150/170;) Designed to blend into a hillside of eucalypts, these A-frame retreats are a magnet for cheeky cockatoos. Cottages sleep four or six and have basic mod cons, but bland décor.

Other recommendations:

Ocean Lodge Motel (☎ 5289 1330; 6 Armytage St; d low/high season $95/145) Ocean views.

Whispering Gums (☎ 5289 1368; 43 Richardson Bvld; d low/high season $80/150) Comfy studio, steep walk.

Sandridge Motel (☎ 5289 2180; www.sandridgemotel.com.au; 128 Mountjoy Pde; d low/high season $145/225;) Beach and main-street frontage.

Cora-Lynn Apartments (☎ 5289 2288; www.smythestateagent.com.au; Mountjoy Pde; studio from $140) Centrally located, functional studios.

Eating

Lorne is the munching capital of the Great Ocean Rd with heaps of good (if overpriced) cafés and restaurants along Mountjoy

Pde. Most are open day and night during summer, but in winter most have shorter trading hours according to the number of visitors in town; some close altogether. It's hard to find a bad coffee in Lorne.

ba ba lu BAR (☎ 5289 1808; 6a Mountjoy Pde; mains $18-28; ☻ breakfast, lunch & dinner daily, closed Tue & Wed in low season) Millionaires mix with backpackers indoors and out at this unpretentious place, always set on cruise control. Flavoursome, organic (where possible) nosh is served, from authentic tapas to eclectic à la carte. It closes June and July.

Mermaids Cafe (☎ 5289 2422; 22 Great Ocean Rd; mains $10-14; ☻ breakfast & lunch daily, closed Tue & Wed winter) At the quiet end of town, Mermaids has ace views, a relaxed outdoors area and funky interior. Very tasty fare, from the nut pancake with muesli, yoghurt and fruit to its tofu, lentil and vegie-patty burgers.

Imperial Rhino (☎ 5289 5215; 44 Mountjoy Pde; mains $15-20; ☻ breakfast, lunch & dinner) It's the long wooden tables and ottoman squats for seats that first impress, but this licensed, contemporary Asian-fest does everything well, from noodles to stir-fries and sushi. A friendly place to chow down.

Kafe Kaos (☎ 5289 2639; 52 Mountjoy Pde; lunch $8-15; ☻ breakfast & lunch) You come here to feel like you're hanging out in a friend's inner-urban retro pad, except it's by the beach. Standard Mod Oz lunch fare prepared with excellent bread, and a good place for vegetarian options.

Louttit Bay Bakery (☎ 5289 1207; 46b Mountjoy Pde; mains $3-8; ☻ breakfast & lunch) Cakes! Say no more. OK, good ones. Sandwiches and rolls made to order, with essential complements like capers. Yes, pies, pastries and bread are available too.

Arab (☎ 5289 1435; 94 Mountjoy Pde; mains $20-24; ☻ breakfast, lunch & dinner) They're doing something right, having opened in 1956! It's a bustling eatery that ploughs on in quiet seasons, offering simple, tasty food with no-fuss presentation and ambience to match.

Reif's (☎ 5289 2366; 84 Mountjoy Pde; dinner mains $19-25; ☻ breakfast, lunch & dinner daily Oct-May, closed Sun dinner & Thu in winter) Good vibe. Fronted by tiered decks, Reif's menu offers adventure with kangaroo carpaccio, and crowd-pleases with curry or yumtious chickpea-and-cumin battered fish and chips.

Other recommendations:

Lorne Ovenhouse (☎ 5289 2544; 46a Mountjoy Pde; mains $20-25; ☻ lunch & dinner all year, breakfast Nov-Apr) Gourmet wood-fired pizza, and pasta and focaccias; family friendly.

Moon's Cafe (☎ 5289 1149; 108 Mountjoy Pde; mains $6.50-11; ☻ breakfast & lunch) Coffee-and-newspaper nook.

Tiramisu Ristorante (☎ 5289 1004; 1a Grove Rd; mains $19-25; ☻ dinner all year, lunch in summer) Basic, busy, good Italian.

Salty Dog Fish & Chippery (☎ 5289 1300; Shop 1 Cumberland Resort; ☻ lunch & dinner) Fresh-looking fish.

Entertainment

Over summer, a number of Lorne's restaurants add acoustic music to their menus.

ba ba lu BAR (☎ 5289 1808; 6a Mountjoy Pde; ☻ to 1am, closed Tue-Wed in low season) Serves up world music in a chilled atmosphere. Perch at the bar or grab an outdoor table; the vibe here works for just about everyone. Closed June and July.

Martians Cafe Bar (☎ 5236 3350; 12 Lorne Rd, Deans Marsh; ☻ 9am-9pm daily in summer, Wed-Sun in winter) It's a big old shed with great coffee, booze, and live music on weekends, but it's a 44km round trip from Lorne (see p205).

Grand Pacific Hotel/Motel (☎ 5289 1609; 268 Mountjoy Pde) Striving for beachside sophistication with its sleek bar, it has cool jazz on Saturday nights all year, and solo artists on Sundays in peak season.

Lorne Ovenhouse (☎ 5289 2544; 46a Mountjoy Pde; mains $20-25; ☻ to late Nov-Apr) The Ovenhouse is a stylish, but casual, eatery and bar with a lounge out back showing music videos.

Lorne Hotel (☎ 5289 1409; cnr Mountjoy Pde & Bay St) Bands play in the bottom bar most weekends, and more often in peak season, but the shaded terrace overlooking Lorne is entertainment enough on summer nights.

Lorne Theatre (☎ 5289 1272; cnr Mountjoy Pde & Grove Rd; adult/child $12/8; ☻ closed Jul & Aug) Movies daily during the peak season, less often other times.

Getting There & Around

V/Line (☎ 13 61 96) has daily bus services along the Great Ocean Rd which stop at the Commonwealth Bank on Mountjoy Pde – to/from Melbourne costs $26.20, including train fare. The bus service to/from Geelong costs $12.60, and Apollo Bay $5.50.

You can hire a car through **Avis** (☎ 5521 1332; per day from $55) in Geelong and, availability pending, they will deliver it on the same day to **Lorne Automotive Services** (☎ 5289 2593; 2 Beaurepaire Dr, Lorne).

From late December through January, a free shuttle bus runs the length of Mountjoy Pde (10am to 6pm, every 30 minutes).

If you want a taxi, call **Lorne Taxi Service** (☎ 0409-892 304).

SHIPWRECK COAST

LORNE TO APOLLO BAY

This is probably the most spectacular section of the Great Ocean Rd, besides the Twelve Apostles near Port Campbell. The narrow, twisting roadway carves higher and higher into sheer cliffs that drop away into the ocean. It's dangerously distracting though, and difficult to see around corners, so do pay attention to the road and beware the meanderings of other drivers. Accommodation options along here are also wonderfully diverse for those who enjoy less bustle and more bush.

From Lorne, you'll pass through the small towns of Wye River, Kennett River and Skenes Creek and it's certainly worth taking the picturesque, roller-coaster road up and over the Otways into the wee settlement of Forrest.

Cumberland River

☎ 03

Six kilometres southwest of Lorne, **Cumberland River** is the prettiest camping ground along this coast. On one side is the craggy, blackened rock face of **Mt Defiance** plunging into clear, shallow waters, with campsites nestled in grassy verges beside it. And there's a fabulous beach right across the road. The **Cumberland River Holiday Park** (☎ 5289 1790; stay@ cumberlandriver.com.au; 2680 Great Ocean Rd; camp sites per 2 people low/high season $16/24; d cabins with bathroom $65/115) allows campfires and has 'Skip', the local kangaroo.

Wye River

☎ 03

A further 8km on is **Wye River** and the much bigger **Wye River Valley Tourist Park** (☎ 5289 0241; www.wyerivervalleypark.com.au; 25 Great Ocean Rd; powered/unpowered sites low season $32/25, high season

$39/29, d cabins with bathroom low/high season $85/95), which is short on shade, but has a superb beach across the road. Also here is the **Rookery Nook Hotel** (☎ 5289 0240; 19 Great Ocean Rd; mains $15-22; ☷ lunch noon-2pm, dinner 6-8pm; dm $15, d low/ high season $95/135, studio $110/150; ☐), perfectly poised on the hillside, with rugged ocean views from its outdoor tables; or snaffle the public picnic tables below. The Nook's vibrantly decorated motel units, all with views, are top value. Bunks beds are available, and there's a cosy studio for couples. Breakfast? You'll have to make do with a toasted sandwich or burger from the general store.

Kennett River to Skenes Creek

Another 5km along is **Kennett River**, which has the best **koala spotting** on the southwest coast. Behind the caravan park, walk 200m up Grey River Rd and you'll see bundles of the sleepy bears clinging to branches. The cute factor is very high.

Be camera-ready for stunning **Cape Patton lookout**, about 4km beyond Kennett River. From here to Skenes Creek, the land rolls and folds dramatically in camel-hump hills.

Wongarra, 8km south of Cape Patton, has a moody, windswept quality that appeals to the recluse within. Quaint, secluded and unique, **Patrick's By the Sea B&B** (☎ 03-5237 0267; 50 Beattie Lane; d low/high season $120/150) is a former railway caboose lovingly refurbished with a cosy ocean-front lounge, wide timber decking, wood fire and claw-foot bath; it's an experience worth savouring. **Points South Cottages** (☎ 03-5237 0296; www.points-south.com.au; 5260 Great Ocean Rd; d $250) is run by retired Australian cycling champ Phil Anderson and his wife Christy, who offer an isolated hilltop getaway in 200 acres of animal-dotted farmland. Their two luxuriant, contemporary cottages have a minimum two-night stay on weekends. Pets are welcome. From its summit, **Wongarra Heights B&B** (☎ 03-5237 0267; wongarra_bb@iprimus.com.au; 65 Sunnyside Rd; d low/high season $110/160) has sweeping Southern Ocean views, east and west, that any artist would die for. It's a traditional homestead with neatly kept rooms in 1930s country style.

Skenes Creek

☎ 03

From **Skenes Creek**, Skenes Creek Rd (route C119 signposted to Colac) winds steeply into the heart of the Otways to Forrest. Its

SOUTHWEST

languid curves reveal dramatic valley views, rolling pasturelands and graveyard vistas of culled pine plantations before plunging into mossy rainforest. About 15km in you'll see a left-hand turn-off to Beech Forest via the narrow, unsealed, corrugated and potholed Turtons Track, which leads to more Otways waterfalls and townships. Hold it! The track is only advisable for 4WDs, and it's off-limits to all vehicles in winter. In summer, conventional vehicles might attempt it, but it's *very* rough going.

A few minutes further along Skenes Creek Rd is the **Mt Sabine Falls** turn-off, on the right. From the car park, it's a 3.6km moderate-to-steep walk that takes about 2½ hours return. The next settlement, **Barramunga**, has a walk to **Stevensons Falls** and the back-to-basics **Barramunga Cabins** (☎ 5236 3302; www .barramungacabins.com.au; Upper Gellibrand Rd; cabins for 8-10 people from $240), surrounded by state forest. These are terrific for families, groups and *Blair Witch Project* die-hards.

V/Line (☎ 13 61 96) buses between Skenes Creek and Geelong cost $19.70.

Forrest
☎ 03

Finally, 32km from Skenes Creek is the township of Forrest where the air is sweet with the scent of log fires and cut grass. There's a general store, pub and tea-rooms, but for a truly memorable night, stay at the **Forrest Country Guesthouse Restaurant** (☎ 5236 6446; 16 Grant St; d low/high season $130/150). A clutter of bric-a-brac from the region adorns every nook of this place and creates themes in each guest room (which has disabled facilities, too). Your hosts prepare fine, home-cooked meals (rates include breakfast) and they have the Otways' cosiest country bar. You'll be sad to leave.

If you want to feel like a real local, the **Little Mill Cottage** (☎ 5236 3302; Turner St; d low/high season $90/100) is a timber shack with creaking floors and lingering log-fire smells; nothing flash but very area-authentic.

From Forrest, it's a 7km drive and 25-minute moderate-to-steep walk to tranquil **Lake Elizabeth**, where the platypus play for those up early enough to see them. There are three other lake walks you can do here. Alternatively, you can book a four-hour paddle on the lake with **Otway Natural Wonders and Platypus Tours** (☎ 5236 6345; 10 Blundy St; per person $85) in the early morning or afternoon. Dawn is the best time to go, and trips are limited to a minimum of two and a maximum of six people.

APOLLO BAY
☎ 03 / pop 1400

Ridiculously picturesque Apollo Bay is a fishing town and popular summer beach drop zone. It's a little more relaxed than Lorne and a lot less trendy, but you can sniff development at its heels and an air of resignation among its eclectic populace of fishing folk, artists, musicians and sea-changers who have kept its secret well.

Majestic rolling hills, reminiscent of northern Scotland, provide a postcard backdrop to the town – although you can see them filling fast with new homes and accommodation options – while broad, white-sand beaches dominate the foreground. It's also an ideal base for exploring magical Cape Otway and Otway National Park.

Information

Cafe Nautigals (☎ 0402-825 590; 57 Great Ocean Rd; ☽ 8.30am-11pm) The Internet is available at this place on the main drag.
Great Ocean Road Visitors Centre (☎ 5237 6529; Great Ocean Rd, Apollo Bay; ☽ 9am-5pm) On the left as you arrive from Lorne. In the same building, there's an impressive 'eco-centre' with displays on Aboriginal history, rainforests, shipwrecks and the building of the Great Ocean Rd.

Sights & Activities

There's plenty of action and adventure in and around Apollo Bay, much of it focussed on the area's natural delights (for attractions inland of Apollo Bay, see p211). You could easily base yourself here for a week and still wish for more time.

It's 1.5km from town to **Marriners Lookout** (signposted) for spectacular views of the town and back along the coast toward Cape Patton – from the car park it's about 20 minutes to the lookout (return) with lots of huff-and-puff. No pain, no height gain.

Having paid your respects to the gods of nature, you may indulge in some frivolous activity. Horse-riding along the beach is always a respectable alternative: **Wild Dog Trails** (☎ 5237 6441; 225 Wild Dog Rd; ☽ 9am-6.30pm) has 1½- to three-hour horse rides (from $45). Or, you might enjoy meeting the slippery crew banished to the **Marengo Reef Seal Colony**, who are visited regularly by **Apollo Bay Sea Kayaking** (☎ 0405-495 909) at 10.30am and 2pm most days.

Dudes seeking 'amplitude' can tandem hang-glide or paraglide from Marriners Lookout with **Wingsports Flight Academy** (☎ 0419-378 616), or else at **Cape Otway Aviation** (☎ 0407-306 065; 3 Telford St; flights per person $145) join Vic Bongiorno and his Cessna 206 in dive bombing the Twelve Apostles (kidding).

Otway Expeditions (☎ 5237 6341) runs two- to three-hour, cop-out (mainly downhill), mountain-bike rides through the Otways ($55), as well as some gentle bush-bashing adventure in the cross-terrain-and-water Argo Buggies (from $35).

Museum! Yawners, read no further. The **Old Cable Station Museum** (☎ 5237 7441; Great Ocean Rd; admission $2.50; ☷ 2-5pm Sat & Sun, school & public holidays), has a huge collection of photographs and local artefacts relating to the 1859 submarine telegraph cable from Cape Otway to Tasmania (see p213). Another cable was laid to Tassie in 1936, this time from Apollo Bay. It was capable of carrying *six* telephone conversations – some people will do anything for a natter.

Meet the locals at their Saturday **community market** (☷ 8.30am-4.30pm) along the main strip. Keep an ear cocked for the self-made celebrity and talented flautist Howlin' Wind, who is usually about; his CD with the Great Ocean Rd tribute track is worth a listen.

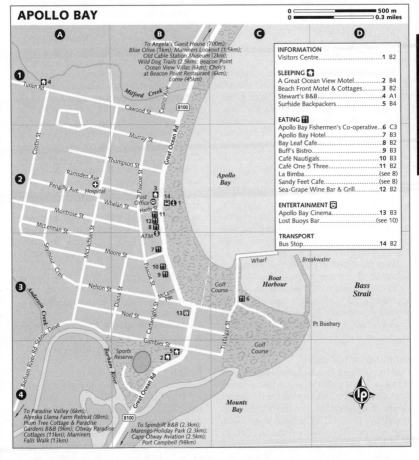

APOLLO BAY

INFORMATION	
Visitors Centre	1 B2

SLEEPING 🏠	
A Great Ocean View Motel	2 B4
Beach Front Motel & Cottages	3 B2
Stewart's B&B	4 A1
Surfside Backpackers	5 B4

EATING 🍴	
Apollo Bay Fishermen's Co-operative	6 C3
Apollo Bay Hotel	7 B3
Bay Leaf Cafe	8 B2
Buff's Bistro	9 B3
Café Nautigals	10 B3
Café One 5 Three	11 B2
La Bimba	(see 8)
Sandy Feet Cafe	(see 8)
Sea-Grape Wine Bar & Grill	12 B2

ENTERTAINMENT 🎭	
Apollo Bay Cinema	13 B3
Lost Buoys Bar	(see 10)

TRANSPORT	
Bus Stop	14 B2

Festivals & Events

Apollo Bay Music Festival (☎ 5237 6761; www.apollo
baymusicfestival.com; adult weekend pass $100; late Apr),
held over a weekend in late April, features
blues, jazz, classical, rock and folk music,
plus street performers, buskers and markets.
As far as festivals go, it's an intimate affair,
attracting about 3000 locals and blow-ins.
Sunday morning's Gospel Grooves are ace.

Sleeping

Accommodation has mushroomed in recent
years, particularly in the B&B market, with
many gems tucked in the Otways. The pesky
two-night minimum stay on weekends is
popular here, as are week-long bookings for
summer and Easter holidays. There are loads
of motels in town, but ask to see a room first;
they're not all on par.

BUDGET

There are several caravan parks and backpackers in town.

Angela's Guest House (☎ 5237 7085; 7 Campbell Crt;
d low/high season $60/100) Readers gave glowing
reports of Angela and Denis's large family
home and their genuine, warm welcome.
Spotless, well equipped, double and family
rooms have bright, cheerful décor. Some
share a bathroom (prices are the same with or
without; it's first in, first served), most have
balconies, and they're all excellent value.

Surfside Backpackers (☎ 5237 7263; cnr Great
Ocean Rd & Gambier St; dm low/high season $18/22,
d $55/60) Of the three backpackers, this ram-
bling, old, white weatherboard affair is the
largest. It's a homely place to hang out with
other folk and listen to retro records in the
lounge with its views of tumbling surf.

Marengo Holiday Park (☎ 5237 6162; www.marengo
park.com.au; Off Great Ocean Rd; powered/unpowered sites
per 2 people low season $32/17, high season $36/18, d cabin
low/high season $80/160) Just 2km west of town on
a rise by the beach, this very well run park
has incredibly spacious, motel-quality deluxe
cabins. Light on shade for campers though.

MIDRANGE & TOP END

Plum Tree Cottage & Paradise Gardens B&B (☎ 5237
6939; www.paradisegardens.net.au; 715 Barham River Rd;
d from $130-210; ⚥) This turreted mini manor
overlooks a pretty dam and the fairytale hills
of Barham River Rd, 9km from town. Giant
beds, sumptuous fabrics and shades of dusky
blue, husk and pearl make this a polished,

self-contained getaway that can be divided
into a bedsit. There's a B&B room available
in the homestead.

Stewart's B&B (☎ 5237 6447; 2 Tuxion Rd; d low/high
season $140/190) Perched on a rolling hillside
dotted with sheep, these lovely rooms have
grand views of the town and ocean and are
fresh, with lively yellow and sailor-blue décor.
Rate includes continental breakfast, or there's
hot nosh for $10 more; it's 1km from town.

Alyeska Llama Farm Retreat (☎ 5237 6138; www
.llama.asn.au/alyeska; 355 Killala Rd; loft low/high season
$125/150) Getting to know their guests is these
llamas' favourite pastime, so prepare for
inquisitive company. The Loft is an idyllic
couples' retreat with king-size bed upstairs,
kitchen and lounge downstairs. Continental
breakfast provided the first morning.

Spindrift B&B (☎ 5237 7410; spindrift@vicnet.net.au;
2 Marengo Cres; d $100) Who wants dibs on this
incredible ocean vista? Windswept views of
Mounts Bay dominate two very spacious,
spotless rooms that bookend a generous
guests' lounge room. Your cheery hosts provide continental breakfast, plus eggs.

Beacon Point Ocean View Villas (☎ 5237 6218;
www.beaconpoint.com.au; 270 Skenes Creek Rd; d from
$150-250; ⚥) These hilltop deluxe and premium
villas have great bush and ocean views, wood
fires, a sensual feel and contemporary edge.
Cheaper suites have spas and daggy fabrics.

Beach Front Motel & Cottages (☎ 5237 6666;
www.beachfrontmotel.com.au; 163 Great Ocean Rd, Apollo
Bay; d low/high season $89/215) Perfectly located
at the top of the main drag, these rooms
with brown-brick walls, exposed beams and
slanted ceilings feel rather 'ski-lodge', with
views onto rolling highlands. Beds piled
with plump cushions are a plush extra.

Other recommendations:

Otway Paradise Cottages (☎ 5237 7102; www.otway
-paradise-cottages.com.au; 935 Barham River Rd;
d low/high season $140/160) Basic, pine-panelled digs in
wondrous bushland.

A Great Ocean View Motel (☎ 5237 6527; www.great
oceanview.com.au; 1 Great Ocean Rd; d low/high season
$125/180) New, bland furnishings; fabulous views.

Eating

In winter local eateries operate very much
on flexi-time, according to the amount of
trade (which is particularly affected by dis-
mal weather).

Bay Leaf Cafe (☎ 5237 6470; 131 Great Ocean Rd; lunch
mains $10-16; ☯ breakfast, lunch & dinner) Excellent

DETOUR: APOLLO BAY–LAVERS HILL–BEECH FOREST

Hiding in the back blocks of Apollo Bay are forest 'flying', special sleepovers, fairytale landscapes, giant biscuits (really!) and inimitable meet-the-native (animal and human) encounters. Fuel up, it's time to explore.

A beaut half-day to long-day drive (if you do all side trips) is from Apollo Bay to Beech Forest via Lavers Hill and Melba Gully State Park. It becomes a loop if you take the **Aire Valley Rd** (which becomes Binns Track) from Beech Forest back to Apollo Bay, but be warned: this narrow, logging-truck route is not advised for conventional vehicles. It is badly corrugated, mushy clay, arduous driving and certainly no short cut! In winter, it's out of bounds to everyone.

Lavers Hill: is 48km from Apollo Bay. This often mist-shrouded hilltop was once a thriving timber town but today it's a stuff-your-face stop with two cafés. Zoom 1.5km further towards Port Campbell for the **McDuff's Bakehouse** (☎ 03-5237 3123; ♥ breakfast & lunch) experience: a fabulous rainbow lounge with brilliant coffee, giant lamingtons and biscuits, and incredible pies and breads. Should you decide to linger, two hilltop bistros compete for dinner business: **Lavers Hill Roadhouse** (☎ 03-5237 3251; Lavers Hill; mains $14-24) and **Otway Junction Motor Inn** (☎ 03-5237 3295; www.otwaymotorinn.com; Lavers Hill; d low/high season $88/125; mains $15-26; ☒) both offer fairly standard menus, but include several vegetarian options.

As for beds, the Motor Inn's rooms are ready for a refurb, but have good hilly views, while **Southern Heights B&B** (☎ 03-5237 3131; 5159 Great Ocean Rd; d low/high season $110/140) 3km out of town has quality rooms, with lush views from one. International folk love the **Fauna Australia Wildlife Retreat** (☎ 03-5237 3234; www.faunaaustralia.com.au; d low/high season $100/150) where almost-tame native animals (bred on the property) snoop about at night. The cabins are spacious, but very dull.

Seven kilometres southwest of Lavers Hill is tiny **Melba Gully State Park** with a lovely picnic area below the car park. The marked **Madsen's Track** rainforest nature walk has an eerie canopy of blackwoods and myrtle beeches and the fat, 300-year-old 'Big Tree', an unimaginatively named messmate eucalypt that is 27m in circumference. After dark, **glow-worms** (the larvae of the fungus gnat) glimmer in the park. Handy accommodation is 600m away at quaint **Cottage Flower Farm B&B** (☎ 03-5237 3208; Melba Gully Rd; d low/high season $100/120) with landscaped gardens and a duck pond.

You won't escape the well signposted **Otway Fly** (☎ 03-5235 9200; Phillips Track; www.otwayfly.com; adult/child/family $15/9/39; ♥ 9am-5pm), 5km from Beech Forest. It's an elevated steel walkway in the forest canopy with a lookout tower that affords great views for the 700 to 2000 people pumped through it each day. Arrive before 10am and it's *virtually* all yours. The total walk is 2.5km and tuckers out many, but a buggy is available for anyone with limited mobility. The café is charmless, but the outdoor sausage sizzle is a ripper.

Triplet Falls, further along the same road as the Fly (Phillips Track), is also worth the hike. The walk is 900m long and includes a historic timber site. The **Beauchamp** and **Hopetoun Falls** are just past Beech Forest, down the unsealed and troublesome Aire Valley Rd, mentioned earlier (above).

For a real slice of Otways' life, meet the locals by staying overnight in **Beech Forest**. Amid rolling mists, the **Beechy Pub** (☎ 03-5235 9220; Beech Forest; d $85; mains $15-18; ♥ lunch & dinner, closed Mon & Tue) is a welcoming shelter that goes by the motto 'Great Food, Great Beer, Great Pub'. Rooms are clean but basic. Another curious option is the restored old school turned **Otways School House B&B** (☎ 03-5235 9227; 1560 Old Beech Forest Rd; d low/high season $130/150; ☒). Couples looking for seclusion in a neat little rust-red and storm-grey, self-contained, spa-cottage plonked in a plush-green farmland dell, can dial **Dinmont House** (☎ 03-5237 3181; Old Colac Rd; d low/high season $135/165).

spot for any meal, but the morning's pancake stacks and evening's chicken-and-leek pie are wizard. A favourite with locals for its innovative menu, real coffee and buzzy, friendly atmosphere at fair prices. Outside Christmas and Easter, dinner is served Tuesday to Saturday.

Cafe Nautigals (☎ 0402-825 590; 57 Great Ocean Rd; mains $14-16; ♥ breakfast, lunch & dinner; ▣) There's a great selection of tasty, satisfying Asian noodle, rice and curry dishes, and tofu plates for vegetarians, but it's the wildly warm colours and magnetic vibe that drags you in and keeps you here. A backpackers' menu includes free drink and Internet with your meal.

Buff's Bistro (☎ 5237 6403; 51 Great Ocean Rd; mains $19-25; ◷ lunch & dinner) This BYO and licensed restaurant looks far cosier at night, when the exciting menu presents almond-and-ricotta gnocchi or prawn spring rolls with chilli jam, alongside gourmet bangers and mash.

La Bimba (☎ 5237 7411; 125 Great Ocean Rd; mains $16-23; ◷ breakfast, lunch & dinner, closed Tue & Wed) At night it's a moody candlelit lair for romance and meaningful conversation. This inviting licensed, upstairs bistro, café and wine-bar does a Mod Oz menu, a kiddie's menu, and has a limited, but choice, wine list.

Cafe One 5 Three (☎ 5237 6518; 153 Great Ocean Rd; mains $4-10; ◷ breakfast & lunch) Light and bright with wraparound windows, there's great people-watching here. Breakfast runs all day and the dried-fruit compote with home-made muesli and yoghurt is a healthy start. Lunches are a bread fest: turkish, focaccia, bagels, rolls, bruschetta, toasted sandwiches.

Blue Olive (☎ 5237 7118; Great Ocean Rd; mains $15-25; ◷ lunch & dinner, breakfast Sat & Sun) Overlooking the rolling surf, 1km before town, the Olive has the best eating views around and a really innovative menu of international flavours. Friday nights they have jam sessions and there's live music on Sunday.

Chris's at Beacon Point Restaurant (☎ 5237 6411; Skenes Creek Rd; mains $30-35; ◷ lunch & dinner) A hilltop fine-dining sanctuary that over-looks Apollo Bay, 6km away. It's a beau-tifully designed restaurant, from its stone feature walls, sandstone floors and vaulted ceilings to its panoramic views. You'll be treated well, but your $33 eye fillet sits alone on its wide white plate.

Other recommendations:

Apollo Bay Hotel (☎ 5237 6250; 95 Great Ocean Rd; mains $18-24; ◷ lunch & dinner) Excellent-value bok choy this and pesto mash that.

Sea-Grape Wine Bar & Grill (☎ 5237 6610; 141 Great Ocean Rd; mains $25-28; ◷ breakfast, lunch & dinner) Terrific wine list.

Sandy Feet Cafe (☎ 5237 6995; 139 Great Ocean Rd; mains $4.50-8; ◷ breakfast & lunch) Tofu, tempeh *and* vegie burgers.

Apollo Bay Fishermen's Co-operative (☎ 5237 6591; Nelson St; ◷ 9.30am-4.30pm) Buy and barbecue fresh fish.

Top Pub (Great Ocean Hotel; ☎ 5237 6240; 29 Great Ocean Rd) Does cheap bar meals.

Entertainment

Half of Cafe Nautigals (p211) is the **Lost Buoys Bar** (◷ 10am-7pm Sun-Thu, 10am-1am Fri & Sat), a rainbow-coloured joint with cushions, bar stools and lounges for chatty nights. It stays open till late throughout January and on pub-lic holidays, including Easter and Christmas.

The Top Pub and Apollo Bay Hotel (left) have live bands during summer and on weekends, and packed outdoor terraces in good weather.

During holidays, a **cinema** (cnr Great Ocean Rd & Nelson St) operates from the local hall.

Getting There & Away

Daily **V/Line** (☎ 13 61 96) buses travel along the Great Ocean Rd to Apollo Bay from Geelong ($21.60) or from Melbourne (including con-necting train fare, $32.30). Buses stop at the visitors centre. At 9.20am on Friday, there's a V/Line bus service from Warrnambool to Apollo Bay ($24.90) via Port Campbell. It departs Apollo Bay for Warrnambool at 1.40pm. There's also a service on Monday during the Christmas holidays.

AROUND APOLLO BAY

Head 6km southwest of Apollo Bay along the Great Ocean Rd to the signposted **Shel-ley Beach** turn-off. It's an unsealed road, and part 4WD track toward the end. There are toilets and wood barbecues in the reserve, a short walking track leading down to the beach or the 4km **Elliot River Walk**.

There are tonnes of excellent short and long walks in the area, like the remarkable **Great Ocean Walk**, a 33km trek from Apollo Bay to Cape Otway along wild coast and windswept heathland. It can be done in shorter sections with help from obliging accommodation hosts who might agree to pick-ups or drop-offs at various points. Ask the visitors centre for maps.

Note this down: from Apollo Bay you must drive the unreasonably pretty 12km up the narrow (take care) **Barham River Road Scenic Drive** to its very end (see p209). Prom-ise to marvel at the rolling scenescape of velvet grass, unusually fluffy sheep and co-lossal eucalypts in this Land of Biodynamic Milk and Honey.

Before returning to town, you will saun-ter along the enchanted **Marriners Falls** walk, which follows the babbling Barham River, and stone-step over five, crystal-clear, creek crossings. Digicam is very busy recording this afternoon. Will also pop in to aptly named **Paradise Valley** picnic area.

Seventeen kilometres past Apollo Bay is **Maits Rest Rainforest Boardwalk**, an easy 20-minute walk through a gripping (yes, gripping) rainforest gully. Tree ferns unfurl their *Alien* spawn under a thick canopy of ancient myrtle beeches that have their roots in the evolution of the Gondwana continent 50 million years ago. The mountain ash here are gargantuan.

CAPE OTWAY

The Cape Otway coastline is a particularly beautiful, rugged and dangerous place, having snapped plenty of ships wide open. It's part of the Otway National Park. To get to Cape Otway, drive 21km along the Great Ocean Rd from Apollo Bay to the turn-off, which heads down Lighthouse Rd.

About 8km down Lighthouse Rd is a sign-post that points down an unsealed road leading to **Blanket Bay**, **Parker Hill**, **Point Franklin** and **Crayfish Beach**. These are all gorgeous, secluded spots for beach ambling (absolutely no swimming!) but the road to Blanket Bay is 4WD territory only. **Bush camping** (per 2 people low/high season $10/$20) is allowed here; book through **Parks Victoria** (☎ 13 19 63) in Apollo Bay, and the visitors centre (p208) has walking maps.

THE AUTHOR'S CHOICE

Cape Otway Centre for Conservation Ecology (☎ 03-5237 9297; www.capeotway centre.com.au; 635 Lighthouse Rd; d $190) Womby, the adorable, boofhead dog, leads you to the post-and-beam mudbrick homestead run by his folks: Lizzie, the zoologist, and Shayne, the natural resources manager. This attractive retreat with broad pastoral views practices sustainable living, from its solar power down to its recycled loo paper and locally made, natural shampoo. You're likely to find an orphaned joey or baby koala slung in a woolly hat on the back of a lounge chair. Or meet Big Buck, the eastern grey roo who mentors the many orphans lovingly nursed here until they are ready to rejoin the wild. The guided nature walks and gourmet meals are special, but the total experience, promoting this environment as nature intended, is unique.

You can climb to the top of **Cape Otway Lighthouse** (☎ 03-5237 9240; Lighthouse Rd; adult/child/family $10.50/5.50/26; ☉ 9am-5pm) for amazing views. It's absolutely reviving up here – tingly fresh. This stately beacon bearer was built in 1848 by more than 40 stonemasons. Grounds are open to picnickers, and the café serves good-value, super-tasty home cooking. Tours, well worth taking, run at 11am, 2pm, 3pm and 4pm. Part of the lighthouse complex is a Telegraph Station, which displays fascinating (yes, fascinating) stuff on undersea cable links with Tasmania (the first telegraph cable from Victoria to Tasmania ran from Cape Otway). Imagine the logistics of submerging 100km of telecom cable to the ocean floor in 1859! The entry fee to the lighthouse includes a tour of the station.

You can stay on these windswept, grassy mounds at the **Lighthouse Keeper's Residence** (☎ 03-5237 9240; www.lightstation.com; B&B d low/high season $145/165) in an airy, sandstone place with austere older-style furnishings in keeping with the times. It's a self-contained cottage sleeping up to four ($300 per night) that can be divided into a B&B for two, or there's the West Studio (doubles low/high season $135/145), which is part of the café. Single-night stays are OK.

Or, there are the wonderfully secluded **Shearwater Cottages** (☎ 03-5237 9290; www.shear watercottages.com; 760 Lighthouse Rd; d low/high season $165/175). These spacious, well-appointed log cabins are very relaxing and doggy friendly, but there's a minimum two-night stay, even midweek.

Bimbi Park (☎ 03-5237 9246; www.bimbipark.com .au; Manna Gum Dr; powered/unpowered sites per 2 people low season $22/15, high season $26/18, dm low/high season $16/20, d cabins $56/75), about 3km before the lighthouse, is a horse-riding ranch with great climbing trees, and shade. There are some good bushwalking tracks here leading to remote beaches, and 1½-hour trail rides ($40) are available.

CAPE OTWAY TO PORT CAMPBELL NATIONAL PARK

After Cape Otway, the Great Ocean Rd straightens out somewhat and runs in a series of sweeping curves around the large and fertile Horden Vale flats, which are occupied by farmers selling souvenirs: 'sheep poo for sale – $2', or horse poo if you prefer. The road returns to the coast briefly at

MUM-LESS MARSUPIALS

'Hang on a sec! I've got an armful of joeys.' Annie Fraser sounds swamped as she answers the phone. Annie is one of more than 350 volunteer wildlife carers around Victoria who offer their homes as temporary shelter for injured or orphaned animals. 'Actually, I've got two maggies, four joeys and three ringtail possums. This always happens in spring.' Come spring, eager travellers hit the road, as does local wildlife, stirred from the winter chill. Road kill is a big problem along the Great Ocean Rd and the Otway Ranges hinterland. People aren't aware they need to drive slowly and be extremely watchful in the early morning, early evening, all night, and especially down quieter unsealed roads, says Annie.

'Always get someone like a wildlife carer to check the pouches of animals,' she begs, having nursed more orphans to adulthood than she can remember. In her 60s now, it's tough work feeding 'pinkies' (jellybean-sized baby roos without fur) three-hourly, 24 hours a day, until they are strong enough to manage four-hourly feeds of the substitute Wombaroo milk. Fancy having nine mouths to feed at once!

But her reward is when her young 'uns return for a visit after being released back into the bush, as they often do, sometimes with a joey of their own. 'I'm a grand-kangaroo-parent several times over,' Annie says proudly.

If you do hit an animal or bird, call **Wildlife Line** (☎ 0500-540 000). You will be put in touch with a wildlife carer who will either take the animal in or, if things are grim, will organise to have the animal euthanased. Or contact the nearest police station.

Glenaire (a hill with a few buildings) after a long and steep climb past a lookout point.

From Glenaire, the road returns inland and begins the climb up to Lavers Hill (see p211). But before you get there, six kilometres north of Glenaire, take the 5km detour down the Red Johanna Rd. It winds through magnificent rolling hills dotted with grazing cows to **Johanna beach**, known for its wild, thrashing surf (forget swimming). The world-famous Rip Curl Pro surfing competition (see p199) comes here when Bells Beach is misbehaving. It's a mesmerising beach walk beside these heaving, surging breakers.

There are a few self-contained cottages tucked down the Red Johanna and Blue Johanna Rds (which make a loop back to the Great Ocean Rd). Of these, the **Boomerangs** (☎ 03-5237 4213; cnr Great Ocean Rd & Red Johanna Rd; d $200) wins on novelty value alone: boomerang-shaped cabins with vaulted ceilings, jarrah floorboards, ceramic pottery basins, leadlighting, spas, gorgeous views of the Johanna Valley and starry nights. The builder has a house shaped like a gum leaf (seriously). A minimum two-night stay applies most weekends.

Back at Lavers Hill, the road heads south again towards the coast. About 16km from Lavers Hill is the turn-off to the romantically named Moonlight Head, a lumpy, 5km dirt-

and-gravel road that forks near the coast: to the left is the **Moonlight Head cemetery** and a walking track along the cliff-tops; to the right is a car park with a track leading down to **Wreck Beach** – you can see the anchors of two of the many ships that met their fate along this coast. The *Marie Gabrielle* sank off here in 1869, and in 1891 the *Fiji* was driven aground in a storm and 12 sailors were drowned.

The **Shipwreck Trail** walk follows this unforgiving coastline 110km from Moonlight Head to Port Fairy. Commemorative plaques have been mounted at points overlooking the sites of 25 shipwrecks (for more wreck information, see opposite). Ask for more information at the Apollo Bay visitors centre.

Port Campbell National Park

A little further and finally, the **Port Campbell National Park** – the most famous and most photographed stretch of the Great Ocean Rd. It's a narrow coastal stretch of low heathlands from Princetown to Peterborough, where sheer limestone cliffs tower 70m over fierce seas, and waves and tides relentlessly thrash soft rock in an ongoing process of erosion and undercutting. Over thousands of years, natural sculptures have been carved out of this soft tertiary limestone, creating a fascinating series of rock stacks, gorges, arches and blowholes.

THE SHIPWRECK COAST

The Victorian coastline between Cape Otway and Port Fairy was a notoriously treacherous stretch of water in the days of sailing ships. Navigation was a fearsome task due to hidden reefs and frequent heavy fog. More than 80 vessels came to grief on this 120km stretch in just 40 years.

The most famous wreck was that of the iron-hulled clipper *Loch Ard*, which foundered off Mutton Bird Island at 4am on the final night of its long voyage from England in 1878. Of 37 crew and 19 passengers on board, only two survived. Eva Carmichael, a nonswimmer, clung to wreckage until she was rinse-cycled into the gorge where apprentice officer Tom Pearce rescued her. Tom heroically climbed the cliff the next day (wait till you see it!) and raised the alarm at a local farmhouse, but no other survivors were found. Eva and Tom were both 19 years old, leading the press to gossip about the possibility of romance, but nothing actually happened. Eva soon returned to Ireland, they never saw each other again, and James Cameron made *Titanic*, the movie, instead of *Loch Hard II: Eva and Tom Tie the Knot*.

Four of the victims of the *Loch Ard* are buried in a small **cemetery** here, and a sign at the gorge relates its story. Allow your goose pimples free reign along the short walking trails around it. On an average day, the heaving waves that churn foam and plumes of sea spray make you wonder how anyone survived at all. Past the cemetery are more formations: the **Blowhole**, **Elephant Rock** and **Mutton Bird Island**, which is home to a large colony of short-tailed shearwaters (called mutton birds by the early settlers).

Another Shipwreck Coast story engages historians in fiery debate. It surrounds the sighting of a Portuguese vessel nicknamed the 'Mahogany Ship', which is said to have run aground off Warrnambool in the 1500s. If it's true, it makes Captain Cook's discovery of our shores a tad retro. Fact or fable? The Portuguese *Deliens World Map*, published in 1567, includes a mysterious landmass called 'Java La Grande' in the vicinity of the then-unknown Australian continent, and in 1836, two shipwrecked sailors reported having seen the remains of a large mahogany ship in the sand dunes near Armstrong Bay, between Warrnambool and Port Fairy. Sightings were reported up until 1870, when it is thought the ship may have been covered by shifting sand dunes. Perhaps it doesn't want to be found (cue scary music).

Falls of Halladale, yet another casualty, was a Glasgow barque that foundered in 1908 on its way from New York to Melbourne. There were no fatalities, but it lay on the reef, fully rigged and with sails set, for a couple of months, to the delight of locals. Other notable wrecks were the *Newfield* in 1892 and *La Bella* in 1905.

Divers have investigated these wrecks and their relics are on display at the terrific **Flagstaff Hill Maritime Village** in Warrnambool, which also runs a nightly sound-and-laser show that re-enacts, with stupendous special effects, the Loch Ard's sinking (see p219).

The **Gibson Steps**, carved by hand into the cliffs in the 19th century (and more recently replaced by concrete steps), lead down to feral Gibson Beach. This beach, and others along this stretch of coast, are not recommended for swimming – you can walk along the beach, but be careful not to be stranded by high tides or nasty waves. Opposite Gibson Steps is the 1869 **Glenample Homestead** (admission adult/child $4/2; 🕙 11am-4pm Sat & Sun Dec-Mar, 11am-4pm Mon-Fri Jan & Easter) where the survivors of the famed *Loch Ard* shipwreck recovered (see above).

The **Twelve Apostles** is the best-known rock formation in Victoria. These lonely rocky stacks have been abandoned to the ocean by eroding headland. Today, only seven apostles can be seen from the viewing platforms: the fate of the missing apostles is unknown. Either there were originally 12, and five have been consumed by the sea, or the formation was named by a drunk with double vision.

The **display centre** (Great Ocean Rd, 🕙 9am-5pm) at the Twelve Apostles, 6km past Princetown, is fairly useless (save the public toilets). However, there's access to the viewing platforms and car park from here at all times. Timber boardwalks run around the clifftops, providing viewing platforms and seats. Pedestrian access to the Twelve Apostles is via a walking trail running beneath the Great Ocean Rd. About 200m up the road, the friendly crew at **12 Apostles Helicopters** (☎ 03-5598 6161; www.12apostleshelicopters.com.au)

offer a range of tours from $80 per person for eight-minute flights. They also record a 'Skycam' video of your trip for $25.

Take your imagination (and a handkerchief) to nearby Loch Ard gorge where the Shipwreck Coast's most haunting tale of woe awaits.

PORT CAMPBELL

☎ 03 / pop 460

This small, windswept village is poised on a dramatic, natural gorge that almost looks artificial, it's so perfectly rectangular in shape. At the end of the inlet, a pleasant sand beach is a superb spot for picnics, and one of the few safe swimming beaches along this tempestuous coast. But once you've enjoyed the natural wonders and a helicopter flight, there's not much else to do here.

Information

Port Campbell Visitors Centre (☎ 5598 6089; 26 Morris St; ☉ 9am-5pm) This well organised office has stacks of regional information and helpful photographs of local accommodation. At the front of the centre is the anchor from the *Loch Ard*, which was salvaged by divers in 1978.

Sights & Activities

In calm seas, a rarity around here, there is stunning **diving** in the kelp forests, canyons and tunnels of the Arches Marine Sanctuary and to the *Loch Ard* wreck, as well as **boat tours** to the Twelve Apostles. Ask at **Port Campbell Marine Services** (☎ 5598 6411; 32 Lord St) at the Mobil Service Station.

The 4.7km **Discovery Walk**, with signage, gives an introduction to the area's natural and historical features. It's just out of town on the way to Warrnambool.

Sleeping & Eating

There's a bunch of motels paying homage to the '60s and '70s and some slick, self-contained accommodation has sprung up in recent years, but digs fill quickly in holiday periods and on weekends. Eating rates in the OK zone only. There's one pub, a couple of cafés and takeaways catering for the passing parade of tourists.

Ocean House Backpackers (☎ 5598 6492; campin port@datafast.net.au; Cairns St; dm low/high season $20/25) Occupies the best chunk of real estate in town. Smack bang overlooking the main beach, this hot-pink, pine-panelled house has a warm ambience and cosy guest lounge

with open fireplace. The kitchen's a little small, but you'll cope.

Port Campbell Cabin and Camping Park (☎ 5598 6492; campinport@datafast.net.au; Morris St; powered/unpowered sites per 2 people $23/20, cabins with bathroom low/high season $80/105) Neat, small and a two-minute walk to the beach and bottom end of town, these new cabins are a good option, although camp sites lack shade.

Daysy Hill Country Cottages (☎ 5598 6226; daysy hill@gatewaybbs.com.au; d garden ste low/high season $125/135; 🐾) Just a few minutes from town, these lovely hillside cedar suites are decked out in modern colonial-style country comfort. The rooms are part of one building or there are more private, self-contained cottages.

Eastern Reef Cottages (☎ 5598 6561; eastern.reef@bigpond.com; Great Ocean Rd; d low/high season $90/120; 🐾) Hooray, they accept single-night stays in these warm, woody, open-plan A-frame cabins. No views, but great for short stays. It's 600m out of town.

Portside Motel (☎ 5598 6084; portsidemotel@big pond.com; d low/high season $75/145) These 10 spacious and light units are 200m from town. The motel is only five years old. It has a pleasant outlook and beachside feel, with private decks looking onto coastal-inspired native gardens.

Loch Ard Motor Inn (☎ 5598 6328; cnr Cairns & Lord Sts; d low/high season $80/150) Creamy green and wattle colours gives these smallish rooms a relaxed vibe and the balcony views of the beach open things up considerably. It's also right in the heart of this teensy township.

Waves (☎ 5598 6111; 29 Lord St; mains $20-26; ☉ breakfast, lunch & dinner) It's the only flash-looking eatery in town and manages a good breakfast at reasonable prices. At night, the seafood menu is as enticing as the contemporary ambience buoyed by the rich coral hues of the décor. Mainly fish-fillet dishes, with just a couple of meat options.

Nico's Pizza and Pasta (☎ 5598 6131; 25 Lord St; mains $15-19; ☉ dinner all year, lunch in summer) This pizza-and-pasta joint is the tasty-food 'n' chatty-ambience option. It offers schnitzels, cray and steak, and unusual pizza toppings, eg 'the Persian': walnuts, feta, pears and tomato topped with cumin.

Getting There & Away

On Fridays at 9.55am (and Mondays during summer holidays), a **V/Line** (☎ 13 61 96) bus departs from Geelong and arrives at Port

Campbell ($37.80) at 3.35pm after stopping in Apollo Bay for lunch. The **Wayward Bus** (☎ 1300 653 510; www.waywardbus.com.au) stops here as part of its Melbourne to Adelaide trip (see also p411).

PORT CAMPBELL TO WARRNAMBOOL

West of Port Campbell, the next ocean sculpture is **The Arch**, a rocky archway offshore from Point Hesse. Nearby is **London Bridge**, albeit fallen down. It was once a double-arched, rock platform linked to the mainland and visitors could walk out across a narrow section over one of the arches and reach the other side. But in 1990, one of the arches collapsed into the sea, stranding two astounded tourists on the newly formed island – they were eventually rescued by helicopter. On clear moonlit evenings, this is a good spot to view penguins as they retire for the night. Next are **The Grotto** and the aptly named **Crown of Thorns** rock.

You'll pass by the old-fashioned coastal township of Peterborough, which is just a pub and general store built around the mouth of the Curdies River; a great spot for fishing and swimming. Eight kilometres west of Peterborough is the **Bay of Islands**, where a two-hour walk from the car park takes you

along the coastline to magnificent lookout points over the bay of rocky island clumps.

Then it's time for a teary farewell. The 'Great' part of the Great Ocean Rd effectively ends at the Bay of Islands. From here, the road heads inland through unspectacular flatlands and farming communities all the way to Warrnambool.

There is one important detour however, about 16km from Peterborough. **Timboon Farmhouse Cheese** (☎ 03-5598 3387; Ford & Fells Rd; ⏰ 10.30am-4pm daily Oct-Apr & school holidays, Wed-Sun May-Sep) has generous (free) tastings at the 'Mousetrap' where you nibble your way through award-winning, biodynamic cheeses such as their camembert, brie, feta and triple creams. Cheese platters, a selection of sandwiches, Devonshire teas and wine are all sold here, and may be scoffed politely in the pleasant garden, especially if the weather is dandy.

WARRNAMBOOL

☎ 03 / pop 26,840

These days, Warrnambool feels like the major industrial and commercial centre that it is, although its historic buildings, waterways and streets lined with Norfolk Island pines and pohutukawas (New Zealand Christmas trees) add appeal. It has good sheltered swimming beaches and open surf beaches, and blossoms with families in summer.

Anglers dribble over the fishing prospects here, with a choice of fishing from the Merri and Hopkins Rivers, or more adventurous ocean fishing.

There's also a large student population attending the Warrnambool campus of Deakin University, which means you can party if the mood takes you.

Warrnambool was originally settled as a humble whaling and sealing station and was first named 'Warnimble', an Aboriginal word meaning 'plenty of water', which figures, given the outer edges of town are prettily situated on Lady Bay between the two rivers. It was chosen as a settlement site because of the supposedly safe and sheltered harbour of Lady Bay – but the ghosts of more than 30 shipwrecks off the coast are gargling their protest.

If you're in a hurry to head back to Melbourne, you'll kiss the Great Ocean Rd goodbye here, and head inland to the speedy Princes Hwy (see p232).

PRANKS AHOY!

In March 1882 Port Campbell was practically the end of the earth and, as such, became the convenient stage for a hoax. Around that time, there was a fear that Australian shores would be invaded by bearded, vodka-slamming Russians. Henry Bryant, a bit of a wag, pumped up the hype by convincing the *Age* newspaper that a Russian fleet was ready to attack, and the invasion was to take Melbourne by surprise via the rather lengthy route of Port Campbell. Panic spread and rumours flourished – 'Canons fired!', 'Horses snaffled!' – the troops were city-bound. Finally, someone managed to contact the windswept nether region to discover the closest thing to a foreign fleet near Port Campbell was a humble ketch. According to Jack S Fletcher's *The Infiltrators: A History of the Heytesbury 1840–1920*, Henry Bryant ended up doing hard labour for his foray into false pretences. That sure fixed his little red sails.

SOUTHWEST

WARRNAMBOOL

INFORMATION
Visitors Centre....................1 C3
Warrnambool Library............2 F1

SIGHTS & ACTIVITIES
Botanic Gardens...................3 C1
Flagstaff Hill Maritime Village....4 C3
Lake Pertobe Adventure Playground..5 C3
Logans Beach Whale-Watching
Platform..........................6 F4
Mahogany Walking Trail Starting
Point.............................7 B4
Warrnambool Art Gallery..........8 F1

SLEEPING
All Seasons Motor Inn.............9 D3
Attwood Motor Inn................10 C2
Bayside Lodge....................11 B4
Bonnie's Cottage at Ban Kor House..12 F1
Comfort Inn on Raglan............13 D3
Girt By Sea......................14 C2
Lady Bay Apartments..............15 B4
Ocean Beach Holiday Village......16 B3
Olde Maritime Motor Inn..........17 F2
Warrnambool Beach Backpackers....18 B4

EATING
Balenas..........................19 F1
Beach Babylon....................20 F1
Bojangles.................(see 24)
Fishtales Cafe...................21 F1
Images Family Restaurant...(see 28)
Malaysia.........................22 F1
Pippies by the Bay.........(see 1)
Supermarket......................23 C2
Whaler's Inn.....................24 F1

ENTERTAINMENT
Cinema...........................25 E1
Fish Bowl Lounge Bar......(see 27)
Hotel Warrnambool................26 F1
Loft.............................27 F1
Seanchaí.........................28 F1
Warrnambool Performing Arts
Centre...........................29 F1

Information

Warrnambool Library (☎ 5562 2258; 25 Liebig St; ☽ 10am-5pm Mon-Thu, to 8pm Fri, to noon Sat) You can access the Internet here, or at Warrnambool Beach Backpackers (see p220).

Warrnambool Visitors Centre (☎ 5559 4620; Merri St; ☽ 9am-5pm) This office, signposted off the Princes Hwy (A1), produces a handy *Warrnambool Visitors Guide*, which has detailed information on sights, accommodation, eating and transport, as well as regular 'what's on' listings.

Sights

FLAGSTAFF HILL MARITIME VILLAGE

Warrnambool's major tourist attraction is the impressive **Flagstaff Hill Maritime Village** (☎ 5564 7841; Merri St; adult/child/family $14/5.50/35; ☽ 9am-5pm), modelled on an early Australian coastal port. The lighthouse, keeper's cottage and chartroom were moved here from Middle Island (near the mouth of the Merri River) in 1872, and you can see the original cannon and fortifications built in 1887 to withstand the perceived threat of Russian invasion.

It's a terrific couple of hours' exploration through the Ship Chandler's office, a shipwreck museum and the Public Hall, in which the superb *Loch Ard* Peacock is displayed. This magnificent earthenware statue was made in England by Minton Potteries and was on its way to Melbourne for the Great International Exhibition when the *Loch Ard* was tragically shipwrecked in 1878 (see p215). Only two teenagers and the delicate peacock, washed ashore in its packing crate, survived.

A small theatre continually screens old maritime films and documentaries such as the brilliantly narrated 1929 classic *Around Cape Horn*, and at night there's **Shipwrecked** (adult/child/family $23/12.50/63), a sound-and-laser show of the *Loch Ard's* plunge. Special effects are stunning; no wonder, the show was designed by the team who envisaged the 2000 Sydney Olympics' opening ceremony.

There's also a working blacksmiths' shed and shipwrights' workshop, two restored historic ships and a gift shop.

WARRNAMBOOL BOTANIC GARDENS

These genteel **gardens** (cnr Queen & Cockman Sts), with their velveteen-like lawns, are a superb spot for a leg stretch beneath exotic trees. There's a fernery, a band rotunda and a small lake where kids can annoy the ducks.

William Guilfoyle designed the gardens in 1879, not long after he completed the Royal Botanic Gardens in Melbourne.

OTHER SIGHTS

The *numero uno* drawcard for many are the **southern right whales**, the mums, with their new calves, and proud dads breaching and fluking within sight of Warrnambool from July to September (see p220). It's a real family affair!

Warrnambool has some excellent beaches such as the main swimming beach, sheltered **Lady Bay**. **Logans Beach** is the best surf beach, but there are other good breaks at **Levy's Beach** and **Second Bay** (near the golf course). A walk out along the blustery breakwater (very *French Lieutenant's Woman*), at the end of Viaduct Rd at the southern end of town, is sure to clear foggy minds and hangovers.

Southern Right Charters and Diving (☎ 5562 5044; www.southernrightcharters.com.au) has too many whale-watching and boat tours (per hour from $35), diving (per dive $40), fishing charters (per 3½ hours $60), and shuttle services and day tours (per person from $20 to $150) to nearby attractions to mention. If you're car-less, or up for some water play, call them. They even do balloon animals (kidding).

You're on holiday, which means you must play: give **Lake Pertobe Adventure Playground** a go. On weekends and during the holidays, you can hire canoes, paddleboats and mini power boats, walk across suspension bridges to islands on the lake, play minigolf and lose the kids in the maze. It's picnic and barbecue friendly. Access is via Pertobe Rd at the southern end of town.

Art fetishists shouldn't miss the **Warrnambool Art Gallery** (☎ 5564 7832; 165 Timor St; adult/student/child under 16 $4/2/free; ☽ 10am-5pm Mon-Fri, noon-5pm Sat & Sun). It has a large permanent collection that includes early Australian colonial paintings, a collection from the Melbourne modernism period (1930–50), 19th-century European salon paintings and more than 600 contemporary prints.

The visitors centre (left) has maps and brochures of some of the **walking trails** in and around Warrnambool, like the 3km **Heritage Trail** that takes you past historic sites. The short **Thunder Point** stroll shows off the best coastal scenery in the area; it's also the starting point for the 22km coastal

SOUTHWEST

SOUTHERN RIGHT WHALES

Warrnambool's Logans Beach is a major breeding ground and nursery for southern right whales. Each year around July, these majestic whales migrate to the ocean waters around Port Fairy and Warrnambool and stay until September or October. See them from the car park and several lookout platforms on the sandy cliff-tops above Logans Beach – a pair of binoculars comes in handy.

The southern right whale was hunted from whaling stations in Victoria and Tasmania from the earliest days of European settlement. It was considered the 'right' whale for hunters for several reasons – it was an easy target due to its slow swimming speed and preference for shallow water, and as an added benefit, it floated after being killed.

By 1940 it was estimated that there were fewer than 1000 southern right whales left in the world. Although the species has been protected since 1935, today these whales still number only around 1200 to 1500, with about 980 estimated to be using Australian waters. You can be fined up to $100,000 for interfering with whales; boats have to keep at least 100m away, and you can't swim or dive within 30m.

For the latest information on sightings, you can contact the **Warrnambool visitors centre** (☎ 03-5559 4620).

Mahogany Walking Trail. The first to spot the fabled Mahogany shipwreck (p215) will rewrite Australian history.

Midway between Warrnambool and Port Fairy on the Princes Hwy (about 14km from Warrnambool), you'll find the **Tower Hill State Game Reserve** (admission free; ☼ 9.30am-dusk), a huge wetland based around the remains of an extinct volcanic crater; it's great for wildlife spotting in the early morning or late afternoon. The reserve's mostly viewable residents include koalas, grey kangaroos and peregrine falcons, and the emus are always trying to join your picnic. There's a loop drive around it, and walks that range from five minutes to one hour.

Hopkins Falls, known locally as 'mini Niagara', is 13km northeast of Warrnbool.

Festivals & Events

Wunta Festival (Feb) 'Wunta' is a local Aboriginal word for fish, and the festival celebrates the fishing industry with a wine and seafood fair, a whaleboat race, and concerts.

Mortlake Buskers Festival (☎ 5599 2616; Feb) Mortlake, 50km northwest of Warrnambool, is where more than 100 buskers from around the country come to compete, on eight undercover stages, for the Australian Busking Championship: nonstop entertainment and plenty of market stalls too.

May Racing Carnival (May) A three-day horse-racing festival that starts on the first Tuesday in May. It features Australia's longest horse race, the gruelling Grand Annual Steeplechase. This hellish 5.5km jumps race and carnival draws huge crowds; you'll need to book accommodation well in advance.

Sleeping

BUDGET

Atwood Motor Inn (☎ 5562 7144; atwood@hotkey.net.au; 8 Spence St; d low/high season $88/102; ☒) The Atwood is in a quiet side-street, yet only a three-minute walk from all the action in Liebig St. The doubles are small, but attractively furnished, and it's excellent value in this location. It's intimate though: noisy neighbours are easily heard.

Bayside Lodge (☎ 5562 7323; 30 Pertobe Rd; d $85) At these prices, you can't whinge about the uninspired refurbishment of this '70s building of self-contained units. The new couches are plump and the beach is at your back door, plus it's just 2km from the shopping area.

Warrnambool Beach Backpackers (☎ 5562 4874; david_gilllane@hotmail.com; 17 Stanley St; dm/d $20/60; ☒) Close to the sea, this place has a huge living area, bar and Internet access, and offers free pick-up from train and bus stations. It's a good place to hook up with others, plus use of the mountain bikes and canoes is free.

MIDRANGE

There's no shortage of motels in Warrnambool but there is a deficit of accommodation with charm.

Girt by Sea (☎ 5562 3162; www.girtbyseabandb.com.au; 52 Banyan St; tw/d/suite $110/130/150) The exception: this restored sandstone home built in 1856 is refurbished with exquisite flair from its large bathrooms with antique vanities and red Baltic pine floors to crisp bed linen. The Southern Cross suite is a particular joy: huge brass bed, lavish proportions and private garden decking. There's a large, bright guest lounge and breakfasts to pine for: Bircher muesli and ricotta hot cakes, mmm.

Bonnie's Cottage at Ban Kor House (☎ 5562 9461; www.bankorhouse.com.au; cnr Banyan & Koroit Sts; cottage low/high season $100/175) Bonnie's is your home away from home. Yippee, they accept overnight stays too. It's a very snug, quaintly renovated sandstone cottage with many original features: love the African bedroom with its zebra cushions, pith helmet and fur throw. One block from town, two blocks from the beach.

Whale Bay B&B (☎ 5562 2204; www.whalebay.com; 234 Hopkins Point Rd; d $110, ste $130) A few kilometres out of town, set on bald hills overlooking the mighty Southern Ocean, is this relaxing getaway with cheery hosts and resident alpacas and sheep. The suite is very large, with a fabulous dark wood, hand-carved, four-post bed and elegant parlour lounge setting. You'll love the ocean and hill views, and the chance to do some whale-spotting in season.

Comfort Inn on Raglan (☎ 5562 2755; www.comfort innonraglan.com.au; 349 Raglan Pde; low/high season executive d $110/130; ☒) A slick, corporate-style refurbishment in shades of coffee, aubergine and mushroom will assuage the reality of having succumbed to digs on the neon motel strip entering town.

Lady Bay Apartments (☎ 5562 1662; www.ladybay apartments.com.au; 2 Pertrobe Rd; studio low/high season $125/135, 2-bedroom apt from $150; ☒ ☒) If you plan to stay a few days, this new, colourful, cardboard cut-out townhouse complex by the breakwater has functional and fresh one- to three-bedroom digs in modern, minimalist style. The studios are viewless on the ground floor. Be warned, construction doesn't finish until 2006.

Other recommendations:

Ocean Beach Holiday Village (☎ 5561 4222; www .oceanbeachvillage.com.au; Pertrobe Rd; powered sites per 2 people low/high season $25/36, studio $82/98, d cabin with bathroom $70/125; ☒) By the beach; some cabins are care-worn.

Olde Maritime Motor Inn (☎ 5561 1415; www.olde maritime.com.au; cnr Merri & Banyan Sts; d low/high season $99/110; ☒) Mock colonial suites; close to town.

All Seasons Motor Inn (☎ 5561 2833; 367 Raglan Pde; d low/high season $110/130; ☒) At last, a mini bar!

Eating

Liebig St is Warrnambool's main strip and many of the eateries are along here, but for

a town this size, you feel there should be plenty of outstanding options.

Fishtales Cafe (☎ 5561 2957; 63 Liebig St; mains $8-15; ☺ breakfast, lunch & dinner) Don't let this suspiciously large menu put you off. This upbeat, friendly eatery/takeaway has deliciously prepared fare, from a dozen different types of burgers to fish and chips, vegetarian specials, seafood and Asian dishes, as well as good breakfasts. There are nooks for lone eaters, a hint of Art Deco with wrought iron and retro chairs, and a cheery courtyard out back. Vegetarians: go the tofu, pesto and roast-vegie stack.

Beach Babylon (☎ 5562 3714; 72 Liebig St; mains $19-24; ☺ dinner) The eclectic exoticism of this interior works beautifully: a touch Mediterranean and Middle Eastern, blending stormy blues, claret, and burnished-wheat feature walls with opulent adornments. Likewise, the menu is an adventure of zesty and curious flavour combos. It's a memorable experience.

Bojangles (☎ 5562 8751; 61 Liebig St; mains $12-20; ☺ lunch & dinner) Bojangles has been here forever but the feel-good ambience never tires thanks to vibrantly coloured enclaves, crannies and appealing wall murals. It's also a three-time finalist in the 'Best of the Best' national pizza awards, for good reason. Gourmet wood-fired pizza aside, there's pasta and à la carte to tempt diners.

Pippies by the Bay (☎ 5561 2188; Merri St, Flagstaff Hill; mains $26-30; ☺ lunch & dinner daily, breakfast Sat & Sun) A real slow-food mood consumes you in this classy space cushioned by deep plum walls and dark wood. The menu offers Mod Oz cuisine, finely executed. The wine list is exceptional, as is gazing over Lady Bay with a ratatouille tart and a crisp white for company: nice, very nice. It's in the same complex as the visitors centre.

Whaler's Inn (☎ 5562 8391; cnr Liebig & Timor Sts; mains $12-16; ☺ lunch & dinner) It's a family-friendly set-up here with a kids' playpen and banquette seating. Meals are tasty and served in generous portions. Try the Greek chicken breast with tomato, parsley, feta and olive sauce; simple, rich and satisfying. Prices include visits to the all-you-can-eat salad bar.

Other recommendations:

Balenas (☎ 5562 0900; 158 Timor St; mains $20-26; ☺ lunch Mon-Fri, dinner Mon-Sat) Understated, elegant dining, with friendly service.

Images Family Restaurant (☎ 5562 4208; 60 Liebig St; mains $16-19; ☯ lunch & dinner) So '80s, from its chandeliers to camembert chicken with plum sauce.
Malaysia (☎ 5562 2051; 69 Liebig St; mains $13-17; ☯ dinner) Star-struck owner displays wall-to-wall memorabilia of dubiously 'famous' customers.

Entertainment

For quiet nights, there's always the **cinema** (Kepler St), but if you're up for a big one there's plenty of raw, acoustic and rock music from the smoky, local pub scene on weekends – as well as two nightclubs.

Hotel Warrnambool (☎ 5562 2377; cnr Koroit & Kepler Sts; ☯ 10.30am-midnight Mon-Tue, to 1am Wed-Sat, to 10pm Sun) This is one smoky pub you shouldn't miss. It's the most welcoming place in town: an earthy, cavernous affair with exposed mud bricks and railway sleepers, lounge areas for slouching, a billiard table and enough moods to pull a big night or cosy evening in. The art of conversation lingers here.

Loft (☎ 5561 0995; 58 Liebig St; ☯ 5.30pm-1am Wed, Fri & Sat, daily in summer) This place was just about to open and promised a relaxed, contemporary vibe with laid-back live music on weekends – one of Warrnambool's few smoke-free zones.

Fish Bowl Lounge Bar (☎ 5562 9753; 56 Liebig St; ☯ 5.30pm-1am) Poor fish trapped in a tank watch uni students down fish-bowl margaritas ($24) in this funky little nook next door to the Loft. Black vinyl couches, a jukebox and video screen attract a young-ish crowd for drinks.

Seanchai (☎ 5561 7900; 62 Liebig St; ☯ 2pm-1am Wed-Sun) Seanchai encourages original live music, but on Sundays reverts to the traditional Irish jig. It's the usual vibe of lads sipping pints with elbows at rest and bums on knobbly wood furniture. It's pronounced 'shannakee' and it's Gaelic for storyteller.

Warrnambool Performing Arts Centre (☎ 5564 7885; cnr Liebig & Timor Sts) This is a major venue for live theatre, ballet and music. Phone to find out what's on.

Getting There & Away

Warrnambool's **V/Line** (☎ 13 61 96) train station is on Merri St at the southern end of Fairy St. There are daily services between Melbourne and Warrnambool (economy/1st-class $41/58, three trains daily, 3¼ hours) via Geelong, Birregurra, Colac, Camperdown and Terang. There are also two

Sunday bus services ($41) that follow this route.

Connecting V/Line buses continue west to Port Fairy ($5.10), Portland ($14.60) and Mt Gambier ($32.30). There are also weekday bus services to Ballarat ($21.60) and Hamilton ($7.30).

At 9.20am on Friday, a bus heads along the Great Ocean Rd to Apollo Bay ($24.90), with connections to Geelong ($29.40 from Warrnambool), and returns from Apollo Bay at 1.40pm. There's also a service on Monday during the Christmas holidays.

PORT FAIRY
☎ 03 / pop 2600

If you haven't arrived on a gusty, cold day (of which there are many), you'll feel immediately at peace in hospitable Port Fairy. It's one of the earliest settled areas in Victoria, dating back to 1835. The town has a tranquil, salty feel with its old bluestone and sandstone buildings, whitewashed cottages, colourful fishing boats, and streets lined with toilet-brush pines. If you're not into history or shipwrecks, it is definitely a place to burrow in, eat well, take reviving sea or river walks, nap lots and snuggle into a ripper book.

Buckets of investment bucks here threaten to snuff out Port Fairy's homely quaintness however, as the merchants of slick renovate properties and tweak menus to attract a sophisticated market. Fortunately, the National Trust has classified about 50 of the fine old buildings here, so they're safe; like the rambunctious Caledonian Hotel, which claims to be Victoria's oldest licensed premises. There are several unfinished rooms at the hotel – apparently, during the 1850s the workers downed tools and joined the rush to the goldfields, and the work was never completed.

The first arrivals were whalers and sealers, and you can still walk along picturesque Fisherman's Wharf by the glassy Moyne River and check out the fishing boats as they unload their crayfish and squid catch.

Information
Electric Dreams (☎ 5568 3288; 47 Sackville St; ☯ 9am-6pm) Internet access is available here.
Port Fairy Visitors Centre (☎ 5568 2682; Railway Pl; ☯ 9am-5pm) The town centre is along Sackville St but the tourist office is at the ocean end of Bank St.

Sights

Port Fairy has a rich and sometimes gloomy heritage that enraptures local history buffs. A brochure from the visitors centre shows a popular **Shipwreck Walk**, actually it's three short walks, highlighting some of the wreck sites along the coastline.

Then you can do the signposted **History Walk** around town, using a walk map (20c) available from the visitors centre, in combo with its *Historic Buildings of Port Fairy* booklet ($2.20). The **Port Fairy History Centre** (Gipps St; adult/child $3/50c; 2-5pm Wed, Sat & Sun, daily in school holidays), housed in the old bluestone courthouse (complete with dusty mannequins acting out a courtroom scene), has shipping relics, old photos and costumes,

and a prisoner's cell. On **Battery Hill** there's a lookout point, and old canons and fortifications that were positioned here in the 1860s.

Next, hold your nose and visit **Griffiths Island**. In the 1830s local whaling operations were based on the island, which is joined to the mainland by a narrow strip of land. A bluestone lighthouse built here in 1859 still shines its beacon to warn local ships. Today, the island is home to a colony of smelly mutton birds (short-tailed shearwaters). These birds, a protected species in Victoria, have a remarkably regular life cycle, returning to their nesting grounds on the island within a few days of 22 September each year. Amazing! Birds return to the same nest burrow occupied the previous year,

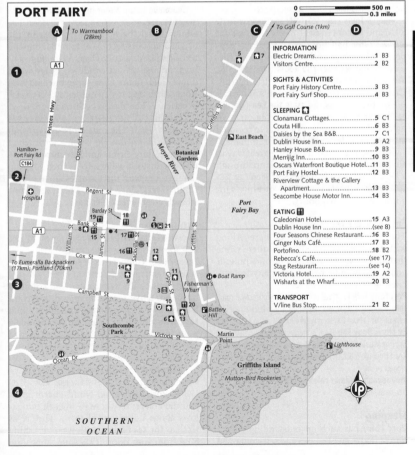

PORT FAIRY

INFORMATION	
Electric Dreams	1 B3
Visitors Centre	2 B2

SIGHTS & ACTIVITIES	
Port Fairy History Centre	3 B3
Port Fairy Surf Shop	4 B3

SLEEPING	
Clonamara Cottages	5 C1
Couta Hill	6 B3
Daisies by the Sea B&B	7 C1
Dublin House Inn	8 A2
Hanley House B&B	9 B3
Merrijig Inn	10 B3
Oscars Waterfront Boutique Hotel	11 B3
Port Fairy Hostel	12 B3
Riverview Cottage & the Gallery Apartment	13 B3
Seacombe House Motor Inn	14 B3

EATING	
Caledonian Hotel	15 A3
Dublin House Inn	(see 8)
Four Seasons Chinese Restaurant	16 B3
Ginger Nuts Café	17 B3
Portofino	18 B2
Rebecca's Café	(see 17)
Stag Restaurant	(see 14)
Victoria Hotel	19 A2
Wisharts at the Wharf	20 B3

TRANSPORT	
V/line Bus Stop	21 B2

and generally mate with the same partner throughout their breeding life. The birds lay their eggs in November (the eggs hatch in January), and leave with their young for the Kamchatka Peninsula in Siberia every April. When they're in town, you can see the memorable sight of tens of thousands of birds returning to their nests at dusk to feed their young. Take a torch and stick to the tracks, or you will collapse the birds' nests if you stray and walk across the dunes.

Activities

East Beach is the place to go for **swimming** and it is patrolled daily over the warmer months.

If you must trip about, take the very worthwhile **Codrington Wind Farm tour** (☎ 5568 1853; adult/child/family $7/5/19); see p226.

Mary S Tours (☎ 5568 1480; adult/child under 12 $11/1) and **Mulloka Cruises** (☎ 5568 1790; adult/child $10/free) offer half-hour scenic cruises peppered with shipwreck tales and port history, while **Michael J IV Tours** (☎ 5568 2816), along with the other two, runs fishing trips. Cruises depart from Fisherman's Wharf.

For the car-less, **B-Beside the Sea** (☎ 5568 1670; www.b-besidethesea.com) has a big range of half- and full-day minivan tours to regional attractions as far away as the Grampians.

Because it's so flat, a bike is a great way to zip about, providing you can pump through a head wind: visit **Port Fairy Surf Shop** (☎ 5568 2800; 33 Bank St; bike hire per hr $5). Note: hire's for a minimum of two hours.

Festivals & Events

They're a little festival-struck here. Along with the festivals listed below there's one that showcases local artists in mid-June. If you're likely to be here during any festival, book beds well in advance.

Port Fairy Folk Festival (www.portfairyfolkfestival.com; early Mar) One of Australia's foremost music festivals, held here on the Labour Day long weekend.

Ex-Libris Book Fair (Sep) A literary festival.

Spring Music Festival (mid-Oct) Classical and jazz music. Apart from the folk fest, this sophisticated affair is the town's biggest event.

Moyneyana summer celebration festival (late Dec–late Jan)

Sleeping

Port Fairy has such an outstanding collection of B&Bs, guesthouses and self-contained cottages that it's difficult to recommend one over another. Accommodation is heavily booked during holidays and festivals. The visitor centre offers a booking service for $2, or check out **My Port Fairy** (www.myportfairy.com) for more.

BUDGET

Port Fairy also has three caravan parks, but Belfast Cove's cabins, on the highway just as you enter town, have the prettiest gardens.

Port Fairy YHA (☎ 5568 2468; 8 Cox St; www.portfairy hostel.com.au; dm $20/24, d $50/57; ☐) In the rambling 1844 home of merchant William Rutledge, this friendly, relaxed and well run hostel has a large kitchen, peaceful gardens and free cable TV. The dorms have a cosy ski-lodge feel. You'll want to stay longer.

Seacombe House Motor Inn (☎ 5568 1082; www .seacombehouse.com.au; cnr Cox & Sackville Sts; d $40) The whitewashed 'backpacker' doubles in the original upstairs section of this 1847 inn are terrific value and quite clean. With high ceilings, original paned windows, heavy wood doors, and floors that have buckled and sloped with age, it's an authentic Port Fairy experience. The shared bathrooms are new.

Couta Hill (☎ 5568 2412; herrma2@bigpond.com; 14 Gipps St; d/f $75/85) The outside is modern but the huge main double room's dark-wood furniture, floral prints and lace curtains capture the historic village feel. There's also a family room with three singles and en suite. Couta's very close to the wharf, and your friendly hosts speak German.

MIDRANGE

Riverview Cottage & The Gallery Apartment (☎ 5568 2964; www.riverviewonthemoyne.com.au; 17 Gipps St; r per 2 people $130) Choose between a street-front country cottage or riverfront contemporary apartment, both self-contained, adjoined by an attractive sandstone-paved courtyard framed by weeping myrtle and silver birch for privacy. Both interiors are exceptionally well styled. You'll love the cottage's French Provincial kitchen. Riverview sleeps four; the Gallery suits two.

Daisies by the Sea B&B (☎ 5568 2355; jmrahilly@ bigpond.com.au; 222 Griffiths St; d low/high season $120/ 150) If Port Fairy's old-world charm gives you the creeps, try these two beach bungalows about 1.5km out of town. They're as fresh as the sea breeze, with waves crashing 50m from your door. It's a snug, appealing getaway for couples, complete with fluffy robes.

Merrijig Inn (☎ 5568 2324; www.merrijiginn.com; cnr Campbell & Gipps Sts; attic d $130, queen ste $170) There's no room for bulky blokes or luggage in these adorable, doll's-house attic rooms; you'll breathe better in the liberty-print queen suites though. Merrijig feels like a hunter's lodge; it smells wood-fire sweet and wee guest lounges are tucked into every spare corner. An afternoon by the teensy bar appeals, as does breakfast in the airy conservatory.

Dublin House Inn (☎ 5568 2022; dublin@standard .net.au; 57-59 Bank St; d low/high season $75/90, self-contained ste $100/140) A cheese platter, a mellow red and a sheltered sunny afternoon in this large paved courtyard with flower garden would be bliss, but come for the rooms decked in honeyed contemporary tones for restful rehab too.

Clonmara Cottages (☎ 5568 2595; www.clonmara .com.au; 106 Princes Hwy; cottage low/high season $110/125; studio $125/140) Clonmara is a hideaway spot for couples. There's a weeping willow with a swing and fresh vegie patch from which all meals are catered, if you wish. Two cottages are decked in modern country style, while the historic cottage offers yesteryear romance with its cosy dimensions and brass bed. Ask about the wicked chocolate package!

Hanley House B&B (☎ 5568 2709; 14 Sackville St; d $110) For a home-away-from-home experience, stay at this peaceful place dating from the mid-1850s. It has spacious bedrooms, a cluttered, comfy guest lounge, set around a huge log fire, and a friendly host. The gardens are bliss on a sunny day, and it's two secs from town.

TOP END

Oscars Waterfront Boutique Hotel (☎ 5568 3022; www.oscarswaterfront.com; 41b Gipps St; d $250, premium ste $275; 🐾) Think gracious Southern Belle mini mansion. Imagine huge, wrought-iron chandeliers, parquetry floors and so much liberating height and space as you waft along wide, white-tiled corridors that you arrive at the broad, shaded veranda, quite refreshed. The veranda overlooks the boat-speckled wharf, of course. Here, you will nibble giant, star-shaped shortbread and sip quality tea in the morning sun. Presidents and princesses stay at places like Oscars.

Eating

This town could do with more moderately priced eating options, but you can be sure its few cafés and takeaways do fresh seafood, and there's a great bakery for home-made hot stuff.

Ginger Nuts Cafe (☎ 5568 2326; cnr Bank & Sackville Sts; mains $19-24; 🕑 7am-late) Ginger's is one of too few moderately priced dining options. Risotto this, shaved Parmesan that, gourmet African sausages and mash, it's the usual Mod Oz fare but delectably prepared. The Guinness and beef pie with steamed veg is a winner and the wine list is good.

Rebecca's Cafe (☎ 5568 2533; 72 Sackville St; mains $5-12; 🕑 breakfast & lunch, closes 6pm) The chunky fruit toast is as light as fairy floss and the poached eggs perfect at this excellent breakfast spot. Light lunches are reasonably priced too, and Rebecca's has the best muffins, slices, scones, biscuits and home made ice-cream (butterscotch with peanut brittle!) in town.

Victoria Hotel (☎ 5568 2891; 42 Bank St; mains $20-25; 🕑 lunch & dinner) Very schmick; the Victoria's paved outdoor area covered by sail shades and vine canopy is the spot for sampling cleverly devised modern Mediterranean dishes, and it's great to see a regional wine list.

Stag Restaurant (☎ 5568 3058; cnr Cox & Sackville Sts; mains $22-30; 🕑 dinner) Dulcet lighting, fine fabric chairs and starched linen set in a refined parlour secure the Stag's reputation for fine dining. Each meal is wine-matched to enliven the palette. Try the lemon-infused Western District rack of lamb or their specialty, crayfish, any time.

Portofino (☎ 5568 2251; 28 Bank St; mains around $28-31; 🕑 dinner daily, lunch Sun) The menu is limited but the emphasis here is on exquisite execution. At Portofino, wine is served in Buddha's-belly glasses and the dishes suit sophisticated, appreciative palettes. If you pass on the pigeon pie, there's always venison or Portland Bay bugs.

Wisharts at the Wharf (☎ 5568 1884; 29 Gipps St; mains $17-23; 🕑 lunch & dinner) Wharf-side dining doesn't come prettier than this. Plump, juicy fish 'n' chips are always assured here, or how does a seafood curry or herb-encrusted local catch sound? Adventurous presentation and flavours in very relaxed surrounds.

Other recommendations:

Caledonian Hotel (☎ 5568 1044; 41 Bank St; mains $12-18; 🕑 lunch & dinner) Local favourite for no-frills nosh.

Four Seasons Chinese Restaurant (☎ 5568 1889; 58 Sackville St; mains $9-15; ☒ dinner) Recommended by locals.
Dublin House Inn (☎ 5568 2022; dublin@standard.net .au; 57-59 Bank St; mains $20-26; ☒ dinner) Tantalising menu in refined surrounds.

Getting There & Around

There are daily buses between Port Fairy and Warrnambool ($5.10), connecting with trains to/from Melbourne (economy/1st class $43.80/60.40). **V/Line** (☎ 13 61 96) has daily buses heading west to Portland ($10.20) and Mt Gambier ($24.90). Buses arrive and depart at Bank St, next to the visitors centre.

DISCOVERY COAST & PRINCES HIGHWAY

PORT FAIRY TO PORTLAND

Signposted off the Princes Hwy 12km west of Port Fairy are **The Crags**, wild and ragged, and worth an 'oooo-ahhh' snap. You can also see the flat-topped, volcanic **Lady Julia Percy Island** from here. It's known by local Aboriginal tribes as 'Deen Maar' and is important in Aboriginal mythology as the resting place of the spirits of the dead from the Gunditjmara tribe.

You'll hit the blink-and-it's-gone town of **Yambuk** 17km northwest of Port Fairy. There's a good lake for fishing and clean, spacious **Eumeralla Backpackers** (☎ 03-5568 4204; fram@standard.net.au; High St, Yambuk; dm $16.50, d $33) in the old Yambuk school. Run by a local Aboriginal trust, it has good facilities and canoes can be hired (per day $5) to paddle down the Eumeralla River to the lake. Yambuk does have a claim to fame however, as the proposed home for a wind farm: stage one of the huge, controversial **Portland Wind Project** run by Pacific Hydro. When finished, the project will have cast a total of 120 wind wavers as far as pristine Cape Sir William Grant, Cape Nelson and Cape Bridgewater, making it one of the biggest wind projects in the world.

The flat farming land along this stretch is already strikingly punctuated by 14 graceful wind turbines at **Codrington**, also owned by Pacific Hydro. Renewable energy is such a big issue, the **Codrington Wind Farm tours** (☎ 03-5568 1853; tcb@surftheworld.com.au; admission adult/

child/family $7/4/19; ☒ 10am-4pm Thu & Sat) are a quick way to come up to speed and to decide for yourself just how noisy, ugly or dangerous the turbines are. Sadly, Victoria expels the most greenhouse gases of any state through its coal-generated electricity. More tours are conducted in the school holidays.

PORTLAND

☎ 03 / pop 9600
Portland is the site of Victoria's first European settlement, but these days it prefers the moniker 'Gateway to the Great South West Walk'. It's a strange blend of the historic and the industrial – behind its landscaped foreshore dotted with bluestone buildings are the soaring silos of the port and massive woodchip heaps awaiting export.

It's the only deep-water port between Melbourne and Adelaide, handling everything from huge tankers and carriers to small fishing boats. And on a narrow headland 5km out of town is the Portland Aluminium Smelter (not visible from the foreshore), which produces about 340,000 tonnes of aluminium ingots each year, making it one of Australia's biggest export earners. But Portland is also a good base from which to explore the incredibly pristine wonderlands of Cape Nelson and Cape Bridgewater.

From early in the 19th century, this was a main base for seasonal whaling and sealing operations. The first permanent settler was Edward Henty, who brought his family here from Van Diemen's Land (Tasmania) in 1834.

Information

Municipal library (☎ 5523 1497; 40 Bentinck St; ☒ 10am-5.30pm Mon-Thu, to 6pm Fri, to 1pm Sat) Internet access is available here.
Parks Victoria (☎ 5522 3441; 8-12 Julia St; ☒ 9am-5pm) For those attempting the Great South West Walk or visiting national parks.
Portland Visitors Centre (☎ 5523 2671; Lee Breakwater Rd; ☒ 9am-5pm) This office, at the impressive-looking Maritime Discovery Centre, has loads of stuff on Portland and its surrounds.

Sights

The Portland **cable tram** (adult/child/family $12/6/30; ☒ 10am-4pm) plies a 3.5km route linking the vintage car museum, botanic gardens, Maritime Discovery Centre and WWII memorial water tower by way of the waterfront. Pas-

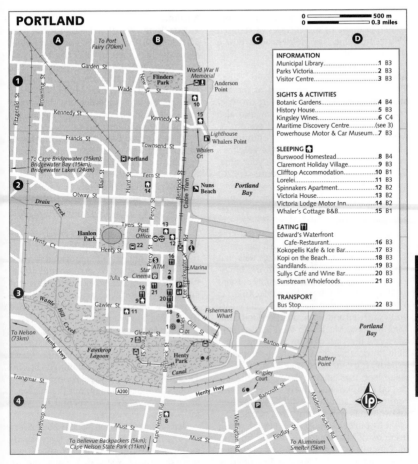

PORTLAND

INFORMATION	
Municipal Library	1 B3
Parks Victoria	2 B3
Visitor Centre	3 B3

SIGHTS & ACTIVITIES	
Botanic Gardens	4 B4
History House	5 B3
Kingsley Wines	6 C4
Maritime Discovery Centre	(see 3)
Powerhouse Motor & Car Museum	7 B3

SLEEPING	
Burswood Homestead	8 B4
Claremont Holiday Village	9 B3
Clifftop Accommodation	10 B1
Lorelei	11 B3
Spinnakers Apartment	12 B2
Victoria House	13 B2
Victoria Lodge Motor Inn	14 B2
Whaler's Cottage B&B	15 B1

EATING	
Edward's Waterfront Cafe-Restaurant	16 B3
Kokopellis Kafe & Ice Bar	17 B3
Kopi on the Beach	18 B3
Sandilands	19 B3
Sullys Café and Wine Bar	20 B3
Sunstream Wholefoods	21 B3

TRANSPORT	
Bus Stop	22 B3

SOUTHWEST

sengers can hop on and off as they please and it's a great way to get acquainted with the town.

The **Powerhouse Motor & Car Museum** (☎ 5523 5795; cnr Glenelg & Percy Sts; adult/child/family $5/1/10) has about 25 vintage Australian and American vehicles and motorbikes dating from the 1920s, as well as some very cool motoring paraphernalia. Car-club members on hand are happy to chat about their babies.

If history hooks you, visit **History House** (☎ 5522 2266; Cliff St; admission $2; ☒ 10am-noon & 1-4pm) in the old Town Hall for Portland's inside story; it's crammed with old photos and records of the town's past; Portland's whaling days are captured at the **Maritime Discovery Centre** (Lee Breakwater Rd; adult/child $5/

free; ☒ 9am-5pm), which is part of the visitors centre.

Lovers of manicured nature must sniff through the 300 varieties of roses at the **Portland Botanic Gardens**. In 1857 the gardens' first curator, William Allitt, borrowed 80 Chinese prisoners from the Portland prison to help him prepare the site. Colourful dahlias reach their spectacular peak in March. Also, **Fawthrop Lagoon**, a tidal water area south of the city centre, is the bees knees for bird watching. There's a barbecue area and walking track that leads around the lagoon to the botanic gardens.

Burswood Homestead (☎ 5523 4686; 15 Cape Nelson Rd) This grand old manor, built for Edward Henty in 1850 with 5.5 hectares of **gardens**

(adult/child $3/free; ◷ 10am-5pm), remains a beguiling example of the excesses of civilised 19th-century life. The homestead is now a B&B (see right).

Activities

There are free, two-hour tours of the **aluminium smelter** (☎ 5523 2671) at 10.15am every Monday, Wednesday and Friday and also at 1pm during holidays. You'll see an informative video, handle raw aluminium and drive through some of the smelter's operation rooms. It's well worth your time. Bookings through the visitors centre (p226) are essential.

There are some good **surfing** spots around this coast, especially at sublime **Bridgewater Bay** (see opposite).

DIY tours are big here, thanks to the visitors centre's walking and driving maps. There's a **cemetery walk**, a **heritage walk** that passes 48 of the town's 200 historic buildings, or the self-guided *Walk in the Footsteps of Mary MacKillop* tour. Mary MacKillop is a sneeze away from being Australia's first saint; she lived and worked in Portland from 1862 to 1866. MacKillop worked two miracles, and the Vatican is investigating a possible third, which may result in sainthood. Otherwise, try the **Wood, Wine & Roses drive** – a 90km loop that takes in the region; the circuit takes in Barretts Winery, the Heathland Nature Walk and the town of **Heywood** best known for its waft-worthy beds of roses.

Pretty pink Kingsley House (1893), which overlooks Portland and the harbour from up on Bancroft St, is now the home of **Kingsley Wines** (Bancroft St; ☎ 5523 1864; ◷ 1-4pm), offering tastings and sales.

Sleeping
BUDGET

Claremont Holiday Village (☎ 5521 7567; 37 Percy St; d cabin with/without bathroom low season $60/45, high season $90/65) This orderly park, two secs from town, has cabins that are more fresh and comfy than crummy pub rooms – with a microwave and TV thrown in! One has disabled facilities too.

Bellevue Backpackers (☎ 5523 4038; Sheoke-Yellow Rock Rd; d $20) Fancy a double bed or two bunks in a dinky backyard caravan run by a lovely older couple? One for the young and young at heart, five minutes from town off the Cape Nelson Rd.

MIDRANGE

Victoria House (☎ 5521 7577; vichouse@hotkey.net.au; 5 Tyers St; d $130) This excellent two-storey bluestone dwelling built in 1853 has been stylishly renovated and has nine heritage-style guestrooms with bathrooms, a comfy lounge, open fires and a gorgeous garden. Enjoy the ragtime music, complimentary sherry and chocolates, and super satisfying breakfast. It's the sparkler amid birthday candles.

Whalers Cottage B&B (☎ 5521 7522; 12 Whalers Crt; d $90-130) You can't help but slide into the buff Chesterfields that adorn this old-fashioned guest lounge. Whalers is a shadowy, bluestone home that has three rooms available, all with shared bathrooms, but the blue room (with matching bathrobes) appeals most.

Spinnakers Apartment (☎ 5526 7257; 123 Bentinck St; d low/high season $130/150) It looks old from the outside but is well renovated within, with a Tuscan-style living room and waterfront views. Spinnakers is a self-contained and most comfortable option if you plan to stay a few days; it's also walking distance from town. They do accept overnighters.

Clifftop Accommodation (☎ 5523 1126; clifftop@dodo.com.au; 13 Clifton Crt; d low/high season $125/130; ⊠) On a sunny day the panoramic views from your balcony are blindingly bright. These sparsely furnished rooms feel big enough to roller blade in, but the big brass beds look snuggly. Continental breakfast for two costs $15 extra.

Victoria Lodge Motor Inn (☎ 5523 5966; 155 Percy St; d $90, deluxe d $120; ⊠) These larger-than-average, well appointed motel rooms are more smartly decorated than some, and are an easy walk into town.

TOP END

Burswood Homestead (☎ 5523 4686; 15 Cape Nelson Rd; low/high season s $105/125 master d $165/200) Built for Edward Henty in 1850 and set amid beautiful gardens, this resplendent place is a formal, indulgent, antique-laden mini mansion. Master rooms are the most spacious and have bathrooms. All prices include a buffet breakfast, and you enjoy a Devonshire tea on arrival.

Lorelei (☎ 5523 4466; www.lorelei.com.au; 53 Gawler St; d $160) This beautiful, lavishly furnished home is a good spot for a luxury weekend. Depending on your taste, you might prefer a spa or claw-foot tub, the room with a four-poster bed or another with veranda access. Room 3 is wheelchair friendly.

Eating

Sullys Cafe and Wine Bar (☎ 5523 5355; 55 Bentinck St; mains $15-18; ☼ 8am-late) 'Safe, Sustainable Cuisine' is the catchphrase at Sullys, a narrow and pleasant nook across from the waterfront. Its produce is organic and humanely farmed, but it's also damn good. The catch of the day crumbed in shredded coconut or macadamia nuts and served with zesty jams and salsas is super. It also has menus for the chronologically advanced (seniors) and challenged (kids).

Edward's Waterfront Cafe-Restaurant (☎ 5523 1032; 101 Bentinck St; mains $22-25; ☼ 7am-late) The wine list is mammoth, the menu choices wide, the ambience cheery, and the cake selection will make grown women cry, especially after they've scoffed a filling entree of ricotta torta or spicy Tunisian omelette. Edward's is the locals' favourite and fills quickly – understandably.

Sunstream Wholefoods (☎ 5523 4895; 49 Julia St; mains $4-6; ☼ lunch, closed Sun) It'd be hard to beat Sunstream for good-value, healthy tucker like mountain-bread rolls, home-made lentil burgers, satay vegie burgers, fresh juices and smoothies. Open from 9.30am, but the emphasis is on lunch.

Kopi on the Beach (☎ 5523 1822; 49 Bentinck St; mains $4-7; ☼ breakfast & lunch Mon-Sat) It's the hot-pink walls, dangling crystal mobiles, mandalas and bushcraft furniture that make you want to linger a little longer over a good latte at Kopi's. It's so reasonably priced, and the toasted tortilla sandwiches are a great light snack.

Kokopelli's kafe & ice bar (☎ 5521 1200; 79 Bentinck St; mains $19-26; ☼ breakfast, lunch & dinner) There's an alluring mix of contemporary cool and self-conscious hip happening at Kokopelli's – a little like its name. The look is James Bond meets *Thunderbirds*, the feel is urban edge, but the wine list is uninspired, and the food just average.

Sandilands (☎ 5523 3319; Percy St; mains $16-24; ☼ dinner, closed Tue & Sun) This elegant manor's imposing facade suggests scary sophistication, but reception-centre chairs tone it down a notch. Vegetarians are well catered for here with stir-fries, pasta and risotto dishes.

Getting There & Away

There are daily **V/Line** (☎ 13 61 96) buses between Portland and Port Fairy ($10.20), Warrnambool ($14.60) and Mt Gambier ($13.30). Buses operate from Henty St, near the corner of Percy St.

AROUND PORTLAND

Cape Nelson

☎ 03

Here's a wee detour worth taking. Head 11km out of Portland along the Cape Nelson Rd and take the scenic Sheoke Rd turn-off into the **Cape Nelson State Park**. There are several excellent coastal lookouts along the road – **Volcanic Isles lookout** has a dramatic view of the smelter atop plunging cliffs – as well as nice walks, like the 3km scrub to cliff-top **Sea Cliff Nature Walk** (Parks Victoria supplies interpretive brochures at the car park) and the 45-minute **Enchanted Forest Walk** through dense, lush, almost rainforest-type growth.

You can only view the National Trust–classified 1884 **Cape Nelson Lighthouse** from the car park; it's still operational and not tour-friendly.

Cape Bridgewater

☎ 03

Even if you see nothing else in this area, do make the 18km detour west to Cape Bridgewater. Not only is it a pretty drive, lined with saltbush, that passes through sand dunes and paddocks, but it delivers you to glorious **Bridgewater Bay**, a dramatic 4km arc of cresting waves along a fine white-sand beach. A surf life-saving club operates here over summer (on weekends and public holidays). It's a must-visit spot. The visitor centre in Portland (p226) has a guide to 15 surf breaks.

The road climbs around the cape to the top of a hill, with great views back along the coast. For a stunning coastline panorama and exhilarating walk, attempt the steep, two-hour walk to the **seal colony**; there's usually dozens of these adorable sea doggies flapping about the rocks (apparently 650 seals live around here). Or, you can get closer by taking a **Seals by Sea** (☎ 5526 7247; adult/child/family $25/15/70) rubber Zodiac to their ocean playground. Prepare for bumps and splashes; the trip takes 45 minutes.

Blowholes Rd continues out to a car park at **Cape Duquesne**, from which walking tracks lead to a platform that overlooks

SOUTHWEST

GREAT SOUTH WEST WALK

Remote, blustery and wild, this walk's conquerors discover a solitude broken only by acrobatic birds and wallowing fur seals. The **Great South West Walk** is a doozy, covering 250km of coastal wilderness between Portland and the South Australian border. It starts from the Portland visitors centre and follows the coast all the way to the small township of Nelson, where it heads inland along the course of the Glenelg River to the South Australian border, before looping back to Portland.

To walk the full distance you'd need at least 10 days, but here are a couple of shorter sections that can be done in a day. Talk to **Parks Victoria** (☎ 03-5522 3441; Portland) or the **visitor centres** (Portland ☎ 03-5523 2671; Nelson ☎ 08-8738 4051) for more itinerary options, or help with drop-offs, as these walks are both one-way. These offices also sell copies of *The Great South West Walk* ($3) and *Short Walks on and Around The Great South West Walk* ($4.50).

There's an 18km, five-hour, easy-to-medium section that starts at **Bridgewater Lakes**, which is about 24km from Portland if you take the turn-off from the Cape Bridgewater road. The walk passes by serene lakes, natural springs, blowholes and barren headlands, winding its way along a solid, grassy path toward superb cliff-top tracks that have excellent views of the cape's fur-seal colony and vast waters. It's somewhat steep in sections, and often quite close to the cliff's edge, but it's worth every effort to 'summit' Victoria's highest coastal cliff (130m); see Lonely Planet's *Walking in Australia* for full coverage of this walk.

From Nelson, another option is the medium-level **Glenelg River Gorge Walk**. It's a 10km hike that takes about 3.5 hours. The track is set high and keeps fairly close to the rim of these chalky orange -and-grey limestone cliffs that are composed of tiny marine critters that were part of the seabed up to 25 million years ago. It provides satisfying views of the snaking river and gorge, and when those are concealed, the native shrubbery appeals, it is so prettily placed (and splotched with wildflowers in spring). Overhead, wrinkled stringy-barks contort themselves to eerie effect.

---

rocky **blowholes** spouting water into the air during high seas. Another track leads to the remains of a **petrified forest** on the cliff-top.

There's plenty of self-contained accommodation available at the cape (and the visitors centre has a good photographic log of most), but friendly **Sea View Lodge B&B** (☎ 5526 7276; Bridgewater Rd; d $90, spa d $130) is special. It's a two-storey beach house, bright and comfortable, with wonderful wide verandas from which to contemplate its spectacular sea views (love the slate-lined spa en suite). Or **Cape Bridgewater Holiday Camp** (☎ 5526 7267; dm $15, cabins $60) has backpacker dorms and a couple of tidy cabins on offer.

The only meal stop is the **Bridgewater Bay Cafe** (☎ 5526 7155; mains $7-12; ⏰ breakfast & lunch), which serves eggs, burgers, open sandwiches and the delectable Mars Bar latte. Sea View Lodge does dinner for guests.

There is no public transport between Portland and Cape Bridgewater, although the **Wayward Bus** (☎ 1300 653 510; www.waywardbus .com.au) comes here as part of its itinerary (see p411).

PORTLAND TO SOUTH AUSTRALIA

From Portland, you can either head north to Heywood to rejoin the Princes Hwy to head toward South Australia, or you can head northwest along the slower, beautiful, coastal route known as the Portland–Nelson road. This road runs inland from the coast, but along the way there are turn-offs leading down to the beaches and into some great national parks.

Mt Richmond National Park

Stop. Walkies. This is your first port of call along the Portland–Nelson road. There are four main walking tracks through the park: **Benwerrin Nature Walk**, **Noel's Walk**, **West Walk** (all one hour), and the **Ocean View Walk** (45 minutes), which gives good views of Cape Bridgewater and Discovery Bay. You may spot koalas feeding on manna gums along this track, and a guide to the local flora and fauna is available from a box at the start of the Benwerrin walk. Rest assured, there are picnic areas with tables and wood barbecues, as well as a lookout tower with views to Discovery Bay and Lady Julia Percy Island.

The park is on the site of an **extinct volcano** (Mt Richmond last erupted about two million years ago). The vegetation is mainly hardy native species such as brown stringybark and manna gums, and the park is known for its glorious spring wildflowers and unusual plants: over 450 species recorded, including 50 different species of orchid! No yawning please.

If you're lucky, you'll meet a few of the residents: kangaroos and wallabies, koalas, shy echidnas and snakes, and that invisible member of the kangaroo family, the potokangaroo (it's nocturnal). Birdies are in abundance, as always.

Lower Glenelg National Park

Canoeists, bushwalkers and anglers get particularly excited about this playground with its deep **gorges,** brilliant **wildflowers**, and tranquil waters. The snaking, bogbrown **Glenelg River**, which originates in the Grampians and travels more than 400km to the coast at Nelson, is at its most impressive during its last 35km – to reach the ocean, the river waters have carved colourful gorges through soft, limestone cliffs, which makes for very pretty flat-water canoeing.

Incidentally, the best way to see the park is by canoe – the river is navigable for more than 75km from Nelson – and there are nine **canoeists' camping sites** between Nelson and Dartmoor that provide basic facilities such as fresh water, toilets and fireplaces, but most manage the full trip in five days. Canoe-camping permits costs $3 and are issued by **Parks Victoria** (☎ 08-8738 4051; Nelson; ☼ 9am-5pm).

You can hire canoes, boats and fishing gear in Nelson (see right).

Over 700 different plant species have been recorded in this park, which means that bushwalkers have many other distractions than the path they're stumbling along (see opposite). Grass trees – the inspiration for those fibre-optic, glow-dome lamps from the '70s – are in fine, fuzz-ball form throughout. The wildlife includes kangaroos, wallabies, echidnas and brushtail possums. Birds are ubiquitous and include emus, herons, ducks, kingfishers and quail. You'll see them along the unsealed roads that lead to camping spots, and along the network of walking tracks throughout the park.

Nelson

☎ 08 / pop 200

Nelson is a riverside village with a few houses, a cute general store, a friendly pub with the lingering scent of fried food, and a handful of accommodation that includes three caravan parks and a motel. It's a popular holiday and fishing spot because of its great setting on the coast and at the mouth of the poo-brown Glenelg River, and because it's out of the way, it hasn't yet been spoiled by commercialisation and development. A well-stacked signpost by the bridge directs you to everything around town.

INFORMATION

The visitors centre and **Parks Victoria** (☎ 8738 4051; ☼ 9am-5pm) share an office and you can also access the Internet here.

SIGHTS & ACTIVITIES

Nelson Beach is one of many remote stretches that are part of the **Discovery Bay Coastal Park**; a long walk along its endless spine of sandy dunes and rolling surf cures a churning mind of all ills.

Exercise-challenged folk can book a leisurely 3½-hour cruise up the Glenelg River with **Nelson Endeavour River Cruises** (☎ 8738 4191; adult/child $23/10). The cruise stops at the **Princess Margaret Rose Cave** (adult/child/family $9.50/5/25), but tickets for the cave tour cost extra. Cruises depart daily in summer at 1pm, but don't operate Mondays and Fridays during the rest of the year. If you travel to the caves under your own steam, it's about 17km from Nelson, heading toward the border. And if you've never experienced the Tolkienesque wonderland of a cave, do take the 45-minute tour; they leave every hour between 10am and 4pm.

Nelson Boat & Canoe Hire (☎ 08-8738 4048; www .nelsonboatandcanoehire.com.au) can rig you up for serious camping expeditions. Canoe hire is from $36 a day. They also do upriver canoe deliveries and pick-ups for an extra fee.

SLEEPING & EATING

Accommodation-wise, there are some decent options.

Simpsons Landing B&B (☎ 8738 4232; d $80) Two cheery rooms, that share a bathroom, in an A-frame, loft set-up .

Casuarina Cabins (☎ 08-8738 4105; www.casuarina cabins.com.au; cabins with bathroom $60; ⌘) Gorgeous

SOUTHWEST

bush setting, which contrasts sharply with the stark, fluorescent-lit interior of the cabins by night.

Nelson Cottage (☎ 8738 4161; cnr Kellett & Sturt Sts; d $80) Cosy enough rooms for short stays.

Ambience Gallery Cafe (☎ 8738 4378; 10 Isle of Bags Rd; mains $5-12; ☪ lunch, closed Tue) A cute, corrugated-iron shed, displaying vibrant local art and crafts, that dares to posit salmon-and-lime cakes, and bean-and-celery patties to folk more familiar with fried steak. Meals are definitely of the light-lunch variety, but it opens from 10am to 6pm.

Nelson Hotel (☎ 8738 4011; Kellett St; d $45; mains $13-17; ☪ lunch & dinner) That's not to scoff at the Nelson, which has a good range of vegetarian options alongside its crumbed and fried fare, and a good salad bar. The accommodation available here is fine for a brief stay.

Getting There & Away
The only public transport option along the coastal route is the **Wayward Bus** (☎ 1300 653 510; www.waywardbus.com.au) – see p411.

ALONG THE PRINCES HIGHWAY
If you're in a hurry, taking the Princes Hwy (A1) from Melbourne to Portland is a good way to combine a speedy trip to the South Australian border without missing *all* the southwest's sensational bits. The trade-off is that you miss the Great Ocean Rd, but the alternative is hardly shabby. Instead, you pass through the heartland of the Western District, with its countryside scarred by ancient volcanic activity, via Colac and Camperdown, before heading south to Warrnambool, then west to Portland, taking the Portland–Nelson Rd to the South Australian Border. Be assured, enchanting Port Fairy, dramatic Cape Bridgewater (see p229) with its seal colony and stunning Discovery Bay (see p231) are ample compensation.

After completing the Great Ocean Rd in Warrnambool, travellers often scoot back to Melbourne along the Princes Hwy via Terang, Camperdown, Colac and Geelong.

Colac
☎ 03 / pop 9800
Colac is a bit of a melting pot. Here, old-fashioned cake shops serve bursting cream buns and a sizeable yarn store declares the talents of crafty locals, but there's also a

growing Sudanese community and a vortex of alternative therapists gathering.

Colac's greatest assets are its position on Victoria's largest freshwater lake, and its proximity to the sumptuous Otway Ranges. The closest townships to Colac are Birregurra, Gellibrand and Forrest. The area has some truly unique experiences on offer.

Before European settlers came in 1837, the Coladgin Koorie tribe lived peacefully beside Lake Colac, but the town quickly grew into a regional centre, fuelled by combined wealth from the pastures of the Western District and the forest timbers of the Otway Ranges.

INFORMATION
Colac Visitors Centre (☎ 5231 3730; cnr Murray & Queen Sts; ☪ 9am-5pm) This office has oodles of info about Colac, the Otway Ranges and the Great Ocean Rd. It's at the beginning of Murray St, the main shopping strip. You can access the Internet here too.

SIGHTS & ACTIVITIES
Within Colac, **Lake Colac** is a playground for water sports and has good fishing – although you're as likely to catch carp as redfin. Part of the lake borders the **botanic gardens** (Queen St), which is a great place to unwind if you're passing through. There are picnic and barbecue facilities here, or you can cheat and visit the café at the gardens' northern edge.

You must spare a half-day to head into the Otways. Fifteen kilometres south of Colac, along the Colac–Lavers Hill road, you'll come to the **Old Beechy Line** rail trail. There's either a short 15-minute walk to the picnic area, or an 8km loop walk, along which you'll spy remnants of the railway that first opened in 1902 for the transport of pulpwood and farm animals.

Here's one for the scrapbook. Hire a **gypsy wagon** and spend a couple of days clomping up and down the unsealed roads of the Otways with your dependable Clydesdale for company. Your hosts leave you to it, but return to harness and unharness the horsies each morning and night. Camping is under brilliant starry skies by your own private lake. **Otway Gypsy Wagons** (☎ 5233 4606; www.otway gypsywagons.com.au; 70 Bushbys Rd, Barongarook) charge $180 a day, and the wagons sleep three or five people.

Seven kilometres south of the Old Beechy Trail is the 'oldest original pub in the Otways', the **Gellibrand River Hotel** (☎ 5235 8499;

Lavers Hill Rd, Gellibrand; meals $12-19). No pokies here, just good steaks and absolute tranquillity in a pleasant beer garden overlooking rolling hills.

SLEEPING
Elms B&B (☎ 5231 5112; www.elmsbb.com; 14-16 Gellibrand St; s/d $65/95) Carmen, a delightful host, warmly welcomes guests to her large, lovingly restored home (c 1880) with its manicured gardens. Once through the front door, you enter another space in time. There are four large rooms available, one with a four-poster bed, and a very relaxed atmosphere. Centrally located, too.

Prince of Wales Guesthouse (☎ 5231 3385; sleepy teapot@iprimus.com.au; 2-6 Murray St; s/d $60/77) This B&B by Barongarook Creek has a snug guestroom, albeit very dark, with a beautiful Federation-era bed. It's also a tea parlour that opens 10.30am to 5pm Wednesday to Sunday. There's a ramshackle garden, and shops are just around the corner.

Bogandeena Studio (☎ 5231 5273; 75 Colac–Lavers Hill Rd, Elliminyt; d $100) It's only 4km out of town to this two-bedroom studio nestled in idyllic gardens with weeping willows for shade. The studio is bright and comfortably furnished, with a reassuring wood heater for chilly nights.

Lake Colac Caravan Park (☎ 5231 5971; lakecolac@telstra.com; 51 Fyans St; powered/unpowered sites per 2 people low season $22/18, high season, $26/21, d cabins with bathroom low/high season $60/75) There are several waterfront cabins, but ask for number three, set right by the lake, with weeping willows and

a grassy knoll out front. It's so pleasant here, you'll want to stay longer. Resident ducks expect breakfast to be served by 10am.

EATING
Duffs Licensed Cafe (☎ 5232 2229; cnr Dennis & Gellibrand Sts; lunch mains $12-17; ☷ lunch daily, dinner Thu-Sat) Wow, the fanciful restoration of this 1870 Oddfellows Hall is as enticing as the menu is varied. An arched, wood-panelled ceiling offsets a spidery gold chandelier, with angel wings in plaster relief along one feature wall, while stencilled vines twine around the rest. It's a beguiling eyeful, so kick back in a comfy lounge with an excellent coffee, or glass of the region's best vino, and appreciate it.

Country Foodstore (☎ 5231 5442; 136 Murray St; lunch mains $4-8; ☷ breakfast & lunch) Perhaps a gluten-free frittata or soup, maybe a soy-lentil patty wrap or just a toasted sanga and flourless poppy-seed cake to finish? You can eat in, but it's much nicer to take away and stretch out in Murray St's shady green gardens.

Nu-Deli (☎ 5232 2227; Shop 186, Murray St; dinner mains $17-27; ☷ breakfast, lunch & dinner) Nu-Deli is just around the corner from the Safeway supermarket on Carangamite St. It feels slightly more upmarket at night and has a wide, tempting menu, with a pretty good wine list. Bit of a crowd pleaser.

Culture Cafe Lounge Bar (☎ 5231 4111; 62-62 Murray St; mains $15-20; ☷ lunch & dinner Mon-Sat, closed Sun) Culture is Colac's only hip joint: deep, dark and garishly orange. In daylight hours, it still feels like a sultry lounge bar. The menu is Mod Oz, and it has live music most weekends.

GETTING THERE & AWAY
Trains travelling between Melbourne and Warrnambool stop in Colac ($23.30).

Colac to Camperdown
The road from Colac to Camperdown skirts a series of volcanic lakes and craters, but to appreciate their breathless beauty, take the 17km detour to **Red Rock Lookout**. The turn-off is 5km west of Colac, near the town of Coraguluc. Drive to the summit of twin volcanic peaks for a top-of-the-world feeling as you pan endless pasturelands and velvet-green rims that plunge into crater bowls. Sunset, when the lakes glint in last light and barren craters cast deep shadows, is an exceptional time.

From here you can see **Lake Corangamite** in all its majesty. It's the largest permanent saltwater lake in Victoria; because it has no outlet or overflow, its salt concentration is three times that of seawater. There's another turn-off to the lake along the lookout road; it's a top spot for bird-watching.

At Pirron Yallock, 17km west of Colac, is the **Floating Islands Reserve**, in which six large peat islands float in a lagoon and move about according to the wind. The islands sound more exciting than they are – it has to blow a gale (or you have to be very patient) for any noticeable movement to occur. A walking trail leads from the car park to the reserve.

South of the town of Weerite, **Lake Purrumbete** is a huge, 45m-deep, freshwater-filled volcanic crater that is home to schools of rainbow trout and chinook salmon. The no-frills caravan park on its banks is a haven for anglers, but you're allowed to drive in and picnic on its shores.

Camperdown
☎ 03 / pop 3200

Camperdown is set prettily at the foot of two camel-hump hills called Mt Leura and Mt Sugarloaf. Both are remnants of volcanic activity in the area just 20,000 years ago – embryonic in geological terms.

INFORMATION
Court A'Fair (☎ 5593 3144; 179 Manifold St; 10am-4.30pm Mon-Thu, to 7pm Fri-Sun) A café, gift shop and gallery in the old courthouse hands out visitor information, including a heritage trail brochure and excellent leaflets on the area's crater and lake highlights.

SIGHTS & ACTIVITIES
The main street is divided by English elm trees and presided over by a storybook red-brick **clock tower**, constructed in 1897, that punctuates the days with beefy tolls. Camperdown's streetfront of chunky historic buildings makes a good spot for a leg-stretch, and you can be sure of a decent cuppa.

You can also drive up to the **Mt Leura lookout** for a terrific view of the surrounding lakes and farmland – turn off the Princes Hwy at Adeney St and it's 1.5km to the top.

SLEEPING & EATING
Your budget options are limited unless you enjoy basic pub digs.

Timboon House B&B (☎ 5593 1003; www.innhouse .com.au/timboonhouse.html; Old Geelong Rd; d $140) Timboon is an exquisite, elegant mini-manor, all bluestone and polished floors and genuine antique furnishings, about 3km north of town. You could easily spend a couple days among its pretty gardens and gracious guest areas and pretend you're travelling royalty.

Old Mill (☎ 5593 2200; www.camperdownmill.com .au; 3-5 Curdie St; s/d $95/130) There's something twee-tourist-village about this uniquely renovated mill set-up, but the nine self-contained apartments offer restful digs with some eccentric touches: a little Tudor lodge here, hunter's den there, and some '80s furnishing flair too.

Manifold Motor Inn (☎ 5593 2666; 295 Manifold St; d low/high season $90/102;) It looks like a motel, smells like a motel, and by golly, it is a motel; a well cared for one, with good size rooms and free cable TV.

Cafe One Fifty Three (☎ 5593 1335; Manifold St; mains $17-19; breakfast & lunch Tue-Sun, dinner Thu-Sat) A warm, amiable interior with high ceilings and hushed, leafy courtyard out back make this an appealing choice. You can choose between lighter snacks and meaty mains. It's licensed, too.

Madden's Bistro (☎ 5593 1187; 115 Manifold St; mains $14-18; lunch & dinner) Eighties-inspired, filo-wrapped delights and chicken Kiev sit alongside risotto and stir-fry staples at this unusual, almost ranch-style bistro. It's a jovial place to tuck into a steak and red wine chaser.

GETTING THERE & AWAY
V/Line (☎ 13 61 96) trains travelling between Melbourne and Warrnambool stop in Camperdown ($29.40).

Central West

Gold fever forms the thrilling history of much of Victoria's central west. It's left a legacy of grand architecture, with all towns boasting classic Victorian buildings. There are also fabulous attractions linked to the era. Sovereign Hill, in Ballarat, is one of Australia's most popular tourist spots; Bendigo's reminders of the past include the famous Chinese dragons, Old Loong and Sun Loong. Castlemaine, an impressive gold town, is surrounded by charming, historic hamlets, or head north to the Golden Triangle and pick up a nugget or two.

The Pyrenees Ranges near Avoca, the Heathcote region and the Bendigo district are major wine-producing areas. The twin towns of Daylesford and Hepburn Springs, in the scenic central highlands, are famous for their mineral spas. Along with the waters are masseurs and naturopaths, gardens and craft shops, restored old guesthouses and cottages, and plenty of great eateries. The Wimmera is a surprising mix of attractions from expanses of wheat and sheep properties, to national parks such as the Little Desert and Mt Arapiles. Pretty little communities like Dimboola contrast with bustling Horsham. The Grampians, an adventurer's paradise, stand majestically over the idyllic Wartook Valley and cute, touristy Dunkeld.

South of the Grampians is some of the best grazing pasture in the country and Hamilton, the major town, is known locally as the 'Wool Capital of the World'. However, the district's volcanic features are probably the most interesting. It's the third largest volcanic plain in the world, with volcanic parks at Mt Napier and Mt Eccles.

HIGHLIGHTS

- Bubbling in a hot tub in a treehouse overlooking the lake in **Daylesford** (p246)
- Deciding to go straight after spending a night in the old gaol at **Castlemaine** (p251)
- Covering your back as a trooper rams gunpowder into his pistol at Ballarat's **Sovereign Hill** (p239)
- Seeing the desert the easy way, by cruising up the idyllic Wimmera River from your accommodation in **Dimboola** (p276)
- Dreaming of untold wealth down a cold, dark goldmine in **Bendigo** (p240)
- Enjoying country hospitality in a winery resort near **Moonambel** (p255) in the heart of the Pyrenees
- Hanging by a thread (OK a rope) on a towering cliff in the **Grampians** (p269)
- Scaling **Mt Arapiles** (p275), a world-renowned rock-climber's mecca

Dimboola ★
Mt Arapiles State Park ★
★ Halls Gap
★ Grampians
Moonambel ★
Bendigo ★
Castlemaine ★
Daylesford ★
Ballarat ★

CENTRAL WEST

- www.visitvictoria.com
- www.goldfields.org.au

THE GOLDFIELDS

One of the state's most interesting areas, the Goldfields region features reminders of the rich heritage of the gold-rush days wherever you go. It's a blend of quaint townships, impressive regional centres and pretty countryside, but also a place of dramatically contrasting landscapes, from the green forests of the Wombat Ranges to the red earth, bush and granite country up around Inglewood. Take to the back roads and go exploring: it's also a great area for bike touring or horse riding, or you can hire a horse-drawn gypsy-style caravan (see p256) and go prospecting. The old diggers dug up most of the gold,

but even today stories are told of significant nuggets being unearthed.

Highlights for bushwalkers include the numerous trails around Daylesford, the rugged granite countryside of the Kooyoora State Park, the Pyrenees Ranges, and the hills and forests around Maldon and Bendigo. There are fine golf courses, lots of good freshwater fishing spots and numerous horse-riding ranches.

Ballarat and Bendigo are the two major 'hubs', with most of the main highways intersecting at one or the other.

Getting There & Around

If you have your own transport, the well-signposted Goldfields Tourist Route makes

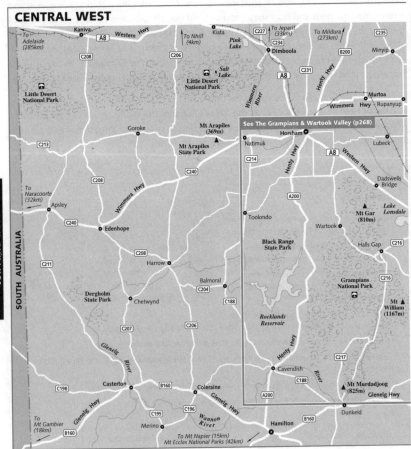

an interesting excursion that takes in all the major gold-rush centres. A route map is available from most of the visitors centres along the way.

There are two main train lines through the Goldfields: the Melbourne–Swan Hill train line (via Kyneton, Castlemaine and Bendigo) and the Melbourne–Ballarat–Adelaide line.

V/Line (☎ 13 61 96) buses cover most of the regional centres, with the majority of services radiating out of Ballarat and Bendigo.

BALLARAT

☎ 03 / pop 83,000

The area around present-day Ballarat was known to the local Koories as 'Ballaarat', meaning 'resting place'. When gold was dis-

covered at nearby Buninyong in August 1851, the rush was on and thousands of diggers flooded into the area. Ballarat's alluvial gold-fields were but the tip of the golden iceberg, and when deep shaft mines were sunk they struck incredibly rich quartz reefs. About 28% of the gold unearthed in Victoria came from Ballarat.

The original shanty town of canvas tents and bark and timber huts was gradually re-placed with a wealth of gracious Victorian architecture, a reminder of the prosperity of the days of gold.

Ballarat's main drag, Sturt St, is a wide boulevard lined with some impressive old buildings and divided by central plantations. They say it had to be three chains wide (60m)

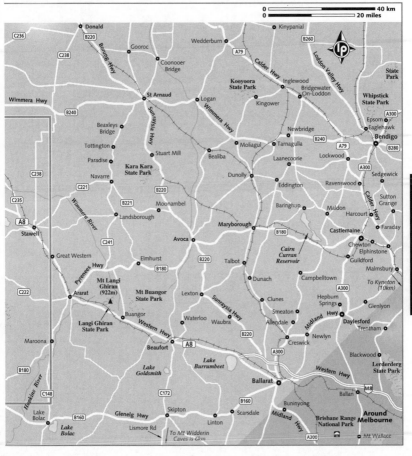

www.lonelyplanet.com

CENTRAL WEST

BALLARAT

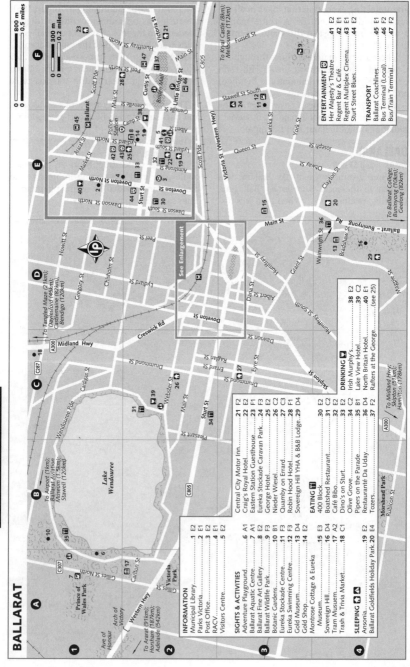

to allow for the turning circle of bullock wagons. Lydiard St is a historic precinct with some of the finest examples of Victorian architecture.

Sovereign Hill is the main attraction, but there are plenty of other points of interest, such as the Camp St arts precinct which buzzes with student activity and includes a public open space for the performing arts.

Information

Accommodation booking service (☎ 5320 5741; 1800 446 633) At the information centre.

Municipal library (cnr Sturt & Camp Sts) Check your emails here.

Parks Victoria (☎ 5333 6782; cnr Doveton & Mair Sts)

Post office (Sturt St) In the shopping mall.

Royal Automobile Club of Victoria office (RACV; ☎ 5332 1946; 20 Doveton St North) Has an information section and accommodation-booking service.

Visitors centre (☎ 5320 5741; 1800 446 633; www .visitballarat.com.au; 39 Sturt St; ⏱ 9am-5pm) You'll be very well looked after here.

Sights

SOVEREIGN HILL

Allow at least half a day to visit this fascinating re-creation of an 1860s gold-mining township. **Sovereign Hill** (☎ 5331 1944; www.sovereignhill .com.au; Magpie St; adult/child/family $29/14/75; ⏱ 10am-5pm) has won numerous awards. The site was mined back in the gold-rush era and thus much of the equipment is original, as is the mine shaft, and there are above-ground and underground diggings. You can pan for gold in the stream – maybe you'll find a speck or two.

The main street features a hotel, post office, blacksmith's shop, printing shop, bakery and a Chinese joss house. It's a living history museum with people performing their chores dressed in costumes of the time.

There are at least four places around the 'town' offering food, from pies and pasties at the Hope Bakery to a three-course lunch at the United States Hotel.

Sovereign Hill is well worth the price. It opens again at night for the impressive sound-and-light show **'Blood on the Southern Cross'** (☎ 5333 5777; adult/child/family $35/19/97; ⏱ summer 9.15 & 10.30pm winter 6.45 & 8pm), which is a simulation of the Eureka Stockade battle (see p241). Bookings are essential.

Your ticket also gets you into the nearby Gold Museum.

GOLD MUSEUM

Sitting on a mullock heap from an old mine, the excellent **Gold Museum** (☎ 5331 1944; Magpie St; adult/child $7.50/3.50; ⏱ 9.30am-5.20pm) has imaginative displays and samples from all the old mining areas, as well as gold nuggets, coins and a display on the Eureka Rebellion. You can get in for free with a Sovereign Hill ticket.

BALLARAT FINE ART GALLERY

This **gallery** (☎ 5320 5858; 40 Lydiard St North; adult/ child $5/free; ⏱ 10.30am-5pm) houses a wonderful collection of Australian art, which includes early colonial paintings, works from noted Australian artists (including Tom Roberts, Sir Sidney Nolan, Russell Drysdale and Fred Williams) and contemporary works from artists such as Howard Arkley. A separate section is devoted to the multitalented Lindsay family who lived in nearby Creswick. You can also see remnants of the original Eureka flag. The gallery is the jewel in the crown of Ballarat's historic and architecturally intriguing Camp St precinct.

LAKE WENDOUREE

Formerly the Black Swamp, this large artificial lake is a focal point for the town and was used as the rowing course in the 1956 Olympics. Wendouree Parade, which circles the lake, boasts much of Ballarat's best residential architecture. There are old timber boatsheds along the shore and you'll often see rowing boats being stroked across the water. The jogging and walking track around the lake is also popular, and a favourite training venue for local hero and Olympic marathon runner Steve Moneghetti.

BOTANIC GARDENS

These beautiful and serene gardens were first planted in 1858. Stroll through the 40 hectares of immaculately maintained rose gardens, wide lawns, old trees and the colourful Conservatory. The cottage of the poet Adam Lindsay Gordon is here. Or you may come face-to-face with John Howard in the Prime Ministers' Avenue, a collection of bronze portraits.

A tourist tramway operates around the gardens, departing from the tram museum south of the gardens. Close by, on the other side of Wendouree Parade, is a fantastic, wooden children's playground. Drive slowly. The swans step gracefully across the road at unexpected moments.

EUREKA STOCKADE CENTRE

On the site of the Eureka Rebellion is the **Eureka Stockade Centre** (☎ 5333 1854; Eureka St; adult/child/family $8/4/22; ☽ 9am-5pm) – look out for the huge Eureka sail (see also opposite). It takes you through multimedia galleries simulating the battle. If you're exhausted after all the fighting, you can move into the 'contemplation space' to be soothed by the sound of running water.

BALLARAT WILDLIFE PARK

This most attractive **zoo** (☎ 5333 5933; www.wild lifepark.com.au; cnr York & Fussell Sts; adult/child/family $15.50/9/42; ☽ 9am-5.30pm, tour 11am) gives you the opportunity of walking among the sweet little King Island wallabies in a tranquil park. Happily the crocodiles are in a compound. Other native species include: Tasmanian devils, emus, quokkas, snakes, eagles and a giant tortoise. On weekends, regular programmes include a koala show, wombat show and crocodile-feeding.

OTHER SIGHTS

Montrose Cottage & Eureka Museum (☎ 5332 2554; 111 Eureka St; adult/child $6/3; ☽ 9am-5pm) is an historic cottage dating from gold-rush times. The interior is practically the original and there is fascinating memorabilia that forms a social history of the Eureka Rebellion.

Lydiard St is one of Australia's finest and most intact streetscapes of Victorian architecture. A walk along here will take you past Her Majesty's Theatre, the art gallery and Craig's Royal Hotel. The *Historic Lydiard Precinct* brochure is available from the information centre.

The **Ballarat Aviation Museum** (Ballarat airport, Sunraysia Hwy; ☽ 1-5pm Sat & Sun) houses a collection of vintage and military aircraft, and associated bits and pieces. Also at the airport, you can take scenic flights or just pretend in the flight simulator at the **Warbird Flight Centre**.

Not surprisingly, the 'medieval' **Kryal Castle** (☎ 5334 7388; Western Hwy; adult/child $20/10; ☽ 9.30am-5pm) has a torture display and medieval re-enactments with the odd whipping. The castle is 8km east of Ballarat.

At the Ballarat Showgrounds there's a fine **Trash & Trivia market** (Creswick Rd; ☽ 8am-2.30pm) every Sunday morning.

Activities

If you want to try gold prospecting, visit the **Gold Shop** (☎ 5333 4242; 8a Lydiard St North) in the old Mining Exchange building. It has a metal detector for hire ($25 per day) and can tell you where to buy detectors and miner's rights.

Despite its notoriously hardy climate, Ballarat has four large outdoor pools. The heated **Eureka Swimming Centre** (☎ 5331 2820; cnr Stawell & Eureka Sts) has a giant water slide and minigolf. The indoor **Ballarat Aquatic Centre** (☎ 5334 2499; Gillies St North; adult/child/family $5/3/12; ☽ 6am-9pm Mon-Fri, 8am-6pm Sat & Sun) has several pools and a gym.

Tours

Timeless Tours (☎ 5342 0652) offers half-day guided tours for $30 around Ballarat's heritage sites, and trips to destinations further afield, including the Brisbane Ranges (p151) and Lerderderg Gorge (p167).

Festivals & Events

Military tattoo (late Jan) Held over the Australia Day long weekend.

Begonia Festival (www.ballaratbegoniafestival.com; early Mar) This 100-year-old festival attracts thousands of visitors. Highlights include sensational floral displays, a street parade, fireworks, art shows and music.

Eureka Jazz Festival (www.ballarat.com/events; Apr)

Royal South St Eisteddfod (www.visitballarat.com.au; Sep/Oct) If you learnt music as a child, you were probably dragged off to this, Australia's oldest eisteddfod.

Sleeping

Ballarat's grand old pubs, B&Bs and cottages all offer gracious accommodation, and there are many motels and holiday resorts, all with budget through to luxury units. Contact the free **Accommodation Booking Office** (☎ 1800 446 633) for more information.

Accommodation is scarce in September/October, when the Royal South St Eisteddfod takes place.

BUDGET & MIDRANGE

Sovereign Hill YHA & B&B Lodge (☎ 5333 3409; www.sovereignhill.com.au; Magpie St; dm/s/d $19/28/44; lodge B&B s/d/f from $105/126/180; ☒) Walk straight into Sovereign Hill or enjoy the surrounding pine forest. The Lodge has gorgeous heritage rooms and the guest lounge is cosy, with fireplace and bar. The YHA house is a separate cottage and quietly fantastic. All the facilities are excellent (and it's often fully booked).

CENTRAL WEST

THE EUREKA REBELLION

As the easily won gold began to run out, Victorian diggers realised the inequality between themselves and the privileged few who held the land and governing power.

The limited size of claims, the brutality of police licence hunts and the fact that the miners were allowed no political representation, all fired the unrest that led to the Eureka Rebellion.

In September 1854 Governor Hotham ordered that the hated licence hunts be carried out twice a week. A month later a miner was murdered near the Ballarat Hotel after an argument with the owner, James Bentley. When Bentley was found not guilty by a magistrate (who just happened to be his business associate) miners rioted and burned his hotel down. Though Bentley was retried and found guilty, the rioting miners were also jailed, which enraged the diggers.

They created the Ballarat Reform League calling for abolition of licence fees, the introduction of miners' rights to vote and increased opportunities to purchase land.

On 29 November about 800 miners tossed their licences into a bonfire during a mass meeting and then built a stockade at Eureka, led by an Irishman called Peter Lalor, where they prepared to fight for their rights.

On 3 December the government ordered the troopers to attack the stockade. There were only 150 diggers within the makeshift barricades and the fight lasted only 20 minutes, leaving 25 miners and four troopers dead.

Though the rebellion was short-lived the miners won the sympathy and support of Victorians. The government deemed it wise to acquit the leaders of the charge of high treason.

The licence fee was abolished and replaced by a Miners' Right, which cost one pound a year. This gave them the right to search for gold; to fence in, cultivate and build a dwelling on a piece of land; and to vote for members of the Legislative Assembly. The rebel miner, Peter Lalor, became a member of Parliament some years later.

There are larger dorm rooms in the complex which usually house school groups.

Robin Hood Hotel (☎ 5331 3348; www.robinhood hotel.com.au; 33 Peel St North; dm/s/d $20/30/40) Right in the centre, this down-market old local pub has spacious, high-ceilinged rooms upstairs, with good beds and crooked, cracked, clean bathrooms. Just beware the karaoke on Friday and Saturday.

Ballarat Goldfields Holiday Park (☎ 5332 7888; 1800 632 237; www.ballaratgoldfields.com.au; 108 Clayton St; camp sites per 2 people from $22, d cabins from $60; ✦) Close to Sovereign Hill, there's a good holiday atmosphere here and the park has won several tourism awards. The cabins are like miners' cottages, some with three bedrooms.

Eastern Station Guesthouse (☎ 5338 8722; www .ballarat.com/easternstation.htm; 81 Humffray St North; s/d/f $35/60/80; Ⓟ) Built in 1862, this corner pub now only opens on weekends. The accommodation area has fresh and spacious rooms, a grand kitchen opening onto a deck, off-street parking and two large games and TV rooms.

George Hotel (☎ 5333 4866; www.ballarat.com/george; 27 Lydiard St North; s/d from $50/65; ✦) This gorgeous pub in historic Lydiard St was rebuilt in 1902 with towering ceilings and sweeping walnut staircases – the rooms are a bit more modern and include breakfast that you can enjoy on the balcony.

Central City Motor Inn (☎ 5333 1775; www.ballarat .com/centralcity.htm; 16 Victoria St; s/d/f from $90/ 100/130; ✦ ✦) Up on Bakery Hill, this place is nice and central, and there's a very little heated pool along with large fresh rooms. If you need more space, the attractive un-cluttered **terrace house** (r from $250) has two bedrooms, spacious spa bathroom and a small garden.

Eureka Stockade Caravan Park (☎ /fax 5331 2281; 104 Stawell St South; camp sites per 2 people from $16, d cabins from $48; ✦ ✦) This place is really convenient, but there's still plenty of grass and trees, a heated pool next door, barbecue areas, games room, cots, pleasant cabins and a disabled room.

TOP END
Ansonia (☎ 5332 4678; www.ballarat.com/ansonia.htm; 32 Lydiard St South; d from $142) An upmarket retreat, this place exudes calm with its minimalist design, polished cement floors and light-filled atrium. The café serves breakfast

CENTRAL WEST

THE AUTHOR'S CHOICE

Nieder Weisel (☎ 5331 8829; www.ballarat
.com/niederweisel; 109 Webster St; B&B d from
$140) You'll think you're a star, walking
through the stained-glass, walnut-trimmed,
arched double doors and along the Persian
carpet hall-runner. Your magnificent room,
bay windows, enormous bed and decadent
bathroom add to the notion. Then the antique white cotton nightclothes, for your
bedtime, make you wonder if you'll ever
want to be yourself again.

The guest sitting rooms, private courtyards, the silver service breakfast and warm
hospitality all concur. Then go below to the
dungeon, and hear the interesting (not
gruesome truly) stories linked to it.

Hosts Sam and Greg have several room
options (an extra person costs $25) and pack-
ages. They'll find one to suit you.

all day. Rooms range from studio apartments for two to family suites.

Quamby on Errard (☎ 5332 2782; www.heritage
homestay.com/quamby_on_errard.htm; 114 Errard St;
B&B s/d from $87/135) If you're after an intimate
experience, try this very sweet cottage, with
its delicate antiques and gourmet breakfast.

Craig's Royal Hotel (☎ 5331 1377; www.craigsroyal
.com; 10 Lydiard St South) This grand old pub is
being renovated. It is expected to have five-
star accommodation but contact the information centre for details.

Eating

Tozers (☎ 5338 8908; 101 Bridge Mall; mains $23-29.50;
⏲ lunch Sat, dinner Tue-Sat) Why go anywhere
else? This has to be the best fine-dining
venue, with fabulous food by Alan, the Irish
chef. Try his eggs stuffed with coriander
and garlic, or eye fillet with caramelised
shallots.

Cafe Bibo (☎ 5331 1255; 205 Sturt St; mains $10.50-
20; ⏲ breakfast & lunch) This retro café is lined
with copies of 1960s *Women's Weekly* and
shelves of decorated coffee cups belonging
to the regulars. The breakfast is so good
you'll be back for the chicken pilliard with
coriander couscous at lunch.

Dino's on Sturt (☎ 5332 9711; www.ballarat.com
/dinos; 212 Sturt St; mains $12-26; ⏲ breakfast, lunch &
dinner) A welcoming, child-friendly, sophisticated and new restaurant with a menu that

you'll love. Try traditional tomato and bread
soup, or lamb shanks with kumera chips.

Olive Grove (☎ 5331 4455; 1303 Sturt Street; meals
$10-14) Up towards the lake is this fantastic
deli, full of gourmet delights, including pies,
focaccias, cakes and cheeses – the perfect
place to stock up.

Boatshed Restaurant (☎ 5333 5533; www.boatshed
-restaurant.com; Lake Wendouree; mains $17.50-27;
⏲ breakfast, lunch & dinner) Sit on the deck over
the lake or stay inside with the open fire and
armchairs. Either way there's a lovely atmosphere, excellent coffee and an exciting menu
that doesn't include duck, fortunately for the
dozens waddling around the grounds.

Pipers on the Parade (Lake Wendouree; mains $9-18;
⏲ breakfast & lunch) This 1890 Lakeside Lodge
was designed by WH Piper. It now has huge
windows so you can look out over the lake
and watch the swans and ducks. The beef
and Guinness pie is great, but you can't get
past the scallops in a caramelised leek and
saffron risotto.

Restaurante Da Uday (☎ 5331 6655; 7 Wainwright
St; mains $12-26; ⏲ lunch & dinner) Come to this
pretty converted cottage and enjoy the intoxi-
cating aromas, or collect takeaway – Indian,
Thai or Italian.

The main café scene, praised in the *Age*
'Good Food Guide', is the **400 Block** (Sturt St),
where tables spill out, along with the coffee aroma. The cafés along here are open
all day:

L'Espresso (☎ 5333 1789; 417 Sturt St) Stylish, friendly
and atmospheric.

Gee Cees Cafe Bar (☎ 5331 6211; 427 Sturt St) Large
and popular.

Europa Cafe (☎ 5331 2486; 411 Sturt St) Turkish,
Spanish, Mediterranean.

Ruby's (☎ 5333 3386; 423 Sturt St) Bright red and funky.

Drinking

Irish Murphy's (☎ 5331 4091; 36 Sturt St; ⏲ to 3am
Wed-Sun) This atmospheric place is a good
option; the live music draws people of all
ages. There's plenty of Guinness on tap and
a good **bistro** (mains $8-17; ⏲ lunch & dinner).

Rafters at the George (☎ 5333 4866; 27 Lydiard St
North; ⏲ to late Fri & Sat) This is a good venue to
kick back, with live bands of general appeal.

Lake View Hotel (☎ 5331 4592; www.thelakeview
.com.au; 22 Wendouree Parade) With its modern
spaces in a truly gorgeous old pub with buzzy
atmosphere and great views over the lake,
you'll enjoy the odd drink or two here. The

DETOUR: CRESWICK TO TALBOT

There are some cute spots to fossick out, just minutes from Ballarat. **Creswick**, an old gold-mining town and the home of **forestry** (www.creswickforestryfiesta.com), is a quiet agricultural centre. Centred around a rotunda, its main road sweeps past cafés, knick-knack shops and an **historical museum** (68 Albert St; admission $2; ☼ 1.30-4.30pm Sun). Creswick produced some famous Austra-lians, including John Curtin (prime minister in 1941), Lady Millie Peacock (first female member of Parliament, 1933) and artist Norman Lindsay.

North of Creswick there are interesting scenic drives through historic hamlets and tumbledown towns with hidden treasures. Along the Castlemaine Rd is **Springmount Pottery** and the quirky **Tangled Maze** (adult/child/family $7/6/26; ☼ 10am-5.30pm). Another 2km north is **Hillview Host Farm** (☎ /fax 5345 2690; Spittle Rd; cottage $98). The cottage overlooks a spectacular valley.

Kirkside Cottages (☎ 5345 6252; fax 5345 6200; 1 Church Parade, Kingston; B&B d $170) has an enchant-ing bluestone chapel in the grounds of its self-contained old miner's cottages.

In **Smeaton** the impressively restored **Anderson's Mill** (☼ noon-4pm Sun) is a gigantic blue-stone flour mill beside Birch Creek. Built in 1862, it has been fully restored and is a great spot for a picnic. Nearby, at the **Tuki Trout Fishing Complex** (☎ 5345 6233; fax 5345 6377; Stoney Rises; r $130-200; adult/child fish-and-meal $22.50/10.50; ☼ 11am-6pm) you can go fishing, then have your catch barbecued and served in the shearing shed restaurant. If you'd like to stay, self-contained cottages overlook the trout ponds.

Clunes, a charming little town, sprawls 32km north of Ballarat. It was the site of Victoria's first significant gold discovery in June 1851 (see p260). There are many fine buildings, and the **William Barkell Arts & Historic Centre** (36 Fraser St) in a double-storey bluestone building.

The small hills around Clunes are extinct volcanoes. Nearby **Mt Beckworth** is noted for its orchids and birdlife, and you can visit the old gold diggings of **Jerusalem** and **Ullina**.

Arrive in quaint, quiet Talbot at night (don't speak too loudly) and visit the **Talbot Observa-tory** (☎ 5463 2029; 9 Camp St; adult/child $5/2.50; ☼ summer/winter 9pm/7pm Fri & Sat). You'll not only see the rings of Saturn and learn about Brown Dwarfs, but you can also join in a star-b-que. Ring to inquire or to arrange your own times.

---

bistro (mains $12.50-24; ☼ breakfast, lunch & dinner) is also popular, with good pub food.

North Britain Hotel (☎ 5331 1291; 502 Doveton St North) Drink in this corner hotel, where the English pub atmosphere is helped by the antiques and collectables.

Entertainment

With its large student population, Ballarat has a lively nightlife. You can club till 5am, but you cannot enter a venue after 3am.

Regent Bar & Cafe (☎ 5331 5507; 71 Lydiard St North; ☼ Wed-Sun) This is an upbeat place for young trendies, who'll love the mainstream music.

Sturt Street Blues (☎ 5332 3676; cnr Sturt & Dove-ton Sts) A popular venue for blues fans of all ages, with live music most nights.

Her Majesty's Theatre (☎ 5333 5800; 17 Lydiard St South) Ballarat's main venue for the perform-ing arts is a wonderful building. Ring to find out what's on while you're in town.

Regent Multiplex Cinema (☎ 5331 1399; 49 Lydi-ard St North) This is Ballarat's main cinema complex.

Getting There & Away

Ten trains a day run from **Ballarat train station** (Lydiard St North) to Melbourne ($17, 1½ hours) via Bacchus Marsh. Buses continue on from Ballarat to Ararat ($16) and Stawell ($18).

V/Line (☎ 13 61 96) has daily bus services from Ballarat to Geelong ($12) and Mildura ($48) via St Arnaud ($20), and weekday ser-vices to Hamilton ($30), Maryborough ($10) and Bendigo ($22) via Daylesford ($11) and Castlemaine ($16).

Greyhound Australia (13 14 99; www.greyhound.com .au) has Melbourne–Adelaide buses that stop at the coach bay at Ballarat train station.

The **Airport Shuttlebus** (☎ 5333 4181; www.air portshuttlebus.com.au) goes direct to Melbourne airport from Ballarat train station ($23, seven times daily).

Getting Around

Davis Bus Lines (☎ 5331 7777; www.kefford.com.au) uses two main terminals: Curtis St and Little Bridge St. Timetables are available from the visitors centre or the train station. Bus No 2 goes to the train station, and Bus No 15 to the botanic gardens and Lake Wendouree. Nos 9 and 10 go to Sovereign Hill.

The Visitor Shuttle Bus (free) leaves the information centre on three different routes. If you stay on at a venue, catch a local bus back for $1.25.

For a cab, call **Ballarat Taxis** (☎ 13 10 08).

DAYLESFORD & HEPBURN SPRINGS
☎ 03 / pop 3500

Set among the scenic hills, lakes and forests of the central highlands, delightful Daylesford and Hepburn Springs together form the 'spa centre of Victoria'. The health-giving properties of the area's mineral springs were first claimed back in the 1870s, attracting droves of fashionable Melburnians. It was claimed that the waters could cure any complaint, and the spas and relaxed scenic environment could rejuvenate even the most stressed-out 19th-century city-dweller.

These days both towns are popular relaxation and rejuvenation centres that boast everything you need to promote health and well-being, including fabulous foodie places.

The well-preserved and restored buildings show the prosperity that visited these towns during the gold rush, as well as the lasting influence of the many Swiss-Italian miners who expertly worked the tunnel mines in the surrounding hills.

The area is also an increasingly popular home for escapees from the city; its population is an interesting blend of alternative-lifestylers and old-timers. There's also a thriving gay and lesbian scene.

Orientation & Information

Daylesford is set around pretty Lake Daylesford. Its two main streets, Raglan and Vincent, are major café strips. Vincent St turns into Hepburn Rd at the roundabout and takes you straight through Hepburn Springs and down to the original spa resort.

Book Barn (☎ 5348 3048; notlob@netconnect.com.au; Leggatt St, Daylesford; ⏰ 11am-5.30pm) Vague out happily at this book shop, where there's an unbelievable range of quality second-hand books for sale.

Visitors centre (☎ 5321 6123; www.visitdaylesford.com; 98 Vincent St, Daylesford; ⏰ 9am-5pm) The staff here are very knowledgeable and helpful.

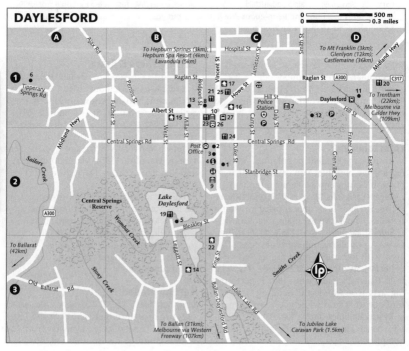

Sights

Daylesford's popular attraction, the **Convent Gallery** (☎ 5348 3211; Daly St; admission $4.50; ☼ 10am-6pm), is a massive 19th-century convent brilliantly converted into a craft and art gallery with soaring ceilings, grand archways, winding staircases and magnificent gardens. The gallery is on Wombat Hill and has an elegant café at the entrance.

Pantechnicon Art Gallery & Antiques (☎ 5348 3500; www.daylesfordartgallery.com.au; 34 Vincent St, Daylesford; ☼ 11am-5pm Thu-Mon) and **Corner Stone** (☎ 5348 4440; 115 Main Rd, Hepburn Springs; ☼ 9am-5pm Thu-Sun) both showcase local artists. You'll find fascinating work, from baskets of woven lily to streamlined sculptures and fine art.

Wombat Hill Botanic Gardens (Central Springs Rd, Daylesford), on top of the hill, is well worth a visit. There's a great picnic area and a lookout tower with fine views of the countryside.

Lake Daylesford is a popular fishing and picnicking area close to the centre of town; boats and kayaks are available for hire. Even prettier is **Jubilee Lake**, about 3km southeast of town, another good picnic spot where you can hire canoes.

There's an excellent **Historical Society Museum** (☎ 5348 3242; 100 Vincent St, Daylesford; adult/child $3/50c; ☼ 1.30-4.30pm Sat & Sun) beside the fire station.

At the **Wreford International Hot Art Glass Studio** (☎ 5348 1012; www.hotartglass.com; 39 Albert St, Daylesford; ☼ 11am-5pm) you can watch glass being turned or blown and see the exquisite results. Don Wreford's work includes the Royal Vase presented to Crown Prince Frederik and Princess Mary of Denmark.

Daylesford Spa Country Tourist Railway (☎ 5348 1759; Daylesford Station; adult/child/family $7/4/18.50; ☼ 10am-2.45pm Sun) operates rides on old railway trolleys and restored trains along the line that used to connect Daylesford with Carlsruhe. Five trips leave from Daylesford station and last about one hour. On the first Saturday of the month, the **Silver Streak Champagne Train Journey** (☎ 5348 3622; per person $18) leaves Daylesford at 5.30pm and returns at 7pm. Champagne and finger food are served on board. **Daylesford Sunday Market** (☼ 8am-2pm Sun) is held at the train station. There's a rich variety of crafts, home-made goods and fresh vegies.

Lavandula (☎ 5476 4393; www.lavandula.com.au; Hepburn–Newstead Rd, Shepherds Flat; ☼ 10.30am-5.30pm, adult/child $3/free) is a Swiss-Italian farm and stone cottage, 5km north of Hepburn Springs, where you can meet the farm animals, check out the gardens and produce, wander between lavender bushes and enjoy lunch in the Ticinese grotto. Fun festivals are held on three Sundays in January, the first weekend in May and the last weekend in October.

Activities

Daylesford and Hepburn Springs are all about health, relaxation and the inner-self (see p246). You'll find plenty of local operators offering traditional massage, reiki, shiatsu, spiritual healing, tarot readings and all sorts of other services. A booklet, *Bliss*, available at the information centre lists many of the town's healers.

The **Hepburn Springs Golf Club** (☎ 5348 2185; Golf Links Rd, Hepburn Springs) is a very pleasant 18-hole public course.

There are wonderful long and short **walking trails** to and from places like Sailors Falls, Tipperary Springs and the Central Springs Reserve; the information centre has maps and walking guides. Other trails around the extinct volcanic crater of **Mt Franklin**, 10km north of Daylesford, take you through lush vegetation, a beautiful picnic area and a lookout. For **hiking trails**, including the Great Dividing Trail, between here and Castlemaine, contact **Parks Victoria** (☎ 13 19 63).

Horse lovers will find interesting trails signposted through the region, including the **Major Mitchell Trail**. Or head to the **Boomerang Holiday Ranch** (☎ 5348 2525; http://users.netconnect.com.au/~b_ranch/intro.htm; Tipperary Springs Rd, Daylesford; adult/child dm $20/15; 1-hr rides $20), which runs leisurely trail rides in the state forest. It has dorm accommodation and group packages that include meals and horse riding.

Sleeping

There are so many charming guesthouses, cottages and B&Bs that most arrangements are made through agencies. The major ones:

Daylesford Getaways (☎ 5348 4422; www.dayget.com.au; 123 Vincent St, Daylesford)

Daylesford Accommodation Booking Service (DABS; ☎ 5348 1448; www.dabs.com.au; 94 Vincent St, Daylesford)

Daylesford Cottage Directory (☎ 5348 1255; www.thespacountryholidayshop.com.au; 86 Vincent St, Daylesford)

Budget accommodation is limited, so in peak periods you should book ahead. Also, many places charge about 30% more on weekends and stipulate a minimum two-night stay. Make sure you inquire.

DAYLESFORD

Lake House (☎ 5348 3329; www.lakehouse.com.au; King St; B&B d from $320; ⚡) Set in rambling gardens with bridges, waterfalls and cockatoos, these welcoming units around the lake make you feel like just staying put, enjoying the feeling and the view. There's a guest lounge, tennis court and the ultimate pampering of Salus healing waters (see below).

Daylesford Hotel (☎ 5348 2335; fax 5348 1083; cnr Albert & Howe Sts; B&B r from $55) This old pub has small rooms upstairs that are prettily painted. Bathrooms are crisp and tiny, and there's a cosy guest TV room. The balcony is fantastic.

Jubilee Lake Caravan Park (☎ 5348 2186; Lake Rd; camp sites for 2 people $13, d cabins from $65) Sitting beneath tall gums beside beautiful Jubilee Lake, this quaint park makes you feel quiet and mellow.

TAKING TO THE WATERS

Communities have always enjoyed bathing in sensual ways – consider the gorgeous bathhouse ruins in Pompeii and Ephesus – so why break the tradition? Simply come to Daylesford and Hepburn Springs, and enter a world of calm and sensual indulgence. Wrap yourself in the fluffy white dressing gown, slip your feet into the hydrotherapy sandals. Sit back. Relax. You're about to be bubbled and scrubbed, oiled and steamed, your every whim attended to before you've thought of it.

At **Salus** (☎ 5348 3329; www.lakehouse.com.au; King St, Daylesford) the magic starts as you walk through a small rainforest to your exotic jasmine flower bath in a cedar-lined tree house overlooking the lake. Then you might choose a lime and ginger salt polish before a steam and waterfall, a rejuvenating facial and a full-body drizzle of warm Japanese camellia oil.

At **Daylesford Day Spa** (☎ 5348 2331; www.daylesforddayspa.com.au; 25 Albert St, Daylesford) you might start with a vitamin-rich mud coat and steam in a Neoqi cocoon, before a scalp massage and Vichy shower.

At **Spa House** (☎ 5348 2202; www.thesprings.com.au; 124 Main Rd, Hepburn Springs) you can have an algae gel wrap, based on an ancient Chinese treatment, then move into the lavender steam room, or take a soft pack float.

The **Hepburn Spa Resort** (☎ 5348 2034; Hepburn Mineral Springs Reserve, Hepburn Springs), where it all began in 1896, is being revamped during 2005. It has plunge pools, floatation tanks, saunas, a swimming pool, salt pool and aero spa – every way of taking to the waters. Finally add, say, a milk and honey wrap. Mmm. Contact the resort about what is open during the extensions.

The waters in the underground cavities of the area have been absorbing minerals and carbon dioxide for a million years. They're as pure as can be and Salus bottles the spring water. Take a container and fill it at the public springs in the parks. After a drink, you'll sparkle both inside and out.

There are other boutique providers; ask for the booklet *Bliss* at the information centre. And taking to the waters doesn't cost too much. Start with an outdoor sundeck hot tub (per hour $15), graduate to a treatment (per hour from $105) then extend your holiday so you can try them all. Enjoy!

Also recommended:

Ambleside B&B (☎ 5348 2691; www.spacountry
.net.au/ambleside; 15 Leggatt St; B&B d from $175) This
restored Victorian cottage overlooks Lake Daylesford. It
has three bedrooms with bathrooms – ask for one with
a view.

Daylesford Central Motor Inn (☎ 5348 2029; 54
Albert St; s/d/f from $65/78/90; 🐾) Just an easy stroll
from everything, the inn is comfortable and pretty.

Double Nut Chalets (☎ 5348 3981; www.doublenut
.com; 5 Howe St; B&B d from $120) The four chalets are
spacious and tasteful with gable ceilings, in a lovely garden
right in town. Each has its own kitchenette.

HEPBURN SPRINGS

Continental House (☎ 5348 2005; www.continental
house.com.au; 9 Lone Pine Ave; dm/s/d $30/40/70) This
old, rambling, timber guesthouse has a laid-
back alternative vibe, a **vegan cafe** (banquet
$15; 🍴 dinner Sat) serving excellent buffets, a
superb open-veranda sitting room and a
music room. BYO linen.

Daylesford Wildwood Youth Hostel (☎ 5348
4435; www.mooltan.com.au/ww/wildwood.htm; 42 Main
Rd; dm/s/d from $19/32/44) In a charming cot-
tage with a grand lounge room, you'd
never know it was a youth hostel. The
dorm rooms are average, but other rooms
have grand bathtubs and views of the lovely
garden.

Springs Retreat (☎ 5348 2202; www.thesprings.com
.au; 124 Main Rd; B&B s/d from $170/185) This charm-
ing 1930s mansion has been brought into
this century in great style. Many rooms have
private balconies, garden rooms have their
own courtyards and pampering packages are
available.

Mooltan Guesthouse (☎ 5348 3555; www.mool
tan.com.au; 129 Main Rd; B&B s/d from $55/85) An in-
viting Edwardian country home, Mooltan
has grand lounge rooms, a billiard table,
a tennis court and a terrific topiary hedge.
Bedrooms open onto a broad veranda
overlooking the Mineral Springs Reserve.
There are special weekend packages and
spa rooms.

Shizuka Ryokan (☎ 5348 2030; www.shizuka.com
.au; Lakeside Dr; midweek package s/d $204/275) In-
spired by ryokan inns, traditional places
of renewal and rejuvenation in Japan, this
serene, minimalist getaway has rooms with
private Japanese gardens, tatami matting
and plenty of green tea. Packages include
a superb Japanese dinner and Japanese or
Oz breakfast.

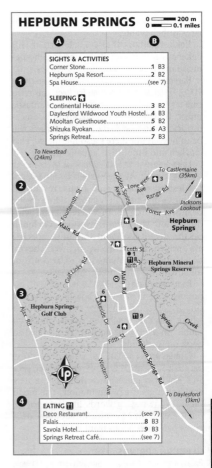

HEPBURN SPRINGS

SIGHTS & ACTIVITIES	
Corner Stone	1 B3
Hepburn Spa Resort	2 B2
Spa House	(see 7)

SLEEPING 🏠	
Continental House	3 B2
Daylesford Wildwood Youth Hostel	4 B3
Mooltan Guesthouse	5 B2
Shizuka Ryokan	6 A3
Springs Retreat	7 B3

EATING 🍴	
Deco Restaurant	(see 7)
Palais	8 B3
Savoia Hotel	9 B3
Springs Retreat Café	(see 7)

Eating

DAYLESFORD

Vincent St has a great range of food joints,
but go around the side streets for more
treats.

Wild Food Cafe (☎ 5348 1030; 11 Howe St; mains
$5.50-9; 🍴 breakfast & lunch Tue-Sun) This tiny
place has gone all organic and specialises
in Australian food. So the quiche has a wild
lime and quandong (that's a fruit, not a
small fluffy animal) salsa. The wine is regional and takeaways are possible.

Sweet Decadence at Locantro (☎ 5348 3202;
87 Vincent St; meals $5-12; 🍴 breakfast & lunch) If
your sugar levels have dropped from all
the hydrotherapy continue your pampering here, where the meals are light, the

setting mellow and the home-made chocolates unbelievable.

Not Just Muffins (☎ 5348 3711; 26 Albert St) This bakery is famous for its sensational home-made muffins ($2.50) and shortcakes.

Harvest Cafe (☎ 5348 3994; 29 Albert St; dinner mains $15-22; ⊙ breakfast, lunch & dinner Thu-Mon) This retro café takes you back to student days. Fantastic music, timber floors and blackboards, amazing prices and food to die for. Vegetarians will be in heaven but there's also marinated Thai chicken and innovative 'aquatic' cuisine.

Lake House (☎ 5348 3329; www.lakehouse.com.au; King St; mains $31-33; ⊙ breakfast, lunch & dinner) Daylesford's famous Lake House restaurant is among the best in Victoria. Dine in the beautiful dining room where picture windows show you Lake Daylesford. Or lunch on the deck (ask about the lunch special) and watch the birds fly by. Whichever, don't miss menu items like roast *confit* of duck with fig and ginger chutney.

Boat House Cafe (☎ 5348 1387; mains $15-19) This popular café is in an old boatshed. The setting is gorgeous, especially out on the deck where you can watch the swans while you nibble on a plate of nachos. You'll need to book on weekends.

Farmers Arms (☎ 5348 2091; www.farmersarms.com.au; 1 East St; mains $21-27.50; ⊙ dinner nightly, lunch Sat & Sun) This place has a new look, a new chef and a great new reputation. The menu includes interesting words like *salmariglio*, but there's nothing confusing about the delicious pan-fried ocean trout.

HEPBURN SPRINGS

Palais (☎ 5348 4849; www.thepalais.com.au; 111 Main Rd; mains $14.50-24.50; ⊙ dinner Thu-Sun) A dazzlingly atmospheric 1920s theatre with a restaurant, café and cocktail bar, enjoy the osso bucco or moussaka then relax in lush lounge chairs, play pool or even have a boogie. Performance nights include well-known bands, or there are locals' nights when meals are $10.

Springs Retreat Café (☎ 5348 2202; 124 Main Rd; mains $13.50-24) This spacious and bustling café fits in with the relaxed elegance of the Springs Retreat, with an eclectic menu that takes in lamb tagine.

Deco Restaurant (mains $23.50-30) Across the hall from the Springs Retreat Café, the elegant Deco has a fabulous menu with items like spiced fillet of wild barramundi

on brandade with *sauce vierge*. Anything sounding that good must taste amazing.

Savoia Hotel (☎ 5348 2314; 69 Main St; mains $14-24.50; ⊙ lunch & dinner) If you like your steak big and your chicken roasted, this is the place. The food is as traditional as the surroundings, with the open fire, pool table and dart board.

Entertainment

d'bar (☎ 5348 2982, 0417 544 035; 1st fl, 74 Vincent St, Daylesford; ⊙ 8pm-1am Fri, 10pm-1am Sat) This lounge, club and bar is a favourite in Daylesford. The DJ plays dance music and R&B on Saturday while the dinner crowd can listen to live jazz on Friday.

Hepburn Springs' Palais (left) hosts bands and shows.

Getting There & Away

There are daily buses connecting Daylesford with the train station at Woodend ($5), from where you can continue to/from Melbourne by train ($15, two hours).

V/Line (☎ 13 61 96) has weekday buses from Daylesford to Ballarat ($11), Castlemaine ($6) and Bendigo ($11). The buses run from **Little's Garage** (45 Vincent St, Daylesford).

Getting Around

A free shuttle bus runs back and forth between Daylesford visitors centre and Hepburn Springs spa complex four times a day (weekdays only). **Taxis** (☎ 5348 1111) include a six-seater in the fleet.

DAYLESFORD TO MALMSBURY

The Daylesford–Malmsbury road takes you through rolling paddocks and bumps of timbered hills. **Glenlyon** is a sleepy hollow 12km along this scenic road with its own mineral spring.

Signposted just northeast of Glenlyon is the magnificent **Holcombe Country Retreat** (☎ 03-5348 7514; www.holcombe.com.au; Holcombe Rd; d from $275; ☒). A grand country homestead built in 1891 on a large sheep property, it's been meticulously restored and is fully self-contained. The facilities available here include a pool, tennis court and trout-stocked dam.

Back just a kilometre northeast from where Malmsbury Rd leaves the road to Castlemaine, a signpost directs you due north to **Tarascon Village** (☎ 03-5348 7773; www.tarasconvillage

.com.au; 530 Porcupine Ridge Rd; B&B d from $160). This is a cluster of high-pitched, self-contained cottages set apart in a peaceful country setting. Each cottage has its own character. There's a licensed café and minigolf course.

MALMSBURY
☎ 03 / pop 500

This tiny settlement on the Calder Hwy, boasts distinctive and solid bluestone buildings, which include a magnificent **bluestone viaduct**, built in 1859 across the Coliban River. The **botanic gardens**, first planted in 1863, have elegant shady old trees and a small ornamental lake. There's a good picnic area beside the **Malmsbury Reservoir**.

Sleeping & Eating
Hopewell Cottage (☎ 5423 2470; fax 5423 2145; 19 Ross St; B&B s/d $100/140) This sweet three-bedroom miner's cottage has an open fire and cooking facilities.

Merchants of Malmsbury Cafe (☎ 5423 2229; Calder Hwy; mains $6-12; ☽ lunch Thu-Sun) This intriguing little place has tables among a mix of toys and collectables, and regular jazz afternoons.

Mill (Calder Hwy) This bluestone flour mill has been a gallery and restaurant with classy B&B units. Contact the Kyneton visitors centre (p263) to see if it has reopened.

Malmsbury Hotel (☎ 5423 2322; Calder Hwy; r without/with spa $75/95) This place has recently been scrubbed up, and you can now enjoy the large country-style motel rooms, with views out over this breathtaking countryside. The equally scrubbed and attractive **restaurant** (mains $8.50-14.50; ☽ lunch & dinner Wed-Sun) has a new chef who prepares wholesome country fare with local produce. Best to book, it's becoming popular.

CASTLEMAINE
☎ 03 / pop 7580

These days Castlemaine is a relaxed country town, home to a diverse group of artists, and splendid architecture and gardens. Its claims to fame include being the original home of the Castlemaine XXXX beer-brewing company (now based in Queensland), producing 'Castlemaine Rock', a popular sweet dating back to the gold-rush days, and being the 'Street Rod Centre of Australia', where hotrods have been built since 1962.

Farmers moved into the Castlemaine district in the 1830s. However the pastoral landscape was totally changed when gold was discovered at Specimen Gully in 1851. The Mt Alexander Diggings had 30,000 diggers working there and Castlemaine became the thriving marketplace for all the goldfield. But its importance waned as the surface gold was exhausted by the 1860s. The centre of the town has been virtually unaltered since then.

Information
Library (cnr Templeton & Baker Sts) Offers Internet access.
Visitors centre (☎ 5470 6200; 1800 171 888; www .maldoncastlemaine.com; Mostyn St; ☽ 9am-5pm) This office is in the magnificent Castlemaine Market building. The friendly staff will help you find what you need, including useful information on historic town walks and vehicle tours. You can buy gold-panning kits here for $6.50.

Sights
BUDA HISTORIC HOME & GARDEN
Dating from 1861, **Buda** (cnr Hunter & Urquhart Sts; adult/child $9/7; ☽ noon-5pm Wed-Sun) combines interesting architectural styles of the original Indian-villa influence and the later Edwardian-style extensions. Home to a Hungarian silversmith and his family for 120 years, the house has permanent displays of the family's extensive art and craft collections, furnishings and personal belongings. The impressive gardens feature a massive, clipped cypress hedge.

CASTLEMAINE ART GALLERY & HISTORICAL MUSEUM
This impressive **gallery** (☎ 5472 2292; 14 Lyttleton St; adult/student/family $4/2/8; ☽ 10am-5pm Mon-Fri, noon-5pm Sat & Sun) in a superb Art Deco building, has a collection of colonial and contemporary Australian art, including work by well-known Australian artists, such as Frederick McCubbin and Russell Drysdale. The museum, in the basement, provides a unique insight into the history of the region, with costumes and china, and relics of gold mining.

CASTLEMAINE BOTANIC GARDENS
These majestic **gardens** (Walker St), among the oldest in Victoria, strike a perfect balance between sculpture and wilderness. Get back to nature among the awe-inspiring National Trust–registered trees. Electric barbecues are available, along with a children's plastic playground.

OLD CASTLEMAINE GAOL

This imposing **sandstone building** (☎ 5470 5311; cnr Bowden & Charles Sts; adult/child $7/3.50; ☺ 10am-3pm) provides excellent views of the town from a hilltop on Bowden St. There's a lingering eerie atmosphere to the place even though it's been renovated and looks almost attractive. Guided tours of the gaol (adult/child $4/2) can be arranged. And if you'd like to do some time, see how in the Sleeping section (opposite). There are often theme nights and mystery weekends.

OTHER SIGHTS

Castlemaine Market (Mostyn St), the town's original market building, is fronted with a classical Roman-basilica façade with a statue of Ceres, the Roman goddess of the harvest, on top. The stunning nave is flanked by side stalls where you'll find the visitors centre, a diggings interpretive display, those gold-panning kits and a kiosk.

An institution in itself, the **Restorers Barn** (Mostyn St; ☺ 10am-5.30pm) is chock-full of interesting bric-a-brac and collectables. It's an ideal place to while away an hour or five.

Festivals & Events

Festival of Gardens (www3.visitvictoria.com; Nov odd years) Over 50 locals open their properties to the public.
State Festival (www.castlemainefestival.com.au; Apr odd years) One of Victoria's leading arts events, featuring theatre, music, art and dance.

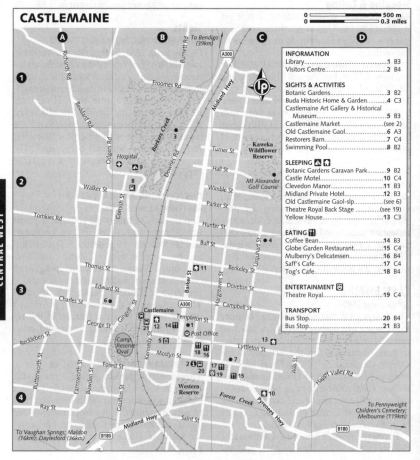

CASTLEMAINE

0 _____ 500 m
0 _____ 0.3 miles

CENTRAL WEST

Sleeping

The information centre and Mt Alexander Shire Council provide a free **accommodation booking service** (☎ 5470 5866, 1800 171 888; www .mountalexander.vic.gov.au). Booking accommodation is essential at festival times.

Castle Motel (☎ 5472 2433; www.visitvictoria.com /castlemotel; Duke St; s/d/f 79/89/109; 🗷) Enjoy spacious rooms in soft colours and timber features, sparkling bathrooms, delightful little pool and spa, grass and trees. And friendly people.

Midland Private Hotel (☎ 5472 1085; www.hotel midland.net; 2 Templeton St; B&B s/d from $80/120) This lace-decked hotel, which has been sheltering travellers since 1879, features a magnificent Art Deco foyer and dining room, and a lounge with open fireplaces and a belvedere ceiling. Breakfast comes with homemade produce, courtesy of the friendly Sicilian owner. There are also apartments (doubles from $180) that are equally attractive.

Yellow House (☎ 54723368; www.castlemaine.au.com /yellow/; 95 Lyttleton St; s/d $120/130) The pseudo-French-provincial Yellow House is perched on the top of Lyttleton St between towering gums with excellent views of the town. Its rooms are stunning white with large doors onto private balconies. It also houses a contemporary art gallery and the resident artist's studio.

Botanic Gardens Caravan Park (☎ /fax 5472 1125; 18 Walker St; camp sites per 2 people from $13, d cabins from $50) This is right next to the fabulous gardens, perfect for early morning strolls. And the public swimming pool (open December to March) is on the other side. There's a camp kitchen, electric and wood barbecues, recreation hut and plenty of grassy space.

Other wonderful sleeping experiences can be had in a cell at the **Old Castlemaine Gaol** (☎ 54705311; www.gaol.castlemaine.net.au; cnr Bowden & Charles Sts; B&B per person $55); in bed with the stars at **Theatre Royal Back Stage** (☎ 54721196; www.castle mainetheatre.com; Hargreaves St; B&B d $195) where the rate includes as many movies as are screening; or nestled among the antiques at **Clevedon Manor** (☎ 5472 5212; clevedon@netcon.net.au; 260 Barker St; s/d from $70/100).

Eating

Saff's Cafe (☎ 5470 6722; 64 Mostyn St; mains $16.50-22.50; 🕑 breakfast, lunch & dinner) This is a fun place with friendly people, excellent home-made bread, cakes and savouries, the best coffee in town and interesting meals like the roti bake topped with tomato and hummus crust.

Tog's Cafe (☎ 5470 5090; 58 Lyttleton St; mains $16-25; 🕑 breakfast & lunch daily, dinner Fri & Sat) This cosy place, with its scruffed floorboards and open fireplaces, is the perfect place for a Kashmiri lamb curry. It has great soups and salads, but don't miss the hot chocolates – they're an artwork.

Mulberry's Delicatessen (56 Lyttleton St) You can load up with whole meals or little goodies at this place next door to Tog's.

Coffee Bean (☎ 5472 4838; 209 Barker St; meals $3.50-8.50; 🕑 breakfast & lunch Mon-Sat) A café and deli with tables spilling onto the street, Coffee Bean has a range of home-baked pastries.

Globe Garden Restaurant (☎ 5470 5055; 81 Forest St; mains $23-32; 🕑 dinner nightly; lunch Sun) Try this popular place, set in an historic building with a superb garden courtyard. It's a fine choice for summer dining. The menu incorporates a range of international cuisine, and the side room is a **café** (mains $15-18) where the steaks are great. Bookings are advisable on weekends.

Entertainment

Theatre Royal (☎ 5472 1196; www.castlemainetheatre .com; 30 Hargreaves St; 🕑 from 1.30pm daily, to 3am Fri & Sat) This historic place is a cinema with a difference. Patrons can dine while the movie is showing, then don their clubbing gear afterwards. There's a small bar (the mulled wine is a must in winter), live bands, performances and functions. Visit the website to see which movies are showing.

Getting There & Away

Castlemaine train station (Kennedy St) has 11 daily trains from Melbourne ($19, 1¾ hours) that continue on to Bendigo ($7) and Swan Hill ($34).

V/Line (☎ 13 61 96) also has weekday bus services from Castlemaine to Daylesford ($5), Ballarat ($15) and Geelong ($29). **Castlemaine Bus Lines** (☎ 5472 1455) provides two bus services each weekday only to Maldon ($5). Buses leave from the train station and the market.

AROUND CASTLEMAINE

Castlemaine was the central hub of the scattered Mt Alexander Diggings, and the town is now surrounded by former gold-mining communities. Off the road heading southeast to Chewton is the sombre **Pennyweight**

Children's Cemetery, a small cluster of tiny graves of children who died during the gold-rush years. **Chewton** is a charming and historic township, with some interesting antique and bric-a-brac shops and a very sweet town hall. Nearby, you can visit the **Forest Creek Historic Gold Digging**. If you've brought your pan you can try it out in the old sluicing site.

Just north of Chewton is **Garfield's Water Wheel**, the remains of Victoria's largest water wheel, which provided power for an ore-crusher at the Garfield Mine.

Also near Chewton is the remarkable **Dingo Farm** (www.wwwins.net.au/dingofarm) Sadly, owner Bruce Jacobs died in 2004. Please visit the website for further information on the farm's operation.

MALDON

☎ 03 / pop 1250

The population of Maldon is a scant reminder of the 20,000 who used to work the local goldfields. Nevertheless, the whole town is a well-preserved relic of the gold-rush era with many fine buildings constructed from local stone.

In 1966 the National Trust named Maldon Australia's first 'notable town', an honour given only to towns where the historic architecture was intact and valuable. In fact Maldon is so important in the history of Victoria that special planning regulations were implemented to preserve it for posterity. Consequently, the whole town oozes charm and is now a very popular tourist spot.

Information

Visitors centre (☎ 5475 2569; www.maldoncastlemaine .com; High St; ☼ 9am-5pm) Has Internet access. Pick up its *Information Guide* and a *Historic Town Walk* brochure, which guides you past some of the most historic buildings.

Sights & Activities

Interesting places along High Street include **Dabb's General Store** (now the supermarket) and the **Maldon**, **Kangaroo** and **Grand** hotels. You'll soon notice the 24m-high **Beehive Chimney**, just east of Main St, and it's worth taking the short trip south along High St to the **North British Mine**.

On the edge of town is the excellent **Penny School Gallery & Cafe** (☎ 5475 1911; www.pennyschool gallery.com.au; 11 Church St; dishes $6-11; ☼ 10am-5pm). Exhibitions of well-known artists' work look

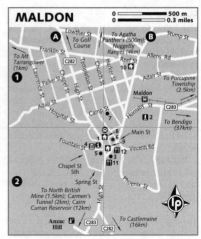

splendid against the original old school walls, with the wood-lined ceilings. Stay for lunch and discuss the work with the knowledgeable owners over Vietnamese chicken.

Carmen's Tunnel (☎ 5475 2667; off Parkin's Reef Rd; adult/child $5/2; ☼ 1.30-4pm Sat & Sun) is 2km south of town. The 570m-long tunnel was excavated in the 1880s. It took two years to dig, yet produced only $300 worth of gold. The tours are candle-lit and you can ring ahead for a guide outside of weekend hours.

Maldon's train station was built in 1884. For rail enthusiasts, the local **Victorian Goldfields Railway** (office ☎ 5470 6658; station ☎ 5475 2966) runs **steam-train trips** (adult/child/family return $16/8/40; ☼ 11.30am & 1pm Wed & Sun, also 2.30pm Sun) along the original track into the Muckleford Forest and back. If you want to get closer to the steam, ask for a ticket in the engine or guard's van.

The **historical museum** (☎ 5474 1633; High St; ⏱ 1.30-4pm Mon-Fri, to 5pm Sat & Sun) is in the town's former marketplace. It has relics from Maldon's past and is popular with the many people who come to Maldon to research their family trees. Nearby, the **Old Post Office** (High St) built in 1870, was the childhood home of Henry Handel Richardson. Her autobiography, *Myself When Young* (1950), happily relates this time, when her mother was Maldon's postmistress.

Mt Tarrangower has a great lookout tower, and good picnic areas and walking tracks. There are other good walks at **Anzac Hill**, where you'll pass a memorial avenue of trees and a Turkish field gun; and in the **Nuggetty Ranges**, 4km north of the town, you'll also find the historic cemetery. Take the dirt road off Church St, signposted to Rock of Ages, and keep left through the Nuggetty Ranges, to the **Rock of Ages** lookout, a beautiful spot and an Aboriginal site.

Historic **Porcupine Township** (☎ 5475 1000; www .porcupinetownship.com.au; Bendigo Rd; adult/child/family $9/5.50/25; ⏱ 10am-5pm), on the Bendigo road, is a quaint re-created gold-mining village with old slab buildings, built on the site of the original township.

Festivals & Events

Maldon Easter Fair (www.maldon.org.au/EasterFair; Mar/Apr)

Maldon Folk Festival (www.maldonfolkfestival.com; early Nov) Maldon's main event is this excellent festival, featuring a wide variety of world music.

Sleeping

There are plenty of self-contained cottages to rent, and charming B&Bs in restored old buildings. Many are managed by **Heritage Cottages of Maldon** (☎ 5475 1094; www.heritagecottages .com.au; 41 High St).

Central Service Centre (☎ 5475 2216; Main St; s/ d $40/65; ⏱) This place looks odd from the outside, being in a petrol station. But inside, the sweet cottagey rooms have views of the main street through the lace curtains. All rooms have a fridge, TV and small bright bathrooms.

Maldon's Eaglehawk (☎ 5475 2750; fax 5475 2914; 35 Reef St; s/d from $90/100; ⏱ ⏱) Even motels in this town have loads of appeal. This has beautiful heritage units in delightful grounds, with little alcoves overlooking the pool, barbecue nooks and wide, vine-trimmed verandas.

Calder House (☎ 5475 2912; www.calderhouse .au; 44 High St; s/d from $90/110) Step back in time at this formal and grand, yet very inviting, place right in the centre of town. It has superb features and guestrooms with four-post beds and claw-foot baths.

Agatha Panther's (☎ /fax 5475 1066; 87 Church St; 1-/2-bedroom cottages $96/109) There are two recently-built but quaint, old-looking cottages on this property, at the turn-off to Rock of Ages lookout. You'll certainly enjoy a country experience, just 2km from town.

Maldon Caravan Park (☎ /fax 5475 2344; Hospital St; camp sites per 2 people from $17, d cabins from $60; ⏱) This old park straggles up through the bush. It's friendly and homely, with bush kitchen, barbecues and a **swimming pool** (⏱ Dec-Mar) right next door.

Eating

There are several cafés and tearooms along the main street that serve good coffee and snacks.

Berryman's Cafe & Tearooms (☎ 5475 2904; 30 Main St; meals $4-9.50; ⏱ breakfast & lunch) Enjoy a light meal, snack or full-on lunch in an old tea-room environment. Or sit outside in the sun. You must try the yummy yabby pie. Yabbies are farmed in the area.

Cafe Maldon (☎ 5475 2022; 52 Main St; mains $9; ⏱ breakfast & lunch) This trendy little place is where the locals read their papers while they watch the visitors' antics. Tables are set between unusual giftware for sale and couches, and with luck you'll catch some live music. The gourmet pastries are highly regarded.

Ruby's at Calder House (☎ 5475 2912; 44 High St; mains $20-27; ⏱ dinner) This is one of the state's best restaurants. Set in an elegant Victorian dining room, it serves 'creative country cuisine' using only fine local produce. Make sure you book.

McArthur's Restaurant and **Maldon Bakery** (☎ 5475 2519; 43 Main St) are on the site of a bakery, believed to have been baking around 1854, and the original oven is still being used. The current brick building was built around 1890. Enjoy a meal here in historic surroundings.

Getting There & Away

Castlemaine Bus Lines (☎ 5472 1455) runs two buses each weekday between Maldon and Castlemaine ($5), which connect with the trains to and from Melbourne. Buses leave

CENTRAL WEST

from the **depot** (145 High St) and stop at the Grand Hotel. The total journey takes about two hours.

Castlemaine taxis (☎ 13 10 08) offer service in Maldon.

MARYBOROUGH

☎ 03 / pop 8000

The district around Charlotte Plains was already an established sheep run, owned by the Simpson brothers, when gold was discovered at White Hills and Four Mile Flat in 1854. A police camp established at the diggings was named Maryborough. By the time gold mining had stopped being economical, Maryborough had developed a strong manufacturing base and is today one of the district's major industrial and production centres. Its alluvial goldfields still attract prospectors from far and wide.

The Ballarat–Bendigo road runs north through the centre of town, and out past Lake Victoria. A block east, the railway line follows the road, but runs behind the lake.

The **visitors centre** (☎ 5460 4511, 1800 356 511; www.centralgoldfields.com.au; cnr Alma & Nolan Sts; ☻ 9am-5pm) has loads of helpful maps and friendly staff, as well as Internet access.

Sights

Maryborough boasts plenty of impressive Victorian-era buildings, but the local train station leaves them all for dead. Built back in 1892, the magnificent and inordinately large **Maryborough Railway Station** (Burns St; ☻ Wed-Mon) was described by Mark Twain as 'a train station with a town attached'. It now houses a mammoth antique emporium, gallery and café. These days, the station is used only by goods trains.

Worsley Cottage (☎ 5461 2800; 3 Palmerston St; ☻ 10am-noon Tue & Thu, 2-5pm Sun) is the local historical society museum, built in the 1800s. Every room is furnished with pieces of the times, which were often donated by local people, and there's a large photographic collection.

Festivals & Events

Highland Gathering (☎ 5460 4508; 1 Jan) Have a fling at Maryborough's Scottish festival with races, stalls etc, held every New Year's Day since 1857.

Gold 'n Wattle Festival (☎ 5460 4511; Sep) A three-day fest with tours, exhibitions, dance performances, brass bands and a good old sausage sizzle.

Energy Breakthrough Festival (☎ 5461 1566; late Nov) This event focuses on alternative energy sources. School groups from all over bring their inventive vehicles for the 24-hour and 16-hour (for juniors) RACV Energy Breakthrough grand prix. About 6000 students compete.

Sleeping

Bella's Country House B&B (☎ 5460 5574; www.cgold .com.au/bellas; 39 Burns St; B&B budget from s/d $55/70, deluxe r from $110) This is an impressive red-brick Victorian homestead with a magnificently restored interior, complete with comfy lounges and open fires. The deluxe rooms are elegant, with lashings of white linen.

Bristol Hill Motor Inn (☎ 5461 3833; 1 High St; s/d $85/95, spa room $140; ☒ ☒) The very central Bristol Hill has spacious new rooms, a pretty courtyard, gym and pleasant pool with outside heated spa. A deluxe townhouse comes with packages that include wine tours.

Bull & Mouth Hotel (☎ 5461 1002; cnr High & Nolan Sts; s/d $30/40) Dance up the glorious staircase under a soaring roof and ornate skylight to these basic little rooms, each with a Juliet balcony from where you can watch all the action on Maryborough's two main streets.

Maryborough Caravan Park (☎ /fax 5460 4848; 7 Holyrood St; camp sites per 2 people from $15, dm from $20, d cabins from $44; ☒) Right in town, by Lake Victoria, this family park is walking distance to the council swimming pools around the back of the lake.

Eating

There's a good foodie scene along High St, with cafés, restaurants, bakeries, takeaways, pubs and clubs.

b&m Restaurant (☎ 5461 1002; cnr High & Nolan Sts; mains $9.50-18; ☻ lunch & dinner) Hosts Tracy and Shaun have scrubbed and polished this old Bull & Mouth Hotel, so the restaurant looks great, with real tablecloths! They serve the best steaks in town or quirky dishes like Venetian prawns in white wine. There's a DJ on weekends playing dance, country and R&B till 3am.

Café Beto (☎ 5460 4331; 95 Nolan St; mains $8-16.50; ☻ breakfast & lunch Mon-Sat, dinner Thu-Sat) This is a bright and cheerful café and wine bar that offers modern food with friendly service. Dine alfresco in summer and try the speciality – local wines.

Old Vault (☎ 5460 5164; 106 High St; mains $10-19; ☻ breakfast, lunch & dinner) There's a great new look here in the Art Deco bank building.

Enjoy the excellent coffee, try an Old Vault beef burger, then kick on till late.

Getting There & Away
The trip from Melbourne ($28, three hours) involves a train/bus changeover at either Ballarat or Castlemaine. The bus stop is at the Maryborough visitors centre's car park.

AVOCA & THE PYRENEES
The town of Avoca is the centre of one of Victoria's most rapidly expanding wine-growing regions (p62). It is also the gateway to the Pyrenees Ranges, so named by Major Thomas Mitchell in 1836 because they reminded him of the Spanish Pyrenees. However, the mountains are distinctively Australian, their covering eucalypts giving them a bluish tinge. Mt Avoca, the highest peak, reaches 760m. There are plenty of good walking tracks and waterfalls throughout the ranges, including the 18km **Pyrenees Trail**, which starts from the Waterfall Picnic Area 7km west of Avoca, along Vinoca Rd.

The helpful **visitors centre** (☎ 03-5465 3767, 1800 206 622; www.pyreneesonline.com.au; 122 High St; ☺9am-5pm) has an excellent brochure, *The Great Grape Road,* a wine-touring trail.

Festivals & Events
There are three annual race meetings which feature local wines and foods, as well as the horses, of course. This is also the home of *pétanque* festivals, with two held every year – over the third weekend in March and the last weekend in November.

Sleeping
Victoria Hotel (☎ 03-5465 3362; 138 High St; s/d $40/75) This pleasant, recently-renovated pub has basic but nicely painted rooms.

Pyrenees Motel (☎ 03-5465 3693; fax 5465 3584; 102 High St; s/d from $60/70) You really feel welcome. The themed rooms are clean and comfortable.

Avoca Heritage School B&B (☎ 03-5465 3691; fax 5465 3735; 124 Rutherford St; d from $130) This renovated old school building bears no resemblance to its past. It has a guest wing, with three guestrooms, in a charming cottage garden.

Avoca Cottages (☎ 03-465 3677, 1800 123 355; fax 5465 3688; 33 Napier St; B&B s/d from $125/165) These self-contained cottages are behind the historic 1854 Avoca jail, and feature large living areas and kitchens. Each has a veranda with views of the Pyrenees ranges. There is wheelchair access.

Eating
Avoca Bakehouse & Cafe (☎ 03-5465 3388; 114 High St; meals $2-4; ☺ breakfast & lunch) This charming place, in an old bank building, offers a good selection of freshly baked goodies.

Times of Yore (High St; meals $8-14; ☺ lunch Thu-Sun) This place is in an interesting old building and serves great coffee with the light meals.

Rokers Restaurant (☎ 03-5465 3618; www.pyrenees manor.com.au; 119 High St; d from $150; mains $24-28; ☺ breakfast Sun, lunch Sat & Sun, dinner Fri & Sat) This lovely restaurant is in the elegant Pyrenees Manor, behind an amazing Italianate Palazzo façade (circa 1912). It is the locals' favourite for fine dining. The Manor offers luxury suites for lovers of fine things, or just lovers.

Getting There & Away
V/Line (☎ 13 61 96) has bus services from Melbourne every night except Saturday ($26, four hours) on the overnight service to Mildura, arriving in Avoca in the wee hours. There's also a train/bus service via Ballarat on Friday (three hours). They leave from outside the town hall.

MOONAMBEL
☎ 03
The tiny township of Moonambel is surrounded by 17 vineyards and wineries (p62), known for their soft earthy reds. You'll find charming B&Bs hidden among the vines, so you don't need to drive after a day of researching some of Australia's greatest cool-climate wines.

Warrenmang Vineyard (☎ 03-5467 2233; www.baz zani.com.au; Mountain Creek Rd; set dinner $55; ☺ lunch & dinner) is an award-winning restaurant at this winery is one of the best in Victoria. The dining room is sophisticated but relaxed, with a large open fire and windows giving views of the valley filled with vineyards. The food is always superb and imaginative, making use of local produce, including rabbit, yabbies and trout. Stay on at **Warrenmang Resort** (B&B s with dinner from $155; ☒) You'll also enjoy winery tours and use of the tennis and *pétanque* courts, pool and spa.

The unique mudbrick **Moonbeam Cottages** (☎ 03-5467 2350; www.ballarat.com/moonbeam; Mountain

CENTRAL WEST

Creek Rd; s/d $100/140) are nestled in the bushland, with views of the vineyards.

Sheltered Paddock Vineyard (☎ 03-5467 2353; shelteredpaddockvineyard@iinet.net.au; 42 Walter's Lane, Warrenmang; B&B d $100) is open every day for tasting and sales, Sheltered Paddock is off the road to Moonambel and offers barbecue and picnic facilities as well as a cosy B&B. Wines are made and bottled from grapes grown on the property.

The old **Moonambel Pub** (☎ 03-5467 2273; Brooke St; mains $15-22; 🕑 lunch & dinner) is a fun place, famous for its spit roasts on Saturday night and Sunday lunch.

MOLIAGUL, TARNAGULLA & DUNOLLY
☎ 03

The rich alluvial goldfields in this area, known as the Golden Triangle, produced many gold nuggets, including the world's largest, the 72kg Welcome Stranger. The Stranger was found in Moliagul in 1869 by John Deason and Richard Oates, who hid it for two days before concealing it in a wagon and taking it to Dunolly, where it was cut into pieces because it was too big to fit on the scales!

Moliagul is now a tiny, tumbledown village with a memorial near the site of the discovery of the Welcome Stranger. Another memorial commemorates the Reverend John Flynn,

founder of the Royal Flying Doctor Service, who was born here in 1880.

Tarnagulla also has some interesting architectural relics from the gold-rush days, including an inordinate number of churches and the **Victoria Hotel & Theatre**, a former dance hall and vaudeville theatre. The town's **historic reserve** features more churches and a charming timber pavilion at the local cricket ground.

Dunolly, the largest town, has the **Goldfields Historical Museum** (Broadway; 🕑 1.30-5pm Sun) with interesting mining relics, equipment, weapons, photos and replicas of some nuggets. In front of the museum is the anvil on which the Welcome Stranger was cut up.

Finders Prospecting Supplies (☎ 5468 1333; 90 Broadway), in the main street, hires out prospecting equipment and metal detectors (just in case you think the old-timers left anything behind).

ST ARNAUD
☎ 03 / pop 3050

This solid country town is bordered by both the mountains and the goldfields. Beyond the town, the flat wide-open Mallee district stretches north all the way to Mildura.

St Arnaud's main street, Napier St, is now a heritage precinct and has been classified by the National Trust. The street is

CENTRAL WEST

DETOUR: WEDDERBURN TO BRIDGEWATER-ON-LODDON

If you're interested in gold mining, this is a glorious golden route with a few other delights thrown in. First, from St Arnaud head up to **Wedderburn**, one of the richest areas during the early days of the gold rush. The ramshackle **museum** (☎ 03-5494 3493; 51 High St; adult/child $2/1; 🕑 9am-5.30pm Tue-Sun) is set up as a late-19th-century store, with cluttered and dusty displays of snake-oil remedies, and old buggies and carts.

Christmas Reef Mine (☎ 03-5494 3002; tours adult/child $8/4; 🕑 noon-3pm), 5km east of Wedderburn, is a working mine. Walk through and see the ore crusher in operation.

Next turn south down the Calder Hwy, where **Inglewood** has an old distillery that has been producing eucalyptus oil for more than 100 years. The town sadly remembers the day in 1862 when a bushfire burnt its 10 pubs down in 30 minutes. West of Inglewood is **Kingower**, known as the 'potato diggings' because finding nuggets was like plucking spuds. The 49kg Blanche Barkly nugget was found here in 1857 and the 27kg Hand of Faith nugget in 1980.

Kingower is on the edge of **Kooyoora State Park**, 3500 hectares of striking contrasts – a great place for bushwalking and rock climbing. In the western section are the **Melville Caves**, named after Captain Melville, a bushranger who hid here – from the lookout he could see anyone coming for him.

Finally, **Bridgewater-on-Loddon** is the base for an amazing way to go exploring: Hire a gypsy-style caravan pulled by Clydesdales from **Colonial Way** (☎ /fax 03-5437 3054; Serpentine Rd; per week $740-950). The caravans sleep up to five and the owners visit each day to check on your progress.

There are motels and caravan parks in most of the towns, and bush camping in the State Park.

lined with old pubs and veranda-fronted shops that date back to the gold-rush days. There are also plenty of other interesting old buildings scattered around the town and an extensive lawn-tennis complex. The **visitors centre** (☎ 5495 1268, 1800 014 455; 4 Napier St; ☺ 9am-5pm) is next to the old post office.

Sleeping & Eating
La Cochon Rose (☎ 5495 3244; www.greatplacestostay .com.au/lacochonrose; 123 Napier St; s/d from $55/65; ☒) These attractive units are behind the historic hotel. Inside the hotel is a café, wine-bar, delightful art gallery and fabulous **restaurant** (mains $14-21; ☺ lunch & dinner Thur-Sun). Have the curry, or perhaps the shami kebabs. Or anything – all the food is excellent.

    Country Road (☎ 5495 2255; cnr Ballarat & Bendigo Rds; s/d/f $63/68/78; ☒) It's friendly here, the Colonial-style rooms are spacious and the aspect bright. And it's an easy stroll down to the shops.

    Botanical Hotel (☎ 5495 1336; fax 5495 3178; cnr Napier & Inkerman Sts; s/d $30/55) This historic hotel with magnificent cast-iron lacework, has pub accommodation and is also a great place for **meals** (mains $14-21; ☺ lunch & dinner Mon-Sat).

    St Arnaud Caravan Park (☎ 5495 1447, 0419 386 344; Alma St; camp sites per 2 people from $16, d cabins d from $50) This is a very pretty spot on Wilsons Hill next to Lord Nelson Park. The views are magnificent.

BENDIGO
☎ 03 / pop 87,000
The solid, imposing and extravagant Victorian-era architecture of Bendigo is a testimony to when gold was discovered at Ravenswood in 1851. Diggers converged on the fantastically rich Bendigo Diggings, which covered more than 360 sq km, to claim the surface gold. As this ran out they turned their pans and cradles to Bendigo Creek and other waterways around Sandhurst (as Bendigo was then known).

    The arrival of thousands of Chinese miners in 1854 caused racial tension and had a lasting effect on the town. It is one of the few places in Victoria where reminders of the Chinese diggers can be seen.

    By the 1860s the scene changed again as independent miners were outclassed by the powerful mining companies, with their heavy machinery. The companies poured money into the town and some 35 quartz

reefs were found. The ground underneath Bendigo is still honeycombed with mine shafts. The last of the mines was worked until the mid-1950s.

    Today Bendigo is a busy and prosperous provincial city, with an interesting collection of mines, museums, historic buildings, one of the best regional art galleries in Australia, and some great wineries in the surrounding district.

Information
Accommodation booking service (☎ 5444 4445, 1800 813 153) At the information centre.
Parks Victoria office (☎ 5444 6620; cnr Taylor St & Midland Hwy, Epsom)
RACV office (☎ 5443 9622; 112 Mitchell St)
Visitors centre (☎ 5444 4445, 1800 813 153; www .bendigotourism.com; 51 Pall Mall; ☺ 9am-5pm) In the historic former post office.

Sights
CENTRAL DEBORAH GOLDMINE
The 500m-deep **Central Deborah Goldmine** (☎ 5443 8322; 76 Violet St; adult/child/family $16.90/9.90/ 46; ☺ 9.30am-5pm), worked on 17 levels, became operational in the 1940s and was connected with two Deborah shafts that date back to the 1860s. About 1000kg of gold was removed before it closed in 1954. The mine is now being reworked and developed as one of Bendigo's major tourist attractions, with exhibits and photographs from the mid-1800s onwards. After donning hard hats and lights, you're taken 61m down the shaft to inspect the ongoing operations, complete with drilling demonstrations.

    A combined ticket for the mine tour plus a ride on the Talking Tram (below) costs $26/14 per adult/child.

BENDIGO TALKING TRAM
A vintage **tram** (☎ 5443 8322; 76 Violet St; adult/ child/family $12.90/7.50/37; ☺ 9.30am-3.30pm) runs with a commentary from the Central Deborah Goldmine, through the centre of the city, out to the **tramways museum** (admission free with tram ticket) and on to the Chinese Joss House (below). It leaves the mine every hour or five minutes later from Alexandra Fountain in Charing Cross.

CHINESE JOSS HOUSE
The **Chinese Joss House** (☎ 5442 1685; Finn St; North Bendigo; adult/child $3/1; ☺ 10am-5pm Thu-Mon),

BENDIGO

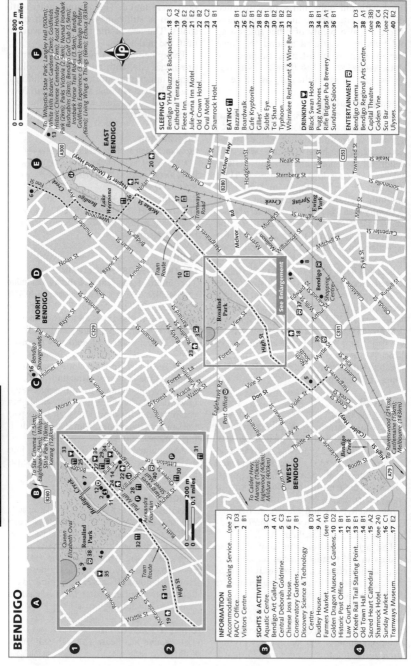

a temple where idols are worshipped, is one of the few practising joss houses in Victoria. It is built of timber and handmade bricks and painted red, the traditional colour for strength. The entrance is guarded by a pair of *kylin* – mythical guardian beasts. Exhibits include embroidered banners, figures representing the 12 years of the Chinese solar cycle, commemorative tablets to the deceased, paintings and Chinese lanterns. Admission is free for worshippers.

The **Goldfields Historical Chinese Cemetery** (White Hills Cemetery, Holdsworth Rd) is the oldest and most significant one in Australia, with a prayer oven where paper money for the spirits of the dead was burnt.

SACRED HEART CATHEDRAL

Construction of the massive **Sacred Heart Cathedral** (cnr Wattle & High Sts) began in the 19th century and was completed in 2001 with the installation of bells in the belfry. It's worth a visit – inside, there's a magnificently carved bishop's chair, some beautiful stained-glass windows and wooden angels jutting out of the ceiling arches. The pews in the cathedral are made from Australian blackwood and the marble is Italian.

BENDIGO ART GALLERY

The **Bendigo Art Gallery** (☎ 5443 4991; www.bendigo artgallery.com.au; 42 View St; admission by donation; ☉ 10am-5pm) is the largest and definitely one of the best provincial galleries in the state. It has an outstanding collection of colonial and contemporary Australian art, including work by Louis Buvelot, Fred Williams, Clifton Pugh, Rupert Bunny and Lloyd Rees. It also has a surprising and valuable collection of 19th-century European art. There are guided tours of the permanent collection at 2pm daily and there is a swish café.

SHAMROCK HOTEL

The magnificent **Shamrock Hotel** (cnr Pall Mall & Williamson St), built in 1897, is a fine four-storey example of elaborate Italianate late-Victorian architecture. Its size and opulence give some indication of how prosperous Bendigo was when, so the story goes, the floors were regularly washed down to collect the gold dust brought in on the miners' boots (see also p261).

GOLDEN DRAGON MUSEUM & GARDENS

The excellent **Golden Dragon Museum** (☎ 5441 5044; Bridge St; adult/child/family $7/4/20; ☉ 9.30am-5pm) has several glorious dragons on display, including the Imperial Dragons Old Loong (the oldest in the world) and Sun Loong (the longest in the world). Old Loong arrived in 1892 to feature in the Easter Procession, a major part of the Bendigo Easter Festival. Sun Loong took over in 1970 when Old Loong retired.

The museum has an amazing collection of Chinese heritage items and costumes, and classical Chinese gardens with bridges, water features and ornamental shrubs. The tearoom serves light meals, including simple, Chinese-style dishes.

GARDENS

Rosalind Park (just north of Pall Mall) features open lawns, big old trees and the fabulous 'Cascades' fountain, which was excavated after being buried for 120 years. You can climb to the top of a lookout tower for sensational 360-degree views, or go for a stroll through the shady green fernery. The **Conservatory Gardens** (Rosalind Park) has a wonderful rose garden, sculptures and a flower conservatory. The **White Hills Botanic Gardens** (Midland Hwy, White Hills) features many exotic and rare plant species, a small fauna park and aviary, and barbecue facilities.

OTHER SIGHTS

The city's impressive Victorian architecture is first seen in Pall Mall, where the **Shamrock Hotel**, **law courts** (☉ 9.30am-4pm Mon-Fri) and former **post office** (now the information centre) form a splendid trio. Wander inside all three – the interiors are just as elaborate as the exteriors. The old **town hall** (Bull St) is also impressive. In the old post office is a permanent **exhibition** (admission by donation; ☉ 10am-4pm) commemorating the city and its role in Federation.

View St, which runs uphill from the Alexandra Fountain in Charing Cross, is a historic streetscape with some fine buildings, including the **Capital Theatre**, which houses the Bendigo Regional Arts Centre, and **Dudley House**, classified by the National Trust.

Much of the town's best **residential architecture** was built along the ridge of a hill just north of the city centre, and it's worth

CENTRAL WEST

VICTORIA'S GOLD RUSH

When gold was discovered in New South Wales in May 1851, Victoria was still being established as a separate colony. If its workforce had been lost to the goldfields it would have been disastrous. So a reward was offered to anyone who could find gold within 300km of Melbourne. A significant discovery was soon made at Clunes and prospectors headed to central Victoria.

Over the next few months, the rush north across the Murray was reversed as fresh gold finds were made almost weekly in the Pyrenees, the Loddon and Avoca Rivers, at Warrandyte and Buninyong. Then in September 1851 the greatest gold discovery ever known was made at Ballarat, followed by others at Bendigo, Mt Alexander, Beechworth, Walhalla, Omeo and in the Great Dividing Range.

By the end of 1851 hopeful miners were coming from England, Ireland, Europe, China and the failing goldfields of California (USA). During 1852 about 1800 people a week arrived in Melbourne.

While the gold rush had its tragic side, as epidemics swept through the camps, and its share of rogues, including notorious bushrangers who attacked the gold shipments, it ushered in a fantastic era of growth and material prosperity for Victoria and opened up vast areas of country previously unexplored by Europeans.

Within 12 years, Victoria's population had increased from 77,000 to 540,000. Mining companies invested heavily in the region over the next couple of decades. The development of roads and railways accelerated, and huge shanty towns were replaced by Victoria's modern provincial cities, most notably Ballarat, Bendigo and Castlemaine, which reached the height of their splendour in the 1880s.

going along streets like Barkly, Forest, Vine and Rowan.

The huge **Discovery Science & Technology Centre** (☎ 5444 4400; Railway Place; adult/child/family $9.50/7/30; ☽ 10am-5pm) has a wide range of interesting and educational exhibits.

Activities

Bendigo has several golf courses, the best at **Bendigo Golf Club** (☎ 5448 4206; 18-holes $15, club hire $10) in Epsom, about 6km north, which has a population of resident kangaroos.

There are four excellent outdoor swimming pools – the **Aquatic Centre** (☎ 5443 6151; Barnard St) is the closest to the centre of town. There are also ice skating rinks, an outdoor skating park and an indoor go-kart track – ask at the visitors centre for details.

Ironbark Horse Trail Rides (☎ 5448 3344; Watson St; 1/2hr $30/55) organises various horse rides including the Great Australian Pub Ride to Allies Hotel in Myers Flat (with lunch $75). In the Ironbark complex, **Bendigo Goldfields Experience** (☎ 5448 4140; www.bendigogold.com.au; Watson St; half-day $130) has fossicking and detecting tours into the bush with metal detectors, or gold panning at the **mobile gold-panning centre** (per hr $10).

The **O'Keefe Rail Trail** is a 19km (one way) hike-and-bike trail along a disused railway line. It starts near the corner of Midland Hwy and Baden St and continues through bushland to Axedale – allow 3/5½ hours to ride/walk one way.

Bendigo Showgrounds is the venue for the weekly **Sunday Market** (☽ 8.30am-3pm) and, on the 2nd Saturday each month, the **Farmers Market** (☽ 8am-1pm).

See p62 for information about the local wineries.

Festivals & Events

Gold and Opal Athletics Carnival (www.vic.cycling.org .au; Mar) This carnival attracts large crowds.

Easter Festival (www.bendigoeasterfestival.org.au; Mar/ Apr) Bendigo's major festival is this annual event which attracts thousands of visitors with its carnival atmosphere and colourful and noisy procession of Chinese dragons.

Bendigo Agricultural Show (www.bendigoshow.org .au; Oct)

Bendigo Cup (www.racingvictoria.net.au/vcrc/bendigo; Nov) This race meeting is part of the Spring Racing Carnival.

Swap Meet (www.bendigoswap.com.au; Nov) Perhaps Bendigo's most curious attraction is this annual meet for enthusiasts in search of that elusive vintage-car spare part. It actually draws in tens of thousands of people, so accommodation is at a premium.

Sleeping
BUDGET

Bendigo YHA/Buzza's Backpackers (☎/fax 5443 7680; 33 Creek St South; dm/s/d/f $19/32/48/60; ☐) This is a small hostel with a homely feel in a weatherboard cottage that has been opened up inside to make bright cheery rooms with all the usual amenities.

Fleece Inn (☎ 5443 3086; 139 Charleston Rd; B&B dm/s/d $30/45/65; 🐾) What a find. A 140-year-old pub turned into accommodation only. The dorm rooms have partitioned-off beds, there are spacious bathrooms, a carpeted balcony and a back courtyard with barbecues. Go up the grand original timber staircase to the smart upstairs rooms.

Old Crown Hotel (☎ 5441 6888; fax 5441 6294; 238 Hargreaves St; B&B s/d $36/58) This place is great because it's right in the middle of everything. It has little old pub rooms with shared bathrooms and a TV lounge. Continental breakfast is served in the dining room.

Oval Motel (☎ 5443 7211; www.ovalmotel.com.au; 194 Barnard St; s/d/f $60/70/95; 🐾) This very central motel is opposite the aquatic centre and performing arts centre. The fresh and comfortable units have a pleasant barbecue area and playground out the back.

Ascot Holiday Park (☎ 5448 4421, 1800 062 340; www.ascotholidaypark.com.au; 15 Heinz St; camp sites per 2 people from $20, d cabins from $65; 🐾 🐾) With its little, and big, cabins nestled between the gardens, this excellent park has a glow about it, plus heated spa, camp kitchen and barbecues, minigolf, TV lounge, everything, just north of town!

MIDRANGE

Shamrock Hotel (☎ 5443 0333; www.shamrockbendigo .com.au; cnr Pall Mall & Williamson St; r/ste from $70/145) No matter which of the rooms and suites you choose, you'll feel pampered. Sit out on the grand balcony and lord it over the street. Ask for the Rosalind Suite and you'll swan about like one of the famous guests who've been here before you. They say Dame Nellie Melba ordered that the noisy post office clock be stopped. Thank goodness the chimes stop at midnight and start again next morning.

Cathedral Terrace (☎ 5441 3242; 81 Wattle St; B&B s/d from $105/150; 🐾) For an intimate experience in olde-worlde classic Victoriana you must stay here, among the antiques which even include a claw-foot bath, and lush furnishings. A full breakfast is served in the lounge, from where you can see the Sacred Heart Cathedral.

TOP END

Langley Hall (☎ 5443 3693; www.langleyhall.com.au; 484 Napier St; B&B s/d from $120/155; 🐾) Built in 1904 for the first bishop of Bendigo, Langley Hall offers unfussy opulence. Sweep up the grand staircase to magnificent suites opening onto expansive verandas. Downstairs, enjoy the elegant and comfortable parlour, drawing room or billiard room, or wander across the lawns to the fountain. Breakfast is cooked by your hosts Allan and Anne.

Julie-Anna Inn Motel (☎ 5442 5855; fax 5441 6032; 268 Napier St; s/d/f from $117/128/177; 🐾 🐾) This upmarket motel is just across from lovely Lake Weeroona. The spacious units open onto an attractive central courtyard, with a grand dining room at the end.

Eating

Bendigo has an excellent range of cafés, pubs and restaurants. Bull St (off Pall Mall) has a great café scene.

Subtle Eye (☎ 0402 328 339; 68 Bull St; mains $6.80-9; 🕑 breakfast & lunch) A funky modern place with a tiny menu and top coffee, at night the tables go outside and it turns into a **Cocktail Bar** (🕑 to 1am Tue-Sat).

Gillies' (Hargreaves St Mall) The pies here are among the best in Australia. A Bendigo institution, you queue at the little window, order one of their five or so varieties, then sit in the mall to eat it.

Boardwalk (☎ 5443 9855; Nolan St; mains $14.50-23.50; 🕑 breakfast, lunch & dinner) This is a special place on the shores of Lake Weeroona. Feel serene while eating pancakes and watching the moorhens on the lake. Or enjoy fine dining with the city lights flickering gold off the water. There's an excellent menu to match the lovely surrounds.

Bazzani (☎ 5441 3777; www.bazzani-bendigo.com; 2 Howard Place; mains $24.50-29; 🕑 lunch & dinner) This stylish, friendly venue has a pleasant outdoor eating area. The menu is diverse and innovative with, for example, organic pork rotolo. There's a separate bar and smoking room, and local wines are sold from the cellar.

Typhoon (☎ 5443 3111; cnr Myers & Mitchell Sts; mains $14-16; 🕑 dinner) This is a cosmopolitan restaurant with a metal-and-glass contemporary look. The exciting menu shows Southeast Asian influences, such as lamb shanks with Massaman curry on roast potato.

Whirrakee Restaurant & Wine Bar (☎ 5441 5557; 17 View Point; mains $13-28; 🕑 dinner Tue-Sat) Owner/head chef Nikki serves excellent modern Australian cuisine (yes, like kangaroo

CENTRAL WEST

sirloin with creamed parsnip!). Downstairs is a small wine bar with cosy sofas.

Toi Shan (☎ 5443 5811; 67 Mitchell St; mains $10-16.80; ☼ lunch & dinner) It has to be good because the Toi Shan has been owned and operated by the same family since 1892.

Cafe Kryptonite (☎ 5443 9777; Pall Mall; mains $14.50-28; ☼ lunch & dinner) No wonder it's popular, with a good buzz. The food's great. Tuscan pork sausages with apple will warm the belly.

Drinking

Pugg Mahones (☎ 5443 4916; 224 Hargreaves St) With Guinness (and many beers) on tap, Pugg's has a great atmosphere, a beer garden and live music every Thursday, Friday and Saturday night.

Rifle Brigade Pub Brewery (☎ 5443 4092; 137 View St; mains $16-20) This popular old pub brews its own beers, including ironbark dark, old-fashioned bitter and rifle lager. There's a shady courtyard and the bistro serves top pub food.

Sundance Saloon (☎ 5441 8222; cnr Pall Mall & Mundy St) This historic pub has a Western-style pool hall with live bands on the weekend playing mainly rock, drawing an older crowd.

Black Swan Hotel (☎ 5444 0944; 6 Howard Pl) This is a trendy place for a drink in a very old pub with a very big TV screen.

Level 2 (☎ 5444 0944; Howard Place; ☼ Fri & Sat) This place, above the Black Swan, plays house dance for 18-35 year olds.

Entertainment

Scu Bar (☎ 5441 6888; 238 Hargreaves St) This is the place to be on Friday and Saturday night if you're into mainstream dance music.

Golden Vine (☎ 5443 6063; 135 King St) One of the best venues, the Vine has popular jam sessions on Tuesday and top bands like The Whitlams playing on Wednesday, Friday and Saturday.

Ulysses (☎ 5441 8711; cnr Williamson & Queen Sts) A huge warehouse-style multilevel high-tech nightclub, Ulysses has smoke machines and pool tables, mainstream music and sometimes live bands.

Bendigo Regional Arts Centre (☎ 5441 5344; www .bendigo.vic.gov.au; 50 View St) In the beautifully restored Capital Theatre, this is the main venue for the performing arts, with hundreds of performances and exhibitions each year.

Bendigo Cinema (☎ 5442 1666; www.cinema.bendigo .net.au; 107 Queen St) This cinema shows mainstream Hollywood films in lovely surroundings several times a day.

Star Cinema (☎ 0408 337 277; http://starcinema.ben digo.net.au; Old Town Hall, Peg Leg Rd, Eaglehawk; adult/child $11/6.60) Sit back in lounge chairs, sip wine and watch classic and arthouse movies at this grand old building in Eaglehawk, just 10 minutes' drive north of town.

Getting There & Away
BUS
V/Line (☎ 13 61 96) buses from Bendigo include daily services to Castlemaine ($6); weekday services to Ballarat ($21) and Geelong ($35); and Monday to Saturday services to Echuca ($8). There are also daily buses to Mildura ($55) via Swan Hill ($28).

Bendigo Airport Service (☎ 5447 9006) is a direct bus service from Melbourne Airport, making three trips daily. Bookings are essential.

TRAIN
V/Line runs 11 trains from Melbourne ($25, two hours). One train continues on to Swan Hill ($28). Other stops include Castlemaine ($7) and Kyneton ($12).

Getting Around
Bendigo and the surrounding area are quite well serviced by public buses. There are two companies operating in the region: **Walkers Buslines** (☎ 5443 9333) and **Christian's Buslines** (☎ 5447 2222). Route maps are available from the visitors centre; tickets cost $1.30 and are valid for two hours.

For a taxi call **Bendigo Associated Taxis** (☎ 13 10 08).

AROUND BENDIGO
Bendigo Pottery
Six kilometres north of Bendigo, **Bendigo Pottery** (☎ 03-5448 4404; Midland Hwy, Epsom; ☼ 9am-5pm) is the oldest pottery works in Australia. It was founded in 1857 and is classified by the National Trust. The historic kilns are still used to produce fine pottery. There's a café and sales gallery, or you can watch potters at work in the studio. Also on site is **Bendigo Living Wings & Things** (☎ 03-5448 3051; adult/child/family $7/4.50/.18), where you walk among butterflies, native birds, dingoes and wallabies, or look at reptiles behind glass.

Whipstick State Park

North of Bendigo is the 2300-hectare Whipstick State Park, which conserves the distinctive whipstick mallee vegetation and protects the abundant birdlife. There are picnic areas, old eucalyptus distilleries, walking tracks and if you have a Miners' Right you can fossick for gold. **Hartland's Eucalyptus Oil Factory** (☎ 03-5448 8270), close to the Whipstick Forest, was established in 1890; buy your soaps and oils here. There are bicycle rides through the park and also a couple of designated camping sites – contact **Parks Victoria** (☎ 03-5444 6620) in Bendigo for more details.

KYNETON

☎ 03 / pop 3750

During the gold rush, Kyneton developed as the main coach stop between Melbourne and Bendigo, and the centre of the local agricultural industry that supplied the diggings with fresh produce. This is another town with a rich architectural heritage and many buildings are built from local bluestone. **Piper St** is a historic precinct lined with tearooms, antique shops, museums and restaurants.

Information

Visitors centre (☎ 5422 6110; Bourke St; ⊙ 9am-5pm) This is just off High St, on the southeastern outskirts of town.

Sights

The **Kyneton Historical Museum** (☎ 5422 1228; 67 Piper St; adult/child $3/1; ⊙ 11am-4pm Fri-Sun) is an old bank building (1855) that now houses a display of local history items, farming machinery, furniture and ornaments – the upper floor is furnished in period style.

Kyneton's **Botanic Gardens** (Clowes St), beside the Campaspe River, were established in the 1860s by Baron Ferdinand von Mueller, and are a wonderful place to stroll and appreciate the wonders of nature. There's a good picnic and barbecue area beside the river. The **Campaspe River Walk** is the highlight of a visit to Kyneton – ask for the route at the visitors centre.

Kyneton Fine China & Wattle Ceramics (☎ 5422 3337; www.wattleceramics.com.au; ⊙ 9.30am-4.30pm Mon-Fri) has a Studio Gallery where you can see artists at work or buy fine bone-china figurines and flowers.

Kyneton's **mineral springs**, 4km north of town, are another good picnic spot, and the **Lauriston Reservoir**, 9km west, has barbecues, a playground and good fishing and water sports.

Festivals & Events

Kyneton is famous for its daffodils. The annual **Kyneton Daffodil & Arts Festival** (www .kynetondaffodilarts.org.au/index.htm) is held each September, with 10 days of gala evenings, markets, concerts, fairs and flower shows.

Sleeping

Kyneton and the surrounding area is dotted with B&Bs and self-contained cottages, each one more elegant, peaceful and luxurious than the last – ask at the visitors centre for details.

Gainsborough (☎ 5422 3999; www.babs.com.au/gains borough; 66 Jennings St; B&B d $140) Newly established, this restored National Trust–classified homestead stands majestically in a rambling English garden just up from the Campaspe. Ask about the murder mystery night or the special packages.

Kyneton Motel (☎/fax 5422 1098; 101 Piper St; s/d from $48/55) This is the cheaper of the town's two motels but quite adequate, with clean spacious rooms around a courtyard.

Kyneton Ridge Estate (☎ 5422 7377, 0409 017 310; www.kynetonridge.com.au; 90 Blackhill School Rd; B&B d from $100) It's part of a vineyard, so you can enjoy your country breakfast on the veranda looking over the rows of grapevines. The gardens are open during Kyneton's Daffodil & Arts Festival (see above).

Kyneton Caravan Park (☎ 5422 1612; www.kcp .com.au; Clowes St; camp sites per 2 people from $15.50, d cabins from $55) This is in a lovely setting beside the river and the botanic gardens.

Eating

Quintessence Café (☎ 5422 6582; 35 High St; ⊙ lunch daily, dinner Fri & Sat) This is a top spot, famous for its seafood platter and kangaroo with roast beetroot.

Club Hotel (☎ 5422 1280; 41 Mollison St; mains $16-25; ⊙ lunch & dinner) Head here for excellent pub meals; there's also Guinness on tap.

Cafe Zulu (☎ 5422 6249; 70 High St; mains $10-18; ⊙ breakfast & lunch Wed-Mon, dinner Fri & Sat) Don't miss this bright-orange little spot that serves wonderful things like marinated steak strips on couscous, baked ham and chilli prawns.

Getting There & Away

Kyneton has a lovely old **train station** (Mollison St). There are 16 daily trains to Melbourne ($14, one hour).

THE WIMMERA

The major attraction of the Wimmera is the spectacular Grampians National Park, with four rugged granite and sandstone mountain ranges renowned for their flora and fauna, colourful wildflowers, fine bushwalks, superb mountain lookouts and excellent rock climbing. Come here to try abseiling, bike-riding, horse riding, or simply to visit waterfalls. Another natural feature is the Mt Arapiles State Park, known as the 'Ayers Rock of the Wimmera' and Australia's most famous rock-climbing venue.

The Little Desert National Park is a wonderful wilderness area. There are extensive walking and 4WD tracks, and a fascinating array of hardy native species that have adapted to the extremes of this harsh environment.

Horsham is the Wimmera's largest town. Stawell and Ararat, east of the Grampians, have a gold-mining heritage and Stawell still has a functioning commercial goldmine.

There are numerous wineries to visit (see p63) and if you're into fishing you'll find some pretty good places to dangle a line – surprisingly, Horsham hosts one of the country's richest fishing competitions.

Getting There & Around

The *Overland*, the Melbourne–Adelaide train, runs through the Wimmera, stopping at Ararat, Horsham and Dimboola (for confirmed bookings only), four times a week between 1am and 3am. **V/Line** (☎ 13

61 96) has train/bus services between Melbourne and major towns.

From Horsham, you can take a bus north to Mildura, west to Naracoorte (South Australia; SA) or south to Hamilton.

LANGI GHIRAN STATE PARK

This small park is carpeted with huge granite boulders and native vegetation including red gums, yellow box, banksias and wattles, and in spring, colourful wildflowers. The dominant features are the two granite mountains, **Langi Ghiran** (950m) and **Gorrin**. It's a full-day trek to the summit of Mt Langi Ghiran, where you'll get great views across to the Grampians; or you can do a short walk to the Langi Ghiran reservoir.

Langi Ghiran is the Aboriginal name for the yellow-tailed black cockatoo. Other species found here include corellas, robins, honeyeaters and finches. Spring is the best time for bird-watching. This area was significant for local Aboriginal clans, and there are several rock-art sites, shelters and scar trees. For more information, contact **Parks Victoria** (☎ 03-5349 2404) in Beaufort.

On this same road is **Wilde's Caravan Museum** where the oldest exhibit dates back to 1910 and looks like a Coolgardie safe on wheels.

ARARAT

☎ 03 / pop 7000

Chinese miners travelling from Adelaide to the Ballarat goldfields found gold in Ararat in 1857. They mined here until the early 1860s and the town continued to grow as a commercial centre for the surrounding agricultural district. The town has another two museums and a massive wine school – it's an emerging wine-producing region to keep an eye on.

The **visitors centre** (☎ 1800 657 158; www.ararat .vic.gov.au; 91 High St; ☉ 9am-5pm) is at the train station.

Sights & Activities

Several historic buildings have been classified by the National Trust. Some of the better examples are **Pyrenees House** (Girdlestone St) beside the hospital and **Ararat Town Hall** (Vincent St), which was built in 1898.

J Ward (☎ 5352 3357; Girdlestone St; adult/child $10/4; ☉ hourly tours 10-11am & 1-2pm Mon-Sat, 10am-3pm Sun) was a gaol for the criminally insane. It was originally built in 1861 and closed

---

CENTRAL WEST

YUMMY IN YOUR TUMMY

As you wander through the townships of the region, check out the displays of 'local produce' prepared by the Grampians Produce Group. Most unusual are the green eggs. Then there are jars of Pomonal berry preserves, lavender honey, locally grown and processed tea, olives and olive oil products.

in 1991. Get a chilling glimpse of what was kept secret for 100 years. Surrounding the awful bluestone building are the delightful **Alexandra Gardens** (cnr Girdlestone & Vincent Sts), set around a central lake and with picnic facilities, an orchid glasshouse, playground and garden fernery with waterfalls.

Gum San Chinese Heritage Centre (☎ 5352 1078; www.gumsan.com.au; 31 Lambert St; adult/child/family $8/5/20; ☽ 10am-4.30pm) is an authentic re-creation of a two-storey Chinese pagoda and a fascinating memorial to the arduous journey of the town's Chinese founders.

Next to the town hall is **Ararat Gallery** (☎ 5352 2836; cnr Barkly & Vincent Sts; admission $2; ☽ 11am-4pm Mon-Fri, noon-4pm Sat & Sun), which is mainly devoted to the works of contemporary artists working with fibres and textiles.

Langi Morgala Museum (☎ 5352 4858; 48 Queen St; adult/child $2/50c; ☽ 1-4pm Sat & Sun), just off Barkly St, is the local historical museum, a dusty jumble of bric-a-brac. Of particular interest is the Mooney collection of Aboriginal artefacts.

The **YMCA Recreation Centre** (78 High St; swim $3.50; ☽ 6am-9pm Mon-Fri, 8am-5pm Sat, 1-5pm Sun) was the old Common School. It now has a basketball stadium and 25m indoor pool with a host of other facilities.

Festivals & Events

Ararat is one of the hosts of the **Grampians Great Escape** (May), when Montara Winery holds a 'Scarecrows in the Vineyard' competition. Entrants from all over the country submit their scarecrows, which are displayed throughout the vineyard. For details contact the visitors centre (opposite).

Sleeping

Ararat Hotel (☎ 5352 2477; 130 Barkly St; B&B s/d/tw from $35/40/45) The rooms are small but bright, and the comfortable guest room has TV and free tea and coffee.

Orchid City Motor Inn (☎ 5352 1341; 96 High St; s/d $98/110; ⊠) It's so new the plants are just poking up their heads. But the rooms are mellow and peaceful with a modern design.

Statesman Motor Inn (☎ 5352 4111; statflag@net connect.com.au; Western Hwy; s/d from $80/95; ⊠) It doesn't look that good, but the rooms are spacious, the beds sound and it's very convenient to the local attractions.

Acacia Caravan Park (☎ 5352 2994; www.acacia touristpark.com; 6 Acacia Ave; camp sites per 2 people from $18.50, d cabins from $45; ⊠ ⊞) It's getting a bit worn but the central location is a big advantage.

Eating

Vines (☎ 5352 1744; stnicholas@ozisp.com.au; 74 Barkly St; mains $16-24; ☽ breakfast & lunch daily, dinner Fri & Sat) All cane and cushions with local artwork on display, Vines is recommended everywhere you go. Vines uses local produce, organic vegies, and fish from Warrnambool, served perhaps on a raft of asparagus with white bean purée. Yum. It's so popular you should book ahead!

Sicilians (☎ 5352 2627; 102 Barkly St; mains $10-15; ☽ lunch & dinner Mon-Sat) This large, open place is a café, bar and restaurant with an interesting menu of Lebanese delights like kofta, good pizzas (delivered free) and steak. Or settle in if you just want a drink.

Waack's Bakery (☎ 5352 1618; 170 Barkly St; meals $4.50-9) This is the place for a cheap lunch or snack.

Kerry's Cafe (☎ 5352 1205; 96 Barkly St; banquets $15-20; ☽ breakfast & lunch Thu-Sun) You have to go to Kerry's to try the specials of the day: soups, risottos, pasta, pies or curry.

Getting There & Away

Ararat train station (Queen St) is at the northern end of the street. Daily services from Melbourne include the *Overland*, two **V/Line** (☎ 13 61 96) trains and four bus/train services changing at Ballarat ($40, three hours).

STAWELL

☎ 03 / pop 6250

Born of the gold rush of the 1850s and still a substantial producer of gold ($70 million dollars worth was extracted in 2000), Stawell is actually best known as the home of the Stawell Gift, a world-famous foot race.

The 1870s were the boom years for Stawell and many of the most impressive buildings, including the town hall and most of the pubs, date back to these times. Stawell is a popular base for visitors to the nearby Grampians, and a bus service links the defunct train station with Halls Gap.

The excellent **visitors centre** (☎ 1800 330 080; 50-52 Western Hwy; ☽ 9am-5pm) is before the turn-off to Halls Gap. The main shopping area is in and around the Gold Reef Mall in the centre of Main St.

Sights & Activities

Central Park, the local football and cricket ground, has been the venue for the Stawell Gift since 1898. The impressive set of iron entrance gates were erected in 1903 in memory of the local men who served in the Boer War, and a Victorian timber grandstand, built in 1899, has been restored.

The unassuming **Stawell Gift Hall of Fame** (☎ 5358 1326; Main St; adult/child $4/2; ☺ 9-11am Mon-Fri) has a collection of videos, photos and memorabilia documenting the history of the Stawell Gift race meeting. There are also a few souvenirs for sale.

Attracting tourists by the busload, **Casper's World in Miniature** (☎ 5358 1877; London Rd; adult/child $10/4; ☺ from 9am) is an extensive park, with spreading pavilions housing displays devoted to different countries, cultures and eras. There are things like a pyramid, a miniature Eiffel Tower and a replica goldmine, and there's also a souvenir gallery.

When trains stopped coming to Stawell in 2002, the station residence was put to good use as the **Railway Station Gallery** (☎ 5358 3304; Napier St; ☺ 10am-4pm Thu-Sun), a quaint little gallery showcasing local arts and crafts.

Bunjil is the creator spirit of the Koories of this region and **Bunjil's Shelter** (Pomonal Rd), 11km south of Stawell, is one of the most significant Aboriginal rock art sites in the state. The painting is enhanced by the contours of the rock and makes sense only within its context. Two dimensional sketches of the painting suggest a 'primitive' quality that doesn't exist in the original.

Named after two sisters who once owned this property, **Sisters Rocks** (Western Hwy), 6km south of Stawell, is a collection of huge granite rocks painted with colourful graffiti.

Stawell Aviation Services (SAS; ☎ 5358 3822, 0428 501 600) offers scenic flights over the Grampians ($150 for three people, 40 minutes).

Festivals & Events

The **Stawell Gift** (www.stawellgift.com; Mar/Apr) has been run here on Easter Monday since 1878. The race meeting features a variety of sprint and distance-running events, but the prestigious 120m dash is the main event. It's the richest foot race in the country, attracting up to 20,000 visitors, so if you're planning to visit during the Gift, you'll need to book your accommodation – preferably, a year in advance.

Sleeping

BUDGET

Town Hall Hotel (☎ 5358 1059; fax 5358 3355; 62 Main St; B&B s/d from $25/40, penthouse $150) This grand old pub has good, basic rooms with pressed-tin ceilings, a cosy guest room with TV, reasonable shared bathrooms and a back deck.

Coorrabin Motor Inn (☎ /fax 5358 3933; 7 Western Hwy; s/d/f $55/66/90; ☒) Of the string of motels along the Western Hwy, this is one of the cheapest, yet its units are spacious, sparkling and quiet.

Stawell Park Caravan Park (☎ 5358 2709; fax 5358 2199; Western Hwy; camp sites per 2 people from $15, d cabins from $66; ☒ ☒) This park on 48 hectares of attractive bushland has a pool and recreation room.

MIDRANGE & TOP END

Magdala Motor Lodge (☎ 5358 3877; fax 5358 4176; 30 Western Hwy; s/d/f from $99/105/160; ☒ ☒) This is a resort. Truly. Lovely rooms look out over the small lake or the large central court. Golf, tennis and canoeing are all free for guests, and the **restaurant** (mains $15-24, ☺ dinner Mon-Sat) serves country dishes like all-day simmered lamb shanks.

Walmsley Guest House (☎ /fax 5358 3164; 19 Seaby St; B&B s/d from $60/85, deluxe $130) This beautiful 130-year-old building has been tastefully restored to its old grandeur. Guests enjoy two gorgeous lounge rooms, a veranda made for lounging, and a cooked breakfast.

Stawell Holiday Cottages (☎ /fax 5358 2868; www .stawellholidaycottages.com; Errington Rd; s/d $55/70; ☒ ☒) Off the Western Hwy, 2km from Stawell, these cottages are on a small bush property. Six simple and comfortable, self-contained cottages sleep up to six people. The facilities include a playground, pool and barbecues.

Eating

Café 102 (☎ 5358 4400; 102 Main St; light meals $5-9; ☺ breakfast, lunch & dinner) This buzzy little café in the centre of town churns out fresh light meals. You'll find the Grampians Produce Group goodies here too.

Pleasant Creek Cafe (☎ 5358 2834; 54 Longfield St; mains $14-17; ☺ breakfast & lunch Wed-Sun, dinner Thu-Sat) In an old house next to the information centre, with tables on the veranda, this place serves pastas and tarts, cooked breakfasts and soups.

Diamond House Motor Inn Restaurant (☎ 5358 3366; 24 Seaby St; mains $17-26; ☾ dinner Mon-Sat) This is an excellent choice, in an amazing building that's a local landmark, and the cellar is full of local wine.

Getting There & Away

The old **train station** (Napier St) is about 1km south of the centre. There are five buses daily to Ararat or Ballarat connecting with the train to Melbourne ($36, 3½ hours).

A bus service connects Stawell with the Grampians (see p272).

GRAMPIANS NATIONAL PARK

Major Thomas Mitchell named the spectacular mountain ranges the Grampians after the mountains in Scotland. In 1836 he eloquently described them as:

> ...a noble range of mountains, rising in the south to a stupendous height, and presenting as bold and picturesque an outline as a painter ever imagined.

The Grampians are one of Victoria's most outstanding natural features and a wonderland of flora and fauna. The array of attractions includes an incredibly rich diversity of wildlife and plant species, spectacular wildflower displays, unique and unusual rock formations, Aboriginal rock art, fine bushwalking, an extensive network of creeks, streams, cascades and waterfalls and excellent abseiling and rock climbing.

Over 900 species of native trees, shrubs and wildflowers have been recorded here, with everything ranging from fern gullies to red-gum forests. There are almost 200 species of bird, 35 different mammals, 28 reptiles, 11 species of amphibian and six types of freshwater fish; so you never know what you might see in your wanderings.

The mountains are at their best in spring, when the wildflowers (including 20 species that don't exist anywhere else in the world) are at their peak. The Grampians are worth visiting at any time of year, although it can often be extremely hot in summer and very wet in winter.

The rock art sites (nearby Bunjil's Shelter is one of Victoria's most sacred indigenous sites – see opposite) indicate the esteem in which these mountains are held by local indigenous communities, whose name for the region is Gariwerd.

Orientation

The four greatest mountain ranges of the Grampians are Mt Difficult in the north, Mt William in the east, Serra in the southeast and Victoria in the southwest. They spread from Ararat to the Wartook Valley and from Dunkeld up almost to Horsham. The township of Halls Gap lies in the Fyans Valley between the Mt William and Mt Difficult ranges. The smaller Wonderland Range, close to Halls Gap, has some of the most spectacular and accessible scenery. There are good scenic drives, picnic grounds and excellent walks ranging from a half-hour return stroll to Venus Baths to a four-hour loop walk to the Pinnacle.

Mt Stapylton in the north is renowned as an abseiling and rock-climbing spot. Mt Zero affords great views. Along the way there are walks from Roses Gap to Beehive Falls or Briggs Bluff and the ruins of Heatherlie Quarry, the origin of the sandstone in many of Melbourne's Victorian-era buildings.

The Victoria Ranges are the most remote, and have good walking and climbing areas such as the Fortress and the Chimney Pots. The scenic Buandik camping ground here is popular.

The forested valley between the Serra and Victoria Ranges is known for its wildlife, and is a popular area for seeing magnificent displays of wildflowers.

HALLS GAP

This small township in the heart of the Grampians is a popular base. It has some shops, adventure activity offices, restaurants, cafés and a wide range of accommodation.

Information

The Halls Gap newsagency, general store and post office has some banking facilities: ATM, Eftpos, an **ANZ agency** (☾ 1.30-3pm Mon) and a Commonwealth Bank agency.

Parks Victoria (Map p245; ☎ 03-5356 4381, 13 19 63; www.parkweb.vic.gov.au; ☾ 9am-5pm) This office has a building at the excellent Brambuk – The National Park Cultural Centre (see p269), a large complex 2.5km south of Halls Gap. There are plenty of maps and brochures, and the rangers can advise you about where to go, where to camp and what you might see. They also issue camping permits and fishing licences.

THE GRAMPIANS & WARTOOK VALLEY

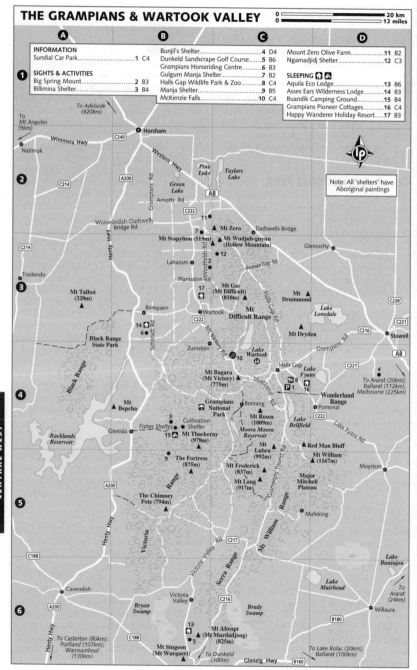

0 _____ 20 km
0 _____ 12 miles

INFORMATION
Sundial Car Park.................................**1** C4

SIGHTS & ACTIVITIES
Big Spring Mount.............................**2** B3
Billimina Shelter..............................**3** B4

Bunjil's Shelter................................**4** D4
Dunkeld Sandscrape Golf Course....**5** B6
Grampians Horseriding Centre..........**6** B3
Gulgurn Manja Shelter.....................**7** B2
Halls Gap Wildlife Park & Zoo..........**8** C4
Manja Shelter..................................**9** B5
McKenzie Falls...............................**10** C4

Mount Zero Olive Farm..................**11** B2
Ngamadjidj Shelter.........................**12** C3

SLEEPING
Aquila Eco Lodge...........................**13** B6
Asses Ears Wilderness Lodge..........**14** B3
Buandik Camping Ground...............**15** B4
Grampians Pioneer Cottages...........**16** C4
Happy Wanderer Holiday Resort.....**17** B3

Note: All 'shelters' have
Aboriginal paintings

Visitors centre (Map p245; ☎ 03-5356 4616, 1800 065 599; Grampians Tourist Rd, Halls Gap; ⏱ 9am-5pm) This office is housed in Centenary Hall. You can book all tours and activities here, and use the free accommodation booking service.

Sights

BRAMBUK – THE NATIONAL PARK CULTURAL CENTRE

You'll be drawn to the amazing, award-winning building of **Brambuk – The National Park Cultural Centre** (Map p245; ☎ 03-5356 4452; admission free; ⏱ 9am-5pm). The flowing roof represents the open wings of the cockatoo. Inside are Koorie symbols: the curved seat is the caring embrace of Bunjil, the creator spirit; the ramp the eel dreaming; the theatre ceiling the southern right whale (totem of the Gundjitmara people). The centre is run by five Koorie communities, together with Parks Victoria. Displays and examples of Koorie art, clothes, weapons and tools all aim to raise visitors' awareness of their history.

There's a souvenir shop and **café** (⏱ lunch). Outside are the native plants used by Aboriginal people for food and medicine.

The **Gariwerd Dreaming Theatre** (adult/child $4.50/2.50), in the complex, presents both Dreamtime stories of Gariwerd and modern informative films about the region. There are demonstrations of Koorie music and dance, organised tours of the rock art sites (see below), and education and holiday programmes.

The front building, where you'll find the rangers, has interesting educational displays covering the natural features and history of the Grampians.

ABORIGINAL ROCK ART

There is an extensive collection of rock art (Map p268) within the Grampians National Park. In the Northern Grampians near Mt Stapylton the main sites are Gulgurn Manja Shelter and Ngamadjidj Shelter. In the Western Grampians near the Buandik camping ground the main sites are Billimina Shelter and Manja Shelter. These paintings, in protected rock overhangs, are mostly hand prints, animal tracks or stick figures.

HALLS GAP WILDLIFE PARK & ZOO

This small **wildlife park** (Map p268; ☎ 03-5356 4668; Pomonal Rd; adult/child/family $9/5.50/25; ⏱ 10am-5pm Wed-Mon), southeast of Halls Gap, houses an interesting variety of animals in a natural bush setting. Wallabies, grey kangaroos and peacocks can get up close and personal, while you can view animals like wombats, possums, deer and monkeys. There are free tours of the property but you must book ahead.

ZUMSTEIN

This reserve (Map p268) in the Western Grampians is named after Walter Zumstein, a beekeeper and naturalist who settled in the area in 1910 and developed it into a wildlife reserve. There are picnic facilities, free electric barbecues and a walking track follows the river to the base of the spectacular McKenzie Falls.

Activities

ROCK CLIMBING & ABSEILING

The Grampians and Mt Arapiles region are the best in Victoria for these fantastic adventure activities that people of any age can enjoy. The following members of Australia's Climbing Instructors Association (ACIA) offer everything from basic instruction to advanced guided climbs.

Hangin' Out (☎ 03-5356 4535, 0407-684 831; www .hanginout.com.au; groups per person from $22.50) will get you started on the cliff faces, with options that give you a 'total' Grampians experience. Tours include lively interpretations of the surrounding country and Earl will show you wildflowers as you go – perhaps to distract you from what lies ahead! He runs adventure walks too. Prices depend on the size of your group and the type of adventure.

The **Grampians Mountain Adventure Company** (GMAC; ☎ 03-5383 9218, 0427-747 047; www.grampians adventure.com.au; instruction from $50) promises a rock climbing or abseiling adventure tailored to suit you.

GENERAL ADVENTURE

Grampians Adventure Services (GAS; ☎ 03-5356 4556; www.g-adventures.com.au; YHA Eco-Hostel), along with Adventure YMCA, offers a full range of outdoor activities. Rock-climb, abseil, canoe, bushwalk, go wildlife-spotting, caving and mountain biking – motorcycles aren't permitted in the park. Most activities cost $35 for beginners, more for things like caving!

BUSHWALKING

There are more than 150km of well-marked walking tracks, ranging from half-hour

CENTRAL WEST

strolls to overnight treks through rough and difficult terrain. Drop into Brambuk – The National Park Cultural Centre and have a chat to one of the rangers. They'll recommend walks, depending on your interests.

The walks all start from the various car parks, picnic grounds and camping areas. Wear appropriate footwear, take a hat and sunscreen, always carry water and let someone know where you're going (preferably the rangers).

OTHER ACTIVITIES

Parks Victoria produces three easy-to-read maps of the most popular and accessible natural attractions and **short walks** throughout the park; you can buy these at both the visitors centre and the Parks Vic office (p267).

Permits ($12), required for **fishing** in local streams and creeks, are available from Brambuk – The National Park Cultural Centre and local petrol stations.

The **Grampians Horseriding Centre** (Map p268; ☎ 03-5383 9255; www.grampianshorseriding.com.au; Schmidt Rd, Brimpaen, Wartook Valley; 2hr rides $50; ☼ 10am & 2pm) offers great horse riding adventures around a grand property with sweeping views, lakes and idyllic bush tracks. Ask about the luxury accommodation. You can choose a mountain bike if it looks more stable.

Morning balloon flights are offered by **Bendigo Ballooning** (☎ 03-5358 5222; www.bendigoballooning.com.au; rides $175) and **Stawell Aviation Services** (☎ 03-5357 3234; flights for 3 people from $150) offers joy flights by plane.

Tours

Grampians Personalised Tours & Adventures

(☎ 03-5356 4654, 0429-954 686; www.grampianstours.com; tours/walks from $59/175) Offers a range of 4WD tours (with off-road options), or use your feet on the discovery walks. Tours include stop-offs at picturesque locations, and lots to eat. Two- to four-day walks are available.

Brambuk – The National Park Cultural Centre

(☎ 03-5356 4452; ☼ 9am) Offers a two-hour tour to Bunjil's Shelter (adult/child $15/8) and a half-day tour to other rock art sites ($27/17). Bookings are essential.

For other tours from Melbourne, see under tour operators in the Directory, p406.

Festivals & Events

Halls Gap is the focal point for some good local festivities:

HALLS GAP

CENTRAL WEST

Grampians Jazz Festival (www.jazz.adelaide.onau.net/othfests.htm; early Feb)

Grampians Gourmet Weekend (☎ 03-5352 3868; May) On the first weekend in May.

Halls Gap Wildflower Exhibition (www.visithallsgap.com.au; Oct)

Halls Gap Film Festival (☎ 03-5356 4616; Nov)

Sleeping

The helpful **Booking Service** (☎ 1800 246 880) at the visitors centre in Halls Gap can find the accommodation you'd like and tell you the rates, which vary with the season.

CAMPING

Parkgate Resort (Map p245; ☎ 03-5356 4215; www.grampians.com; Grampians Rd; camp sites per 2 people from $24, cabins/cottages d from $75/105; 🏊 🎮) This fabulous resort has everything for the kids, including a jumping pillow and playground. For adults there are tennis courts, a camp kitchen, games and lounge rooms and free barbecues.

Parks Victoria maintains more than 10 camp sites in the park, with toilets, picnic tables and fireplaces, most with limited water. There's no booking system, but permits are required and you can self-register or pay at **Brambuk – The National Park Cultural Centre** (Map p245; ☎ 03-5356 4381; camp sites per 2 people $12).

Bush camping is permitted anywhere except in the Wonderland Range area, around Lake Wartook and in parts of the Serra, Mt William and Victoria Ranges. Check with the rangers before heading off.

Pay close attention to fire restrictions – apart from the damage you could do to yourself and the bush, you can be jailed for lighting *any* fire, including fuel stoves, on days of total fire ban. For more information see p397.

BUDGET

Grampians YHA Eco-Hostel (Map p245; ☎ 03-5356 4544; www.yha.com.au; cnr Grampians Rd & Buckler St; dm/s/d/f $23/52/57/77) This place is designed to use less power and water. So feel good as you enjoy the light, the views, the interesting spaces and very smart kitchen. And keep an eye on the kitchen bench. Your host puts out freshly baked bread, freshly-laid eggs, freshly-picked herbs, all those eco-goodies for free.

Halls Gap Motel (Map p245; ☎ 03-5356 4209; hg motel@netconnect.com.au; Grampians Tourist Rd; s/d/f $64/76/91) This is one of the cheaper motels of the half-dozen or so in Halls Gap.

Grampians Motel (Map p245; ☎ 03-5356 4248; fax 5356 4491; Dunkeld Rd; s/d/spa unit $69/79/115) With its good views, cute wildlife and budget prices, you'll find this a good option.

MIDRANGE & TOP END

Mountain Grand Guesthouse (Map p245; ☎ 03-5356 4232; www.mountaingrand.com; Grampians Tourist Rd; s/d B&B with dinner $133/176) It's a gracious, old-fashioned timber guesthouse, peaceful and friendly, with welcoming guest lounges. The bedrooms are fresh and colourful with their own spacious bathrooms. The Indulgence Getaway package is great value at $218 a double.

Pinnacle Holiday Lodge (Map p245; ☎ 03-5356 4249; www.pinnacleholiday.com.au; Heath St; s & d from $89; 🏊 🎮) Right in the centre of Halls Gap, this gorgeous property sits stylishly behind the Stony Creek shops. It has everything: indoor pool, tennis courts, spacious modern units and a great range from self-contained basic up to deluxe spa suites with gas log fires.

D'Altons Resort (Map p245; ☎ 03-5356 4666; www.daltonsresort.com.au; 48 Glen St, Halls Gap; standard/deluxe cottages from $100/120) These delightful timber cottages spread up the hill between the gums and kangaroos. The cottages have cosy fires, big lounge chairs and little verandas.

Grampians Pioneer Cottages (Map p268; ☎ 03-5356 4402; Birdswing Rd; d $125-145; 🏊) Midway between Halls Gap and Pomonal are these gorgeous rustic stone or red-gum cottages. They're set in quiet bushland, some with open fires, others with spiral staircases up to bedroom attics.

Eating

There are some great eateries along Grampians Tourist Rd in Halls Gap.

Darcy's (☎ 03-5356 4344; Grampians Rd; mains $23-28; 🕐 dinner) An elegant burgundy-and-white restaurant, D'Arcy's has an interesting menu – you'll love the 'roo coated with bush spices – and an excellent range of wines from the Grampians and Pyrenees wineries.

Morningside (☎ 03-5356 4344; mains $8.50-15; 🕐 breakfast & dinner) Walk behind Darcy's to this great café. From the deck you can watch the browsing kangaroos. Inside is art work by local artists and a blackboard menu suggesting goodies like a yum cha platter.

Balconies (☎ 03-5356 4232; mains $16-23) This upstairs restaurant at the Mountain Grand Guesthouse serves fine cuisine and has live jazz on weekends. But you may need to avoid 'Polly's wicked rum & ginger pudding'. The café downstairs is more casual.

Kookaburra Restaurant (Map p245; ☎ 03-5356 4222; mains $15-27; ⏲ lunch Sat & Sun, dinner nightly) Still popular after many years, you'll need to book if you want to try dishes like the duckling risotto. And leave room for the desserts!

A Toast to Us (Map p245; ☎ 03-5356 4858; Stony Ck; mains $14-29; ⏲ breakfast, lunch & dinner) All new and sparkling in a great position to watch the creek gurgling past, you'll find traditional home-baked country fare like Guinness pie here.

Around on the boardwalk along pretty Stony Creek, the bakery makes the best vanilla slices ever, and the ice-creamery and cafés will help you recharge after your adventure activities.

Take a 15-minute drive out to **Namaskaar Indian Restaurant** (Map p268; ☎ 03-5359 5251; noel masla@bigpond.com.au; Western Hwy, Dadswells Bridge; mains $6-22; ⏲ lunch & dinner) where you'll eat possibly the best Indian dishes ever, plus the Italian and French meals are fabulous. And if you don't feel like driving back, stay in the Namaskaar Motel, right next to the **Giant Koala** (☎ 03-5359 5230; Dadswells Bridge).

Getting There & Away

V/Line (☎ 13 61 96) has a daily train/bus service from Melbourne to Halls Gap ($48; four hours). Trains leave Melbourne every morning for Ballarat; a connecting bus takes you to Stawell and another on to Halls Gap.

There are three daily buses from Halls Gap back to Stawell ($12), departing from opposite the newsagent.

The road from Stawell to Halls Gap is flat so it's an easy cycle of about 25km. You can take your bike on the train to Ararat; it's a longer and hillier ride from Ararat to Halls Gap (via Moyston) but still fairly easy.

Getting Around

The major roads through the Grampians include Grampians Tourist Rd from Dunkeld to Halls Gap and on to Stawell; Mt Victory Rd from Halls Gap to Wartook, where it becomes Northern Grampians Rd; and Silverband Rd, which does a loop around the Wonderland area. These roads are all sealed.

The unsealed roads are in good condition, although some are closed during winter and after heavy rain.

WARTOOK VALLEY

You can enjoy spectacular views of the mountains as you travel through lush Wartook Valley. The unsealed roads and tracks lead past little creeks, spectacular waterfalls and idyllic picnic spots. There are several sites with Koorie rock paintings (see p269), canoe trees and middens. Many of the attractions along the valley also offer fascinating B&Bs.

Big Spring Mount (Map p268; ☎ 03-5383 8235; Winfields Rd, Laharum) can take you on a tour of their native flower shed and the nearby olive plantation. Tours are by appointment only.

See p270 for information on horse riding.

Mt Zero Millstone Cafe (Map p268; ☎ 03-5383 8280; Winfields Rd, Laharum; meals $7.50-9; ⏲ lunch Thu-Mon) is a gorgeous café at Mt Zero Olive Farm, set among the olive groves below the towering mountains. It features a 150-year-old stone olive crusher in the courtyard of two old school houses. Enjoy excellent home-cooked meals, and stock your pantry from the **cellar door** (⏲ 10am-4.30pm). Love it? Stay the night in the small B&B.

Asses Ears Wilderness Lodge (Map p268; ☎ 03-5383 9215; www.assesearslodge.com.au; Schmidt Rd, Brimpaen; B&B d/q from $22/66; ▣ ▣), so named because it sits below the Asses Ears Mountain Range, offers cosy cabins that are popular with backpackers and adventurers. There's a large room for **dining** (set menu $12; ⏲ dinner), bar, and plenty of wildlife to watch.

Happy Wanderer Holiday Resort (Map p268; ☎ 03-5383 6210; www.grampians.net.au/wanderer; North Grampians Rd, Wartook; camp sites per 2 people from $19, d cabins from $66; ▣ ▣) is a lovely caravan park with fabulous mountain views. Facilities include barbecues, playground, pool, tennis courts and nine-hole bush golf course.

Wartook Bush Cafe (☎ 03-5383 6377; North Grampians Rd, Wartook; meals $6-15; ⏲ 10am-5pm Wed-Sun) is a charming coffee shop that serves divine Devonshire teas in a native garden.

HORSHAM

☎ 03 / pop 13,200

The area around Horsham was first settled in 1841. In 1849 a post office and general store were built, and from these humble beginnings the town has become the main commercial centre of the Wimmera, servicing the surrounding wheat and sheep farms. It's a good base for exploring the nearby Little Desert National and Mt Arapiles State Parks, and a short hop to the Grampians.

Orientation & Information

Firebrace St, which runs off the Western Hwy, is the main shopping strip, with postal and banking facilities, supermarkets and plenty of other shops and eateries.

The **visitors centre** (☎ 5382 1832, 1800 633 218; www.horshamvic.com.au; 20 O'Callaghan's Parade; ☉ 9am-5pm) has information on Horsham and all the surrounding areas.

Sights & Activities

The **Horsham Regional Art Gallery** (☎ 5382 5575; www.horsham.net.au/gallery; 80 Wilson St; admission by donation; ☉ 10am-5pm Tue-Fri, 1-4.30pm Sat & Sun) houses the Mack Jost Collection of significant Australian artists that includes works by Rupert Bunny, Sir Sidney Nolan, John Olsen and Charles Blackman. A new extension holds exciting temporary exhibitions.

The wide, brown **Wimmera River** meanders through the town, its banks are lined with red gums. The **Botanic Gardens** (Firebrace St) were established in the 1870s and designed by the curator of Melbourne's Royal Botanic Gardens, William Guilfoyle. Behind the entrance gates is a large bunya pine, shady lawns, rose gardens and picnic facilities.

The **Wool Factory** (☎ 5382 0333; 134 Golf Course Rd; adult/child $5/1.50; ☉ 8.30am-4.30pm) provides employment and skill development for handicapped people. It produces ultrafine Merino wool, and there's a walk-through sheep shed, café and shop where you can buy wool products. Tours run at 10.15am, 11am, 1.30pm and 2.30pm.

Festivals & Events

Contact the visitors centre (above) for details of the following festivals.

Horsham's Fishing Competition (Mar) Held on the Labour Day long weekend. Organisers of the first contest, in 1972, got a surprise when around 3500 anglers turned up. Since then, the competition has grown into one of the richest and most popular in the country.

Agricultural Show (Sep/Oct)

Horsham Spring Garden Festival (Oct)

Kannamaroo Festival (Nov) Includes a raft race.

Sleeping

Royal Hotel (☎ 5382 1255; fax 5381 1939; 132 Firebrace St; B&B s/d $30/50) This historic hotel is a good choice, although it's the in place to be on Friday and Saturday, when everybody hangs out till 5am. The popular **bistro** (mains $14-22; ☉ lunch & dinner) serves traditional steaks and pasta dishes.

Country City Motor Inn (☎ 5382 5644, 1800 808 490; 11 O'Callaghans Pde; s/d $99/109; ☒ ☒) This inn has attractive units spread around a small central garden. It's off the main drag but just a few minutes' walk to everything.

Horsham Motel (☎ 5382 5555; fax 5381 1710; 5 Dimboola Rd; d $59; ☒ ☒) This pleasant motel is on the main highway, but is very peaceful and you'll enjoy the little pool.

Horsham House (☎ 5382 5053; fax 5382 3540; 27 Roberts Ave; B&B s/d $105/120, d cottage $140; ☒) This beautiful residence, c 1905, has been lovingly restored and sits grandly beneath a sycamore tree among rose gardens. Guests have a pool room, sun room and barbecue area, and there's a self-contained cottage.

Stronsay (☎ 5382 6247; www.stronsay.wimmera.com.au; Plozza's Rd, Haven; B&B s/d from $85/120; ☒ ☒) This charming place, three minutes south on the Henty Hwy, is very close to the Grampians and Mt Arapiles. Set on two hectares of gardens, you can contemplate the far horizon, out past the wheat plains. Your hosts arrange tours and adventure activities.

Horsham Caravan Park (☎ 5382 3476; fax 5381 2170; 190 Firebrace St; camp sites per 2 people from $20, d cabins from $60) This is a great little spot between the botanic gardens and the river, with shady sites and good facilities.

Wimmera Lakes Caravan Resort (☎ 5382 4481; Western Hwy; camp sites per 2 people from $22.50, d cabins from $85; ☒ ☒) Spread over lovely parkland, this resort has a playground and tennis court, kiosk and laundry and beautiful pool.

Eating

Brills (☎ 5382 1555; 77 Pynsent St; mains $24.50-31; ☉ breakfast Sat & Sun, lunch Tue-Sun & dinner Wed-Sat) Everyone's talking about Brills. Fine dining from a small exclusive menu is in a glorious room with sweeping ceilings, but there's an intimate cellar, atrium and casual front café as well.

Fig Tree Cafe (☎ 5381 1523; 59 Firebrace St; mains $8-11; ☉ breakfast & lunch) This is a good spot for coffee, cake or a steak sandwich.

THE ASCENT OF NATIMUK David Burnett

Fifteen years ago the sleepy town of Natimuk looked certain to play out the familiar story of a late-20th-century agricultural hamlet in decline: secondary industry gone, shops closing, young folk leaving for the big smoke, tumbleweeds spotted in Main St. The one thing it had going for it was Mt Arapiles, brooding enigmatically on the otherwise flat horizon and attracting a trickle of scruffy weirdos who flopped for months in the pine-dotted camping ground and climbed the mountain's crenulated orange flanks. A less likely kernel for a town's revival you couldn't imagine – many were 'dole bludgers', evading the government's employment bureaucrats, or drifters escaping who-knew-what-lives in Europe or New Zealand.

But as any of these newcomers could have told you, if you'd been able to track them down in a fleeting moment of horizontality and sobriety, Mt Arapiles is not your average mountain, and those it attracted were not your average campers. By the late 1980s, Mt Arapiles was already known in rock-climbing circles as a nexus of spectacular yet subtle natural wonders – buttressed crags, hidden gullies, soaring walls – and lizards, 'roos, echidnas, birds and other animals like Dreamtime totems made flesh; and the camping-ground regulars had woven a culture of decadence and spirituality in equal measures.

With house prices and job prospects at an all-time low in the early 1990s, some of the climbers began to migrate to run-down houses in Natimuk, scratching an income from seasonal grape-picking, climbing instruction and a cottage industry of climbing-gear manufacture. With plenty of time on their hands, and primed by an intimacy with the bush and its creatures, Natimuk's new residents festooned their sprawling yards with sculpture and architectural oddities; empty town buildings hosted art exhibitions; eccentric postcards and 'zines appeared on the climbing shop's counters; and cross-cultural links between the climbing and farming communities began to emerge, rooted in a shared love of the shimmering landscape.

In recent years, this trend has made Natimuk a centre of artistic creativity entirely out of proportion to its humble size and remoteness. The town now boasts a dance company, an annual arts festival – **Nati Frinj**, held in spring and featuring a street parade and spectacular aerial choreography on the town wheat-silos – and is home to writers, animators, painters and film makers, some with impressive international awards to their names. No longer a declining backwater or climber's pit-stop, Natimuk's future is assured.

Cafe Bagdad (☎ 5382 0068; 48 Wilson St; meals $9-16; ☺ lunch Tue-Fri, dinner Tue-Sat) The decor is relaxed, the menu a mix of Indian, Asian and Oz, and the coffee excellent. It's a popular spot for climbers heading to Mt Arapiles.

Olde Horsham Restaurant (☎ 5382 6999; Western Hwy; mains $24; ☺ dinner Mon-Sat) The glorious dining room is full of olde-worlde charm. Or if you prefer a little less elegance, there's fine dining in the old Melbourne tram out the back. The menu has a touch of nostalgia too – definitely go for the swagman's roast.

Getting There & Away
BUS
Bus services from Horsham include: south along the Henty Hwy to Hamilton (7.45am Monday to Friday) and west along the Wimmera Hwy to Naracoorte, SA (1.45pm Monday to Friday). There are also **buses** (☎ 5381 1871) north along the Henty Hwy to Mildura on Tuesday, Thursday and Friday and **buses**

(☎ 5352 1501) north to Rainbow via Dimboola on Thursday. All these buses leave Horsham from the **old Police Station** (24 Roberts Ave).

To get to the Grampians, take the **V/Line** (☎ 13 61 96) bus to Stawell (p267) and another bus from there.

TRAIN
The **train station** (Railway Ave) is about 1km north of the town centre. The *Overland* from Melbourne stops here (at 2am!) Thursday to Sunday. There are four train/bus services daily from Melbourne changing at Ballarat ($50, 4½ hours), and two changing at Ararat.

MT ARAPILES STATE PARK
Australia's best venue for rock climbing, Mt Arapiles has more than 2000 routes, ranging from basic to advanced climbs, with colourful names such as Violent Crumble, Punks in the Gym and Cruel Britannia. Rock climbers come here from all around the world and

on most days you can see them – or join them – scaling the mountain. The park is also popular for walks and picnics, and has over 500 species of native plants plus kangaroos, possums, goannas and some rare bird species, including the peregrine falcon. Dogs should not be taken into the park.

The nearby sleepy town of **Natimuk** is home to several climbers who have brought with them an interesting range of tastes and attitudes (see opposite).

Mt Arapiles looms up on the horizon as you approach from the Wimmera Hwy – it's known as the 'Ayers Rock of the Wimmera'. You can drive to the summit along the sealed Lookout Rd.

Centenary Park is a picnic area and camping ground at the foot of the mountain, named in 1936, 100 years after Major Mitchell climbed and named the mountain. The pine trees that were planted at the time provide good shade and protection. There are picnic tables, fireplaces, bore water and toilets.

There are two short and steep walking tracks from Centenary Park to the top of Mt Arapiles, and another rough road leads around the boundary of the park.

Rock Climbing
Several operators, including the **Climbing Company** (☎ 03-5387 1329; www.wimmera.com /users/climbco) and **Arapiles Climbing Guides** (☎ 03-5387 1284; users.netconnect.com.au/~climbacg), offer climbing and abseiling instruction. A group instruction and climb costs from $50 for a half-day.

Sleeping & Eating
Duffholme Cabins & Museum (☎ 03-5387 4246; Natimuk–Goroke Rd; dm/d $6/44) This extraordinary cottage in natural scrub is fully self-contained. The museum shows the story of three children rescued from the bush. There's plenty of wildlife around and scenic views of Mt Arapiles. Ring to make arrangements (it's not staffed) and get directions.

National Hotel (☎ 03-5387 1300; fax 5387 1297; 65 Main St; s $22, cabin d $66; ☷) This Natimuk hotel has comfortable little rooms and self-contained cabins. The pub serves **counter meals** (mains $10-15; ☽ lunch Mon-Sat, dinner Wed-Sat).

Camping ground (Centenary Park; camp sites per 2 people $2) Known locally as 'the Pines', this is a popular spot at the base of the mountain,

with toilets and a washbasin. Dogs are not allowed.

Natimuk Lake Caravan Park (☎ 03-5387 1462; fax 5387 1567; Lake Rd; camp sites per 2 people from $12, d onsite caravans from $35) This is beside Lake Natimuk about 4km north of Natimuk. It offers full facilities like barbecues and laundry.

Getting There & Away
The weekday bus service between Horsham and Naracoorte will drop you at Mt Arapiles ($7.50).

DIMBOOLA
☎ 03 / pop 1550
Cute and attractive Dimboola is on the idyllic Wimmera River. The river is lined with red gums making shady picnic spots all along its banks. It is a historic town, made famous in 1969 by Jack Hibberd's play *Dimboola*, about a country wedding, and the subsequent film. It has some fine old buildings, but most importantly it's the 'Gateway to the Little Desert' (the park starts 4km south).

The **visitors centre** (☎ 5389 1588; dimboola@net connect.com.au; 109 Lloyd St; ☽ 9am-5pm Tue & Fri, 6-8pm Mon, Wed & Fri, 10am-noon Sat; ☐) is in the Dim E-Shop. At other times visit Ron and Jill at the caravan park.

Pink Lake is a colourful salt lake beside the Western Hwy about 9km northwest of Dimboola.

Ebenezer Aboriginal Mission Station was established in Antwerp, 18km north of Dimboola, by Moravian missionaries in 1859. The historic buildings have been classified by the National Trust. You can visit the small cemetery and take in the eerie, haunting beauty of the mission and the disused farm buildings. The mission is signposted off the Dimboola–Jeparit road.

Nicolas Olive Estate (☎ 5389 1073; Horseshoe Bend Rd; ☽ 8am-7pm), a short distance south across the river, is a producer of extra virgin olive oil, with tastings and cellar-door sales.

The enthusiastic owners of Pomponderoo Bush Retreat (p276) run **Oasis Desert Adventures** (☎ 0419-824 618), a fun way to see the desert and learn about it. Tours and prices can be catered to your needs.

Festivals & Events
The **Dimboola Rowing Regatta** (Nov) has been held here on the Wimmera River since 1884. It's the biggest regatta in country Victoria.

Sleeping

Pomponderoo Bush Retreat (☎ 5389 1957, 0419-824 618; www.takeabreak.com.au/PomponderooBushRetreat .htm; Horseshoe Bend Rd; B&B d/f from $85/105; ❂ ❂) Get the feel of the bush in this very natural retreat, but enjoy all the luxuries in the delightful timber cottages. The owners also run desert tours (see p275).

Victoria Hotel (☎ 5389 1630; fax 5389 2050; Lochieal St; B&B s/d from $35/50) This well-preserved 1920s pub with fantastic lacework-trimmed, vine-covered veranda and renovated rooms is family owned and run. The **bistro** (mains $12-18; ❂ lunch & dinner) serves basic pub food.

Riverside Host Farm (☎ 5389 1550; Riverside Rd; camp sites per 2 people $18; cabins from s/d $55/77; ❂) The cabins at this lovely property are on the Wimmera River – you'll be treated to a short boat trip when you arrive. There's a lavender-oil still, camp kitchen, barbecue area, canoes for hire (per hour $10) and a camping ground. You can take a boat tour from here into the Little Dessert (per person $8 an hour). Or take a horse-drawn wagon ride (per group $50).

Dimboola Riverside Caravan Park (☎ 5389 1416; dimboolapark@telstra.com; 2 Wimmera St; camp sites per 2 people from $18, d cabins from $68) This is a beautiful park in a scenic setting beside the Wimmera River with grounds that are shaded by an assortment of eucalyptus and pine trees.

Getting There & Away

The *Overland* will stop, by request when you buy your ticket, at Dimboola at about 2.30am. Otherwise from Melbourne there's the **V/Line** (☎ 13 61 96) train to Ballarat or Ararat and bus to Dimboola ($52.50). The bus stops in Main St behind the Town Shire office.

NHILL

☎ 03 / pop 1900

Although Nhill is an Aboriginal word meaning 'mist over the water', there's not much water around these parts. Lake Nhill is usually a dry lakebed. The town is a wheat industry centre, as evidenced by the huge grain silos and flour mills.

Nhill was the setting of the 1996 film *The Road to Nhill*, about the impact of a car accident on the community. It was also once the home of the lyric poet John Shaw Neilson, and the cottage he was born in (in Penola, South Australia) has been restored and erected on the highway west of town.

The Nhill–Harrow road heads south through the centre of the Little Desert National Park. The **Stringybark Nature Walk** starts just off this road about 20km south of Nhill (see below).

The **visitors centre** (☎ 5391 3086; www.hindmarsh .vic.gov.au; Victoria St; ❂ 9am-5pm; ▣) is in the centre strip by the rotunda.

Sleeping & Eating

Little Desert Lodge (☎ 5391 5232; www.littledesert lodge.com.au; camp sites per 2 people $13; bunk r $15; B&B s/d from $70/95; ❂) Run by Whimpey Reichelt (one of Victoria's 'living treasures'), this retreat 16km south of Nhill, is on the edge of the Little Desert National Park. The complex includes a camping ground and bunk rooms (you must supply your own linen). There's a **dining room** (set dinner from $22; ❂ breakfast, lunch & dinner), barbecue area, campfire and a mallee-fowl aviary (tour $8). The lodge runs park tours (½-/¾-day $40/65) and evening spotlight walks.

Union Hotel (☎ 5391 1722; fax 5391 1688; 41 Victoria St; B&B s/d $25/45) In the centre of Nhill, this old hotel has basic rooms upstairs, with guest lounge, breakfast room and a gorgeous veranda. Downstairs, the **bistro** (mains $14-22; ❂ lunch & dinner) serves interesting meals like Tahitian chicken, or you can tuck into an $8 meal in the bar.

Wimmera Motel (☎ 5391 1444; wimmeramotel@ yahoo.com.au; 103 Victoria St; s/d/f from $49/62/85; ❂) This motel on the western side of town has bright rooms set around a courtyard.

Zero Inn (☎ 5391 1622; fax 5391 1552; Western Hwy; s/d from $66/84; ❂ ❂) Enjoy the pool here. The restaurant serves dinner Monday to Friday.

Nhill Caravan Park (☎ 5391 1683; www.caravan parksvictoria.com; camp sites per 2 people from $18, d cabins from $45; ❂ ❂) You can have a relaxing stay in this quiet spot after your desert experiences.

Caffe Kudos (☎ 5391 1467; 24 Victoria St; meals $5-12; ❂ breakfast & lunch Mon-Sat) Pretty in blue, this is a relaxed place for pastas, soups, cake and coffee.

LITTLE DESERT NATIONAL PARK

Visitors expecting rolling sand dunes are in for a surprise: like most Australian deserts, this one is well-vegetated because the native flora is so well adapted to these conditions. The soil is mainly sandy, but the park is rich in flora and fauna that thrive in the dry environment. There are over 670 indigenous plant species and in spring and early summer the landscape is transformed into a colourful wonderland of wildflowers. Over 220 species of birds have been recorded here, and you may also see possums, kangaroos and reptiles such as the bearded dragon and stumpy-tailed lizard. The best-known resident is the malleefowl, an industrious bird that can be seen in an aviary at the Little Desert Lodge. See p283 for more on this unusual bird.

The park covers a huge 132,000 hectares and the vegetation varies substantially due to the different soil types, climate and rainfall in each of its three blocks (central, eastern and western). The rainfall often reaches 600mm per year, but summers are dry and very hot.

In the late 1960s the state government announced a controversial plan to clear the area for agriculture. Conservationists and environmentalists protested, and the Little Desert became a major conservation issue. Finally, it was declared a national park and was expanded to its present size in 1986.

There are two sealed roads: the Edenhope–Kaniva and Harrow–Nhill roads. The road from Dimboola into the park is gravel, but the tracks are mostly sand only suitable for 4WD vehicles or walking; some are closed to 4WDs in the wet season (July to October).

If you want a brief introduction to the park there are several well-signposted walks: south of Dimboola the **Pomponderoo Hill Nature Walk**, south of Nhill the **Stringybark Nature Walk** and south of Kiata the **Sanctuary Nature Walk**. Other longer walks leave from the camping ground south of Kiata, including a 12km trek south to the Salt Lake. Always carry water and notify the rangers at **Parks Victoria** (☎ 03-5389 1204) before you set out. The rangers will also give you advice on where to go and what to look for at different times of the year.

Little Desert Lodge (see opposite) and Pomponderoo Bush Retreat (see opposite) offer guided tours and walks in the park.

Sleeping

Parks Victoria has **camping grounds** (camp sites per 2 people $12) at Horseshoe Bend and Ackle Bend, both on the Wimmera River south of Dimboola, and another one about 10km south of Kiata. All sites have drinking water, toilets, picnic tables and fireplaces.

You can **bush camp** if you're doing overnight walks in the central and western blocks, but speak to the rangers first at the

Parks Victoria (☎ 03-5389 1204; Wail Nursery Rd) office, south of Dimboola.

See entries under Nhill (opposite) and Dimboola (opposite) for excellent accommodation options just outside the park.

Getting There & Away

There is no public transport from Dimboola into the Little Desert National Park. The only way in, if you don't have a car, is to take an organised tour or contact the information centres in Nhill and Dimboola for maps of signed tracks.

SOUTH OF THE GRAMPIANS

The plains below the Grampians have dramatic signs of a volcanic past: craters and lakes, eroded lava flows, lava tubes and caves, and miles of stone walls made of volcanic rocks. There was a period of violent volcanic activity some 19,000 years ago, when the earth's crust split and volcanoes such as Mt Eccles and Mt Napier erupted.

The local Dhauwurd wurrung Koorie tribe first saw European settlers around 1810. Within a few years settlers had moved inland, grazing their sheep on rich pastures, many of which were traditional meeting places and sacred sites of the local clans. This led to bloody conflict and many Aborigines were massacred. In 1841 the local Koorie population was estimated to be 7900; 22 years later, it was only 500.

After the 1840s, much of this area was owned by a select few families, such as the Hentys and Whytes, who amassed enormous wealth, especially during the heady days of the gold rush when there was a high demand for food. They were the Australian 'aristocrats', nicknamed the 'squattocracy'. After WWII the land was divided and today many properties are owner-operated holdings of around 400 hectares.

SKIPTON

☎ 03 / pop 450

The small rural town west of Ballarat and beside Mt Emu Creek has a few interesting buildings such as the **Skipton Hotel** (1859) and an old Gothic Presbyterian church complete with gargoyles. There's also an eel farm, **Eels Australis** (Cleveland St), where you can usually buy freshly smoked eels – coming from Ballarat, turn right at the bridge.

The **Mt Widderin Caves** (☎ 5340 2010; Lismore Rd; admission $1) are 6km south of Skipton. Part of a group of seven volcanic caves between Bacchus Marsh and Hamilton, the caves are actually lava tubes, formed as streams of lava cooled and the outer crust solidified, leaving a hollow centre. They are privately operated; you can explore it unaccompanied. Take a torch (flashlight) and old clothes, as some clambering and climbing is necessary at the entrance. Once you're inside, a 200m-long walk leads to an underground lake. It's open most days, ring ahead to check.

Mooramong Homestead (☎ 5340 6556; mooramong@netconnect.com.au; adult/child $8/4; s $20; B&B s cottages $55; 🅿 🖳), west of Skipton, is a gorgeous National Trust–classified building built in the 1870s for Claire Adams, a Hollywood actress. There's a great opportunity to stay in the lovely gardens, at the farmstay or cottages. Guests can use the tennis court and glamorous pool. Mooramong is signposted off the Glenelg Hwy, 3km west of Skipton.

DUNKELD
☎ 03 / pop 403

Picturesque Dunkeld has Mt Abrupt and Mt Sturgeon sitting behind it, like two benevolent sisters, with the Piccaninny Range between. The Grampians Tourist Rd from Dunkeld is one of the most scenic routes into the Grampians. Dunkeld has an amazing hotel, great café scene, craft shops and lots of accommodation options. In fact, it's one cute little tourist spot.

The town was established in the 1860s, but many of the buildings were destroyed by bushfires in 1944. The bright **historical society museum** (Templeton St; admission $2; 🕐 1-5pm Sun) in an old bluestone church has a local history collection, including Aboriginal artefacts and old photographs.

The **visitors centre** (☎ 5577 2558; www.sthgrampians.vic.gov.au; Parker St; 🕐 9am-5pm) has lots of useful information.

Sleeping & Eating
Southern Grampians Cottages (☎ 5577 2457; www.grampianscottages.com.au; 35 Victoria Valley Rd; d $90-185) These nine self-contained log cabins in a bush setting are well equipped with TVs, open fires and barbecues.

Aquila Eco Lodges (☎ 5577 2582; www.ecolodges.com.au; Manns Rd, Victoria Valley; cottages d from $190; 🅿) Like to be surrounded by luxury, natural bushland with flora and fauna tours, and a fabulous range of wild orchids? These lodges are sculptured into the bush among pieces of sculpture, between Dunkeld Sandscrape Golf Course and the national park. Local red-gum floors, picture windows, and worm-based waste management are all part of eco-sustainable luxury living.

Royal Mail Hotel (☎ 5577 2241; www.royalmail.com.au; Parker St; mains $14-31; 🕐 breakfast, lunch & dinner) This stylish place has a remarkable restaurant that people drive to from Halls Gap. The imaginative menu boasts dishes like *gado-gado* with sesame-spiced eggs.

Outside, and joined by a river walk, are three fabulous accommodation options: **Mt Sturgeon Backpackers** (dm $20), a house on a working sheep property; **Bluestone Cottages** (d from $140), delightfully squat little shearers quarters (you can bet they didn't get luxury like this!); and **Hotel Units** (s/d $100/115; 🅿 🖳), with totally modern decor, private decks and mountain views.

Griffins Hill (☎ 5577 2499; Grampians Rd; B&B d $130) Enjoy a gourmet breakfast among the time-capsule sculptured cows, while looking out over a beautiful garden – part of the Australian open garden scheme. The guest rooms are a delight.

Caffe Kittani (☎ 5577 2288; 109 Parker St; meals $8-20; 🕐 breakfast & lunch daily, dinner Fri & Sat) This is a pretty tearoom with Devonshire teas, hearty country meals and a **Cottage** (☎ 5577 2588; B&B d $85; 🅿).

Izzy's (☎ 5577 2677; www.izzys.com.au; mains $17.50-23; 🕐 lunch Wed-Sun & dinner Tue-Sun) Great Mediterranean atmosphere; Italian, French, Oz cuisine; Greek banquets with plate smashing; live entertainment Friday and Saturday; Mongolian beef, Beijing prawns; what more can one say?

HAMILTON
☎ 03 / pop 9250

The 'Wool Capital of the World' is the commercial and retail centre for one of the richest and the most intensively grazed wool-growing areas in the world.

The **visitors centre** (☎ 5572 3746, 1800 807 056; hvic@sthgrampians.vic.gov.au; Lonsdale St; 🕐 9am-5pm) is in the centre of town. One block south is the main shopping precinct along Gray St.

Sights & Activities

Hamilton Art Gallery (☎ 5573 0469; Brown St; admission by donation; ⏰ 10am-5pm Mon-Sat, 2-5pm Sun), known for its Australian Colonial art, depicting Western Victoria, also features a fine collection of silver, porcelain and Oriental ceramics and some interesting Tibetan and Indian pieces.

The **Big Woolbales** (☎ 5571 2810; Coleraine Rd; ⏰ 9.30am-4pm), looking like, guess what! oversized wool bales, contains wool-related displays, such as wool samples and shearing demonstrations.

The outstanding **Botanic Gardens** (cnr Thompson & French Sts) were designed by William Guilfoyle. It has trees such as Californian redwoods and weeping elms, that date back to 1870, and the grounds sweep around a pond, walk-through aviary, Victorian band rotunda and playground.

Large, artificial **Lake Hamilton** has a cycling/jogging track circling it. There's a barbecue and picnic area, and a playground at the end of Rippons Rd.

For garden lovers some of the properties in and around Hamilton open their **gardens** to the public. The information centre has the useful brochure *Gardens, Homesteads and Unique Properties.*

Sir Reginald Ansett began his aviation empire in Hamilton in 1931, with a passenger service to Ballarat. In 1937, backed by local money, he launched Ansett Airlines, which became one of Australia's major airlines. The **Sir Reginald Ansett Transport Museum** (☎ 5571 2767; Ballarat Rd; adult/child $4/2; ⏰ 10am-4pm) is in an original aircraft hangar housing displays relating to the Ansett empire, including a replica Fokker Universal aircraft.

The **Hamilton History Centre** (☎ 5572 4933; 43 Gray St; ⏰ 2-5pm Sun-Fri), in the old Mechanics Institute Hall next to the post office, has items of local history, photos and records.

Hamilton is the last refuge of the eastern barred bandicoot, an endangered Australian marsupial. It looks a bit like a bush rat and the colony on the banks of Grange Burn Creek is the last on mainland Australia. The **Hamilton Institute of Rural Learning** (333 North Boundary Rd) is trying to establish new colonies. It has a nature trail where you can see different examples of native flora and fauna.

Festivals & Events

The **Hamilton SheepVention** (early Aug), a trade show featuring wool products and related farming inventions, is held on the first Monday and Tuesday of August and attracts crowds of up to 20,000.

Sleeping

BUDGET

George Hotel (☎ 5572 1844; george-hotel@bigpond.com.au; 213 Gray St; B&B s/d from $54/65) This hotel has basic small units behind the hotel, right in the centre of things. Inside, the **restaurant** (mains $8-19; ⏰ lunch & dinner) uses local produce (you must order Merino chicken!). Meals can be served on the lacy veranda.

Lake Hamilton Caravan Park (☎ /fax 5572 3855; 8 Ballarat Rd; camp sites per 2 people from $15, d cabins from $50; ❷ ❷) It's lovely here, by the Grange Burn, and very close to everything.

MIDRANGE

Lenwin on the Lake Motel (☎ 5571 2733; fax 5572 3817; 24 Ballarat Rd; s/d/f from $62/72/98; ❷) The perfect spot for an early morning walk is this attractive, freshly painted place looking out over the lake.

Bandicoot (☎ 5572 1688; bandicootmi@ansonic.com.au; s/d/f from $60/79/101; ❷) This cheerful place with the ugliest looking animal out the front (sorry conservationists) has pleasant, quiet units, a bar and restaurant.

Garland Cottage (☎ 5572 1054; summerbridge@ansonic.com.au; B&B s/d $90/100) Walk out into a lovely cottage garden, then stroll along a pretty street into town. The cottage is self-contained.

TOP END

Mourilyan (☎ 5572 4347; goldsmithmotel@hotkey.net.au; 22 Pope St; B&B d from $110) This stunning period house glittering with crystal has a billiards room, guest lounge and 1870s four-post beds, but the gourmet breakfast is totally modern.

Botanical Comfort Inn (☎ 5572 1855; fax 5571 2295; cnr Thompson & French Sts; s/d $103/116; ❷) Opposite the botanic gardens is this upmarket motel with units around a car park.

Eating

The corner of Thompson and Gray streets is where the foodie scene happens.

Gilly's (☎ 5571 9111; gillys@hotkey.net.au; 106 Gray St; mains $14-19; ⏰ breakfast & lunch daily, dinner Tue-Sat) This buzzing place has great decor, big lounge chairs, an interesting menu including eye fillet on colcannon mash, friendly staff and fresh yummy breakfasts.

Health on Gray (☎ 5572 4550; 109 Gray St; mains $4-6.50; ☺ breakfast & lunch Mon-Sat) Catering for everyone, including those with special needs, you can enjoy pastas and Tuscan tarts, or buy pure juices, local produce, cakes and takeaway.

Strand (☎ 5571 9144; 100 Thompson St; mains $23-32; ☺ lunch & dinner) Known for its excellent food, extensive wine list and superb atmosphere, the Strand has formal separate dining rooms with high ceilings and chandeliers. Or dine in the garden on meals like Moroccan spatchcock on couscous. There are lunch specials and, on Sunday, live music on the lawn.

Court Lantern (☎ 5572 2818; 144 Thompson St; mains $10-18; ☺ dinner Tue-Sun) Come here for good standard Chinese food and authentic noodle dishes, for eating in or takeaway.

Getting There & Away

V/Line (☎ 13 61 96) has a bus service from Melbourne ($47) that operates twice daily. There are also weekday services south to Warrnambool and north to Horsham.

Buses leave from beside the **train station** (Brown St).

AROUND HAMILTON

South of Hamilton are the Mt Napier and Mt Eccles National Parks. You can walk up to the summit of **Mt Napier** (447m) which last erupted 7000 years ago. It's known for its great diversity of volcanic features: the volcanic cone, with 25m deep crater, the lava flow and the lava tubes or caves. Most interesting are the **Byaduk Caves**, a series of lava tubes that were formed as the outer crust of the lava flow cooled and solidified. The caves can be explored by climbing down holes at ground level. You'll need a decent torch – look for the interesting ferns and mosses. The largest cave is **Church Cave**, which is about 50m long and 7m high.

Mt Eccles erupted 19,000 years ago, and the lava flow covered the countryside in all directions, with one massive tongue flowing 30km to the coast and on another 19km out to sea. Lady Julia Percy Island is a formation of this flow (see p226).

This park includes very scenic **Lake Surprise** (a great swimming spot, rimmed by three craters), several lava caves, a series of vents and craters, a huge koala population and a number of marked walking tracks. The **crater nature walk** (one hour) follows the rim of the craters, and another walk follows the lava canals to **Tunnel Cave** (four hours return).

Both parks are managed by Parks Victoria. There are no camping facilities at Mt Napier, but Mt Eccles has good camping, picnic and barbecue facilities. Ask for maps at the visitors centre in Hamilton (p278), the **ranger's station** (☎ 03-5576 1338) in Mt Eccles National Park, or **Parks Victoria Office** (☎ 03-5576 1014; 21 Huntly St) in Macarthur; ring for camping bookings and inquiries.

West of Hamilton on the Glenelg Hwy are the two pleasant towns of Coleraine and Casterton. In **Coleraine**, the **Tourist & Exhibition Centre** (☎ 03-5575 2733; ☺ 9am-5pm) is housed in the beautifully restored old train station. It has a selection of local arts and crafts. The 1884 **Matthew Cooke Blacksmith Shop** (91 Whyte St; ☺ 10am-noon Sat) still operates as a blacksmith's shop, using all the original equipment. Helena Rubenstein started her famous cosmetics empire here when she came to work in her uncle's grocery shop and started importing cosmetics. That grocery shop is now an antique and gift shop on the main street. Nearby is **Glenelg Fine Confectionery** which makes totally divine traditional hand-made chocolates.

The **Peter Francis Points Arboretum** (Portland Rd), 2km south of Coleraine, is an excellent walking spot with barbecues and playground. In 1968 the local community planted this 37-hectare quarry, and today the site has the largest number of eucalypt species in the southern hemisphere.

Casterton is known as Kelpie country – the birthplace of the Kelpie breed. It celebrates each June long weekend with the **Australian Kelpie Muster** (Jun). Casterton's **visitors centre** (☎ 03-5581 2070; castertonciv@glenelg.vic.gov.au; ☺ 9am-5pm) can give you details of accommodation available in both towns.

Bailey's Rocks, in Dergholm State Park 30km northwest of Casterton, is a scenic picnic area which features enormous green granite boulders.

Northwest

Victoria may seem green, densely populated, cold, busy… Then you reach the northwest and the land extends forever, skies are vast, rivers lazy and the sun is always meltingly hot. And it's dry, although the creekbeds and lake beds did fill three times in the last century.

Coming from the city, or from a region where trees are tall and the odd hill breaks the sky-line, the Mallee appears all horizon and endless, undulating, twisted mallee scrub. It includes the one genuinely empty part of the state – the semi-arid wilderness known as 'Sunset Country'. Nature lovers can delight in it, although it's frighteningly inaccessible except to experienced bushmen with wide hats and wider water bottles, in their high-clearance 4WDs.

Driving through windswept deserts and pale golden wheat fields, you reach a thriving regional centre – a true oasis town: Mildura (milld-*yoo*-ra), meaning 'red soil, where paddle-steamers on the Murray River take you back to the grand old pastoralist era. Foodies, club-bers, shoppers and lazeabouts have great holiday resorts, wineries, markets, boutique or budget shopping, and famous chefs running fabulous eateries on, or around, the river.

And through it all runs the splendid Murray. Follow the river along the state border. Sit on its banks and feel the strength of Australia's most important waterway, laugh at the antics of people enjoying it in steamers, cruisers, canoes, dinghys, inflated tyre tubes and speed boats, or get wet yourself. The weather up here allows it all.

HIGHLIGHTS

- Breezing down Australia's longest river, the Murray, on a **houseboat** (p290)
- Becoming enthusiastic about irrigation history at magnificent **Rio Vista** (p287)
- **Water skiing** (p293) forever, well 80km anyway, along the Murray
- Staying at the shearers' quarters in the **Murray-Sunset National Park** (p286)
- Picnicking on the banks of picturesque **Yarriambiack Creek** (p284)
- Gazing at the spangled night sky from an **outback observatory** (p285) out bush
- Touring Victoria's desert country with an **indigenous guide** (p289)
- Discovering that 'Life is too short to drink bad wine' on the **Golden Mile Wine Trail** (p294)
- Losing the shirt off your back at the **Manangatang races** (p285)

- www.murrayriver.com.au

THE MALLEE

The Mallee takes its name from the mallee scrub that once covered the entire area. A mallee is a hardy eucalypt with multiple slender trunks. Its roots are twisted, gnarled, dense chunks of wood, famous for their slow-burning qualities and much sought after by wood-turners. Mallee gums are canny desert survivors – root systems over 1000 years old are not uncommon – and for the Aborigines the region yielded plentiful food, including waterbirds and fish in the huge but unreliable lakes, kangaroos and other marsupials, emus, and the many edible plants that thrive in this environment. 'Mallee scrub' is actually a diverse and rich biosystem.

When the railway line from Melbourne to Mildura was completed in 1902, much of the region was divided into small blocks for farming. The first Europeans had terrible problems trying to clear it. They used mullenising – crushing the scrub with heavy red-gum rollers pulled by teams of bullocks, then burning and ploughing the land. But after rain, the tough old mallee roots regenerated and flourished. Farmers also had to deal with rabbit and mouse plagues, sand drifts and long droughts. Many pioneers gave up. However, today the Mallee is a productive sheep-grazing and grain-growing district. 'Sheep-wheat' is a common description of a farm here, but more exotic crops, such as lentils, are appearing.

Overclearing and bad irrigation practices have left significant areas of Mallee farmland battling salinity, as underground saltwater table levels reach the surface and make the soil useless. Farming's a tough business in the Mallee.

The attractions (other than huge horizons and friendly little towns) are the semi-arid wilderness areas, such as Wyperfeld National Park, Big Desert Wilderness Park and Murray-Sunset National Park. Collectively these parks cover over 750,000 hectares, and are particularly notable for their abundance of native plants, spring wildflowers and birds.

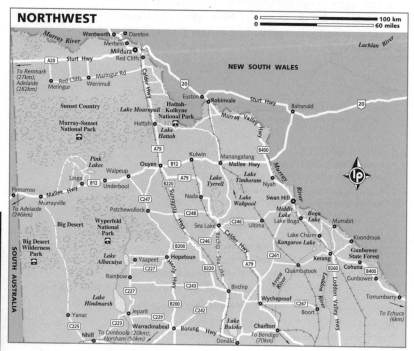

NORTHWEST

CHARLTON

☎ 03 / pop 1100

This small town started as a crossing point on the Avoca River. An inn was built here in 1863, and four years later a bridge was constructed across the river. The town frequently floods when the river spills its banks, but it's a great place for water sports.

Charlton is a pretty town, with some interesting historic buildings and churches. Trees line the river and main streets, and huge grain silos dominate the skyline. The **Golden Grain Museum** (☎ 5491 1359; High St; admission $2; ☺ by request) is in the old Mechanics Institute building (1882). It has local memorabilia, photos and historical items. Call in at the shire offices, or phone one of the telephone numbers displayed at the museum entrance, and someone will show you through. Stay on to enjoy a screening at the **Rex Theatre** (High St), an original old theatre in the centre of town.

Sleeping & Eating

Charlton Motel (☎ 5491 1600; fax 5491 1650; 158 High St; s/d/f $55/65/80; ☒ ☒) Just past the shops is this attractive motel with a pool and barbecue area, and bright spacious rooms.

Vale of Avoca B&B (☎ 5491 1999; fax 5491 2345; cnr Calder & Borung Hwys; B&B s/d $89/99; ☒) You'll love your olde-worlde guestroom upstairs in this historic hotel, and your perfectly cooked breakfast. Downstairs is **Cazza's Cafe** (☎ 5491 2324; meals $6-10), where you can enjoy home-cooked lasagne and the like, or pick up a dinner pack.

Charlton Caravan Stopover (caravan sites per 2 people $20) This interesting space has a central block of eight bathrooms with toilets for caravans to link into. Keys are available from the **East Charlton Hotel** (☎ 5491 1613; 53 High St). The Stopover is behind the pleasant **Travellers Rest** (51 High St), a public eating area, with a playground and toilets.

Across from Cazza's Cafe is a spacious river bank with facilities for **camping** (sites per 2 people from $8). Just pull in and find a spot.

DONALD

☎ 03 / pop 1400

This small highway town on the banks of the Richardson River has the **Bullock's Head**; a tree, in the middle of the river, with a bole that looks exactly like a bullock's head in profile, horns and all. It's signposted off the main road. In the heart of Donald are **historic buildings**, including the Banyenong Police Camp (1874), a slab-timber shepherd's hut (1850s), a colonial brick oven (1880s) and an old police lock up. Nearby a footbridge crosses the

---

A RARE OLD BIRD

The rare malleefowl is one of Australia's most fascinating birds. The mature birds are about the size of a small turkey, with wings and backs patterned in black, white and brown, which helps to camouflage them in the mallee scrub. They can fly short distances if necessary. Until the establishment of the Mallee's national parks, the malleefowl was threatened with extinction.

The life cycle of the malleefowl is an amazing story of survival and adaptation. It is the only one of the world's 19 mound-building birds that lives in an arid area, and it has developed incredibly sophisticated incubation methods to maintain its egg mounds at stable temperatures until the eggs hatch.

The male bird spends up to 11 months preparing the mound for the eggs. First he digs a hole, or opens up an old mound, fills it with leaves, bark and twigs, and covers the lot with sand to create the main egg chamber. When the mound has been saturated by rain and the organic material has started to decompose, he covers the mound with more sand – by now it can be up to 1m high and 5m in diameter – and tests the core temperature daily by sticking his beak inside. Once the temperature is stable at 33°C, he lets the female know that she can start laying her eggs.

The female lays between 15 and 20 eggs, which hatch at various stages over spring and summer. The male continues to check the mound temperature daily, and if it varies from 33°C he adjusts it by covering the mound or removing sand.

After hatching, the chicks dig their way up to the surface, can run within a few hours and fly on their first day out. However, the mortality rate is very high. The parents don't recognise or help their own young and, while an average pair of malleefowl will produce around 90 chicks in their lifetimes, only a few will survive to reproduce.

river to a small picnic area on **Scilleys Island**, which has tables and toilet facilities.

The **visitors centre** (Byrne St) is in the old police station that dates from 1865.

Sleeping

Donald Hotel (☎ 5497 1410; fax 5497 1736; 126 Woods St; B&B s/d $25/35; 🖳) This beautiful hotel has attractive rooms at the back with two guest rooms, both with TV. At the front is a **bistro** (meals $9-18; ☯ dinner Mon-Sat).

Donald Motor Lodge (☎ 5497 1700; fax 5499 1799; Cnr Borung & Sunraysia Hwys; s/d from $74/82; 🐾) The lodge, in a pleasant tree-shaded setting, has a playground, barbecue area and a **restaurant** (meals $12-22; ☯ dinner).

Donald Caravan Park (☎ /fax 5497 1764; cnr Borung Hwy & Moore St; camp sites per 2 people from $12, on-site d caravans from $32) Right on the lake, north of town. Perfect if you're into water sports.

WARRACKNABEAL
☎ 03 / pop 2500

Warracknabeal ('large gum trees by the water') was established in 1867 when a store was built on the banks of Yarriambiack Creek, which is lined with ancient red gums. Six of the town's old buildings are classified by the National Trust. These days it's a commercial centre for the surrounding wheat fields.

There's a **visitors centre** (☎ /fax 5398 1632; warrack@netconnect.com.au; 119 Scott St; ☯ 9am-5pm) next to the startling Tudor-style post office. Ask for the map of the **Yarriambiack Creek Walk**. The walk starts at Apex Park and follows the western bank of the creek past a fauna park, where there is a garden area with picnic and barbecue facilities, and an adventure playground. You'll enjoy the peace, variety of native vegetation and historical points along the way.

The **Warracknabeal Agricultural Machinery Museum** (☎ 5398 1616; Henty Hwy; adult/child $6/4; ☯ 10am-noon & 1-5pm Mon-Sat, till 4pm Sun), 3km south of town, has interesting old tractors, buggies, harvesters and wagons. There's also the **Historical Centre** (☎ 5398 2371; 81 Scott St; adult/child $3.50/1.50; ☯ 2-4pm Sun-Fri) in the old bank house. The **Wheatlands Warehouse** (10 Scott St) has an amazing spread of antiques and collectables.

Sleeping & Eating
Palace Hotel (☎ 5398 1071; 99 Scott St; s/d from $25/30) This is one of four pubs along the main

---

DETOUR: JEPARIT

At the southern end of Lake Hindmarsh, just 45km northeast of Warracknabeal, **Jeparit** is famous as the birthplace of former prime minister Sir Robert Menzies. Wander through the tiny township and think about how one can rise to fame. But don't miss the **Wimmera-Mallee Pioneers Museum** (☎ 5397 2101; 1 Dimboola Rd; adult/child $6/2.50; ☯ 9.30am-4.30pm Mon-Fri, 1-4.30pm Sat & Sun), an amazing place with original furnished homesteads, a cookhouse, interesting antiques and farm machinery.

You can kick back at the grand, stylish and very comfortable **Hindmarsh Hotel** (☎ 5397 2041; 50 Roy St; B&B s/d from $30/45). Its **restaurant** (mains $11-20; ☯ dinner Tue-Sun) is famous for its lamb shanks.

---

street. The basic rooms upstairs are often booked out, so book early. Downstairs the **bistro** (mains $11.50-19; ☯ lunch & dinner Mon-Sat) serves traditional pub meals.

Warrack Motel & Tourist Park (☎ 5398 1633; fax 5394 1488; 2 Lyle St; camp sites per 2 people $16, d cabins $55, motel s/d from $55/65; 🐾 🖳) If you like a restful spot, this park and motel beside the Yarriambiack Creek is perfect. It's a lovely stroll along the creek into town.

Pharmacino (☎ 5398 1713; 106 Scott St; meals $5.50-7.50; ☯ breakfast Mon-Sat, lunch Mon-Fri) Attached to, ho hum, the pharmacy, it's actually a delightful place with wholesome meals that include salads and focaccias.

Danny's Rusty Nail Restaurant (☎ 5394 1811, 0429-981 154; www.dannysrustynailrestaurant.com.au; Dumbuoy Rd; mains $20; ☯ lunch Sun, dinner Wed-Sat) This fun restaurant is 2km south of town. Danny uses local produce to present fine meals, like baked chicken breast stuffed with rusty nails, oops no, cheese and fresh basil.

WYPERFELD NATIONAL PARK
You'll fall in love with this naturalists' piece of paradise. Even the government had to admit, back in 1909, that it should be preserved. Now there's 356,800 hectares of tranquil dry lake beds, woodlands of red gum and black box along dry creek strings, and a glorious rolling sea of ancient mallee gums, with a good network of **walking and cycling tracks**. Emus and kangaroos are plentiful, and there's always lots of birdlife.

If you ever hear that the Wimmera River is in flood, go visit. The waters fill the lakes in turn – Hindmarsh, Albacutya and so on. Then the 450 species of wild flowers display themselves spectacularly. Birds fly in from as far as Western Australia, and tracks turn to mud baths. Great for the complexion.

The visitors centre is at **Wonga Campground** (Main Access Rd; camp sites per 2 people $12), about 7km north of the entrance. **Casuarina Campground** (sites free) is some way north and accessible by 4WD only – or by foot. It would be a good walk along a dry creek bed. Both campgrounds have pit toilets, fireplaces and rainwater. Contact the **ranger's office** (☎ 03-5395 7221) at **Yaapeet**, on the eastern fringe of Lake Albacutya, for more information. There are small **camp sites** (sites free) at Yaapeet Beach and at Western Beach, across the lake.

The atmospheric **O'Sullivan's Pine Plains Lodge** (☎ 03-5084 1216; fax 5084 1218; pineplains@big pond.com; Pine Plains Rd; dm $55), in the heart of the park, 25km west of Patchewollock, offers you a bed in a droplog homestead, with a huge living area, fully equipped kitchen, barbecue area, camp oven and an **astronomical observatory**. Birdwatchers can watch the malleefowls and Major Mitchell cockatoos.

The main access road is signposted off the Dimboola–Hopetoun road, which passes through Rainbow and Jeparit. The access road takes you north past Lake Albacutya into the centre of the park.

BIG DESERT WILDERNESS PARK

Unlike its southern cousin, Little Desert National Park (p276), the Big Desert Wilderness is 113,500 hectares of real desert wilderness. There are no roads, tracks or facilities, and no water. Walking and camping are permitted, but only do so if you are experienced and can use a map and compass. You have to be totally self-sufficient, ie carry your own food and water, take out your rubbish and use a camping stove for cooking. In summer, the temperatures are usually way too high for walking. Notify the **rangers office** (☎ 03-5395 7221) at Yaapeet before going.

The area is mostly sand dunes, red sandstone ridges and hardy mallee. There's an abundance of flora and fauna: 93 species of birds have been recorded, and there are some interesting small mammals, such as the western pygmy-possum and Mitchell's

hopping mouse. Over 50 species of lizards and snakes have also been recorded.

There are no access roads into the Big Desert. A dry-weather road from **Murrayville** (on the Mallee Hwy) to Nhill (on the Western Hwy) separates this park from the Wyperfeld National Park. This dirt road is very rough in sections and it may be impassable after rain. It also has buffer zones from the park, mostly of 5km-wide strips of state forest.

There are **camp sites** (free) on the outskirts of the park: east at Big Billy Bore in the State Forest, southeast at Broken Bucket Reserve and south at Red Bluff. Picnic spots are set up at the Springs and Moonlight Tank, east of the park.

OUYEN
☎ 03 / pop 1250

Ouyen (o-y'n) is a busy transport centre for the produce of the surrounding district – mainly wheat, oats, wool and lambs (the lambs feed on the surrounding saltbush, which gives their meat a distinctive flavour, popular with locals and gourmets alike).

There's a **visitors centre** (☎ 5091 3600; Oke St; ☒ 10am-3pm Mon-Fri) in the courthouse. Oke St is the shopping street.

If you're here in late October, you might catch the **Vanilla Slice Contest**, with competitors from all over the state baking their version of this humble confectionary.

Sleeping & Eating
Victoria Hotel (☎ 5092 1550; fax 5092 2550; 22 Rowe St; B&B s/d/f from $30/45/65) If you've worked up a thirst on the long hot drive, stop at this beauty for refreshment. It's one of Victoria's best examples of a classic country pub – a red-brick, veranda-fronted delight, with

---

IT'S NOT THE MELBOURNE CUP, BUT...

It's the **Manangatang Races** (☎ 03-5035 1440; www.countryracing.com.au; Manangatang Racecourse, Sport St). Manangatang is a one-horse town 55km east of Ouyen, but twice a year this small, sleepy hollow comes to life. All the farmers (and more than a few outsiders) come to town for these famous races. The racecourse is truly a bush track – some of the fairways from the adjacent golf course even pass through it! Race meetings are held in mid-March and mid-October.

NORTHWEST

emerald-green wall tiles and excellent stained glass. Inside, it feels as though time has stood still. But the **bistro** (meals $8-22; ☼ lunch & dinner) has certainly moved on. The salt bush prime Mallee lamb cutlets are a gourmet treat.

Ouyen Motel (☎ 5092 1397; fax 5092 1600; Calder Hwy; s/d from $58/65; ✲ ✧) This is one of a few motels along the highway, all of which charge about the same rates. Margaret, the friendly owner, offers bright spacious rooms.

Ouyen Caravan Park (☎ /fax 5092 1246; Calder Hwy; camp sites per 2 people from $16, d cabins from $58) This park is on the highway on the southern side of town. There's plenty of shade trees, and you'll have no trouble getting the van level. The friendly owners keep the park spotless.

Mallee Bakery (☎ 5092 2128; 29 Oke St; meals $4-12; ☼ from 6am) Claims to be the home of the vanilla slice – they're certainly good enough for that to be true.

WEST OF OUYEN

If you're visiting the Murray-Sunset or Wyperfeld National Parks, you may stop at **Underbool** or **Murrayville** to buy provisions and let someone know your whereabouts if you're going off the beaten track.

The old **Underbool Hotel** (☎ /fax 03-5094 6262; Cotter St, Underbool; s/d $40/55) has basic rooms and serves counter meals from Wednesday to Saturday. The **Mallee Fowl Hotel** (☎ /fax 03-5095 2120; Mallee Hwy, Murrayville; B&B s/d $60/73; ✲) is a lovely hotel near the South Australian (SA) border, with en suite rooms, motel units and a **bistro** (mains $7-16; ☼ lunch & dinner).

MURRAY-SUNSET NATIONAL PARK

Pack your hat, fill your water bottle and prepare to enjoy these stunning 633,000 hectares of mallee woodland that reach from the river red gums of Lindsay Island right down to pretty Pink Lakes (see right) near Underbool. Move slowly in your 4WD to catch glimpses of rare animals, especially at dusk. The park was established to save these unique native fauna, which suffered greatly from the clearing of 65% of the mallee scrub.

It you go for walks along the tracks, leave before dawn and be out of the sun before noon. As the wide, wide sky turns pink at dusk, venture out again to watch the birdlife and the magic of the night sky open before you.

You can go fishing and yabbying in the billabongs and creeks in the Lindsay Island

---

DETOUR: PINK LAKES

The **Pink Lakes**, a group of lakes at the southern edge of the park, are definitely pink, or purplish at times, and most colourful on a cloudy day. They get their colour from millions of microscopic organisms in the lake, that concentrate an orange pigment in their bodies. It's an easy drive from Ouyen – from **Linga**, on the Mallee Hwy, there's a signed, unsealed road that was built when salt was harvested from the lakes. Nearby is a basic camping ground, but beyond that you need a 4WD. Don't go exploring in a 2WD – one hour's driving equals one day's walking, and you won't see any water or passing traffic.

---

surrounds, and marvel at the snow-white sand dunes.

Rich in human history, the **Shearer's Quarters** (☎ 03-5028 1218; groups $55) has hostel-type accommodation on the western side of the park. It's pretty basic (freshwater, hot water and a fridge are supplied), and accessible only by 4WD.

For more information contact the rangers in **Underbool** (☎ 03-5094 6267; Fasham St) on the Mallee Hwy, or in **Werrimull** (☎ 03-5028 1218) on the northern side of the park.

THE MURRAY

Australia's most important waterway flows from the mountains of the Great Dividing Range in northeastern Victoria to Encounter Bay in South Australia – more than 2700km. It's also an unusual river. For very long stretches it collects no water from the country it passes through.

The Murray is a river with a history. It was travelled along by some of Australia's earliest explorers, including Thomas Livingstone Mitchell, Charles Sturt and Edward John Eyre. And long before roads and railways crossed the land, the Murray's paddle-steamers carried supplies and carted wool to and from remote sheep stations and homesteads, travelling for hundreds of miles along the Murray's winding waterways, and up and down the Murrumbidgee, Goulburn and Darling Rivers.

Many of the river towns carry evocative reminders of their riverboat days, including historical museums, old buildings and well-preserved paddle-steamers.

The Murray is of great economic importance. The irrigation schemes of northern Victoria support dairy farms, vineyards, market gardens, orchards and huge citrus groves that provide fresh fruit and supply the thriving dried-fruit industry, which exports its produce around the world. After years of irrigation, however, soil salinity has become a major problem, one that poses a long-term threat to the economic viability of much of this area.

The river is also famous for the magnificent forests of red gum along its banks, the plentiful bird and animal life, and leisurely riverbank camping. It is deemed to be in NSW and there's almost always 'twin' towns on either side, from the days before Federation (1901), when the states levied tariffs on goods carried across their borders: all major river crossings were likely to have customs houses on each bank.

The Murray is one of the state's great watersports playgrounds and is used for a huge range of activities, including fishing, swimming, canoeing, water-skiing, houseboat holidays and boat cruises. The Murray region is also a golfer's paradise, with plenty of excellent riverside courses.

The Murray Valley Hwy links all the major riverside towns, but is mostly separated from the river by flood plains, subsidiary waterways and forests of red gum. However, you can take advantage of the fairly frequent tracks (often marked 'River Access') that lead you to the banks.

MILDURA
☎ 03 / pop 25,000

As well as being one of the richest agricultural areas in Australia, Mildura is a popular tourist destination, with access equally convenient for people from Melbourne, Adelaide and Sydney in search of endless blue skies.

The main road into the town centre, Deakin Ave, is impressively lined with palms and gum trees, and at night is one continuous strip of neon lights from motels and takeaway food shops. It's easy to forget you're in the midst of Victoria's arid region when you see the lush green golf courses, endless orange groves, orchards and vineyards for which Mildura is renowned.

Mildura owes its existence to the Chaffey brothers and their irrigation systems (see p289). The early years were tough and full of frustrations, but when the Melbourne–Mildura railway line finally opened in 1902, the town's future was assured.

Orientation

Central Mildura is compact. Deakin Ave, a wide boulevard, runs east to the Murray River. Langtree Ave, one block north, is a shopping mall between Eighth and Ninth Sts. Farther east is the main café scene. The new Mildura Plaza is at the southern end of Deakin Ave, on the corner of 15th St. It's an ultramodern one-stop retail-therapy spot.

Mildura's urban sprawl extends south as far as Red Cliffs, a quiet little town with a big tractor (see p292).

Information

Accommodation booking service (☎ 5018 8380) At the visitors centre.

Main post office (cnr Orange Ave & 8th St) There's another in the Langtree Ave mall.

RACV office (☎ 5021 3272; cnr 9th St & Lime Ave)

Retro Bar (☎ 5021 3822; 28 Langtree Ave; ☺ from 9am Mon-Sat) Has Internet access.

Visitors centre (☎ 5018 8380; www.visitmildura.com .au; cnr Deakin Ave & 12th St; ☺ 9am-5.30pm Mon-Fri, 9am-5pm Sat & Sun) In the Alfred Deakin Centre; has interesting displays and books tours.

Sights
MILDURA ARTS CENTRE & RIO VISTA

This excellent **complex** (☎ 5018 8322; 199 Cureton Ave; adult/child $3/free; ☺ 10am-5pm) is well worth a visit. It combines an art gallery, a theatre and a historical museum at Rio Vista, the former home of William B Chaffey (see p289). The modern art gallery has a large collection that includes a European section, with various works by Sir William Orpen (a leading British society portrait artist) and Sir Frank Brangwyn, and a most prized painting, *Woman Combing Her Hair at the Bath,* by the French Impressionist painter Edgar Degas. Australian paintings include works by Fred McCubbin and Arthur Streeton, and there is an interesting Australian sculpture collection.

Next door is the historic **Rio Vista**. This grand homestead has been beautifully preserved, and the interior is set up as a series

MILDURA

0 — 0.5 km
0 — 0.3 miles

INFORMATION	
Main Post Office	1 C3
RACV	2 C3
Visitors Centre	(see 5)

SIGHTS & ACTIVITIES	
Mildura Arts Centre & Rio Vista	3 C2
Mildura Golf Club	4 A2
Mildura Waves	5 B4
Old Mildura Homestead	6 C1
Putt Putt Land of Fun	7 D3
Visible Effects Day Spa	8 B3

SLEEPING	
Camellia Court Holiday Apartments	9 C2
Commodore Motor Inn	10 C3
Grand Hotel	11 C3
Mildura Golf Club Resort	12 A2
Mildura International Backpackers	13 C4
Northaven Motel & Backpackers	14 C3
Olive House	15 B3

EATING	
27 Deakin	16 C3
Avoca	17 C3
Coffee House	18 C3
Dining Room One	(see 11)
Folkways Café	19 C3
Hudaks Bakery Café	20 C3
Restaurant Rendezvous	21 C3
Stefano's Restaurant	(see 11)

DRINKING	
Brewery	22 C3
Enjoy Wine	23 C3

ENTERTAINMENT	
Deakin Twin Cinemas	24 C3
Dom's Nighclub & Retro Bar	25 C3
O'Malley's Irish Pub	26 C3
Sandbar	27 C3

TRANSPORT	
Bus Depot	28 C3

of historical displays depicting life in the 19th century, with period furnishings, costumes, photos, and an interesting collection of letters and memorabilia.

OTHER SIGHTS

The information centre has a handy brochure called *The Chaffey Trail*, which guides you around some of Mildura's more interesting sights, including the **Mildura Wharf**, the **weir** and **lock**, **Mildara Winery** and the **Old Psyche Bend Pump Station**.

The **Old Mildura Homestead** (☎ 5018 8322; Cureton Ave; adult/child $2/free; ☒ 9am-6pm), a cottage that was the first home of William B Chaffey, is in a heritage park on the banks of the Murray. There are a few other his-

toric buildings in this pleasant park, which has picnic and barbecue facilities.

Activities

PADDLE-STEAMER CRUISES

The famous **PS Melbourne** (☎ 5023 2200; Mildura Wharf; 2-hr cruise adult/child $22/8) is one of the original paddle-steamers and is the only one still driven by steam power – watch the operator stoke the original boiler with wood. Cruises depart at 10.50am and 1.50pm Sunday to Thursday. The fastest of the riverboats, the **PV Rothbury** (☎ 5023 2200; Mildura Wharf) offers dinner or winery cruises ($48) on Thursday, and a cruise that includes lunch on Tuesday ($21). The winery cruise visits the Trentham Estate Winery.

THE CHAFFEY BROTHERS

The Canadian brothers George and William Chaffey were famous 19th-century irrigation engineers who set up an irrigation colony at Mildura.

A promotional scheme was launched in 1887 that attracted more than 3000 settlers to the area. They cleared scrub, dug irrigation channels and built fences. Two massive pumping-station engines were shipped from England, one of which now stands in front of Rio Vista (the home William built).

The early years of the settlement weren't easy. There was an economic collapse in the 1890s, rabbit plagues and droughts, and clearing the mallee scrub was a nightmare. George became disillusioned, and in 1896 returned to the USA.

In 1889 William built Rio Vista, a grand riverside homestead, to express his confidence in the new settlement. But his wife, Hattie, died during childbirth before it was finished, and their newborn son died five months later. William later married his deceased wife's niece, also named Hattie, and lived in Mildura until he died in 1926 at the age of 70.

Cruises depart from the Mildura Wharf, and run more often during school-holiday periods. Most cruises go through a lock, which is interesting to watch (as the gate shuts and opens, the water levels change). There are also overnight cruises (p290).

ADVENTURE ACTIVITIES

Wild Side Outdoors (☎ 5024 3721; wildsideoutdoors@ bigpond.com) runs walking/mountain-bike/ canoe ecotours (from $25/45/55). These range from two-hour trips to King's Billabong Nature Reserve to two-day experiences to Hattah-Kulkyne National Park. It also has canoe hire (per hour $30).

GOLF

The **Mildura Golf Club** (☎ 5023 1147; 12th St; 18 holes $20, club hire $10) is an excellent course, open to the public, that also offers a pool, barbecue and bistro, all in a beautiful setting. The **Riverside Golf Course** (☎ 5023 1560; Park St, Nichols Pt; 18 holes $18) is also a good course in a lovely setting, with a licensed clubhouse.

HOT-AIR BALLOONING

Hot-air balloon trips are offered daily at dawn by **Camerons Mildura** (☎ 5021 2876; www .cameronsmildura.com.au; 40 min from $240), weather permitting. The price includes champagne afterwards to celebrate your dream trip.

SWIMMING

Mildura Waves (☎ 5023 3747; cnr Deakin Ave & 12th St; adult/child from $5/2.50; ⏰ 6am-9pm Mon-Thu, 6am-7pm Fri, 8am-6pm Sat & Sun) is a modern complex with an artificial wave pool, among many other facilities.

If you are swimming in the mighty, muddy Murray be careful of snags and sudden huge holes, and never jump into water when you can't see what's below the surface. **Apex Beach** is a favourite spot.

OTHER ACTIVITIES

There's a huge range of holiday-oriented entertainment. Stuff like **minigolf**, **tenpin bowls** and **Formula K Go Karts** that are somehow irresistible when you're taking a break. Check with the visitors centre for details, or perhaps head off to **Putt Putt Land of Fun** (☎ 5023 3663; cnr 7th St & Orange Ave; ⏰ 10am-7.30pm), which has to be good, with a name like that.

Afterwards you'll need a few hours at **Visible Effects Day Spa** (☎ 5022 8000; www.visibleeffects .com.au; 157 Lime Ave). Try the mineral mud body mask, followed by a body-butter massage, in a cocoon of music and aromatherapy.

Tours

Several Aboriginal operators run tours concentrating on culture, history (which covers 45,000 years if you go to Lake Mungo) and wildlife. The best-known is **Harry Nanya** (☎ 5027 2076; www.harrynanyatours.com.au), whose tours include an excellent day trip to Mungo National Park (per adult/child $85/45) in New South Wales (NSW), or a fine Wineand-Dine Tour ($75) if that's more your scene – you'll visit several wineries along the Murray and enjoy lunch overlooking the Darling River.

An alternative is **Jumbunna Tours** (☎ 0412-581 699), which also offers a range of tours at similar prices.

Junction Tours (☎ 0408-596 438, 5021 4424; day trips adult/child $120/92) has day trips from Mildura to Broken Hill via Wentworth on Monday, Wednesday and Friday, or outback tours to Menindee from Broken Hill.

Paddleboat Coonawarra (☎ 5023 3366, 1800 645 103; www.pbcoonawarra.com.au; 5-day cruise per person from $515) offers three- and five-day cruises, with all meals provided, or book the whole boat for up to 36 people.

Festivals & Events
Mildura's main festivals:

Mildura Wentworth Arts Festival (Mar)
Mildura 100 Ski Race Held over Easter.
International Balloon Fiesta (Jul) In the first week of that month.
Mildura Country Music Festival (Sep) During the school holidays.
Jazz, Food & Wine Show (Oct/Nov)
Mildura Show (☎ 5018 8380; www.mildura.vic.gov.au; mid-Oct) One of the largest festivals in rural Victoria.

Sleeping
Staying on a houseboat is a great way to see the river. Over 20 companies hire houseboats that range from two- to 12-berth and from modest to luxurious. Most have a minimum hire of three days, with prices from around $100 a night, dramatically more in summer and school holidays. Contact the visitors centre or RACV office (p287) for more details.

See also the houseboat review, right.

BUDGET
There are nearly 30 camping grounds and caravan parks around Mildura.

River Beach Camping Ground (☎ 5023 6879; fax 5021 5390; Cureton Ave; camp sites per 2 people from $8, d cabins/villas from $55/75; 🏊) It's a total outdoor experience, staying in this bushland setting near Apex Beach. There's camp fires, a bush kitchen, barbecue area, boat ramp, good swimming, walking and cycling, and a café.

Golden River Caravan Gardens (☎ 5021 2299; fax 5021 1364; camp sites per 2 people from $24, d cabins from $60) On the river, this is 5km northwest of the town centre, and has excellent facilities.

Mildura International Backpackers (☎ /fax 5021 0133; 5 Cedar Ave; dm $20, weekly rate $120) All the rooms have two beds (not bunks). Your hosts will help you find work, and they cook up a fine barbecue.

Northaven Motel & Backpackers (☎ 5023 4499; 138 Deakin Ave; dm/s/d from $20/55/66; 🏊 🖳 🖵) This rather blue motel set around a swimming pool has four- to six-bunk rooms in one

section (weekly rate $100), so it's popular with fruitpickers. The motel units are rather rundown, but good value, and very quiet – fruitpickers don't party late. There's a barbecue area and games room. Just catch the bus along Deakin Ave to get here.

MIDRANGE
Commodore Motor Inn (☎ 5023 0241; www.commodore -mildura.com.au; cnr Deakin Ave & 7th St; d/f from $90/130; 🏊 🖳) Right in the centre of town, the Commodore has an indoor pool, modern décor, a cocktail garden and a quality restaurant.

Mildura Golf Club Resort (☎ 1300 366 883; www .milduragolfclub.com.au, 12th St; s & d from $77; 🏊 🖳) This is the place for golf enthusiasts, and those who enjoy lazing comfortably while others chase little white balls. The motel units are right on the golf course, and there's a barbecue area, great pools, abundant birdlife, and a bar and bistro.

Camellia Court Holiday Apartments (☎ 5029 1555; camellia@vic.hotkey.net.au; 169 Cureton Ave; d/q/f from $96/114/135; 🏊 🖳) Opposite the river, next to a playground and just along from the Art Centre. Perfect spot. The décor is totally '70s, but apartments are spacious, with a kitchen, laundry, TV and dishwasher, lovely outlooks, and a pleasant pool and barbecue area.

TOP END
Grand Hotel (☎ 5023 0511; www.milduragrandhotel.com; 7th St; B&B s/d from $58/77; 🏊 🖳) Palm-fronted and boasting a few different architectural styles, the Grand reflects Mildura's development. Although it's a gambling venue, there are pleasant rooms upstairs and many suites, like the State Suite (singles/doubles $265/300), open onto a delightful courtyard garden. There are several bars and dining rooms, including a casual wine bar, a bistro: **Dining Room One** (mains $14-35; 🍴 lunch Mon-Fri, dinner Mon-Sat), and the award-winning Stefano's Restaurant (see opposite).

Olive House (☎ 0419-355 748; www.olivehouse.com .au; 170 9th St; B&B d $145, extra person $45) This fine Federation cottage tastefully combines pressed-tin walls and ceilings, and period furnishings with a very modern bathroom, including a spa bath. Your booking gives you the whole cottage, a tranquil cottage garden, breakfast provisions and a few evening luxuries!

Acacia Houseboats (☎ 0428-787 250; www.acacia boats.com.au; d/q minimum 3 nights from $400/530) Acacia has a number of gorgeous houseboats accommodating up to eight people, with everything supplied except food and drink. Prices vary depending on the time of year.

Eating
There's a great café and restaurant precinct along Langtree Ave and around the block, between the mall and the river.

Avoca (☎ 5022 1444; Waterfront; mains $18.50-29; ☺ breakfast Sat & Sun, lunch Tue-Sun, dinner Tue-Sat) This 1877 paddleboat is now a charming restaurant, with food, like seafood skewers or chicken salad, to suit all budgets, local wines, great coffee, and a moving scene of ducks, pelicans and rippling water, or the lights strung along the red gums twinkling and reflecting in the evenings.

Stefano's Restaurant (☎ 5023 0511; Grand Hotel, 7th St; set menu $77; ☺ dinner Mon-Sat) Down in the old cellars of the Grand Hotel is this atmospheric, award-winning restaurant. The set menu is a candle-lit experience of five delightful northern Italian courses, using fresh local produce, and extras like mouth-freshening sorbets. Bookings are essential.

Restaurant Rendezvous (☎ 5023 1571; 34 Langtree Ave; mains $16.50-27; ☺ lunch Mon-Fri, dinner Mon-Sat) A local favourite, the warm, casual atmosphere complements the perfectly prepared seafood, grills or unusual menu items, like stuffed figs, listed on the blackboard. It also features Sunraysia wines, and offers courtyard dining.

Coffee House (☎ 5022 2900; fstrangio@optusnet .com; 26 Langtree Ave; mains $9-13; ☺ breakfast & lunch) The coffees and teas are worth a rave, and breakfast is so good you'll come back for lunch. No wonder it's won awards.

Folkways Cafe (☎ 5023 5655; fax 5023 5566; 136A 8th St; mains $8.50-12; ☺ lunch daily, dinner Mon-Sat) It's tiny, but big on friendliness, with wonderful home-cooked food. The oxtail soup served with Maori bread is the best ever, or enjoy authentic Maori *hangi* (a feast of Maori food cooked over embers) while listening to live music and poetry from Thursday to Sunday.

27 Deakin (☎ 5021 3627; www.stefano.com; 27 Deakin Ave; mains $13-21; ☺ 8am-3pm) Owned by Stefano, an advocate for local produce, this gourmet deli serves cakes, pizza, antipasto or open sandwiches, or you can stock up on oils, jams and other tempting produce.

Hudak's Bakery Café (☎ 5023 1843; 139 8th St; mains $6-16) This bakery is the place to go for a quick snack, pie or sanger, with self-serve ready-to-go food in sparkling clean display cabinets.

Drinking
Enjoy Wine (☎ 5023 7722; www.enjoywine.com.au; 120 8th St) Sit in the old leather couches in the lovely old Hotel Mildura and taste the local wines until you decide which one to buy for dinner. It could take a while, there are 32 vineyards represented – a great way to start your night out. Tastings are free (should you choose to buy, wines per glass cost $4.50 to $7.50).

Brewery (☎ 5022 2988; www.mildurabrewery.com .au; 16 Langtree Ave; snacks $5-10, lunch & dinner $10-16; ☺ 11am-1am) It's no surprise that this microbrewery is the 'in' place. There's lots of glass and slate, and the fabulous stainless steel vats, pipes and brewing equipment really set the scene. Everything kicks on from the moment the doors open. Take a tour, taste and buy a few ales, kick back, eat and be merry. Food is served from 11.30am to 9.30pm Tuesday to Sunday.

Entertainment
Mildura has a small but lively nightlife scene. All the nightclubs are just two minutes' walk apart, so you can check a few out for a change of scene, or band.

Sandbar (☎ 5021 2181; cnr Langtree Ave & 8th St) There's modern mainstream live music from Wednesday to Saturday night, and an intimate courtyard for hanging out.

O'Malley's Irish Pub (☎ 5021 4236; cnr 8th St & Deakin Ave) Kicks on till late, especially Friday and Saturday when there are live bands.

Dom's Nightclub & Retro Bar (☎ 5021 3822; 28 Langtree Ave; ☐) You can enjoy a luscious snack, like roast-vegetable focaccia with goats' cheese, while surfing the Net, then settle in for a while. The music is mostly techno.

Deakin Twin Cinemas (☎ 5023 4452; 93 Deakin Ave) Most films cost $12. There's also a cinema meal deal ($17), which offers the movie of your choice and a meal at the **Workers** (☎ 5023 0531; 90 Deakin Ave), which serves a great range of bistro meals.

Getting There & Away
AIR
Mildura airport is about 10km west of the town centre, off the Sturt Hwy (A20). **Rex**

BIG LIZZIE

Eighteen kilometres southeast of Mildura, **Red Cliffs** is primarily notable as the final resting place of 'Big Lizzie', a huge steam-engine tractor.

The tractor, a massive monument to one man's inventiveness and stubborn persistence, was the brainchild of Mr Frank Bottrill, who designed it to cart wool from the outback sheep stations around Broken Hill in central New South Wales (NSW). It was built in a backyard factory in Richmond, Melbourne, in 1915.

With a travelling speed of two miles (1.6km) per hour and a turning circle of 60m, Lizzie wasn't built for city living and, once finished, Frank and his family set out on the journey north. Two years later they reached the Murray River, where Frank stumbled on the one small flaw in his plan – he couldn't get Lizzie across the border into NSW, as the river was in flood. So instead of Broken Hill, Lizzie was put to work in the Mallee, where she worked for many years clearing scrub and trees.

Lizzie was saved from rusty oblivion and brought to Red Cliffs in 1971, and now stands proudly in a small park on the Calder Hwy, where a taped commentary tells her story.

Airlines (Regional Airlines; ☎ 13 17 13; www.rex.com.au) operates daily services between Melbourne and Mildura, as does **Qantas** (☎ 13 13 13, www.qantas.com.au), with return fares from $240. Smaller local operators fly to other destinations, including Adelaide.

BUS

There is a **V/Line** (☎ 13 61 96; www.vline.com.au) direct overnight bus to Melbourne, leaving from the train station, nightly ($65, 9½ hours), except Saturday, as well as several daily train/bus services with changes at Bendigo or Swan Hill. V/Line also has a four-times-weekly bus service (Murraylink) connecting all the towns along the Murray River – destinations from Mildura include Swan Hill ($36) and Echuca ($42).

Greyhound Australia (☎ 13 14 99; www.greyhound.com.au) has daily services between Mildura and Adelaide ($54) or Sydney ($109).

The **Henty Highway Coach** (☎ 5023 5658) runs between Horsham and Mildura ($46) three times a week, stopping at many towns along the way.

Long-distance buses operate from a depot at the train station on 7th St.

Getting Around

There are regular bus services around town and out to Red Cliffs and Merbein, mostly during the week but there are a few on weekends. The visitors centre has timetables and bus-stop information.

Mildura Taxis (☎ 5023 0033, 13 10 08) operates 24 hours a day. There are several car-hire companies that operate out of the Mildura Airport's main terminal.

HATTAH-KULKYNE NATIONAL PARK

The vegetation of the beautiful and diverse Hattah-Kulkyne National Park ranges from dry, sandy mallee-scrub country to the fertile riverside areas closer to the Murray, which are lined with red gum, black box, wattles and bottlebrush.

When the area was proposed as a park in 1976, it was the most rabbit-infested part of the state. The rabbits were largely eradicated, but it has become evident that the 20,000-odd population of kangaroos are wrecking the fragile environment – the park can only carry around 5000 kangaroos. The sad thing is that while this huge kangaroo population is causing the degradation of the environment, and many of the kangaroos will die during the drought seasons from lack of food, their numbers can't be culled because the issue is too politically sensitive.

The **Hattah Lakes** system fills when the Murray floods, which is great for water birds. The many hollow trees are perfect for nesting, and more than 200 species of birds have been recorded here. There are many native animals, mostly desert types that are active in the cool of the night, as well as wetland species, such as the burrowing frog, which digs itself into the ground during the dry season and waits until there is enough water to start breeding. There are also a few reptiles. One, the mountain devil, is the inspiration for the great Aussie saying 'flat out like a lizard drinking' because it draws surface water into its mouth by lying flat on the ground. The vegetation varies considerably from season to season, and over 1000 plant species have been recorded, 200 of which are listed as rare or endangered.

The main access road is from the small town of **Hattah**, 70km south of Mildura on the Calder Hwy. The visitors centre, 5km into the park, will tell you if the network of tracks are passable. If so, there are two **nature drives**, the Hattah and the Kulkyne, and a network of old camel tracks, which are great for **cycling**, although you'll need thorn-proof tubes. Tell the rangers where you're going, and carry plenty of water, a compass and a map.

There are **camping** (sites per 2 people $12) facilities at Lake Hattah and Lake Mournpoul, but there is limited water and the lake water, when there is any, is undrinkable. Camping is also possible anywhere along the Murray River frontage, which is actually the **Murray-Kulkyne State Park**.

For more information contact **Parks Victoria** (☎ 13 19 63; www.parkweb.vic.gov.au) or the **Hattah ranger's office** (☎ 03-5029 3253).

ROBINVALE
☎ 03 / pop 1750
Robinvale is best known for its 300 days per year of sunshine and great stretch of river. You can water-ski forever, and they do in the annual **80km ski classic** held over two days in March, when the peaceful murmur from the river gums and wafting scent of eucalyptus is swapped for the roar of outboard motors and smell of fuel. Events head off from the boat ramp along Riverside Dr. Sit anywhere on the banks for a bird's-eye view. Or go bird-watching, which is good around here, as is the wine and olive tasting at local farms and vineyards.

There's a **visitors centre** (☎ 5026 1388) at the northern end of the main street.

Sleeping & Eating
Motel Robinvale (☎ 5026 3090; fax 5026 4306; 112 Bromley Rd; s/d/f $66/77/110; ❄ 🖳) Right in the centre of town, this small motel has a dining room serving dinner nightly, a barbecue area and a very welcome swimming pool.

Robinvale Hotel (☎ 5026 3030; rvhotel@iinet.net .au; cnr Perrin & George Sts; s/d/f $25/45/45) This old pub has basic but spacious rooms, and is very popular with fruitpickers (rate per week $100). The **bistro** (❄ lunch & dinner) serves traditional pub food.

Riverside Caravan Park (☎ 5026 4646; river4@ iinet.net.au; Riverside Dr; camp sites per 2 people from $13,

d cabins from $60; ❄) This delightful spot, five minutes from the shops and spread along the banks of the Murray, is the best place to relax. There's a boat ramp, barbecue area, kiosk, camp kitchen and disabled facilities.

Follarchies Cafe, Restaurant, Tavern (☎ 5026 1188; follarchies@iinet.net.au; mains $10-24; ❄ breakfast Sat & Sun, lunch & dinner Wed-Sat) Don't go anywhere until you've been to Follarchies. This fabulous new restaurant has a laid-back bar with old leather couches, and steak sandwiches on order, plus a swish dining area, all metal and glass, and the best menu – the orange-baked salmon ($23.50) is a taste treat. On Friday and Saturday the place buzzes until past 2am.

SWAN HILL
☎ 03 / pop 9700
Swan Hill, the low hill on which the town sits, was named by early explorer and surveyor Major Mitchell in 1836, after he was kept awake by swans in the nearby lagoon. The area was settled by sheep graziers soon after, and the original homesteads of the two major properties in the area, Murray Downs and Tyntynder, are still looking magnificent. Swan Hill is a major regional centre surrounded by fertile irrigated farms that produce grapes and other fruits, yet it has the easy pace of a country town.

The **visitors centre** (☎ 5032 3033, 1800 625 373; www.swanhillonline.com; cnr McCrae & Curlewis Sts; ❄ 9am-5pm; 🖳) is crammed with helpful maps and brochures.

Sights & Activities
SWAN HILL PIONEER SETTLEMENT
Swan Hill's major attraction, the **Pioneer Settlement** (☎ 5036 2410; Horseshoe Bend; adult/child $16/9; ❄ 10am-5pm Tue-Sun) is a re-creation of a riverside port town of the paddle-steamer era, and the entrance to the settlement is through the old *PS Gem*, one of the largest riverboats to have served on the Murray.

The settlement's displays include a blacksmith's workshop, stereoscope, general store (with very tasty boiled lollies), a great collection of old carriages and buggies, and an old-time photographic studio. The paddle-steamer *PS Pyap* makes short **cruises** (adult/child $12/7) along the Murray at 10.30am and 2.30pm. Other attractions include vintage-car and wagon rides. There's an excellent café and gift shop, as well as one of the

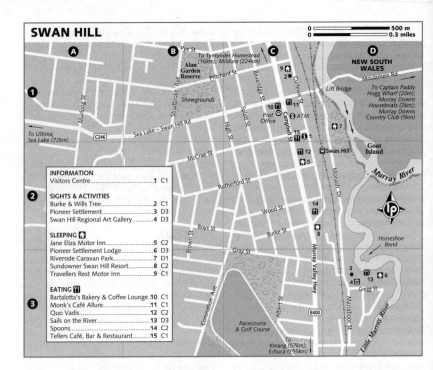

SWAN HILL

0 — 500 m
0 — 0.3 miles

NEW SOUTH WALES

To Tyntynder Homestead (16km); Mildura (224km)

Alan Garden Reserve

To Ultima; Sea Lake (72km)

To Captain Paddy Hogg Wharf (20m); Murray Downs Houseboats (2km); Murray Downs Country Club (5km)

Lift Bridge

Post Office

ATM

Swan Hill

Goat Island

Murray River

Horseshoe Bend

Racecourse & Golf Course

To Kerang (57km); Echuca (155km)

INFORMATION	
Visitors Centre	1 C1

SIGHTS & ACTIVITIES	
Burke & Wills Tree	2 C1
Pioneer Settlement	3 D3
Swan Hill Regional Art Gallery	4 D3

SLEEPING	
Jane Eliza Motor Inn	5 C2
Pioneer Settlement Lodge	6 D3
Riverside Caravan Park	7 D1
Sundowner Swan Hill Resort	8 C2
Travellers Rest Motor Inn	9 C1

EATING	
Bartalotta's Bakery & Coffee Lounge	10 C1
Monk's Café Allure	11 C1
Quo Vadis	12 C2
Sails on the River	13 D3
Spoons	14 C2
Tellers Café, Bar & Restaurant	15 C1

prefabricated houses shipped to Australia en masse to accommodate the dramatic increase in population during the gold rush.

Every night at dusk a 45-minute **sound-and-light show** (adult/child $10/6) is held, a dramatic journey through the settlement in a motorised transporter.

GOLDEN MILE WINE TRAIL

The wine trail is a section along the Murray River from Beverford in the south to Goodnight in the north. Some major wine companies and many boutique wineries along the trail offer cellar-door tastings and lunches overlooking the river. Wine festivals are held in the region every October, including the **Australian Inland Wine Show** on the third weekend in October. The region's motto: 'Life is too short to drink bad wine'.

OTHER SIGHTS & ACTIVITIES

The **Swan Hill Regional Art Gallery** (☎ 5032 9744; Horseshoe Bend; admission by donation; ☺ 9am-5pm Tue-Sun), opposite the Pioneer Settlement, concentrates on the works of contemporary artists.

MV Kookaburra (☎ 5032 0003; Moulamein Rd, Murray Downs; adult/child $35/16) has 1½-hour luncheon cruises leaving from Captain Paddy Hogg Wharf, 500m over the lift bridge on the NSW river bank, at 12.30pm Tuesday, Thursday, Saturday and Sunday.

Tyntynder Homestead (☎ 0428-500 417; Murray Valley Hwy; adult/child $8/4), 16km north of the town, has a small museum of pioneering and Aboriginal relics, and many reminders of the hardships of colonial life, such as the wine cellar! Visits are by appointment only.

Murray Downs Country Club (☎ 5033 1966; www .murraydownsresort.com.au) is considered a Swan Hill club, although it's 5km away across the river. It has a fine **golf course** (bookings ☎ 5033 1427; 18 holes $35), poker machines and cheap bistro meals.

Sleeping

There are no grand hotels or quaint B&Bs in the town at present, but you'll find plenty of very pleasant places to stay.

Pioneer Settlement Lodge (☎ 5032 1093; fax 5032 1096; Horseshoe Bend; dm/d from $25/65) Watch the river flow by at this rambling lodge with

THE BURKE & WILLS TREE

This magnificent Moreton Bay fig tree, the largest in the Southern Hemisphere, was planted in 1860, possibly by Burke himself. It was to commemorate the visit by Burke and Wills as they passed through Swan Hill on their ill-fated journey to the Gulf of Carpentaria. The planting was held at the home of Dr Gummow, who hosted the explorers and their party. Everyone expected the explorers to see the progress of their tree on their return visit, but they never made it. The tree is on Curlewis St opposite the bowling green.

glorious verandas. It's basic, but there are comfortable guest-lounge and dining areas. Other buildings cater to groups, with bunk beds (per person $17.50, linen $6) and leaders' rooms. There's a barbecue pit and spacious grounds.

Jane Eliza Motor Inn (☎ 5032 4411; jeliza@swanhill .net.au; 263 Campbell St; s/d/f from $68/75/165; ✗ ✿) If you've arrived by train, this place, near the station, is so convenient. It has a recreation room, solar-heated pool and barbecue area, and basic rooms on two levels.

Travellers Rest Motor Inn (☎ 5032 9644; www.best western.com.au/travellersrest; 110 Curlewis St; s/d/f $95/105/125) It sits gloriously in the shade of the Burke and Wills Tree, giving you a good feeling, as do the rooms, which are smart and comfortable.

Sundowner Swan Hill Resort (☎ 5032 2726; 405 Campbell St; s/d/f $114/121/217; ✗ ✿) The Sundowner's central courtyard is a landscaped tropical playground. Wander through to indoor and outdoor pools and a spa. Out past the garden is mini-golf, a half-sized tennis court and more.

Murray Downs Houseboats (☎ 5032 2160, 0428-500 066) This is the perfect way to experience the Murray. Houseboats for eight people cost from $700 for two nights, per extra night $150. High-season rates are significantly more – a seven-night cruise over Christmas/ New Year costs $2500. Don't fret. You can always hire a dinghy (two hours for $75).

Riverside Caravan Park (☎ 5032 1494; www.swan hillriverside.com.au; Monash Dr; camp sites per 2 people from $23, d cabins from $62; ✗ ✿) Enjoy this tranquil park set on the grassy river bank, with sensible safety areas for children. There's a

barbecue area, laundry and disabled facilities, and you're still right in the middle of everything.

Eating

There's a great café scene on Campbell St, especially on Sunday morning.

Quo Vadis (☎ 5032 4408; 255 Campbell St; mains $15-29; ✪ dinner) For a good Italian hit, come to this atmospheric, fun place with Italian favourites cooked to perfection. Next door, its takeaway or eat-outside pizza joint buzzes merrily.

Tellers Cafe, Bar & Restaurant (☎ 5033 1383; 223 Campbell St; mains $14-22; ✪ lunch & dinner Mon-Sat) Named Tellers because it's in an old bank, this lively, friendly place uses all-local produce, making dishes like smoked pork kassler. It's Mexican, Asian, Oz, with burgers, sandwiches and other snacks as well.

Spoons (☎ 5032 2601; 387 Campbell St; meals $5-10; ✪ breakfast & lunch) New in town, this small award-winning deli has a charming eating area, and an interesting array of risottos, salads, curries and couscous dishes.

Bartalotta's Bakery & Coffee Lounge (☎ 5033 1662; 178 Campbell St; meals $4-9) This is a cheerful place, offering cooked breakfasts, sandwiches or snacks.

Monk's Café Allure (☎ 5032 4422; 147 Campbell St; mains $7.50-18; ✪ breakfast & lunch) This popular contemporary café has outdoor dining when the weather's appropriate – which is always. There's a range of vegetarian dishes, pastas, stir-fries and steak sandwiches.

Sails on the River (☎ 5036 2410; Horseshoe Bend; meals $6.50-9; ✪ breakfast & lunch) Who can resist a café where you can sit at big log tables and watch the mighty Murray zap past. The food, such as roasts, pies and quiches, is good too, and the service is quick.

Getting There & Away

The **train station** (☎ 5032 4444) is near the centre of town, between Monash Dr and Curlewis St. **V/Line** (☎ 13 61 96; www.vline.com .au) runs several times daily between Melbourne and Swan Hill ($52, 4½ hours) via Bendigo. On some services there's a train between Melbourne and Bendigo and then a bus to Swan Hill, but there's at least one direct train each day.

There are V/Line buses 17 times weekly between Swan Hill and Mildura ($36), Echuca ($22) and Albury-Wodonga ($48).

NORTHWEST

EAST OF SWAN HILL

Travelling east, the highway takes you past a string of 50 or more lakes and swamps, including Lake Boga, Kangaroo Lake, Salt Lake (from where salt is commercially harvested) and Lake Charm. **Lake Boga** is famous for its glorious pelican colony. However, the area is best known for the huge flocks of ibis that breed here. **Middle Lake**, 16km south towards Kerang, is the best place to see the rookeries; there's a small bird hide on the lake.

The superb **Gunbower State Forest**, on Gunbower Island, features forests of magnificent red gums, and large areas of swamps and marshes. The forests have been extensively milled since the 1870s, supplying timber for hundreds of piers and bridges, for house stumps, railway sleepers, fence posts and paddle-steamer fuel in the river-trade days. Red gum is an incredibly beautiful and dense timber, a rich 'tawny port' red in colour, but because of its wide availability in Victoria it has always been taken for granted.

Gunbower also has abundant animal and birdlife, including kangaroos, possums, emus, goannas, turtles and snakes, and more than 160 bird species have been recorded here, including many water birds.

Cohuna is the main access point to the forest, linked by a bridge across Gunbower Creek. The network of marked dirt tracks in from the highway and throughout the forest are all on old river mud and become impossibly slippery after rain – only 4WD access is possible in the wet. There are plenty of walking tracks.

You'll find over 100 numbered riverside camp sites, with fireplaces and picnic tables, in the forest. Or live it up at these options:
Cohuna Caravan Park (☎ 03-5456 2562; fax 5456 2562; Island Rd; camp sites per 2 people from $17, d cabins from $50; 🔀)
Cohuna Hotel/Motel (☎ 03-5456 2604; pgibbs2@bigpond.com; 39 King George St; s/d from $60/65; 🔀)
Cohuna Motor Inn (☎ 03-5456 2974; fax 5456 2547; Murray Valley Hwy; s/d $60/70; 🔀)

North to the Murray

If they could see us now. Powering north on a broad band of bitumen. This used to be a track, the main route to Sydney, with bullock wagons piled with wheat waiting for those ahead to make the next river crossing. Just 40 years ago, heading north was a jostle of sedans, caravans and trucks on a narrow potholed road.

Today the Hume is Victoria's busiest freeway. The country rolls away as you sweep up the hills towards Seymour and as you top the ridge the air is warmer. By the time you reach the mighty Murray you are in endless summer (well it feels like that): pleasant country towns, wineries, galleries, fine food, and adventure sports. The Hume's little sister, the Goulburn Hwy, heads off at Seymour to Victoria's fruit bowl, the Goulburn Valley, a rich agricultural district. And the wineries here include the well-respected Tahbilk and Mitchelton.

The beautiful Goulburn River, the irrigation source that makes intensive agriculture possible, was once a complex of rivers, creeks and billabongs. It's been tamed by dams, levees and channels although you can still find pockets of riverine ecology, and there's still the occasional damaging flood.

Finally the magic of the Murray, Australia's largest river, sweeps you away to a tourist heaven of balmy weather, magnificent Murray red gums, watersports, paddle steamers, birdlife and, of course, wineries.

HIGHLIGHTS

- Going arty-farty in **Benalla Art Gallery** (p301) while your lunch is prepared
- Being cool under the stars at the **Wangaratta Jazz Festival** (p304)
- Bird-watching in the **Chiltern-Mt Pilot National Park** (p305)
- Walking the **Wiradjuri Walkabout** (p306), passing signed Aboriginal sites, at Wodonga
- Cruising by limo to the **wineries** (p307) of Rutherglen
- Steaming it up on a **paddle-steamer on the Murray** (p313) from Echua
- Dwelling on the past as you walk to the ruins of a former gold-mining township in **Whroo Historic Reserve** (p319)
- Lying on the grass watching **skydivers** (p320) drop from above at Nagambie

---

- www.visitvictoria.com

Getting There & Around

BUS

From Melbourne's Southern Cross station (formerly Spencer Street station) there are V/Line Friday buses to Wangaratta, Euroa, Benalla and Wodonga; a daily bus to Murchison, Tatura, Kyabram and Echuca; a weekday bus to Seymour, Murchison, Shepparton, Numurkah and Cobram; a Sunday bus to Seymour, Murchison and Shepparton; and a daily bus to Kyabram, Nathalia and Barmah.

Buses between Bendigo and Albury stop in Shepparton and Wangaratta. The daily Speedlink service between Adelaide and Sydney stops in Shepparton, Benalla, Wangaratta and Wodonga.

Trains connect with several bus services to smaller towns in the region.

TRAIN

The Melbourne–Wodonga **V/Line** (☎ 13 61 96) service follows the Hume Fwy, and daily trains stop at Seymour, Euroa, Benalla and Wangaratta. **CountryLink** (☎ 13 22 32) has its XPT (express) train service to Wangaratta,

Benalla and Albury (Wodonga). You need a reservation.

V/Line has two daily trains which stop at Seymour then branch off to Murchison East, Mooroopna and Shepparton.

MELBOURNE TO WODONGA

The Hume Fwy runs along the eastern edge of the Goulburn Valley, separating the valley from the foothills of the High Country in Victoria's northeast. Wangaratta and Benalla are the main centres. The minor roads and flat terrain make this an excellent region for leisurely cycling. The many country clubs boast excellent golf courses and country race meetings are held throughout the region.

KILMORE

☎ 03 / pop 2700

Kilmore was the first coach stop on the Melbourne to Sydney route, reaching its prime during the gold-rush years. Impres-

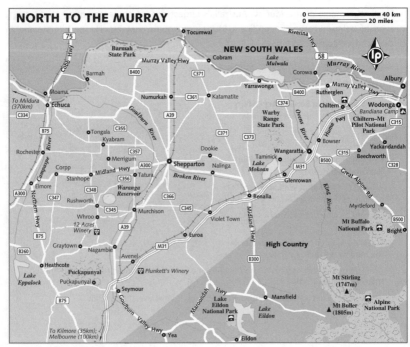

FROM BOLE TO BOWL

When insects burrow into the river red gums, sap builds up to form a bole, that very big growth you see on the trees. Local craftsmen turn the boles into all those clocks, bowls or sculptures you see in gift shops throughout the region. Boles are the only part of a fallen tree that can be removed from the bush. The rest of the tree must stay where it has fallen to provide housing for animals and river life.

---

sive old bluestone and brick buildings from the era include three pubs and the court-house buildings (1863). The **old post office and museum** will soon house a café and the old mill sells antiques and coffee.

The friendly **visitors centre** (☎ 5781 1319; msls@ vicnet.net.au; 🕑 9am-5pm) is in the central library. There's a **market** (☎ 5782 1406; William St) every Saturday and Sunday, and an **Agriculture Show** (East St; Dec), with showbags and all.

Whitburgh Cottage (Piper St; admission free; 🕑 2-4pm Sun) was built in 1857. The simple and solid bluestone cottage, with twin-peaked slate roof, has been preserved as an historic museum. It's on the road to the ruins of the Old Kilmore Gaol which burnt down in 2004.

Sleeping & Eating

Kestrel Motor Inn (☎ 5782 1457; 99 Powlett St; s/d $58/68) On the way into town is the Kestrel, with two wings of simple but sparkling rooms around a courtyard.

Red Lion Hotel (☎ 5782 1411; 45 Sydney St; s/d/f $35/60/80) This old hotel offers basic rooms off the typically squeaky upstairs corridor. It's very clean and the shared bathrooms are fine.

Bindley House (☎ 5781 1142; 20 Powlett St; bindley _house@mailcity.com; B&B s/d $130/160) Welcome to a cosy, rustic cottage, set in a pretty garden. It's all early-Australian till you see the spa and lush dressing gowns. Packages can include massages, and meals by your personal chef.

Kilmore Town Hall Restaurant (☎ 5782 1991; 16 Sydney Rd; mains $17-27; 🕑 dinner Fri & Sat) Dine like a lord mayor on seared swordfish with *dukkah* (a mix of ground spices, nuts and seeds) in a grand room with carved timber fireplaces and high ceilings. Downstairs, the **Town Hall Cafe** (mains $8.50-10; 🕑 lunch daily, dinner

Thu-Sun) offers pasta and risotto in charming little rooms.

SEYMOUR

☎ 03 / pop 6300

Come off the freeways to stroll along the banks of the Goulburn River, passing the historic New Crossing Bridge, vineyards, majestic old gums and abundant native wildlife. Seymour is known for industry and agriculture. It's also central to many activities.

The **visitors centre** (☎ 5799 0233; Emily St; 🕑 9am-5pm) will set you up with fun activities which won't disappoint – like walking up Mt Disappointment!

Sights & Activities

Riddy's Trawool Valley Tours (☎ 5792 3641, 5792 1654; riddys@eck.net; 8366 Goulburn Valley Hwy; adult/child $25/15) offers 4WD tours of waterfalls, reservoirs and to the summit of Mt Pleasant, which overlooks a National Trust–registered river valley.

Seymour Railway Heritage Centre (☎ 5799 0515; info@srhc.org.au; Victoria St; admission $2; 🕑 10am-3pm Tue, Thu, Sat & Sun) has a fantastic collection of heritage Victoria Railway locomotives and carriages.

The **RAAC Tank Museum** (☎ 5735 7285; atm@ancc .com; Hopkins Barracks, Puckapunyal; adult/child/family $6/3/12; 🕑 10am-4pm Wed-Fri, noon-5pm Sun) is 18km west of Seymour. It houses vintage armoured vehicles and tanks, including the Vicker MKII, anti-tank weapons and historic army displays. From here you can start the **Military Heritage Trail** (tourist drive 65; 107km) to Murchison which takes in points like the Graytown War Camps and Italian Ossario Memorial (see p319).

Sleeping

There are six motels along Emily St, and three caravan parks in Seymour.

Saratoga Lodge (☎ 5799 2669; www.saratogalodge .com.au; 110 Kobyboyn Rd; d from $125; 🐾 🖳) You'll totally relax here, among the gum trees, with wild ducks, kangaroos, and even a small racing stable. Luxurious cottages give you a heritage feeling, or is it the port and chocolates? Winner of a 'Best Accommodation Experience' award, the lodge is just past Seymour Racecourse – so include a country race day, with all its character and charm. Visit http:// tourism.net.au/victoria/macedon/events. html for a calendar of race days.

Auto Lodge Motor Inn (☎ 5792 1700; Emily St; s/d/f $52/63/85; ❄ ⬛) You can't miss the sign to this place. The Auto is set back from the road, behind trees, with its old rooms freshly painted, good bed arrangements for families, a camp kitchen and barbecue.

Terminus Hotel (☎ 5792 1827; s $22) Across from the station, the Terminus is dusky and squeaky with small rooms and shared old bathrooms, a kitchen and TV room. Beware the disco on Friday and Saturday.

Goulburn River Caravan Park (☎ 5792 1530; www .goulburnrivercp.com; Progress St; camp sites per 2 people from $14, d cabins from $55; ❄) It nestles around a bend of the Goulburn River, so watch the waters drift past. There are barbecues between the gums, and a playground next door.

Eating

Old Post Office Seymour (☎ 5792 3170; www.artsey mour.com.au/index.html; 50 Emily St; mains $15-25; ☾ lunch & dinner) Browse around the fine art gallery with paintings by Australian artists, while the chef prepares a rack of lamb, teamed perhaps with a bottle of local wine.

Somerset Crossing Vineyard Restaurant (☎ 5799 0330, 0407-368 8171; 1 Emily St; mains $14-26; ☾ lunch & dinner Thu-Sun) Enjoy elegant dining in an octagonal restaurant or vine-covered courtyard. There's baked salmon, good veg choices, and country fare like, no kidding, 'Mum's Pav'. Next door, **Somerset Crossing Vineyard** (☎ 5792 2445; Emily St; ☾ 10am-5pm Fri-Sun) has wine tastings and sales.

Caravan Café (☎ 5792 2463; Emily St; hamburger $6) It's just a window across from the Royal Hotel, but it's an institution – selling burgers for 40 years.

Araminta's Tea Rooms (☎ 5792 1886; 56 Tallarook St; mains $8-18; ☾ breakfast & lunch) For more history, enjoy the hospitality at the beautifully restored Araminta where you can also buy local art and crafts.

Getting There & Away

Eighteen **V/Line** (☎ 13 61 96) trains and one coach stop at Seymour Monday to Friday, on their way from Melbourne to Albury or Shepparton. There are fewer on weekends.

SEYMOUR TO BENALLA

As you head up the freeway, turn off to **Plunkett's Winery and Restaurant** (☎ 03-5796 2150; Lambing Gully Rd, Avenel; ☾ 11am-5pm). The wines are excellent, especially the merlot. And from the stunning **dining room** (☾ lunch Thu-Mon) you look across the vineyard to the Strathbogie Ranges.

Four kilometres north is the turnoff to **Avenel Maze** (☎ 03-5796 2667; Upton Rd, Avenel; ☾ 10am-5pm Thu-Mon). There are five amazing mazes which include the only rock labyrinth in Australia. There's also a licensed café and barbecue area.

Next turn is to **Euroa**, so pretty sitting at the foot of the Strathbogie Ranges that it need do little else. Its late Victorian and Edwardian red-brick buildings have been put to good use: the Farmers Arms Hotel (1876) is now the **Farmers Arms Museum** (admission free; ☾ 1-4pm Fri-Mon) with local memorabilia, farm machinery and old buggies; while the court house (1892) is now **Court House B&B**

OCTOBER, WHEN THE FUN BEGINS

A small shire that includes places like Kilmore, Seymour and Tallarook State Forest, **Mitchell** (www.mitchellshire.vic.gov.au), is just an hour's easy drive north from Melbourne. Here the activities are action packed, crafts varied and exquisite, food and wine superb and the countryside rich in rivers, plantlife, wildlife and sweeping plains. Then comes October, when the special events, exhibitions, race days and festivals will keep you away from home all month.

Go to the calendar on the shire's website or contact any regional information centre. There's bound to be a must-do for you. A selection:

Festival of Arts Offers art and craft fairs, music and plays all month, at venues right through the shire.

Seymour Show Features agricultural delights.

Wine and Food Festivals, shows and tastings are held at local wineries.

Southern Classic Festival Motorcycles rule, with a swap meet, trade show, rally and racing.

Classic Car Day Vintage cars from all over Victoria, live music and gourmet food-and-wine stalls on the course.

Seymour Cup Premier spring racing meeting; has food and wine, live music, children's entertainment, dinner packages and fashions on the field.

(☎ 03-5795 1436; Binney St; d $120; ⊠), where you sleep in the judge's chambers, prepare food in the cell, and kick back in the courtroom.

Seven Creeks Hotel (☎ 03-5795 3034; Old Hume Hwy; s/d $25/45) has lots of lacework and small rooms with sparkling shared bathrooms.

Skydive Euroa (☎ 9432 2419; Drysdale Rd) is open weekends. The **Miniature Steam Train** (Turnbull St) holds rides on the fourth Sunday of the month.

As you come off the freeway the Old Hume Hwy runs along the eastern edge of town. Enjoy a leisurely meal at **Haygun's** (☎ 03-5795 2187; Old Hume Hwy; mains $16-23; ♥ lunch & dinner Wed-Sun). Or call into **Jumping Jumbuck** (☎ 03-5795 1181; Old Hume Hwy; mains $10-14; ♥ breakfast & lunch daily, dinner Fri-Sun) The quick-service gourmet meals and excellent coffee will set you happily back onto the freeway.

BENALLA
☎ 03 / pop 8600

Benalla is probably a variation on a local Aboriginal word meaning 'crossing place'. It's a relaxed country town on the banks of the Broken River, which has been dammed to make an attractive lake.

The first European settlers camped at Winding Swamp, an Aboriginal hunting ground, with several thousand sheep and cattle. On 10 April 1838 the 18 settlers were attacked by some 300 Aborigines, with an awful number of casualties.

Benalla also has associations with the Ned Kelly legend: Ned made his first court appearance here in 1869 when, aged 14, he was charged with robbery and assault. In 1877 he was again being escorted to the Benalla court when he escaped and hid in a saddle-and-boot maker's shop in Arundel St. It was here he told police trooper Thomas Lonigan that if ever he shot a man, it would be Lonigan, which he did a year later (see p303).

The **visitors centre** (☎ 5762 1749; Mair St; ♥ 9am-5pm) is by the lake.

Sights & Activities

Most of Benalla's attractions are centred around Broken River. The **Benalla Ceramic Mural**, overlooking the river, is a terracotta sculpture wall inspired by the Catalan architect Antonio Gaudi. From the mural, there's a 4km-long **walking path** around Lake Benalla past Jaycee Island and the art gal-

lery (pick up a free map and guide at the information centre).

Benalla's **botanic gardens**, on the western side of the river, have large expanses of lawns and shady old trees, fronted by a colourful stretch of rose gardens. Facing the main road, is the **Weary Dunlop Memorial**. Sir Edward 'Weary' Dunlop, born in Benalla, was an army doctor who tended fellow POWs in the appalling Japanese camps on the Thai–Burma railroad during WWII. He was regarded as a saint by the men he helped.

Also here, the **Benalla Art Gallery** (☎ 5762 3027; ♥ 10am-5pm) has a good collection of Australian art, including paintings from the Heidelberg School, and more recent works by artists such as Leonard French, Fred Williams and John Brack. **Gallery Cafe** (meals $8-14; ♥ lunch), inside, serves an artistic Caesars salad, and you may hear a local band playing.

Ned Kelly's cell and a **period costume museum** (adult/child $4/1), which has an impressive range of old costumes and uniforms, is at the visitors centre. **Mrs Stell's House in Miniature** from Wangaratta is expected to be housed here soon.

Benalla is known worldwide for its fabulous thermal activity. The **Gliding Club of Victoria** (☎ 5762 1058; Samaria Rd Aerodrome; joy flights $80-140) has a base at the airport, 2km from Benalla.

Northwest of Benalla, the **Winton Motor Raceway** (☎ 5766 4235) is one of Victoria's main motor-racing circuits, and has events almost every weekend. Ring to find out what's on.

The heated indoor **Benalla Aquatic Centre** (☎ 5762 2154; adult/child/family $4/2.50/10; ♥ 6.30am-8pm Mon, Wed & Fri, 9am-8pm Sat, Sun, Tue & Thu) is a water-lover's dream, with all sorts of pools and activities.

Festivals & Events

Benalla's **Rose Festival** (early Nov), held over 10 days, features the botanic rose gardens, parades and fireworks.

Sleeping

Belmont B&B (☎ 5762 6575; www.belmontbnb.com.au; 80 Arundel St; s/d from $95/135) Enjoy a taste of total luxury. Lush beds piled with pillows and wraps nestle in high-ceilinged rooms with gorgeous en suites. Arts and crafts sit prettily between the antique furniture. Just steer clear of the brandied apricots at breakfast if you're racing out at Winton later.

Benalta Family Inn (☎ 5762 5600; 27 Bridge St; s/d/f $50/65/83; ⊠ ⊠) This is one of the cheapest of the many motels in town. Two blocks back, by the lake, it's a pleasant stroll down to the water.

Top of the Town Motel (☎ 5762 4866; 136 Bridge St; s/d from $78/89; ⊠ ⊠) This motel has gorgeous, shiny clean rooms with video, microwave and just about everything, including a supermarket across the street.

Trekkers Rest (☎ 5762 3535; www.trekkersrest.com.au; Kilfeera Rd; s/d from $25/50; ⊠ ⊒) An amazing complex of different-sized, prefabricated apartments, bathroom blocks and kitchens, all set among wide open spaces. The friendly managers will pick you up from the station and rent you a bicycle.

Eating

Café Lago (☎ 5762 2035; Bridge St; meals from $7; ⊠ Mon-Sat) This perfect lunch spot looks out over the lake where peaceful pelicans breeze past.

Raffertys (☎ 5762 4066; 55 Nunn St; mains $18-25; ⊠ lunch Wed-Fri, dinner Tue-Sat) The super-friendly staff will skip to your table with your order (eye fillet with Swiss mushrooms?) from a very good menu. Enjoy. The wines are local, and if you're lucky there may be a concert out the back.

Georgina's (☎ 5762 1334; 100 Bridge St; mains from $12; ⊠ dinner) This friendly place has a good local reputation. Dishes include pasta, risotto or fish of the day.

Hides Bakery (☎ 5762 2324; 111 Bridge St; breakfast $10; ⊠ breakfast & lunch) You'll get a hearty breakfast inside or alfresco, from 6am. Or indulge in a gourmet pie.

Getting There & Away

The Benalla train station is on Mackellar St. There are daily **V/Line** (☎ 13 61 96) trains to/from Melbourne ($30) and V/Line buses connect with Wangaratta ($5) and Yarrawonga ($9).

GLENROWAN

☎ 03 / pop 350

Ned Kelly's legendary bushranging exploits came to their bloody end here in 1880. The story of Ned and his gang has since become something of an industry. You can't drive through Glenrowan without being confronted by the legend.

Sights

KELLYLAND

The highlight of Glenrowan's attractions is this **theatre** (☎ 5766 2367; Gladstone St; adult/child/family $16/10/45; ⊠ 9.30am-4.30pm) where original props include the bar of McDonell's Tavern, a hand-gun owned by Ned, Sgt Kennedy's hitching post and a rare copy of the findings of the Royal Commission into the Kelly manhunt. You move through different rooms while the story is told (every 30 minutes) by a cast of surprisingly lifelike computerised characters (it may be too scary for young children). There's a souvenir shop and an information section. If you're a Ned Kelly buff, ask for the brochure titled *An Easy Self Guided Walk Around the Kelly Siege Site*.

WINERIES

There are three wineries near Glenrowan, all well worth a visit for tastings and sales: **Bailey's of Glenrowan** (☎ 5766 2392; Gap Rd; ⊠ 9am-5pm Mon-Fri, 10am-5pm Sat & Sun), about 10km north in Taminick; **Auldstone Cellars** (☎ 5766 2237; www.auldstone.com.au; Booth's Rd; ⊠ 9am-5pm Thu-Sat, 10am-5pm Sun), a further 5km, with lunches on the weekend; and **Booth's Taminick Cellars** (☎ 5766 2282; Booth's Rd; ⊠ 10am-5pm), nearby.

See also the Victorian Wineries chapter, p64.

Sleeping & Eating

Glenrowan Kelly Country Motel (☎ 5766 2202; Main St; s/d/f from $55/70/90; ⊠ ⊠) Spacious yellow rooms look out on a small garden and barbecue area, in the centre of town.

Glenrowan Hotel (☎ 5766 2255; Main St; mains $7.50-15; ⊠ lunch & dinner) It's free of Kelly paraphernalia, but you'd swear the air was the same that Kelly breathed. Fortunately there's a courtyard.

Glenrowan Bushland Caravan Park (☎ 5766 2288; Warby Range Rd; camp sites per 2 people from $15, d cabins from $38) In a relaxed bushland setting 2km north of town, this place is interesting, with its many long-term residents. Turn just north of Kellyland.

Getting There & Away

V/Line (☎ 13 61 96) has a daily bus service here.

WARBY RANGE STATE PARK

The 400-million-year-old Warby Range extends about 25km north of Glenrowan and

THE KELLY GANG

Ned Kelly is probably Australia's greatest folk hero. His life and death have been embraced as a part of the national culture – from Sidney Nolan's famous paintings to Peter Carey's Booker prize–winning novel *True History of the Kelly Gang*. Ned himself has become a symbol of the Australian rebel character.

But before he became a cult hero, Edward 'Ned' Kelly was a common horse thief. Born in 1855, Ned was first arrested when he was 14 and spent the next 10 years in and out of jails. In 1878 a warrant was issued for his arrest for stealing horses, so he and his brother Dan went into hiding. Their mother and two friends were arrested and sentenced to imprisonment for aiding and abetting. Family members had always felt persecuted by the authorities and the jailing of Mrs Kelly was the last straw.

Ned and Dan were joined in their hide-out in the Wombat Ranges, near Mansfield, by Steve Hart and Joe Byrne. Four policemen – Kennedy, Lonigan, Scanlon and McIntyre – came looking for them and, in a shoot-out at Stringybark Creek, Ned killed Kennedy, Lonigan and Scanlon. McIntyre escaped to Mansfield and raised the alarm.

The government put up a £500 reward for any of the gang members, dead or alive. In December 1878 the gang held up the National Bank at Euroa, and got away with £2000. Then, in February 1879, they took over the police station at Jerilderie, locked the two policemen in the cells, and robbed the Bank of New South Wales wearing the policemen's uniforms. By this time the reward was £2000 a head.

On 27 June 1880 the gang held 60 people captive in a hotel at Glenrowan. A train-load of police and trackers was sent from Melbourne. A plan to destroy the train was foiled when a schoolteacher warned the police. Surrounded, the gang shot it out from the hotel for hours while wearing heavy armour made from ploughshares. Ned was shot in the legs and captured, and Dan Kelly, Joe Byrne and Steve Hart, along with several of their hostages, were killed.

Ned Kelly was brought to Melbourne, tried and hanged on 11 November 1880. On her last visit, his mother told him to die like a Kelly. He met his end bravely and his last words were something like, 'Such is life'.

His death mask, armour and the gallows on which he died are on display in the Old Melbourne Gaol, see p92.

---

probably provided Ned Kelly and his gang with many vantage points. It's a low range of steep, granite slopes preserved as a state park because of its scenic value (and, probably, because it wasn't farmable). Features include fast-flowing creeks and waterfalls after rain, wildflowers in spring, some great picnic spots and an abundance of birdlife.

The views from **Ryan's Lookout** are exceptional. There are good sealed roads (a short trip starts at Ryan's Lookout, goes along Gerrett Rd, links up with Adam's Track and then Thoona Rd), and also good walking tracks, picnic areas and a campsite – ask for the map and brochure at the visitors centre in Wangaratta (see right).

WANGARATTA

☎ 03 / pop 15,500

Wangaratta (or just plain old 'Wang') is at the junction of the Ovens and King Rivers. Its name comes from two local Abori-

ginal words meaning 'resting place of the cormorants'.

The first buildings, in the 1840s, were based around a punt service which operated until 1855. The Wangaratta Woollen Mills and Bruck Mills were established here after WWII, allowing Wangaratta to become an industrial centre and a major textile town. Today the town is a modern rural centre.

Wangaratta is the turn-off point for the Great Alpine Rd, which leads to Mt Buffalo, Myrtleford, Bright and the northern ski resorts of the Victorian Alps (see p322).

Orientation & Information

As with most towns off the freeway, Wangaratta's main street, Murphy St, was once the old Hume Hwy.

Coles supermarket (Greta Rd; 🕒 6am–midnight)

Department of Sustainability & Environment office (DSE; ☎ 5721 5022; Tara Court, Ford St) See them if you're going bushwalking.

Royal Automobile Club of Victoria (RACV; ☎ 5722 1292; 10 Templeton St)

Visitors centre (☎ 5721 5711, 1800 801 065; Murphy St; ⏰ 9am-5pm; 🖥️) In the old library. Pick up the informative *Discover Adventure, Legends & Indulgence* brochure while you're here.

Your Computer Zone (☎ 5721 4677; 64a Murphy St; per 5min $1) For Internet access.

Sights

At the Wangaratta Cemetery, south of town, is the grave of **Dan 'Mad Dog' Morgan**, one of Australia's most notorious and brutal bushrangers. It contains most of Morgan's remains – his head and scrotum were cut off after he was fatally shot at nearby Peechelba Station in April 1865. The head was taken to Melbourne for a study of the criminal mind; the scrotum was supposedly fashioned into a tobacco pouch.

Holy Trinity Anglican Cathedral (cnr Ovens & Norton Sts) is a most impressive church, begun in 1909 and finally finished in 1965. **Apex Park**, beside the Ovens River bridge, has a market on weekends, barbecues, a new toilet and shower block and a new playground.

Activities

The **Murray to the Mountains Rail Trail** starts in Bowser (8km northeast of Wangaratta) and heads southeast all the way to Bright in the Great Dividing Range, with a spur to Beechworth. The trail is suitable for walking or mountain biking (because it was a rail route, the grades are never too severe). A brochure with a map is available at the information centre. There are plans to extend the trails north to Wahgunyah and south to Whitfield.

Festivals & Events

ANA Carnival (☎ 5721 8708; late Jan) An athletics meeting featuring the Wangaratta Gift foot race.

Wangaratta Jazz Festival (www.wangaratta-jazz.org .au/docs/festival.php; Oct/Nov) First held in 1990, this is one of Australia's premier music festivals, and features a program of traditional, modern and contemporary jazz. It's held on the weekend before the Melbourne Cup, with hundreds of musicians and acts, and many awards and workshops.

Sleeping

Pinsent Hotel (☎ 5721 2183; 20 Reid St; s/d $35/70) This pub has had major renovations so the old rooms upstairs are as swish as any motel. The bistro serves well presented pub meals.

Billabong Motel (☎ 5721 2353; 12 Chisholm St; s/d from $40/55; ❄️) You can walk from town to this old but homely warren of fresh little rooms with very old but clean bathrooms. It's the cheapest motel in town, and nice.

Millers Cottage (☎ 5721 5755; 26 Parfitt Rd; s/d from $62/68; ❄️ 🏊) This motel, on the northern side of town, has small comfortable rooms in a large garden, with a pool, playground and barbecue.

Gateway Wangaratta (☎ 5721 8399, 1800 033 439; www.wangarattagateway.com.au; 29-37 Ryley St; s/d/f from $109/119/144; ❄️ 🏊) At this modern motel there are good standard rooms and more expensive suites with spas. Rooms are spacious, or head for the cocktail lounge, restaurant, dance floor, gym, spa or sauna. Disabled facilities are available.

Painters Island Caravan Park (☎ 5721 3380; Pinkerton Crescent; camp sites per 2 people $19, d cabins $50; ❄️) Set in 25 acres of lovely grounds on the banks of the Ovens River, you can lose yourself in this friendly place, just two minutes from town. There's a playground, barbecue and camp kitchen.

Eating

There's a great café scene along Murphy St and Reid St, in the centre of town.

Scribblers Coffee Lounge (☎ 5721 3945; 66 Reid St; meals $8-16; ⏰ breakfast & lunch) This friendly spot with outdoor seating has a varied menu, including pastas, country-veg and other interesting quiches, pies and cakes.

Rusty Dog Cafe (☎ 5722 4392; cnr Reid & Ovens Sts; mains $12-25; ⏰ breakfast & lunch daily, dinner Tue-Sat) You'll feel right at home in this modern café, and you'll love the fresh salads, steaks, seafood baskets, and the variety of local wines.

Cafe Martini (☎ 5721 9020; 87 Murphy St; mains $10-22; ⏰ lunch Mon-Sat, dinner nightly) This big and bustling restaurant is known for its wood-fired pizzas. Eat upstairs or down, the food will still be good.

Peter's Cellar 47 (☎ 5721 6309; 54 Ryley St; mains $16-28; ⏰ dinner Mon-Sat) This place is a popular dinner spot, with its long bar and open fire. The menu offers great pastas, or try the famous steaks and seafood.

Vine Hotel (☎ 5721 2605; www.tourismInternet.com .au/wgvine.htm; Detour Rd; mains $12-24; ⏰ lunch & dinner Wed-Sun) This charming old pub hasn't changed since Ned Kelly and his gang used to drink here, except the food's much better! After your meal, go down to the basement to the small history museum and cellars. The Vine is about 3km north of town, on the road to Eldorado.

Getting There & Away

Wangaratta **train station** (Norton St) is just west of the town centre. Daily **V/Line** (☎ 13 61 96) trains from Melbourne ($36) continue on to Wodonga ($14).

V/Line buses run daily to Rutherglen ($6).

CHILTERN

☎ 03 / pop 1100

Tiny Chiltern is one of Victoria's most historic and charming colonial townships. The entire streetscape is so quaint and authentic that the town is often used as a film set for period pieces, including the early Walt Disney classic, *Ride a Wild Pony*. Originally called Black Dog Creek, it was established in 1851 and prospered when gold was discovered here in 1859.

Beryl, at the Chiltern **visitors centre** (☎ 5726 1611; 30 Main St; ✆ 10am-4pm) is knowledgeable about the region and passionate about bird-watching in the nearby Chiltern-Mt Pilot National Park (see right).

Sights

The National Trust–classified **Lake View Homestead** (☎ 5726 1317; Victoria St; ✆ 10am-4pm Sun) was built in 1870 and overlooks Lake Anderson. It was the home of Henry Handel (Florence Ethel) Richardson, who wrote of life here in the book *Ultima Thule* (1929), the third part of her trilogy *The Fortunes of Richard Mahony* (1930). Richardson's other works touch on her time in Maldon (see p252), as well as *The Getting of Wisdom* (1910) about her schooldays at Presbyterian Ladies College in Melbourne.

Atheneum Library & Museum (☎ 5726 1467; Conness St; admission $2.50; ✆ 10am-4pm Sat & Sun) is housed in the former town hall (1866) and has a collection of memorabilia, art, photos and equipment from the gold-rush days.

Star Hotel/Theatre (☎ 5726 1395; cnr Main & Conness Sts; adult/child $4.50/1.50; ✆ by appointment), once used for plays and dances, was the centrepiece of Chiltern's social and cultural life. It is now a museum filled with memorabilia. The grapevine in the courtyard is the largest in Australia.

Sleeping & Eating

Chiltern Colonial Motor Inn (☎ 5726 1788; fax 5726 1131; 1 Main St; s/d $61/72; ⊠) A modern motel with good units, the Colonial has its own **restaurant** (mains $14-22; ✆ dinner Fri & Sat), and owner Jim arranges packages for bird-watchers.

Mulberry Tree (☎ 5726 1277; www.tourismInternet .com.au/chmulb.htm; 28 Conness St; s/d $100/130) This B&B is in an old bank. The front room is a lacy **tea room** (dishes $7-12; ☎ breakfast & lunch) serving soup and focaccias.

Lake Anderson Caravan Park (☎ 5726 1298; www .tourismInternet.com.au/chcara2.htm; Alliance St; camp sites per 2 people from $15, d cabins from $65) It's peaceful here by the lake, with attractive little cabins between the trees. Just laze about or go fishing and bird-watching.

Quinny's Wine Bar & Cafe (19 Conness St; mains $9.50-14; ✆ breakfast, lunch & dinner) It sounds posher than it is. The retro look, with corrugated tin bar, is a backdrop for loud music and home-made pastas.

AROUND CHILTERN

Almost 4500 hectares around Chiltern, on either side of the Hume Fwy, is the **Chiltern-Mt Pilot National Park**, in which both the environment and relics of early mining activities are conserved. The **Chiltern Historic Drive** starts from Chiltern and takes you through the park past the old open-cut Magenta Mine, the remains of the Indigo Cemetery and Donkey Hill. You can also hike through the park, but if you leave the main tracks watch out for old mine shafts.

The **Pilot Range** is where Ned Kelly and his gang are thought to have holed up for months before his capture at Glenrowan. The views from **Mt Pilot** are spectacular, as is the Aboriginal art site **Yeddonba**.

There are picnic areas, and you can camp, but contact the local **Parks Victoria office** (☎ 03-5726 1234) first. This is the last remnant of box-ironbark forest in this part of the state. There's a colourful display of wildflowers each spring and over 150 species of birds. People come here from all over the world to **bird-watch**. Ask Beryl at the Chiltern visitors centre (left) for the *Chiltern Bird List* and the booklet *Bird Trails of Chiltern*.

WODONGA

☎ 02 / pop 31,000

Wodonga looks out on the lovely Sumsion Gardens and a lake formed off Wodonga

Creek. Wodonga is a commercial centre, also know for its sporting facilities, with bike trails, sports and aquatic facilities that are world class.

Information

The Lincoln Causeway runs from the city centre across Wodonga Creek to the border at the Murray River. The Causeway is lined with tourist attractions.

Gateway visitors centre (☎ 6051 3750, 1300 796 222; www.destinationalburywodonga.com.au; ☒ 9am-5pm) You'll easily spot this very informative centre. It has a 24-hour touch-screen information service, in case you need it.

Activities

Harveys Fish and Fun Park (☎ 6021 2070; www.hffp .com.au; Lincoln Causeway; adult/child $8.50/6.50; ☒ 9am-5pm Wed-Mon) keeps the kids amused with water slides, playgrounds and mini golf. For bigger kids, the **Indoor Go Karts** (☎ 6041 3933; www .tourisminternet.com.au/abcart.htm; Lincoln Causeway; per 10min $20; ☒ Fri-Sun) should be a goer. The Gateway shopping area, farther along the Causeway, has art and craft shops where you can watch timber pieces being carved, or buy fine china, dolls, whatever.

There are signed trails for the **Gateway Island Bicycle and Walking Tracks** (www.tourisminter net.com.au/wdbike1.htm) and **Wiradjuri Walkabout, Aboriginal River Walk** (which is the first 3km of the track). Display signs include details of Aboriginal bush food and medicine plants, Aboriginal cooking sites, camp sites, carving in trees and a birdlife sanctuary. There is a display of didgeridoos and canoes and how they are made and used. The path goes underneath the Hume Hwy to join the bicycle track along the Lincoln Causeway, named after Merv Lincoln, a Wodonga athlete who represented Australia at the 1954 Olympic Games.

The **Army Museum Bandiana** (☎ 6055 2525; Murray Valley Hwy, Bandiana; adult/child $5/2; ☒ 9.30am-4pm Sun-Fri) displays a variety of war weaponry and documents. The old cars are magnificent – Buick and Holden staff cars, Chevvy and Dodge trucks, a grand display well worth the visit.

Sleeping

You'll see the main cluster of motels as you drive into town, and along the main street.

Sanctuary Park Motel (☎ 6024 1122; www.sanctuary parkmotel.com.au; 11 High St; s/d/f $60/72/88; ☒ ☐ ☒)

This bright and friendly place also has a self-contained cabin (doubles $110) with wheelchair access, a spa and delightful views of pelicans wandering by the lake.

Stagecoach Motel (☎ 6024 3044; 188 Melbourne Rd; s/d from $77/87) A few blocks west of the town centre, set in a quiet location, this friendly place has pleasant, modern rooms and suites.

Blazing Stump Hotel (☎ 6056 3433; www.blazing stump.com.au; Tallangatta Rd; d/f from $101/160; ☒ ☐ ☒) If you like country-style luxury – spacious rooms, expansive views, loads of facilities like pool, spa, gym, playground – the Blazing Stump on the eastern edge of town is for you. Family suites have enclosed gardens and executive suites feature spas.

Wodonga Caravan & Cabin Park (☎ 6024 2598; www.tourisminternet.com.au/wdcabin.htm; 186 Melbourne Rd; camp sites per 2 people from $17, d cabins from $38; ☒ ☒) About 2km west of the town centre, there's plenty of breathing space here with gum trees, grassy areas, pool and playground. But the real joys are the luxurious cabins.

Eating

Black Duck Cafe (☎ 6024 6955; Wright Rd, Lincoln Causeway; meals $7.50-13; ☒ breakfast & lunch Sat & Sun) Sit by the fountain and watch the waterbirds coming up from the lake as you tuck into the Royal Duck breakfast.

Zilch Food Store (☎ 6056 2400; 8/1 Stanley St; mains $6.50-12; ☒ breakfast & lunch Mon-Fri) Enjoy freshly made soups and gourmet sandwiches in the courtyard, or stock up on Zilch's great local produce and go picnic.

Steak Pit (☎ 6024 1262; 51 Elgin St; mains $22-30; ☒ lunch Wed-Fri, dinner Tue-Sat) When you try the steak you'll forgive them the name.

Three Monkeys Tavern (☎ 6041 2626; Lincoln Causeway; mains $16-23; ☒ breakfast, lunch & dinner) That huge castle houses a family restaurant specialising in seasonal local produce. You have to try the fillet of beef with confit of tomato and local olives.

Getting There & Away

Wodonga's train station is in the centre of town near the intersection of the Hume Fwy and Murray Valley Hwy. There are daily **V/Line** (☎ 13 61 96) services to/from Melbourne ($47).

V/Line buses connect Wodonga with Yarrawonga ($10) and Mildura ($64).

ALONG THE MURRAY

RUTHERGLEN

☎ 02 / pop 1900

This quaint little town is at the centre of one of Victoria's major wine-growing districts, a food-and-wine buff's paradise (see also Victorian Wineries, p59). But as well as being a popular base for touring the wineries, the town has a Main St that is an historic precinct, lined with weathered timber buildings, antique and bric-a-brac shops, tearooms and veranda-fronted pubs.

Information

Visitors centre (☎ 6033 6300, 1800 622 871; info@ rutherglenvic.com.au; 57 Main St; ⏱ 9am-5pm) A fun place where you'll get all the help you need.

Sights & Activities

The **Common School Museum** (☎ 6033 6300, 1800 622 871; 57 Main St; admission $2; ⏱ 9am-5pm Sun) has an amazing range of weights and measures, local inventions, period pieces and school equipment.

A great way to make your winery tour is with **Rutherglen Stretch Limousine** (☎ 6032 9588; www.motelwoongarra.com.au). The limo takes up to seven passengers, picnic hampers can be provided, and half- or full-day tours arranged.

Festivals & Events

There's special events on almost every weekend, all featuring a wide range of activities, especially focussed around eating and drinking. Contact the visitors centre (above) for what's on when you're here, or go to the **Rutherglen Wine Experience** (www.rutherglenvic.com /events/regular.asp) events page.

Some not-to-be-missed events:

Tastes of Rutherglen (Mar)
Winery Walkabout Weekend (Jun)
Hot & Spicy Festival (Sep)
Rutherglen Agriculture and Wine Show (late Sep) Don't miss this: a cowbell is rung at 7am to signal a mad rush as all wines are $8.
Winemakers' Legends Weekend (mid-Nov)

See also p59.

Sleeping

Accommodation is likely to be tight during major festivals and rates are, of course, higher. They're also seriously higher on weekends and public holidays.

RUTHERGLEN

Victoria Hotel (☎ 6032 8610; www.victoriahotelrutherglen.com.au; 90 Main St; s/d from $35/40) This beautiful old National Trust–classified place has several little old rooms. But grab a front room with bathroom and views over Main St, and live like a king. The wide lace-trimmed balcony is the perfect spot to discuss wine. The downstairs **restaurant** (meals $9-16; ⏱ lunch & dinner Wed-Sun) has an interesting menu with meals like Mediterranean chicken with olives and fetta ($16) – or splurge on a bar meal ($7).

Motel Woongarra (☎ 6032 9588; www.motelwoongarra.com.au; cnr Main & Drummond Sts; s/d from $58/66) The Woongarra is nearest to the centre of town. Its rooms are spacious and the grounds and pool are gorgeous. Packages are available that include winery tours in a stretch limousine (left).

Carlyle House (☎ 6032 8444; www.carlylehouse.com.au; 147 High St; B&B r/ste from $140/185) Spread your wings in a garden apartment, or nestle among the antiques inside the beautifully restored house. Either way, you'll enjoy an excellent breakfast served by your host.

THE AUTHORS CHOICE

Brimin Floating Lodge (☎ 6035 7245; www.briminlodge.com.au; Brimin Rd; lodges $80; ⌘) On a billabong, where the river red gums keep watch and the kookaburras laugh as you skinny dip, this is the perfect Aussie getaway. Walk along the levee and across the ramp, and you're in your own little old houseboat.

Step onto the pontoon, and you can pull yourself across the billabong by a rope and walk through the bush to the river. That's if you can drag yourself from your rooftop lounge chair, where lunch is sizzling on the electric barbecue.

There again, you can hightail it down to **Bundalong Tavern** (☎ 5726 8586; Murray Valley Hwy; mains $12-20; ⏱ lunch & dinner) for a traditional meal, with fresh vegetables, in an old Aussie pub.

Tuileries (☎ 6032 9033; www.tuileriesrutherglen .com.au; 13 Drummond St; B&B d from 165; 🔌 🖵) Tuileries offers boutique accommodation, with gloriously coloured modern rooms, guest lounge and even a tennis court. Such bright, uncluttered luxury. See also review under Eating, right.

Rutherglen Caravan & Tourist Park (☎ 6032 8577; www.grapevinegetaways.com.au; 72 Murray St; camp sites per 2 people $13, d cabins $40) A pretty place on the banks of Lake King, there's budget or luxury cabins, well spaced sites (true) and sparkling amenities blocks. It's next to a golf course, bowling club, playground and swimming pool. And there's ducks and turtles in the lake.

AROUND RUTHERGLEN

There are some excellent accommodation houses around, all in locations with unique features and a range of options, from fully self-contained or B&B to full packages.

Mt Ophir Estate (☎ 6032 8920; www.mount-ophir .com; Stillards Lane; B&B d from $180) This historic 75-hectare property, 6km southeast of Rutherglen, is also an emu-and-elk farm growing organic produce and grapes. There's a homestead and old winery as well. Self-contained packages are available.

House at Mount Prior (☎ 6026 5256; www.houseat mountprior.com; Howlong Rd; B&B d from $130) The marble fireplace in your room will be enough, but of course the whole place is elegant, warm and friendly. The historic mansion has two gourmet restaurants.

Eating

There's a great café scene all along Main St, and take-away places to fill a picnic hamper.

Café Shamrock (☎ 6032 8439; 121 Main St; dishes $18-27; 🕑 lunch Thu-Sat, dinner nightly) The Shamrock

is an upbeat restaurant and piano/wine bar offering an interesting menu and live music most evenings.

Rendezvous Courtyard (☎ 6032 9114; 68 Main St; mains $17-24; 🕑 dinner Thu-Tue) This place has a Mediterranean-influenced menu to match the Mediterranean décor.

Tuileries Restaurant (☎ 6032 9033; 13 Drummond St; mains $25-29; 🕑 dinner) There's lots of glass around a fountain and fine dining includes dishes like lamb loin crusted with walnut and Milawa blue. Yum. The **café** (meals $12-16; 🕑 breakfast & lunch Wed-Sun), on the other side of the fountain, has equally exciting meals like chicken luxor and roast-beef baguettes. See also Sleeping review, left.

WINERIES

All the major wineries (see also p59) have restaurants and cafés in superb settings overlooking their vineyards, lakes and rivers. They are mostly open for lunch and snacks. The food is always outstanding, and menus choices cover all budgets. Some examples:

House at Mount Prior (☎ 6026 5256; www.houseat mountprior.com; 1790 Howlong Road; 🕑 lunch & dinner) At the Mount Prior winery.

Terrace (☎ 6033 1922; www.eldtrain.com.au/allsaints .htm; All Saints Rd, Wahgunyah; 🕑 lunch & dinner Sat) At All Saints.

Lazy Grape (☎ 6033 1004; www.stleonardswine.com .au; St Leonards Rd, Wahgunyah; 🕑 lunch) At St Leonards.

Pickled Sisters Café (☎ 6033 2377; Distillery Rd, Wahgunyah; 🕑 lunch Wed-Mon, dinner Fri & Sat) At Cofield.

Gehrig's Courtyard (☎ 6026 7296; Murray Valley Hwy, Barnawartha; 🕑 lunch Thu-Sun) At Gehrig Estate.

Getting There & Around

The **V/Line** (☎ 13 61 96) bus to Wangaratta ($5.50) connects with the train to Melbourne on Wednesday, Friday and Saturday.

DETOUR: WAHGUNYAH

Just northeast of Rutherglen is this idyllic little township on the Murray River. At the height of the riverboat era Wahgunyah was a thriving port town and trade depot. Now, renowned wineries such as All Saints, St Leonards and Pfeiffers surround it, so wining and dining is fantastic.

In town is the fabulous old **Wahgunya Empire Hotel** (☎ 02-6033 1094; 6 Foord Street), where **Fairy's** (mains $10-18) serves traditional fare with fresh vegies. The perfect place to stay is **Riverside Waterfront Motel** (☎ 02-6033 1177; www.riversidemotel.com.au; Cadel Terrace; s/d/f $65/70/110; 🔌) where sparkling units feature sliding doors that lead out onto the grassy banks of the Murray. Rates include a light breakfast, plus there's a communal kitchen and barbecue – and a courtesy car.

A **V/Line** (☎ 13 61 96) bus service linking Wangaratta and Corowa in New South Wales (NSW) stops in Wahgunyah on Wednesday and Friday evening.

V/Line's Murray Link bus connecting Wodonga with Mildura stops at Rutherglen. The bus stop is at the western end of Main St.

You can hire bikes for leisurely bicycle tours from the visitors centre (p307).

YARRAWONGA
☎ 03 / pop 4600

Part of the sun country on the Murray – the entertainment and lifestyle destination. Tourist blurb, but it is actually true. If you like fine and sunny weather, activities like windsurfing, swimming, power boating and water-skiing, and a laid back, slightly surreal atmosphere, then Yarrawonga is for you. It has more sunshine hours than mostly anywhere else in Australia.

Information
Visitors centre (☎ 5744 1989, 1800 062 260; Irvine Pde; ⊙ 9am-5pm) This office is on the shores of Lake Mulwala, just beside the bridge. You can book accommodation and tours here.

Sights
Byramine Homestead (☎ 5748 4321; Murray Valley Hwy; admission $5; ⊙ 10am-4pm Thu-Mon) is the former home of Elizabeth Hume, sister-in-law of the explorer Hamilton Hume. She was the first permanent European settler in this area and built this substantial homestead, 14km west of town, in 1842.

The **Clock Museum** (☎ 5744 1249; 21 Lynch St; admission $5.50; ⊙ 10am-4.30pm), inside a simple Tudor-style house, has hundreds of clocks simultaneously ticking and tocking – it's an ominous sound, your life ticking away.

Activities
Lake Mulwala, the centre of much activity and entertainment, has great parks along its shores with picnic and barbecue areas. The lake was formed during the project to harness the waters of the Murray for irrigation. Every few years the lake is drained for weir maintenance purposes – the empty lake is an eerie sight.

Two cruise boats, the **Lady Murray** (☎ 0412 573 460) and the **Paradise Queen** (☎ 0418 508 616) operate daily cruises along the lake and the Murray River. Both have 1½-hour barbecue cruises ($18) at noon and a scenic cruise ($12) at 2pm. There are dinner cruises during summer.

Yarrawonga Outdoors (☎ 5744 3522; www.yarrawongaoutdoors.com.au; 7 Witt St) has kayaks, bikes and kites for sale or hire. Or to really discover the lake and river, take a half-day guided kayak tour ($60).

Many watersports companies are across the Murray in Mulwala. So pop into NSW to **Phil and Val Smith's Ski Rides** (☎ 0419-211 122; www.skirides.com.au; foreshore, Mulwala). It offers a huge array of water craft for hire, from canoes ($30) to fishing boats ($70) – costs are per half-day. It also offers water-skiing ($50 per 30 minutes) and other boat-towed thrills.

Mulwala Waterski School (☎ 03-5744 2777; www.mulwalawaterski.com.au; Melbourne St, Mulwala) offers water-skiing instruction and parasailing. It has ski equipment for sale and hire.

Sleeping
There are about 10 caravan parks, 20 motels and plenty of time-share resorts in Yarrawonga. The visitors centre (left) has a free booking service.

Lakeview Motel (☎ 5744 1555; fax 5743 1327; 1 Hunt St; s/d/f $80/85/105; ⊠ ⊛) This place is lovely. It looks out onto the lake, has spacious attractive rooms, gardens, it's opposite the information centre, and the rates are very reasonable. It has a large pool and cable TV.

Murray Valley Resort (☎ 5744 1844; www.murrayvalleyresort.com.au; s/d from $100/125; ⊠ ⊛) The amazing range of facilities include a gym, indoor and outdoor pools, tennis courts, billiard tables and spas. The accommodation is modern, with interesting architecture, soft colours and lots of space.

Terminus Hotel (☎ 5744 3025; fax 5743 2725; 95 Belmore St; r $40) This great old pub is popular with the locals. But tourists will like the spacious rooms and grand balcony. The bathrooms gleam and the lounge area has a TV, kettle, microwave and toaster. Downstairs, the **bistro** (meals $9-20; ⊙ lunch & dinner) serves good counter meals.

Yarrawonga Holiday Park (☎ 5744 3420; info@yarrawongaholidaypark.com.au; Piper St; camp sites per 2 people from $18, d cabins from $59; ⊠ ⊛) On the banks of the Murray River around an oval and tennis courts, this pretty park has plenty of sporty options. The cabins range from basic to new luxury ones near the boat ramp.

Eating
There's a fantastic café scene on Belmore St, with lots of outdoor seating to enjoy

sunshine and people-watching while modern, fresh food is prepared for you.

GJ's (☎ 5744 1450; 40 Belmore St; mains $16-28; ☺ breakfast, lunch & dinner) Setting the standard for top eating, GJ's is in a charming historic building with several dining areas including a chandelier room and pretty courtyard. The dinner menu will keep you coming back – the eye fillet with horseradish risotto is a must.

Slug & Lettuce (☎ 5743 1922; 137 Belmore St; mains $14-26; ☺ breakfast & lunch daily, dinner Tue-Sat) New to town, the building is spunky glass and metal with a pleasant bar area. The menu has plenty of country favourites and adventurous items like pepper-crusted kangaroo.

Left Bank Bistro (42 Belmore St; mains $12-23; ☺ breakfast, lunch & dinner) It's not Paris, but a real bank, left over perhaps. Enjoy sandwiches, roasts, burgers and cakes, or the evening BYO bistro.

Gusto 171 (☎ 5744 1800; 171 Woods Rd; mains $16-26; ☺ dinner Thu-Mon) This restaurant is in a grand old homestead and serves modern cuisine and some strange dishes like buffalo medallions with beetroot bake, teamed with local wines.

Lussino's (☎ 5743 2982; 132 Belmore St; mains $10-24; ☺ lunch & dinner) This is a popular pasta bar and Italian restaurant, where you can get favourites like scotch fillet on garlic potatoes.

Getting There & Away

There are daily **V/Line** (☎ 13 61 96) train/bus services from Melbourne ($39) with a change at Benalla. V/Line's Murray Link bus service which runs along the Murray Valley Hwy from Mildura to Wodonga stops near the Shire Hall.

COBRAM

☎ 03 / pop 4600

With Cobram being so close to the Murray, the township, local economy and tourism all revolve around the big river. The surrounding area produces peaches, citrus fruit, tomatoes, wheat, grapes, wool and much more.

The **visitors centre** (☺ 5872 2132, 1800 607 607; cnr Main & Station Sts; ☺ 9am-5pm) offers lots of help and a free accommodation booking service.

The main tourist attraction is the river itself, and Cobram has some excellent sandy 'beaches', the best of which is **Thompson's Beach** just north of the town.

Cobram is known as the 'Home of Peaches and Cream' because of the weekend **Peaches and Cream Festival** (late Jan, odd-numbered years).

Sleeping

Royal Victoria Hotel (☎ 5872 1009; fax 5872 1059; 1 Mookarii St; s/d from $25/40) This has simple pub rooms off the upstairs corridor, with shared old but clean bathrooms.

Charles Sturt Motor Inn (☎ 5872 2777; 3 Mookarii St; s/d $75/85; ☒ ☒) It's a very 1980s motel, all dark brick, but the rooms are spacious, and there's an attractive pool with a spa. Besides you can't go past the reasonable rates.

Tokemata Retreat (☎ 5873 5332; www.tokemata .com.au; s & d $125; ☒) This is a golfer's paradise. You can play on any of the nearby courses, take a tuition package, or throw the clubs away and enjoy the beautiful surroundings.

RACV Club Cobram (☎ 5872 2467; gary_hunt@racv .com.au; Campbell Rd; camp sites per 2 people from $21, d cabins/apt from $45/100; ☒ ☒) A large family-style holiday complex, the club has tennis courts, playground, recreation room and a gorgeous swimming pool.

Eating

Tuscanny on High (High St; mains $4-12; ☺ breakfast & lunch Mon-Sat) There's good coffee here, but make sure you don't miss the pancakes with maple syrup for breakfast.

Vine Leaf Cafe (☎ 5871 1871; 87 Punt Rd; meals $4-9; ☺ breakfast & lunch) This café's specialty is gourmet sandwiches, but the warm chicken salad is a close second.

Chefoo (☎ 5872 2845; 87 Punt Rd; mains $7.50-12; ☺ lunch & dinner) Next door to the Vine Leaf, this licensed restaurant has good Chinese food at reasonable prices.

Old Currency (☎ 5872 2990; cnr Main & Station Sts; mains $18-27; ☺ dinner) This is an upmarket, very pleasant BYO restaurant in the former State Bank of Victoria building. Bookings are essential.

BARMAH STATE PARK

Known as the Kakadu of the south, but without the crocodiles, **Barmah State Park** is a significant wetland area created by the flood plains of the Murray River. It's the largest remaining red-gum forest in Australia (and thus the world), and the swampy understorey is usually flooded in winter, creating a complex wetland ecology which is important as a breeding area for many fish and bird species.

Dharnya Centre (☎ 03-5869 3302; admission by donation; ☒ 10.30am-4pm) is the visitors centre and includes a small museum with displays on Aboriginal heritage and on the park. It is run by members of the Yorta Yorta people in partnership with Parks Victoria.

Evidence dates Aboriginal occupation at a thousand years or so; not long, probably because floods have destroyed older evidence. Not far away, on drier land, evidence of more than 40,000 years of occupation has been found. However, the Yorta Yorta people's Native Title claim (the right to claim title to traditional lands) for the area was rejected in 1998.

The park starts 9km north of the small town of **Barmah**, along a good dirt road which leads to the Dharnya Centre and camping areas. Beyond, there's a forest **nature drive** and a network of walking tracks, but they may be flooded so check on road conditions at the centre, which also has track notes for the walks.

The park is popular for **bird-watching, fishing** and **walking**, although in the wet season a canoe is the best way to get around.

Gondwana Canoe Hire (☎ 03-5869 3347), 4km past Barmah, hires canoes ($60 per day) and can advise on canoe trails. Staff can pick you up from as far afield as Echuca (for a fee; see p313).

The cruise boat **Kingfisher** (☎ 03-5869 3399; www.kingfishercruises.com.au; adult/child/family $20/14/64; ☒ 11am Mon, Wed, Thu, Sat & Sun) runs two-hour cruises along the waterways. Benita will point out local birds and tell you about the history of the Murray and how come the river is higher than the surrounding land in some places (true).

Sleeping

You can camp for free anywhere in the park or at the Barmah Lakes camping area (near the Dharnya Centre) which has tables, barbecue areas and pit toilets.

Barmah Hotel-Motel (☎ 5869 3270; Murray St, Barmah; s/d from $50/60) There are good, basic rooms with single and queen beds, in this very sleepy little corner that hardly seems like a town.

Barmah Caravan & Camping Park (☎ 5869 3225; fax 5869 3485; Murray St, Barmah; camp sites per 2 people $12, d cabins from $45) Right on the river, this serene and beautiful park has clean and comfortable cabins.

ECHUCA

☎ 03 / pop 10,100

Echuca is right where three great rivers meet – the Goulburn, Campaspe, and the Murray. So, guess what – *Echuca* (e-*choo*-ka) is an Aboriginal word meaning 'the meeting of the waters'.

Echuca is one of the state's most popular tourism centres, with the recreational benefits of the Murray River including waterskiing, swimming, paddle-steamer cruises and houseboat holidays. There are also some excellent tourist attractions, most notably around the old port.

The town was founded in 1853 by ex-convict Harry Hopwood who was transported to Australia for receiving stolen goods. He settled on the banks of the Murray, converted some rough sheds into an inn and store, then established punt and ferry crossings over the Murray and Campaspe Rivers. With his transport monopoly and the gold rush in full swing, he profited handsomely. Hopwood built the Bridge Hotel in 1858, and lived his remaining years in Echuca as a wealthy man, watching his town grow into the busiest inland port in Australia.

At the peak of the riverboat era there were more than 100 paddle-steamers carting wool, timber and other goods between Echuca and the outback sheep stations. The famous red-gum wharf was just over 1km long and lined with shops and hotels. But the Melbourne–Echuca railway line opened in 1864, and within a decade the boom years of the riverboat trade had ended.

Information

Accommodation booking service (☎ 1800 804 446) At the information centre.

Coin laundry (Darling St) Near the corner of Hare St.

Visitors centre (☎ 5480 7555; www.echucamoama.com; 2 Heygarth St; ☒ 9am-5pm)

Sights

HISTORIC PORT OF ECHUCA

The best feature of the **old port area** (adult/child/family passport $12/7.50/33, with a paddleboat cruise $24/13/60; ☒ 9am-5pm) is that everything is original, so you're exploring living history. The attractions are spread along the waterfront, and you buy a 'passport' that admits you to the three main sections: the wharf, the Star Hotel and the Bridge Hotel.

The booking office is at the entrance to the **Echuca wharf** via the old train station building, which has interesting vintage trains, carriages and a railway crane. In the wharf's cargo shed, there's an audiovisual presentation and dioramas depicting life on the riverboats.

Walk along the various levels of the massive wharf and onto the restored historic **paddle-steamers**: *Pevensey* (which featured in the TV series *All the Rivers Run*) and *Adelaide,* which are moored alongside. The wharf was built with three tiers because of the changing river levels, and there are gauges marking the highest points the river has reached.

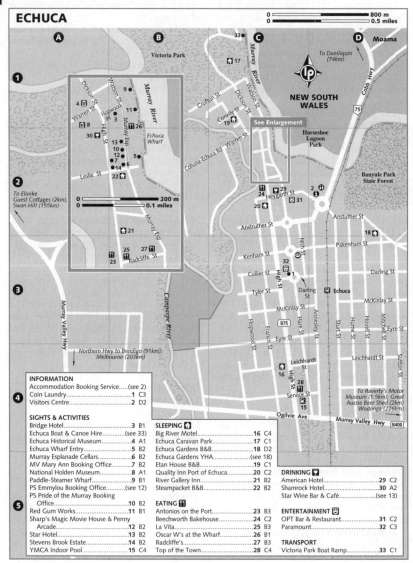

INFORMATION
Accommodation Booking Service.....(see 2)	
Coin Laundry.....................................**1** C3	
Visitors Centre....................................**2** D2	

SIGHTS & ACTIVITIES
Bridge Hotel..**3** B1	
Echuca Boat & Canoe Hire.............(see 33)	
Echuca Historical Museum................**4** A1	
Echuca Wharf Entry............................**5** B2	
Murray Esplanade Cellars...................**6** B2	
MV Mary Ann Booking Office............**7** B2	
National Holden Museum...................**8** A1	
Paddle-Steamer Wharf........................**9** B1	
PS Emmylou Booking Office.........(see 12)	
PS Pride of the Murray Booking	
Office...**10** B2	
Red Gum Works...............................**11** B1	
Sharp's Magic Movie House & Penny	
Arcade..**12** B2	
Star Hotel...**13** B2	
Stevens Brook Estate.......................**14** B2	
YMCA Indoor Pool...........................**15** C4	

SLEEPING 🏠
Big River Motel.................................**16** C4	
Echuca Caravan Park........................**17** C1	
Echuca Gardens B&B.........................**18** D2	
Echuca Gardens YHA.....................(see 18)	
Etan House B&B................................**19** C1	
Quality Inn Port of Echuca...............**20** C2	
River Gallery Inn...............................**21** B2	
Steampacket B&B..............................**22** B2	

EATING 🍽
Antonios on the Port.......................**23** B3	
Beechworth Bakehouse.....................**24** C2	
La Vita...**25** B3	
Oscar W's at the Wharf......................**26** B2	
Radcliffe's..**27** B3	
Top of the Town...............................**28** C4	

DRINKING 🍷
American Hotel.................................**29** C2	
Shamrock Hotel................................**30** A2	
Star Wine Bar & Café....................(see 13)	

ENTERTAINMENT 🎭
OPT Bar & Restaurant.......................**31** C2	
Paramount.......................................**32** C3	

TRANSPORT
Victoria Park Boat Ramp...................**33** C1	

Across the road at the **Star Hotel** (1867) you can escape through the underground tunnel which helped drinkers avoid the police during the years when the pub was a 'sly grog shop' (see reviews under Eating, p315 and Entertainment, p315).

At the **Bridge Hotel** (1 Hopwood Pl), your ticket admits you to an historic upstairs gallery. This pub is now a restaurant and bistro.

PORT AREA SIGHTS

Attractions in the area include **Red Gum Works** (Murray Esplanade; admission free; ☎ 9am-4pm) an historic sawmill that recreates the timber-milling days. You can watch woodturners and blacksmiths at work with traditional equipment, and purchase red-gum products.

Sharp's Magic Movie House & Penny Arcade (☎ 5482 2361; Murray Esplanade; adult/child $14/8; ☎ 9am-5pm) has authentic and fully restored penny-arcade machines that accept pennies, included with the admission fee. Another blast from the past is the free fudge tasting! The movie house shows old movies using original equipment; programs include Australian films, archival footage, and Buster Keaton or Laurel and Hardy classics. Your ticket is valid all day so you can come and go.

You can take a tour in a horse-drawn coach with **Billabong Carriages** (☎ 5483 5122; www.justhorses.com.au; adult/child $5/3). Get your tickets on the coach. For other carriages, see the *PS Pride of the Murray* booking office or the visitors centre.

There are free tastings of local wines at the port, at **Murray Esplanade Cellars** (☎ 5482 6058; Old Customs House, Murray Esplanade; ☎ 10am-5.30pm) and at **Stevens Brook Estate** (☎ 5480 1916; 620 High St) around the corner.

OTHER SIGHTS

Echuca Historical Museum (☎ 5480 1325; 1 Dickson St; adult/child $2/1; ☎ 11am-3pm) is in the old police station and lock-up buildings, classified by the National Trust. It has a collection of local history items, charts and photos from the riverboat era, and early records.

The **National Holden Museum** (7 Warren St; adult/child $6/3; ☎ 9am-5pm) has over 40 restored Holdens and associated memorabilia – one for the car buffs. Then head off to **Raverty's Motor Museum** (☎ 5482 2730; Murray Valley Hwy; adult/child $5/1; ☎ 10am-5pm) where there are 40 vehicles dating from 1900.

The **Great Aussie Beer Shed** (☎ 5480 6904; 377 Mary Ann Rd; ☎ 9am-5pm Sat & Sun) is in a huge shed that's wall-to-wall different beer cans – mostly cans of Aussie beer. One dates back to Federation. There's also an interesting display of old equipment.

Activities

As you enter the pedestrians-only Murray Esplanade, you can buy tickets for a cruise, or to explore the historic buildings along the esplanade. A paddle-steamer cruise along the Murray is almost obligatory, and at least four steamers offer cruises; head down to the river and check out the sailing times. **PS Emmylou** (☎ 5480 2237; 1-hr cruise adult/child $15/7.50) is a fully restored paddle-steamer driven by an original engine. Other cruises include a two-day, one-night cruise departing Wednesday evening (from $395). She sleeps 18 – book the whole boat to receive a discount.

One-hour cruises are offered by **PS Alexander Arbuthnot** (☎ 5482 4248; adult/child $16/6), **PS Canberra** (☎ 5482 2711; adult/child $13/6), **PS Pevensey** (☎ 5482 4248; adult/child $16/6) and **PS Pride of the Murray** (☎ 5482 5244; adult/child $13/6).

PS Adelaide is the oldest wooden-hulled paddle-steamer still operating anywhere in the world, and occasionally takes passengers on a cruise. **MV Mary Ann** (☎ 5480 2200) is a cruising restaurant, offering lunch and dinner cruises.

Echuca Boat & Canoe Hire (☎ 5480 6208; Victoria Park boat ramp) has motor boats, kayaks and canoes for hire, or you can be driven upstream to places like Barmah State Park and paddle back. Take a four-hour paddle ($40), three-day trip ($154) or a 10-day marathon from Yarrawonga to Echuca ($310). Prices are for two people.

Several operators offer **water-skiing** trips and classes – ask about them at the visitors centre (p311).

For horse-riding, contact **Billabong Trail Rides** (☎ 5480 1222; per hr $20), which also has rides for kids every second Sunday.

The **YMCA Indoor Pool** (☎ 5480 2994; cnr High & Service Sts; adult/child $4.50/2.60; ☎ 6am-8pm Mon-Fri, 9am-6pm Sat & Sun) is new and crystal bright, with heated pool, spa, sauna and gym.

Festivals & Events

There are so many events and activities that there are two calendars on the web to

consult: the **Murray River Website** (www.murray
-river.net/events/echuca) and **Echuca-Moama** (www
.echucamoama.com/html/whatson.htm).

Club Marine Southern 80 (☎ 5480 6754; Feb) The
world's largest ski race on the second Sunday of February.

Riverboats Jazz Food and Wine Festival (1800 804
446; late Feb) Music, food and wine by the Murray.

Steam, Horse & Vintage Rally (☎ 5482 4126; Jun)
On the Queen's Birthday weekend; features classic and
historic vehicles powered by all imaginable methods.

Sleeping

Echuca has accommodation everywhere,
from quaint B&Bs to spacious caravan parks,
huge brick motels and lace-trimmed old
hotels. They all outdo each other to please
you.

Hiring a houseboat is a great way to experience river life. The boats generally sleep
from four to 12, and are fully equipped with
facilities including sundecks and TVs etc.
Some boats provide linen. Rates vary according to season and size of boat. For example,
a boat with two double bedrooms may cost
$950 per week between May and Novem-
ber, but up to $3000 in January. The visitors
centre (p311) has full details and a booking
service. See p313 for overnight cruises on
PS *Emmylou*.

BUDGET

Big River Motel (☎ 5482 2522; fax 5480 2223; 371 High
St; s/d from $58/68; 🆒 🖳) This budget place
close to the town centre has attractive clean
rooms, barbecue areas, some nice trees to sit
under and a playground across the road.

Echuca Gardens YHA (☎ 5480 6522; echucagardens@
iinet.net.au; 103 Mitchell St; dm/d $20/40) This small
hostel is a 135-year-old workers' cottage with
tiny bedrooms, clean old bathrooms, country
kitchen and TV room. Outside is an exotic
garden with ponds, statues, veggie patch,
chooks, fruit trees. But wait, there's the even
more exotic B&B (below).

Echuca Caravan Park (☎ 5482 2157; fax 5480 1551;
51 Crofton St; camp sites per 2 people from $23, d cabins
from $70; 🆒 🖳) This is beside the river and
still close to everything. The facilities are
amazing, with new timber camp kitchens,
resort pool, large grassy areas and magnificent shady river red gums.

MIDRANGE

Echuca Gardens B&B (☎ 5480 6522; echucagardens@
iinet.net.au; 103 Mitchell St; s/d from $90/130; 🖳)

Doubles with bathroom and private balconies are art works in progress. Breakfast is
amid potted plants with fountains tinkling
below. Owner Kym can tell you where to go
(there are bikes for hire for $15 per day) and
entertain you with local anecdotes.

Steampacket B&B (☎ 5482 3411; fax 5482 3408; cnr
Murray Esplanade & Leslie St; B&B s/d/f from $75/85/160)
What a gem, right by the old port, in a
National Trust–classified building. The
rooms are quaint, with brass bedsteads and
little windows with views of the activities
on the wharf. The lounge room is cosy and
downstairs is the tearoom where meals are
served on fine china. It's even kid-friendly.

Quality Inn Port of Echuca (☎ 5482 5666; fax 5482
5682; 465 High St; s & d from $130; 🆒 🖳) This huge
luxury motel looks unappealing with its car-
parking areas, but the rooms are swish, the
pool large and heated, and there's a gym, as
well as barbecue areas.

TOP END

Elinike Guest Cottages (☎ 5480 6311; www.elinike
.com.au; 209 Latham Rd; B&B d from $170) These are
quaint little mudbrick cottages set in rambling gardens on the Murray River. Inside,
the rooms are all white and lacy, with a
small sitting room in which to enjoy your
gourmet breakfast.

Etan House B&B (☎ 5480 7477; www.etanhouse.com
.au; 11 Connelly St; B&B d from $180; 🆒 🖳) For the
luxury you deserve, stay in this elegant B&B
in a beautifully restored homestead. It's in
a quiet street, with friendly owners, grand
and comfortable lounges, your own country
kitchen, a grass tennis court and pool.

River Gallery Inn (☎ 5480 6902; www.rivergalleryinn
.com; 578 High St; B&B d from $160) Downstairs is a
gallery. Upstairs the Inn has eight elaborately
decorated rooms. Choose between Colonial
Australian or French Provincial, an Early
American spa room or perhaps the Scottish
en suite room.

Eating

High and Hare Sts both have a collection
of bakeries, cafés, restaurants, pubs and
takeaways.

Beechworth Bakehouse (☎ 5480 1057; 513 High
St; meals $4.50-8; 🕑 breakfast & lunch) An open,
cheerful place with delicious toasted sandwiches and home-baked goodies. Find a
seat on the deck overlooking the prettily
rippling Campaspe River.

Star Wine Bar & Cafe (☎ 5480 1181; 45 Murray Esplanade; mains $17-22; ⊗ breakfast & lunch daily, dinner Fri & Sat) In the historic Star Hotel, the seafood salads are popular, or call in for a snack and just soak up the atmosphere. See Entertainment review, below.

Oscar W's at the Wharf (☎ 5482 5133; www.oscarws .com.au; 101 Murray Esplanade; dinner mains $24-29; ⊗ lunch & dinner) Right on the wharf, Oscar W's bustles with people enjoying the only restaurant in the whole world that overlooks the Murray. No longer really true, but still. The food is magic. The baked pork had a tiny brandied cumquat on top. Prices are particularly reasonable, and the wine list extensive.

Radcliffe's (☎ 5480 6720; 2 Radcliffe St; mains $24-29; ⊗ dinner Wed-Sun) An atmospheric place, Radcliffe's has an extensive modern menu with items like spiced spatchcock with chilli paprika lime. The Tuscan courtyard is perfect in summer.

La Vita (☎ 5482 6688; cnr Radcliffe & High Sts; mains $17-24; ⊗ lunch Wed-Sun, dinner daily) This smart Italian place has tasty Oz meals, as well as traditional pastas at reasonable prices.

Antonios on the Port (☎ 5482 6117; 527 High St; mains $19-29; ⊗ dinner) Light bounces of the wine glasses at this sparkling Italian place with starched tablecloths. It backs onto the lovely Campaspe. Gourmet pizzas are a specialty.

Top of the Town (☎ 5482 4600; cnr High & Service Sts) This claims to be the best fish-and-chip shop in the state. Maybe so. It has a good range of the piscine, including river fish such as redfin and yellowbelly; it isn't often that you get the chance to sample these.

Drinking

There are quite a few good pubs in town:

Shamrock Hotel (☎ 5482 1036; 583 High St) Has a big welcome, Guinness and live music.

Bridge Hotel (☎ 5482 2247; 1 Hopwood Place)

American Hotel (☎ 5482 5044; cnr Hare & Heygarth Sts).

Entertainment

OPT Bar & Restaurant (☎ 5480 0150; 272 Hare St; ⊗ bar from 5pm Tue-Sat, nightclub to 4am Fri & Sat) This is the in place to be with its mezzanine dining and pool table. Downstairs is a dance band, upstairs a DJ.

Star Hotel (☎ 5480 1181; 45 Murray Esplanade) Has a duo singing on Friday and Saturday. With its open fireplace and ghosts of the past, it appeals to the over-30s but closes at midnight. See also Eating review, above.

Paramount (☎ 1900 931 166; 392 High St) Has daily screenings of mainstream movies and occasional live shows.

A courtesy coach will ferry you to the gambling clubs across the river in Moama. Some show free movies – ask your host where you're staying.

Getting There & Away

V/Line (☎ 13 61 96) has daily train services to/ from Melbourne ($33, 3½ hours). V/Line's Murray Link buses run daily from the train station, connecting Echuca with Wodonga ($39), Swan Hill ($22) and Mildura ($41). A daily service is available to destinations in southern NSW.

GOULBURN VALLEY

The 'Food Bowl of Australia' is an important centre for fruit, dairy, food processing and some of Australia's oldest and best wineries. The waterways, the Goulburn, Broken and Murray rivers are the lifeblood of the region and their wetlands are the habitat for diverse wildlife. Shepparton is the major town, and the visitors centre there has advice, pamphlets and maps for all of the valley's attractions.

KYABRAM
☎ 03 / pop 5700

Kyabram is a bustling commercial centre, with modern retail facilities for the surrounding farming communities. 'Kyabram' (ky-*ab*-r'm) is a local Koorie word meaning 'dense forest'.

The main point of interest is the **Kyabram Fauna Park** (☎ 5852 2883; Lake Rd; adult/child $8.50/6; ⊗ 9.30am-5.30pm), devoted to native species. It has modern enclosures and natural habitats for kangaroos, koalas, Tasmanian devils and dingoes. There's a large number of bird species in aviaries and a variety of water birds in the wetlands section. It's 1km south of the town centre, and very well signposted.

River Country Adventours (☎ 5852 2736; www.ad ventours.com.au; 57 Lake Rd, Kyabram; 2-day safaris per person from $145) rents out canoes and organises camping trips.

The indigenous people of this area called the Murray River the Tongala. Northwest of Kyabram, the nearby town of **Tongala** boasts the **Golden Cow centre** (☎ 5859 1100; cnr Henderson & Finlay Rds, Tongala; adult/child $5/2.50) with displays

---

DETOUR: MERRIGUM

Aboriginal for 'little clearing', **Merrigum** is 10km southeast of Kyabram. Dr John Saunders, who developed the intra-operative MRI machine used to track anatomical changes to the brain during brain surgery, grew up here. The town was originally named Andrews after his maternal great-grandfather. The **Merrigum Historical Society Museum** (☎ 03-5855 2330; 111 Waverley Ave; admission by gold coin; ⦿ daily by appointment) has details of Saunders' career. Other displays and memorabilia date back to the 1870s and there is a period house, blacksmith shop and old general store.

---

on the dairy industry (including a small farm), and the best milkshakes in Australia.

Sleeping & Eating

Echoes (☎ 5852 2379; www.theechoes.com.au; 245 Cooma Rd; B&B s/d $90/110) For a bit of luxury, spend a night or 10 in this gracious homestead on 2.5 hectares of parkland. Breakfast is served on the veranda, so you start your day watching the peaceful waters of the lake.

Commercial Hotel (☎ 5852 1005; 217 Allan St; s/d $50/60; ⊠) The basic motel-like rooms behind the pub are large and nicely furnished. Go into the hotel grounds for a barbecue, or the **bistro** (mains $11-19) serves standard pub meals.

Kyabram Hotel (cnr Allen & Union Sts; mains $11-19; ⦿ lunch & dinner Mon-Sat) This blue-painted pub has good-quality food, like garlic tiger prawns on rice. The front room is **Coronalas Tea Rooms** (meals $3.50-6; ⦿ lunch Mon-Fri) with, we're talking country pub here, lace curtains! The zucchini slice is to die for.

Getting There & Away

V/Line (☎ 13 61 96) has a daily bus service from Melbourne, and a coach service that runs every day except Wednesday between Albury and Mildura. Both stop at the **transit centre** (Union St).

Kyabram Transit (☎ 5952 1497) provides a local taxi service.

SHEPPARTON

☎ 03 / pop 56,500

Where the Goulburn and Broken Rivers meet is Shepparton, the regional centre of the Goulburn Valley, a modern town at the junction of the Midland and Goulburn Valley Hwys.

It started out in 1850, when McGuire's punt and inn were built beside the Goulburn River. In 1912 irrigation technology came to the Goulburn Valley, leading to a sudden influx of settlers and a steady growth in the local agricultural industries. Today, the city's major industrial employers are SPC Ardmona Fruit Products and Campbell's Soups.

You'll know you've arrived when you see the extraordinary cows alongside the road. So colourful. Perhaps they produce flavoured milk.

Orientation & Information

The Goulburn Valley Hwy becomes Wyndham St as it passes between Princess Park and the main shopping precinct around the Maude St mall.

McPherson Media (☎ 5832 8000; 194 High St) Offers Internet access (per hour $6.60).

RACV (☎ 5821 9522; 330 Wyndham St)

Visitors centre (☎ 5831 4400, 1800 808 839; Wyndham St; ⦿ 9am-5pm) Shepparton's excellent information centre is at the southern end of the Victoria Park Lake.

Sights

Shepparton City Historical Museum (cnr High & Welsford Sts; adult/child $2/1; ⦿ 1-4pm Sun, or by appointment) is so good it ought to be open every day! It is divided into sections devoted to transport, local agriculture, colonial clothing, shopping and communications. A highlight is the huge 100-year-old, four-faced post office clock, in full working order, which chimes on the hour.

The museum is close to the original site of McGuire's punt. A volunteer at the information centre will happily show you around.

Shepparton Art Gallery (☎ 5832 9861; Eastbank Centre, 70 Welsford St; ⦿ 10am-4pm) is between the town hall and the municipal offices. Its permanent collection of Australian art includes ceramics and paintings by Margaret Preston, John Perceval, Arthur Boyd, Frederick McCubbin, Arthur Streeton and Rupert Bunny. *Goulburn River near Shepparton* (1862) by Eugene von Guèrard is an early landscape that depicts McGuire's punt across the river. A separate gallery has temporary and touring exhibitions.

The **Bangerang Keeping Place** (Parkside Dr; ⦿ 9am-4pm Mon-Fri), about 2.5km northwest, has displays on the area's original Aboriginal owners.

Activities

Just south of town is the **Victoria Park Lake** (Wyndham St), a popular venue for watersports, surrounded by trees and pleasant picnic and barbecue areas. Beside the lake is **Aquamoves** (☎ 5831 8188; Tom Collins Dr; adult/child $4.50/3; ☻ 6am-9pm Mon-Fri, 8.30am-5pm Sat & Sun), a health and fitness extravaganza with several pools, including a rapid-river simulation pool and a hydrotherapy pool, gym and a large water-slide.

Ardmona KidsTown (☎ 5831 4213; Midland Hwy/ Mooroopna Causeway; admission by donation; ☻ dawn-dusk) is for kids under 98 years old, with flying fox, miniature railway, barbecues, café, giftware shop, a giant playground and more, just a few minutes east out of Shepparton.

Shepparton Golf Club (☎ 5821 2717; www.shep partongolf.net.au; Golf Links Dr) is a sand-belt course with great dining areas, alfresco drinks on the deck, spacious motel accommodation right on the course, and a long bar.

Sleeping

BUDGET

Hotel Australia (☎ 5821 4011; cnr Maude & Fryers Sts; s/d $33/55) This grand yellow pub with its wide protected verandas has basic old rooms upstairs with their own exit down to a little courtyard. Live bands play here Thursday to Saturday nights.

Victoria Hotel (☎ 5821 9955; cnr Wyndham & Fryers Sts; hotel s/d $35/45, motel $50/60) Upstairs, the hotel has small clean rooms with shared facilities. Out the back are newish motel units that are also great value.

Victoria Lake Holiday Park (☎ 5821 5431; info@ viclakeholidaypark.com.au; Wyndham St; camp sites per 2 people $18, d cabins from $62) Right beside Victoria Lake, across the lake from Aquamoves, this friendly place has plenty of grass and trees, bicycle paths and walkways. New luxury cabins have balconies out to the lake.

MIDRANGE

There are almost 20 motels in Shepparton, so enjoy.

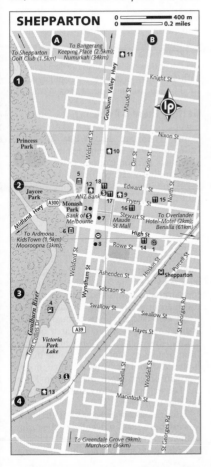

SHEPPARTON   0 |————| 400 m   0 |————| 0.2 miles

Overlander Hotel-Motel (☎ 5821 5622; overland@cv .quik.com.au; 97 Benalla Rd; s/d from $63/73; 🖴 🕾) This looks like any big pub, but the motel units are spacious and quiet, with views out to rolling paddocks. The central courtyard has a small pool and picnic area and the popular dining room has a kid's play area.

Tirana Motel (☎ 5831 1766; 33 Wyndham St; s/d $78/ 88; 🖴) This clean, well-run motel has very friendly hosts, and the high wall along the street blocks traffic noise.

Sherbourne Terrace Motel (☎ 5821 4977; 109 Wyndham St; s/d from $99/110; 🖴 🕾) Large and modern, the Terrace also has standard and VIP spa rooms, bistro and cocktail bar. Upstairs rooms have attractive balconies and there's an outdoor pool in a pleasant garden.

Eating

There are lots of bakeries and takeaways in and around the Maude St Mall and along Wyndham St. And all those grand hotels along Fryers St serve lunches and dinners.

Lemon Tree Cafe (☎ 5822 2300; 98 Fryers St; mains $13-19; 🕙 breakfast & lunch Mon-Sat) It's an oh-so-friendly place with wonderful breakfast items like French toast with bacon and maple syrup, and an interesting lunch menu including meals like spicy lamb kofta.

Spaghetti Hollow (☎ 5821 0771; 247 Wyndham St; mains $12-18; 🕙 lunch & dinner) Locals love this place for its filling portions of creative pasta dishes.

Letizia's Cafe, Bar & Restaurant (☎ 5831 8822; 67 Fryers St; mains $18-24; 🕙 breakfast, lunch & dinner) This open friendly place has a pleasant casual air, but there's nothing casual about its Asian-influenced food. If you want Oz, try the grilled pesto chicken.

Cellar 47 (☎ 5831 1882; 170 High St; mains $20-25; 🕙 lunch & dinner Mon-Sat) With its sleek black-and-glass décor and black bar, this smart restaurant has been a long-standing favourite. The menu includes Italian and Australian dishes.

Friars Cafe/Restaurant (☎ 5822 2181; 127 Fryers St; mains $19-23; 🕙 breakfast & lunch daily, dinner Wed-Sat) You'll feel quite blessed in this old church when you taste the food. The veal with sage-and-bocconcini polenta is heavenly.

Entertainment

There are cinemas, touring artists at the Eastbank Centre, which is Shepparton's arts centre, and many clubs. For a drink:

Hotel Australia (p317)
Flanigan's Irish Bar Part of Victoria Hotel (see p317).
Sports Bar (Sherbourne Terrace) You could catch a live band (Saturday) at this place (see left).

Or kick on at **Station One** (🕙 10pm-5am Fri & Sat) where the DJ plays dance music for the young and trendy.

Shopping

Shepparton is the area's shopping centre, with plenty of stores in and around the Maude St Mall. It's a pleasant way to shop – unhurried with friendly service.

Greendale Grove (☎ 5823 2785; info@greendale olives.com.au; 7230 Goulburn Valley Hwy; 🕙 10am-5pm) This mansion, 10km south of Shepparton, is actually a fabulous retail therapy stop, with all types of olive products, gifts and homewares, local produce, tastings and a gourmet restaurant.

SPC Ardmona (☎ 5825 2444; www.ardmonafactory sales.com.au; McLennan St, Mooroopna 🕙 9am-5pm) Has cash-and-carry discounts of popular Aussie food brands: Masterfoods, Heinz, Mars etc.

Getting There & Away

Shepparton train station is east of the town centre. There are daily **V/Line** (☎ 13 61 96) trains and buses to/from Melbourne ($28); and buses to/from Cobram ($10).

V/Line buses also connect with Wodonga ($29) and Benalla ($9) daily, and with Mildura ($48) and Bendigo ($12) three times a week.

TATURA
☎ 03 / pop 2800
A small farming community, Tatura has an interesting history. At the outbreak of WWII, all 'enemy aliens' in Australia were confined to internment camps and more than 25,000 prisoners of war (German, Italian and Japanese) were held in camps throughout Australia. Camps set up in the area between Tatura, Rushworth and Murchison ranged from temporary tent camps to the historic homestead at Dhurringile, which housed German officers from the Afrikan Korps, the Luftwaffe and sailors and officers from the ship *Cormoran*.

Tatura's **museum** (cnr Hogan & Ross Sts; 🕙 2-4pm Sat & Sun) has a section devoted to the history of this area's camps, with fascinating photos, records, books and memorabilia. The origi-

GOLD & YELLOW, WITH A DUSTING OF BROWN

There's no tourist buses here yet the area is famous. It was a stopover for travellers between the Beechworth and Bendigo gold diggings, that is until some local Koories took a couple of travellers to see the 'pretty stones' in a gully. By the 1880s there were more than 50 reefs being mined.

The town is **Rushworth**. Its High St, classified an historic precinct, is divided by a central plantation and a Victorian band rotunda. But don't think boulevard. Just as it was a hundred or so years ago, this sleepy, sprawling little precinct lazes dustily in the sun. The two hotels, the Rushworth and the Criterion, have certainly seen better days. You hardly need to visit the **Historical Museum** (High St; admission by donation; ☺ 10am-noon Sat, 2-5pm Sun) in the old Mechanics Institute, to get a feel for this town's past.

The surrounding box ironbark country is known as 'golden ironbark', since it provided wealth after the gold ran out. At one stage these forests supported seven sawmills. Some people see ironbark gums as scruffy. Well, neat they're not. But let your eyes adjust to their raggedy-tag limbs and you'll soon grow to love this harsh bush.

You can bide a while, to soak up the past, at **Miners Pick Caravan Park** (☎ 5856 1550; Neill St; sites/cabins from $14/38), or cute little **Rushworth Motel** (☎ 5856 1090; 4 School St; s/d/f from $59/69/90; ⊠), owned by a young couple. And the coffee at the Bakery is decidedly modern.

Just 7km south of Rushworth is **Whroo Historic Reserve** in the centre of the Rushworth State Forest. The new **visitor information centre & café** (☎ 5856 1561) is staffed by Doris who is passionate about the area. But there's a note on the door. *'Sorry. On call. Injured wildlife'*. It's not written with a thumbnail dipped in tar, but it's just as evocative.

The bush is spangled with wildflowers. And the quiet is cut only by the sound of birdsong. **Whroo** (pronounced 'roo') is an old gold-mining ghost town, with relics of the gold-rush era: old mine shafts, cyanide vats (used for dissolving and separating the gold from quartz) and puddling machines. Although the town once had over 130 buildings, the ironbarks and native scrub have reclaimed it. Just the Balaclava open-cut mine is open for inspection – go through the tunnel.

Whroo's old **cemetery** (nearby on Spring Hill and National Trust–classified) is an evocative place with headstone inscriptions that bear testimony to the hard life experienced by the diggers and their families.

There are walking tracks and signed nature trails through the scrub; one leads to Ngurai-Illum-Wurrung rock well, a small waterhole used by the Koories who lived here. There's also a signposted **camp site** (free) with toilets, picnic area and open fireplace.

And just to bring you back to the present, half-way along the dusty road to Nagambie you pass **12 Acres Winery** (☎ 5794 2020; ☺ 10am-6pm Thu-Mon) where you can taste and buy the 12 Acres reds.

nal section of the museum is devoted to local history with special displays on the history of irrigation.

Signposted off the Midland Hwy, 2km west of Tatura, is the **German Military Cemetery**. This cemetery was established by the German government in 1958, when the remains of all German prisoners of war and internees who died in Australia during WWI and WWII were reburied here.

The small **Whim-Inn Motel** (☎ 5824 1155; cnr Hogan St & Dhurringile Rd; s/d/f from $66/80/114) has a charming fresh look and cheerful rooms, on a large grassy property.

With a wide range of cabins and caravans, the well-maintained **Country Gardens Caravan Park** (☎ 5824 2652; 270 Rushworth Rd; camp sites per 2 people $11, d cabins from $20) is a good choice. It's about 2km west of town.

V/Line (☎ 136196) buses to/from Melbourne and Echuca stop in Fraser St.

MURCHISON

☎ 03 / pop 630

Murchison is beautiful, spreading along the banks of the Goulburn River, with pleasant picnic parks every few metres. There are also a number of historic buildings. The **Murchison Backpackers Hostel** (see p320) was built in 1860.

South of town, **Murchison Wines** (☎ 5826 2294; www.murchisonwines.com.au; Old Weir Rd; ☺ 10am-5pm Thu-Mon) has tastings and sales. Guido is the winemaker, and his wife Sandra the

---

WINERIES

For more details on wineries and wine touring in the Murchison, Nagambie and Heathcote areas see the Victorian Wineries chapter (p61).

---

cheesemaker, so calling in here is one way to get the best of both worlds. The winery also sells gifts and souvenirs and has a gorgeous picnic area under a vine-covered pergola.

In the local cemetery is the **grave of King Charles Tattambo**, leader of the Goulburn tribe at the time of white arrival. Also here is the **Italian Ossario**. This mausoleum, with its rows of cypress pines, houses remains of Italian prisoners of war and detainees. There is a campanile and an altar of Italian marble. Each year, on Remembrance Day, Mass is celebrated before a large gathering. There is also an Italian war memorial and chapel.

East of town, you'll find the friendly **Murchison Motel** (☎ 5826 2488; 111 High Rd; s/d/ f from $50/65/83) It has classic motel rooms and a small restaurant. **Murchison Backpackers Hostel** (☎ 5826 2655; backpacker@iinet.com.au; 17 Stephenson St; dm per night/week $22/110; 🖳) is a homely hostel with barbecues, kitchen and TV room. Keith, the owner, offers loads of information about the region. There are three caravan parks around the outskirts of town.

V/Line (☎ 13 61 96) buses stop in the main street, on their way to/from Melbourne and Echuca.

NAGAMBIE

☎ 03 / pop 1300

Nagambie (pronounced 'na-*gam*-bi') is on the shores of pretty Lake Nagambie, which was created by the construction of the Goulburn Weir back in 1887. This area's main attractions are its wineries and watersports.

Information

Visitors centre (☎ 5794 2647, 1800 444 647; www .nagambielakestourism.com.au; 145 High St; ⏰ 9am-5pm) The Nagambie Lake visitors centre is in the nut house. It's true. But you'll still get a great range of information on the region and the local wineries, along with many nutty goodies. There's a free tasting of the many different types of nuts every weekend, and a small shop sells souvenirs and maps.

Sights & Activities

Lake Nagambie and **Goulburn Weir** are popular for **watersports** such as water-skiing, rowing, canoeing, sailing, fishing and swimming. There's an International Rowing Course on Lake Nagambie where the **World Masters Rowing** (Mar) competitions are held and many rowing camps do much splashing around.

Two of the best-known wineries in Victoria are just south of town: **Tahbilk Winery** (☎ 5794 2555; Off Goulburn Valley Hwy; ⏰ 9am-5pm Mon-Sat, 11am-5pm Sun) and **Mitchelton Wines** (☎ 5794 2710, 5736 2222; Mitchellstown Rd; ⏰ 10am-5pm); see also p61. A great way to visit both these wineries is to take a cruise with **Goulburn River Cruises** (☎ 5794 2877; per person $19; ⏰ Sep-May). Meals are available, and group cruises can be arranged.

Nagambie is the place to try skydiving. **Skydive Nagambie** (☎ 5794 2626, 1800 266 500; www.sky divenagambie.com; 1232 Kettles Rd) offers tandem dives from $280, but you can just go out there, grab a hot dog from the kiosk, and watch. Perhaps they're floating down from the nut house.

Sleeping & Eating

Nagambie Lakes Entertainment Centre (☎ 5794 2747; www.nlec.com.au; per person $20) If you want to bunk down there's beds upstairs in bright but tiny rooms with many shared bathrooms and a great glass-walled community room. It's used by rowing camps in summer. Downstairs, the **bistro** (mains $14-25; ⏰ lunch & dinner) serves upmarket food like a vegetable stack layered with goats' cheese. Grab yourself a table on the deck overlooking the lake.

Lakeside Resort Nagambie (☎ 5794 2833; 185 High St; r $99-135) For awesome accommodation, ask for a spa room with views of the lake. There's exclusive dining in the restaurant.

Other options:

Nagambie Goulburn Highway Motel (☎ 5794 2681; 143 High St; r/units from $60/70) A small motel with fresh blue rooms. Next door to the Nagambie Caravan Park.

Nagambie Caravan Park (☎ 5794 2681; 143 High St; camp sites from $17) A friendly, well-run place.

HEATHCOTE

☎ 03 / pop 1550

Pleasant little Heathcote, by the Valley of the Liquidambars, is a great starting point for walks in the surrounding box ironbark forests. One walk is to **Pink Cliffs Reserve**, a unique moonscape of pinks and ochres, formed by the sluicing activities of goldminers. Another goes up past an **historic powder magazine** to the **Devil's Cave** and up to the **Viewing Rock Lookout**.

Another great lookout spot is atop **Mt Ida Flora Reserve**, where wildflowers are best from July to February. It's 5km north of Heathcote on the road to Echuca.

Happily, Heathcote is also a wine centre (see p62), so you can kick back with an interesting drop after all the walking. Unless you're heading off to the excellent local golf course.

Heathcote's **visitors centre** (☎ 5433 3121; www .heathcote.org.au; cnr High & Barrack Sts; ☒ 9am-5pm) has maps of forest and winery trails, and details of the B&B, motel and holiday park accommodation.

Sleeping & Eating

Wattle Gully B&B (☎ 5433 2362; bundy2@iinet.net.au; 4440 McIvor Hwy; B&B s/d from $70/105; ☒ ☒) Enjoy total relaxation in this gorgeous limestone home with a barbecue rotunda next to a lily pond.

Heathcote Motor Inn (☎ 5433 2655; 257 High St; s/d $58/68; ☒ ☒) In a pleasant garden, just a short walk to local wineries, this motel is a great spot.

Emeu Inn (☎ 5433 2668; www.emeuinn.com.au; 187 High St; mains $25-29; ☒ lunch & dinner Thu-Mon) The food reflects the chef's passion for bush tucker, the delightful décor is European, the rabbit tagine an exciting taste sensation. Enjoy the regional wines, then ask about the Inn's luxury accommodation.

Queens Meadow Caravan Park (☎ 5433 2304; april wood@bigpond.com; Barrack St; camp sites per 2 people $13, d cabins from $55) This is a quiet park, shaded by grand trees, and very popular with holidaymakers.

A Gaggle of Geese (☎ 5433 2981; 97 High St; meals $6-11; ☒ lunch & breakfast) For the best quiche you've ever tasted, pop into the quaint little Gaggle.

LAKE EPPALOCK

This large rockfill lake on the Campaspe River, 8km from Heathcote on the McIvor Hwy, is usually fantastic for watersports and is known for its fishing, but the drought has left it almost dry. There are four caravan parks and a motel, dry swimming spots and several sad boat-launching ramps. Fortunately it still has its interesting cycling and motorbike tracks, an outdoor cinema, two golf courses nearby and plenty of local wineries. For information about the lake's condition call **Fisheries Victoria** (☎ 13 61 86).

The High Country

Grab your bike, throw the skis on the roof and get set for an action-packed trip to the High Country, where the air is clear, the scenery spectacular and there's a thousand different ways to enjoy this superb region. It's greatest asset is its unspoilt, natural beauty.

The High Country isn't particularly high in world terms – the highest point, Mt Bogong, reaches 1986m. But it's a diverse, fragile and beautiful environment, at the southern end of the Great Dividing Range. The region has Victoria's largest national park, the Alpine National Park, and other parks include Mt Buffalo and Baw Baw national parks.

Highlights include resorts and snowfields for both downhill and cross-country skiing in winter, and horse riding and walking in summer; the attractive former gold-mining towns in the northeast, especially Beechworth and Yackandandah; and the all-seasons towns at the foothills of the mountain ranges – particularly Mansfield, Bright and Mt Beauty. The thriving Milawa gourmet region is also worth a stop, with exciting restaurants, acclaimed wineries and an impressive range of local produce.

Away from the mountains, Lake Eildon National Park is a watersports paradise. Spend a few days on a houseboat, do some fly fishing or just take in the gorgeous surroundings at one of the many attractive B&Bs in the region.

HIGHLIGHTS

- Getting your heart pounding with a double-black-diamond rush down the powder bowls at the back of **Falls Creek** (p341)
- Leaving the car at home to explore by bicycle; follow the Murray River to the Mountains Rail Trail or take on **Mt Buller** (p334) in summer
- Enjoying a taste of the region at one of the acclaimed restaurants in **Bright** (p344)
- Soaking up some gold-mining history at the historical precinct in **Beechworth** (p350)
- Making like *The Man from Snowy River* with horse rides in spring near **Mansfield** (p331)
- Skiing cross country at **Lake Mountain** (p327)
- Going off-road on the drive from **Jamieson to Walhalla** (p331) via Woods Point
- Taking in the summer blossoms and spectacular views of the **Alpine National Park** (p337)

- www.legendswinehighcountry.info

THE HIGH COUNTRY

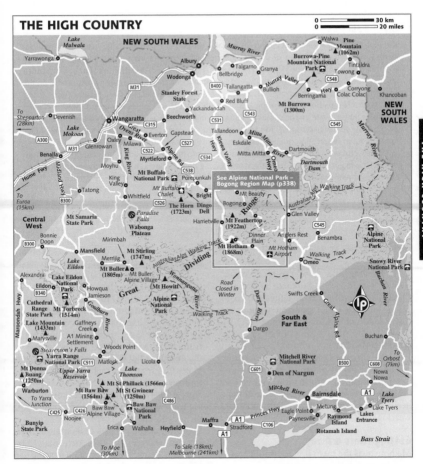

Climate

As this is an alpine environment, weather conditions can change dramatically and without warning any time of year. In winter, which runs from June to September, most of the higher mountains are snowcapped and frosts are frequent. A fine sunny day can deteriorate into blizzard conditions, so make sure you have access to protective clothing on the slopes. If you are driving up to the ski fields, you are required by law to carry chains (see right). In the height of summer, you can walk or bike all day in the heat without finding water, and then face temperatures below freezing at night. Bushwalkers should be self-sufficient, with a tent, fuel stove, warm clothes, a sleeping bag and plenty of water. Sunburn is also a serious problem, even on cloudy days, so slap on a high-SPF sunscreen and wear goggles or sunnies.

Dangers & Annoyances
ALPINE DRIVING

During winter take care when driving in this area as roads can be slick with ice and snow, and some can become impassable. Check road conditions with the **Official Victorian Snow Report** (☎ 1902 240 523; www.vicsnow report.com.au) before heading out. Snow chains must be carried during winter even if there's no snow – heavy penalties apply if you don't. These can be rented from most service stations and ski hire shops in gateway towns,

---

ON THE SLOPES

The High Country provides the setting for arguably the best skiing in Australia. Victoria may not rival North America for its amount of snow or Europe for its length of runs, but if you like your skiing and boarding with sun, blue skies and gum trees, head to the northeast of the state for impressive resorts and a rocking après-ski scene. The ski season officially launches, with or without snow, on the June Queen's Birthday long weekend and runs until mid-September. The best deals are to be found in June and September (low season), with late July to August (high season) the busiest and most expensive time. For a report on snow conditions, contact the **Official Victorian Snow Report** (☎ 1902 240 523; www.vicsnowreport.com.au). The call is charged on a per-minute basis. The website has winter road-condition reports, information, accommodation links and 'snow cams', even in summer.

Come October and the alpine ski trails transform into fine walking and mountain-biking environments. The major ski resorts have their own Alpine Resort Management Boards, which generally also offer on-mountain information offices (most are open year-round). There are no dedicated banks in any of the ski resorts, but Eftpos is widely available.

In most of the alpine resorts a limited number of places to stay and restaurants remain open over summer. This information is given in the text under specific towns.

---

such as Mansfield, Harrietville, Bright and Omeo.

If travelling in a diesel-powered vehicle, it's also a good idea to purchase 'alpine mix' diesel (with antifreeze) at either Omeo or Harrietville – it could save you a call to the Royal Automobile Club of Victoria (RACV).

OTHER DANGERS

Extreme climatic conditions are to be expected in the High Country, so come prepared (see p323 for more information). March flies are also a problem in summer. Take along a healthy supply of insect repellent and avoid wearing dark-coloured clothing.

Getting There & Away

Melbourne is the main link for public transport to the High Country.

BUS

Bus service to major alpine towns is available with **V/Line** (☎ 13 61 96; www.vline.com.au), and there are also connecting services from Benalla and Wangaratta. Many small private local services run from the alpine base towns to the resorts. Most of these services vary seasonally.

BAW BAW NATIONAL PARK

This national park is a southern offshoot of the Great Dividing Range, encompassing the Baw Baw Plateau and the forested valleys of the Thomson and Aberfeldy Rivers. The highest points are Mt St Phillack (1566m) and Mt Baw Baw (1564m). The subalpine

vegetation ranges from open eucalypt stands to wet gullies and tall forests on the plateau.

There are long and short **walking tracks** through here, including the 3km **Mushroom Rocks Walk**, leading to huge granite tors (great blocks of granite broken off from the massif by the expansion and contraction of ice in winter and other weathering effects) from Mt Erica car park, and a section of the **Australian Alps Walking Track** (www.netc.net.au /bushwalking/alpswalk), which starts its 655km journey at Walhalla. There is a camping area at **Aberfeldy River**, in the northeastern section, with picnic tables, fireplaces and pit toilets. Eastern Tyers camping area, in the south of the park, is a designated camp site for walkers on the Australian Alps Walking Track. Dispersed **bush camping** (sites free) is also allowed on the Baw Baw Plateau (fuel stove only).

The main access roads are the Baw Baw Rd from Noojee and the Moe–Rawson Rd via Erica. If you're heading up this way, taking a detour to Walhalla (p359) is highly recommended.

The higher sections of the park are covered with snow in winter, and the Mt Baw Baw ski resort and Mt St Gwinear cross-country skiing area are both within the park.

MT BAW BAW VILLAGE

☎ 03 / elevation 1564m

This small downhill ski resort in the centre of Baw Baw National Park is a relaxed option for beginners and families, and is seldom overcrowded. The Australian Alps Walking

ALPINE TOURS

While you can't beat the thrill of discovering a place for yourself, there are some excellent tour options in the alpine country – anything from horse riding through spring blossoms to sampling regional wine and food. Note that most 4WD tours or walking tours only run from November to late May. Most prices quoted here are all-inclusive of accommodation and meals. Other tours and activities are listed under specific towns.

Adrenalin (☎ 1800 800 445; www.whitewaterrafting.com.au; Lake William Hovel Rd, Cheshunt; from $155) The only onsite white-water rafting facility in Australia that offers rafting and sled tours on the King River, Lower Mitta and Mitta Gorge; tours last from five hours to five days.

Australian Photographic Tours (☎ 02-9922 4092; www.phototours.com.au; 7-day tours $2780) This Sydney-based outfit runs week-long remote-area 4WD photography tours of the High Country.

Ecotrek (☎ 08-8383 7198; www.ecotrek.com.au; 6-day cycling tour $1490, 5-/8-day walking tours $895/$1390) Has a range of overnight trips, including an eight-day traverse across Victoria's three highest peaks, and a gourmet cycle tour.

Epicurious (☎ 0407 261 510; www.epicurioustravel.com.au; 4-/5-day tour $1020/1690) Offers luxury all-inclusive cycling and walking holidays that combine spectacular High Country scenery with fine food and even finer accommodation.

Mountain Top Experience (☎ 5134 6876; www.mountaintopexperience.com) Can provide food parcel drop-offs and car shuttles (per person $25) for walkers on the Australian Alps Walking Track (see p44). It also has a range of 4WD tag-along tours (per day $90), as well as 4WD hire.

River Mountain Guides (RMG; ☎ 1800 818 466; www.rivermountainguides.com.au; 2-day adventures from $300) A specialist snow-sports guiding company that runs back-country snow adventures and summer walking trips. All tours are centred around Falls Creek and the Bogong High Plains.

Stirling Experience (☎ 5777 3541; www.stirling.au.com; 1-day tour from $75, 2-/3-day tour $275/395) 4WD day trips run to Mt Stirling, Craig's Hut and the Howqua Valley. Overnight trips explore the King Valley or Wonnangatta area.

Track (p44) passes by a few kilometres from the village.

There are good beginner to intermediate runs, and several harder runs. The downhill skiing area is 25 hectares with a vertical drop of 140m. Baw Baw is also an excellent base for **cross-country skiing**, with plenty of trails, including one that connects to the Mt St Gwinear trails on the southern edge of the plateau. Ski patrols operate on weekends and during peak midweek periods.

Information

In the centre of the village, **Mt Baw Baw Alpine Resort Management Board** (☎ 5165 1136; www.mountbawbaw.com.au) offers general tourist information and can make accommodation bookings.

Several ski-hire places operate during the season, including **Mt Baw Baw Ski Hire** (see right) **IDS Snowsports** (☎ 5165 1155), based in the Alpine Hotel (right).

Costs

Ski season admission fees are $26 per car for the day car park. The ski lifts only operate if there is snow and cost $63/33 a day per adult/child; lift-and-lesson packages cost $85/60 per

adult/child. Mt Baw Baw's most recent addition is the Frantic Frog Super Tube Park ($20 per five-ride ticket), a thrilling slide down the mountain on an oversized tube.

Sleeping & Eating

Mt Baw Baw Central Accommodation Booking Service (☎ 5165 1120; 1800 629 578; www.bawbawskihire.com.au), based at Mt Baw Baw Ski Hire, books accommodation. In the ski season, ski-club accommodation is available midweek/weekends from $30/50 per person per night (minimum two nights).

Kelly's Lodge (☎ 5165 1129; www.kellyslodge.com.au; Frosti Lane; in summer $60, ski season $77-180) A super friendly place and one of the few lodges open year-round. The rooms are standard Baw Baw–style: no frills, but comfortable enough with a cosy lounge. You can cook in the shared kitchen or have a meal in the café.

Alpine Hotel (☎ 1300 651 136; Currawong Rd; midweek/weekend dm $25/30, d $120/140, cabins $288/360) During the ski season the pub has motel-style accommodation as well as a back-packer dorm on the top floor. It also runs brand-new self-contained cabins that sleep up to six people. In winter the bar-café is a good spot to hang while local bands belt out schnapps-fuelled rock covers to the après-ski crowd.

Kelly's Cafe (☎ 5165 1120; dishes $8–$16; breakfast, lunch & dinner winter, 8am-7pm Sat & Sun summer) If you're ravenous after a day on the slopes, Kelly's ski-in café is a favourite for its pizza, pasta and healthy stir-fries. Savoury crepes, burgers and baked potatoes fill up the troops during the day. If you're too exhausted to move, it will deliver.

Getting There & Away

Mt Baw Baw is 176km east of the centre of Melbourne – an easy three-hour drive. You can either take the Princes Hwy (A1), or go via Yarra Junction and Powelltown to Noojee, from where you take Baw Baw Rd. The last section of the drive from Noojee is steep and winding, but very scenic.

Mountain Top Experience (☎ 5134 6876; www .mountaintopexperience.com) meets V/Line trains at Warragul and has a bus service to Mt Baw Baw (one way or same-day return $50).

MT ST GWINEAR

☎ 03 / elevation 1250m

Mt St Gwinear is a cross-country skiing area, ideal for intermediate and advanced touring, in the Baw Baw National Park. Managed by **Parks Victoria** (☎ 5165 3204) and the Department of Sustainability & Environment (DSE), a 9km link trail starts from the car park and heads across the Baw Baw Plateau, via the Australian Alps Walking Track, connecting to Mt Baw Baw Alpine Village. This is a popular walk in the warmer months. Mountain biking is not permitted in the area due to the fragile peat-bog environment.

The Walhalla Star Hotel (p360) has good information on Mt St Gwinear on its website (www.starhotel.com.au/snowreport). Facilities are limited and ski patrols operate only on weekends. Accommodation, ski equipment and chain hire are available at Erica. The day admission fee is $9.30 per car during the ski season. No fees apply for overnight snow camping.

From Melbourne the main access route is via the Princes Hwy (A1) to Moe, then north via Erica.

MARYSVILLE

☎ 03 / pop 625

Small, sleepy-town Marysville was originally established as a private mountain re-

treat back in 1863 and by the 1920s was known as Melbourne's honeymoon capital. Today its beautiful mountain setting still attracts weekend visitors and is the main base for the cross-country ski fields of Lake Mountain.

Information

The **visitors centre** (☎ 5963 4567; www.marysvilletour ism.com; Murchison St; 9am-5pm) has Parks Victoria notes on the area's natural attractions. There is an ATM in the Marysville Hotel/Motel on Murchison St. Cross-country ski hire and toboggans are available at several places on Murchison St.

Sights & Activities

A unique collection of vintage and classic vehicles is on display at **Marysville Museum** (☎ 5963 3777; 49 Darwin St; adult/child aged 12-18/child under 12 $8/5/free; 10am-5pm Sat & Sun), just behind the general store. The highlight is the exquisite 19th-century Romany caravan.

In a rainforest setting, the life-size terracotta statues at **Bruno's Art & Sculptures Garden** (☎ 5963 3513; 51 Falls Rd; adult/child $5/free; garden 10am-5pm daily, gallery 10am-5pm Sat & Sun) have an element of otherworldliness, but they probably won't appeal to everyone.

Spectacular **Steavenson's Falls**, 3.5km from Marysville, are Victoria's highest waterfalls at 82m. A short walk from the car park ($2 parking fee) leads to the falls, which are floodlit until midnight nightly. There are several bushwalks from here, many quite steep, including **Nicholl's Lookout** and **Keppel's Lookout**.

Lady Talbot Drive, which starts in Marysville, is a 48km scenic loop past some of the area's prettiest spots, camp sites and most spectacular features, including **Phantom Falls**. Popular walks on the drive include the 2km return **Keppel Falls Walk** and the 4km **Beeches Rainforest Walk**. The road is unsealed, but should be fine for 2WD vehicles in the dry months. A Parks Victoria note is available. **Cumberland Scenic Reserve**, with numerous walks and the Cora Lynn and Cumberland Falls, is 16km east of Marysville.

The Steavenson, Taggerty and Acheron Rivers have great **fishing** and magnificent settings. Pick up the '10 Best Fishing Spots' notes from the visitors centre or try **Mystic River Fly-Fishing Adventures** (☎ 5963 4316 or 5772 1771).

Sleeping

Karami Guesthouse (☎ 5963 3260; karamihouse@virtual
.net.au; 7 Karami Cres; d $140-245) With its Tudor ex-
terior and leafy grounds, filled with magno-
lias, waratahs and pines, this friendly 1920s
guesthouse is reminiscent of an English
country inn. Billiards anyone? There's a full-
size table. The hosts also serve first-rate dinners using mainly regional produce.

Moondai Farm B&B (☎ 5774 7319; www.moondai
.uni.cc; 182 Marysville Rd, Buxton; d midweek/weekend
$150/180) On a small alpaca stud, 9km north
of Marysville, the private B&B wing is perfect
for a romantic retreat, with gorgeous views of
the Steavenson River and a double spa bath.
There's plenty of great fishing on the property, and a barbecue to cook up your catch.

Dalrymples (☎ 5963 3416; 18 Falls Rd; d midweek/
weekend from $140/190) Choose between the
chintzy garden cottage or the two-storey
loft house, both well equipped with generous
breakfast provisions (freshly baked bread
and home-made jams), open fires and corner spas. But the real pleasure of staying here
is the peaceful surrounds and lush garden.

Marysville Caravan and Holiday Park (☎ 5963
3443; 1130 Buxton Rd; powered/unpowered sites for 2 people
from $23/20, d cabins $52-85, linen extra) The Steavenson River runs through this popular cara-
van park, right in the centre of town, which
has an attractive barbecue area and a well-
equipped laundry.

Eating

Fraga's Café (☎ 5963 3216; 19 Murchison St; mains $8-
15; ☾ 10am-3.30pm Sun-Tue, lunch & dinner Thu-Sat) A
refreshingly non–olde-worlde surprise with
a creative café-style menu and good coffee,
which can be enjoyed in the sunny art-filled
dining room or from the outside seats while
people watching.

In Neutral (☎ 5963 3666; 6 Murchison St; mains $12-
25; ☾ breakfast, lunch & dinner) As they like to say
at this American-style roadhouse, restaurant and bar, 'get your butt in gear and park
it In Neutral', and while you're here, dig into
the eccentric cuisine where Tex-Mex meets
Aussie road kill. Run by bikers, this place is
for bikers and anyone else who enjoys warm
service, a heavily stocked bar and a comfortable lounge to sink into by the fire.

Gilberts at Fruit Salad Farm (☎ 5963 3232; www
.fruitsaladfarm.com.au; Aubrey-Couzens Dr; mains $21-27;
☾ dinner Fri-Mon, lunch Sat) Gilberts has an attractive rainforest setting, great views and a

reputation for good food, although it's well
and truly time for an update of the tweesville
interior! Locals rave about the seared fillet of
kangaroo ($22). It also has comfortable self-
contained cottages from $125 per double.

Marysville Patisserie (☎ 5963 3368; 18 Murchison St;
☾ 10am-6pm Wed-Sat, 10am-5pm Sun) This bustling
café gets fab reports from Melbourne weekenders who love the Belgian truffle mousse,
fresh salads and mouthwatering home-made
pastries.

Getting There & Away

Bus service to/from Marysville is available
with **McKenzie's Bus Lines** (☎ 9853 6264; www
.mckenzies.com.au). It departs from the coach terminal at Southern Cross station (formerly
Spencer St station) in Melbourne ($13.30,
2¼ hours, daily), and continues to Alexandra and Eildon.

LAKE MOUNTAIN

☎ 03 / elevation 1433m

Renowned as the premier cross-country ski
resort in Australia, this part of Yarra Ranges
National Park has world-class facilities, with
an extensive system of 37km of trails that
are groomed daily, including several toboggan runs. Ski patrols operate daily during
the season. Walkers and mountain bikers
are encouraged to make use of the ski trails
in summer.

Summer walks include the 4km (two hours
return) **Summit Walk**, which crosses alpine
bog and granite rock faces. The walk starts
from Gerraty's Car Park, the main parking
area. Parks Victoria notes are available from
the Marysville visitors centre (opposite) or
the spanking-new **Alpine Visitor Centre** (☎ 5963
3288; www.lakemountainresort.com.au; ☾ 7am-6pm during ski season, 8am-4.30pm Mon-Fri rest of year), which
houses a café, and has ski hire, a ski school
and undercover barbecue areas.

The daily admission fee is $25 per car
during the ski season. The daily trail fee per
adult/child costs from $10/5.50.

There's no accommodation on the mountain. Summer and snow camping are allowed –
there's no fee, but you *must* notify the Alpine
Visitors Centre of your intentions before
heading out.

Getting There & Around

No public transport operates to Lake Mountain. A daily bus service travels between

Melbourne and Marysville (see p327), the nearest major town. **Country Touch Tours** (☎ 5963 3753; adult/child $20/15) runs a weekend winter shuttle between Marysville and Lake Mountain, which includes resort entry. It departs from Marysville at 10.30am and Lake Mountain at 3pm. Pickup from Melbourne may also be arranged.

CATHEDRAL RANGE STATE PARK

The Cathedral Range State Park is roughly 10km northwest of Marysville, and offers excellent walking, rock-climbing, fishing and camping. Dominated by the 7km-long razorback ridge of the ranges, which reach a height of over 800m, the park is quite small at only 3500 hectares. Its vegetation varies dramatically – from tall open forests to damp sheltered gullies, so a wide variety of animal and birdlife (including lyrebirds and satin bower birds) inhabits the park. Pick up Parks Victoria notes from the visitors centre in Marysville.

Popular short walks include the **Canyon Track** (one hour return), from Sugarloaf Saddle to Sugarloaf Peak, which involves some rock scrambling but rewards with fine views, or the easier **Little River Track** (1¼ hours return), which follows the river between Ned's Gully and Cook's Mill. Well-known rock-climbing areas include Sugar Loaf and North Jawbone. Little River runs through the park and is a popular trout-fishing spot.

There are three camp sites in the park – at Ned's Gully, Cook's Mill (both with pit toilets) and the Farmyard (accessed on foot only and without any facilities). Camping fees apply to all sites; you must BYO firewood and boil all drinking water. Bunkhouse accommodation is also available at Taggerty (below).

Several roads access the park off the Maroondah Hwy (B360) and Marysville Rd, although you should check road conditions during winter and spring. All roads within the park are gravel and 2WD accessible.

TAGGERTY

☎ 03

At the foot of the Cathedral Ranges, the tiny farming township of Taggerty is home to the pioneer-style **Australian Bush Settlement** (☎ 5774 7378; www.green.net.au/australian_bush_settlement; Maroondah Hwy; tent sites $10 per person, dm $19-25, d $45-60), a rambling collection of cottages on 32 hec-

tares of farmland, and a Willing Worker on Organic Farms (Wwoof) member (see p393). There are walks, open campfires and plenty of wildlife, including a shelter for orphaned native animals. In the town itself, **Willowbank at Taggerty** (☎ 5774 7503; www.willowbankattaggerty.com.au; 29 Coomb St; d $160) has well-appointed accommodation, with a particularly lovely garden, as well as an excellent, lantern-fringed **bistro** (mains $15-30; ☽ lunch & dinner Thu-Sun). The **Old Woolshed Cafe** (☎ 5774 7523; Webbs Lane; meals $4-12; ☽ 10am-4pm Thu-Sun), within **Clearstream Olive Farm**, showcases local produce, including gingko elixir.

ALEXANDRA

☎ 03 / pop 1850

Alexandra has a gentle small-town air, with trout fly fishing on the Acheron and Goulburn Rivers, water sports on Lake Eildon and many lovely B&Bs. It was once the heart of a thriving timber industry, and an extensive narrow-gauge steam railway system built through the area's forests once linked the network of bush sawmills to the town.

The **visitors centre** (☎ 5772 1100, 1800 652 298; Grant St; ☽ 9am-5pm), opposite Rotary Park, can book accommodation.

Train spotters might enjoy the **Timber Tramway & Museum** (☎ 5772 1035; Station St; adult/child $2.50/1; ☽ 10am-4pm every 2nd Sun) in the old station. **Totally Trout Fishing Centre** (☎ 5772 2662; 42 Downey St) supplies bait, sells rods and dispenses fishing tips.

Australian Adventure Experience (☎ 5772 1440; www.ausadventures.com) runs a wide range of outdoor adventure activities, including whitewater rafting and rock-climbing.

Sleeping

Old Convent (☎ 5772 3220; www.who.net.au/theoldconvent; 32 Downey St; s/d $105/145; ☒) This elegant timber home has three beautifully restored suites and a great wraparound veranda to relax on. An interesting four-course set menu is available for dinner at $39 per person, with standout dishes, such as rabbit sausage with carrot and fennel purée.

Athlone Country Cottages (☎ 5772 2992; 266 UT Creek Rd; d $175 incl breakfast; ☒ ☒) Only five minutes from Alexandra, these cheerful self-contained cottages have a wonderful outlook over the green hills. The dam is well stocked with trout and there's a barbecue to grill your catch.

Bushwalker, Grampians National Park (p267)

SALLY DILLON

Central Deborah Goldmine (p257), Bendigo

RICHARD I'ANSON

Loch Ard Gorge (p215), Port Campbell National Park

GRANT DIXON

Wine casks, Morris winery,
Rutherglen (p60)

Rio Vista (p287), Mildura

PS *Melbourne* (p288), Murray River, Mildura

Mittagong Homestead & Cottages (☎ 5772 1586; www.countrycottages.biz; 462 Spring Creek Rd; d midweek/weekend $165/185 incl breakfast; ⬛ ⬛) Nestled on a 1200-hectare grazing property, 11km north-west of Alexandra, the comfortable cottages and homestead suite have gorgeous views and a host of facilities, including a tennis court and sauna. Pets are also welcome.

EILDON
☎ 03 / pop 700

The small, one-pub town of Eildon is a popular recreation and holiday base for both Lake Eildon and the surrounding national park. It was originally built in the early 1950s to house Eildon Dam project workers. From the town centre, you can drive across the top of the dam's massive retaining wall. On the other side is a **lookout point**, boat-launching ramps and the national park. A road leads around the lake to Jerusalem Inlet.

Information
Opposite the shopping centre on Main St, there's a small **visitors centre** (☎ 5774 2909; www .visitlakeeildon.com; ☼ 10am-2pm Sat-Mon, 10am-5pm Fri). Mansfield's **visitors centre** (☎ 5575 1464, 1800 060 686) can book accommodation and houseboats.

Sights & Activities
Kids will love the touch-and-feel tanks at the **Freshwater Discovery Centre** (☎ 5774 2208; Snobs Creek; adult/concession/child $5.50/3/3; ☼ 11am-4pm Fri-Mon, 11am-4pm daily during school holidays), a trout farm and hatchery run by the DSE that releases over one million fish each year. The centre is on the Goulburn Valley Hwy, 5km southwest of Eildon.

Based at Thornton, southwest of Eildon, horse trails are run by **Rubicon Valley Horseriding** (☎ 5773 2292; www.rubiconhorseriding.com.au; Rubicon Rd, Thornton; 2/3hr $55/75).

LAKE EILDON
In 2003, after the worst drought in a century, Lake Eildon looked more like a moonscape than Victoria's second biggest water storage and popular holiday spot. Though rain did eventually fall, the lake, created as a massive reservoir for irrigation and hydroelectric schemes, is still only 40% full. A $50-million-dollar project (www.eildonproject.com.au) to refill the lake and strengthen the dam wall is now underway.

Originally called Sugarloaf Reserve, the lake was constructed from 1915 to 1929 and flooded the town of Darlingford, as well as surrounding farm homesteads. Capacity was increased in 1951 and today the lake covers 14,000 hectares.

Despite six years of drought, there's plenty of action to keep you wet all day long. Try the **Goulburn Valley Fly-Fishing Centre** (☎ 5773 2513; www.goulburnvlyflyfishing.com.au; RMB 1270 Goulburn Valley Way) or **Blackridge Flyfishing School** (☎ 5774 2825; www.flyflickers.com; 785 Back Eildon Rd) if you want to practise your angling. **Eildon Lake Charters** (☎ 5774 2871; 55 Joe Taylor Rise) rents anything that floats, as well as organising water-skiing and sightseeing trips around the lake.

On the northern arm of the lake is **Bonnie Doon**, a popular weekend base, which reached pop-culture icon status as the nondescript spot where the working-class family in the satirical 1997 Australian film *The Castle* enjoyed the serenity.

Sleeping & Eating
Robyn's Nest (☎ 5774 2525; 13 High St; d $100-140) This plush 'adults-only' B&B swears it has the most comfortable beds in Eildon. If you decide to get up, the private balconies have superb views of the Eildon Valley and Mt Torbreck.

Golden Trout Hotel/Motel (☎ 5774 2508; 1 Riverside Dr; s/d from $60/70) If you can secure a room with a Goulburn River view, this is a good option. The pub has a decent bistro (meals $8 to $30) with a nice sundeck.

There are plenty of camping options at caravan parks in and around Eildon, as well as camp sites in Lake Eildon National Park.

Eildon Caravan Park (☎ 5774 2105, 1800 651 691; Eildon Rd; powered/unpowered sites for 2 people $19/17, d cabins $50-80) This roomy camping ground beside the Eildon Pondage has volleyball and tennis courts. There's excellent fishing, and a well-stocked kiosk sells tackle and bait if you want to have a dabble.

Blue Gums Caravan Park (☎ 5774 2567; www.blue gums.com.au; 746 Back Thornton Rd; powered/unpowered sites for 2 people from $19/16, bunkhouse per bed $16.50, d cabins from $75; ⬛) This camping ground has sites and a bunkhouse on the banks of the Goulburn River, as well as an array of family-friendly extras, such as a kids' play-ground, volleyball courts and two pools.

Lake Eildon Marina & Houseboat Hire (☎ 5774 2107; www.houseboatholidays.com.au; 190 Sugarloaf Rd) and **High Country Houseboats** (☎ 5777 3899; www .ahch.com.au) both hire 10- to 12-berth houseboats from around $2100 to $4500 per week during the high season.

For a bite to eat try **Coco's Restaurant & Bar** (☎ 5774 2866; mains lunch $9-13, dinner $17-23; ☺ lunch & dinner Wed-Sun), overlooking the boat harbour, or **Taste of Eildon** (☎ 5774 2642; 7 High St; mains $8-16; ☺ 9am-5pm Thu-Mon, dinner Summer), a café-cum-gallery selling gourmet food and wine in the old general store.

Getting There & Away
Bus service is available with **McKenzie's Bus Lines** (☎ 9853 6264), which travels from Melbourne to Eildon ($21.60, 3¼ hours, daily), Marysville and Alexandra (three hours, Monday, Wednesday and Thursday).

LAKE EILDON NATIONAL PARK
Surrounding the southern and central sections of Lake Eildon, Lake Eildon National Park covers an area of over 27,000 hectares, and provides excellent opportunities for walking and camping.

From the middle of the 19th century, the areas around Lake Eildon were logged and mined for gold, so much of the vegetation is regrowth eucalypt forest.

There are several very busy lakeside **camping areas** (sites per night for up to 4 people $15) at Coller Bay in the Fraser section that are equally popular with kangaroos; showers and pit toilets are available. No bookings are taken.

In the Jerusalem section, the main camping areas are at **Jerusalem Creek** (site per night for up to 4 people $11), which has pit toilets, and along the Eildon–Jamieson road, which forms the southern boundary of the park. This road is steep, winding and unsealed in sections, but particularly scenic. Various **4WD tracks** lead off the road into the park and across to the lake.

A kiosk sells basic supplies at the gate to Coller Bay; the admission fee is $6.50 per car. There are walking tracks throughout the park, including **Candlebark Nature Walk**.

HOWQUA
☎ 03
So tiny you could quite easily drive right on by, the Howqua area is famous for the **Howqua Dale Gourmet Retreat** (☎ 5777 3503; www .gtoa.com.au), an exclusive cooking school and an epicurean's dream weekend getaway. A

two-night package, including all meals and an open bar, costs $880 per person.

Regular holiday-goers, however, head to **Howqua Valley Caravan Park** (☎ 5777 3588; www .howquaholidays.com.au; Mansfield-Jamieson Rd; powered/ unpowered sites for 2 people from $18/16, d cabins without shower from $50; ☒), by Lake Eildon. Fishing-boat (half-/full day $55/90) and canoe (half-/full day $20/35) hire is available.

Peace and birdsong are the attractions at **Calm Waters Retreat** (☎ 5777 3725; www.calmwaters .com.au; d cottage/chalet from $175/210; ☒), a grouping of self-contained cottages in a secluded location. Guests can use the free mountain bikes to explore the area.

JAMIESON
☎ 03
Jamieson is a deliciously peaceful, remote backwater in a scenic setting at the junction of the Goulburn and Jamieson Rivers. The village attracts 4WD tourers and bushwalkers who come for the abundance of back roads and tracks through this spectacular and unspoiled mountain countryside.

The **Historic Jamieson Courthouse** (Nash St; adult/ child $2.50/1; ☺ 10am-4pm Sat, Sun & public holidays Nov-Easter) has a local gold-mining exhibit and an outdoor display area.

On the road to Eildon, just outside Jamieson, **Protea Australia Farm** (☎ 5777 0727; admission $2.50; ☺ 11am-4pm) grows 16 different varieties of the prehistoric-looking protea flower. Tours are available or you can wander at your leisure. On the same road, **Jamieson Brewery** (☎ 5777 0515), within the Lakeside Hotel, runs brewery tours on demand, but offers no free tastings. The brewery produces stout, brown and pale ales, and a raspberry beer.

Sleeping & Eating
Emerald Park Holiday Farm (☎ 5777 0569; Licola Rd; d $75) There are chooks to feed and ponies to ride at this small mixed farm just outside Jamieson. The cottages are all self-contained.

Jamieson Caravan Park (☎ 5777 0567; Grey St; powered/unpowered sites for 2 people $18/15, onsite d cabins $50-85; ☒) Right by the Jamieson River, this is a relaxed and leafy camping ground, but it's without a camp kitchen.

Lakeside Hotel (☎ 5777 0515; Eildon Rd; s/d $35/ 60) Right on the edge of the Goulburn River, this is a great place to stop for lunch. The pub's **bistro** (mains $12-23; ☺ lunch & dinner) serves

---

DETOUR: JAMIESON TO WALHALLA

The spectacular 135km drive south from Jamieson to Walhalla is one of the best in the whole state. The road is unsealed and rough in sections, winding alongside the Goulburn River, through forests and hills, and past a series of derelict gold-mining settlements, many of which were destroyed by the tragic bushfires of 1939. About 15km south of Jamieson, the **Tunnel Bend Reserve** has a **camping ground** (sites free) with picnic facilities, and some good swimming spots in the Goulburn River. **Woods Point**, 55km south of Jamieson, is a tiny and historic gold-mining town set in a valley on the upper reaches of the Goulburn River. The friendly **Commercial Hotel** (☎ 5777 8224; B&B per person $50) is a great pub with a bistro. **Matlock**, 8km southwest of Woods Point, has stunning views. From there, you can head 55km west to **Cumberland Junction** (and from there either west to Warburton or northwest to Marysville), or continue east and then south, down to Walhalla. Conventional vehicles are OK for the main road, but you'll need a 4WD if you want to head off the beaten track.

---

interesting dishes, making good use of the onsite brewery, such as beef-and-beer pie and lamb shanks in stout. It also offers motel accommodation.

Getting There & Away

For bus travel, **Stewarts Bus Service** (☎ 5775 2630) leaves from Mansfield post office at 1.45pm on weekdays ($9, 1¼ hours) and continues to Woods Point ($21.60). Call to book a seat.

The road from Jamieson to Eildon is spectacular, climbing and twisting through the edge of Lake Eildon National Park. Sections of it are unsealed, although it's regularly graded.

MANSFIELD

☎ 03 / pop 2550

Mansfield is an all-seasons destination that outdoor enthusiasts really get excited about, offering a plethora of activities from skiing at Mt Buller to late-spring trail rides on horseback through the mountains. With an array of accommodation options, and its proximity to the highlights of the High Country, Mansfield makes a great base for a weekend or a longer stay.

Information

The visitors centre, **Mansfield & Mt Buller High Country Reservations** (☎ 5775 2518, 1800 039 049; www.mansfield-mtbuller.com.au; Maroondah Hwy; ☼ 9am-5pm, 8am-9pm in ski season), is at the Old Railway Station. The centre can book ski accommodation for you, and also sells lift tickets.

The Commonwealth and National Australia Banks have ATMs on the main street.

Connect Cafe (☎ 5775 1464; High St; ☼ 2-6pm Tue-Thu, Fri 2-10pm) is more community centre than cybercafé. **Devil's River Book Café** (☎ 5775 2978;

12 High St) has a decent range of second-hand books, and there's a laundry and supermarket in the same complex.

Sights & Activities

The graves of the three Mansfield police officers killed by Ned Kelly and his gang in 1878 at Stringybark Creek rest in **Mansfield Cemetery**, at the end of Highett St. There's also a monument to the slain officers, erected in 1879, in the centre of the roundabout on the corner of High and Highett Sts.

Make like the *Man from Snowy River* and take a trail ride on the Great Dividing Range, 22km from Mansfield at **Watson's Mountain Country Trail Rides** (☎ 5777 3552; www.watsonstrail rides.com.au; 3 Chains Rd, Booralite; 1hr/2hr $30/50). One of the highlights is the downhill area featured in the 1982 film.

Rides around Merrijig or overnight trips across Mt Stirling, camping in a cattleman's hut at Razorback, are on offer at **High Country Horses** (☎ 5777 5590; www.highcountryhorses.com.au; 10 McCormacks Rd, Merrijig; 2hr/half-day ride $50/75, full-day ride $140-180, overnight trip $400).

Adventure bike tours are run by **Mansfield Mountain Bike Tours** (☎ 5775 2380, 1800 815 810; 2hr/half-day rides $35/80; ☼ Oct-Apr).

High Country Camel Treks (☎ 5775 1591; Rifle Butts Rd; per hr $20), 7km south, offers hourly and overnight treks.

If you want to get off-road, join a **High Country Scenic Tour** (☎ 5777 5101; www.highcountry scenictours.com.au; ☼ Nov-May), which has exciting day tours from $110 per person.

You can enjoy spectacular sunrise views of Mt Buller from a hot-air balloon during a one-hour flight with **Global Ballooning** (☎ 9428 5703; www.globalballooning.com.au; $285 incl

THE HIGH COUNTRY

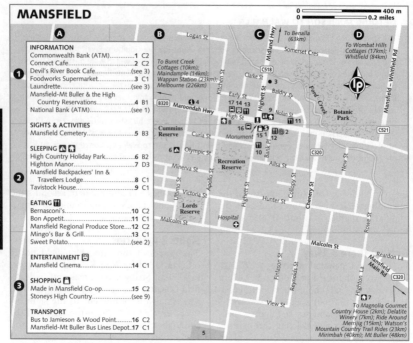

MANSFIELD

0 ——————— 400 m
0 ——————— 0.2 miles

INFORMATION
Commonwealth Bank (ATM).............1 C2
Connect Cafe...............................2 C2
Devil's River Book Cafe...............(see 3)
Foodworks Supermarket.................3 C1
Laundrette................................(see 3)
Mansfield-Mt Buller & the High
  Country Reservations.................4 B1
National Bank (ATM)....................(see 1)

SIGHTS & ACTIVITIES
Mansfield Cemetery.......................5 B3

SLEEPING
High Country Holiday Park..............6 B2
Highton Manor...........................7 D3
Mansfield Backpackers' Inn &
  Travellers Lodge.......................8 C1
Tavistock House.........................9 C1

EATING
Bernasconi's.............................10 C2
Bon Appetit..............................11 C1
Mansfield Regional Produce Store....12 C2
Mingo's Bar & Grill.....................13 C1
Sweet Potato.............................(see 2)

ENTERTAINMENT
Mansfield Cinema.........................14 C1

SHOPPING
Made in Mansfield Co-op.................15 C2
Stoneys High Country....................(see 9)

TRANSPORT
Bus to Jamieson & Wood Point........16 C2
Mansfield-Mt Buller Bus Lines Depot.17 C1

To Benalla (63km);
To Wombat Hills Cottages (17km); Whitfield (84km)

To Burnt Creek Cottages (10km); Maindample (14km); Wappan Station (23km); Melbourne (226km)

To Magnolia Gourmet Country House (2km); Delatite Winery (7km); Ride Around Merrijig (15km); Watson's Mountain Country Trail Rides (23km); Mirimbah (40km); Mt Buller (48km)

---

champagne breakfast). **Kestral Aviation** (☎ 0428 376 619) runs helicopter joy flights.

Festivals & Events

Mansfield and Mt Buller run the **High Country Festival**, held annually over the week leading up to the Melbourne Cup in early November; it features a mountain-horse race, art exhibitions and bush markets; call the visitors centre (p331) for information. A **Balloon Festival** (www.mansfieldballoonfestival.com) is held in April, and the food and wine lovers' **Harvest Festival** (☎ 5777 3447; www.uppergoulburnwine.org.au) is held over the Labour Day weekend in early March.

Sleeping

BUDGET

High Country Holiday Park (☎ 5775 2705; www.high countryholidaypark.com.au; 1 Ultimo St; bunkhouse $12, powered/unpowered sites for 2 people from $23/20, onsite d cabins $63-73, cottages $128; 🖭) Close to the centre of town, this shady holiday park has all sorts of well-maintained accommodation, along with a kiddie's pool, games room and tennis court.

Mansfield Backpackers' Inn & Travellers Lodge (☎ 5775 1800; www.mansfieldtravellodge.com; 112 High St; dm $23, d $85-95, ste $125-35; 🖭) There's superior dorm accommodation in this restored heritage building. The modern motel rooms are large and offer excellent value (price drops midweek). There's a well-stocked kitchen and discount coupons for local restaurants if you prefer to eat out.

MIDRANGE

Burnt Creek Cottages (☎ 5775 3067; O'Hanlons Rd; d from $125; 🖭) About 10 minutes' drive from the town centre are these attractive cottages with all the creature comforts you would expect, perched on a hill overlooking Lake Eildon. Select a bottle of local wine from reception and take in the view from the veranda, ignoring the occasional alpaca that may cross your path.

Wappan Station (☎ 5778 7786; www.wappanstation .com.au; Royal Town Rd, Maindample; shearers' quarters adult/child $30/15, cottage d from $90; 🖭) If you want to experience life on a 4000-hectare sheep and cattle property, Wappan Station on the banks of Lake Eildon has newly renovated

---

TOP FIVE 'MAN FROM SNOWY RIVER' MOMENTS

You've seen the film, you've watched the TV series and you might even have read Banjo Paterson's famous poem (or had it drummed into you at school), but now it's time to see where the legend was born and never dies.

Craig's Hut, Mt Stirling (p336) The number-one seller on every walking, cycling, 4WD and horse-riding tour in the High Country – for a reason.

Downhill Slope (p331) If you can ride, if you can really ride, it's still as scary as it looks in the movie.

Man from Snowy River Bush Festival, Corryong (p355) Grab the Akubra and get set for four days of whip-cracking and yarn-spinning good fun.

Telstra Country Wide Challenge, Corryong (p355) It seemed like so much fun in the film, the locals just had to try it – mountain horse racing where 'the hills are twice as steep and twice as rough'. See this true test of horse-riding prowess during the Man from Snowy River Bush Festival.

Jack Riley's Grave, Corryong (p354) Was this tailor turned mountain hero the real 'man' of the story?

---

self-contained cottages and more basic twin-share rooms. Guests are welcome to observe seasonal activities on the farm or just take it all in from the great decks.

Tavistock House (☎ 5775 1024; www.tavistockhouse .com.au; cnr High & Highett Sts; d midweek/weekend $120/135 incl bottle of wine) With so many banks closing down in regional Australia, it's a pity not more of them are restored as well as this excellent conversion of the former Westpac into a handsome guesthouse, right in the centre of town. Its three spacious rooms are decked out in Victorian-era style (no TV, phone or radio here) with high ceilings and heavy furnishings.

TOP END

Highton Manor (☎ 5775 2700; www.hightonmanor.com .au; 140 Highton Lane; d stable/manor $120/$235 incl breakfast; 🕲) Built in 1896 for Francis Highett, a tennis champion and tenor who sang with Dame Nellie Melba, this stately two-storey manor (which took 20 years to complete) has motel-style rooms in the former stables, and lavish period-era rooms in the main house. The impressive gardens are great for a stroll.

Wombat Hills Cottages (☎ 5776 9507; Lochiel Rd; d $195-225 incl breakfast) It's worth driving the 17km from Mansfield to these luxurious stone cottages set in a tranquil valley. Enjoy the views of Mt Buller from your hammock or the lakeside gazebo. If you fancy a swim, there's a jetty with steps down into the lake.

Eating

Magnolia Gourmet Country House (☎ 5779 1444; 190 Mt Buller Rd; mains $24-26; 🕲 dinner Thu-Sat) This well-regarded country restaurant is the locals' pick for fine dining in Mansfield. If you need warming up on a winter's night, try the robust High Country beef with mash and mushrooms. Magnolia House is also a B&B – a good thing to remember after demolishing one of the signature desserts, as there's no way you'll be able to move!

Mansfield Regional Produce Store (☎ 5889 1404; 68 High St; mains $7-15; 🕲 breakfast & lunch daily, dinner Fri) This rustic store is a great place to shop if you're self-catering, with its array of delicious home-made produce and artisan breads. If not, take a seat by the fire or get to know the locals over a coffee and baguette at the communal tables.

Sweet Potato (☎ 5775 1955; 50 High St; mains $10-18; 🕲 10.30am-2pm & dinner Thu-Mon) There's a relaxed vibe at this cosy licensed café, which serves Mod Oz cuisine with highlights like the lunch-time roast pumpkin and fetta *quesadillas* ($14), while dinner gets a little spicier with some Asian fusion dishes.

Bernasconi's (☎ 5779 1600; 28 Highett St; mains $14-18; 🕲 dinner Mon-Sat) It's best to book a table on weekends if you want to try the Swiss-Italian inspired cooking at this local favourite.

Bon Appetit (☎ 5775 2951; 39-41 High St; 🕲 9.30am-6pm Mon-Fri, 9am-5pm Sat) This inexpensive deli-café serves gourmet surprises in a sunny courtyard. The vanilla slices are justifiably famous.

Entertainment

Mansfield Cinema (☎ 5775 2049; www.mansfieldcinema.com.au; 117 High St) Recent-release movies are screened on Tuesday and Saturday at 8pm (and more regularly in January).

Shopping

Made in Mansfield Co-op (☎ 5775 1893; High St) This great little gallery exhibits some fine ceramics, bush furniture, wood-turned pieces and textiles.

Stoneys High Country (☎ 5775 2212; www.stoneys .com.au; 93 High St) Stoney's is the spot to stock up on moleskins, Blundstones, Akubras, and books and videos on the High Country.

Getting There & Away

Bus service is available with **V/Line** (☎ 13 61 96), which operates twice daily (once on Sunday) from Melbourne ($32.30). In the ski season **Mansfield-Mt Buller Bus Lines** (☎ 5775 2606) has daily buses from Mansfield to Mt Buller ($34.90 return).

MANSFIELD TO MT BULLER

The **Delatite Winery** (☎ 03- 5775 2922; Stoney Rd; ☽ 10am-5pm) is off Stoney's Rd about 7km east of Mansfield, and showcases some premium cool climate wines, the region's speciality.

Farther along the same road, about halfway to Mt Buller, **Merrijig**, near the Delatite River, is a small settlement with several accommodation options, including **Buttercup Cottage & Guesthouse** (☎ 03-5777 5591; www.buttercup.com.au; Buttercup Rd; d cottage/guesthouse wing from $170/150 incl breakfast), a well-appointed stone cottage with full wheelchair access and fine views of the mountains. There is also a private guesthouse attached to the main homestead.

Off-mountain accommodation includes the **Arlberg Merrijig Resort** (☎ 03-5777 5633; fax 5777 5780; cnr Omega St & Mt Buller Rd; d summer/ski season from $75/95; 🏊).

MT BULLER

☎ 03 / elevation 1805m

Less than three hours' drive from Melbourne, Mt Buller is Victoria's largest and busiest ski resort. There's an extensive lift network on the mountain, including a chairlift that begins in the car park and ends in the middle of the ski runs. The downhill skiing area is 180 hectares (snow-making covers 44 hectares), and runs are divided into 25% beginner, 45% intermediate and 30% advanced, with a vertical drop of 400m. **Crosscountry trails** link Mt Buller and Mt Stirling.

It's a well-developed resort with a complete range of facilities. **Night skiing** on the Bourke St run generally operates on Wednesday and Saturday nights.

Information

The **Mt Buller Resort Management Board** (☎ 5777 6077; www.mtbuller.com.au; ☽ 8.30am-5pm Mon-Fri during ski season, 10am-4pm Sat & Sun outside ski season) shares premises in the village with the post office on Summit Rd. In winter the information office is 100m farther along Summit Rd, opposite the Village Centre Building. There's Internet access in the **Abom complex** (☎ 5777 6091; Summit Rd).

Costs

Gate admission fees to the resort are $27 per car, for the day car park only, during the ski season (an overnight fee also applies). Lift tickets for a full day cost $82/44 per adult/ child. Combined lift-and-lesson packages start at $122. University students get discounted tickets Wednesday to Monday and a whopping 50% off on Tuesday. A sightseeing ticket costs $16/9 per adult/child.

Sights & Activities

The **Sports Centre at La Trobe University Mt Buller** (☎ 5733 7080; www.latrobe.edu.au/mtbuller) has a huge variety of adventure activities operating year-round, including rock-climbing, abseiling and fly fishing. Tours include 4WD day trips, mountain-bike tours, and ecotours led by environmentalists. Mountain-bike hire is also available (one hour/half-/full-day $20/40/60), and the Horse Hill chairlift operates during January and most weekends from February to April. All-day access to the lift and trails costs $25.

The first and only alpine museum in Australia, the **National Alpine Museum of Australia** (NAMA; ☎ 5733 7000; www.nama.org.au; Level 1, La Trobe University; admission free; ☽ Sun & Mon) has a dynamic collection highlighting the fascinating history of this area, which is well hidden beneath the razzle-dazzle of the big resorts.

Breathtaker on High Spa Retreat (☎ 1800 088 222; massages per hr $90) Soak and revive at this fancy spa, which offers the usual range of treatments as well as the intriguing hydrotherapy geisha tub (per 20 minutes $45)!

Festivals & Events

You can hear the roar of the engines all the way to Mansfield during the **Porsche Mt Buller Sprint** (☎ 9817 2152; www.mtbullersprint.com) held in January, while there are Irish jokes aplenty at the **Craic Irish Music & Comedy Festival** (www .mtbuller.com/events) held at the end of March.

Sleeping

There are over 7000 beds on the mountain, with rates depending on high and low seasons. **Mt Buller Central Reservations** (☎ 1800 039 049) books accommodation in lodges costing from around $75 per person. There's generally a two-night minimum stay on weekends.

Mt Buller YHA Lodge (☎ /fax 5777 6181; The Ave; midweek dm $62, weekend dm $67) Open only during winter, this is one of the least expensive places on the mountain and it makes a great place to crash if you're skiing on the cheap. While the dorms are on the small side, there's good-quality bedding, facilities (kitchen, drying room, TV etc) and friendly staff. At the time of writing there was talk of major renovations taking place here.

Duck Inn (☎ 5777 6236; www.duckinnmtbuller.com; 18 Goal Post Rd; dm/tw/d from $70/95/100 incl breakfast) An intimate guesthouse with a range of accommodation from dorm rooms to doubles. There's a good restaurant (guess what its special is!), as well as a ski- and clothing-hire store.

Andre's at Buller (☎ 5777 6966; www.andresatbuller.com; Cobbler Lane; d summer/ski season from $140/240 incl breakfast) The luxurious Andre's is open year-round depending on whether you want to take advantage of the excellent ski-in/ ski-out position during winter, or the glorious summer sunsets from this architecturally designed chalet.

Mercure Grand Chalet (☎ 5777 6566; www.mtbuller chalet.com.au; Summit Rd; d summer $180-210, ski season $240-380; ☒) Certainly Buller's smartest option, with a range of swanky suites, a library with billiard table, and several well-regarded eateries. Tired bodies who have spent more time on the snow than on their skis will love the impressive sports centre.

Eating

Breathtaker Signature Restaurant (☎ 5777 6377; Breathtaker All Suite Hotel, 8 Breathtaker Rd; mains $17-33; ☒ dinner year-round) The food at this fine-dining restaurant lives up to the magnificent views, with a fusion of Asian, European and Mod Oz cuisine. Highlights include smoked-duck pie and a stellar version of the standard ski-lodge fave, sticky-date pudding with butterscotch sauce.

Pension Grimus (☎ 5777 6396; Breathtaker Rd; mains $25-30; ☒ dinner nightly, lunch Sat & Sun winter only) Of the numerous restaurants, Pension Grimus,

next to the Bourke St Ski School, is one of the best. Sit by the roaring fire, throw back some schnapps and indulge in a two-course meal for $50. Wiener schnitzel with vegetable rice pilaf and cranberry marmalade followed by a sumptuous Salzburger Nockerl (hazelnut and chocolate-chip soufflé); close your eyes and you could be in Klosters! It also has very comfortable boutique apartments.

Uncle Pat's Lounge Café (☎ 5777 6494; Cow Camp Plaza; mains $8-15; ☒ lunch & dinner) If you can't find a table, the easygoing crew will let you perch at the bar over a beer and pizza while they take on the hordes at this affordable, family-friendly restaurant that doles out generous portions of pasta, burgers and stir-fries.

Cattleman's Café (☎ 5777 7800) For breakfast or coffee, locals recommend this café at the base of Bourke St.

Supermarket (☒ closed in summer) There's a licensed supermarket in Moloney's building in the village centre.

The restaurants, bars and cafés at the **Mercure Grand Chalet** (☎ 5777 6566; Summit Rd) and the **Arlberg Hotel** (☎ 5777 6260) are open year-round.

Drinking & Entertainment

Kooroora Hotel (☎ 5777 6188) Inevitably, this is where everyone turns up at the end of the night. This pub rocks hard and late, with cheesy tunes, snowboarders playing drinking games and ski instructors looking for action. There's live music on Wednesday nights and most weekends, with the occasional top-line act making an appearance during the ski season.

Ski Club of Victoria (☎ 1300 554 709; Summit Rd) Locals heartily recommend the 'Whitt' (Ivor Whittaker Memorial Lodge), which is popular year-round. Bands play during winter, and there are pool tables, a bar and restaurant.

Abom/Moosehead Bar (☎ 5777 6091; Summit Rd) For a quiet drink, try the Moosehead Bar downstairs at Abom, which has plenty of atmosphere, snazzy cocktails and tapas.

Mt Buller Village Cinema (☎ 5733 7000; La Trobe University; admission adult/child $12.50/8.50) Australia's highest cinema runs two sessions nightly.

Getting There & Around

From Melbourne to Mansfield, **V/Line** (☎ 13 61 96; www.vline.com.au) has buses twice daily ($32.30). **Mansfield-Mt Buller Buslines** (☎ 5775 2606, winter 5775 6070) has daily buses year-round that run up to Mt Buller (adult/child $38/25 return).

Ski-season car parking is below the village. A 4WD taxi service transports people around the village (with luggage adult/child $7.50/5.50, without luggage $5/4) and from the overnight car park (adult/child $12/8).

If you're coming just for the day, you can take the quad chairlift from the Horse Hill day car park into the skiing area and bypass the village – ski hire and lift tickets are available at the base of the chairlift. However, there is a free day-tripper shuttle bus service between the day car park and the village.

For the ultimate rock-star arrival, chopper into Mt Buller with **Helicopters Victoria** (☎ 9416 9999; $2950 return for up to 7 people). Be on the slopes within 45 minutes of leaving Melbourne; the price includes lift passes.

MT STIRLING
☎ 03 / elevation 1747m

A near neighbour to Mt Buller, the alpine woodland and meadows of Mt Stirling make for an excellent cross-country area in winter, while in summer and autumn it's popular with walkers and 4WD tourers. There is a range of over 60km of cross-country ski trails, though the summits leading to the peak of Mt Stirling are not for beginners. Ski patrols operate daily on the main trails. In warmer weather, the unsealed **Circuit Rd** is the start of 4WD trips (though 2WD touring is possible), providing access to **Bindaree Falls** and **Craig's Hut**, of *The Man from Snowy River*

CATTLE COUNTRY

When the National Trust bluntly stated in 2004 that mountain cattlemen are not as culturally important as the environment their activities damage, High Country graziers were hoofing mad. Then in May 2005 the state government stepped in, announcing a permanent ban on cattle grazing in the Alpine National Park. There was an immediate outcry from cattlemen. As this book went to press the Cattlemen's Association of Victoria was appealing to the federal government for an emergency heritage listing, in a bid to protect the 170-year-old practice of grazing.

While the romance of the bush is all very well, the 8000 cattle grazing in Victoria's alpine areas each summer puts huge pressure on an already stressed environment after six years of drought and severe, widespread bushfires in 2003.

The damage caused by grazing cattle in Australia's alpine regions has long been recognised. Because of their effect on water quality for the Snowy Mountains Hydroelectric Scheme, cattle were taken out of Mt Kosciuszko National Park in NSW during the 1950s. Areas of the Victorian High Country, such as Mts Feathertop, Hotham and Bogong, were phased out for cattle grazing during the 1960s, but current licences, at $5.50 per head of cattle, cover about a third of the Alpine National Park. The state government will not renew these licences, making a transitional payment to licence holders over the next three years.

Cattle grazing has been responsible for dramatically increasing the spread of weeds, as well as the massive erosion of moss-beds, bogs and stream banks from cattle trampling the fragile peaty soils. The National Parks Association says that about 20 plants and animals are listed as threatened by grazing in northeastern Victoria.

Grazing is also no longer economically viable. The government gets a return of around $30,000 from the licences, while park management and the taxpayer spend over $500,000 on conservation measures directly related to grazing.

The main argument cattlemen use is that grazing reduces fires. During the bushfires of 2003 most of the alpine meadows between Falls Creek and Anglers Rest apparently didn't burn, even though the wooded slopes all around were blackened. However, a state inquiry into the fires found that 'a decision regarding cattle grazing should not be based on the argument that 'grazing prevents blazing'.

The other issues raised are 'bush lore' and the 'good old days' when the high plains were there for the taking, be it for timber, grazing, shooting or fishing. But any visitor to the High Country will see that if this complex, fragile environment has a future it will be based on sustainable management and not romantic tales of the past. Left unprotected it will resemble a cow paddock, not a national park.

fame. Several 4WD tour operators also run trips through the area (see p325). There's no accommodation on the mountain, but camping is possible in the nearby Alpine National Park at King Hut and Pineapple Flat.

Facilities are limited. **Mt Stirling Alpine Resort Information Office** (☎ 5777 0815; www.mtstirling.com .au) and **Mt Stirling Ski Hire & Ski School** (☎ 5777 6441; www.stirling.au.com), as well as a bistro and kiosk, operate in winter only. The daily admission fee is $23 per car during winter only ($9 overnight). The daily trail fee is $9.50/4.65/25 per adult/child/family. The main access route is via the Mansfield–Mt Buller Rd. The ski school runs a daily return bus service in winter from Mansfield (40km), Merrijig and the park entrance gates at Merimbah.

ALPINE NATIONAL PARK

Declared a national park in December 1989, the Alpine National Park covers an area of 646,000 hectares, a substantial proportion of the High Country of the Great Dividing Range, and joins the High Country areas of NSW and the Australian Capital Territory (ACT). It is divided into four separately managed units: the Bogong, Wonnangatta-Moroka, Cobberas-Tingaringy and Dartmouth areas.

There are plenty of access roads to and through the park, although in winter a number of roads are closed. The opportunities for recreation and ecotourism in the area are outstanding. Dispersed **bush camping** (sites free) is allowed in areas running off 4WD and walking tracks, but on principal roads visitors are encouraged to use designated camping areas (and to camp at least 100m from waterways) and to observe fire bans. The area's many walking tracks include the Australian Alps Walking Track, which extends 655km through the park from Walhalla to the outskirts of Canberra.

The park is a spectacular and fragile environment, and the vegetation throughout is quite diverse. Eucalypt forests are typical, ranging from stringy-bark and peppermints in the lower reaches, to blue gum, mountain ash, alpine ash and snow gums in the higher areas. In spring and summer the areas above the snowline are carpeted with beautiful wildflowers. More than 1100 plant species have been recorded in the park, including 12 that are unique to Australia.

Visitors centres can provide Parks Victoria notes, while Parks Victoria has a number of offices in the region for more specific queries.

HARRIETVILLE

☎ 03

Harrietville is a picturesque little town nestled at the foot of Mt Feathertop. During ski season a bus shuttles between the town and Mt Hotham, so it's a good spot for slightly cheaper off-mountain accommodation.

Ski and wheel-chain hire is available from Harrietville Hotel/Motel and **Hoy's** (☎ 5779 2658).

Harrietville is the starting and finishing point for various **alpine walking tracks**, including the popular Mt Feathertop, Razorback Ridge and Dargo High Plains walks. Several small companies, including **Higher Ground Adventures** (☎ 5759 2754), lead day walks to Mt Feathertop (per four-person group $150) but Higher Ground specialises in longer overnight trips that are self-catering (two nights, including equipment $250).

In late November the annual **Blue Grass Festival** (bluegrass.org.au/festivals/harrietville) takes over the town. Early December heralds the **Lawnmowing Grand Prix**, a classy affair of lawnmower and snowmobile races.

Sleeping & Eating

Pick & Shovel Cottage (☎ 5759 2627; 1 Pick & Shovel Rise; d midweek/weekend $125/140 incl breakfast; 🐾) Professionally run by a helpful couple, who have heaps of advice on walking and fishing in the area, this lovely cottage retains great style despite its old-world charm (claw-foot bath, cast-iron beds etc). A generous breakfast and complimentary bottle of fizz are an added bonus.

Shady Brook Cottages (☎ 5759 2741; www.shady brook.com.au; Mountain View Walk; d midweek/weekend from $110/30 incl breakfast) Shady Brook is in 4.85 hectares of secluded landscape and bush at the foot of Mt Hotham, bordered by state forest on the Ovens River. There are two alpine-style cottages, both with spas and spacious verandas for contemplating the stunning surroundings.

Big Shed Café (☎ 5759 2672; Great Alpine Rd, Smoko; 🕙 10am-5pm Wed-Mon) A popular spot a few kilometres down the road towards Bright, this tobacco shed, with great views of the snowcapped Mt Feathertop, started

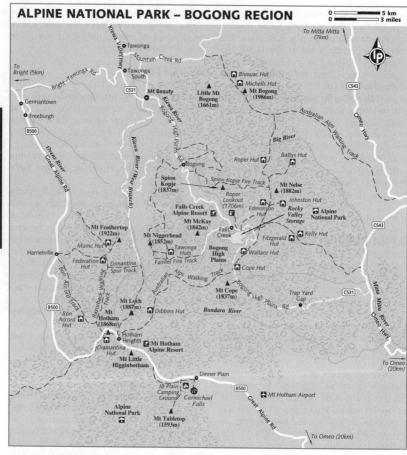

out as a fruit and veggie store before reinventing itself as a gourmet café.

Getting There & Away
No public transport operates to Harrietville.
During the ski season a bus connects Harrietville to Mt Hotham ($20 return, twice
daily). **Mountain View Holiday Retreat** (☎ 5759
2530) sells tickets and is the pick-up point.
The road to Mt Hotham is sometimes
closed because of snow in winter.

MT HOTHAM
☎ 03 / elevation 1868m
Serious hikers and skiers head to Mt
Hotham, which is the starting point for
some stunning alpine walks from November

to May, and home to 245 hectares of downhill runs. About 80% of the ski trails are
marked as intermediate or advanced, with
double black diamonds marking the most
challenging terrain. The Big D lift is open
for **night skiing** every Wednesday and Saturday, and the village chairlift runs from late
December to early January and at Easter.

Off-piste skiing in steep and narrow valleys is good. **Cross-country skiing** is also good,
with 35km of trails winding through tree-
lined glades. Cross-country skiing on the
Bogong High Plains, which can be crossed
to Falls Creek, is excellent. Below the village,
on the eastern side, is a series of trails that
run as far as Dinner Plain (p340). All these
and other trails can also be hiked during

summer when Mt Hotham becomes an excellent base for High Country walking.

Information

Mt Hotham Alpine Resort Management Board
(MHARMB; ☎ 57593550; www.mthotham.com.au; ☻ 8am-5pm daily in ski season, Mon-Fri rest of year) is at the village administration centre.

Costs

The ski-season admission fee is $26 per car. Lift tickets cost $82/69/43 per adult/student/child. Lift-and-lesson packages are $120 for adults.

Activities

You can obtain good walking notes from Parks Victoria in Omeo and Bright. The most popular walk is to Mt Feathertop, but there are many others to choose from. The **Razorback–Mt Feathertop Walk** requires good walking shoes (and strong knees and ankles!). The 22km-return walk crosses the ridge linking Mt Hotham and Mt Feathertop (1922m). The walk starts at the Diamantina Hut (2.5km from Mt Hotham village, on the Harrietville side). It passes the junction of the easterly **Diamantina Spur Track** at Twin Knobs (1798m). At the Cross, the **Bungalow Spur Track** heads in a westerly direction. The summit is 1.5km north of the Cross.

Sleeping

Three booking agencies offer the best route to finding suitable accommodation, be it in a lodge, chalet or apartment: **Mt Hotham Reservation Centre** (☎ 1800 354 555; www.hotham.net.au; Hotham Central; ☻ year-round); **Mt Hotham Accommodation Service** (☎ 5759 3636, 1800 032 061; www.mthothamaccommodation.com.au; Lawlers Apartments; ☻ in ski season); and **Mt Hotham Central Reservations** (☎ 5759 3522, 1800 657 547; www.mthotham-centralres.com.au), which can book local and off-mountain accommodation throughout the year.

Ski-season accommodation generally has a minimum two-night stay.

Hotham Heights Chalets (☎ 5759 3522, 1800 354 555; Great Alpine Rd; chalets summer $280, low/high ski season $750/1600) Sleeping up to 13 of your nearest and dearest, these ultramodern apartments have all the cherries on top – entertainment system, spa, views, fully equipped kitchen, open fire and wonderfully soft lounges, so you can kick back after a day on the slopes.

Gravbrot Ski Club (☎ 5759 3533; www.gravbrot.com; Great Alpine Rd; d low/high ski season $90/190) The price at this homey place includes all meals and pre-dinner nibbles, making it startlingly good value for the ski fields. You need to bring your own linen or sleeping bag.

Karnulurra Ski Club (☎ 5759 2517; karnbook@dragnet.com; d low/high ski season $110/150) A laid-back lodge with a well-equipped kitchen for self-caterers and a great location next to the Big D lift.

Arlberg (☎ 5986 8200; www.ski.com.au/arlberg.htm; Great Alpine Rd; s & d ste per 2 nights $600-760; ☎) Smack bang in the centre of all the action, the multi-level Arlberg has a family bistro, and a heated indoor pool, sauna and spa. There's also organised activities for the kids.

Eating & Drinking

Some of the better eateries in winter (all closed in summer) are **Swindlers** (☎ 5759 4421; Hotham Central), which is also the place for an après-ski *gluhwein* (mulled wine); the Austrian-inspired **Zirky's** (☎ 5759 3542; Great Alpine Rd); and **Chiones** (☎ 5759 3626; Hotham Central), which features an impressive Mod Oz menu and a lovely deck.

General (☎ 5759 3523; Great Alpine Rd; mains $11-16; ☻ lunch & dinner) This pub does tasty pizzas and counter meals, and is one of the more popular watering holes during the ski season. It's usually the only place to stay open over part (not all) of the summer.

Snowbird Inn (☎ 5759 3503; Great Alpine Rd) The Summit Bar at this inn can get rather raucous during its daily Jug Frenzy sessions, as it's the bar of choice for the young snowboarding pack.

If you're staying somewhere with kitchen facilities, there's a small supermarket next to the Big D lift, plus a few kiosks and takeaways, including AJ's next to the ticket counter, where everyone gets their mitts on hot roast-beef rolls and overpriced coffee.

Getting There & Around

AIR

The **Mt Hotham Airport** (☎ 5159 6777) services Mt Hotham and Dinner Plain. **Qantas Link** (☎ 13 13 13) flies throughout the week in the ski season from Melbourne and Sydney, and on weekends from Brisbane via Newcastle. No services operate in summer. Transport to/from the airport meets every flight.

The Helicopter Lift Link takes six minutes to fly to Falls Creek ($94 return, not including lift ticket), but only operates on clear days.

BUS

In winter **Trekset** (☎ 9370 9055; www.mthothambus .com.au) has daily buses from Melbourne to Mt Hotham. It also has daily services between Hotham and Myrtleford, Bright and Harrietville. A separate shuttle service also operates to Dinner Plain.

A free shuttle runs frequently around the resort from 7am to 3am; the free 'zoo cart' takes skiers from their lodges to the lifts between 8am and 6pm.

CAR

Mt Hotham is located 373km northeast of Melbourne, and can be reached either via the Hume Fwy (M31) and Harrietville (4½ hours), or via the Princes Hwy (A1) and Omeo (5½ hours). In winter contact **Mount Hotham Resort Managmenet Board** (MHRMB; ☎ 5759 3550) to check road conditions before deciding which route to take (note that wheel chains must be carried).

DINNER PLAIN

☎ 03 / elevation 1520m

The stylish alpine resort of Dinner Plain is a lovely place in both winter and summer, with attractive High Country architecture and an endless list of outdoor activities. The entire village was built in the mid-1980s from corrugated iron and local timber and stone, all inspired by the early cattlemen's huts, with a few quirky additions. Information can be obtained from Dinner Plain's **visitors centre** (☎ 1300 734 365; www.dinner-plain.com).

During the ski season the village is a popular base, and there are some excellent cross-country trails around the village itself, including the **Hotham–Dinner Plain Ski Trail** (10km one way), which closely follows the main road. There is one lift for skiers and one-day tickets cost $35/30 per adult/child. **Molony Ski Hire** (☎ 5159 6450; ⏱ 7.30am-6pm) has full hire options, and **Dinner Plain Ski School** offers ski and snowboard packages. About 12km from Mt Hotham, it's a short 20-minute drive away or visitors can use the convenient shuttle-bus service between the two resorts. In August there's the **Crystal Creek Resort Sled Dog Challenge** (www.sleddogchallenge.com), with over 100 teams competing with their malamutes on a 10km track through the village.

In summer the village has more facilities open than the ghostlike Mt Hotham village, and is an ideal base for horse riding. Try **Dinner Plain Trail Rides** (☎ 5159 7241; www.dinnerplain trailrides.com; 1hr/half-/full-day $50/110/160; ⏱ Nov-Jun).

There is great summer hiking here, and notes are available from Parks Victoria in Mt Hotham and at various other alpine visitor centres in the region. A 10km intermediate return walk to **Mt Tabletop** starts at JB Plain Camping Ground, 1.5km from Dinner Plain (towards Mt Hotham), with stunning views.

Contact Dinner Plain Central Reservations (see below) about tennis-court hire.

There's Internet access at **Dinner Plain Hotel** (☎ 5159 6462; Big Muster Dr).

Sleeping

With so many chalets and lodges to choose from, it might be easier to leave it with the experts at **Dinner Plain Central Reservations** (☎ 03-5159 6451, 1800 670 019; www.dinnerplain.com; Big Muster Dr).

Crystal Creek Resort (☎ 51596422; www.crystalcreek resort.com; Big Muster Dr; summer s/d $80/110, winter $145/210; ▣) This sprawling complex was originally an Australian army retreat, but it's now a well-run hotel that's as popular with families as it is with weekender couples. There's all the comforts you would expect (spa, sauna, restaurant/bar and Samoyed snow dog), but a definite lack of pretension compared with flashier accommodation at the big ski resorts.

Currawong Lodge (☎ 5159 6452 summer, 1800 635 589 winter; www.currawonglodge.com.au; Big Muster Dr; per person summer/winter from $40/65) The Currawong is a cosy place, especially in the spacious lounge, which features a huge stone-surround fireplace and rough timber ceilings. There's a well-equipped kitchen, a games room (table tennis and pool table) and lots of bubbles in the 10-person spa.

High Plain Lodge (☎ 5159 6455; www.highplains .au; d $90-130 summer, d from $110-170 ski season incl breakfast) Superior, comfy, motel-style rooms and cable TV. There's a decent bar and restaurant here (see opposite).

There is a camping ground at JB Plain.

Eating & Drinking

Dinner Plain Hotel (☎ 5159 6462; Big Muster Dr; mains $9-18) This is a great place to hang out. It looks somewhat like an overgrown mountain hut, with its split-level interior of huge timber poles and slabs, plus roaring open fires. The bistro has had good reports, particularly the pizza.

High Plain Lodge (☎ 5159 6455; mains lunch $6.50-15, dinner $18-25; ⊗ year-round) Expect delicious options, such as pan-fried cod served with laksa ($22). The bar is also a fine spot for a drink and spills out into a lovely garden in summer.

Getting There & Away

The **Mt Hotham Airport** (☎ 5159 6777) is a 10-minute drive east of Dinner Plain. In winter, a shuttle bus operates from the airport, and another runs to Mt Hotham from Dinner Plain.

FALLS CREEK

☎ 03 / elevation 1780m

Falls Creek is arguably the most fashion-conscious and upmarket ski resort in Australia, combining a picturesque alpine setting among snow gums with impressive skiing and infamous après-ski entertainment. Hordes of city folk make the 4½ hour journey from Melbourne on weekends during the snow season.

The skiing is spread over two main areas, the Village Bowl and Sun Valley. There are 19 lifts and the downhill area covers 451 hectares, with 17% beginner, 60% intermediate and 23% advanced runs. The vertical drop is 267m. Experienced skiers and boarders can push on beyond the resort to Mt McKay (1842m) and Rocky Knolls where there is an additional 200 hectares of untouched mountain. **Night skiing** in the Village Bowl operates several times a week. The Summit chairlift also runs from late December to early January and during the Easter holiday.

You'll also find some of the best **cross-country skiing** in Australia here. A **trail** leads around Rocky Valley Pondage to old cattlemen's huts, and the more adventurous can tour to the white summits of Nelse, Cope and Spion Kopje. These also provide walking routes in summer.

Information

The **visitors centre** (☎ 5758 3490, 1800 033 079; www .fallscreek.com.au; bottom of Gully chairlift; ⊗ 9am-5pm), on the right-hand side as you enter the resort, has plenty of information on the whole region, including Mt Buffalo.

Costs

The daily admission fee is $24 per car during the ski season only. Lift tickets for a full day cost $82/69/43 per adult/student/child. Combined lift-and-lesson packages cost $121/90/83.

Activities

If you're after a double-black-diamond rush, try **Kat Skiing/Boarding** ($69 return) where you hitch a lift on a heated Kassbohrer (snow kat) up Mt McKay and take on the powder bowls of the Rocky Knolls and Dam Site.

Some of the best **hiking** trails start at Falls Creek, including the walk to **Wallace Hut**, built in 1889, and said to be the oldest cattleman's hut in the High Country. Mountain bikers can hire bikes from the **Viking Lodge** (☎ 5758 3247) for a half-/full day ($25/35). Focusing on the High Country ecosystem, **Alpine Nature Rambles** (☎ 5758 3492) has three-hour snowshoe walks ($35 per person in winter), and longer walks in both summer and winter ($100 for a minimum of four people).

Festivals & Events

Early January brings the **Taste of Falls Creek Festival** (☎ 1800 232 557), while in August, Australia's premier long-distance cross-country ski event, the **Kangaroo Hoppet** (☎ 5754 1045; www .hoppet.com.au), is raced.

Sleeping

Accommodation may be booked via several agencies, including **Falls Creek Central Reservations** (☎ 5758 3733, 1800 033 079; www.fallscreek.com .au; Bogong High Plains Rd); **Mountain Multiservice** (☎ 5758 3499, 1800 465 566; www.mountainmultiservice .com.au; Schuss St); and **Go Snow Go Falls Creek** (☎ 9873 5474, 1800 253 545; www.albury.net.au/~gosnow).

All accommodation at Falls is above the snowline, which means the lodges are truly ski in, ski out.

Frueauf Village (☎ 1300 300 709; www.fvfalls.com .au; d 2 nights summer from $300, low/high ski season $400/950; 🖳) It's been called an 'oasis of cool on the slopes' and these 25 luxurious, architect-designed apartments certainly live up to the reputation. They have everything an alpine chalet needs and more, with free Internet access and private outdoor hot tubs in every unit, plus the funky Milch Cafe Wine Bar, and Cinema Glo downstairs in the same complex.

Julians Lodge (☎ 5758 3211; www.julianslodge.com; 18 Slalom St; low ski season dm/d $85/95, high ski season dm/d $140/160; ☒) Great value is to be had at this warm, laid-back lodge, which has been in the same family for the last 45 years. The price includes dinner and breakfast, plus a justifiably talked-about spread of pre-dinner nibbles in the decidedly retro lounge.

Astra Alpine Lodge (☎ 5758 3496, 1800 033 079; www.astralodge.com.au; 5 Sitzmark St; d low/high ski season from $155/270; ☒) The Astra has luxurious private doubles and great facilities, including a heated indoor pool, spa, sauna and private masseuse. It's only open from December to January and in winter.

Alpha Lodge (☎ 5758 3488; www.alphaskilodge.com .au; 5 Parallel St; bunk room $90, d from $105) No worries about tripping over your mates' ski paraphernalia at this spacious lodge, which is set up with a sauna and a large lounge with panoramic views. Self-caterers will have a field day in the communal kitchen, which has eight cooking stations.

Eating

Mo's Restaurant at Feathertop (☎ 5758 3232; 14 Parallel St; mains $14-30; ◷ dinner) This inviting restaurant with its red-gum furniture, private alcoves and mood lighting is the most celebrated in Falls Creek. Bookings are recommended if you want to feast on freshly shucked oysters and boutique beer.

Summit Ridge (☎ 5758 3800; 8 Schuss St; mains $14-30; ◷ dinner) A great dinner option is this rustic restaurant in the Summit Ridge apartments. High Country fine dining meets crisp Asian flavours, with dishes like double cutlet of lamb with garlic mash and Vietnamese mint glaze. But the real strength is the extensive wine list: feel free to scan the shelves yourself. Bookings are essential.

Milch Cafe Wine Bar (☎ 5758 3770; 4 Schuss St; mains $12-18; ◷ 8am-1am) The hip place to see and be seen. Flavoursome Middle-Eastern *mezze* and a bottle or two from the expansive wine list are the order of the day.

Café Max (☎ 5758 3347; 27 Falls Creek Rd; ◷ breakfast, lunch & dinner) This very social café in the Village Bowl serves tasty Mod Oz dishes all day. Après drinks are served between 4pm and 6pm.

In the **Snowland Shopping Centre** (☎ 5758 3318; 9 Slalom St) at the bottom of Halleys Comet chairlift a licensed supermarket and the **Wombat Cafe** (☎ 5758 3666) are open year-round. In the ski season the usual kiosks are open.

Drinking & Entertainment

Man (☎ 5758 3362; 37 Telemark St) This hotel has been around forever and is one of the main nightspots in winter, operating as a club, cocktail bar and live-music venue where top Aussie bands thrash it out most weeks.

Astra Vodka Bar (☎ 5758 3496; 5 Sitzmark St) Thirty-nine different types of vodka to try before your ski holiday ends. It's a challenge, but staff at this classy new bar, upstairs in the Astra Lodge, have seen it done before.

Cock 'n' Bull (☎ 5758 3210; 10 Slalom St) Locals head to this English-style pub for a quiet drink.

Cinema Glo (☎ 5758 3407; Frueauf Village; adult/child $12/8) If you can nab a seat (there's only 35), this is quite the movie experience, with surround sound and wildly comfortable chairs. But forget the popcorn, how about kicking back with a picnic from Milch Cafe upstairs?

Getting There & Around

Falls Creek is 375km and a 4½-hour drive from Melbourne. In winter **Pyle's Coaches** (☎ 5754 4024; www.buslines.com.au) operates buses daily between Falls Creek and Melbourne (one way/return $78/125), and to/from Albury ($44/70) and Mt Beauty ($25/40).

If you want to ski Mt Hotham for the day and have a valid lift ticket, jump on the Helicopter Lift Link for $94 return.

The Over-Snow Taxi service operates between the car parks and the lodges ($25 return) from 8am to midnight (2am Friday night). Car parking for day visitors is at the base of the village, next to the ski lifts.

MT BEAUTY & KIEWA VALLEY

☎ 03 / pop 1650

Nestled at the foot of Mt Bogong (Victoria's highest mountain), Mt Beauty and its twin town of Tawonga South are the gateway to the Falls Creek ski resort and the Bogong High Plains. The town was built in the 1940s as a base for workers on the Kiewa Hydroelectric Scheme. It's a handy base for Falls Creek for skiers in winter and for a range of activities in other seasons. The Kiewa Valley is also making a name for itself as a wine region – see the Victorian Wineries chapter (p65) for more information.

Information

The **Alpine Discovery Centre** (☎ 1800 808 277; www .visitmtbeauty.com.au; 31 Bogong High Plains Rd; ◷ 9am-5pm) has an **accommodation booking service** (☎ 1800 033 079; accommodation@mtbeauty.com.au). The brand-new visitors centre also incorporates extensive displays highlighting the history and nature of the region.

The Commonwealth (with ATM) and ANZ Banks have branches in the Mt Beauty shopping centre.

Sights & Activities

One for the kids: handfeed the alpacas and llamas at picturesque **Erindale Alpacas** (☎ 5754 5330; Reids Lane; ◷ 10am-5pm Wed-Sun & school holidays). To find it, turn off Kiewa Valley Hwy onto Red Bank Rd, 5km north of Tawonga. **Annapurna Wines** (☎ 5754 4517; Simmonds Creek Rd, Tawonga South) has tastings.

The pretty 2km **Tree Fern Walk** and slightly longer **Peppermint Walk** both start from Mountain Creek Picnic & Camping Reserve on Mountain Creek Rd, off Kiewa Valley Hwy. For information on longer walks in the area, visit the Alpine Discovery Centre (above). **Huts of the High Country** (☎ 0419 396 293; www.hutsofthe highcountryguidedwalks.com.au) runs relatively easy three-day guided walks through the Bogong High Plains with stops at cattlemen's huts along the way. The price ($550 per person) includes accommodation in a comfortable local lodge, breakfast and lunch. Join a day walk from $79.

Tracks through the mountains that were once used in the hydroelectricity works have been cleared and mountain bikers now make good use of them. Trips on different routes that cater to varying levels, from 1½-hour beginner rides ($25) to advanced runs (eg a downhill run from Falls Creek to Mt Beauty; $95), are organised by **Rocky Valley Bikes** (☎ 5754 1118; www.rockyvalley.com.au; Kiewa Valley Hwy). Bike hire is also available from $22 per day.

If you're not so energetic, experience these beautiful tracks on the back of a horse with **Bogong Horseback Adventures** (☎ 5754 4849; www .bogonghorse.com.au; Mountain Creek Rd, Mt Beauty; half-/full-/3-/5-day $70/$140/825/1375). It runs excellent trips over the Bogong High Plains; longer trips head as far as the NSW High Country.

The Kiewa Valley is a world-renowned **trout-fishing** area, and during spring, summer and autumn is the best time to hook

one. Well-recommended fly-fishing trips are run by **Peter Panozzo Guided Fishing Tours & Lessons** (☎ 5754 4522; 18 Nelse St; Mt Beauty; per hr for 2 people $40).

Sleeping

Dreamers (☎ 5754 1222; www.dreamers1.com; Kiewa Valley Hwy, Tawonga South; d $160-290; ☒) If you're seeking High Country luxury accommodation at its best, we recommend this enchanting collection of superbly designed timber and stone cottages built around a peaceful lagoon. The chalets are quite close together, but there is an overriding feeling of privacy, and the cheerful hosts have a great eye for detail.

Braeview (☎ 5754 4756; www.braeview.com.au; 4 Stewarts Rd; B&B s/d $99/110, spa cottage s/d from $160/190) Choose between traditional B&B rooms with a scrumptious country breakfast served on the balcony overlooking the gardens, and a self-contained cottage or apartment with spa and white fluffy bathrobes.

Springfield Cottage (☎ 5754 1112; springfield@netc .net.au; 186 Simmonds Creek Rd, Tawonga South; s/d $90/125) This Japanese themed B&B is curiously furnished, but has a sun-drenched garden and views to Mt Bogong.

Tawonga Caravan Park (☎ 5754 4428; Mountain Creek Rd; powered/unpowered sites for 2 people $20/18, d cabins from $55) This caravan park is in a beautiful setting by the Kiewa River; turn off the Kiewa Valley Hwy at the Bogong Hotel in Tawonga to find it.

Mountain Creek Picnic & Camping Reserve (Mountain Creek Rd) Located 10km along Mountain Creek Rd.

Eating & Drinking

Roi's Diner Restaurant (☎ 5754 4495; 177 Kiewa Valley Hwy, Tawonga; mains $18-25; ◷ dinner Thu-Sun) Roi's, an unassuming timber shack on the highway, is an award-winning restaurant that offers exceptional modern Italian cuisine. The menu changes daily, but expect delights like risotto with roast pumpkin and sage prosciutto followed by poached pear and macadamia crumble.

Mt Beauty Bakery & Café (☎ 5754 4870; Hollands & Kiewa St; meals $4-8; ◷ 6.30am-6.30pm) *The* place for a bite for lunch, this swish bakery-bar-café has a sunny outdoor area, and a big range of cakes, focaccias and antipasto plates.

Bogong Hotel (☎ 5754 4482; 169 Kiewa Valley Hwy; ◷ lunch Sun, dinner Thu-Mon) The obvious

GET ONYA BIKE

The **Murray to the Mountains Rail Trail** (☎ 03-5751 1283; www.railtrail.com.au) is one of the best ways to experience the High Country as you ride (or walk) through spectacular rural scenery, including river gums, mountain ash, spring blossoms and snowcapped ranges. The 94km trail follows the path of disused railways between the townships of Wangaratta, Beechworth, Myrtleford, Porepunkah and Bright. If you break up the journey, this is a leisurely way to explore the area, especially if you stop off for a cold beer in a country pub, feast on some regional produce, or spend a day or two in one of the many comfortable B&Bs. Aficionados say the 16km between Everton and Beechworth is the best part of the trail, despite the challenging uphill part of the ride, as you are cycling through the bush. However, all the landscape and views along the way are tremendous. There is good signage, so navigation isn't generally a problem, and there are several toilets and water stops, plus all towns have bike hire. If you are coming car-free and don't want to repeat the same route, think about catching the train to Wangaratta, then hop on the bus to Bright or Beechworth and ride back to Wangaratta.

spot for a beer (if you get a taxi, the first drink is free), this place also has a relaxed bistro with lovely views of the snowcapped mountains. Bookings are recommended.

Getting There & Away

In Tawonga South **Pyle's Coaches** (☎ 5754 4024; www.pyles.com.au) operates buses to Albury ($14.50) from Monday to Friday and to Falls Creek daily in winter ($20). **V/Line** (☎ 13 61 96) operates a train/bus service via Wangaratta ($50) twice weekly.

BRIGHT

☎ 03 / pop 1900

Most spectacular in autumn when its leafy avenues and gardens are really showing their colours, this picturesque holiday town in the foothills of the Alps is a popular base year-round. Bright is perfectly placed to provide access to the wonders of the Alpine National Park, the Falls Creek and Mt Hotham ski resorts, and a wide range of outdoor adventure activities.

To top it off, the abundance of great local produce, coupled with the savvy ski tourists passing through, has made for a sophisticated restaurant scene well worth staying the night for.

Information

The **visitors centre** (☎ 1300 551 117; www.brightescapes .com.au; 119 Gavan St; ☯ 9am-5pm) has a very busy accommodation booking service, as well as Parks Victoria information.

There are plenty of banking facilities in Bright. A National Australia Bank ATM is on the corner of Camp and Barnard Sts, and the Commonwealth Bank is opposite the ANZ Bank (both with ATMs) on Gavan St. **Bright Internet Café** (☎ 5750 1244; 4 Ireland St; per 10 min $2.50; ☯ 10am-9pm) is at Bright Hikers Backpackers' Hostel (opposite).

Activities

There are plenty of **walking trails** around Bright, including the 3km loop **Canyon Walk**, which starts from Star Rd Bridge and follows the Ovens River. The 4km **Cherry Walk** heads in the other direction along the Ovens and starts from Centenary Park, and a 6km track to **Wandiligong** follows Morses Creek.

The **Murray to the Mountains Rail Trail** (above) starts at Bright, behind the old train station, and continues an easy 30km to Myrtleford via Porepunkah. Bikes can be rented from **Cyclepath Adventures** (☎ 5750 1442; 74 Gavan St; per hr/half-/full-day $12/18/24; ☯ 9am-5pm Mon-Fri, 10am-4pm Sat & Sun). Cyclepath also leads bike tours, the most popular being the Bright Single-track route ($65), which takes you through the hills around Bright.

If you want to get airborne, **Alpine Paragliding** (☎ 5755 1753; www.alpineparagliding.com; 100 Gavan St; ☯ Oct-Jun) has 20-minute tandem flights for $150 around Bright, and one-to two-day intro courses for $225 per day. Also for the adventurous are powered hang-glider flights with **Bright Microlights** (☎ 5750 1555), where 10-minute/half-hour flights cost $70/155.

Festivals & Events

The **Bright Autumn Festival** (☎ 5755 2275; www .brightautumnfestival.org.au) is held over the last week of April and the first week of May.

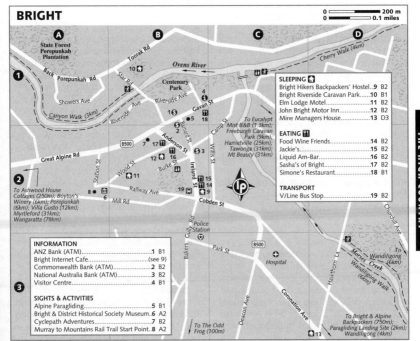

BRIGHT

0 ——— 200 m
0 ——— 0.1 miles

SLEEPING 🏠
Bright Hikers Backpackers' Hostel..**9** B2
Bright Riverside Caravan Park.....**10** B1
Elm Lodge Motel.........................**11** B2
John Bright Motor Inn..................**12** B2
Mine Managers House..................**13** D3

EATING 🍴
Food Wine Friends......................**14** B2
Jackie's...................................**15** B2
Liquid Am-Bar...........................**16** B2
Sasha's of Bright.......................**17** B2
Simone's Restaurant...................**18** B1

TRANSPORT
V/Line Bus Stop.........................**19** B2

INFORMATION
ANZ Bank (ATM)...........................**1** B1
Bright Internet Cafe....................(see 9)
Commonwealth Bank (ATM)...........**2** B2
National Australia Bank (ATM).......**3** B2
Visitor Centre.............................**4** B1

SIGHTS & ACTIVITIES
Alpine Paragliding........................**5** B1
Bright & District Historical Society Museum.**6** A2
Cyclepath Adventures...................**7** B2
Murray to Mountains Rail Trail Start Point.**8** A2

THE HIGH COUNTRY

Highlights include open gardens, scenic convoy tours and a popular gala day.

Sleeping

There's an abundance of accommodation, but rooms are scarce during the holiday seasons so book ahead.

BUDGET

Bright Hikers Backpackers' Hostel (☎ 5750 1244; backpackers@brighthikers.com.au; 4 Ireland St; dm/s/tw $21/30/44; 🖳) We love an efficient, clean, well-set-up hostel, and this little gem in the middle of town justifies the good reports. There's a cosy lounge for winter nights, and a huge veranda perfect for a summer day lazing in the hammock. Knowledgeable staff are an added bonus.

Elm Lodge Motel (☎ 5755 1144; elmlodge@bigpond .net.au; 2 Wood St; s $55-75, d $70-130; 🖳) There are rooms to suit all budgets in this restored 1950s pine mill, just a few minutes' walk from the centre of town. The beautifully landscaped gardens are the real attraction, as are the super-friendly owners, who can help you plan activities in the area.

Bright & Alpine Backpackers (☎ /fax 5755 1154; www.brightbackpackers.com.au; 106 Coronation Ave; powered/unpowered sites for 2 people $16/14, bunks $15) This decent budget option on 3 hectares of bushland, 2km southeast of Bright's centre, has two-bed bunkrooms and doubles. This place is fine in summer, but feels a little damp during the colder seasons.

There are several caravan and camping grounds alongside the Ovens River between Bright and Harrietville, including **Freeburgh Caravan Park** (☎ 5750 1306; www.free burghcabins.com.au; 1099 Great Alpine Rd; powered sites $20-30, bunkhouse $16, d cabins $60-120; 🖳), 9km from Bright, which has fine views of Mt Feathertop. Closer to town is **Bright River- side Caravan Park** (☎ /fax 5755 1118; riversideholiday park.com.au; 4-10 Toorak Ave; powered sites $22-36, d cabins $70-112).

MID RANGE

Eucalypt Mist B&B (☎ 5755 1336; 152A Delaney Ave; d $115-135) There's only two elegantly decorated suites in this attractive B&B, but you either share with friends or have the whole place to yourself. It's a short walk into town –

if you can leave the veranda overlooking the gorgeous bird-filled garden.

Ashwood House Cottages (☎ 5755 1081; ashwood@ netc.net.au; 22A Ashwood Ave; d $145; ⚄) No, it's not an outdoor dunny, it's a unique, corrugated-iron cottage set in bushland down by the Ovens River. And there are three of them, all with creature comforts, such as an entertainment system, double spa and log fires, as well as some interesting touches, like curved ceilings and leadlight windows.

John Bright Motor Inn (☎ 5755 1400; 10 Wood St; s/d from $80/90; ⚄ ⚐) If you're passing through town on your way to the snowfields, this busy motel is a good place to stop for the night. The rooms are comfortable – despite the red-velvet overkill – and all have bathtubs. It's on a quiet street in the middle of town.

TOP END

Odd Frog (☎ 5755 2123; www.theoddfrog.com; 3 McFa-dyens Lane; d $130-180) Designed and built by the young architect/interior designer owners, expect to be impressed with these contemporary, ecofriendly studios, made with natural materials, that welcome the bush landscape indoors with light, breezy spaces and fabulous outdoor decks.

Mine Managers House (☎ 5755 1702; 30 Coronation Ave; s/d $130/155) Restored to its former 1892 glory, this lovely guesthouse is gracefully furnished and has a gorgeous English-style garden.

Eating & Drinking

Simone's Restaurant (☎ 5755 2266; 98 Gavan St; mains $26-30; ⊗ dinner Tue-Sun) There aren't many restaurants in regional Victoria where you have to book a table on a Tuesday night, but Simone's is certainly one of them. Owner and chef Patrizia Simone serves outstanding Italian food with a focus on local ingredients and truly seasonal produce in the rustic dining room of a heritage-listed house.

Sasha's of Bright (☎ 5750 1711; 2d Anderson St; mains $18-30; ⊗ dinner) Sasha's serves up seriously good and incredibly hearty European cooking; if you don't fancy the smoked pork neck with sauerkraut pikelet, the Chateaubriand is highly recommended. There's also a reasonably priced regional wine list.

Liquid Am-Bar (☎ 5755 2318; 8 Anderson St; mains $14-25; ⊗ dinner Thu-Tue) Locals and visitors pack into this cosy shopfront for a relaxed family meal. Have a pre-dinner cocktail and chat with the friendly staff at the bar before taking a look at the tasty specials board. The food isn't Bright's best, but its appealing menu features great pasta choices and lots of robust mountain fare.

Jackie's (☎ 5750 1303; 6 Ireland St; dishes $5-12; ⊗ 8am-3pm) A great pit stop for adrenaline seekers who are off for a day on the mountain, Jackie's fresh juices are delicious instant health hits, and the breakfasts are excellent and generous – one bowl of porridge would serve an army! Lunches aren't as exciting, but it's a cosy place to sit.

Food Wine Friends (☎ 5750 1312; 2/6 Ireland St; dishes $8-15; ⊗ 10am-5pm) It's one for me and one for the pantry at this foodie haven where you can shop for regional goodies while tucking into light dishes, such as smoked-trout bruschetta, and downing an espresso.

Getting There & Away

From Melbourne to Wangaratta, **V/Line** (☎ 13 61 96) has a train and a connecting bus service continues to Beechworth and Bright ($46.70, daily). During the ski season a bus operates from Bright to Hotham (one way/return $25/35; twice daily Saturday to Thursday, three times daily Friday; 1½ hours).

AROUND BRIGHT

The idyllic former gold-mining town of **Wandiligong**, or Wandi as locals call it, is 6km south of Bright's centre. Kids (including big ones) will enjoy **Wandiligong Maze** (☎ 03-5750 1311; admission adult/child/family $8/5.50/24; ⊗ 10am-5pm Wed-Sun, daily in school holidays, closed Aug), allegedly the largest of its type in Australia. The

---

THE AUTHOR'S CHOICE

Villa Gusto (☎ 5756 2000; www.villagusto .com.au; 630 Buckland Valley Rd, Buckland; d $220-325 incl breakfast) The owners of this exquisite Tuscan-inspired villa are so into Italy that they named the suites *cioccolato*, *limone* and *arancia*. The décor is Italian bourgeois and the in-house cinema presumably shows *Deserto Rosso* on the days it doesn't screen *La Dolce Vita*. But after removing one's tongue from the cheek, what you have here is a class joint run by enthusiasts who will stop at nothing to ensure you are well cared for. And that includes the superb **restaurant** (⊗ dinner Thu-Sun) – Italian, natch!

café and impressive rotunda is a pleasant spot for coffee. It's signposted off Morses Creek Rd. The **Mountain View Hotel** (Wandi Pub; ☎ /fax 03-5755 1311; s/d $35/50, cottage per night from $70) is a bit of a find, with a great lost-in-time atmosphere, a fine **kitchen** (mains $7-20; ☺ lunch & dinner Fri-Sun) and regular outdoor music gigs.

Boynton's Winery (☎ 03-5756 2356; Great Alpine Rd, Porepunkah; ☺ 10am-5pm), about 8km northwest of Bright, is worth a visit. The tasting room sits on a rise overlooking the vineyards and the road. There's also a **café** (☺ 11am-4pm Thu-Sun).

MT BUFFALO NATIONAL PARK

The oldest national park in the Victorian Alps was declared back in 1898, and since then it has always been one of the state's best loved and most popular. It covers an area of 31,000 hectares.

Apart from Mt Buffalo itself, the park is noted for its spectacular scenery of huge granite outcrops, pleasant streams and waterfalls, an abundance of birdlife and some fine walks. The mountain was named in 1824 by the explorers Hume and Hovell on their trek from Sydney to Port Phillip; from a distance they thought its bulky shape resembled a buffalo.

The mountain is surrounded by huge granite tors. There's abundant plant and animal life around the park, and over 90km of walking tracks. The **Big Walk**, an 11km (or 16km with a side trip to Rollasons Falls), four- to five-hour ascent of the mountain starts from Eurobin Creek Picnic Area, north of Porepunkah, and finishes at the Gorge Day Visitor Area by the Mt Buffalo Chalet. Self-guided nature walks include the 2.5km-return **Gorge Nature Walk**, the 4km-return **View Point Nature Walk** and the 4km-return **Dickson's Falls Nature Walk**. A road leads to just below the summit of the Horn (1723m), the highest point on the massif.

In summer Mt Buffalo is a **hang-glider's** paradise and the near-vertical walls of the Gorge provide some of the most challenging **rock climbs** in Australia. **Lake Catani** is excellent for **swimming** and **canoeing**, while in winter Mt Buffalo turns into a ski resort with downhill and cross-country skiing (see right).

The park is located 333km northeast of Melbourne – about a four-hour drive. The main access road leads off the Great Alpine Rd at Porepunkah.

MT BUFFALO

☎ 03 / elevation 1500m

Mt Buffalo is Victoria's smallest ski resort. While Parks Victoria manages the Mt Buffalo National Park, a private operator manages Mt Buffalo Chalet and Cresta Lodge, the ski lifts, the handful of downhill runs, along with some more challenging cross-country skiing areas that are popular with beginners and families.

There are two skiing areas: Cresta Valley and Dingo Dell. Cresta is the main area, with five lifts – the downhill skiing area is 27 hectares, and the eight runs are predominantly beginner and intermediate, with fewer advanced runs and a vertical drop of 157m. Within Mt Buffalo's Cresta Lodge there's a café, kiosk and ski hire. Cresta Valley is the starting point for many of the **cross-country trails**. Dingo Dell is ideal for beginners, and has a day-visitor shelter with a kiosk and ski school. It's usually only open on weekends.

Information

Track information, camping permits and payments can be organised at the **Entrance Station** (☎ 5756 2328). **Parks Victoria** (☎ 5755 1466) has an office at Porepunkah for further information.

Costs

The admission fee to Mt Buffalo National Park is $9.30 per car ($12.90 in winter, but only if ski lifts are operating) and payable at the Mt Buffalo Entrance Station. Lift tickets are priced according to the amount of lifts open, but cost $25/12.50 to $50/25 per adult/ child. Lift-and-lesson packages cost $55/39 per adult/child.

Activities

Adventure Guides Australia (☎ 5728 1804; www.adventureguidesaustralia.com.au) offers abseiling, caving and rock-climbing alpine style, meaning the worse the conditions (rain, snow etc) the better – though you're only 200m from a hot coffee at Mt Buffalo Chalet! It also offers ski touring/snow camping and other activities from $77 to $100 per half-day.

Horse riding, climbing, abseiling, guided walks and hang-gliding can be arranged through **Mt Buffalo Chalet** (☎ 1800 037 038), which rents mountain bikes.

Eagle School of Microlighting (☎ 5750 1174; www.eagleschool.com.au) offers tandem flights for $250 and powered hanggliding from $95 to $155.

Sleeping & Eating

Mt Buffalo Chalet (☎ 5755 1500, 1800 037 038; www .mtbuffalochalet.com.au; s & d per person with/without shower from $125/116; ☒) This rambling mountain guesthouse was built in 1909 and retains a wonderfully old-fashioned feel, with simple bedrooms, large lounges and games rooms with open fires. There are four different types of rooms – the standard rooms have shared bathrooms – and during the ski season and January all accommodation includes dinner and breakfast. Ask also if the year-round special deals (room, breakfast and dinner per person from $99) are available. The Mt Buffalo Chalet Café is open daily to the public, while the chalet's dining room, in the former ballroom, is reserved for house guests. The café offers a high tea (per person $12) between 11.30am and 4pm with scones and jam.

Cresta Lodge (r per person from $96, high season $160) The refurbished lodge, 8km from Mt Buffalo Chalet, was due to reopen in late June. There are free shuttles between the lodge and the chalet.

Remote **camping** (sites free) is possible at Rocky Creek, which has pit toilets only. Strict conditions apply – organise a permit through **Parks Victoria** (☎ 5756 2328) at the Mt Buffalo Entrance Station. **Lake Catani** (tent sites for 2 people per night $16.50) also has a summer camping ground, with toilets and showers. You must book during peak periods.

Getting There & Around

There is no public transport to the plateau, though the **V/Line** (☎ 13 61 96) bus from Melbourne to Bright stops at Porepunkah ($43; one per day Monday, Tuesday, Thursday and Friday), near the base of the mountain. Transport from Wangaratta train station can be arranged for chalet and lodge guests.

MYRTLEFORD
☎ 03 / pop 2700

At the foot of Mt Buffalo, Myrtleford is yet another 'gateway to the alps', making it a handy overnight stop en route to the High Country or the snowfields. The helpful **Alpine Visitor Centre** (☎ 1800 991 044; www.alpinevic.com .au; Great Alpine Rd) has information and a book-

ing service for the alpine valley area and all the ski fields.

Myrtleford is a good place to jump on the **Murray to the Mountains Rail Trail** (p344), which follows a path close to the Great Alpine Rd from Gapstead, northwest of Myrtleford, and south to Bright. **Myrtleford Cycle Centre** (☎ 5752 1511; 59 Clyde St; ☒ 10am-5.30pm Mon-Fri, 9am-1pm Sat) rents bikes and helmets for $25 per day or $40 for the weekend.

Two local wineries are **Michelini Wines** (☎ 5751 1990; Great Alpine Rd; ☒ 10am-5pm) and **Gapsted** (☎ 5751 1383; Great Alpine Rd, Gapsted; ☒ 10am-5pm). For more information, see p64.

Sleeping & Eating

Golden Leaf Motor Inn (☎ 5752 1566; 186 Great Alpine Rd; s/d from $75/90; ☒) Well-furnished rooms and a pleasant garden are on offer at this motel. Bike hire is available for guests.

Myrtle Creek Farmstay Cottages (☎ 5753 4447; www.myrtlecreekcottages.com; d $150 incl breakfast, extra child $25) Feed the horses and get up close and personal with some fluffy alpacas at this hands-on farm stay. Bed down in self-contained log cabins, which come with a spa and well-equipped kitchen.

Ovens Hotel (☎ 5751 1628; Great Alpine Rd, Ovens; mains $10-25; ☒ lunch Tue-Sun, dinner Wed-Sun) A popular place for a drink, especially when there's a blues band jamming in the beer garden. The Ovens also gets top marks for its pub grub.

Alpine Enoteca Restaurant (☎ 1800 9910 44; Great Alpine Rd; mains $9-16; ☒ lunch daily, dinner Wed-Sun) Locals love this casual bistro, which is in the Alpine Visitor Centre (left). With its airy ambience and chilled music, it's a great place to hoe into risotto or a big bowl of pasta.

South of town, off the Buffalo River Rd and on the edge of Mt Buffalo National Park, Nug Nug Reserve has a picnic and camping area.

MILAWA GOURMET REGION & THE SNOW ROAD

Milawa, a one-pub town, has had a renaissance as a regional gourmet centre. Good food is a normal part of life here, and the superior attitudes you may encounter elsewhere are refreshingly absent. Notable wineries, fine restaurants, the impressive Milawa Cheese Company, and several other small-scale local food producers are well worth a stop and a graze.

> **WINERIES**
>
> For more details on wineries and wine touring in the Milawa and Ovens Valley area, see the Victorian Wineries chapter (p64).

The main points of interest along the route are to be found around the twin towns of **Milawa** and **Oxley** on the Snow Rd, which runs from the Hume Fwy near Glenrowan east to the Great Alpine Rd near Myrtleford.

The most famous of these is **Brown Brothers Vineyard** (☎ 03-5720 5500; www.brown-brothers.com.au; Bobbinawarrah Rd, Milawa; ☒ 9am-5pm). The winery's first vintage was in 1889, and the winery has remained in the hands of the same family ever since. As well as the tasting room, there's an excellent restaurant (see right), and pleasant picnic and barbecue facilities.

In the town itself is **Milawa Mustards** (☎ 03-5727 3202; Old Emu Inn; The Cross Roads; ☒ 10am-5pm), which has tastings of all 18 of its handmade seeded mustards, while the **Olive Shop** (☎ 03-5727 3887; oliveshop@ozemail.com.au; Snow Rd; ☒ 10am-5pm Thu-Mon) is an olive 'gallery'. Locally produced olive oil and delicious olive tapenade are on sale and can be sampled.

At Oxley, there are several wineries, including **John Gehrig Wines** (☎ 03-5727 3395; ☒ cellar door 9am-5pm). At **King Valley Cellar** (☎ 03-5727 3777; Snow Rd, Oxley), part of the King River Café (right), tastings of Pizzini, Chrismont and Moyhu wines are encouraged, and other King Valley wines are also on sale.

The **Milawa Cheese Company** (☎ 03-5727 3588; milawacheese@netc.net.au; Factory Rd; ☒ 9am-5pm) is 2km north of Milawa. From humble origins, it now produces a mouthwatering array of cheeses. It excels at soft farmhouse brie and pungent washed-rind cheeses. It's possible to sample, but there are no tours. The **Wood Park** (☎ 03-5727 3367; ☒ Wed-Mon 10am-5pm) label also has wine tastings.

Sleeping

Will Oak B&B (☎ 03-5727 3292; www.willoaks.com.au; Tetleys Lane; d $120-$140) City slickers will no doubt enjoy the small touches at this attractive B&B on a working cattle property 3km west of Oxley. Art books, glossy magazines, herbal teas and real coffee can all be found in the modern timber cottage with views to Mt Buffalo. The two-course breakfast gets fantastic reports.

Lindenwarrah Country House (☎ 03-5720 5777; www.lindenwarrah.com.au; Bobinawarrah Rd; d $280-360 incl breakfast; ☒) Set among vineyards, this sublime Moroccan-inspired boutique hotel has simple but impeccably stylish rooms eclectically decorated with French tapestries and contemporary art. The onsite **Restaurant Merlot** (mains $26-32; ☒ breakfast daily, lunch Fri-Sun, dinner Thu-Sun) garners good reports.

Old Emu Inn (☎ 03-5727 3202; Old Emu Inn, The Cross Roads; d $105 incl breakfast) B&B accommodation is also available at this comfy guesthouse run by the owners of Milawa Mustards.

Eating

Milawa Factory Bakery & Restaurant (☎ 03-5727 3589; Factory Rd, Milawa; mains $20-25; ☒ lunch daily, dinner Thu-Sat) An absolute must stop on the Gourmet Rd is this fabulous bakery and restaurant. For dinner there's a great range of options, from rump steak to pan-fried sardines with chickpea purée. The old loading dock outdoor area is fringed by grapevines, and makes a pleasant place to stop for a simpler lunch from the stone-oven bakery.

Epicurean Centre (☎ 03-5720 5540; www.brownbrothers.com.au; Brown Brother's Vineyard, Bobbinawarrah Rd; 2-4 courses plus wine per person $34-55; ☒ 11am-3pm) The rustic Epicurean Centre sees itself as a total wine and food experience. Brown Brothers wines are carefully matched with each dish, with an emphasis on regional produce and contemporary Asian and Mediterranean flavours.

King River Café (☎ 03-5727 3461; www.kingrivercafe.com.au; Snow Rd, Oxley; mains $15-22; ☒ 10am-3pm Mon, 10am-late Wed-Sun) Drive too fast and you'll miss this inviting café, an old general store that is now *the* place to stop en route to the snow for coffee or a reasonably priced meal of local produce, featuring specialties like Milawa blue soufflé and sinfully good homemade gnocchi.

KING VALLEY
☎ 03

South of Oxley, the Wangaratta–Whitfield Rd takes in several small towns, cool-climate wineries and produce growers. Past Whitfield there is excellent 4WD touring and walking country in the Wobonga Plateau/Mount Cobbler area of the Alpine National Park. Highlights include **Paradise Falls**, 20km south of Whitfield, which has a straight drop of 31m. Bush **camping** (sites free) is possible at

> **WINERIES**
>
> For information on wineries and wine touring in King Valley and the Alpine Valleys area, see the Victorian Wineries chapter (p63).

Bennies by Rose River and at **Lake Cobbler**. To reach **Lake Cobbler** and beyond, including **Dandongadale Falls**, with a 225m drop, the highest in Victoria, a 4WD vehicle is recommended. The King River is known for excellent trout fishing.

King Valley hosts the bumper annual **La Dolce Vita** (☎ 1800 801 065), in mid-November, which celebrates the region's wine and produce. Informal visitor information is available in Whitfield from **Mountain View Hotel** (☎ 5729 8270; s/d $50/80; pub meals $8-16, dining-room meals $14-25; ☉ lunch Tue-Sun, dinner Tue-Sat), a great country pub known for its Mediterranean-focused restaurant. Blackboard-menu pub meals include tasty options, such as pizza with roast pumpkin and Milawa Gold; King Valley wines are available by the glass. Bookings are recommended on weekends. The pub also has spotless motel accommodation, and includes a continental breakfast.

On the Whitfield–Mansfield Rd, 20km south of Whitfield, is **Powers Lookout** named after the bushranger Harry Power, a contemporary of Ned Kelly, who sheltered here while on the run in 1870. There are striking views of Mt Feathertop and the Upper King Valley. The **Kelly Tree** at **Stringybark Camping Reserve** (Tatong–Tolmie Rd), 36km from Mansfield, marks the spot where the gunfight between Ned Kelly and three Mansfield policemen occurred in 1878. The tree is 100m south of the day-visitors' area.

BEECHWORTH

☎ 03 / pop 2950

Rated by the National Trust as one of Victoria's two 'notable' towns (although these days it feels more like yet another wealthy Melbourne suburb), Beechworth is a living legacy of the 1860s gold-rush era. The impressive historical and cultural precinct remains, with many of the public buildings built in distinctive honey-coloured local granite, including the jail where both Ned Kelly and his mother Kate were imprisoned, and the courthouse where Kelly

was charged and remanded for trial for the murder of two Mansfield policemen.

The scenic countryside surrounding the town is also excellent for activities, such as walking and cycling. Some of the region's best wines are also grown around Beechworth. For more information, see the Victorian Wineries chapter (p65).

Information

The helpful **visitors centre** (☎ 1300 366 321, 5728 8065; www.beechworth.com; 103 Ford St; ☉ 9am-5pm), in the Old Shire Hall, books accommodation and activities, and has information on walks and wineries in the area.

Parks Victoria/DSE (☎ 5720 8190) has an office at La Trobe University's Beechworth campus on Albert Rd.

For bicycle repairs head to **Beechworth Cycles** (☎ 5728 1402; 17 Camp St).

Sights

HISTORIC PRECINCT

Beechworth's **historic and cultural precinct** (☎ 1300 366 321; www.beechworthprecinct.com.au; adult/child/family $12.50/5.50/30) consists of many interesting old buildings, including the excellent **Burke Museum** (☎ 5728 8067; Loch St; adult/child/family $5.50/3/15; ☉ 9am-5pm), named after the hapless explorer Robert O'Hara Burke, who was Beechworth's superintendent of police before he set off on his historic trek north with William Wills. The museum has gold-rush relics and an arcade with 16 shopfronts preserved as they were over 140 years ago.

The **Beechworth Courthouse** (Ford St; adult/child/family $4/2/10; ☉ 9am-5pm) is notable as the site of Ned Kelly's first court appearance, where he was committed to trial for the murders of constables Scanlon and Lonigan in August 1880. Across the road and in the basement behind the **Shire Hall**, you can see the cell where Ned was held. You can send a telegram to anywhere in the world from the **Telegraph Station** (Ford St), the original morse-code office.

The new **Chinese Cultural Centre** (☎ 5728 2866; adult/child/family $3/1/8; ☉ 10am-4pm Wed-Mon) displays the history of the 6000 Chinese gold seekers from Guangdong province who arrived in the Ovens district in the 1850s to strike it rich.

Also, check out the **Powder Magazine** (Gorge St; adult/child/family $2.50/1.50/6), an 1859 storage area for gunpowder. The *Echoes of History* video can be viewed at the 1858 **town hall** (Ford St), approximately every half-hour.

The precinct admission ticket covers the whole experience.

Ask the visitors centre about free tours and the Ned Kelly trial re-enactments.

OTHER SIGHTS

Old brewery paraphernalia is on display at **MB Historic Cellars** (☎ 5728 1304; 29 Last St; admission $1; ☒ 10am-4pm), a former brewery that now produces traditional cordial mixers. Within the same premises and open the same hours is the **Carriage Museum**.

The **Golden Horseshoes Monument** (cnr Sydney Rd & Gorge Scenic Dr) is near the spot where, in 1855, a horse was shod with golden shoes and ridden into town by candidate Donald Cameron on the nomination day of Victoria's first parliamentary elections. The Victorian-era PR stunt seemed to work and Cameron was duly elected to parliament.

The local **La Trobe University** (Albert Rd) campus used to be the Beechworth Lunatic Asylum for over 130 years; there's an excellent walking tour through the heritage gardens and buildings, which date from the 1860s.

The **Left Bank Artists' Co-operative** (☎ 5728 1988; Sub-Treasury Bldg, Ford St; ☒ 10am-5pm Thu-Mon) has some unique, affordable pieces on show.

The work of local potters is on display at **Potters of Beechworth & District** (☎ 5728 2636; 56 Ford St; ☒ 10am-5pm), a folksy ceramics store. Changing exhibitions take place in the space upstairs.

Activities

On the northern outskirts lies **Beechworth Historic Park**, an area that was once potholed with gold-mining activity. The Gorge area has 12km of **walking tracks**, and most points of interest have self-guided information. A good starting point for walks is the 1859 Powder Magazine; from it to Wool Shed Falls is 9km return. Also within the park is the **Gorge Scenic Drive**, a 5km tour, which starts at Wodonga Rd and finishes at Newtown Falls.

The **Murray to the Mountains Rail Trail** (p344), from Wangaratta to Bright, detours east to Beechworth at Everton.

Tours

Two-hour **Historic Town Tours** (adult/child/family $12.50/7.50/37.50) run twice a day and can be booked through the visitors centre.

Festivals & Events

Beechworth's three major annual festivals are the **Golden Horseshoe Festival**, held over Easter, which is a celebration of local history; the **Harvest Celebrations**, held in May, when food and wine workshops take to the streets of Beechworth; and the **Celtic Festival**, held in mid-November. Contact the visitors centre (opposite) for more information.

Sleeping
BUDGET

Old Priory (☎ 5728 1024; 8 Priory Lane; dm/s/d $40/50/80, cottage $105 incl breakfast) This historic convent has lovely gardens and a range of accommodation; it's the most atmospheric you'll get at this price. It can often be overrun by school groups, so check first when booking.

Silver Creek Caravan Park (☎ 5728 1597; Stanley Rd; powered/unpowered sites for 2 people $21/18, d cabins $50-70; ☒) In grassy surrounds, the park has good facilities, including a solar-heated pool and a decent camp kitchen. Dogs are allowed.

MIDRANGE & TOP END

There are an infinite number of B&Bs and self-contained cottages in the area. The visitors centre will book for you, but if you can, drop in and check out its glossy photo albums!

Bank Mews (☎ 5728 2223; www.thebankrestaurant .com; 86 Ford St; d $160; ☒) The original stables and coach house of this historic building have been renovated to house four swish B&B suites overlooking an attractive courtyard and garden.

Kinross (☎ 5728 2351; kinross@dragnet.com.au; 34 Loch St; s $125-135, d $150-165; ☒) A former Presbyterian minister's house from the 1850s, this elegant B&B retains many of its original features while allowing for modern trappings, such as TV and Internet facilities.

Beechworth House (☎ 5728 2322; 5 Dingle Rd; s $110-150, d $150-185 incl breakfast) If you can leave the glorious gardens – a lake, birds, roses and views – you'll find a peaceful guesthouse with very comfortable rooms and delicious breakfasts, such as pancakes with butterscotch bananas and maple syrup. One of the owners is a chef and will make dinner on request.

Country Charm Swiss Cottages (☎ 5728 2435; www.swisscottages.com.au; 22 Malakoff Rd; d $170-215 incl breakfast) These private self-contained timber cottages are ideal for families, and have excellent views of the Beechworth Gorge and Woolshed Valley.

Eating

Gigi's (☎ 5728 2575; 69 Ford St; mains $17-26; ✆ breakfast, lunch & dinner Mon-Tue & Thu-Sat, breakfast & lunch Sun) This shopfront café and produce store can be on the snooty side, but hearty Italian dishes, such as spinach and scallop risotto, are deservedly popular. Slow-braised goat is a speciality worth trying.

Bank (☎ 5728 2223; 86 Ford St; mains $20-28; ✆ lunch Sun, dinner nightly) Sophisticated dining amid the antique interior of this former bank building, which is not as austere as it first looks, makes for a culinary experience. Duck, ostrich and buffalo all feature on the creative Mod Oz menu. There's a number of regional wines by the glass, or check out the cellar, which is housed in the old vault.

Green Shed Bistro (☎ 5728 2360; 37 Camp St; mains $18-25; ✆ lunch Fri-Sun, dinner Wed-Thu) This former printery is now a cosy place to warm your hands by the fire and check out the busy open kitchen, where thin-crust pizzas are rushed out of the oven and tasty delights, such as spicy Moroccan lamb on couscous, are prepared.

Beechworth Bakery (☎ 5728 1132; 27 Camp St; ✆ 6am-7pm) We've heard talk of this bakery two states away, and it's certainly worth elbowing the locals and tourists out of the way so you can get your hands on a delicious pie, though the coffee is definitely ordinary.

Beechworth Provender (☎ 5728 2650; 18 Camp St) Absolutely crammed with delectable local produce, such as Milawa cheeses, wines, chutneys and antipasto, this is a great spot for gourmet bush-picnic supplies.

Getting There & Around

From Melbourne, **V/Line** (☎ 13 61 96) has daily services to/from Beechworth ($41). **Wangaratta Coachlines** (☎ 5722 1843) runs to major centres nearby. Tickets for V/Line, Country-Link and Greyhound Australia buses can be booked at **Beechworth Animal World** (☎ 5728 1374; 36 Camp St).

YACKANDANDAH

☎ 02 / pop 600

Set amid beautiful hills and valleys, the entire town of Yackandandah has been classified by the National Trust, which could explain why it still has a 'drapery' store!

Visitor information (High St) is available in the church hall. Pick up the free *A Walk in High Street* brochure, which details the history of the shops. There's also a glossy *Yackandandah Touring Guide* with information on the wider area. A **Folk Festival** (☎ 6027 1447) is held in mid-March.

Other options apart from curio shopping (try Vintage Sounds Restoration on Wyndham St) are **trout fishing** on Yackandandah Creek; a visit to the **Lavender Patch** (☎ 6027 1603; Beechworth Rd; ✆ 9am-5.30pm) for some lavender ice cream; or a trip to the studio-gallery **Kirby's Flat Pottery** (☎ 6027 1416; ✆ 10.15am-5.30pm Sat & Sun), 4km south of Yackandandah.

The unsealed 14km **Yackandandah Scenic Forest Drive** begins at Bells Flat Rd and travels over former gold-mining territory, much of which is now Stanley State Forest. There are six bush camping sites along Yackandandah Creek. There are also **4WD drive tracks** in the area.

Built in 1863, **Star Hotel** (☎ 6027 1493; 30 High St; d $45 incl breakfast) is an old country pub with renovated rooms and good meals (try Scotch fillet with Milawa blue cheese) for lunch and dinner (from $8.50 to $19).

About 5km from town, the homestead of **Karililla** (☎ 6027 1788; Ben Valley Lane; d $130) offers genuine country hospitality, a generous breakfast and lovely gardens.

Getting There & Away

From Monday to Friday, **Wangaratta Coachlines** (☎ 5722 1843) travels between Beechworth, Yackandandah and Wodonga, but only on Tuesday and Thursday during January.

OMEO HIGHWAY

Stretching almost 300km on its journey from the coast to the Murray River, the Omeo Hwy (C543) passes through the heart of the High Country, and takes in some of Victoria's most scenic and diverse countryside. The highway is unsealed in several sections (between Anglers Rest and Mitta Mitta) and snow often makes it difficult to pass in winter, but at any time it is a memorable drive.

The first section of the road, from Tallangatta to Mitta Mitta, follows the flatlands of the Mitta Mitta River. **Mitta Mitta** is a former gold-mining settlement, and a track leads from the highway to the former Pioneer Mine site, an open-cut mine that was one of the largest hydraulic sluicing operations in Victoria, yielding some 15,000oz (425.25kg) of gold over 16 years. For unique accommodation, head to **Bharatralia Jungle Camp** (☎ 02-6072 3621; cgotto@msn.com; Omeo Hwy). The comfortable tented camp costs $25 per person, and there's a camp kitchen, and barbecues and meals are available. Seventy kilometres south of Mitta Mitta, a turn-off leads to the Bogong High Plains and the Falls Creek alpine village – this road is closed during the ski season.

At **Anglers Rest**, beside the Cobungra River, is the **Blue Duck Inn Hotel** (☎ 03-5159 7220; Omeo Hwy; d from $65), which is popular with anglers, canoeists and bushwalkers. Self-contained units sleep up to six people; there's also a bar that serves meals and a good barbecue area right by the river.

About 30km south of Anglers Rest is Omeo, the only sizable town along the highway, and the turn-off point for Dinner Plain and Mt Hotham.

OMEO
☎ 03 / pop 300
Nestled among hills thick with bushland, Omeo is a particularly pretty little town. It's the southern access route to Mt Hotham, although the road is sometimes snowbound in winter; always check conditions before heading this way. Omeo's origins date back to the gold-rush days of the 1850s, when it was one of the toughest and most remote goldfields in the state. The area once had a very busy **Chinatown** in the area behind the Omeo Service Station.

There's an unofficial visitors centre in the **German Cuckoo Clock Shop** (☎ 5159 1552; Great Alpine Rd; ☼ 9.30am-5.30pm). The Historical Park has a mud map to the **Oriental Claims Walk**.

Omeo Service Station (BP; ☎ 5159 1312) has snow-chain hire; drop-off is possible at **Hoy's** (☎ 5779 2658) in Harrietville.

Sleeping & Eating
Omeo Bankhouse (☎ 5159 1405; http://omeoregion.com .au/bankhouse; 154 Day Ave; up to 10 people $200) A real find for a group ski trip, this restored two-storey bank easily accommodates up to 10 people with its airy rooms (ceilings are 14ft high!), well-equipped kitchen and large backyard.

Golden Age Motel & Bar (☎ 5159 1344; Day Ave; s/d from $70/90) This Art Deco pub has been converted into B&B-style en-suite accommodation. Its **restaurant** (mains $13-18; ☼ Mon-

Sat) serves reliable fare of steaks, salads and soups.

The scenic Victoria Falls Camping Area, off the Great Alpine Rd, 18km west of Omeo, has pit toilets and a picnic area, while **Omeo Caravan Park** (☎ 5159 1351; Old Omeo Hwy; powered/ unpowered sites for 2 people $18/15, d cabins from $55) is alongside the Livingstone River.

Gracie's Tea Rooms (☎ 5159 1428; 174 Day Ave; dishes $8-13) You won't need dinner after hoeing into a veggie bake at this great little lunch stop.

Getting There & Away
From Monday to Friday **Omeo Bus Lines** (☎ 5159 4231) runs between Omeo and Bairnsdale ($28, two hours). During the ski season **O'Connells Bus Lines** (☎ 5159 1377) operates a winter service to Dinner Plain and Mt Hotham from Friday to Sunday; it also has inexpensive bunkhouse accommodation in Omeo.

SWIFTS CREEK
☎ 03
The small town of **Swifts Creek** is 27km south of Omeo. **The Great Alpine Gallery** (☎ 5159 4445; ☼ 10am-4pm Wed-Mon) is a bright, modern space showcasing the labour of local artists and craftspeople. **Club Secondhand Bookshop** (☎ 5159 4354; Great Alpine Rd; ☼ 11am-5pm 26 Dec-30 Apr or by appointment) stocks a wide range of secondhand books, specialising in Gippsland. It's also the base for the small, independent **Ngarak Press** (www.users.bigpond.com/ngarak), fuelled along by writer and publisher Peter Gardner. Ngarak publishes a range of provocative historical titles focusing on the genocide of the Kurnai (Gunai/Kurnai) Aboriginal tribes, as well as more benign titles on historical place names.

High Plains Bakery (☎ 5159 4208; McMillan Ave) is well known in the local area for its woodfired breads and pies.

THE NORTHEAST

WODONGA TO CORRYONG
East of Wodonga the Murray Valley Hwy continues through **Tallangatta**, a small township with an interesting history. In the 1950s, following construction of Hume Weir, Tallangatta was flooded by the rising waters of the Mitta Mitta River, a tributary of Lake Hume. Most of the township had already been relocated to what is now known as

New Tallangatta. Seven kilometres east of town, there's a lookout point from where you can see the streetscape of Old Tallangatta, especially if the waters are low.

Fifteen kilometres west of Tallangatta, there's a turn-off to the town of **Granya**. The road to the north rejoins the Murray River and follows it all the way around to Towong and Corryong, via **Tintaldra**, which is worth a detour if you have a day or two to spare. Rupert Bunny (1864–1947), an Australian artist with an international reputation, spent time here in the 1920s, painting *The Murray at Tintaldra* during that period. The **Tintaldra Hotel** (☎ 02-6077 9261; Main St; basic d $30, motel d $65) is only 100m from the banks of the Murray River. It has a fine beer garden, tasty meals, basic rooms and a motel room. Camping is also an option. The main road also leads to Corryong, but by a slightly quicker and more direct route.

BURROWA-PINE MOUNTAIN NATIONAL PARK

This rugged and remote area, in the northeastern corner of Victoria, was always considered too rocky and steep for farming, making it a significant wildlife and vegetation reserve. It's popular for a range of outdoor activities, including walking and rock-climbing.

The park covers an area of 18,400 hectares and is in two separate mountainous sections. The northernmost section is centred around the red-granite **Pine Mountain** (1062m), which is covered in black cypress pines. A walk leads to its summit, which has great views of the Snowy Mountains and Murray River. This section of the park is botanically significant for its large number of rare plant species, such as the phantom wattle, branching grevillea and pine-mountain grevillea.

The southern or Burrowa section is dominated by the volcanic rock of **Mt Burrowa** (1300m). The vegetation is mainly eucalypts, with peppermint and blue gums in the lower areas, and alpine ash and snow gums higher up. Wildlife is abundant, with kangaroos, wallabies, wombats and more than 180 species of birds, including lyrebirds.

The main access road into the park is the Cudgewa–Tintaldra Rd, which runs off the Murray Valley Hwy about 15km west of Corryong. The other tracks through the park are 4WD-only roads. The facilities in the park are limited, with a picnic and camping area

at **Bluff Creek**, with pit toilets, and two other small camping areas at **Blue Gum Camp** and **Hinces Creek**. Some good walking tracks start from these areas, and park notes are available from Parks Victoria. If you want to go on an extended walk and hike overnight, it's best to notify the ranger of your intentions; contact **Parks Victoria/DSE** (☎ 02-6071 2602; 34 Towong St) in Tallangatta for more information.

CORRYONG

☎ 02 / pop 1200

The Victorian gateway to the Snowy Mountains and Mt Kosciuszko National Park in NSW, Corryong is a pretty township ringed by mountains. The surrounding area is a natural playground, perfect for trout fishing (the two best trout waters are the Cudgewa and Nariel Creeks) and canoeing on the Murray River, cycling and bushwalking.

Information

Corryong Visitor Information Centre (☎ 6076 2277; www.towong.com; 50 Hanson St; ☼ 9am-5pm)
National Park Visitors Centre (☎ 6076 9373; Scott St, Khancoban)

Sights
JACK RILEY'S GRAVE

Widely believed to be the real man from Snowy River, Corryong's most famous son is buried with a simple **memorial** of stone and timber engraved with the words: 'In memory of the Man from Snowy River, Jack Riley, buried here 16th July 1914'. The town's pretty hillside cemetery is at the top of Pioneer Ave and is signposted off the main road.

THE MAN FROM SNOWY RIVER MUSEUM

This **museum** (☎ 6076 1114; 105 Hansen St; adult/child $4/0.50; ☼ 10am-noon & 2-4pm) isn't actually dedicated to the legend, but is more of a local history museum. Still, it houses a fascinating collection of memorabilia. Standouts include snow skis dating from 1870, an amazing flying jacket that was handmade from scraps by a prisoner of war during WWII, and the Jarvis Homestead, a 19th-century slab timber hut.

Activities

Across the border in Khancoban (27km west of Corryong), you'll find quite a few outdoor adventure companies. The area around Corryong and Khancoban is great for canoeing, and **Alpine Hideaway** (☎ 02-6076 9498; Spillway, Khancoban) rents canoes for $50 per day.

Festivals & Events
Get on that horse and make tails to the **Man from Snowy River Bush Festival** (☎ 6076 1992; www.manfromsnowyriverbushfestival.com.au), held at the end of March. Highlights include bush poetry, a ute muster and a tribute trail ride to Jack Riley. The festival also features the Country Wide Challenge, one of Australia's ultimate tests of horse-riding prowess.

Sleeping & Eating
Jardine Cottage on the Park (☎ 6076 1318; 23 Jardine St; d $95, spa room $115) Just off the main road, this B&B is in a modern Victorian-style building.

Its café, **Jardine Cottage** (mains $10-21; ☿ lunch & dinner), in a former miner's cottage, is great for a warm salad or the popular rainbow trout ($16.50). It accepts bookings only.

Corryong Country Inn (☎ 6076 1333; www.corryong countryinn.com; 7 Towong Rd; s/d $70/87) An 1889 building fronts this modern inn, giving it an atmospheric feel. There's genuine country hospitality, and a decent **restaurant** (☿ dinner Tue-Sat) serving mainly local produce.

There are two very pleasant camping areas, both in scenic settings: **Mt Mittamatite Caravan Park** (☎ 6076 1152; powered/unpowered sites for 2 people $15/12, d cabins $36-46; ☒), 1km west of town; and **Corryong Creek Caravan Park** (☎ 6076 1520; Murray Valley Hwy; powered/unpowered sites for 2 people $15/12, d cabins $37-48) by Corryong Creek.

THE HIGH COUNTRY

South & Far East

Gippsland sprawls across the southeastern corner of Australia and is packed full of national parks, lakes and deserted coastline, and has some of the most diverse wilderness, scenery and wildlife on the continent. There are also plenty of hamlets with lively pubs and friendly locals, and towns with thriving arts scenes and a sprinkling of contemporary bars and restaurants.

Breathe the fresh air up in the mountains at the historic gold-mining town of Walhalla, once one of Australia's biggest-producing gold reefs, before heading to South Gippsland, the land of rolling hills. Valleys of giant tree ferns and towering mountain ash once covered this area; revel in the remnants of this extraordinary landscape at Tarra Bulga National Park. South Gippsland's rugged coastline boasts some of the best diving and snorkelling in Australia. And this is home to Victoria's most popular national park, Wilsons Promontory, a walking and swimming paradise. Heading east, the Lakes District, Australia's largest inland waterway system and a rich haven for birds, is separated by coastal dunes from the long and lonely stretch of Ninety Mile Beach, which has some quirky little towns dotted along its length.

Farther east is the sparsely populated corner pocket of the state, which has five major national parks: Cape Conran with beautiful beaches; Croajingolong with coastal walks, and an abundance of birdlife and wildlife; Snowy River with bush and mountain scenery, and river gorges; Errinundra with sensational cool temperate rainforests; and Coopracambra with its sense of isolation.

HIGHLIGHTS

- Hike through isolated wilderness at **Wilsons Promontory** (p368) or **Croajingolong National Park** (p390)
- Hang out with penguins at lighthouse accommodation on **Gabo Island** (p389)
- Relax, swim, or charter a boat lakeside at **Metung** (p376), **Paynesville** (p374) or **Mallacoota** (p389)
- Indulge in the fine food, bars, and art scene in and around up-and-coming **Sale** (p371)
- Discover the tiny town of **Walhalla** (p359)
- Visit **Krowathunkoolong Keeping Place** (p373) in Bairnsdale for Gippsland's Aboriginal history
- Catch a wave at **Lake Tyers Beach** (p379), with or without a surf instructor
- Lunch in the gardens at the revered **Koonwarra Store** (p363) before heading to local wineries

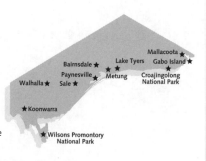

- www.gippslandinfo.com.au
- www.ausemade.com.au/vic

Getting There & Around

Melbourne is the main link for bus and train services to Gippsland.

BUS

There are daily **V/Line** (☎ 13 61 96; www.vline.com .au) buses along the Princes Hwy (A1) from Bairnsdale to Narooma in NSW, as well as one to two bus services per day from Bairnsdale to Lakes Entrance and to Lake Tyers. Another service, which runs twice weekly, follows the Princes Hwy as far as Cann River, then proceeds north to Canberra in the Australian Capital Territory (ACT).

    Premier (☎ 13 34 10; www.premierms.com.au) has daily services from Melbourne, travelling along the Princes Hwy to Sydney.

    From Bairnsdale there are private bus services north to Omeo and Buchan, and south to Paynesville.

    There are also regular V/Line buses from Traralgon to Sale via Maffra; Melbourne to Yarram, which stop along the South Gippsland Hwy; and Melbourne to Inverloch, which stop along the Bass Hwy.

    For those using the **Oz Experience** (☎ 1300 300 028, 02-9213 1766; www.ozexperience.com) hop-on, hop-off bus, you can hop off at Foster, Bairnsdale, Lakes Entrance and W Tree (near Buchan).

CAR & MOTORCYCLE

The two major routes through Gippsland are the Princes Hwy, which runs through the centre of the region, and the South Gippsland Hwy, which heads southeast before rejoining the Princes Hwy at Sale.

    Many of the special out-of-the-way places in Gippsland require a 4WD for ease of access (although 2WD access is often possible during the summer months). Many roads are unsealed and of varying standards, and some of the roads (especially those through national parks) will be closed during the wetter winter months. Check road conditions with visitors centres and **Parks Victoria** (☎ 13 19 63; www.parkweb.vic.gov.au) before heading onto unsealed roads. Also keep an eye out for logging trucks.

TRAIN

Bairnsdale is the end of the **V/Line** (☎ 13 61 96; www.vline.com.au) train link from Melbourne. Daily services from Melbourne to

---

> **SEASONAL VARIATIONS**
>
> During the high season of mid-December to January, Easter and long weekends, accommodation prices increase, restaurants stay open longer, and organised tours and activities run more regularly. Accommodation prices and restaurant opening hours quoted in this chapter are for the low season.

Bairnsdale stop at all major towns along the Princes Hwy.

WEST GIPPSLAND

Escape from the highway to enjoy West Gippsland. Detour to stock up at fruit farms, lose yourself in time at historic Walhalla or, if there's no time to deviate that far, take a breather at busy Gumbayah Park or creative Yarragon. Then brace yourself for unexciting stretches of cleared farmland and the industrial heartland of the West Gippsland between Moe and Traralgon, where you can't miss seeing the massive Loy Yang power station at Morwell belching out noxious fumes. It's almost worth it for the contrast a couple of hours farther down the highway.

PRINCES HIGHWAY – TYNONG TO YARRAGON

An hour's drive from Melbourne, at Tynong, **Gumbayah Park** (☎ 03-5629 2613; 2705 Princes Hwy; adult/child/family $8.50/4.60/25; 🕙 10am-6pm) is a large bushy wildlife park with emus, kangaroos, wallabies, a lone caged dingo, and birds in walk-through aviaries, including peacocks that strut their stuff. Picnic tables abound and there's a children's playground; avoid the park on weekends unless you love crowds. The amusement rides will be a winner with older children (per ride $4).

    The excellent **Wild Dog Winery** (☎ 03-5623 1117; South Rd; 🕙 9am-5pm) is 3km off the Princes Hwy on the Warragul-Korumburra Rd. This winery was one of Gippsland's first, and produces a range of stellar reds and whites, all grown and bottled on its 30 acres.

YARRAGON & AROUND

If you stop anywhere along the highway to shop, make it Yarragon. The town has successfully reinvented itself over the years

SOUTH & FAR EAST

into a Gippsland mecca for quality art, gifts and gourmet produce.

The **Town & Country Gallery** (03-5634 2229; 111 Princes Hwy) is a must, with a quality display of Australian paintings, hand-blown glassware, ceramics and woodwork for sale, while **Gippsland Food & Wine** (☎ 03-5634 2451; www.yarragonvillage.com; 123 Princes Hwy) is a large deli and café, showcasing gourmet produce and wine from Gippsland's 25 wineries. It also triples as a visitor centre, with a reasonable selection of brochures. The Commercial Hotel, on the Princes Hwy, can help out with its ATM if you've just parted with large quantities of cash.

Yarragon's shiny new image has been accompanied by the arrival of some quality cafés and accommodation. The star among the eateries is **Sticcado** (☎ 03-5634 2101; The Village Walk; breakfast $4.50-9, lunch mains $9.50-17.50; ✌ breakfast & lunch Wed-Mon), specialising in beef dishes from its own cattle farm, but also providing a classy space to have a cuppa.

A short stroll from the centre of town is **Yarragon Villas** (☎ 03-5634 2623; www.yarragonvillas.com.au; 16 Campbell St; s/d from $125/140 Mon-Thu, s & d with breakfast $170-250 Fri-Sun; ✲). These self-contained villas are bound to be featured in *Vogue Living* magazine before this guide is even published. Decked out with spas and wood fires, each villa is decorated in a different theme: French provincial, modern Asian, and completely over the top pink-and-green chintzy floral; they are all luxuriously stylish.

SOUTH & FAR EAST

For a complete bliss-out, next door there's **Santoshi Bodyworks** (☎ 5634 2314; 18 Campbell St) offering massage, private yoga classes and body balancing (all per hour $50; by appointment only).

The area surrounding Yarragon is dubbed 'Gippsland Gourmet Deli Country' (www .gourmetgippsland.com) and there are a few places close together that make a fun country jaunt; all are signposted from the highway:

Drouin West Fruit & Berry Farm (☎ 03-5628 7627; 315 Fisher Rd; ⏰ 10am-5pm, till 3pm in winter, closed Jul-mid Aug) is a pick-your-own berry and fruit orchard, and has the great little **Berry Good Cafe** (lunch mains $10.50), where you can tuck into focaccias, pies and platters featuring local produce, and some berry delicious deserts.

A few kilometres away is **Piano Hill Cheese Farm** (☎ 03-5628 5377; Main Neerim Rd; ⏰ 11am-4pm Fri-Tue, in winter Fri-Sun) for, er, cheese tastings.

Sunny Creek Fruit and Berry Farm (☎ 03-5634 7526; 69 Tudor Rd, Chiltern; ⏰ school holidays & weekends Dec-Apr) has certified organic berries. It's a beautiful 7km drive from the highway through remnant rainforest to pick a bucketful of organic raspberries, strawberries or gooseberries.

WALHALLA

☎ 03 / pop 23

Tiny Walhalla, 46km north of Moe, is one of Victoria's most historic and charming towns (so charmingly authentic that it was only connected to the electricity grid at the

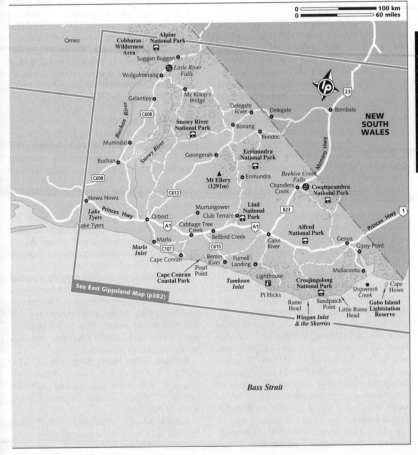

close of the 20th century!). Gold was dis covered here in 1862 by Ned Stringer. Between 1885 and 1890 there were over 4000 people living in the town, serviced by 10 pubs and five churches. They pulled 74 tonnes of gold out of Walhalla, worth about $1.4 billion in today's money. By the time the railway from Moe came into service in 1910, the population was (and still is) in decline. There's still plenty to see in Walhalla, and the drive up to the town is beautiful (mind the hairpin bends). Stringers Creek, encircled by a cluster of historic buildings set into the hillsides, runs through the centre of the town, which is in an idyllic valley.

The visitors centre in Traralgon (opposite) stocks Walhalla tourist information.

Sights & Activities

Many of Walhalla's attractions are open year-round, but there's even more happening on weekends and during the high season. The best way to see the town is on foot – take the circuit walk that leads from the car park by the information shelter as you enter the town. It passes the main sights before climbing up the hill to follow the old timber tramway back to the car park. There are many mine shafts in the area so keep to the marked tracks, and allow a couple of hours.

Guided tours of the **Long Tunnel Extended Gold Mine** (☎ 5165 6259; off Walhalla-Beardmore Rd; adult/child/family $9/6.50/27) give you a look at Cohens Reef, once one of Australia's top producers of reef gold, from which miners extracted more than 13 tonnes of gold. Tours also include the mine museum and take place at 1.30pm Monday to Friday, and noon, 2pm and 3pm Saturday and Sunday.

You can also take a very scenic 25-minute ride between Thomson Station and Walhalla on the **Walhalla Goldfields Railway** (☎ 9513 3969, 5126 4201; return adult/child/family $15/10/35). Train departure times on Wednesday, Saturday and Sunday, and public and schools holidays are at 11.30am, 1.20pm and 3.10pm from Thomson station; and 12.10pm, 2pm and 3.50pm from Walhalla station. The train snakes along Stringers Creek Gorge, passing lovely forested gorge country and crossing a number of trestle bridges. Back in town, steps lead up a steep hillside to **Walhalla Cricket Ground**. Check out the famous sign at the step's base about renowned Australian cricket captain Warwick Armstrong.

On the way back down to town, **Walhalla Cemetery** gives a more sombre insight into the history of the area; the terrain is so steep that some were buried sideways.

There's a group of restored shops on the main street, including **Walhalla Corner Store & Gold Era Museum** (☎ 5165 6250; 10am-4pm), which offers 1¼-hour **ghost tours** ($15) on the first Saturday of each month.

The southern trail head of the **Australian Alps Walking Track**, which goes all the way to Canberra and takes six weeks to hike, starts in Walhalla. For the less intrepid, it's also possible to do one-day return walks along it.

For some rugged mountain adventuring, there's the **Copper Mine Adventure** (☎ 5134 6875; www.mountaintopexperience.com; adult & child $15, family $50), which operates a 1½-hour 4WD trip, on most weekends and Wednesdays, along old coach roads to a disused mine. **Wheels to Walhalla** (☎ 5165 3212; bike hire $10, 2hr-trip $20) runs tailored small-group mountain-bike excusions along the bush tracks around Walhalla during the warmer months.

Sleeping & Eating

Camping in Walhalla is free; there are good bush camping areas along Stringer's Creek, as well as a designated camping area, with toilets, at the northern end of the town.

Walhalla Star Hotel (☎ 5165 6262; www.starhotel .com.au; Main Rd; d from $169) The rebuilt, historic Star offers stylish boutique-hotel accommodation with sophisticated designer décor and king-size beds. In the hotel there's **Parker's Restaurant** (mains from $19-23; dinner); non-guests should reserve a table.

Windsor House (☎ 9882 5985, 5165 6237; www.wind sorhouse.com.au; d from $150) The clock turns back more than a century when you step into this B&B with four-poster beds, open fires and a library of old books. This building was a guesthouse in Walhalla's heyday, and has been restored to its former glory.

Walhalla Lodge Family Hotel (☎ 5165 6226; mains $12-15; lunch daily; dinner Wed-Mon) This is a cosy one-room pub decked out with prints of old Walhalla. It serves good enough pub fare.

Miner's Cafe (☎ 5165 6227; $4.50-10.50; lunch) A small café, next to the general store, serving takeaway food.

RICHARD NEBESKY

Beechworth Bakery (p352), Beechworth

Horse riding (p331), Mansfield

JOHN HAY

PABLO GARCIA GASTAR

Tobogganers, Lake Mountain (p327)

Sunset on snow gums, Alpine National Park (p337)

RICHARD NEBESKY

Beachcombing, Lake Tyers Beach (p379)

Waiting for the ferry to Raymond Island, Paynesville (p374)

Historic advertisements at Walhalla (p359)

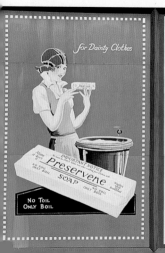

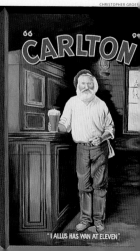

Getting There & Away

There's no public transport to Walhalla. For drivers, the exit is signposted on the highway near Moe, 46km away.

TRARALGON

☎ 03 / 19,600

Traralgon is the centre of the state's paper and pulp industry, and a major electricity-generating centre. **Latrobe visitors centre** (☎ 51 74 3199, 1800 621 409; www.latrobefirst.com.au; Princes Hwy) is in front of the train station. **Parks Victoria** (☎ 5172 2111; 71 Hotham St), off Franklin St, has information on national parks in the area.

SEAL Diving Services (☎ 5174 3434; www.sealdiving services.com.au; 27 Princes Hwy, Traralgon; introductory dive $99, PADI 4-day course $495) is bursting with local knowledge and is well worth seeking out. It offers PADI training, as well as full hire facilities, and shore- and boat-diving tours for certified divers to Wilsons Prom and Bunurong Marine Park.

Traralgon is linked by rail to Melbourne ($23.40) and Bairnsdale ($16.40). There are regular services from Melbourne, but only two daily on to Bairnsdale.

TRARALGON TO SALE VIA MAFFRA

This route is a peaceful alternative to the Princes Hwy and is dotted with small towns that sprang up during the gold-rush era.

Just before you reach the small township of **Cowwarr**, you'll find **Cowwarr Art Space** (☎ 03-5148 9321; www.cowwarr.com; Main Rd; ⊙ 11am-5pm Fri-Mon, or by appointment) exhibiting contemporary art in a magnificent heritage-listed butter factory. Sit back with an espresso and admire the exhibition, which changes monthly. Stroll across the garden to the **Australian Marble Sculpture Studio** where you can see Clive Murray-White at work on his portraiture sculptures. His work is included in the collections of the National Gallery of Victoria and National Gallery of Australia.

In Cowarr, the **Cricket Club Hotel** (☎ 03-5148 9233; helenho@net-tech.com.au; Main St; s/d $30/50) is a nice old pub. The bar downstairs is a real locals' bar, with well-worn carpet. The accommodation upstairs has had a makeover, with antique furnishings and smart doona covers for the queen-size beds.

Four kilometres southwest of **Heyfield** is **Abington Farm B&B** (☎ 03-5148 2430; cogs@i-o.net.au; Coghlan's Rd; s/d from $70/90) for a bit of luxury

farm living. The dairy has been converted into a stylish family cottage, the old barn is now a classy glass-and-wood number complete with spa, the pump house is now a sleek modern studio where you wake up looking at the river, and there are also a couple of comfortable guest rooms in the 80-year-old homestead.

Heading north from Heyfield on the Licola road leads you to **Lake Glenmaggie**, an arrestingly beautiful lake, fringed by snow gums. You can camp on the shores at **Lake Glenmaggie Caravan Parks** (☎ 03-5148 0202; powered/unpowered sites per 2 people $20/15) and enjoy the serenity – in holiday periods expect to have the peace shattered by boaters and skiers.

Just down the road is Gippsland's newest winery, **Glenmaggie Wines** (☎ 03-5145 1131, 0417-560 432; McLachlans Rd, off Weir Rd; ⊙ 11am-4pm Sun & public holidays, or by appointment), where the friendly Dawkins family handcraft their quality wine.

At **Tinamba**, east of Heyfield, the old colonial-style **Schoenmaeker's Tinamba Tavern** (☎ 03-5145 1484; www.dstbusiness.com.au/tinamba; mains $12.50-$21.50; ⊙ lunch & dinner; s/d with breakfast $75/100; ⊠) is brimming with character. The tavern bistro specialises in Dutch and Indonesian dishes. Try the *bitter ballen* ($5) – meat croquettes that take three days to make. Rooms in the wooden house out the back overlook the garden. It has a bathhouse feel with rooms built around a heated indoor swimming pool and spa.

MAFFRA

☎ 03 / pop 4200

Maffra is the centre of the local dairying community, and its wide, tree-lined main street is dotted with historic buildings and a few interesting shops.

Maffra visitors centre (☎ 5141 1811; maffrainfo@hot key.net.au; Johnson St; ⊙ 10am-5pm Thu-Tue) is in the old court house. It's worth stopping by to gaze at the **Pino Deriu Gemstone Collection**, gathered from around the world by a collector who retired in Maffra and bequeathed his collection to the local shire.

Don't be put off by the floral bedspreads at the **Maffra Motor Inn** (☎ 5147 2111; fax 5145 1450; 184 Johnson St; s/d $65/75; ⊠ ⊠); these are clean, comfortable brick motel units, breaking out of the mould with cathedral-style ceilings, and only a short stroll from the town centre.

Cambrai Backpackers (☎ 5147 1600; www.south easthostel.com; 117 Johnson St; dm/d with breakfast $25/55; 🖂) is a haven for backpackers, and one of Gippsland's best. It's in a 120-year-old building that was once a doctor's residence and is now a relaxed hostel, with a licensed bar, open fire and pool table in the cosy lounge, a small self-catering kitchen and clean, cheerful rooms. It's family friendly, with a set of bunks in the double rooms, and there's wheelchair access.

Foster Place (☎ 5147 1335; 17 Foster St; dishes $5-8.50; 🕙 lunch Mon-Fri), a café, gallery and nursery, staffed by people with disabilities, is the best place to lunch in Maffra. It has outdoor seating in a large leafy garden, and a children's playground. Expect friendly but sometimes haphazard service, and great cakes.

From Monday to Friday, **V/Line** (☎ 13 61 96) buses connects Maffra with Sale three times daily ($2.50) and with Traralgon via Heyfield ($5.90) twice daily. There is one service to Traralgon and Sale from Maffra on Saturday.

SOUTH GIPPSLAND

From Melbourne, the South Gippsland Hwy passes through the green, rolling hills of the Strzelecki Ranges and is the quickest route to Wilsons Promontory. An alternative coastal route, via Wonthaggi, Inverloch and Bunurong Marine Park, is even more scenic, with some stunning ocean views.

KORUMBURRA

☎ 03 / pop 3040

Korumburra is a sleepy town on the South Gippsland Hwy, where all the attractions take you back in time. It became a coal-mining centre in the 1870s and that history is now kept alive at the town's main drawcard, Coal Creek Heritage Village. The mining boom lasted only a few decades, and since then the town has survived as a dairy centre.

Information

On the way out of town next to Coal Creek, the **Prom Country Information Centre** (☎ 5655 2233, 1800 630 704; www.promcountrytourism.com.au; South Gippsland Hwy) is a large, efficient visitors centre, and the main office for information on Wilson's Promontory and South Gippsland.

Sights & Activities

Coal Creek Heritage Village (☎ 5655 1811; www.coal creekvillage.com.au; adult/child/family $11/6/30; 🕙 10am-4.30pm), next to the information centre, is a reasonable re-creation of a 19th-century mining town. It has a mine tour and 50 buildings, some staffed by volunteers, in period costume, who are knowledgeable about this period in the town's history and good at answering questions from curious children. The friendly, low-key atmosphere at this long-running heritage village is appealing. There's lots of shade for picnics.

South Gippsland Railway (☎ 5658 1111, 1800 44 22 11; adult/child/family return $12/7/35) runs heritage diesel trains along scenic tracks, with plenty of sharp curves and steep gradients for some moderate thrill seeking, from Korumburra to neighbouring towns on Sunday and public holidays (four services).

There are several wineries in the area, including the award-winning **Paradise Enough** (☎ 5657 4241; 175 Stewart's Rd, Kongwak; 🕙 10am-5pm Thu-Mon), 16km from Korumburra and signposted off the Korumburra-Inverloch Rd. There are friendly owners, good homemade wine, picnic and barbecue facilities, and a couple of pets to keep the children amused while you have a tipple.

Six kilometres from Korumburra, **Gooseneck Pottery** (☎ 5655 2405; Kardella Rd, Kardella; 🕙 11am-4pm Sat, Sun & public holidays; phone for weekday times) is a studio in an idyllic bush setting, where you can see the Asian-influenced work of potter Robert Barron, as well as one of the largest wood-fired kilns in Australia.

Sleeping & Eating

Kardella Homestead (☎ 5659 8252; www.members.dcsi .net.au/alert; 355 One Chain Rd, Kardella; s $130, d $180-220) Just down the road from Gooseneck Pottery, this homestead has plush antique-adorned rooms in pretty gardens, with great views of those rolling hills.

Divas (☎ 5655 1139; 27 Bridge St; mains $15-26; 🕙 lunch Wed-Sun, dinner Thu-Sat) This classy contemporary restaurant is friendly and relaxed enough that you'll feel comfortable bringing along the kids, who are well-catered for with a children's menu and box of toys. The grown-ups menu is select and inspired, featuring dishes like chicken with cranberry and camembert ($18.50).

Lyn's Café (☎ 5655 1021; 34 Bridge St; mains $12-20; 🕙 lunch & dinner) You know you've hit cat-

---

DETOUR: GRAND RIDGE ROAD

Between the Latrobe Valley and the South Gippsland coastal areas are the beautiful 'blue' rounded hills of the Strzelecki Ranges. These areas fiercely resisted early agricultural development, and were less-than-affectionately nicknamed the 'Heartbreak Hills' by pioneer farmers.

The winding **Grand Ridge Rd** traverses the top of these ranges, running from midway between Warragul and Korumburra to midway between Traralgon and Yarram, providing a fabulous excursion through fertile farmland that was once covered with forests of giant mountain ash trees. The road is mostly gravel, and rough and bumpy in sections as it twists through the hills. Take a good road map with you, as it's almost impossible not to get lost at some stage (it can get confusing – the logging tracks are in better condition than the road).

You can easily get onto the panoramic road by going north from Korumburra, or south from either Trafalgar or Moe via the lovely little townships of Narracan or Thorpdale. Alternatively use the road to get to or from Tarra Bulga National Park (see below).

The only place of any size along the route is the pretty township of **Mirboo North**, home to the unassuming **Grand Ridge Brewery** (☎ 03-5668 1647) in the historic Butter Factory building. This is Gippsland's only beer brewery and it has a **bistro** (☾ lunch & dinner Thu-Sun). There are also some good picnic areas and walking tracks in and around the town, including the 13km **Rail Trail** walking and cycling track that winds its way to Boolara.

---

tle country at Lyns, in the Austral Hotel, when one of the seasonal bistro offerings is 400g of Angus beef rump steak ($20).

There are also a few takeaway places in town.

Getting There & Away

Daily **V/Line** (☎ 13 61 96) buses from Melbourne to Yarram ($16.50) make two stops in Korumburra, one at the start of the main street shopping strip and the other outside Coal Creek Heritage Village

KOONWARRA
☎ 03

This tiny town is barely a blip on the South Gippsland Hwy, but produces a surprising abundance of fine food and wine. It has a refreshingly relaxed but happening feel about it. You'll need a car to visit, as there's no public transport to Koonwarra. There are a couple of stores in Koonwarra and some wineries a few minutes' drive away.

The café **Koonwarra Store** (☎ 5664 2285; South Gippsland Hwy; lunch $10.50-15.50, dinner $19.50-32; ☾ breakfast & lunch daily, dinner Fri & Sat) is a destination in its own right. Local produce and wines are on sale in the renovated timber store, and simple but very tasty food, such as roasted vegetable pie with orange salad ($10) for lunch, is served in relaxed surroundings, which include a garden with a children's cubby house.

In August the **Prom Country Slow Food Festival** (☎ 5674 2094) celebrates slow food – food that is neither processed nor mass produced.

Lyre Bird Hill Winery & Guest House (☎ 5664 3204; www.lyrebirdhill.com.au; 370 Inverloch Rd; ☾ 10am-5pm Thu-Mon; cottage d $110, guesthouse s/d $100/150) a popular winery with an old-fashioned B&B, has light-filled rooms overlooking the garden. There's also rooms in a faded country cottage. A three-course dinner ($60) can be arranged, accompanied by the house wines.

TARRA BULGA NATIONAL PARK

At the eastern end of Grand Ridge Rd and about 30km south of Traralgon, Tarra Bulga National Park is one of the last remnants of the magnificent forests that once covered the whole of southern Gippsland. This small park (2015 hectares) is an absolute delight to visit, and a relief to get to after the drive there through the environmental war zone of logged pine plantations and dead wildlife (watch out for wombats).

A canopy of towering mountain ash trees encloses areas of cool temperate rainforest. Below the mountain ash are sassafras, myrtle beech and mulberry trees, and the ground is covered with a mass of tree ferns, Christmas bush and mosses. Birds, including lyrebirds, parrots, robins and honeyeaters, revel in the lush environment.

There are two main picnic areas in the park. The Tarra Valley picnic ground is on the west side, off Tarra Valley Rd. A

1.4km walking track leads from here to **Cyathea Falls**. The Balook picnic and barbecue area is next to **Parks Victoria** (☎ 03-5196 6166; ☒ 10am-4pm Sat, Sun & school holidays), and the 2.4km return **Fern Gully Nature Walk**, crossing the Bulga suspension bridge, starts here. Camping isn't permitted in the park.

Tarra-Bulga Guest House (☎ 03-5196 6141; www .tarrabulgaguesthouse.com; Grand Ridge Rd, Balook; B&B s with/without dinner $100/80, d with/without dinner $150/110) is near the park entrance. It's an old-fashioned guesthouse, built in the 1930s, with simple rooms with shared bathrooms, central heating and a lounge with an open fire. There is also a **café** (☒ closed Tue). In the cold winter of 1954, the famous Russian defectors Vladimir and Evdokia Petrov spent a weekend at the guesthouse (then called 'Fern Gully') as a break from the rigours of the Petrov Royal Commission. It does get remarkably cold here in winter, as Mrs Petrov noted in the visitors book: 'A pleasant rest from the Royal Commission. Weather not unlike Siberia.'

KILCUNDA
☎ 03 / pop 230

Overlooking the ocean, on the Bass Hwy, Kilcunda with its rugged cliffs and pounding surf offers breathtaking views. Gawk too long at the ocean views and you'll miss the town centre: a pub, general store and café (with Internet facilities). The **George Bass Coastal Walk**, a 7km one-way walk from Kilcunda Caravan Park west to Punchbowl Rd in San Remo (the town before you cross the bridge to Phillip Island), is a popular trek, although the beaches along the walk have dangerous undertows and rips, and swimming is not an option (Parks Victoria track notes are available from its office in Wonthaggi). The mouth of the **Powlett River**, 3km east of Kilcunda, enclosed by high sand dunes, is also worth exploring.

Ocean Walk B&B (☎ 5678 7419; oceanwalk@waterfront.net.au; 8-14 Gilbert St; s/d from $120, cottage d $170; ☒) is a friendly B&B, with superb views over Bass Strait. Antiques adorn the rooms, and there's the option of a home-cooked three-course meal ($35).

Kilcunda Caravan Park (☎ 5678 7260; Bass Hwy; powered/unpowered sites per 2 people $17.50/14, d cabins from $55), perched on the cliff top, has sensational views from faded cabins. There's grassy sites for tents, and some overlook the ocean.

Mario's Ocean View Bistro (☎ 5678 7011; mains $15-32; ☒ lunch & dinner) in the 'Killy Pub' is where locals come to eat for the superb pub food, so book ahead. If the stylish bistro is full you can order from a reduced menu with reduced prices in the bar. The sunset from the pub balcony is divine.

Daily **V/Line** (☎ 13 61 96) buses operate from Melbourne ($15.60, 2½ hours) and continue to Inverloch ($4).

WONTHAGGI
☎ 03 / pop 6100

Wonthaggi originally ran to the rhythm of the coal mine when a steam-operated whistle rang through the town 17 times a day, marking the start and finish of shifts. The tradition continues at noon daily when the **State Coal Mine Whistle** blows from a platform in the town centre. In 1937 Wonthaggi was the scene of one of Victoria's worst mining disasters. During a miners' strike, a naked flame set off an underground methane gas fire, killing 18 maintenance workers. The events were portrayed in the 1984 Australian film *Strikebound*.

The **Wonthaggi visitors centre** (☎ 5671 2444, 1300 854 334; www.basscoast.vic.gov.au; Watt St) can book accommodation.

A surprisingly fascinating place to visit is the **State Coal Mine** (☎ 5672 3053; www.parkweb.vic .gov.au; admission free; ☒ 10am-4.30pm). Its highlight was the underground mine tours, but these have temporarily stopped because of safety concerns about the underground cable-car system that visitors travelled in, but you can still check out the open-air museum and view a couple of short movies that are screened. Check its website or with the local visitors centre for updates on when mine tours are likely to resume. The mine is 2km south of the town centre.

There's a particularly good children's **playground** in Graham St, opposite the Coal-fields Caravan Park.

Sleeping & Eating

Wonthaggi has two caravan parks, several motels and a B&B.

Caledonian Hotel (☎ 5672 1002; Graham St; mains $9-22; ☒ lunch & dinner) The revamped Caledonian has a happening vibe and good pub fare, and there's an action-packed children's room where kids can expend energy playing with hundreds of plastic balls.

DIGGING FOR DINOSAURS

In **Bunurong Marine Park**, which covers 17km of coast between Wonthaggi and Inverloch, you'll find an array of rock pools, tidal platforms, cliffs and sandy coves backed by coastal scrub. Over 115 million years ago the rock platforms formed a channel across a floodplain between present-day Australia and Antarctica; as the two continents began to separate the rocks moved north. Fossils were first found in the Bunurong park area 100 years ago at Eagles Nest, and in 1991 a research team found Victoria's most prolific dinosaur-bone site at Flat Rocks. The area is now a significant excavation site for many species of dinosaur remains; however, it was the discovery of the jawbone of *Ausktribosphenos nyctos* that caused the most excitement. This tiny placental mammal lived in a polar habitat, and the fossil is more than twice as old as the oldest marsupial or monotreme fossil previously found in Australia.

The **Monash Science Centre Dinosaur Dreaming dig team** (☎ 03-9905 5161; www.earth.monash .edu.au/dinodream) spend each summer, from late January to early March, diligently excavating the area – not an easy task when you consider that the main site lies beneath the high-tide line. The university welcomes volunteers on the digs, but you'll need to contact the team by November the prior year and also undertake a training program in December.

Mega Bites (☎ 5672 3344; 132 Graham St; meals $6-14; ⏰ lunch) The best place for lunch with decent food including curries, pasta, burgers and roll-ups. There's a children's menu.

Getting There & Away
Daily **V/Line** (☎ 13 61 96) buses from Melbourne travel to Wonthaggi ($18.20, three hours) and continue to Inverloch ($3.20).

BUNURONG MARINE PARK & CAPE PATERSON
The car parks along the Cape Paterson–Inverloch Rd provide access to the 17km coastal strip of Bunurong Marine Park, which starts at Harmers Haven, just south of Wonthaggi, and goes east to Inverloch. Many areas within the park are great for **snorkelling**, including the Caves, which is a sheltered rock pool. Eagles Nest, Shack Bay, Cape Paterson and Flat Rocks are also popular **scuba-diving sites**. This unassuming patch of marine park is also a significant excavation site (see boxed text, above).

SEAL Diving Services, in Traralgon, has diving tours here (see p361).

There's no accommodation or other facilities available at the marine park; they're all at nearby Cape Paterson and Inverloch. At Cape Paterson, the shop across the road from the caravan park offers Internet access and has an ATM.

Sleeping & Eating
The following recommendations are located in Cape Paterson, which is smaller and

quieter than its action-packed sibling, Inverloch, and the few accommodation options tend to book up quickly over summer.

Ibis Inn (☎ /fax 5672 2555; ibisinn@nex.net.au; Cape Paterson Rd; d $100, 2-night minimum) On a Protea farm, and named for the winter visits from flocks of ibis on nearby wetlands, this place has loft doubles in homey self-contained timber cottages. It's a five-minute drive to the coastal park.

Cape Paterson Caravan Park (☎ 5674 4507; www .cpcp.com.au; powered sites per 2 people $19.50, d cabins $72) A peaceful spot to stay adjoining the beach with lots of coastal tea trees.

Cape Tavern (☎ 5674 8122; Surf Beach Rd; mains $14-22; ⏰ lunch Sun, dinner Tue-Sat, lunch & dinner daily in high season) is a modern pub with large glass windows overlooking the extensive coastal scrub.

INVERLOCH
☎ 03 / 3740
Inverloch is part retirement village, part seaside resort and is getting ritzier each year. It's a popular destination with good ocean beaches and safe swimming spots, and is ideal for beginner surfers.

Information
Inverloch visitors centre (☎ 5671 2233; invyinfo@ basscoast.vic.gov.au; 6 A'Beckett St) is a shopfront in the town centre with oodles of information about the local area. The **Bunurong Environment Centre** (☎ 5674 3738; Ramsey Blvd; ⏰ 10am-4pm Thu-Sun, daily in peak season) offers conservation information.

Sights & Activities

Beginning at Inverloch Foreshore Reserve at the eastern end of the beach, **Screw Creek Nature Walk** is an easy 40-minute return walk that offers refreshing views from the bluff and plenty of birdlife.

You can take lessons year-round with **Learn to Surf Offshore Surf School** (☎ 5674 3374; 45 Beach Ave; 2-hr lesson $40). Everything is provided, so you just need to book and turn up at the beach.

There's an assortment of tourist town shops; one of the more interesting is **Inverloch Antique Centre** (☎ 5674 3003; 36 Bear St, ☿ 10am-5pm Wed-Sun), a warehouse and gallery of old and exotic furniture and bric-a-brac, which also has a museum section displaying 19th-century dresses.

Festivals & Events

Every March Inverloch hosts an annual **jazz festival** (☎ 5674 3141).

Sleeping & Eating

Holiday houses and apartments can be booked through local real-estate agents.

Lofts (☎ 5674 3656; www.stockdaleleggo.com.au /Inverloch; Ramsay Blvd; s, d & f $150; ☒) You'll feel very zen in these classy Japanese-influenced self-contained apartments in the town centre. Some have water views.

Moilong Express (☎ 0439-842 334; fax 5674 3710; 405 Inverloch–Venus Bay Rd; d $80) Train lovers will be in heaven in these two converted guards vans, which features many original features and some new ones, like a kitchen and bathroom, added. Sleeping on a train has never been so comfortable. They accommodate up to five people and have views over Anderson's Inlet. No credit cards.

Inverloch Foreshore Reserve (☎ 5674 1236; cnr Esplanade & Ramsay Blvd; powered/unpowered sites per 2 people $19/17) You're separated from the beach only by coastal scrub. The reserve is managed by the neighbouring Inverloch Holiday Park. Prices increase by 50% during the Christmas school holidays.

Kiosk Cafe by the Sea (☎ 5674 3611; meals $3-14.50; ☿ breakfast & lunch) This little red shack about 1km or so from the town centre is a friendly, relaxed café perched opposite the beach, serving good food and coffee.

Cafe Tsunami (☎ 5674 2129; 8 Williams St; mains $15-25; ☿ lunch & dinner) This café caters for everyone, with classy dining in its timber-

and-corrugated-iron-look venue, as well as takeaway gourmet pizzas ($10 to $12.50) nightly for the masses.

Getting There & Away

V/Line (☎ 13 61 96) buses to/from Melbourne ($21.60, 3¼ hours) stop in the heart of town on the Esplanade, not far from the visitors centre.

VENUS BAY

☎ 03 / pop 440

Fringed by coastal heathland, this small holiday settlement by **Cape Liptrap Coastal Park** (which stretches from Point Smythe to Waratah Bay) has excellent walking tracks and fine swimming beaches, although watch out for rips (Venus Bay No 1 Beach is patrolled during summer). Its gorgeous dunes give the impression that not a single house could have ocean views.

Anderson Inlet Walk (4km return) starts at the car park at Doyles Rd (6km from the shops), and passes along mudflats and mangroves teeming with crabs and birdlife.

Sundowner Lodge Guesthouse (☎ 5663 7099; www.sundownerlodge.com; 128 Inlet Road; d $130) is an award-winning boutique guesthouse that's just the place for a romantic weekend. There's a large spa, it has its own fully licensed restaurant and your privacy is guaranteed.

The friendly, well-run **Venus Bay Caravan Park** (☎ 5663 7723; venbaycp@tpgi.com.au; 113A Jupiter Blvd; powered sites per 2 people from $23, d cabins from $55; ☒) is 800m from the beach and has a children's playground.

The sleek **Venus Bites** (5663 7887; 114A Jupiter Blvd; dishes $4.50-20; ☿ breakfast, lunch & dinner Thu-Mon) is a cool grey-and-maroon-toned café and wine bar serving tasty food.

WILSONS PROMONTORY NATIONAL PARK

One of the most loved national parks in Victoria, the 'Prom', as it's known by locals, was established in 1898 and covers the peninsula that forms the southernmost part of the mainland. The Prom offers a superb variety of activities, including more than 80km of walking tracks and a wonderful selection of beaches – whether you want surfing, safe swimming or a secluded spot, you can find it at the Prom. Then there's the wildlife, which abounds despite the park's popularity. The wildlife around Tidal River is very tame.

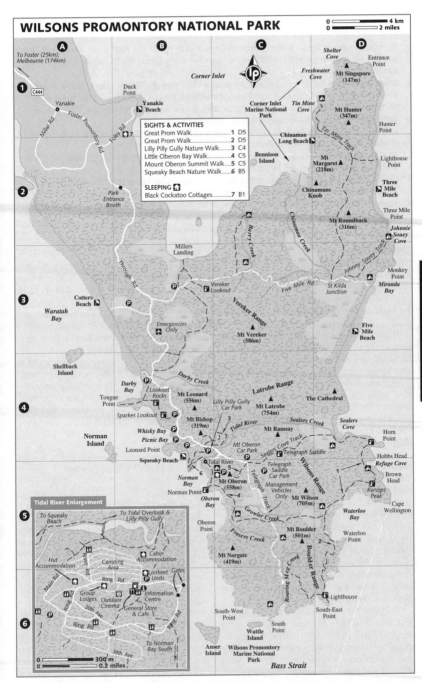

WILSONS PROMONTORY NATIONAL PARK

SIGHTS & ACTIVITIES	
Great Prom Walk.....................1	D5
Great Prom Walk.....................2	D5
Lilly Pilly Gully Nature Walk......3	C4
Little Oberon Bay Walk............4	C5
Mount Oberon Summit Walk....5	C5
Squeaky Beach Nature Walk.....6	B5
SLEEPING	
Black Cockatoo Cottages..........7	B1

SOUTH & FAR EAST

Tidal River Enlargement

TOP FIVE PROM WALKS

From November to Easter a free shuttle bus operates between the Tidal River visitors' car park and the Mt Oberon car park (a nice way to start the Prom Circuit Walk). Return times and distances are given here:

Great Prom Walk This is the most popular long-distance hike, a moderate 45km circuit across to Sealers Cove from Tidal River, down to Refuge Cove, Waterloo Bay, the lighthouse and back to Tidal River via Oberon Bay. Allow two to three days, and coordinate your walks with tide times, as creek crossings can be hazardous. It's possible to visit or stay at the lighthouse (see opposite) by prior arrangement with the park office.

Lilly Pilly Gully Nature Walk An easy 5km (two-hour) walk through heathland and eucalypt forests, with lots of wildlife. Or take the longer route through stringy-bark forest (6km, two to three hours).

Mt Oberon Summit Starts from the Telegraph Saddle car park. A moderate-to-hard 7km (2½-hour) walk, it's an ideal introduction to the Prom, and the panoramic views from the summit are excellent.

Little Oberon Bay An easy-to-moderate 8km (three-hour) walk over sand dunes covered in coastal tea trees; you'll be rewarded with beautiful views over Little Oberon Way.

Squeaky Beach Nature Walk Another easy stroll of 5km returning through coastal tea trees and banksias to a sensational white-sand beach. Go barefoot on the beach to find out where the name comes from.

Information

The **Parks Victoria office** (☎ 03-5680 9555, 1800 350 552; fax 03-5680 9516; www.parkweb.vic.gov.au; ☷ 8am-4.30pm) in Tidal River takes accommodation reservations, and issues camping permits for outside the Tidal River area. It also has walking-track notes.

If you're visiting for the day, the entry cost to the park is $9.30. Otherwise entry is included in your accommodation cost. The one access road into the park leads to Tidal River, which has a park office and education centre, a general store and café (with Internet facilities), and a seasonal open-air cinema; petrol is also available. There's a medical centre operating for limited hours during the high season.

Bushwalking

You don't have to go very far from the car parks to really get away from it all. The walking tracks (see boxed text, above) take you through swamps, forests, marshes, valleys of tree ferns and long beaches lined with sand dunes. If you're staying more than a couple of days, it's worth buying a copy of *Discovering the Prom* ($15) from the park office. Lonely Planet's *Walking in Australia* also has a detailed description of the Great Prom Walk.

The northern area of the park is much less visited, simply because all facilities are at Tidal River. Most walks in this 'wilderness zone' are overnight or longer, and mainly for experienced bushwalkers. Wood fires are not permitted anywhere in the park.

Tours

SEAL Diving Services, in Traralgon, offers diving tours here (see p361). The following places also offer organised tours in the area:

Bunyip Tours (☎ 9531 0840; www.bunyiptours.com; 2-/3-/4-day tour $225/345/425) Eco-friendly company offering hiking tours of the Prom. There's a 10% or more discount for ISIC and IYHA members.

Hiking Plus (1300 138 312; www.hikingplus.com; 2-6 day hikes from $675-1410) This tour company organises hikes to the Prom from nearby Foster, where it has comfortable guesthouse accommodation (including spa) for the start and end of each trip. Packages include meals; some also include massages. Ask about its specials.

Sleeping

All accommodation here should be booked through Parks Victoria (see left)

CAMPING

Tidal River has 480 camping sites, and in the high season booking is essential. In fact, camping applications are accepted in June, and a ballot is held in July allocating sites for Christmas. The park office usually reserves a few camp sites for overseas and interstate visitors during the holiday season, with a two-night maximum stay and no pre-booking allowed. There's usually enough sites, but do call the park in advance to check out whether places are likely to be available. In the high season, sites for up to three adults (or two adults and two children) and one car cost $19.60, plus $4.20 per extra adult and $6 per extra car.

There are another 11 bush-camping areas around the Prom, all with pit or compost toilets and most with water, but nothing else in the way of facilities. Overnight hikers need camping permits (adult/child $6.50/3.25), which should be booked ahead through the park office.

HUTS & UNITS
There are a number of self-contained cabins and units that can accommodate four to six people at Tidal River. The spacious and private self-contained timber cabins (per double $144) have a bush or river outlook. They're simple but very comfortable, and have a bath and large sliding glass doors overlooking the great outdoors. The smaller '60s-style 'Lorikeet Units' (per double $104) are like uninspired motel rooms. The cosy wooden huts ($55 for up to four people) have bunks and kitchenettes, but no bathroom. They're big enough to be comfortable and small enough to want to get outside for the day. There are also group lodges (per night 12-/24-/30-bed $256/516/644) available. All cabins and huts are usually heavily booked, so plan well ahead.

LIGHTHOUSE
The lighthouse-keeper's cottages are magnificent, stone walled, heritage-listed 1850s cottages on a pimple of land that juts out into the wild ocean. The spot has a secluded wild beauty and is a great place to kick back after the 19km hike there, and watch ships or whales passing by. You can usually visit the lighthouse itself, depending on park staff availability. It costs $41 to $65 per person to stay in an eight- to 12-bed cottage; prices increase by 50% on Saturday nights.

Getting There & Away
Unfortunately, there isn't any direct public transport between Melbourne and the Prom, though there are day trips and organised tours (see opposite). Prom Coast Backpackers (see p370) can usually organise a lift to the Prom for its guests for about $10.

AROUND WILSONS PROMONTORY
Waratah Bay
☎ 03
West of the Prom is the half-moon shaped Waratah Bay, with a couple of quiet and remote holiday townships and some won-

---

> **TIPS TO PRESERVE THE PARK & YOURSELF**
>
> ▪ Don't feed the wildlife, they've got plenty in the park to forage on.
>
> ▪ Stay on the marked tracks; there have been a few who have strayed and have never left the park.
>
> ▪ Don't light any fires anywhere in the park at any time of the year.
>
> ▪ Pull off the road when viewing wildlife – even if you've seen a kangaroo many times before.
>
> ▪ Have ambulance cover; an emergency usually requires being airlifted out of the Prom, which can be mighty expensive.

derful long stretches of white-sand beach. You can stay at the **Waratah Bay Caravan Park** (☎ 5684 1339; Freycinet St; powered/unpowered sites per 2 people from $20/17, d cabins from $50). Prices double during the Christmas school-holiday period. There are no shops, although the park office sells supplies.

Waratah Bay is a 30km drive from Foster. There's no public transport to Waratah Bay.

Walkerville & Bear Gully
☎ 03
Overlooking Waratah Bay, and part of Cape Liptrap Coastal Park, Walkerville is a pretty spot with just a handful of holiday houses scattered across the hills. There are some great beach walks in this area, and you can drive the 14km down to the lighthouse at **Cape Liptrap**. Right on the foreshore is **Walkerville Camping Reserve** (☎ 5663 2224; powered/unpowered sites per 2 people $17/14, d caravans $60).

In Bear Gully, 7km southwest of Walkerville, **Bear Gully Coastal Cottages** (☎ 5663 2364; www.beargullycottages.com.au; 33 Maitland Ct; d from $230), overlooking the bay, are gorgeous self-contained cottages. Sliding glass doors open from bedrooms onto the decking, with sensational ocean views. There's a delicious feeling of isolation.

Bush camping is possible at the well-maintained **Bear Gully camp site** (sites free), south of Walkerville. There's no water, so you'll need to bring your own.

Driving is the main transport option here as there's no public transport.

SOUTH & FAR EAST

Yanakie

☎ 03

The nearest settlement to the Prom, Yanakie, an Aboriginal word meaning 'between waters', is a tiny place with gorgeous accommodation nearby. At **Black Cockatoo Cottages** (☎ 5687 1306; www.blackcockatoo.com; 60 Foley Rd; d $120) you can take in glorious views of the Prom without leaving your very comfortable bed; these are private, stylish, modern, black timber self-contained cottages.

Yanakie Caravan Park (☎ /fax 5687 1295; yanakie caravanpark@hotmail.com; 390 Foley Rd; powered sites per 2 people $19, d cabins from $55) has a few light and bright deluxe cabins ($90) with a deck overlooking the Prom; linen is provided.

You need a car to get to Yanakie, which is 25km from Foster.

Foster

☎ 03 / pop 1000

This former gold-mining settlement on the South Gippsland Hwy survives in part on the tourist traffic to and from Wilsons Prom. There's a **Parks Victoria office** (☎ 13 19 63; 3a Main St), and an adjoining tourist information display.

Prom Coast Backpackers (☎ 5682 2171; http://gipps land.com/web/WarraweeHolidayApartments; 40 Station Rd; 4-bed dm/d/f $25/60/75) In a small renovated cottage with polished floorboards, this cosy backpackers has a small kitchen and lounge, and sleeps 10. The friendly owners can usually organise a lift to the Prom (about $10). It also has **Warrawee Holiday Apartments** (d/f from $80/100) next door, which are homey and spacious units with a wood-fired stove, and children's books and toys.

The popular **Exchange Hotel** (☎ 5682 2377; 43 Main St; mains $14-27; ☽ lunch & dinner) has been tastefully renovated and decorated with old sepia-tone prints of Foster in the old days. It has good-quality bistro meals, including smoked-salmon risotto (entree $8.90). Kids will love the padded cell, er, Kidz Korner, where they can literally bounce off the walls.

Foster is connected to Melbourne ($26.20) and Yarram ($5.90) by **V/Line** (☎ 13 61 96) buses.

PORT ALBERT

☎ 03 / pop 220

The quiet little fishing town of Port Albert lays proud claim to the title of being Victoria's first established fishing port. The his-

toric town buildings all have plaques telling a piece of its story as an international port and arrival point for those trying their luck on the goldfields of Dargo and Omeo.

The **Maritime Museum** (☎ 5183 2520; Tarraville Rd; adult/child $4/1; ☽ 10.30am-4pm daily Sep-May, Sat & Sun Jun-Aug) is Port Albert's star act, covering the town's whaling and sealing days, and the boats that used to sail here, as well as an exhibit of the actual top revolving light section of a lighthouse, once used on one of the islands off the coast of the Prom.

Sleeping & Eating

Port Albert Bed & Breakfast (☎ 5183 2525; www .portalbertbedandbreakfast.com; 27 Wharf St, d from $200) This house looks out of place in historic Port Albert, but once inside this boutique accommodation you won't give a toss. It's like stepping onto the film set of *Gone with the Wind*, except for the sweeping views of the Prom and the port. Each tastefully furnished room has a king-size bed and spa. For a romantic weekend, ask for the sublime Lovers Suite ($230).

Port Albert Hotel/Motel (☎ 5183 2212; Wharf St; s/d $55/75) Crowded on weekends with hardy fishing types, this hotel is the oldest licensed pub in Victoria. Its rooms are clean, with faded bedcovers, and the **bistro** (mains $12-17) has decent pub fare.

Boathouse (☎ 5183 2434; ☽ lunch & dinner) It doesn't advertise, doesn't have a business card and staff don't wear a uniform, but the crowds are queuing out the door in summer for the renowned fish and chips – they're delicious.

Getting There & Away

V/Line (☎ 13 61 96) buses will let you off at the turn-off to Port Albert on the South Gippsland Hwy. From the turn-off, it's 7km to Port Albert.

YARRAM TO SALE

A commercial centre on the South Gippsland Hwy, Yarram has several historic buildings lining its main street, including the 1930 **Regent Theatre** (☎ 03-5182 5420), proudly restored by the locals, who are happy for you to have a peek. There are several caravan parks and motels in town. **Rosewood** (☎ 03-5182 5605; Hiho's Lane; d $120, 2-night minimum Fri-Sun) is a bluestone cottage set in traditional, lavishly landscaped gardens abuzz with blue wrens.

Once you get over the bright lights, the friendly and efficient **Paul the Pieman** (☎ 03-5182 6488; dishes $3-4.50; ☺ lunch) has a fabulous selection of pies and cakes and good coffee. The vegetarian roll with seed mix ($4.10) is recommended.

At **Woodside**, head southeast to **Woodside Beach**, at the western reaches of Ninety Mile Beach, or head south to the small holiday shack settlement of **McLoughlin's Beach**, which forms part of Nooramunga Marine and Coastal Park. A worthwhile 2.5km (one-hour) walking trail to Ninety Mile Beach, along a boardwalk and across wetlands, starts from the jetty at McLoughlin's Beach. This quite beautiful place with salt marshes, mangroves and low-lying scrub is preserving its character well, with not a single shop or place to stay.

V/Line (☎ 13 61 96) buses from Melbourne run daily to Yarram ($32.20), but there's no public transport to Woodside or McLoughlin's Beach.

LAKES DISTRICT

Gippsland's Lakes District is the largest inland waterway system in Australia. There are three main lakes: Lake King, Lake Victoria and Lake Wellington. They are all joined, and fed, by a number of rivers that originate in the High Country, including the Mitchell, Nicholson, Tambo and Avon Rivers. The lakes are actually shallow coastal lagoons that were once part of a large bay. Over thousands of years sand has built up in deposits along the coastline, and the lakes are now separated from the ocean by a narrow strip of coastal sand dunes known as Ninety Mile Beach. Most of Ninety Mile Beach, from Woodside Beach to Lakes Entrance, is part of the 17,200-hectare Gippsland Lakes Coastal Park. Within this area is The Lakes National Park, including the bird-watcher's paradise of **Rotamah Island**. Mitchell River National Park is another feature of the area.

The regional centre of Sale is the gateway to the Lakes District.

SALE

☎ 03 / pop 12,850

Until recently a pretty unexciting stop along the Princes Hwy, Sale is getting a more contemporary vibe with the advent of its striking

new entertainment centre, classy restaurants and bars, and the development of the old Port area.

Information

The **Central Gippsland visitors centre** (☎ /fax 5144 1108; www.gippslandinfo.com.au; 8 Foster St/Princes Hwy) has Internet facilities and is the first Victorian tourist office to have an online accommodation booking service. For **Parks Victoria** (☎ 5143 8200; 1 Lacey St; ☺ Mon & Fri) turn right at Foster St onto Guthridge St.

Sights & Activities

The **Sale Wetlands Walk** is signposted from Lake Guthridge. The 4km walking trail skirts around the lake via **Sale Common**, a 330-hectare wildlife refuge, including bird hides, an observatory, boardwalks and other walking tracks, which is part of an internationally recognised wetlands system. The best time to go is early morning or late evening (apply mosquito repellent; they're vicious). Camping is not permitted at the Common, but free camping (no facilities) is allowed in the greater wetlands area as long as you camp 20m away from the water.

The **Gippsland Art Gallery** (☎ 5142 3372; Civic Centre, 68 Foster St; adult/child $3/1.50; ☺ 10am-5pm Tue-Fri, 1-5pm Sat & Sun) is a small gallery always worth a look, exhibiting work by locally and nationally renowned artists. It also hosts touring exhibitions.

Sale's old **Port** has been given a facelift with new timber walkways and picnic tables. There are grand plans for a marina and upmarket accommodation, and eateries overlooking the port, once a busy place during the paddle-steamer heyday.

Sleeping & Eating

Bon Accord (☎ 5144 5555; www.bonaccordb-b.com.au; 153-155 Dawson St; s/d from $135/170) Sleeping in the ironing room suddenly becomes an incredibly attractive proposition at this 1860s homestead, where the original school room and the stables have been restored to offer luxury accommodation. The stables, with a loft upstairs and a claw bath, is more spacious and the best option. A full breakfast is served in the homestead.

Relish@the Gallery (☎ 5144 5044; Gippsland Art Gallery, 68-70 Foster St; dishes $6-19; ☺ dinner Wed-Sat, breakfast & lunch) Relaxed but stylish design and great views of the old Port make this a top

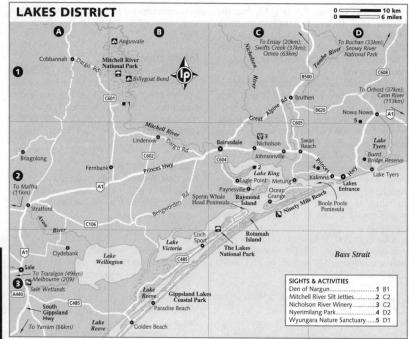

LAKES DISTRICT

SIGHTS & ACTIVITIES	
Den of Nargun............................1	B1
Mitchell River Silt Jetties.............2	C2
Nicholson River Winery................3	C2
Nyerimilang Park.........................4	D2
Wyungara Nature Sanctuary.....5	D1

choice. Breakfast is available all day. Focaccias are good, as is the Thai seafood cakes with Malibu sweet-chilli sauce ($14). There is disabled access, as well as baby-changing facilities.

Bis (☎ 5144 3388; Wellington Entertainment Centre, 100 Foster St; breakfast & lunch mains $8-17, dinner mains $23-31; ⏰ breakfast Sat & Sun, lunch daily, dinner Tue-Sat) Bis is one of Gippsland's best restaurants. The service is relaxed but attentive and the Italian-influenced food is superb. For an exquisite blend of tastes, try the entree of grilled goats cheese with pear, balsamic and rocket ($13), or the pistachio-stuffed chicken with pancetta, parmesan, polenta and jus ($25). You'll probably feel uncomfortable here with children.

Drinking & Entertainment

Phoenix (☎ 5144 4989; 118-24 Raymond St; ⏰ 5pm-1am) With the rising of the Phoenix, Sale has it's first all-night bar and lounge in the Art Deco AMP building – check out the Grecian pillars. This is one classy place to hang out.

Redd Catt (☎ 5143 1911; Raymond St) A velvet ceiling, bold paintings, a friendly vibe and

music from Wednesday to Saturday make this place a good drinking option.

Wellington Entertainment Centre (☎ 5143 3200; www.wellington.vic.gov.au/entertainment; 100 Foster St; tickets $25-45) Top-class state and national theatre productions, comedy shows and music performances make brief appearances at the centre. There's disabled access and a baby-change room available.

Getting There & Away

Sale's train station is in Petit Dr on the western side of town. Trains run twice daily between Melbourne and Sale ($32.20).

STRATFORD

☎ 03 / pop 1330

Stratford is a pretty little blimp on the Princes Hwy, a 15-minute drive from either Maffra or Sale, and has retained its authenticity and appeal without going tourist-kitsch.

There's a vibrant arts community, with the **Eye 2 Eye Theatre Company** (☎ 5145 7088; ⏰ Fri & Sat) presenting regular high-calibre productions, and the contemporary **Red**

River Designs Gallery (☎ /fax 5145 6769; ☺ 10am-4.30pm Wed-Fri & Sun), both on Tyers St (Princes Hwy). The **Shakespeare on the River Festival** is held annually here in April/May.

Based in Stratford, Graham, a third-generation gold miner, runs **Overland Gold Adventures** (☎ /fax 5145 6701; Tyers St; day trip incl lunch per person $100) – tailored 4WD tours exploring the gold-mining areas of Gippsland. Expect to visit old mines and prospect for gold. Overnight trips to the Dargo area are also possible.

Sleeping & Eating

Stratford Motel (☎ 5145 6500; stratfordmotel@ozemail .com.au; 26 Tyers St; s/d/f $55/60/90, spa room $100; ☒) This friendly place has some of the most home-like motel rooms around, with well-chosen fluffed-up doonas. The spa room is spacious and air-conditioned.

Stratford Top Tourist Park (☎ 5145 6588; www.top touristparks.com.au/vic/sttp.html; McMillan St; tent/powered sites per 2 people $15/17, dm from $18, d cabin with bathroom from $53) On the banks of the Avon, this leafy park has a bunk room for backpackers and a separate kitchen.

Wa-de-Lock (☎ 5145 7050; 76 Tyers St; dishes $3-11.50; ☺ breakfast & lunch Sat-Thu) The cool-climate winery has its cellar door at Stratford, and now runs a café where you can try local produce, such as smoked trout and Gippsland cheese, and drink wine by the glass. The bread in the gourmet pizzas, focaccias and sandwiches is all made on-site.

Stratford Bakehouse (☎ 5145 6003; 35 Tyers St; snacks $2-4.50) Justifiably popular for its pies and cakes, and a nice no-frills spot for a quick bite or espresso.

BAIRNSDALE

☎ 03 / pop 10,670

On the banks of the Mitchell River, Bairnsdale is East Gippsland's commercial hub and the last stop for a 24-hour petrol station. The shopping strip along the highway demands your attention, but it's worth going beyond the main drag for gourmet cafés, an absorbing insight into Aboriginal history, and the quite astonishing contrast to the hubbub of the main street, the Macleod Morass wetlands.

Information

Bairnsdale visitors centre (☎ 5152 3444, 1800 637 060; www.egipps.vic.gov.au; 240 Main St)

East Gippsland Shire Library (☎ 5152 4225; Service St) Free Internet access is available here.

Parks Victoria (☎ 5152 0600; 73 Calvert St)

Sights & Activities

The **Krowathunkoolong Keeping Place** (☎ 5152 1891; 37-53 Dalmahoy St; adult/child $3.50/2.50; ☺ 9am-5pm Mon-Fri) is a Koorie cultural exhibition space that explores Gunai (Kurnai) daily life before and after white settlement. The Aborigines of Gippsland, collectively known as the Kurnai, are estimated to have inhabited Gippsland for over 65,000 years. Descended from their Dreamtime ancestors, Borun the Pelican and his relative Tuk the Musk Duck, the five Kurnai clans lived together in relative harmony. The exhibition covers life at Lake Tyers Mission, east of Lakes Entrance, which is now a trust privately owned by Aboriginal shareholders. Everyday items, such as an impressive 2.5m bark canoe and a trumpet-like woven eel-and-fish basket, reveal the Kurnai's skill in fishing the waterways of the area. The unmitigated massacres of the Kurnai during 1839–49 are also detailed. The Keeping Place is behind the train station.

There's a grand red-brick **St Mary's Catholic Church**, beside the visitors centre, that's notable for its opulent ceiling murals of rosy-cheeked cherubs. Your neck will be aching when you leave (pity the poor artist Italian-Australian Frank Floreani, who painted the murals over four years in the 1930s).

On the edge of town (signposted from the highway at Forge Creek Rd) the **MacLeod Morass Boardwalk** is a stunning internationally recognised wetland reserve with walking tracks and bird hides.

The **East Gippsland Art Gallery** (☎ 5153 1988; 222 Nicholson St; ☺ 10am-4pm Tue-Fri, 10am-2pm Sat) is a bright, open space with regular exhibitions, mostly work of East Gippsland artists.

Howitt Park is a popular playground stop on the highway, and also the starting point for the popular bike and walking track, the **East Gippsland Rail Trail**. The trail leads northeast to **Bruthen**, 30km away, and a new **Discovery Trail** now extends it through state forest to Lakes Entrance.

A few kilometres east of town is the **Bairnsdale Archery, Mini Golf & Games Park** (☎ 5156 8655; www.bairnsdalefunpark.com.au; 459 Princes Hwy), which has Australia's only bungee trampoline.

About 4km northeast of the town of **Nicholson** and signposted from the highway,

Nicholson River Winery (☎ 5156 8241; 57 Liddells Rd, Nicholson; ⊙ 10am-4pm) has tastings ($2, refundable with purchase) in a garden overlooking the river. It's best known for its whites.

Sleeping & Eating

There are numerous motel options on the highway (Main St).

Riversleigh Country Hotel (☎ 5152 6966; fax 5152 4413; 1 Nicholson St; s/d with breakfast from $114/159) This Victorian-era boutique hotel has elegant rooms, with crisp linen, brass beds and antique furnishings that transport you back in the most comfortable way to a bygone era. Disabled facilities are available. Breakfast is served in the sunny conservatory. There's a formal **restaurant** (lunch $12-19, dinner mains $21-25; ⊙ lunch Thu-Fri, dinner Mon-Sat; ✖) here, which uses local ingredients to produce inventive, modern cuisine.

Mitchell Gardens Holiday Park (☎ 5152 4654; http:// gippsland.com/web/MGHP; powered/unpowered sites per 2 people $20/17, d cabins from $44) East of the town centre on the banks of the Mitchell River, this is a friendly park, with shade for cabins and full sun for tents. The holiday units ($74), actually deluxe cabins, have river views.

Larrikin's Cafe Deli (☎ 5153 1421; 2 Wood St; breakfast $6-14, meals $9-16; ⊙ breakfast & lunch Mon-Sat) This smart little café, in converted 1880s stables, has stunning farmland views and is a local favourite. The food options are typical city-café fare, including salads, focaccias, bagels and gourmet offerings, and the coffee is good. Wine is available by the glass.

Getting There & Away

Bairnsdale's V/Line station is on McLeod St, one block south of the town centre. There are two daily train services between Melbourne and Bairnsdale ($41). From Bairnsdale **V/Line buses** (☎ 5152 1711) operate daily to Lakes Entrance ($9.10) and Orbost ($22).

MITCHELL RIVER NATIONAL PARK

About 42km northwest of Bairnsdale is the Mitchell River National Park, which covers over 12,200 hectares. The park's best-known feature is the **Den of Nargun**, a small cave which, according to Aboriginal stories, is haunted by a strange, half-stone creature, the Nargun. According to the legend, the creature would drag passers-by into its cave and, if attacked, was able to deflect spears back onto the thrower. It's believed that the

legend developed from the whistling sound of the wind in the cave, and served the dual purpose of keeping Kurnai children close to camp sites and scaring others away from this sacred place where women's initiation ceremonies were held. A one-hour loop walk leads to a lookout, rainforest gully and the den. It's not possible to enter the cave.

The best walking track is the signposted 18km (two-day) linear one-way track, which follows the Mitchell River. One of the most interesting aspects of this park is the dramatic contrast between the warm temperate rainforest areas in the sheltered river gullies and the sparse vegetation in the open and higher areas of the park. The spectacular deep gorges and valleys carved through rock by the Mitchell River are another feature.

Access tracks lead into the park off Dargo Rd. There are four **camp sites** (sites free), all with toilets, within the park, but not all have drinking water or firewood, so bring your own. **Parks Victoria** (☎ 03-5152 0600) in Bairnsdale has park notes.

EAGLE POINT

☎ 03 / pop 395

Eagle Point is the humble home to the natural wonder of the 8km-long **Mitchell River Silt Jetties**, the second longest in the world (after the Mississippi). There's an information board explaining how they're created at the **Eagle Point Lookout**, just before you drive onto the jetties, where you can marvel at the extensive views across the silt jetties and Lakes King and Victoria. The area is a prime fishing, bird-watching and walking spot, and has the 16-acre **Eagle Point Reserve**, which is great bushland for walks and spotting wildlife.

Eagle Point Caravan Park (☎ /fax 5156 6232; Bay Rd; powered/unpowered camp sites per 2 people $17/13, d cabins from $58; ✖) has camp sites and deluxe cabins by the lake, and a fully equipped camp kitchen.

PAYNESVILLE & RAYMOND ISLAND

☎ 03 / pop 2850

On the edge of Lake Victoria, Paynesville is a relaxed little town which proudly claims the title of boating capital of Victoria.

Information

There's an ATM at the petrol station on the way into town. Paynesville's pub and eateries are all clustered close to the ferry.

Sights & Activities

You can take a boat cruise on **Plover or Karen** (☎ 0417 137 590; Fisherman's Wharf jetty; adult/child $25/12.50, canal trips $15/7.50) around Paynesville's man-made canals or take a three-hour trip across the lake to Ocean Grange on Ninety Mile Beach; on Wednesday, Saturday and Sunday, or by arrangement

Paynesville hosts an annual **jazz festival** each February.

Lake Gallery (☎ 5156 0448; 2a Backwater Ct; admission free; ⏰ noon-5pm Thu-Sun) adds some class to the town with its small but sophisticated modern art collection.

Raymond Island, a skip away across McMillan Strait, is famous for its large colony of koalas, which were relocated from Phillip Island in the 1950s. The koalas are so rampant now and the eucalypts they feed on so denuded that many of the koalas are being relocated elsewhere. The small island has large areas of bush, with some good **walking tracks** and flock upon flock of black swans. Look out for kangaroos on the north end of the island. You can go on a koala-spotting drive with **Clydesdale Carriage Tours** (☎ 0413-028 084; Ferry Park; adult/child $8.50/5; ⏰ 10.30am-3pm Sat, Sun, public & school holidays). The carriage awaits in the small park across from the ferry landing. A car and passenger ferry runs a constant shuttle service from Paynesville to Raymond Island (per car return $7, pedestrians free) from 8am to 10.30pm or later.

Sleeping & Eating

The more flamboyant Paynesville has almost all the accommodation and eating options. Gippsland Lakes **Escapes** (☎ 5156 0432; www.gippslandlakesescapes.com.au; The Esplanade) books midrange and classy holiday homes in Paynesville, Raymond Island and beyond. Prices for holiday accommodation for a two-night minimum start from $280.

Paynesville Hotel (☎ 5156 6442; 75 The Esplanade; s/d with bathroom $55/70) Its rooms will give you '70s flashbacks, but two have brilliant views overlooking the water; one room caters for families.

Lake Gallery B&B (☎ 5156 0448; www.lakegallery bedandbreakfast.com; 2a Backwater Ct; s & d with breakfast $205) Perched on the water's edge, each of the stylish rooms, complete with original art work, king-size bed and en suite spa, have dreamy views and private balconies. There's also a small art gallery (see above).

Fisherman's Wharf Pavilion (☎ 5156 0366; 70 The Esplanade; mains $22; ⏰ breakfast, lunch & dinner Wed-Sun) The light-filled Pavilion is as close to the water as you get. Try the free-range eggs with spinach, mushroom and Gippsland Cheddar ($14.50) for breakfast or the grilled Japanese spiced flathead tails ($19.50) for dinner. You can dine contentedly knowing that you're eating non-genetically modified, fresh local produce. It caters to vegans and those with food allergies, and serves the best coffee in town.

Paynesville Seafoods (☎ 5156 6080; 67a The Esplanade; ⏰ lunch & dinner) On a fine day it's hard to beat sitting on the foreshore with the ultra-fresh fish and chips from this place.

Getting There & Away

Bus services are available with **Paynesville Bus Lines** (☎ 0418-516 405) Monday to Saturday between Bairnsdale train station and Paynesville ($6.10); you can also arrange drop off en route at Eagle Point Caravan Park ($6.10) in Eagle Point.

NINETY MILE BEACH

☎ 03

Ahh, ninety miles of pristine, sandy beaches. This long strip of beach is backed by dunes, swamplands and lagoons, and stretches from McLaughlin's Beach to Marlo. Beaches are great for surf-fishing and walking though they can be dangerous for swimming, except where patrolled at Seaspray and Woodside.

From Seaspray to Lakes Entrance is the **Gippsland Lakes Coastal Park**, where you'll see typically low-lying coastal shrubs, banksias and tea trees, and native wildflowers in spring. There are large numbers of kangaroos and black wallabies so drive slowly, especially at night.

The main access roads are from Yarram to Woodside Beach (see p371), and from Sale to Seaspray, Golden Beach and Loch Sport. The townships along here are small and remote with limited facilities.

For those interested in hiking the length of the Ninety Mile Beach, permission can be obtained from **Parks Victoria** (☎ 13 19 63) for remote camping.

At the western end of Ninety Mile Beach, **Reeves Beach** has a **camping ground** (sites free) with pit toilets.

Seaspray has somehow escaped development and is packed full of holiday shacks.

There's a licensed general store with ATM facilities, a takeaway food store and the **Seaspray Caravan Park** (☎ 5146 4364; powered sites per 2 people $16, d cabins $48), where it's sardine-like, but only a short stroll over the dune to the patrolled beach. **Ronnie's Tea Rooms** (☎ 5146 4420; 13 Trood St; coffee & cake $5.50; ☒ Sat, Sun, public & school holidays) adds a touch of class to Seaspray, and the sunny tea room has views of Ronnie's immaculate tea garden.

On the road between Seaspray and Golden Beach, there are Parks Victoria camp sites, nestled on the beach side and shaded by tea trees – very popular during summer. No camping fees or permits apply – it's first in. Some sites have barbecues and pit toilets, but there's no water or firewood. Avoid camp sites 1 to 6 at Golden Beach if you're not a dog lover, as it's the one spot that permits dogs.

Kangaroos graze on front lawns at **Loch Sport** (really) in this small town surrounded by lake, ocean and bush, with some good swimming areas for children. The bright and friendly **Marina Hotel** (☎ 5146 0666; mains $15-23.50 ☒ lunch & dinner), only metres from the lake, does great sunset views and decent Tuscan seafood. **Gary Powers Real Estate** (☎ 5146 0411; www .garypowersrealestate.com; Lot 217 Lake St), in Loch Sport, has more than 30 holiday houses (per night from $85 to $250), from the mundane to the classy, available for nightly or weekly rental.

Separated from the rest of the world by 7km of dirt track, **90 Mile Beach Holiday Retreat** (☎ 5146 0320, www.90milebeachholidayretreat .com; Track 10, off the Loch Sport–Seaspray Rd; powered/ unpowered sites per 2 people $24/22, caravans $60, d lodge & cottage $100), is on a huge chunk of land with 2.4km of beach frontage. There's plenty of grassy areas for camping, the two ex-Sydney Olympic 2000 lodges are ultra-stylish, and the self-contained cottage is like being at your granny's where the style hasn't changed for a few decades, but it's only a short toddle to the beach.

The Lakes National Park

A spit of land surrounded by lakes and ocean, The Lakes National Park covers 2400 hectares of coastal bushland. You can reach it by road from adjoining Loch Sport or by boat from Paynesville (5km).

Banksia and eucalypt woodland abound with areas of low-lying heathlands and some swampy, salt-marsh scrub. In spring the park is carpeted with native wildflowers and has one of Australia's best displays of native orchids. You're likely to spot kangaroos, as well as wallabies, possums, emus and possibly koalas. There's abundant bird life, with over 190 species sighted, including the rare white bellied sea eagle and the endangered little tern.

There is a **Parks Victoria rangers' office** (☎ 5146 0278; ☒ hours vary) at the park entrance near Loch Sport. A loop-road provides good car access, and there are well-marked **walking trails**, including some short walks, and several picnic areas (BYO water). **Point Wilson**, at the eastern tip of the mainland section of the park (20-minute drive), is the best picnic area and a popular gathering spot for kangaroos (don't even think about feeding them!). The only camping is at **Emu Bight**, which has pit toilets and fireplaces; BYO water. **Camp sites** (up to 6 people $14) can be booked and paid for through the park office.

METUNG

☎ 03 / pop 520

On the shores of Australia's largest waterway, the Gippsland Lakes, Metung is a small, unhurried village whose shoreline is dotted with jetties and small wooden craft. The town, whose Aboriginal name is said to mean 'bend in the lake', is perched on a narrow spit of land, and surrounded by the waters of Lake King to the west and Bancroft Bay to the east. Opposite Metung Yacht Club on the edge of Bancroft Bay is **Legend Rock**, a sacred Aboriginal site. According to Aboriginal oral histories, the rock represents a hunter who was turned to stone for not sharing the food he had caught. There were originally three rocks; the other two were destroyed during road-construction work, and the remaining one was saved when an injunction was issued, after community pressure, under the Heritage Act of Victoria. The road into town shaves past the rock.

Metung is an upmarket base for all sorts of water-based activities – sailing, cruising and fishing.

Information

Diagonally opposite the post office, **Metung Village Store** (☎ 5156 2201; www.metung.com; Metung Rd) is the informal visitors centre, and also sells petrol and bait. There's an ATM at the Metung Hotel on Kurnai Ave.

Sights & Activities

Pelicans crash land in the lake outside the Metung Hotel at noon each day for a feed of fish. For a dip, head to the safe swimming beach by Lake King Jetty.

A historic ketch **Spray** (☎ 0428-516 055; adult/child/family $32/10/74) operates 4½-hour picnic cruises (BYO lunch) to various lake destinations; cruises depart at 11am daily from the jetty at the Metung Hotel. Book tickets at the Metung Village Store (opposite).

Boats and yachts for cruising, fishing and sailing on the 400 sq km of the Gippsland Lakes are available from **Riviera Nautic** (☎ 5156 2243; www.rivieranautic.com.au; 185 Metung Rd; motor boat per day $110, 4-berth yacht per week from $1945). The lake floor is sand and mud, so it's ideal for boating. There are no reefs, rocks or sharks!

If the pace is too slow, there's thrill-seeking opportunities with **Parasailing Victoria** (☎ 5155 3032; single $70, per person tandem $60), which has rides over the lakes.

Sleeping

There are holiday homes and other accommodation available through **Metung Accommodation** (Slipway Villas; ☎ 5156 2861; www.metung accommodation.com).

Anchorage B&B (☎ /fax 5156 2569; www.beautiful accommodation.com/anchorage.html; 11 The Anchorage; d $130) On Chinaman's Creek, the Anchorage is built around views, views, views. It's a pretty cosy spot in winter, especially the sunny glasshouse-like breakfast room. The full breakfast is delicious.

McMillans of Metung (☎ 5156 2283; www.mcmil lansofmetung.com.au; 155 Metung Rd; d from $130; ⚲ ⚳) McMillans won stacks of tourism awards for its lakeside resort of country-style cottages set in eight acres of manicured gardens. Massage, tennis, a games room, and a lagoon with resident birdlife are also on offer here. There's a two-night minimum and rates increase by 10% to 50% in peak periods.

Moorings At Metung (☎ 5156 2750; www.the moorings.com.au; d/f from $125/170; ⚲ ⚳) Towering over Bancroft Bay, this large contemporary apartment complex has rooms and units all with water views. It's a luxuriously comfortable option, with modern rooms, a tennis court and spa, and promises to pander to your every whim. Minimum stays

apply during Christmas and Easter school holidays, when prices increase about 20%.

Arendell Holiday Units (☎ /fax 5156 2507; 30 Mairburn Rd; d/f $66/77; ⚲) It's very '70s and doesn't have water views, but the comfortable timber cottages are a few hundred metres from the beach and a couple of kilometres from the town centre, and it's the cheapest accommodation option in Metung. Prices double during the Christmas school holidays.

Eating & Drinking

Marillee (☎ 5156 2121; 50 Metung Rd; mains $16-46; ⏲ breakfast, lunch & dinner; ⏲ Wed-Mon) If you get in early, or crane your neck, you'll get a water view at this restaurant offering elegantly presented food that's usually delicious. It's the best restaurant food in town. Seafood is the theme; the Atlantic salmon in a white wine and caper sauce ($22) is good. Children are catered for with their own menu and a table with colouring books. On Thursday and Friday nights hang out at the bar or the lounge with the $5 cocktails.

Metung Hotel (☎ 5156 2206; Kurnai Ave; meals $15.50-26; ⏲ lunch & dinner) Perched on the edge of the lakes, with an outdoor deck and garden area overlooking Bancroft Bay, Metung Hotel does good pub food: the scallops and calamari in beer batter with lemon aioli dipping sauce ($19) is worth trying. The children's meals ($4.50) are the cheapest in Gippsland.

Gourmet Appetite (☎ 5156 2877; Shop 3/51 Metung Rd; dishes $3-12; ⏲ breakfast & lunch Tue-Sun) Some of Metung's best food comes out of this tiny café serving gourmet food made from local produce. Don't miss Jan's spinach pie ($7).

Metung Yacht Club (☎ 5156 2315; Metung Rd; ⏲ Wed-Sun) Welcomes visiting yachties and nonmembers. It has a bar and beer garden with great views across the water.

Getting There & Away

From Melbourne, **V/Line** (☎ 13 61 96) buses can drop people off in Swan Reach ($44), from where you can call **Tambo Taxis** (☎ 5156 2222) for the 5km trip to Metung ($18).

AROUND METUNG

A few kilometres from Metung is **Tricia Allen Glass** (☎ 5156 3211; 105 Jetty Rd, Nungurner; ⏲ glassblowing 11am-4pm Sun Nov-Apr), the studio of this renowned Australian glass blower.

Ten kilometres east of Metung, the homestead at **Nyerimilang Park** (☎ 5156 3253;

SOUTH & FAR EAST

Metung–Kalimna West Rd; adult $4; ⊗ 9am-4pm) was originally built in 1892 as a gentleman's holiday retreat. Managed by Parks Victoria and staffed by volunteers, the property has an East Gippsland Garden, showcasing varieties of indigenous vegetation, and a picnic area. Varied walking tracks lead through the property, some offering exceptional views across the lake.

LAKES ENTRANCE
☎ 03 / pop 5500

Lakes Entrance is a brash seaside resort that's home to one of Australia's largest fishing fleets. The town sprawls along the Esplanade (Princes Hwy) with way too many crass developments. It's in stark contrast to the opposite side of the highway, where you'll see the gentle waters of Cunninghame Arm, backed by sand dunes and small fishing boats. Just beyond them is a magnificent stretch of ocean beach. Lakes, as it's known by the locals, is primed to cater to almost every water-related whim you may have.

Information
The **Lakes Entrance visitors centre** (☎ 5155 1966, 1800 637 060; www.lakesandwilderness.com.au; Princes Hwy) is eternally busy.

Internet access is available at **Hai Q** (☎ 5155 4247; cnr of Myer St & Esplanade; per hr $8), a computer business with a quirky gift shop, or for free at the **library** (☎ 5153 9500; 18 Mechanics St).

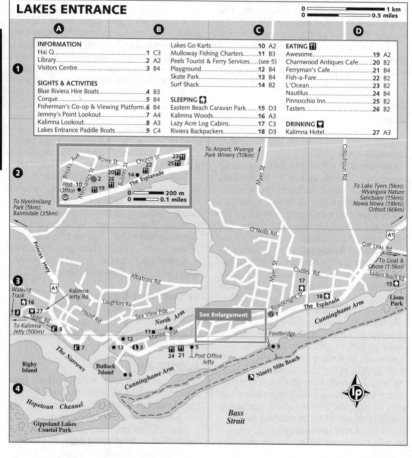

LAKES ENTRANCE

0 _____ 1 km
0 _____ 0.5 miles

INFORMATION	
Hai Q	1 C3
Library	2 A2
Visitors Centre	3 B4

SIGHTS & ACTIVITIES	
Blue Riviera Hire Boats	4 B3
Corque	5 B4
Fisherman's Co-op & Viewing Platform	6 B4
Jemmy's Point Lookout	7 A4
Kalimna Lookout	8 A3
Lakes Entrance Paddle Boats	9 C4
Lakes Go Karts	10 A2
Mulloway Fishing Charters	11 B3
Peels Tourist & Ferry Services	(see 5)
Playground	12 B4
Skate Park	13 B4
Surf Shack	14 B2

SLEEPING	
Eastern Beach Caravan Park	15 D3
Kalimna Woods	16 A3
Lazy Acre Log Cabins	17 C3
Riviera Backpackers	18 D3

EATING	
Awesome	19 A2
Charnwood Antiques Cafe	20 B2
Ferryman's Cafe	21 B4
Fish-a-Fare	22 B2
L'Ocean	23 B2
Nautilus	24 B4
Pinnocchio Inn	25 B2
Tasters	26 B2

DRINKING	
Kalimna Hotel	27 A3

Map labels: Breaks Ave; Rowe St; Church St; Bulmer St; Mechanics St; Post Office; The Esplanade; 0 — 200 m; 0 — 0.1 miles; To Airport; Wyanga Park Winery (10km); Myer St; Colquhoun Rd; To Nyerimilang Park (5km); Bairnsdale (35km); To Lake Tyers (5km); Wyangura Nature Sanctuary (15km); Nowa Nowa (18km); Orbost (60km); O'Neills Rd; Golf Links Rd; To Goat & Goose (1.5km); Eastern Beach Rd; Princes Hwy; Albatross Rd; Kalimna Jetty Rd; Laughtons Rd; Hazel Rd; Sea View Pde; North Arm; Marine Pde; Coates Rd; Roadknight St; The Esplanade; Cunninghame Arm; Lions Park; Walking Track; Hotel Rd; To Kalimna Jetty (500m); The Narrows; Bullock Island; Cunninghame Arm; Post Office Jetty; Footbridge; Ninety Mile Beach; Rigby Island; Hopetoun Channel; Gippsland Lakes Coastal Park; Bass Strait; See Enlargement

Sights & Activities

A footbridge crosses the Cunninghame Arm inlet from the centre of town to the ocean and the magnificent **Ninety Mile Beach**. From there, you can walk along a 2.3km **walking track** to the 'entrance' to the lakes; the current entrance is artificial, the original was near the footbridge. You can return via the **Eastern Beach Walking Track**. A town map, with the track marked, is available from the visitors centre.

Surfing lessons are available from the **Surf Shack** (☎ /fax 5155 4933; 507 Esplanade; 2-hr lesson $40). Qualified instructors lead the surf lessons at **Lake Tyers Beach**, and surf gear is provided.

If you want to explore the lakes independently, three motorboat-hire companies on Marine Parade offer boats at the same price, including **Blue Riviera Hire Boats** (☎ 5155 3113; Marine Parade; 1-hr/4-hr hire $30/80). Ask about its low-season specials.

A vast array of watery activities is offered by **Lakes Entrance Paddleboats** (☎ 0419-552 753; paddleboats/canoes per 30 min $15/10, bodyboards/catamarans per hr $5/40; ☺ Nov-Apr), located at the ocean end of the footbridge.

Wildlife at Night (☎ 5156 5863; adult/child/family $22/13/55) is your chance to play sleuth, armed with a torch, and spot gliders, possums, koalas, wallabies, wombats and owls in the wild. You do this in the company of an experienced naturalist at the Wyungara Nature Sanctuary, 15km from town.

During Christmas school holidays, Buchan Bus 'n' Freight runs day trips from here to the Buchan Caves (see p381).

You can unleash the petrol head inside you at **Lakes Go Karts** (☎ 5155 3981; ☺ 10am-6pm or later, Sat, Sun, public & school holidays) if you're aged five and over. A wet slippery track is created sometimes, for extra excitement.

Can we stop there, mum? Everyone in the know with children from 12 months to 12 years breaks their drive at the enormous playground opposite the tourist office or the popular skate park on the other side of the highway.

On **Bullock Island**, at the western end of the Esplanade, the **Fisherman's Co-op** (☎ 5155 1688; ☺ 9am-5pm) viewing platform provides a bird's-eye view of the daily catch being unloaded. The Fisherman's Co-op also sells lake and ocean fish fresh off the boats. It's the best place to buy fish in East Gippsland.

Signposted off the Princes Hwy on the western side of town, **Jemmy's Point Lookout** has great views of the ocean, lakes and entrance. A **walking track** leads from Kalimna Lookout nearby west to Kalimna Jetty.

CRUISES & FISHING CHARTERS

For boat hire and fishing charters head down Marine Parade. If it's a cruise you're after, you'll find one along the Esplanade.

The **Corque** (☎ 5155 1508; Post Office Jetty; adult $40, child $5 to $18) has a popular all-inclusive 4½-hour lunch cruise (departing at 11.30am) to Wyanga Park Winery, as well as dinner cruises on Friday and Saturday night, a Sunday brunch trip (except in winter), and a lunch trip to Metung on Thursday.

Mulloway Fishing Charters (☎ 5155 3304; 0427-943 154; jetty opposite 66 Marine Parade; adult 3-hr trip $40) has regular fishing cruises on the lake. Children are charged by their age; if they're eight years old, its $8. Rods, tackle, bait and morning or afternoon tea are provided.

Peels Tourist & Ferry Services (☎ 5155 1246; Post Office Jetty; adult/child $25.30/12.65) has several daily two-hour cruises exploring Reeves Channel, Bancroft Bay and Lake King, and also a daily four-hour cruise (with lunch $38.50, departing at 11am) to Metung.

Sleeping

Kalimna Woods (☎ 5155 1957; www.kalimnawoods .com.au; Kalimna Jetty Rd; d $95-140; ☒) Rainforest, gardens, possums, birds, wood fires and spas – this is a very comfortable retreat from the hustle and bustle of the Lakes Entrance town centre 2km away. The log cottages, with quality timber furnishings and fluffy towels, are spacious and very comfortable.

Riviera Backpackers YHA (☎ 5155 2444; www.yha .com.au; 660-671 Esplanade; 4-6 bed dm $22, s/d $33.50/41.50; ☐ ☒) This hostel now adjoins Beaches Family Holiday Units. The YHA rooms are part of the maze of units, each with a couple of bedrooms and a bathroom. There's a big communal kitchen and lounge with pool table, and it offers 5% to 10% discounts on many local activities. Prices are the same year-round.

Goat & Goose (☎ 5155 3079; www.goatandgoose.com; 16 Gay St; B&B d $130-160) The Goat & Goose, a two-storey timber pole-frame B&B, is on the eastern outskirts of town overlooking Bass Strait. The house is unique, the owners are friendly and the rooms (all with spas) are gorgeously quaint. It's well worth a stay – no children, though. Prices increase about 40% in the high season.

Eastern Beach Caravan Park (☎ 5155 1581; powered/ unpowered sites per 2 people $18/15) Close to the beach, this park is refreshingly old style – it has a bush setting by the Eastern Beach Walking Track into town (one way 30 minutes). Prices almost double in the high season.

Lazy Acre Log Cabins (☎ 5155 1323; lazyacre@net -tech.com.au; 35 Roadknight St; d/f $95/120; 🔅 🖳) A friendly, relaxed place to stay, with self-contained small timber cabins shaded by trees. Bicycle hire and a babysitting service are available. Prices are 50% higher in the high season.

Eating & Drinking

Nautilus (☎ 5155 1400; mains $23-47; 🕒 dinner Tue-Sat) This glass-sided barge moored on the water offers fine food and an exclusively Gippsland wine list. Unsurprisingly, seafood is the feature act on the menu, and includes Eden blue mussels in broth and six variations on the oyster theme.

Pinocchio Inn (☎ 5155 2565; 569 Esplanade; dishes $13-25; 🕒 lunch & dinner) This friendly little home-style Italian eatery is a long-time local favourite offering traditional pizza, pasta and seafood dishes. Children will love the collection of Pinocchio dolls and puppets.

Ferryman's Cafe (☎ 5155 3000; Esplanade, mains $8-17; 🕒 lunch & dinner daily; breakfast Sat & Sun) The latest waterside dining option in Lakes is in a converted Raymond Island ferry. It's not as classy as the *Nautilus*, but it offers a good selection of seafood dishes, including bouillabaisse ($21). It does a good coffee, and there's a deck to drink it on. The café's on the western side of the clock tower.

Tasters (☎ 5155 3955; 357 Esplanade; 🕒 Wed-Sun) Offers tastings and sales of delicious gourmet dips and deli produce, and discounted wine.

Charnwood Antiques Cafe (☎ 5155 2348; cnr Esplanade & Bulmer St; 🕒 breakfast & lunch) This is a cosy café nestled between the antiques and crafts parts of the shop. It has a mouthwatering selection of cakes and biscuits.

Kalimna Hotel (☎ 5155 1202) For a drink with views, you can't beat this hotel, off the highway on the Melbourne side of Lakes Entrance.

There are a few excellent fish-and-chip shops in Lakes:

Awesome (☎ 5155 3166; 337 Esplanade) Traditional fare.
Fish-a-Fare (☎ 5155 4535; 509 Esplanade) Bright and efficient.
L'Ocean (☎ 5155 2253; 19 Myer St) Award-winning; caters for the gluten-free and vegetarian crowds.

Getting There & Away

There are daily **V/Line** (☎ 13 61 96) buses between Lakes Entrance and Bairnsdale ($9.10), connecting with trains to/from Melbourne (from Lakes $49.60). V/Line and **Premier** (☎ 13 34 10) also have daily buses continuing along the Princes Hwy into NSW; V/Line also has a bus service to Lake Tyers ($2.50).

AROUND LAKES ENTRANCE

Just east of Lakes Entrance, **Lake Tyers** is a small and peaceful settlement, though growing at a rapid rate. The area is popular with surfers and there are good surf breaks at **Red Bluff**.

With views across to the lake, **Airdrie** (☎ 03-5156 5640; 19 Cross St, Lake Tyers; d from $140) is a comfortable, modern B&B with prices the same year-round. **Lake Tyers Beach House** (☎ 5156 5995; www.laketyersbeachhouse.com.au; 3 Larkins Pl, Lake Tyers; d $150) is an artistically inspired four-bedroom cliff-top house with stunning ocean views and a hot pink retro-chic look. The owners have a yoga studio next door where visitors can join in a class or arrange private tuition. On bushland with beach frontage, the **Lakes Beachfront Holiday Retreat** (☎ 03-5156 5582; www .holidayretreats.com.au; 430 Lake Tyers Beach Rd, Lake Tyers; powered/unpowered sites per 2 people $22/20, d cabins $55-90, beach cottage d $120; 🖳) is a brilliant camp park with tent sites in shady bush sites and a new rock swimming pool, and it's a minute's walk from the ocean. Prices go up 50% to 100% in the high season.

The **Waterwheel Tavern** (☎ 03-5156 5530; 557 Lake Tyers Beach Rd, Lake Tyers; mains $18.50-35) has an inspired bistro menu with offerings such as its famous Big Arse Seafood Platter ($35, or for two people $60), and marinated kangaroo fillets with juniper berries and tomato confit ($19.50). This is not your average pub bistro – there's quality food and stylish presentation, and the views over the lake are fantastic.

At tiny **Nowa Nowa**, at the north arm of Lake Tyers, the stirring **Nowa Nowa Nudes** art exhibition is held annually in November. **Mingling Waters** (☎ 5155 7247; www.lakes-entrance .com/minglingwaters; Princes Hwy, Nowa Nowa; powered/

unpowered sites per 2 people $15/18, 22-bed dm $20, d cottages $60) has a great little café/gallery and plenty of accommodation by the lakeside. A few kilometres east of Nowa Nowa, **Yelens Studio Gallery** (☎ 5155 7277; Nelsons Rd, Nowa Nowa), down a dirt road and overlooking Lake Tyers, is home to contemporary painter Gary Yelen. It's worth a visit to see his vibrant oil paintings and sensuous sculpture, and to have an espresso stop. It's open most days; call to check times.

A **V/Line** (☎ 13 61 96) bus goes to Lake Tyers via Lakes Entrance ($4).

EAST GIPPSLAND

This section of Gippsland contains some of the most remote and spectacular national parks in the state. Unlike the rest of Victoria, much of this region has never been cleared for agriculture. So, instead of the vast and barren sheep pastures that characterise the Western District on the opposite side of the state, or the denuded hills of the Strzelecki Ranges, which were once rich with towering mountain ash and giant tree ferns, this area is a wonderland of dense forests, ranging from the coastal wilderness areas of Croajingolong to the lush rainforests of the Errinundra Plateau.

The Princes Hwy (A1) carves its way through the centre of the region. Happily, the magnificent coastal areas of Cape Conran, Mallacoota and Croajingolong are all uncrowded, unspoiled and undeveloped.

Orbost is the only sizeable town and has a useful visitors centre. There are excellent Parks Victoria visitors centres at Cann River (p387) and Mallacoota (p389).

BUCHAN
☎ 03 / 400

Buchan, a beautiful town in the foothills of the Snowy Mountains, is chiefly known for its spectacular limestone cave system. Less attention is given to its black marble, which was used in notable public buildings, such as the Shrine of Remembrance in Melbourne. Small pieces are on display at **Buchan Black Marble Hut** (☎ 5155 9296; Main St).

Buchan Valley Roadhouse sells petrol, and the general store/post office has Eftpos facilities and local tourist information.

Buchan Caves Reserve

The Caves Reserve is just over 1km from the tiny Buchan township. Underground rivers cutting through limestone rock that formed about 300 to 400 million years ago carved the caves and caverns. The main caves are the Royal and Fairy, but the reserve itself is also a pretty spot with shaded picnic areas, **walking tracks** and grazing kangaroos.

Parks Victoria (☎ 5162 1900), based at the reserve, runs regular guided cave tours (adult/child/family $12/6/30.50). The rangers also offer hard-hat guided tours to Federal Cave during the high season (the Federal is equally as impressive as Fairy or Royal, but doesn't have artificial lighting, like the other caves).

In the Christmas school holidays, **Buchan Bus 'n' Freight** (☎ 5155 0356; adult/child/family $50/30/110) runs day trips from Lakes Entrance to the caves. The price includes caves admission and lunch at the Caves Hotel (p383).

Sleeping & Eating

There are a couple of excellent accommodation options at W Tree, a small community 25km northeast of Buchan.

OFF THE BEATEN TRACK

Most of the Snowy River or Errinundra National Parks can only be explored with a 4WD, and there are just a few companies providing organised trips into this beautiful wilderness area.

Snowy River Expeditions (☎ 03-5155 9353; Karoonda Park, Gelantipy) Runs adventure tours, including one-, two- or four-day rafting trips on the Snowy River (per day $130); half-day/full-day abseiling or caving trips are also available. Costs include transport, meals and camping gear. See also Karoonda Park (p384).

Buchan Bus 'n' Freight (☎ 03-5155 0356; buchanbusnfreight@hotmail.com; 4-day trek $540) Offers an East Gippsland Wilderness Tour visiting Buchan Caves and Snowy River and Errinundra National Parks, camping and staying at Ontos (see p383). The tour starts at Bairnsdale or Lakes Entrance, and operates between November and April.

Echidna Walkabout (☎ 03- 9646 8249; www.echidnawalkabout.com.au; 4-day trek & flight $1325, 5-day trek $1190) Echidna's upmarket treks start in Melbourne, and focus on national parks and wildlife in East Gippsland. All you need to carry is a day-pack – backpacks are delivered to the night's luxury camping spot or B&B.

SOUTH & FAR EAST

EAST GIPPSLAND

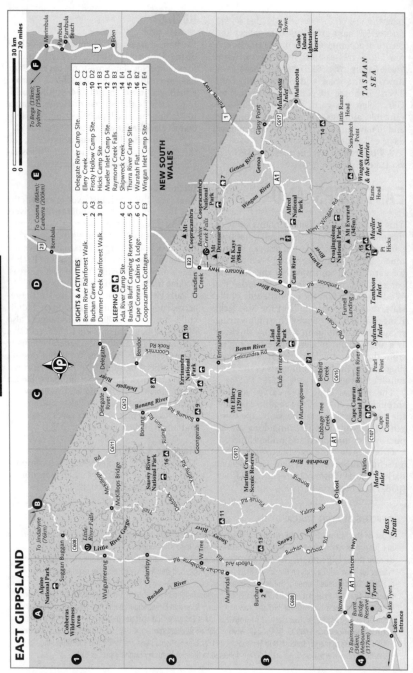

0   30 km
0   20 miles

Natural Healing & Spiritual Centre (☎ 5155-0245; 2337 Gelantipy Rd, W Tree; s/d with all meals $125/250) This is the place for a complete de-stress. Overlooking bush and mountains, you stay in Carol and Hans' lovely timber home, are fed vegetarian meals, taken on bush walks and, as part of the service, given the kinesiology natural healing treatments you need in the adjoining treatment centre (once the W Tree school room).

Ontos (☎ 5155 0275; ontos@net-tech.com.au; Gelantipy Rd, W Tree; s/d cabins $40/50, s/d units $50/80) People used to let out audible sighs of pleasure when you mentioned Ontos, a health retreat that drew people back time and again, until its main building was destroyed by fire. Happily, Ontos is rebuilding. It offers rustic wooden cabins with potbelly stoves, sleeping up to six, and some simple units. The full, healthy breakfast includes homemade bread. A café using organic and local produce should be open for lunch and dinner by the time you read this. Breakfast is included in the rates given here.

Buchan Lodge Backpackers (☎ 5155 9421; www .buchanlodge.com; Saleyard Rd, Buchan; 12-bed dm with breakfast $20) A short walk from the caves and the town centre, and just by the river, this is a friendly, rough-and-ready, timber-lined building, great for lounging about and taking in the country views. Children under 14 can stay by arrangement.

Buchan Caves Caravan Park (☎ 5162 1900; Buchan Caves Reserve; powered/unpowered sites per 2 people $16/12, d cabins $55; ⊠) This picturesque camping ground has a camp kitchen and open fireplaces.

Caves Hotel (☎ 5155 9203; Main St, Buchan; mains $13.50-18.50; ☺ lunch Tue-Sun, dinner daily) A pretty timber pub that cooks a well-recommended steak ($16.50).

Getting There & Away

On Monday, Wednesday and Friday **Buchan Bus 'n' Freight** (☎ 5155 0356) operates a service from Karoonda Park (p384) to Bairnsdale (one way/return $16/25) via W Tree, Buchan, Nowa Nowa and Lakes Entrance.

SNOWY RIVER NATIONAL PARK

This area is one of Victoria's most isolated and spectacular national parks, dominated by deep gorges carved through limestone and sandstone by the mighty Snowy River. The entire park is a smorgasbord of unspoiled

and superb bush, and mountain scenery. It covers over 95,000 hectares and includes a huge diversity of vegetation, ranging from alpine woodlands and eucalypt forests to rainforests and even areas of mallee-type scrub.

For information about camping, road conditions and other details contact the park offices at **Deddick** (☎ 02-6458 0290), Buchan (p381), Orbost (p384) or Bairnsdale (p373).

The two main access roads to the park are the Buchan Jindabyne Rd from Buchan and the Bonang Rd from Orbost. These roads are joined by MacKillops Rd (also known as Deddick River Rd), which runs across the northern border of the park from Bonang to just south of Wulgulmerang. Various access roads and scenic routes run into and alongside the park from these three main roads. The **Deddick Trail**, which runs through the middle of the park, is only suitable for 4WDs.

Along MacKillops Rd you'll come across **MacKillops Bridge**, which crosses the Snowy River. This is a spectacular and beautiful area. Near the bridge are the park's main **camp sites** (sites up to 5 people $12.50), toilets and fireplaces, as well as some sandy river-beaches and swimming spots. There are several good short walks around here, and the **15km Silver Mine Walking Track** starts at the eastern end of the bridge. The views from the lookouts over **Little River Falls** and **Little River Gorge**, the deepest in Victoria, signposted about 20km to the west of MacKillops Bridge, are spectacular.

There are various other bush **camping areas** (sites free) and picnic grounds in the park. **Walking** and **canoeing** are the most popular activities in this area, but you need to be well prepared for both as conditions can be harsh and subject to sudden change. The classic canoe or raft trip down the Snowy River from MacKillops Bridge to a pull-out point near Buchan takes at least four days and offers superb scenery: rugged gorges, raging rapids, tranquil sections and excellent camping spots on broad sandbars.

Good **scenic drives** in and around the park include MacKillops Rd, Rising Sun Rd from Bonang, Tulloch Ard Rd from just south of Gelantipy, and Yalmy Rd; the last is the main access road to the southern and central areas, and places like Waratah Flat, Hicks Camp Site and Raymond Creek Falls. These roads are unsealed and usually closed during winter.

SOUTH & FAR EAST

DETOUR: BALDWIN SPENCER TRAIL

The 262km **Baldwin Spencer Trail** driving tour is a great way to see some of East Gippsland's most interesting and diverse natural features, from ocean to rainforest. It follows the trail of Walter Baldwin Spencer, a noted scientist and explorer who led an expedition through here in 1889. At the time Orbost and Bendoc were the only settlements in the area. The circular route starts in Orbost, heads south to Marlo on the coast, then north through the cool temperate rainforest areas of the Errinundra Plateau and on to Bendoc, from where it returns back along Bonang Rd to Orbost.

There are various camping areas, picnic grounds and short walking tracks along the route. Many of the roads along the trail are unsealed, narrow, winding and steep. They are often impassable in winter, so check out road conditions at Parks Victoria in Orbost (below) before heading out.

At **Gelantipy**, 40km north of Buchan, **Karoonda Park** (☎ 03-5155 0220; www.karoondapark.com; Gelantipy Rd; dm/d with breakfast $24/58, cabins for 6-10 people $95; ✕ ▯ ▣), where you'll receive a friendly country welcome, is a cattle-and-sheep property and horse-riding ranch, and home to Snowy River Expeditions (p381). It has backpacker accommodation, and double rooms, which each have a set of bunks. Cabins are older and more faded but comfortable. A three-course home-cooked meal in the large camp kitchen costs $14; fully catered packages are also available. Activities include abseiling (per hour $20), horse riding (per hour $30), wild caving (per 1½ hours $30) and white-water rafting.

At **Delegate River**, on the Bonang Rd, the **Delegate River Tavern** is in a cleared valley near the NSW border. The pub is popular with trout fishers, bushwalkers and 4WD tourers, and has good bistro dinners, as well as accommodation in the adjacent **Tranquil Valley Lodge** (☎ 02-6458 8009; tranquility_lodge@bigpond.com; d cabins with/without bathroom $71.50/49.50). The resort has camp sites and log cabins. Rates include breakfast.

ORBOST

☎ 03 / pop 2100

Orbost, just off the Princes Hwy and on the banks of the Snowy River, is mainly a service centre for the surrounding farming and forest areas. There's an edgy feel in this town, where tensions between environmentalists and loggers can run high.

The Orbost Newsagent doubles as the **visitors centre** (☎ 5154 2424; 152-156 Nicholson St). Close by, **Parks Victoria** (☎ 5161 1222; cnr Nicholson & Salisbury Sts) has information on road conditions if you're heading up into the forests.

The **Slab Hut** (☎ 5154 2511; cnr Nicholson & Clarke Sts; ✆ 10am-4pm) is a cute historic timber dwelling dating back to 1872, and worth a peek. Watch out for the two resident geese if you're driving by. **Forest Park**, next to the Slab Hut, has picnic tables and a barbecue, and a politically inspired mosaic pathway. The park's name encapsulates the irony of Orbost – there's barely a tree in it. Painter and potter Bronwen Di Bari of **Snowy River Country Craft** (☎ 5154 2296; 110a Nicholson St) has a beautiful collection of work.

Sleeping & Eating

Snowy River Cottage (☎ 0438-083 014; snowyrivercottage@dodo.com.au; 6 Nicholson St; s/d $80/100, 2-night minimum) A refurbished old-style cottage set in a pretty garden opposite Forest Park, this is the nicest accommodation close to the town centre.

Commonwealth Hotel (☎ 5154 1077; 159 Nicholson St; s/d $30/40) This sprawling old hotel has standard pub rooms, and breakfast is included – you'll find the cereal box strategically positioned on the basin.

Shawny's Bistro (mains $14.50-21; ✆ lunch & dinner Mon-Sat) Offers good meals accompanied by '80s music.

A Lovely Little Lunch (☎ 5154 1303; 125a Nicholson St; mains $6-10; ✆ lunch Mon-Sat) A friendly little café serving focaccia, salads and pasta.

Getting There & Away

Daily **V/Line** (☎ 13 61 96) buses go west to Sale and on to Melbourne ($56). From Melbourne, they go east along the Princes Hwy into NSW (from Orbost to Narooma $53.10)

ERRINUNDRA NATIONAL PARK

The Errinundra Plateau is a misty and verdant wonderland that contains Victoria's largest remaining areas of cool temperate rainforest. It's one of East Gippsland's most outstanding natural areas, a battleground

IF YOU GO DOWN TO THE WOODS TODAY...

You'll be in for a big surprise all right. East Gippsland's mighty old-growth forests are being logged at a rapid rate – every day the equivalent of an astounding 13 football fields are lost. East Gippsland contains Victoria's last and largest area of ancient forest; while 35% of the forests are protected by national park, the remainder, under state control, continue to be clear felled. It's a controversial issue that has divided many communities who live, work and play among the forest giants.

Nestled in the very heart of East Gippsland's forest is tiny **Goongerah**. A school, a CFA building and a phone box are the only visible signs of the settlement (population 50), but there's a thriving community here, with its own organic food co-op, probably the only totally 'greenie'-run CFA in Victoria, and two active community environmental organisations: **Environment East Gippsland** (EEG; ☎ 03-5154 0145 www.eastgippsland.net.au) and **Goongerah Environment Centre** (GECO; ☎ 03-5154 0156), which organises ongoing protests and blockades in the forest.

Goongerah is home to Jill Redwood, who spearheads EEG. Jill's name has been synonymous with the fight to save East Gippsland's forest since she moved here more than 20 years ago. She's a gentle, quietly spoken woman, steadfast in her beliefs.

'These original ancient forests are the product of more than 40 million years of evolution, and have a very complex and diverse ecosystem with thousands of species that interact. Clear felling to bare earth, and deliberate hot fire afterwards, destroys everything. It creates a sterile land that is purposely planted with only the commercially useful trees. Publicly owned forests are being turned into single-species tree farms for the use of private logging and woodchipping companies. Eighty to ninety percent of these trees end up as woodchips,' Jill says.

The logging industry catchcry is 'jobs'; towns will be devastated if loggers lose their livelihood. 'It's a complete furphy. About 2% of East Gippsland's workforce relies on logging, it's not the mainstay of the economy. Even in Orbost only about 10% to 12% of the workforce is reliant for an income on the logging industry,' says Jill.

The logging is relentless and the wins are comparatively minor. After years of lobbying by EEG, 2500 hectares of the Ellery Creek area near Goongerah was added to Errinundra National Park. But there are some slivers of hope for the forests. Tourism may be one – it's estimated the logging industry in East Gippsland is worth $11 million, while tourism is worth a whopping $250 million.

Jill Redwood and EEG have pointed out to the government that people come to East Gippsland to see the old-growth forests, yet there's not a single walk where they can do that. In a move that confounds all the stereotypes that portray 'greenies' and loggers as having no common ground, the Orbost & District Community Forum, comprising environmentalists, loggers, farmers, business people and Aboriginal interests, is working on a grand vision to build a 300km world-class walk through East Gippsland's forests, taking in and linking up Errinundra, Snowy River, Croajngalong and Cape Conran National Parks. To date, it's received funding for a feasibility study into shorter walks.

Public education is one of the aims of EEG, and each year it provides people with the chance to explore the forests under the guidance of environmental experts at the **Forests Forever Ecology Camp** (☎ 03-5154 0145; www.eastgippsland.net.au; adult/teenager/child per day $40/20/free) held each Easter at the back of Jill Redwood's property. BYO camping gear and food. Ecologists guide you through the forest, and hope that you'll be awed by their beauty and complexity, and outraged by their destruction and will spread the word.

Donations payable to Environment East Gippsland, Private Bag 3, Orbost 3888 are tax deductible. EEG membership per year is full/concession $15/12 and includes a quarterly 16-page newsletter covering current issues.

between environmentalists and loggers (see boxed text, above), and also one of the least-visited parts of East Gippsland by travellers.

The national park covers an area of 25,000 to 30,000 hectares, and has three granite outcrops that extend into the clouds resulting in high rainfall, deep, fertile soils, and a network of creeks and rivers that flow north, south and east. The park has several climatic zones, with some areas of the park being quite dry and its peaks regularly receiving snow. This is a rich habitat for native birds and animals, which include many rare and endangered species, such as the potoroo.

Errinundra's one of the best examples in the world of 'mixed forest' vegetation. It's dominated by southern sassafras and black oliveberry, with eucalypt forests providing a canopy for the lower rainforests. Some of these giant trees are hundreds of years old.

The main access roads to the park are Bonang Rd from Orbost and the Errinundra Rd from Club Terrace. Bonang Rd passes on the western side of the park, while Errinundra Rd passes through the centre. Road conditions are variable, and the roads are often closed or impassable during the winter months or after floods. Watch out for logging trucks also. Roads within the park are all unsealed, but are 2WD accessible for seven to eight months of the year, though they can deteriorate quickly at any time of the year after rain.

You can explore the park by a combination of scenic drives and short and medium-length walks. **Mt Ellery** offers spectacular views; **Errinundra Saddle** has a rainforest boardwalk; and from **Ocean View Lookout** there are stunning views down the Goolengook River, from where you can see as far as Bemm River. The park also has **mountain plum pines**, some over 400 years old, which are easily accessible from Goonmirk Rocks Rd.

The only camping area within the park is at **Frosty Hollow** on the eastern side of the park, and there are a few basic picnic and **camping** areas on the park's edges – at Ellery Creek on Green's Rd, Ada River and Delegate River. In **Goongerah** a new camp site has opened, featuring a fancy compost toilet. Camping is free at all of these sites.

Jacarri (☎ 03-5154 0145; www.eastgippsland.net.au /jacarri; Bonang Hwy, Goongerah; s/d/f $85/85/95), on Jill Redwood's organic farm, is a gorgeous little cottage made from recycled and plantation timber. It's solar powered, has a slow combustion stove for heating and cooking, and sleeps four.

There's a petrol station and general store at Bonang, a pub at Bendoc, and another pub and cabins at Delegate River (see p384).

For park details, including information on road conditions, contact **Parks Victoria** (Bendoc ☎ 02-6458 1456; Orbost ☎ 03-5161 1222).

MARLO
☎ 03 / pop 350
Marlo is a sleepy little settlement at the mouth of the Snowy River, 15km south of Orbost.

The road from Orbost to Marlo follows the Snowy on the final leg of its journey from the mountains to the ocean. The river flows into a large lagoon before entering the sea, and the area has excellent fishing and abundant birdlife around the inland waterways.

Marlo's general store has an ATM and some tourist information.

French's Narrows Walking Track follows the river to the beach from a starting point about 2km out of the town on the Marine Parade–Cape Conran Rd.

Marlo Bush Races are a major event on New Year's Day. The racetrack is just out of town on the Marlo–Cape Conran Rd.

Sleeping & Eating
Marlo Hotel & Country Retreat (☎ 5154 8201; fax 5154 8493; s/d $120) The adults-only suites in this historic white timber pub come with spas and the choice of a jaw-dropping ocean view or an open fireplace. King-size beds, comfy sofas and antique furniture make this an indulgently comfortable option. Prices go up 25% in peak periods. In the **bistro** (mains $16; ☻ lunch & dinner), which does cater for littlies, the tasty garlic prawns with rice ($14) are worth trying.

Tabbara Lodge (☎ 5154 8231; fax 5154 8430; 1 Marlo Rd; s/d $50; ☒) Wood-lined rooms decorated with country crafts give these family-friendly self-contained units a homey ambience. They're set in a shady garden with a barbecue and playground; it's on the right as you enter town from Orbost. Prices go up 30% in peak periods.

CAPE CONRAN COASTAL PARK
This is a blissfully undeveloped part of the coast. The 19km coastal route from Marlo to Cape Conran is very pretty; it's bordered by banksia trees, grass plains, sand dunes and the ocean.

There are some simply beautiful, remote **white-sand beaches** along this coast. The cape is excellent for **watersports**, like snorkelling, scuba diving, boating and fishing and, in the warmer weather, swimming and surfing.

There are several good picnic areas and loads of short nature walks – **Parks Victoria** (☎ 5154 8438; www.parkweb.vic.gov.au) can provide a brochure. It also manages the accommodation at Cape Conran.

Bring everything you need, as there are no shops at Cape Conran. In fact, there's noth-

THE AUTHOR'S CHOICE

Cape Conran Cabins & Lodge (☎ 5154 84 38; www.parkweb.vic.gov.au; Cape Conran Coastal Park; cabins for up to 4 people $100) These self-contained cabins, which sleep up to eight people, are surrounded by bush, far apart enough to offer some privacy and just 200m from the beach. Built from local timbers, the cabins are like oversized cubby houses with cosy nooks for sleeping. The Hideaway cabin, for two people only, is popular with couples wanting to get away from it all, while Oliveberry Lodge, for group bookings, sleeps up to 17 people. BYO linen. The cabins have rain water.

ing, except the accommodation mentioned here (see also the boxed text, above).

Right on the foreshore and surrounded by banksia woodlands, **Banksia Bluff Camping Area** (tent sites for up to 4 people $15) has toilets, cold showers and a few fireplaces, but you'll need to take drinking water if you don't like the taste of bore water.

ORBOST TO GENOA

There are various rainforest walks, state forests and national parks along this section of the Princes Hwy. Roads leading to the area's four major national parks also lead off this part of the route.

Bemm River

☎ 03

Edged by Cape Conran Coastal Park, Bemm River is a small and friendly holiday hamlet favoured by fisher folk. It's 23km off the Princes Hwy, on the shores of Sydenham Inlet.

Facilities include a pub, a general store, Internet access, a couple of caravan parks and a few holiday flats. The general store has Eftpos facilities, basic food supplies and bait. Fuel is not available. **Sydenham Inlet** is rich with birdlife, including black swans and wading birds, and good bream and perch fishing is possible. There's also access to coastal beaches a few kilometres from town.

Bemm River Holiday Lodge (☎ 5158 4233; bemm riverholidaylodge@net-tech.com.au; 37-41 Sydenham Pde; s/d/f $50/60/100) has old-fashioned units and friendly owners. Boats are available for hire (per day $60).

Bemm River Hotel (☎ /fax 5158 4241; bemmriver hotel@hotmail.com; 3-5 Sydenham Pde; d/f $80/100) has a timber deck with views of the inlet. Generous meals (from $5 to $19) are available for lunch and dinner daily. New modern cabins are well designed, with a double room with bathroom and three or four bunks.

Bellbird Creek

☎ 03

Back on the Princes Hwy, a couple of kilometres past the turn-off to Bemm River, the **Bellbird Hotel** (☎ 5158 1239; s/d pub room with shared bathroom $30/60, motel-style d $70) is an old redtin-roofed timber pub. It's got an old-style pub atmosphere, and bistro meals (from $4 to $19) are available. The pub rooms are ultra-simple. The motel rooms pack in the beds and sleep five or six at a squeeze, but there are three acres of bush to wander, with the chance of spotting a lyrebird. Rates include breakfast.

Lind National Park

Signposted just east off the turn-off from the Princes Hwy to Club Terrace, this small **park** (1365 hectares) was declared in 1926 as a scenic stopover for travellers along the highway. A number of creeks run through the park, and the vegetation ranges from warm temperate rainforests and wet-gully plants alongside the creeks to open eucalypt forests in the drier areas. There are several **walking tracks**, a picnic area in the centre of the park and a **nature drive** that follows the Euchre Creek through the park from Club Terrace back to the Princes Hwy.

Cann River

☎ 03 / pop 250

A small sawmilling centre, Cann River sits at a massive crossroad at the junction of the Princes and Monaro Hwys. **Parks Victoria** (☎ 5158 6351) in the centre of town is the main visitors centre for Croajingolong National Park. Road access information, overnight hiking and camping permits, and walking-trail park notes are available. A range of topographic maps and walking guides are available for purchase.

The town itself has a small supermarket, caravan park and several motels. Filling food is available at the pub and cafés, but this is not the place to stop for quality food. The Mobil petrol station has an ATM.

SOUTH & FAR EAST

From Cann River, the Monaro Hwy heads north to the Coopracambra National Park, and the unsealed Tamboon Rd heads south to Tamboon Inlet and Croajingolong National Park.

Drummer Creek Rainforest Walk
Eleven kilometres east of Cann River, on the northern side of the Princes Hwy, this is a easy half-hour walk that starts at the picnic area and takes you through warm temperate rainforest.

COOPRACAMBRA NATIONAL PARK
Coopracambra is one of the most remote and least developed of the state's national parks. It was declared a national park in 1979 and now covers an area of more than 35,000 hectares. It's bordered in the north by the NSW border and on the west by the Monaro Hwy. The landscape is rugged and spectacular, with the dramatic deep gorges of the Genoa River and a series of smaller creeks running through it. The vegetation is mainly open eucalypt forest, with a few areas of sheltered rainforest, and there are various difficult climbs to high peaks, such as at **Mt Denmarsh**, **Mt Kaye** and at **Mt Coopracambra**.

One 4WD track passes through the centre of the park from the Monaro Hwy to the west of Genoa. Apart from this route, there are no other access tracks, camping grounds or walking trails through Coopracambra, which makes it a great spot for experienced bushwalkers who want to escape the madding crowds. On the Monaro Hwy side, the **Beehive Creek Falls** (signposted) is an idyllic and scenic spot, with small cascades falling into rock pools shaded by the surrounding bush – there are some great swimming holes for the warmer weather.

It's a fascinating journey from Cann River to Bombala in NSW. The Victorian sector of the highway is very pretty, winding through national parks and thick forests, but as soon as you cross the border the landscape changes dramatically into dry, denuded sheep pastures and a landscape that is stripped of its natural vegetation.

The **V/Line** (☎ 13 61 96) bus service from Sale to Canberra travels up the Monaro Hwy.

Coopracambra Cottages (☎ 03-5158 8277; www .mallacoota.com; d $60) is a wonderfully remote getaway set on a scenic farm bordering Coopracambra National Park. The octag-

onal timber cottages, which sleep six, are built of local timbers, with solar power and log-fire heating. Bird-watching and 4WD tours of the area are available, and walking trails are close at hand. The turn-off to the cottage is just outside Genoa, and from there it's 16km on an unsealed road.

GIPSY POINT
☎ 03
Named after the schooner *Gypsy* that tied up here in the 19th century, Gipsy Point is an idyllic settlement at the head of Mallacoota Inlet. It's only 10km off the Princes Hwy, but it has a deliciously remote atmosphere – once you're sitting on the jetty looking out over the inlets, you'll feel like you're a million miles from anywhere (unless, of course, you're here during the Christmas holidays). A resident mob of Eastern grey kangaroos live in the area and you'll often see them, especially at dusk, as they graze by the water.

The friendly **Gipsy Point Lodge** (☎ 5158 8205, 1800 063 556; www.gipsypoint.com; self-contained cottage/ guesthouse with meals per person $105/145; ☒) is in a peaceful setting surrounded by bush and water. The guesthouse rooms have glorious water views. Facilities include a tennis court, use of canoe and rowboats, and motorboat hire (per day $75). Nonguests are welcome for the well-recommended dinner (three-course set meal per person $55), but be sure to book ahead.

Decisions, decisions at **Gipsy Point Luxury Lakeside Apartments** (☎ 1800 688 200; www.gipsy .com.au; s/d from $195; ☒ ☒). Hmmm, darling, shall we go on a boat cruise, hop in our private spa or the free-form pebble-sheen pool, or watch the kangaroos graze on the grass from our deck? This is one of only two five-star accommodation options in Gippsland and it's indulgently luxurious. The modern, spacious, split-level apartments with king-size beds are in a prime location on the edge of the lake. No children under eight.

MALLACOOTA
☎ 03 / pop 1040
Completely surrounded by the internationally acclaimed Croajingolong National Park, Mallacoota is a one-road-in, one-road-out town populated by alternative lifestylers, retirees, abalone fishers and surfers. Everything is fairly low-key and relaxed, and life revolves around the ocean, the inlet, the bush and the

pub. It's been a haven for travellers since the early 20th century when a camp set up by the poet EJ Brady, on the shores of the inlet, attracted notable Australian literary figures, such as Henry Lawson and Katherine Susannah Pritchard.

Mallacoota's attractions are unique: there's access to remote ocean beaches, an extensive estuarine waterway system, the fabulous Croajingolong National Park, an abundance of birdlife, great fishing, bushwalks, surfing and swimming. Mallacoota's character changes in the Christmas school holidays and at Easter, when everyone wants to share its delights – even then you can still find a quietish bit of bush or beach.

Information

Mallacoota Information Shed (☎ 5158 0800; Main Wharf, cnr Allan & Buckland Drs; 🕙 10am-4pm) Operated by friendly volunteers.

Mallacoota Telecentre (☎ 5158 0603; Mallacoota Community House, cnr Genoa Rd & Mattson St; per hr $5; 🕙 9am-5pm Mon-Fri) Offers Internet access.

Parks Victoria (☎ 5161 9500; cnr Buckland & Allan Drs; 🕙 9.30am-noon & 1-3.30pm Mon-Fri) Has an information centre opposite the main wharf, with excellent outdoor displays and information on Croajingolong National Park and Mallacoota.

Sights & Activities

CRUISES & BOAT HIRE

One of the best ways to experience Mallacoota is by boat. The estuarine waters of **Mallacoota Inlet** are completely surrounded by the national park and have more than 300km of shoreline. Fewer cruises operate in winter, so call ahead to check.

Porkie Bess (☎ 5158 0109, 0408-408 094; 2hr-cruise per person $25) is a 1940s wooden boat offering fishing trips and cruises around the lakes. It also acts as a ferry for hikers (per person $10, minimum of four).

Wilderness Coast Ocean Charters (☎ 0418-553 809; Gabo Island $60, Skerries $100) runs trips to Gabo Island (accommodation drop-off is possible) from Bastion Point early in the morning and picks up in the afternoon. The Skerries seal-colony trip views these delightful creatures off Wingan Inlet. Whales are sometimes spotted on trips from September to November.

Mallacoota Hire Boats (☎ 0438-447 558; Main Wharf, cnr Allan & Buckland Drs; motorboats half-/full-day hire $70/110, canoes per hr $15) is centrally located,

and hires out canoes and boats; no licence is required.

GABO ISLAND LIGHTSTATION RESERVE

The windswept 154-hectare **Gabo Island**, 14km from Mallacoota, is home to seabirds and one of the world's largest colonies of little penguins. Whales, dolphins and fur seals are regularly sighted offshore. The island has an operating **lighthouse** (tours per person $8), built in 1862, which is the tallest in the southern hemisphere. Accommodation is available in the self-contained **Assistant Lighthouse Keeper's residence** (bookings ☎ 5161 9500; per night for up to 8 people from $156). Access to the island is possible by boat (see left), or by air with **Mallacoota Air Services** (☎ 0408-580 806; return for up to 3 adults $176).

BEACHES

For good surf, head to **Bastion Point** or **Tip Beach**. There's swimmable surf and some sheltered waters at **Betka beach**, which is patrolled during Christmas school holidays. There's also good swimming spots along the beaches of the foreshore reserve, at Bastion Point and **Quarry Beach**.

WALKING

There are plenty of great short walks around the town, the inlet and in the bush, ranging from a half-hour stroll to a four-hour walk. The easy 5km one-way **Bucklands Jetty to Captain Creek Jetty Walk** starts about 4km north of the town and follows the shoreline of the inlet past The Narrows (and past many patient anglers). The walk can be extended from Captains Creek via eucalypt forests to either Double Creek or the Mallacoota-Genoa Rd (both 3km from Captains Creek). The 7km **Mallacoota Town Walk**, which loops round Bastion Point and combines five different walks, is also popular. Walking notes with maps are available from Parks Victoria and the Information Shed (see left).

SCENIC FLIGHTS

Scenic flights over the inlet, to Gabo Island and as far afield as Eden in NSW are available with **Mallacoota Air Services** (☎ 0408-580 806; flights for 3 adults from $35-250).

Festivals & Events

The biannual **Mallacoota Arts Festival** (☎ 5158 0890) has a different theme each year. It focuses on creative arts, writing, theatre and music workshops, which often lead to performances during the course of the festival. The next festival will be held in 2006.

Sleeping

There are plenty of accommodation options, though during Easter and Christmas school holidays you'll need to book well ahead. At those times expect prices to be about 20% higher than those indicated here (peak prices are mentioned here when they're a whole lot higher).

Karbeethong Lodge (☎ 5158 0411; www.karbeethonglodge.com.au; 16 Schnapper Point Dr; d with/without bathroom from $85/65, f extra $10) It's hard not to be overcome by the serenity as you rest on the broad verandas at this early 1900s timber guesthouse overlooking Mallacoota Inlet. The large guest lounge and dining room are equally comfortable, with an open fire and period furnishings. There's also a mammoth kitchen if you want to prepare meals. The pastel-toned bedrooms are small.

Adobe Mudbrick Flats (☎ 5158 0329; www.adobeholidayflats.com.au; 17 Karbeethong Ave; d/f flats $65/80) These eco-friendly, creative, comfortable mud-brick flats about 5km from the town centre are fun, particularly for families, with birds to feed, a farmyard of ducks and kangaroos, and a lyrebird to look out for. Enjoy the gorgeous inlet views from the comfort of your hammock. Linen costs extra.

Mallacoota Houseboats (☎ 5158 0775; low/high season 3-night minimum $750/1250, subsequently per night $100/200) These houseboats are a divine way to explore Mallacoota's waterways. The clean and cosy boats sleep up to six, and have kitchen, toilet and shower. There's a barbecue on the deck for a bit of alfresco dining.

Mallacoota Hotel Motel & Backpackers (☎ 5158 0455; inncoota@speedlink.com.au; 51-55 Maurice Ave; 2-4 bed dm $22, motel s/d/f from $55/66/75; 🕲 🕮) The backpacker rooms are a bit shabby, but there's a good shared kitchen, use of the motel pool, and it's conveniently located next door to the pub. Simple motel and family units overlook the lawn and pool.

Mallacoota Foreshore Caravan Park (☎ 5158 0300; camppark@vicnet.net.au; powered/unpowered sites per 2 people $17.50/14, d caravans $50) Hundreds of grassy sites extend along the foreshore and have sublime views of the lake, with its resident population of black swans and pelicans. Prices go up 50% at Christmas and Easter.

Eating

Croajingalong Cafe (☎ 5158 0098; Allan Dr; mains $6.50-11; 🕲 breakfast & lunch Tue-Sun) Overlooking the inlet, this friendly café is a perfect place to linger over a latte and watch the world as it moves slowly by. The menu has some inspired offerings and it serves great fruit smoothies. Try the Vegie Brekky – tomatoes, mushrooms, beans and eggs on avocado toast ($10), or the chicken with sage and mushroom on a bed of noodles ($8). No credit cards.

Pub Bistro (☎ 5158 0455; 51-55 Maurice Ave; mains $14-26; 🕲 lunch & dinner) For hearty meals try the pub bistro, where you can sample porterhouse in seafood sauce ($26) and the rich profiterole mousse cake ($7.50). Bands play at the pub regularly in summer.

Tide Restaurant (☎ 5158 0100; 70 Maurice Ave; mains $15-25; 🕲 dinner daily) With a prime lakeside location, the Tide serves quality food and wine. It's sunny outdoor deck is deservedly popular.

Getting There & Away

Mallacoota is 23km off the Princes Hwy. Although buses stop at Genoa, at the time of writing, a shuttle bus from Genoa to Mallacoota was being trialled. Call the **Mallactooa Information Shed** (☎ 5158 0800) to see if this service is currently operating. **Mallacoota Taxis** (☎ 5158 0192) does the Genoa–Mallacoota run for $30.

CROAJINGOLONG NATIONAL PARK

Designated a World Biosphere Reserve by Unesco in 1977, Croajingolong National Park is one of Australia's finest national parks. This coastal wilderness park covers 87,500 hectares and stretches for about 100km along the easternmost tip of Victoria from Bemm River to the NSW border. Magnificent unspoiled beaches, inlets, estuaries and forests make this an ideal park for camping, walking, swimming and surfing. The five inlets, Sydenham, Tamboon, Mueller, Wingan and Mallacoota, are popular canoeing and fishing spots. Mallacoota Inlet is the largest and most accessible (see p389).

Contact **Parks Victoria** (Cann River ☎ 03-5158 6351; Mallacoota ☎ 03-5161 9500) for information, road conditions, overnight hiking and camping permits, and track notes. Lonely Planet's *Walking in Australia* has an excellent detailed description of the walk from Thurra River to Mallacoota.

Two sections of the park have been declared wilderness areas (which means no vehicles, access to a limited number of walkers only and permits required): the **Cape Howe Wilderness area**, between Mallacoota Inlet and NSW border, and **Sandpatch Wilderness area**, between Wingan Inlet and Shipwreck Creek. The **Wilderness Coast Walk**, only for the well prepared and intrepid, starts at Sydenham Inlet, by Bemm River, and heads along the coast to Mallacoota. You can start anywhere in between. Thurra River is a good starting point, making the walk an easy-to-medium 59km (five-day) hike to Mallacoota.

In Mallacoota, Tony Gray runs a **shuttle service** (☎ 03-5158 0472, 0408-516 482), with transport for up to five people to Thurra River costing $190 (you can leave your car at Mallacoota airport).

Croajingolong is a **bird-watching** paradise, with over 300 recorded species, including glossy black cockatoos and the rare ground parrot; while the inland waterways are home to a myriad of water birds, such as the delicate azure kingfisher and the magnificent sea eagle. There are many small mammals here, including possums, bandicoots and gliders, and the reptile population includes a colony of huge goannas at Goanna Bay, to the north of Mallacoota Inlet. The vegetation ranges from typical coastal landscapes to thick eucalypt forests, with some areas of warm-temperate rainforest. The heathland areas are filled with impressive displays of orchids and wildflowers in the spring.

Access roads of varying quality lead into the park from the Princes Hwy. Apart from Mallacoota Rd, all roads are unsealed and can be very rough in winter, so check conditions with Parks Victoria before venturing on, especially during or after rain.

The main camping areas are at Wingan Inlet, Shipwreck Creek, Thurra River and Mueller Inlet.

The serene and secluded **Wingan Inlet camp site** (per camp site up to 6 people $14.50) has the best facilities, with pit toilets, fireplaces, picnic tables and fresh water. **Shipwreck Creek** (per campsite up to 6 people $10) has pit toilets and shared fireplaces. You need to bring your own water.

Other bush camping areas (permits required) lie along the Wilderness Coast Walk, but you may need to bring drinking water.

Point Hicks was the first part of Australia to be spotted by Captain Cook and the *Endeavour* crew in 1770, and was named after his first Lieutenant Zachary Hicks. The remote **Point Hicks Lighthouse** has two comfortable **heritage-listed cottages** (☎ 03-5158 4268; pointhicks@bigpond.com; per night up to 8 people from $210) that originally housed the assistant lighthouse keepers. The cottages have ocean views and wood fires.

Thurra River and Mueller Inlet **camping grounds** (tent sites $13.50) are less than 5km from the lighthouse, with pit toilets, running water and fireplaces.

SOUTH & FAR EAST

Directory

CONTENTS

PRACTICALITIES

- **Electricity** Plug your hairdryer into a three-pin adaptor (not the same as British three-pin adaptors) before plugging into the electricity supply (220–240V AC, 50Hz).

- **Newspapers & Magazines** Leaf through the broadsheet newspaper *The Age*, the tabloid *Herald Sun* or the national *Australian* newspaper. Buy or sell anything in the *Melbourne Trading Post*, published on Thursday.

- **Radio** For something a little different in Melbourne, tune in to 3RRR (102.7) and 3PBS (106.7), two excellent noncommercial stations featuring alternative and independent music, current affairs and talk programmes.

- **TV** Switch on the box to watch the ad-free ABC, the government-sponsored and multicultural SBS, or one of three commercial TV stations, namely Seven, Nine and Ten.

- **Video Systems** Videos you buy or watch will be based on the PAL system.

- **Weights & Measures** Australia uses the metric system. See the Quick Reference page (inside front cover) for a metric conversion chart.

ACCOMMODATION

It's not difficult to get a good night's sleep in this popular southern state, which offers everything from the tent-pegged confines of camping grounds and the communal space of hostels to gourmet breakfasts in guesthouses and lavish resorts, plus the gamut of hotel and motel lodgings.

The **RACV** (www.racv.com.au) publishes a comprehensive *Accommodation Guide* (member/nonmember $10.50/15.95), listing all types of accommodation in the state, which is updated annually. There's also a *Tourist Park Guide* ($9.95/14.95), which lists thousands of camping areas and caravan parks. The *Experience Victoria* guide ($9.95/14.95) offers a good mix of accommodation suggestions, as well as information on tours, attractions and festivals.

The RACV's branch offices around the state also offer accommodation booking services, as do many of the visitor information centres.

The listings in the Sleeping sections of this guidebook are ordered from budget to midrange to top end, with the best options within each category listed first. Any place that charges up to $40 per single or $80 per double has been categorised as budget accommodation. Midrange prices are from $80 to $150 per double, while the top-end tag is applied to places charging more than $150 per double. Inevitably, for more expensive destinations such as Melbourne and the Southwest (see p198), our price ranges differ slightly, with midrange places going as high as $165 per double, and top-end prices categorised above $165.

In many regions of Victoria, prices don't vary dramatically from season to season, and we have simply listed the prices that are charged for most of the year. In other areas there are more dramatic seasonal price variations; in these cases, we have listed both low- and high-season prices. Along the coast, the summer months are high season, particularly the school holidays that begin just before Christmas. The Easter school holidays are another busy time in the holiday hotspots. However, on the ski fields, prices are highest during the winter peak season when the action on the slopes is at its powdery best.

B&Bs & Guesthouses

The local bed and breakfast (B&B) population is climbing rapidly and options include everything from restored miners' cottages, converted barns and stables, rambling old houses, upmarket country manors and beachside bungalows to a simple bedroom in a family home. Tariffs are typically in the $70 to $150 (per double) bracket, but can be much higher. Some extremely luxurious places charge over $300, usually incuding gourmet meals.

Tourism Victoria publishes a great little booklet called *Victoria's Bed & Breakfast Getaways*, which lists 260 properties around the state – for more information, see the **Victoria's Bed & Breakfast Getaways** (☎ 132 842; www.visitvictoria.com/bnb) website. You can get your free copy by calling (from within Australia only), or from visitor information centres. There are also several books dedicated to these places, including *Beautiful B&Bs and Small Hotels Victoria & Tasmania* by Jennifer Lamattina. See **Beautiful Accommodation** (www.beautifulaccommodation .com) for the online version.

For online accommodation information, try the **Bed & Breakfast Site** (www.babs.com.au/vic .htm) and **Bed and Breakfast Australia** (www.ozbedand breakfast.com).

Camping & Caravanning

Whether you're packing a tent, driving a campervan or towing a caravan, camping in the bush is a highlight of travelling in Australia. In some state forests and national parks camping is free, although the more popular parks generally charge a fee of around $10 to $14 per site (for up to six people). There are also countless private camping grounds and caravan parks around the state, charging anywhere between $13 and $23 for two people camping, slightly more for a powered site. When it comes to urban camping, remember that most city camping grounds are miles away from the centre of town.

If you're looking for something with a few more creature comforts, consider hiring one of the self-contained cabins in caravan parks across the state. It's surprising how flash some of these onsite cabins can be, and they're often much better value than your standard faded motel room (though you'll usually have to bring your own linen). In this book caravan parks and tourist resorts are generally categorised as budget accommodation, but often the cabin or cottage accommodation they offer falls quite squarely in the midrange quality and price category. You can enjoy a charming self-contained unit with a modern bathroom, your own deck, a leafy environment, and still have access to the park pool, games rooms and other facilities. Prices generally range from $50 to $110.

Note that caravan park prices are strongly affected by seasonal demand. In any area with a hint of a tourist attraction (usually some sort of water – dam, river, sea), you'll pay much more in January, at Easter and in school holidays. Around Christmas and at Easter there might be a minimum stay of at least a few days.

Host Farms

A number of the state's farms and stations offer a rural getaway. At some you can kick back and watch other people raise a sweat, while others like to rope you in to the day-to-day activities. Most accommodation is very comfortable – in the main homestead (B&B-style) or in self-contained cottages on the property. Other farms provide budget options in outbuildings or former shearers' quarters. Check out options on the websites for **Australian Farmhost Holidays** (www.australiafarm host.com) and **Accommodation Getaways Victoria** (www.agv.net.au).

For travellers who don't mind getting their hands dirty, there's **Willing Workers on Organic Farms** (Wwoof; ☎ 5155 0218; www.wwoof.com.au), which is well established in Victoria. Like the bartering system of old, WWOOF offers travellers the chance to exchange a few hours of toil every day for bed and board. It's a fabulous way of meeting local people, getting into the countryside, learning about the rural culture, picking up some new skills and inexpensively travelling through the country. Membership costs $50/60 for singles/couples, and you can join through the website. Wwoof will send you a membership number and a booklet that lists around 1600 participating places all over Australia.

Hostels

Hostels are a highly social, low-cost fixture of the Victorian accommodation scene. In some areas, hostels are reinventing themselves as 'inns' or 'guesthouses', partly to broaden their appeal beyond backpackers.

YHA HOSTELS

The **Youth Hostels Association** (YHA; ☎ 9670 9611; www.yha.com.au; 83 Hardware Lane, Melbourne; ☻ 9am-5.30pm Mon-Fri, 10am-1pm Sat) is part of the International Youth Hostel Federation (IYHF or HI). If you're already a member of that organisation in your own country, your membership entitles you to YHA rates in the relevant Victorian hostels.

YHA hostels provide basic accommodation, usually in small dormitories (bunk rooms), although more and more are providing twin rooms. Nightly charges are between $19 and $28 for members; most hostels also take non-YHA members for an extra $3.50. In this book, we've listed nonmember prices throughout. Private singles are usually available for $30 to $60 and doubles for $50 to $75. Family rooms may also be available for around $80. Visitors to Australia should preferably purchase an HI card in their country of residence, but can also buy a visitors' card at major Victorian YHA hostels at a cost of $35 for 12 months. Australian residents can become full YHA members for $52/85/115 for one/two/three years; see the **HI** (www.hihostels.com) website for further details.

See the YHA website for a list of all YHA hostels in Victoria and any membership discount entitlements (eg bus transport, car hire, activities, accommodation).

INDEPENDENT HOSTELS

Victoria has a rapidly growing group of independent hostels of varying quality. Fierce competition for the backpacker dollar means that standards are generally kept pretty high –

and there are plenty of bonus enticements, such as free Internet access, courtesy buses, and discount meal and beer vouchers. In Melbourne, some places are run-down hotels trying to fill empty rooms, and the unrenovated ones are often gloomy and depressing. There are also purpose-built hostels with stacks of facilities but some travellers find these places too big and impersonal. If you crave peace and quiet, avoid 'we love to party' places; instead, stay in smaller, more intimate hostels where the owner is also the manager.

Independent backpacker establishments typically charge $20 to $28 for a dorm bed and $50 to $70 for a twin or double room (usually without bathroom), often with a small discount if you're a member of YHA or one of the other hostel organisations, such as Nomad or VIP.

Some places will only admit backpackers from overseas; this is mainly in Melbourne hostels that have had problems with locals looking for a cheap place to crash and bothering the backpackers. Hostels that discourage or ban Aussies say it's only a rowdy minority that makes trouble, and often these hostels will only ask for identification in order to deter potential troublemakers, but it certainly can be annoying, patronising and discriminatory for genuine travellers trying to explore their own country. If you're an Aussie and encounter this kind of reception, tell them you're a genuine traveller.

Hotels & Motels

Except for pubs, the hotels that exist in cities or large centres are generally of the business or luxury variety where you get a comfortable, anonymous and mod-con–filled room in a multistorey block. These places tend to have a pool, restaurant/café, room service and various other facilities. We quote 'rack rates' (official advertised rates) throughout this book, but often hotels/motels will offer regular discounts and special deals.

For comfortable midrange accommodation, motels (or motor inns) are often a reliable option. Almost every country town has at least one, and the larger towns have dozens to choose from. Prices vary and there's rarely a cheaper rate for singles, so they tend to be better for couples or groups of three. Most motels are low-rise and have similar facilities (tea- and coffee-making, fridge, TV, air-con, bathroom) but the price will indicate the standard. The majority of country motels also offer options such as executive suites, rooms with private courtyards, spas in some rooms and other such extras. You'll mostly pay between $50 and $120 for a room.

Pubs

In country towns, pubs are invariably found in the town centre. Many pubs were built during boom times, so they're often among the largest and most ornate buildings in town. In tourist areas some pubs have been restored as heritage buildings, but generally the rooms remain small and old-fashioned, with a long walk down the hall to the bathroom. You can sometimes rent a single room at a country pub for not much more than a hostel dorm, and you'll be in the social heart of the town to boot. But if you're a light sleeper, never book a room above the bar.

Standard pubs have singles/doubles with shared facilities starting from around $35/60, obviously more if you want a private bathroom. Few have a separate reception area – just ask in the bar if there are rooms available.

Staying in these places can be a great way to experience country Victoria, and you'll meet many more interesting locals in the bar than you would if you stayed in a motel.

ACTIVITIES

See the Victoria Outdoors chapter on p43.

BUSINESS HOURS

Standard shop-trading hours are Monday to Thursday from 9am to 5.30pm, Friday from 9am to 9pm, and Saturday from 9am to 12.30pm. Many shops in Melbourne's city centre and other major shopping centres also stay open until 9pm on Thursday and until 5pm on Saturday – especially the larger retailers. Most retail shops close on Sunday, although many shops in tourist precincts are open every day. Places such as delicatessens, milk bars and bookshops often stay open late and open on the weekend. Many of Victoria's supermarkets are open until late at night, and some stay open 24 hours a day.

Most offices and businesses open Monday to Friday from 9am to 5.30pm, although some government departments close at 4.30pm or 5pm. Normal banking hours are Monday to Thursday from 9.30am to 4pm, and Friday from 9.30am to 5pm. Post offices are open from 9am to 5pm Monday to Friday, but you can also buy stamps on Saturday morning at post office agencies (operated from newsagencies) and from Australia Post shops in the major cities.

For general opening hours of restaurants, cafés and other eateries, consider that breakfast is normally served between 6am and 11am, lunch is served from around noon to 3pm and dinner usually starts after 6pm. Cafés tend to be all-day affairs that either close around 5pm or continue their business into the night. Pubs usually serve food from noon to 2pm and from 6pm to 8pm. Pubs and bars often open for drinking at lunchtime and continue well into the evening, particularly from Thursday to Saturday.

CHILDREN
Practicalities

Melbourne and most major towns have centrally located public rooms where parents can nurse their baby or change a nappy; check with the local tourist office or city council for details. While many Australians have a relaxed attitude about breast-feeding or nappy changing in public, others frown upon it.

Most motels and the better-equipped caravan parks have playgrounds and swimming pools, and can supply cots and baby baths – motels may also have in-house children's videos and child-minding services. Top-end hotels and many (but not all) midrange hotels are well versed in the needs of guests who adore children. B&Bs, on the other hand, often market themselves as sanctuaries from all things child-related. Some cafés and restaurants make it difficult to dine with small children, lacking a specialised children's menu, but many others do have kids' meals, or will provide small serves from the main menu. Some also supply high chairs.

Child concessions (and family rates) often apply for such things as accommodation, tours, admission fees, and air, bus and train transport, with some discounts as high as 50% of the adult rate. However, the definition of 'child' can vary from under 12 to under 18 years. Medical services and facilities in Australia are of a high standard, and items such as baby food, formula and disposable nappies are widely available in urban centres. Major hire-car companies will supply and fit booster seats for you, for which you'll be charged around $16.50 for up to three days' use, with an additional daily fee for longer periods.

Lonely Planet's *Travel with Children* by Cathy Lanigan contains plenty of useful information.

Sights & Activities

Victoria is a child's dream destination, with no shortage of active, interesting and educational things to do. Every town or city has at least some parkland, or you could head into the countryside for wide open spaces, bushland or beaches. For more ideas on how to keep kids occupied, see Child's Play (p20). Also see the Melbourne for Children section (p112) for city-based tips.

CLIMATE CHARTS

Victoria has a temperate four-season climate, although the distinctions between the seasons are often blurred by the unpredictability of the weather. There are three climatic regions: the southern and coastal areas, the alpine areas, and the areas north and west of the Great Dividing Range.

The following climate charts give an indication of the average seasonal temperatures and rainfall for Melbourne, Mt Hotham, Cape Otway, Point Hicks and Mildura.

In general the southern and coastal areas are similar to Melbourne, while the alpine areas (including Mt Hotham) are colder and wetter, and the northern and western areas (including Mildura) are warmer and drier.

Rainfall is spread fairly evenly throughout the year, although mid-January to mid-March tends to be the driest period. Victoria's wettest areas are the Otway Ranges and the High Country. Because of exposure to frequent cold fronts and southerly winds, the coastal areas are subject to the most changeable weather patterns.

The weather is generally more stable north of the Great Dividing Range. The Wimmera and Mallee regions have the lowest rainfall and the highest temperatures.

The alpine areas have the most extreme climatic conditions (for more information, see p323). In winter, most of the higher mountains are snow-capped and frosts are frequent, while in summer a warm or hot day might be followed by a night of below-freezing temperatures.

For more information on climate, see also the Getting Started chapter, p15.

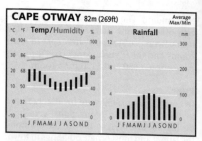

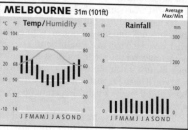

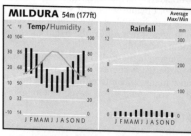

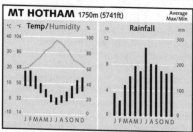

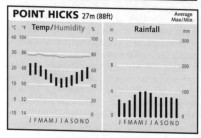

CUSTOMS

For comprehensive information on customs regulations, contact the **Australian Customs Service** (☎ 1300 363 263; www.customs.gov.au).

When entering Australia you can bring most articles in free of duty provided that customs is satisfied they are for personal use and you'll be taking them with you when you leave. There's a duty-free quota per person of 2.25L of alcohol, 250 cigarettes and dutiable goods up to the value of $900.

When it comes to prohibited goods, there are a few things you should be particularly conscientious about. The first is drugs, which customs authorities are adept at sniffing out – unless you want to make a first-hand investigation of Australian jails, don't bring illegal drugs in with you. Note that all medicines must be declared.

The second is all food, plant material and animal products. You will be asked to declare on arrival all goods of animal or plant origin (wooden spoons, straw hats, the lot) and show them to a quarantine officer. The authorities are naturally keen to protect Australia's unique environment and important agricultural industries by preventing weeds, pests or diseases getting into the country – Australia has so far managed to escape many of the pests and diseases prevalent elsewhere in the world.

Weapons and firearms are either prohibited or require a permit and safety testing. Other restricted goods include products made from protected wildlife species (such as animal skins, coral or ivory), unapproved telecommunications devices and live animals.

It's worth mentioning that Australia takes quarantine very seriously. All luggage is screened or X-rayed – if you fail to declare quarantine items on arrival and are caught, you risk an on-the-spot fine of $220, or prosecution which may result in fines over $60,000, as well as up to 10 years imprisonment. For quarantine regulations relating to state border crossings, see p410.

For more information on quarantine regulations contact the **Australian Quarantine and Inspection Service** (AQIS; www.aqis.gov.au).

DANGERS & ANNOYANCES
Animal Bites & Stings

See p421 for information on treating bites and stings from ticks, leeches, mosquitos, snakes and spiders, as well as some methods for avoiding them.

Bushfires & Blizzards

Bushfires happen every year in Victoria. Don't be the mug who starts one. In hot, dry and windy weather, be extremely careful with any naked flame – cigarette butts thrown out of car windows have started many a fire. On a total-fire-ban day it's forbidden even to use a camping stove in the open. Locals will not be amused if they catch you breaking this particular law; they'll happily dob you in, and the penalties are severe.

If you're unfortunate enough to find yourself driving through a bushfire, stay inside your car and try to park in an open space, away from trees, until the danger passes. Lie on the floor under the dashboard, covering yourself with a wool blanket if possible. The front of the fire should pass quickly, and you will be much safer than if you were out in the open. It is very important to cover up with a wool blanket or wear protective clothing, as it is heat radiation which is the big killer in bushfire situations.

Bushwalkers should seek local advice before setting out – be careful if a total fire ban is in place, or delay your trip. If you're out in the bush and you see smoke, even a long way away, take it seriously – bushfires move very quickly and change direction with the wind. Go to the nearest open space, downhill if possible. A forested ridge, on the other hand, is the most dangerous place to be.

More bushwalkers actually die of cold than in bushfires. Even in summer, temperatures can drop below freezing at night in the mountains and the weather can change very quickly. Exposure in even moderately cool temperatures can sometimes result in hypothermia – for more information on hypothermia and how to minimise its risk, see p422.

On the Road

Cows, kangaroos and even wombats can be a real hazard to the driver, especially at dusk and at night. Unfortunately, other drivers are even more dangerous, particularly those who drink. See p413 for more information on driving in Victoria.

Swimming & Boating

Popular Victorian beaches are patrolled by surf life-savers in summer and patrolled

DIRECTORY

areas are marked off by a pair of red and yellow flags. Always swim between the flags if possible.

Victoria's ocean beaches often have dangerous waves and rips. Even if you're a competent swimmer, you should exercise extreme caution and avoid the water altogether in high surf. Children should be watched closely and kept out of the water if conditions are rough. If you happen to get caught in a rip when swimming and are being taken out to sea, try not to panic. Raise one arm until you have been spotted, and then swim parallel to the shore – *don't* try to swim back against the rip, you'll only tire yourself.

A number of people are also paralysed every year by diving into shallow water and hitting a sandbar; check the depth of the water before you leap.

Melbourne's Port Phillip Bay is generally safe for swimming – the closest you're likely to come to a shark is in the local fish and chip shop. The small blue-ringed octopus is sometimes found hiding under rocks in rockpools on the foreshore. Its sting can be fatal, so don't touch it under any circumstances!

Boating on Port Phillip Bay can be hazardous, as conditions can change dramatically and without warning.

Theft

Victoria is a relatively safe place to visit, but you should still take reasonable precautions. Don't leave hotel rooms or cars unlocked, and don't leave money, wallets, purses or cameras unattended, in full view through car windows, for instance. Most accommodation places have a safe where you can store your valuables. If you are unlucky enough to have something stolen, immediately report all details to the nearest police station.

Trams

In Melbourne, be *extremely* cautious when stepping on and off trams – too many people have been hit by passing cars, so don't step off without looking both ways. Pedestrians in Bourke St Mall should watch for passing trams too.

Car drivers should treat Melbourne trams with caution (see p145). Cyclists should be careful not to get their wheels caught in tram tracks, and motorcyclists should take special care when tram tracks are wet.

DISABLED TRAVELLERS

Disability awareness in Australia is reasonably high. Legislation requires that new accommodation must meet accessibility standards and tourist operators must not discriminate. Many of the state's key attractions provide access for those with limited mobility and a number of sites have also begun addressing the needs of visitors with visual or aural impairments; contact attractions in advance to confirm the facilities.

The excellent *Mobility Map* of Melbourne is available from the Melbourne Visitor Information Centre in Federation Square, and from the information booth in the Bourke St Mall (see p68). It's also available to view online at the **Access Melbourne** (www.accessmelbourne .vic.gov.au) website.

Many new buildings incorporate architectural features helpful to the vision impaired, such as textured floor details at the top and bottom of stairs. Melbourne's pedestrian crossings feature sound cues.

Organisations

Access Foundation (www.accessibility.com.au) Includes a guide to Melbourne's accessible sites, as well as useful regional transport information and a full list of Victoria's municipal council websites.

National Information Communication and Awareness Network (Nican; ☎ 1800 806 769; www.nican .com.au) An Australia-wide directory providing information on access issues, accommodation, sporting and recreational activities, transport and specialist tour operators.

Paraplegic & Quadriplegic Association of Victoria (Para Quad; ☎ 9415 1200; www.paraquad.asn.au)

Royal Victorian Institute for the Blind (RVIB; ☎ 9522 5222; www.rvib.org.au)

RTA (☎ 13 11 74; www.vicroads.vic.gov.au) Supplies temporary parking permits for disabled international drivers.

Traveller's Aid (☎ 9654 2600; 2nd fl, 169 Swanston St) A helpful and friendly independent organisation catering to travellers, particularly with special needs. It has loads of information, a lounge, café, wheelchair-accessible toilets, showers and lockers. There is also a disability access service offering minor repairs to wheelchairs and battery recharge, as well as personal care attendance. It has a second location at **Southern Cross Station** (formerly Spencer St station; ☎ 9670 2873; Spencer St).

Victorian Deaf Society (☎ 9473 1111; www.vicdeaf .com.au)

Vision Australia Foundation (☎ 1800 331 000; www.visionaustralia.org.au)

Transport

Accepted only by Qantas, the Carers Concession Card entitles a disabled person and the carer travelling with them to a 50% discount on full economy fares; call Nican (see opposite) for eligibility and an application form. Melbourne airport has dedicated parking spaces, wheelchair access to terminals, accessible toilets and skychairs to convey passengers onto planes via airbridges.

Melbourne's suburban rail network is accessible and the country trains and stations in the **V/Line** (☎ 13 61 96) network are equipped with ramps. Some rural services employ hoist-equipped accessible coaches. Twenty-four hours advance booking is required. Newer buses and trams in Melbourne have low steps to accommodate wheelchairs and people with limited mobility; see also information on Traveller's Aid (opposite). There are many car-parking spaces allocated for disabled drivers throughout the city.

Avis and Hertz offer hire cars with hand controls at no extra charge for pick-up in Melbourne and at the airport in Tullamarine, but advance notice is required.

DISCOUNT CARDS

Carrying a student card entitles you to a wide variety of discounts throughout Victoria. The most common card is the International Student Identity Card (ISIC), which is issued to full-time students aged 12 years and over, and gives the bearer discounts on accommodation, transport and admission to some attractions. It's available from student unions, hostelling organisations and some travel agencies; for more information, see the website of the **International Student Travel Confederation** (ISTC; www.istc.org).

The ISTC is also the body behind the International Youth Travel Card (IYTC or Go25), which is issued to people who are between 12 and 26 years of age and not full-time students, and gives equivalent benefits to the ISIC. A similar ISTC brainchild is the International Teacher Identity Card (ITIC), available to teaching professionals.

EMBASSIES & CONSULATES

Australian Embassies & Consulates

Australian consular offices overseas:

Canada Ottawa (☎ 613-236 0841; www.ahc-ottawa.org; 7th fl, Suite 710, 50 O'Connor St, Ottawa, Ontario K1P 6L2) Also in Vancouver and Toronto.

France Paris (☎ 01-40 59 33 00; www.austgov.fr; 4 Rue Jean Rey, 75724 Cedex 15, Paris)

Germany Berlin (☎ 030-880 0880; www.australian-embassy.de; Wallstrasse 76-79, 10179 Berlin) Also in Frankfurt.

Ireland Dublin (☎ 01-664 5300; www.australianembassy.ie; 7th fl, Fitzwilton House, Wilton Terrace, Dublin 2)

Japan Tokyo (☎ 03-5232 4111; www.australia.or.jp; 2-1-14 Mita, Minato-Ku, Tokyo 108-8361) Also in Osaka, Nagoya and Fukuoka City.

Netherlands The Hague (☎ 070-310 82 00; www.australian-embassy.nl; Carnegielaan 4, The Hague 2517 KH)

New Zealand Wellington (☎ 04-473 6411; www.australia.org.nz; 72-76 Hobson St, Thorndon, Wellington); Auckland (☎ 09-921 8800; 7th fl, Price Waterhouse Coopers Tower, 186-194 Quay St, Auckland)

Singapore Singapore (☎ 6836 4100; www.singapore.embassy.gov.au; 25 Napier Rd, Singapore 258507)

UK London (☎ 020-7379 4334; www.australia.org.uk; Australia House, The Strand, London WC2B 4LA) Also in Edinburgh and Manchester.

USA Washington DC (☎ 202-797 3000; www.austemb.org; 1601 Massachusetts Ave NW, Washington DC 20036) Also in Los Angeles, New York and other major cities.

Consulates in Melbourne

Most foreign embassies are in Canberra but some countries have diplomatic representation in Melbourne. Their opening hours are generally from 8.30am to 12.30pm and 1pm to 4.30pm Monday to Friday. Consular offices in Melbourne include the following:

Canada (Map pp72-4; ☎ 9653 9674; www.canada.org.au; 50th fl, 101 Collins St, Melbourne Vic 3000)

France (Map pp72-4; ☎ 9602 5024; Suite 805, 8th fl, 150 Queen Street, Melbourne Vic 3000)

Germany (Map pp84-5; ☎ 9864 6888; meldiplo@bigpond.net.au; 480 Punt Rd, South Yarra Vic 3141)

Netherlands (Map pp72-4; ☎ 9670 5573; melbourne.consulate@netherlands.gov.au; 4th fl, 118 Queen St, Melbourne Vic 3000)

UK (Map pp72-4; ☎ 9652 1600; www.uk.emb.gov.au; 17th fl, 90 Collins St, Melbourne Vic 3000)

USA (Map pp84-5; ☎ 9526 5900; http://usembassy-australia.state.gov/melbourne; 553 St Kilda Rd, Melbourne Vic 3004)

FESTIVALS & EVENTS

Victoria is rich with cultural and sporting events, ranging from huge international city-based festivals to small regional affairs. There are music festivals, food festivals, ethnic festivals, film festivals, comedy festivals, sporting events, swap meets and agricultural fairs. Victorians treasure their diversity of events, and not a weekend goes by without something to celebrate and some new festival to attend.

Details of festivals and events that are grounded in a single place are provided throughout the destination chapters of this book. For a list of food and wine festivals, see p51. The following are more general events that are celebrated throughout the region.

March

Irish Festival (17 Mar) Held at venues all over Melbourne and the state, this festival is celebrated over several days and reaches a climax on St Patrick's Day with an open-air concert in the Treasury Gardens.

April

Anzac Day Parades (25 Apr) Dawn services are held throughout the state to pay tribute to those who fought and died for their country, but the biggest and most famous is that held at Melbourne's impressive Shrine of Remembrance (see p96) in King's Domain.

May

Sorry Day (www.journeyofhealing.com; 26 May) Each year, on the anniversary of the 1997 tabling of the *Bringing Them Home* report, concerned Australians acknowledge the continuing pain and suffering of Indigenous people affected by Australia's one-time child-removal practices and policies. Events are held in Melbourne and many regional centres.

July

Naidoc Week (National Aboriginal Islander Day Observance Committee; www.naidocvic.com; early Jul) Communities around Victoria celebrate this; events include the annual Melbourne Naidoc Ball, local street festivals and art exhibitions across the state.

November

Spring Racing Carnival (late Oct–early Nov) This series of horse races is one of the highlights of the Victorian sporting and social calendar. The red-letter day of the Spring Racing Carnival is the Melbourne Cup (see p115), held on the first Tuesday in November. You can just about feel the entire state hold its breath as the horses line up at the start. Even if you can't make it to the racecourse, it's worth going to a race party or a pub to catch the action.

December

Carols by Candlelight (24 Dec) Regional centres around the state hold their own carols under the stars, but the traditional televised Carols by Candlelight attracts some of Australia's most popular performers to Melbourne's Sidney Myer Music Bowl each year.

Melbourne to Hobart Yacht Race (27-30 Dec) Although it's called Melbourne to Hobart, this exciting race actually starts from Portsea on the Mornington Peninsula.

For a good extensive list of events in the region, grab a copy of the free monthly publication, *Melbourne Events,* available from the Visitor Information Centre at Federation Square. Also useful is the **Tourism Victoria** (www.visitvictoria.com) website and the *Age* newspaper's Friday *EG* (entertainment guide).

FOOD

The impressive range and quality of food found in Melbourne and regional Victoria is largely thanks to the huge number of immigrants who flooded into the state in the last century, bringing their cuisines with them.

The best value can be found in modern cafés, where a good meal in casual surroundings costs under $20 and a full-cooked breakfast around $10. Some inner-city pubs offer upmarket restaurant-style fare, but most pubs serve standard (often large-portion) bistro meals, usually in the $10 to $19 range. Bar (or counter) meals, which are eaten in the public bar, usually cost between $6 and $10. For business hours, see p395.

See also the Food & Drink chapter (p50).

GAY & LESBIAN TRAVELLERS

Homosexuality is legal and the age of consent is 17. The straight community's attitude towards gays and lesbians is, on the whole, open-minded and accepting.

The gay scene in Victoria is squarely based in Melbourne (for more information, see p114), where there are exclusively gay venues and accommodation options. Around the state, places such as Daylesford and Hepburn Springs, Phillip Island, the Mornington Peninsula and Lorne have accommodation catering for gays and lesbians.

HOLIDAYS
Public Holidays

On public holidays, government departments, banks, offices, large stores and post offices are closed. Victoria has the following public holidays:

New Year's Day 1 January
Australia Day 26 January
Labour Day 13 March 2006
Good Friday (Easter) 14 April 2006
Easter Monday 17 April 2006

Anzac Day 25 April
Queen's Birthday 12 June 2006
Melbourne Cup Day 1st Tuesday in November. Note that Melbourne Cup Day is a holiday only in the Melbourne metropolitan area. Some other urban centres (such as Ballarat, Geelong and Bendigo) have their own cup days which are local holidays.
Christmas Day 25 December
Boxing Day 26 December

When a public holiday falls on a weekend, the following Monday is declared a holiday (with the exception of Anzac Day and Australia Day).

School Holidays
The school year is divided into four terms. Holidays are generally as follows: the longest break is the Christmas holiday from mid-December until the end of January, then there are three two-week holiday periods which vary from year to year, but fall approximately from late March to mid-April, late June to mid-July and mid-September to early October.

INSURANCE
Don't underestimate the importance of a good travel-insurance policy that covers theft, loss and medical problems – nothing is guaranteed to ruin your holiday plans quicker than an accident or having that brand new digital camera stolen. Most policies offer lower and higher medical-expense options; the higher ones are chiefly for countries that have extremely high medical costs, such as the USA. There is a wide variety of policies available, so compare the small print.

Some policies specifically exclude designated 'dangerous activities' such as scuba diving, parasailing, bungee jumping, motorcycling, skiing and even bushwalking. If you plan on doing any of these things, make sure the policy you choose fully covers you for your activity of choice.

See also Insurance (p419) in the Health chapter.

INTERNET ACCESS
Email and Internet addicts will find it fairly easy to get connected throughout Victoria. Connection speeds and prices vary from one place to the next, but they all offer straightforward access to the Internet. All public libraries have limited access (usually for research rather than for checking emails, and you may have to join the library to use the service), or there are loads of Internet cafés with super-fast connections. Access charges range from $4 to $9 an hour. The average is about $6 an hour, usually with a minimum of 10 minutes' access. Most youth hostels and backpacker places can hook you up, as can many hotels and caravan parks.

Some free web-based email services:
Excite (www.excite.com)
MSN Hotmail (www.hotmail.com)
Yahoo (www.yahoo.com)

Hooking Up
If you've brought your palmtop or notebook computer and want to get connected to a local ISP (Internet Service Provider), there are plenty of options, though some ISPs limit their dial-up areas to major cities or particular regions. Whatever enticements a particular ISP offers, make sure it has local dial-up numbers for the places where you intend to use it – the last thing you want is to be making timed STD calls every time you connect to the Internet. If you're based in Melbourne or a large centre, there's no problem. Telstra (BigPond) uses a nationwide dial-up number at local call rates. Some major ISPs:
America Online (AOL; ☎ 1800 265 265; www.aol.com.au)
Australia On Line (☎ 1300 650 661; www.ozonline.com.au)
CompuServe (www.compuserve.com.au) Users who want to access the service locally can check the website or phone **CompuServe Pacific** (☎ 1300 555 520) to get the local log-in numbers.
iPrimus (☎ 1300 850 000; www.iprimus.com.au)
OzEmail (☎ 13 28 84; www.ozemail.com.au)
Telstra BigPond (☎ 13 12 82; www.bigpond.com)

Australia uses RJ-45 telephone plugs and Telstra EXI-160 four-pin plugs, but neither are universal – electronics shops such as Tandy and Dick Smith should be able to help. You'll also need a plug adaptor, and a universal AC adaptor will enable you to plug in without frying the innards of your machine. Most midrange accommodation and all top-end hotels will have sockets but you'll be hit with expensive call charges. In cheaper places you'll probably find that phones are hardwired into the wall.

Keep in mind that your PC-card modem may not work in Victoria. The safest option is to buy a reputable 'global' modem before you leave home or buy a local PC-card modem once you get to Australia.

For a list of generally helpful websites, see p16.

LEGAL MATTERS

Most travellers won't have any contact with the Victorian police or any other part of the legal system. Those that do are likely to experience these while driving. There is a significant police presence on the region's roads, with the power to stop your car and ask to see your licence (you're required to carry it), to check your vehicle for road-worthiness, and also to insist that you take a breath test for alcohol – needless to say, drink-driving offences are taken very seriously here. In 2005 Victorian police conducted a year-long random drug testing trial that enabled them to stop drivers and test them for cannabis and methamphetamines. At the time of writing, it wasn't clear whether drug testing drivers would be permanently adopted in the state.

If you are arrested, it's your right to telephone a friend, relative or lawyer before any formal questioning begins. **Legal Aid** (www .legalaid.vic.gov.au) is available only in serious cases and only to the truly needy (for details see the website). However, many solicitors do not charge for an initial consultation.

MAPS

When you arrive in a new town, the local tourist office can usually be relied upon to dole out a free map, though the quality can vary. For more detailed maps, try the **Royal Automobile Club of Victoria** (RACV; www.racv.com .au), which has a stack of road maps available (including downloadable route maps). Prices for members/nonmembers are gen-

erally $4/7. For a more serious exploration of the state, pick up a copy of RACV's *Vicroads Country Street Directory of Victoria* (members/nonmembers $35/43).

Lonely Planet publishes the *Australia Road Atlas,* an easy-to-use, comprehensive book covering the entire country; and a handy fold-out city map of Melbourne.

Commercially available city street guides, such as the *Melways, Gregorys* and *UBD* are useful for in-depth urban navigation, but they're expensive, bulky and only worth getting if you intend to do a lot of city driving.

If you plan on bushwalking or taking part in other outdoor activities for which large-scale maps are an essential item, the Victorian state government produces the Vicmap Topographic 1:30,000 series, which covers the entire state. Maps in A4 size ($1.50 per mapsheet) are available online from **Land** (http://services.land.vic.gov.au/landchannel/content/).

MONEY

Money isn't a big issue for travellers in Victoria. There are Automated Teller Machines (ATMs) in most towns and all cities, as well as banks that will cash travellers cheques. As usual, the best bet for travellers is to bring a credit or debit card to withdraw money from ATMs, with perhaps a few travellers cheques or some hard cash as a back up.

See the Getting Started chapter, p16, for information on costs.

ATMs, Eftpos & Bank Accounts

ANZ, Commonwealth, National and Westpac bank branches (and branches of affiliated banks) are found throughout Victoria and many of them have 24-hour ATMs attached. Most ATMs accept cards from other banks and are linked to international networks.

Eftpos (Electronic Funds Transfer at Point Of Sale) is a convenient service that many Australian businesses have embraced. It means that you can use your bank card (credit or debit) to pay direct for services or purchases, and often withdraw cash as well. Eftpos is available practically everywhere these days, even in country roadhouses where it's a long way between banks. Just like an ATM, you need to know your Personal Identification Number (PIN) to use it.

COMING OF AGE

For the record:

■ learner drivers (L-platers) must be 16, while provisional drivers (P-platers) must be 18.

■ the legal age for voting in Australia is 18.

■ the heterosexual age of consent is 16.

■ the homosexual age of consent is 17.

■ the legal drinking age is 18.

Cash

Australia's currency is the Australian dollar, which is made up of 100 cents. There are 5c, 10c, 20c, 50c, $1 and $2 coins, and $5, $10, $20, $50 and $100 notes. Although the smallest coin in circulation is 5c, prices are often still marked in single cents, then rounded to the nearest 5c when you come to pay.

Credit Cards

Perhaps the best way to carry most of your money is in the form of a plastic card, especially if that's the way you do it at home. Australia is well and truly a card-carrying society – it's becoming unusual to line up at a supermarket checkout, petrol station or department store in cities and see someone actually paying with cash these days. Credit cards such as Visa and MasterCard are widely accepted for everything from a hostel bed or a restaurant meal to an adventure tour, and a credit card is pretty much essential (in lieu of a large deposit) if you want to hire a car. They can also be used to get cash advances over the counter at banks and from many ATMs, depending on the card, but be aware that these incur immediate interest. Charge cards such as Diners Club and American Express (Amex) are not as widely accepted.

Another option is a debit card with which you can draw money directly from your home bank account using ATMs, banks or Eftpos machines around the state. Any card connected to the international banking network – Cirrus, Maestro, Plus and Eurocard – should work, provided you know your PIN. Fees for using your card at a foreign bank or ATM vary depending on your home bank; ask before your leave.

The most flexible option is to carry both a credit and a debit card.

Moneychangers

Exchanging foreign currency or travellers cheques is usually no problem at banks throughout the state or at a licensed moneychanger such as American Express in Melbourne (see p69). Most large hotels will change currency or travellers cheques for their guests but the rates are generally poor.

The Australian dollar tends to fluctuate a bit against the greenback (US dollar). In recent years it has generally been pretty weak, though in mid-2004 it had peaked at US$0.80. See the Quick Reference page on the inside front cover for the exchange rate at the time of printing.

Taxes & Refunds

The Goods and Services Tax (GST) introduced by the federal government in 2000, amid much controversy, is a flat 10% tax on all goods and services – accommodation, eating out, transport, electrical and other goods, books, furniture, clothing and so on. There are, however, some exceptions, such as basic foods (milk, bread, fruits and vegetables etc). By law the tax is included in the quoted or shelf prices, so all prices in this book are GST-inclusive.

If you purchase new or second-hand goods with a total minimum value of $300 from any one supplier no more than 30 days before you leave Australia, you are entitled to a refund of any GST paid under the Tourist Refund Scheme (TRS). The scheme only applies to goods you take with you as hand luggage or wear onto the plane or ship. Also note that the refund is valid for goods bought from more than one supplier, but only if at least $300 is spent per supplier. For more details, contact the **Australian Customs Service** (☎ 1300 363 263; www.customs.gov.au).

Travellers Cheques

If your stay is short, then travellers cheques are safe and generally enjoy a better exchange rate than foreign cash in Australia. Also, if they are stolen (or you lose them), they can readily be replaced. There is, however, a fee for buying travellers cheques (usually 1% of the total amount) and there may be fees or commissions when you exchange them.

Amex, Thomas Cook and other well-known international brands of travellers cheques are easily exchanged. You need to present your passport for identification when cashing them.

Buying travellers cheques in Australian dollars is an option worth looking at. These can be exchanged immediately at banks without being converted from a foreign currency or incurring commissions, fees and exchange-rate fluctuations.

POST
Letters & Parcels

Australia's postal services are efficient and reasonably cheap. It costs 50c to send a standard letter or postcard within the country. **Australia**

Post (www.auspost.com.au) has divided international destinations into two regions: Asia-Pacific and Rest of the World; airmail letters up to 50g cost $1.20 and $1.80, respectively. The cost of a postcard (up to 20g) is $1.10 and an aerogram to any country is 95c.

There are five international parcel zones; rates vary by distance and class of service.

Sending & Receiving Mail

All post offices will hold mail for visitors, and some city GPOs (main or general post offices) have very busy poste restante sections. You must provide some identification (such as a passport) to collect mail. You can have mail sent to you at city Amex offices if you have an Amex card or travellers cheques.

See p395 for post office opening times.

SOLO TRAVELLERS

People travelling alone in Victoria face the unpredictability that is an inherent part of making contact with entire communities of strangers: sometimes you'll be completely ignored as if you didn't exist, and other times you'll be greeted with such enthusiasm it's as if you've been spontaneously adopted. Suffice to say that the latter moments will likely become highlights of your trip.

Solo travellers are common throughout Victoria and there is certainly no stigma attached to lone visitors. Women travelling on their own should exercise caution in less-populated areas, and will find that guys can be annoyingly attentive in drinking establishments; see also Women Travellers (p406).

TELEPHONE

Victoria's area code is ☎ 03. Dial this number first if calling from outside Victoria, but not for calls within Victoria (or to Tasmania). If dialling Australia from overseas, the country code is ☎ 61 and you don't need to dial the zero in Victoria's ☎ 03 area code.

There are a number of providers offering various services. The two main players are the mostly government-owned **Telstra** (www.telstra.com.au) and the fully private **Optus** (www.optus.com.au). Both are also major players in the mobile (cell) market, along with these others:

AAPT (www.aapt.com.au)

Orange (www.orange.net.au)

Vodafone (www.vodafone.com.au)

Domestic & International Calls
INFORMATION & TOLL-FREE CALLS

Numbers starting with ☎ 190 are usually recorded information services, charged at anything from 35c to $5 or more per minute (more from mobiles and payphones). To make a reverse-charge (collect) call from any public or private phone, just dial ☎ 1800-REVERSE (738 3773), or ☎ 12 550.

Toll-free numbers (prefix ☎ 1800) can be called free of charge from anywhere in Victoria, though they may not be accessible from certain areas or from mobile phones. Calls to numbers beginning with ☎ 13 or ☎ 1300 are charged at the rate of a local call. Telephone numbers beginning with either ☎ 1800, ☎ 13 or ☎ 1300 cannot be dialled from outside Australia.

INTERNATIONAL CALLS

Most payphones allow ISD (International Subscriber Dialling) calls; the cost and international dialling code will vary depending on which provider you're using. International calls from Australia are very cheap and subject to specials that reduce the rates even more, so it's worth shopping around.

Country Direct (☎ 1800 801 800) is a service which connects callers in Australia with operators in nearly 60 countries to make reverse-charge (collect) or credit-card calls.

When calling overseas you need to dial the international access code from Australia (☎ 0011 or ☎ 0018), the country code and the area code (without the initial 0). So for a London number you'd dial ☎ 0011-44-171, then the number. Also, certain operators will have you dial a special code to access their service.

Following is a list of some country codes:

Country	International country code
France	☎ 33
Germany	☎ 49
Japan	☎ 81
Netherlands	☎ 31
New Zealand	☎ 64
UK	☎ 44
USA & Canada	☎ 1

LOCAL CALLS

Calls from private phones cost 15c to 25c while local calls from public phones cost 40c; both involve unlimited talk time. Calls to mobile phones attract higher rates and are timed. Blue phones or gold phones that you sometimes find in hotel lobbies or other businesses usually cost a minimum of 50c for a local call.

LONG DISTANCE CALLS & AREA CODES

For long-distance calls, Australia uses four STD (Subscriber Trunk Dialling) area codes. STD calls can be made from virtually any public phone and are cheaper during off-peak hours, generally between 7pm and 7am. Long-distance calls (ie to more than about 50km away) within these areas are charged at long-distance rates, even though they have the same area code. Broadly, the following are the main area codes in Australia:

State/Territory	Area code
ACT	☎ 02
NSW	☎ 02
NT	☎ 08
Queensland	☎ 07
SA	☎ 08
Tasmania	☎ 03
Victoria	☎ 03
WA	☎ 08

Area code boundaries don't necessarily co-incide with state borders – in some border areas, Victoria uses the neighbouring code.

Mobile Phones

Local numbers with the prefixes ☎ 04xx or ☎ 04xxx belong to mobile phones. Australia's two mobile networks – digital GSM and digital CDMA – service more than 90% of the population, but vast tracts of the country are uncovered. The coastal areas and regional centres get good reception, but away from the major towns it can be haphazard or nonexistent.

Australia's digital network is compatible with GSM 900 and 1800 (used in Europe), but generally not with the systems used in the USA or Japan. It's easy and cheap enough to get connected short-term, though, as the main service providers (Telstra, Optus and Vodafone) all have prepaid mobile systems. Just buy a starter kit, which may include a phone or, if you have your own phone, a SIM card (around $15) and a prepaid charge card. The calls tend to be a bit more expensive than with standard

contracts, but there are no connection fees or line-rental charges and you can buy the recharge cards at convenience stores and newsagents. Don't forget to shop around between the three carriers as their products differ.

Phonecards

A wide range of phonecards is available, which can be bought at newsagents and post offices for a fixed dollar value (usually $10, $20, $30 etc) and can be used with any public or private phone by dialling a toll-free access number and then the PIN number on the card. Once again, it's well worth shopping around, as call rates vary from company to company. Some public phones also accept credit cards.

TIME

Victoria (along with Tasmania, New South Wales and Queensland) keeps Eastern Standard Time (GMT/UTC plus 10 hours).

When it's noon in Melbourne, it's 6pm the previous day in Los Angeles, 2am the same day in London, 4am in Cape Town, 10am in Perth (WA), 11am in Tokyo, 11.30am in Adelaide and Darwin, and noon in Brisbane, Sydney and Hobart. For more on international timing, go to **Time and Date** (www.timeanddate.com/worldclock).

In Victoria, clocks are put forward an hour for daylight-saving time on the last Sunday in October, and put back on the last Sunday in March.

TOURIST INFORMATION

For travel tips and information on Victoria as well as the other states and territories of Australia, contact the **Australian Tourism Commission** (ATC; ☎ 1300 361 650; www.australia.com).

For general state-wide information, try **Tourism Victoria** (☎ 13 28 42; www.visitvictoria.com.au; Federation Sq, Melbourne Vic 3000), which will quickly bury you knee-deep in brochures, booklets, maps and leaflets on places all over the state.

Elsewhere, information is available from regional and local tourist offices; in many cases they are very good, with friendly staff providing invaluable local knowledge are readily available in the city. However, many are underfunded and get by on the smell of an oily rag – so don't expect miracles. Details of local tourism offices are given in the relevant city and town sections throughout this book.

The **Royal Automobile Club of Victoria** (RACV; ☎ 13 19 55; www.racv.com.au; 422 Little Collins St, Melbourne Vic 3000) produces the excellent *Victoria Experience Guide,* full of accommodation and touring information.

TOURS

If you don't feel like travelling solo or you crave hassle-free travels with everything organised for you, there are literally dozens of tours through Victoria to suit all tastes and budgets. Recommended operators such as **Autopia Tours** (☎ 1800 000 507 or 03-9419 8878; www .autopiatours.com.au), **Go West** (☎ 9828 2008; www .gowest.com.au) and **Wild-Life Tours** (☎ 9741 6333; www.wildlifetours.com.au) offer day trips (starting from $65) to similar popular destinations, including the Great Ocean Rd, the Grampians and the Phillip Island Penguin Parade.

Activity-based tours are increasing in both number and popularity; the following is just a sample of the countless options on offer. For a more comprehensive list, contact **Tourism Victoria** (☎ 13 28 42; www.visitvictoria.com.au).

Echidna Walkabout (☎ 9646 8249; www.echidnawalk about.com.au) Runs nature eco-trips (from day trips to five-day expeditions) featuring bushwalking and koala spotting.

Eco Adventure Tours (☎ 5962 5115; www.hotkey.net .au/~ecoadven) Offers fascinating guided night walks in the Yarra Valley and the Dandenong Ranges. Ideal for animal lovers. See p172.

Ecotrek: Bogong Jack Adventures (☎ 08-8383 7198; www.ecotrek.com.au) Runs a wide range of cycling, canoeing and walking tours through the Grampians, Murray River and High Country regions.

Steamrail Victoria (☎ 9397 1953; www.steamrail.com .au) Gives visitors the chance to step back in time, catching heritage steam trains to various country destinations around the state.

If you're travelling between Melbourne and either Sydney or Adelaide and want to visit some of the highlights of Victoria along the way, there are some interesting hop-on hop-off bus tour alternative (see p411 for details). For an extensive list of tour options in Melbourne, see p113.

VISAS

All visitors to Australia need a visa. Only NZ nationals are exempt, and even they receive a 'special category' visa on arrival. The type of visa you require depends on the reason for your visit. Most travellers secure an Electronic Travel Authority (ETA) through their travel agent or overseas airline, valid for three months of holiday travel in Australia. The agent or airline makes the application direct when you buy a ticket and issues the ETA, which replaces the usual visa stamped in your passport – they may charge a fee for issuing an ETA, in the vicinity of US$15. This system is available to passport holders of some 33 countries, including the UK, the USA and Canada, most European countries, Malaysia, Singapore, Japan and Korea. You can also make an online ETA application at the **Australian Electronic Travel Authority** (www.eta .immi.gov.au), where no fees apply.

Check the website of the **Department of Immigration & Multicultural & Indigenous Affairs** (www.immi.gov.au) for information on visas, as well as on customs and health issues. Visa application forms are available on this website, or from Australian diplomatic missions overseas or travel agents, and you can apply by mail or in person.

WOMEN TRAVELLERS

Victoria is generally a safe place for women travellers, although the usual sensible precautions apply. It's best to avoid walking alone late at night in any of the major cities and towns. And if you're out on the town, always keep enough money aside for a taxi back to your accommodation. The same applies to rural towns where there are often a lot of unlit, semideserted streets between you and your temporary home. When the pubs and bars close and there are inebriated people roaming around, it's not a great time to be out and about. Lone women should also be wary of staying in basic pub accommodation unless it looks safe and well managed.

Aussie male culture does have its sexist elements, and sexual harassment does occur. If you do encounter infantile sexism from drunken louts, best you leave and choose a better place.

Lone female hitchers are tempting fate, and we don't recommend it – but if you must, hitching with a male companion is safer.

Transport

CONTENTS

GETTING THERE & AWAY

ENTERING THE COUNTRY

Disembarkation in Australia is generally a straightforward affair, with only the usual customs declarations (p397) and the fight to be first to the luggage carousel to endure. If you're flying in with Qantas, Air New Zealand, British Airways, Cathay Pacific, Japan Airlines or Singapore Airlines, ask the carrier about the 'Express' passenger card, which will speed your way through customs.

Recent global instability has resulted in conspicuously increased security in Australian airports, both in domestic and international terminals, and you may find that customs procedures are now more time-consuming.

AIR
International
AIRPORT & AIRLINES

There are lots of competing airlines and a wide variety of air fares to choose from if you're flying in from Asia, Europe or North America. Because of Australia's size and diverse climate, any time of year can prove busy for inbound tourists so make your arrangements well ahead.

THINGS CHANGE...

The information in this chapter is particularly vulnerable to change. Check directly with the airline or a travel agent to make sure you understand how a fare (and ticket you may buy) works and be aware of the security requirements for international travel. Shop carefully. The details given in this chapter should be regarded as pointers and are not a substitute for your own careful, up-to-date research.

Melbourne airport (www.melair.com.au) is in Tullamarine, 22km northwest of the city centre. While plenty of airlines have direct flights into Melbourne, many flights stop off in Sydney. Sydney's airport is stretched way beyond its capacity and flights are frequently delayed on arrival and departure. If possible, try to organise a direct flight to Melbourne.

Airlines that visit Australia include the following (note all phone numbers mentioned here are for dialling from within Australia).
Air Canada (AC; ☎ 1300 655 767; www.aircanada.ca) Flies to Sydney.
Air New Zealand (NZ; ☎ 13 24 76; www.airnz.com.au) Flies to Melbourne, Sydney, Brisbane, Cairns and Perth.
Air Paradise International (AD; ☎ 1300 799 066; www.airparadise.com.au) Flies to Melbourne, Sydney, Perth, Adelaide and Brisbane.
Australian Airlines (AO; ☎ 1300 799 798; http://australianairlines.com.au) Flies to Melbourne, Sydney, Perth, Cairns and Darwin.
British Airways (BA; ☎ 1300 767 177; www.britishairways.com.au) Flies to Sydney.
Cathay Pacific (CX; ☎ 13 17 47; www.cathaypacific.com.au) Flies to Melbourne, Perth, Adelaide, Sydney, Brisbane and Cairns.
Emirates (EK; ☎ 1300 303 777; www.emirates.com) Flies to Melbourne, Sydney, Perth and Brisbane.
Freedom Air (SJ; ☎ 1800 122 000; www.freedomair.com) Flies to Melbourne, Sydney and Brisbane.
Garuda Indonesia (GA; ☎ 1300 365 330; www.garuda-indonesia.com) Flies to Melbourne, Sydney, Perth and Brisbane.
Gulf Air (GF; ☎ 1300 366 337; www.gulfairco.com) Flies to Melbourne and Sydney.
Japan Airlines (JL; ☎ 03-8662 8333; www.jal.com) Flies to Melbourne, Sydney, Cairns and Brisbane.

TRANSPORT

DEPARTURE TAX

There is a A$38 departure tax when leaving Australia. This is included in the price of airline tickets.

KLM (KL; ☎ 1300 303 747; www.klm.com) Flies to Melbourne and Sydney.

Malaysia Airlines (MH; ☎ 13 26 27; www.malaysiaairlines.com.au) Flies to Sydney, Perth, Adelaide, Brisbane and Cairns.

Qantas (QF; ☎ 13 13 13; www.qantas.com.au) Flies to Melbourne, Sydney, Perth and Brisbane.

Royal Brunei Airlines (BI; ☎ 08-8941 0966; www.bruneiair.com) Flies to Sydney, Perth and Brisbane.

Singapore Airlines (SQ; ☎ 13 10 11; www.singaporeair.com.au) Flies to Melbourne, Sydney, Perth, Adelaide and Brisbane.

South African Airways (SA; ☎ 1800 221 699; www.flysaa.com) Flies to Sydney and Perth.

Thai Airways International (TG; ☎ 1300 651 960; www.thaiairways.com.au) Flies to Melbourne, Sydney, Perth and Brisbane.

United Airlines (UA; ☎ 13 17 77; www.unitedairlines.com.au) Flies to Melbourne and Sydney.

TICKETS

Be sure you research the options carefully to make sure you get the best deal. The Internet is an increasingly useful resource for checking airline prices.

Automated online ticket sales work well if you're doing a simple one-way or return trip on specified dates, but are no substitute for a travel agent with the lowdown on special deals, strategies for avoiding stopovers and other useful advice.

Paying by credit card offers some protection if you unwittingly end up dealing with a rogue fly-by-night agency in your search for the cheapest fare, as most card issuers provide refunds if you can prove you didn't get what you paid for. Alternatively, buy a ticket from a bonded agent, such as one covered by the **Air Travel Organiser's Licence** (ATOL; www.atol.org.uk) scheme in the UK. If you have doubts about the service provider, at the very least call the airline and confirm that your booking has been made.

Round-the-world (RTW) tickets can be a good option for getting to Australia, and Melbourne is an easy inclusion on your ticket.

For online bookings, start with the following websites.

Air Brokers (www.airbrokers.com) This US company specialises in cheap RTW tickets.

Cheap Flights (www.cheapflight.com) Very informative site with specials, airline information and flight searches from the USA and major European destinations.

Cheapest Flights (www.cheapestflights.co.uk) Cheap worldwide flights from the UK; get in early for the bargains.

Expedia (www.expedia.msn.com) Microsoft's travel site; mainly US-related.

Flight Centre International (www.flightcentre.com) Respected operator handling direct flights, with sites for Australia, New Zealand (NZ), the UK, the USA and Canada.

Flights.com (www.tiss.com) Truly international site for flight-only tickets; cheap fares and an easy-to-search database.

STA (www.statravel.com) Prominent in international student travel but you don't necessarily have to be a student; site linked to worldwide STA sites.

Travel Online (www.travelonline.co.nz) Good place to check flights from NZ.

Travel.com (www.travel.com.au) Good Australian site; look up fares and flights into and out of the country.

Travelocity (www.travelocity.com) US site that allows you to search fares (in US$) to/from practically anywhere.

Roundtheworld.com (www.roundtheworldflights.com) This excellent site allows you to build your own trips from the UK, with up to six stops.

ASIA

Most Asian countries offer fairly competitive air fare deals to Melbourne, with Bangkok, Singapore and Hong Kong being the best places to shop around for discount tickets.

Flights between Hong Kong and Melbourne are often heavily booked, and flights to/from Bangkok and Singapore are often part of the longer Europe–Australia route so they are also sometimes full. Plan ahead. Typical one-way fares to Melbourne are A$500 from Singapore, A$435 from Bangkok and A$1200 from Hong Kong.

You can get cheap flights between Melbourne and Denpasar in Bali (around A$890 return), a route serviced by several airlines including Qantas and Air Paradise International.

STA Travel has offices throughout Asia that can help with cheap flights:

STA Travel Bangkok (www.statravel.co.th)
STA Travel Singapore (www.statravel.com.sg)
STA Travel Tokyo (www.statravel.co.jp)

CANADA

Flight possibilities from Canada are similar to those from the USA, with most Toronto and Vancouver flights stopping in one US city such as Los Angeles or Honolulu before they continue on to Australia. Air Canada flies from Vancouver to Sydney via Honolulu and from Toronto to Melbourne via Honolulu.

Canadian discount air-ticket sellers are also known as consolidators and their air fares tend to be about 10% higher than those sold in the USA. **Travel Cuts** (☎ 1866 246 9762; www .travelcuts.com) is Canada's national student travel agency and has offices in all major cities.

Round-trip fares from Toronto to Melbourne cost from around C$1800/2400 in low/high season via the US west coast, while fares from Vancouver to Sydney cost from around C$1600/2000.

CONTINENTAL EUROPE

From the major destinations in Europe, most flights travel via one of the Asian capitals. Some flights are also routed through London before arriving in Australia via Singapore, Bangkok, Hong Kong or Kuala Lumpur.

Fares from Paris in the low/high season cost from €1000/1200. Some agents in Paris:

Nouvelles Frontières (☎ 08 25 00 08 25; www .nouvelles-frontieres.fr) Also has branches outside Paris.

OTU Voyages (☎ 01 40 29 12 12; www.otu.fr) Student/ youth oriented, with offices in many cities.

A good option in the Dutch travel industry is **Holland International** (☎ 070-307 6307; www.holland international.nl). From Amsterdam, return fares start at around €1500.

In Germany, good travel agencies include the Berlin branch of **STA Travel** (☎ 030-311 0950; www.statravel.de). Fares start at around €900/1000 in the low/high season.

NEW ZEALAND

Competition on the trans-Tasman routes has hotted up recently, with several airlines entering the market and offering cheap flights between Australia and NZ. Air New Zealand, Qantas, Emirates and Virgin Blue all offer cheap fares between Melbourne and NZ cities such as Auckland, Wellington and Christchurch. At the time of writing, discounted fares were available for as low as NZ$250 return.

To get good advice on up-to-date trans-Tasman options:

Flight Centre (☎ 0800 243 544; www.flightcentre.co.nz) Has a large central office in Auckland and many branches throughout the country.

Freedom Air (☎ 0800 600 500; www.freedomair.com) Air New Zealand subsidiary that offers flights from Palmerston North, Dunedin and Hamilton to Melbourne.

STA Travel (☎ 0508 782 872; www.statravel.co.nz) Has offices in various cities.

UK & IRELAND

There are two routes from the UK: the western route via the USA and the Pacific, and the eastern route via the Middle East and Asia. Flights are usually cheaper and more frequent on the latter. Some of the best deals around are with Emirates, Gulf Air, Malaysia Airlines, Japan Airlines and Thai Airways International. Unless there are special deals on offer, British Airways, Singapore Airlines and Qantas generally have higher fares but may offer a more direct route.

A popular agent in the UK is the ubiquitous **STA Travel** (☎ 0870-160 0599; www.statravel .co.uk).

Typical direct fares from London to Sydney are UK£400/650 one-way/return during the low season (March to June). In September and mid-December fares go up by as much as 30%, while the rest of the year they're somewhere in-between. High-season fares start at around UK£450/750 one way/return.

From Australia you can expect to pay around A$900/1650 one-way/return in the low season to London and other European capitals (with stops in Asia on the way) and A$1100/2050 in the high season.

USA

Airlines directly connecting Australia across the Pacific with Los Angeles or San Francisco include Qantas, Air New Zealand and United Airlines. There are also numerous airlines offering flights via Asia, with stopover possibilities including Tokyo, Kuala Lumpur, Bangkok, Hong Kong and Singapore; and via the Pacific with stopover possibilities like Nadi (Fiji), Rarotonga (Cook Islands), Tahiti (French Polynesia) and Auckland (NZ).

As in Canada, discount travel agents in the USA are known as consolidators. San Francisco is the ticket consolidator capital of America, although some good deals can be found in Los Angeles, New York and other big cities.

STA Travel (☎ 800-781 4040; www.statravel.com) has offices around the country, and can assist with tickets.

Typically you can get a return ticket to Melbourne or Sydney from the US west coast for US$1300/1700 in the low/high season, or from the east coast for US$1600/1900. Return low/high-season fares from Melbourne to the US west coast cost around A$1750/1850, and to New York A$1800/1950.

Domestic
AIRPORTS & AIRLINES

The major domestic carrier is Qantas, while Richard Branson's highly competitive Virgin Blue also offers flights all over Australia – it's great value if you don't mind the cabin crew's corny scripted jokes and the lack of free food service (though you can purchase light snacks and drinks from an inflight menu). Virgin's success in the early noughties forced Qantas to reassess its competitiveness, and in May 2004 it launched Jetstar Airways, a low-cost airline that competes with Virgin Blue for the lucrative holiday market. Though all three airlines operate regular flights between Melbourne and other capital cities, they do not offer a service within the state (for flights within Victoria, see p412).

Qantas, Virgin and many Jetstar flights depart from **Melbourne airport** (www.melair.com.au) in Tullamarine, but Jetstar also offers some flights from **Avalon airport** (www.avalonairport.com .au) in Melbourne's west. All airports and domestic flights are nonsmoking.

Jetstar (JQ; ☎ 13 15 38; www.jetstar.com.au) Flies to Brisbane, Cairns, Gold Coast, Hamilton Island, Hobart, Launceston, Newcastle, Sunshine Coast and Sydney.

Qantas (QF; ☎ 13 13 13; www.qantas.com.au) Flies to Adelaide, Alice Springs, Brisbane, Cairns, Canberra, Darwin, Gold Coast, Hobart, Perth and Sydney, plus many smaller centres.

Virgin Blue (DJ; ☎ 13 67 89; www.virginblue.com.au) Flies to Adelaide, Brisbane, Cairns, Canberra, Gold Coast, Hobart, Launceston, Newcastle, Perth, Sunshine Coast, Sydney and the Whitsundays.

FARES

Few people pay full fare on domestic travel, as the airlines offer a wide range of discounts. These come and go and there are regular special fares, so keep your eyes open.

Qantas and Virgin Blue both offer similar discounted one-way and return domestic fares. At the time of writing, Jetstar fares were a slightly better deal, but with such strong competition, the situation is likely to keep changing (see the websites for the latest deals).

Advance-purchase deals provide the cheapest air fares. Some advance-purchase fares offer up to 33% discount off one-way fares and up to 50% or more off return fares. You have to book one to four weeks ahead, and you often have to stay away for at least one Saturday night. There are restrictions on changing flights and you can lose up to 100% of the ticket price if you cancel, although you can buy health-related cancellation insurance. The airlines offer discounts to those who purchase tickets over the Internet.

There are also special deals available only to foreign visitors (in possession of an outbound ticket). If booked in Australia, these fares offer a 40% discount off a full-fare economy ticket. They can also be booked from overseas (which usually works out a bit cheaper).

LAND
Border Crossings

The two most commonly used entry points into Victoria from New South Wales (NSW) are Albury/Wodonga on the Hume Hwy; and the Princes Hwy crossing further east on the coast near Victoria's Genoa and NSW's Eden. From South Australia (SA), the most scenic border entry point is on the Princes Hwy near Mt Gambier, but further north there's also a crossing on the Western Hwy between SA's Bordertown and Victoria's Nhill. Other crossing points from regional NSW include Mildura and Echuca.

Before crossing a state border into Victoria, remember to eat or dump any fruit (and vegetables such as cucumbers, chillies, zucchinis and capsicums). This precaution is to avoid the spread of pests and diseases from one part of Australia to another, particularly fruit fly.

Bus

Travelling by bus is often the cheapest way to get to Victoria from other Australian mainland states, but bus travel can be slow and tedious.

Greyhound Australia (☎ 13 14 99; www.greyhound .com.au) runs regular services to the interstate capitals and major regional centres. Major interstate routes/fares (one way) from Melbourne include the following:

Destination	Fare (A$)	Distance (km)
Adelaide	54	741
Brisbane	191	1800
Sydney	64	926
Darwin via Adelaide	503	3876

Another option is **Firefly Express** (☎ 1300 730 740, 9317 9312; www.fireflyexpress.com.au), which operates in Victoria, SA and NSW. Sample fares: from Sydney to Melbourne $60, from Melbourne to Adelaide $50.

BACKPACKER BUSES

If you're travelling between Melbourne and either Sydney or Adelaide, you'll miss some great countryside if you fast-track down the main highways, but there are some fun and scenic alternatives. The hop-on hop-off bus options are a particularly popular way for travellers to get around in a fun, relaxed atmosphere and meet like-minded people on the road.

The tours listed here travel scenic routes, take in the major sights along the way and usually stop at backpacker accommodation. Some of them also allow for stopovers along the way.

Autopia Tours (☎ 1800 000 507; www.autopiatours.com.au) The Sydney to Melbourne tour goes via the Blue Mountains, Canberra and the Snowy Mountains (a fairly packed 3½ days) for $185. There's also a three-day Adelaide to Melbourne tour that goes via the Great Ocean Rd, the Twelve Apostles and the Grampians National Park for $170.

Groovy Grape (☎ 1800 661 177; www.groovygrape.com.au) Has three-day trips between Adelaide and Melbourne, taking in the Great Ocean Rd and the Grampians, for $260.

Oz Experience (☎ 1300 300 028; www.ozexperience.com) This backpackers' bus line is a hop-on hop-off bus with a party atmosphere, suited to young travellers. Offers trips from Sydney to Melbourne and along the coastal road to Adelaide.

Wayward Bus (☎ 1300 653 510; www.waywardbus.com.au) Runs a variety of routes through southeastern Australia, most of them connecting Melbourne with Adelaide or Sydney. Its Classic Coast tour between Melbourne and Adelaide, along the Great Ocean Rd, costs $295 including hostel accommodation.

Wildlife Tours (☎ 9741 6333; www.wildlifetours.com.au) Offers tours between Melbourne and Adelaide from $145, and Melbourne and Sydney from $145.

PASSES

If you're planning to travel around Australia, check out Greyhound Australia's excellent Aussie Passes. The Greyhound Aussie Kilometre Pass is purchased in kilometre blocks, starting at 2000km ($328) and increasing in 1000km blocks up to 10,000km ($1259); 5000km costs $681 and 8000km $1018. You can get off at any point on the scheduled route and have unlimited stopovers within the life of the pass. Backtracking is also allowed.

Australian and international students, VIP and Nomads cards holders and children under 14 receive 10% discounts on passes.

Car & Motorcycle

If you're planning to drive between Sydney and Melbourne you have a choice of either the Hume Hwy (870km, and freeway most of the way) or the coastal Princes Hwy (1039km, much longer and slower but also much more scenic). There's a similar choice if you're travelling between Melbourne and Adelaide, with either the fairly direct Western Hwy (730km) or the slower Princes Hwy coastal route (894km), the first section of which is known as the Great Ocean Rd. If you're travelling between Brisbane and Melbourne, the quickest route is via the Newell Hwy (1890km).

See p413 for details of road rules, driving conditions and information on buying and renting vehicles.

Train

Rail travel in Australia is something you do because you really want to – not because it's cheaper or more convenient, and certainly not because it's fast. That said, trains are more comfortable than buses, and on some of Australia's long-distance train journeys the romance of the rails is alive and kicking.

Great Southern Railway (☎ 13 21 47; www.gsr.com.au) operates the three major long-haul services in the country, including the *Overland* (Adelaide to Melbourne). The *Overland* train runs during the day from Adelaide to Melbourne (per adult/child $59/34, 11 hours, four weekly). You can take your car on this journey for $219. There's also an overnight service from Melbourne to Adelaide (per adult/child seats $59/34, sleepers $149/94; 10 hours; four weekly). From Adelaide, there are connecting rail services to/from Alice Springs and Perth.

Victoria's **V/Line** (☎ 13 61 96; www.vline.com .au) runs train services around the state (see p417), but also offers an economy service to Adelaide (adult/child $62/31) and Canberra ($59/37).

Countrylink (☎ 13 22 32; www.countrylink.nsw.gov .au) runs XPT (express) trains between Melbourne and Sydney (economy/1st class/1st-class sleeper $115/162/243, 11 hours, two daily), with one morning and one evening departure daily in each direction.

SEA
Ferry
The **Spirit of Tasmania** (☎ 1800 634 906; www.spirit oftasmania.com.au) cruises nightly between Melbourne and Devonport on Tasmania's north coast. At 9pm nightly year-round, one ferry departs from Port Melbourne's Station Pier and the other departs from the terminal on the Esplanade in Devonport, with both arriving at their destinations across Bass Strait at around 7am the next morning. Additional daytime sailings are scheduled during the peak summer period (from mid-December to mid-January). These daytime sailings depart at 9am, arriving at 6pm. There is a wide variety of fares available, from hostel accommodation to 1st-class suites. One-way low-season fares range from $108 to $295 per adult and $82 to $295 per child. High-season fares range from $145 to $383 per adult, and $110 to $383 per child. Car fares per low/high season start at $10/55, motorcycles are $5/38, and bicycles are free/$6.

GETTING AROUND

AIR
Because of the state's compact size, scheduled internal flights are somewhat limited. Airlines that link Melbourne with a handful of regional centres around the state include the following:

QantasLink (QF; ☎ 13 13 13; www.qantas.com) Flies to Mildura and Mt Hotham. Also offers flights to Burnie and Devonport. Book through Qantas.

Regional Express (ZL; ☎ 13 17 13; www.regional express.com.au) Regional Express flies to Albury, Mildura and Portland. Also offers flights to Burnie, Devonport, King Island and Mt Gambier.

There are also several small private airlines that fly to selected destinations – see the Getting There & Away sections in the regional chapters for details.

BICYCLE
Victoria is a great place for cycling. There are numerous designated bike tracks in Melbourne, rail trails in several parts of the state, and thousands of kilometres of good country roads that carry little traffic. Especially appealing is that in some areas you'll ride a very long way without encountering a hill. If you're silly enough to *like* hills, the High Country in summer will be paradise.

If you're coming to Victoria specifically to cycle, it makes sense to bring your own bike. Check your airline for costs and the degree of dismantling/packing required. If it's not practical to bring your own, you can buy a reasonable touring bike from about $600. Alternatively, many Melbourne bicycle shops hire out bikes (see p108).

You can get by with standard road maps almost everywhere in Victoria, but these don't show topography so you might want to use 1:250,000 topographic maps. If you're mountain biking off the beaten track you'll want 1:100,000 or 1:50,000 maps. Specialty map shop **Map Land** (☎ 9670 4383; www.mapland .com.au; 372 Little Bourke St, Melbourne) sells an extensive range of topographic maps for sporty types.

It can get very hot in summer, and you should take things slowly until you're used to the heat. Cycling in 35°C-plus temperatures isn't too bad if you wear a helmet with a visor and plenty of sunscreen and drink *lots* of water. Be aware of the blistering hot 'northerlies', the prevailing winds that make a north-bound cyclist's life uncomfortable in summer. In April, when the clear autumn weather begins, the southerly trades prevail.

Note that cyclists are subject to most of the same road rules as drivers in Victoria. Running a red light could cost you a $200 fine and riding in a tramway could set you back $75. You must wear an approved helmet when cycling or you risk a $50 fine. For an overview of relevant road rules, contact **Bicycle Victoria** (☎ 1800 639 634; www.bv.com.au). For more information about cycling options in the state, see p45.

BUS

Victoria's regional bus network is a relatively cheap and reliable way to get around, though it can be a tedious form of transport at times and requires planning if you intend to do more than straightforward city-to-city trips. Most buses are equipped with air-con, toilets and videos, and all are smoke-free zones. The smallest towns eschew formal bus terminals for a single drop-off/pick-up point, usually outside a post office, newsagent or shop.

Along with its limited network of trains, **V/Line** (☎ 13 61 96; www.vline.com.au) operates extensive bus services within country Victoria. In Melbourne, the long-distance buses operate out of the coach terminal at Southern Cross train station (formerly Spencer St station). **Viclink** (www.viclink.com.au) is a comprehensive online guide to public transport throughout the state, and can help with timetables, fares and general information.

There are also many smaller bus companies operating locally – see the Getting There & Away sections in the regional chapters for details. For information on bus travel in and around Melbourne, see p146. Backpacker Buses, p411, are another method of getting around the state.

Unless otherwise specified, we quote one-way bus fares in the regional chapters.

CAR & MOTORCYCLE

There is no doubt that travelling by car is the best option in Victoria, as it gives you the freedom to explore off the beaten track. With several people travelling together, costs are reasonable and there are many benefits.

Motorcycles are a popular way of getting around Victoria. The climate is just about ideal for biking most of the year, though it might not always be dry (bring your rain gear) and winters can get chilly. Favoured motorcycle touring areas include the Great Ocean Rd, the Grampians, the upper reaches of the Murray River, east of Albury-Wodonga, the Grand Ridge Rd (p363) in South Gippsland, and the southeastern coast. The wild mountain country northeast of Melbourne offers hidden townships and stunning scenery to those who don't mind gravel roads. For long, empty roads and big skies, put your feet up on the highway pegs and head for the northwest.

Bringing your own motorcycle into Australia will entail an expensive shipping exercise, valid registration in the country of origin and a *Carnet de Passages en Douanes*. This is an internationally recognised customs document that allows the holder to import their vehicle without paying customs duty or taxes. To get one, apply to a motoring organisation/association in your home country. You'll also need a riders licence and a helmet.

Signposting along the major routes is usually adequate, though if you're planning to explore in any depth you'll need a decent road map or two. The **RACV** (☎ 13 19 55; www.racv.com.au) produces a *Victoria State Map* (member/nonmember $4/7) as well as a comprehensive and accurate series of district maps. For more serious exploration, pick up a copy of RACV's *Vicroads Country Street Directory of Victoria* ($35/43). If you plan on restricting your explorations to the Melbourne area, the best source is the *Greater Melbourne Street Directory* ($37/41).

There aren't many places in Victoria you can't get to in a conventional car. However, a 4WD will give you full access to the more remote national parks and state forests.

Automobile Associations

The **Royal Automobile Club of Victoria** (RACV; ☎ 13 19 55; www.racv.com.au) provides an emergency breakdown service, literature, excellent maps and detailed guides to accommodation. It can advise you on regulations you should be aware of and give general guidelines about buying a car.

There are RACV offices around the state, and almost every town has a garage affiliated with the RACV. Membership to the RACV costs from $66 to $161 per year, depending upon the extent of service you'd like to be eligible for, plus a $38 joining fee.

Driving Licence

You can generally use your own home-country's driving licence in Victoria, as long as it carries your photograph for identification and is in English (if it's not, you'll need a certified translation). Alternatively, it's a simple matter to arrange an International Driving Permit (IDP), which should be supported by your home licence. Just go to your home country's automobile association and it can issue you one on the spot.

The permits are valid for 12 months, and cost approximately $20.

Fuel

Fuel (super, diesel and unleaded) is available from service stations sporting the well-known international brand names. LPG (gas) is not always stocked at more remote roadhouses – if you're on gas it's safer to have dual fuel capacity. Prices vary from place to place and from price war to price war, but basically fuel is heavily taxed and prices continue to rise, much to the shock and disgust of Australian motorists. At the time of writing, unleaded petrol (used in most new cars) was hovering around $1 to $1.15 a litre, even in the cities. Once you get out into the country, prices soar.

Hire

4WD & CAMPERVANS

Renting a 4WD enables you to get right off the beaten track and out to some of the natural wonders that most travellers miss, particularly the Little Desert National Park in the central west, and parts of the high country and Gippsland regions.

Check the insurance conditions carefully, especially the excess, as they can be onerous. Even for a 4WD, the insurance offered by most companies does not cover damage caused when travelling 'off-road', which basically means anything that is not a maintained bitumen or dirt road.

Hertz, Budget and Avis have 4WD rentals. **Britz Rentals** (☎ 1800 331 454; www.britz.com) hires fully equipped 4WDs fitted out as campervans. Several other companies rent out campervans, including **Backpacker Campervans** (☎ 1800 670 232; www.backpackercampervans.com).

CAR

Competition between car-rental companies in Australia is pretty fierce, so rates tend to be variable and lots of special deals come and go. The main thing to remember when assessing your options is distance – if you want to travel far, you need unlimited kilometres.

As well as the big firms, there are a vast number of local firms, or firms with outlets in a limited number of locations. These are almost always cheaper than the big operators – sometimes half the price – but cheap car-hire can often come with serious restrictions.

The big firms sometimes offer one-way rentals, but there are a variety of limitations, including a substantial drop-off fee. Ask plenty of questions about this before deciding on one company over another.

The major companies offer a choice: either unlimited kilometres, or 100km or so a day free plus so many cents per kilometre over this. Daily rates in cities or larger centres are typically about $55 to $60 a day for a small car (Holden Barina, Ford Festiva, Hyundai Excel), about $65 to $80 a day for a medium car (Mitsubishi Magna, Toyota Camry, Nissan Pulsar), or $85 to $100 a day for a big car (Holden Commodore, Ford Falcon), all including insurance. You must be at least 21 years old to hire from most firms – if you're under 25 you may only be able to hire a small car or have to pay a surcharge. It's cheaper if you rent for a week or more and there are often low-season and weekend discounts. Credit card is the usual payment method.

Major companies all have offices or agents in most cities and towns.

Avis (☎ 13 63 33; www.avis.com.au)
Budget (☎ 1300 362 848; www.budget.com.au)
Delta Europcar (☎ 1800 030 118; www.deltaeuropcar .com.au)
Hertz (☎ 13 30 39; www.hertz.com.au)
Thrifty (☎ 13 61 39; www.thrifty.com.au)

Another option for those flying into Melbourne is **Airport Rent A Car** (☎ 1800 331 220; www .airportrentacar.com.au), which offers a small car with limited kilometres from around $55 per day, or $30 per day for a minimum of 10 days.

If you want short-term car hire, smaller local companies are generally the cheapest and are pretty reliable. You can usually get a small car with limited kilometres from $32 a day. **Apex** (☎ 1800 804 392; www.apexrentacar .au) is a good-value company with an office in Melbourne.

MOTORCYCLES

Garner's Motorcycles (☎ 9326 8676; www.garnersmotor cycles.com.au; 179 Peel St, North Melbourne) has Victoria's largest range of trail bikes and large road bikes for rent. Sample daily/weekly rates include $132/545 for a Yamaha TTR 250 trail bike, $132/616 for a Honda SL 250 road/trail bike, and $198/1078 for a Honda Hornet 600 road bike.

Insurance

In Australia, third-party personal injury insurance is always included in the vehicle registration cost. This ensures that every registered vehicle carries at least minimum insurance. You'd be wise to extend that minimum to at least third-party property insurance as well – minor collisions with other vehicles can be amazingly expensive.

When it comes to hire cars, know exactly what your liability is in the event of an accident. Rather than risk paying out thousands of dollars if you do have an accident, you can take out your own comprehensive insurance on the car, or (the usual option) pay an additional daily amount to the rental company for an 'insurance excess reduction' policy. This brings the amount of excess you must pay in the event of an accident down from between $2000 and $5000 to a few hundred dollars.

Be aware that if you're travelling on dirt roads you will not be covered by insurance unless you have a 4WD – in other words, if you have an accident you'll be liable for all the costs involved. Also, most companies' insurance won't cover the cost of damage to glass (including the windscreen) or tyres. Always read the small print.

Purchase

If you're planning a stay of several months involving lots of driving, buying a second-hand car will be much cheaper than renting one. But remember that reliability is all-important. You'll probably get any car cheaper by buying privately through newspaper ads (try the *Age* classifieds on Wednesday or Saturday, or the weekly *Trading Post*) rather than through a car dealer. Buying through a dealer does have the advantage of some sort of guarantee, but this might not be much use if you plan to take the car to another state.

When you come to buy or sell a car, there are usually some local regulations to be complied with. See the **VicRoads** (www.vicroads.vic.gov .au) website for details. In Victoria, a car has to have a compulsory safety check and a Road Worthiness Certificate (RWC) before it can be registered in the new owner's name – usually the seller will indicate if the

car already has a RWC. Don't let yourself be talked into buying a vehicle without a RWC – unless you're a mechanic, it almost *always* turns out to be much more hassle than it's worth. Stamp duty has to be paid when you buy a car; as this is based on the purchase price, it's not unknown for the buyer and the seller to agree privately to understate the price.

There are often cheap cars on offer at hostels and other places travellers hang out. Many of these have been around Australia a few times and haven't exactly been well looked after. To avoid buying a lemon, you might consider forking out some extra money for a vehicle appraisal before purchase. The **RACV** (☎ 13 19 55; www.racv.com.au) offers this kind of check in Melbourne and other large Victorian centres for around $130/170 for members/nonmembers; it also offers a comprehensive *Car Buying Guide* on its website.

If you'd like to buy your own motorcycle and have a little bit of time on your hands, getting mobile on two wheels in Australia is quite feasible. The beginning of winter (June) is a good time to start looking. Good starting points are the monthly *Motorcycle Trader* magazine and the **BikePoint** (http://bikepoint.nine msn.com.au) website.

Road Conditions

On all main routes, roads are well surfaced and have two lanes. You don't have to get far off the beaten track, however, to find yourself on unsealed roads, and anybody who sets out to see the country in reasonable detail should expect some dirt-road travelling. A 2WD car can cope with a limited amount of this, but if you want to do some serious exploration, then you'd better plan on having a 4WD and a winch.

Driving on unsealed roads requires special care – a car will perform differently when braking and turning on dirt. Under no circumstances should you exceed 80km/h on dirt roads; if you go faster you will not have enough time to respond to a sharp turn, stock on the road or an unmarked gate or cattle grid. So take it easy: Take time to see the sights and don't try to break the land speed record!

Motorcyclists should beware of dehydration in the dry, hot air – carry at least 5L of water on remote roads and drink plenty of it, even if you don't feel thirsty. If riding in southern and eastern Victoria, you should be prepared for rotten weather in winter and rain at any time of year. It's worth carrying some spares and tools even if you don't know how to use them, because someone else often does. Carry a workshop manual for your bike and spare elastic (octopus) straps for securing your gear.

Road Hazards

The 'road-kill' that you unfortunately see a lot of alongside roads in many parts of Victoria is mostly the result of cars and trucks hitting animals during the night. Many Australians avoid travelling altogether once the sun drops because of the risks posed by animals on the roads.

Kangaroos and wombats are common hazards on country roads, as are cows and sheep – hitting an animal of this size can make a real mess of your car. Kangaroos are most active around dawn and dusk. They often travel in groups, so if you see one hopping across the road in front of you,

slow right down, as its friends may be just behind it.

If you're travelling at night and a large animal appears in front of you, hit the brakes, dip your lights (so you don't continue to dazzle and confuse it) and only swerve if it's safe to do so – numerous travellers have been killed in accidents caused by swerving to miss animals.

A not-so-obvious hazard is driver fatigue. Driving long distances (particularly in hot weather) can be so tiring that you might fall asleep at the wheel – it's not uncommon. So on a long haul, stop and rest every two hours or so – do some exercise, change drivers or have a coffee.

Road Rules

Driving in Victoria holds few real surprises, other than the odd animal caught in your headlights. Cars are driven on the left-hand side of the road (as they are in the rest of Australia). An important road rule is 'give way to the right' – if an intersection is unmarked (unusual), you must give way to vehicles entering the intersection from your right.

Road Distances (km)

	Albury	Apollo Bay	Ballarat	Bendigo	Bairnsdale	Geelong	Horsham	Mallacoota	Melbourne	Mildura	Morwell	Orbost	Port Campbell	Portland	Sale	Shepparton	Wangaratta	Warrnambool
Albury	---																	
Apollo Bay	564	---																
Ballarat	417	173	---															
Bendigo	297	293	120	---														
Bairnsdale	335	460	389	433	---													
Geelong	382	110	87	207	352	---												
Horsham	530	381	189	233	576	276	---											
Mallacoota	520	703	630	669	231	593	818	---										
Melbourne	306	185	112	151	277	76	300	518	---									
Mildura	622	654	464	408	830	551	313	946	553	---								
Morwell	453	334	258	298	128	223	447	358	149	706	---							
Orbost	376	554	485	525	87	450	674	144	374	802	215	---						
Port Campbell	570	103	153	273	563	166	294	794	286	607	435	650	---					
Portland	671	269	256	349	633	218	216	864	523	523	505	720	166	---				
Sale	399	398	320	360	64	285	509	294	213	766	64	165	499	569	---			
Shepparton	176	423	243	123	411	254	356	600	187	465	336	456	407	470	387	---		
Wangaratta	72	435	345	225	309	310	458	498	250	567	333	354	476	570	443	102	---	
Warrnambool	571	169	178	298	538	188	245	782	264	539	411	638	66	95	473	421	498	---

The general speed limit in built-up areas is 50km/h – keep an eye out for signs. Near schools, the limit is 40km/h in the morning and afternoon. On the open highway it's usually 100km/h or 110km/h. The police have speed radar guns and are very fond of using them in carefully concealed locations – don't exceed the speed limit as the boys and girls in blue may be waiting for you.

Police also use cameras to bust speeders, so you can be fined for speeding even if you're never pulled over, which can be a new experience for foreign visitors. If you're caught for speeding while driving a rental vehicle, the rental company will pass the ticket on to you and charge you an extortionate fee for processing. All told, it's probably better to stick to posted limits.

Oncoming drivers who flash their lights at you may be giving you a friendly warning of a speed camera ahead – or they may be telling you that your headlights are not on. Whatever, it's polite to wave back if someone does this. Try not to get caught doing it yourself, since it's illegal.

Seat belts are compulsory – you'll be fined if you don't use them. Children must be strapped into an approved safety seat. Talking on a hand-held mobile phone while driving is illegal.

Don't drink and drive – the blood-alcohol limit of 0.05% is strictly enforced by the police. Random breath tests occur throughout the state and penalties are severe, including losing your licence and having to pay a heavy fine. Probationary and learner drivers must display 'P' and 'L' plates and maintain a blood-alcohol reading of zero. In 2005 Victorian police ran a year-long random drug testing trial that enabled them to stop drivers and test them for cannabis and methamphetamines. Though described as 'random' testing, the police made no secret of their primary targets – long-distance truck drivers and party guys and gals driving home from raves. At the time of writing, it wasn't clear whether drug testing drivers would be permanently adopted in the state, but it seemed likely.

Melbourne has a notoriously confusing road rule, known as the 'hook turn', for getting trams through the city centre without being blocked by turning cars (see p145 for more information).

PARKING

One of the big problems with driving around big cities like Melbourne is finding somewhere to park. Even if you do find a spot there's likely to be a time restriction: meter or ticket machine, or both. It's one of the great rorts in Australia that overstaying your welcome (even by five minutes) in a space that may cost only a few dollars to park in, will see local councils fining you anywhere from $50 to $120. Also note that if you park in a 'clearway' your car will be towed away or clamped – look for signs. In Melbourne there are large multistorey car parks where you can park all day for between $10 and $25.

HITCHING

Hitching is never entirely safe in any country in the world, and we don't recommend it. Travellers who decide to hitch should understand that they are taking a small but potentially serious risk. People who do choose to hitch will be safer if they travel in pairs and let someone know where they are planning to go.

In Australia the hitching signal can be a thumbs up, but a downward-pointed finger is more widely understood.

LOCAL TRANSPORT

Melbourne's public transport system of buses, trains and trams is privatised. For timetable and fare information, contact **Metlink** (☎ 13 16 38; www.metlinkmelbourne.com.au); see also the Melbourne chapter, p146.

The larger towns and cities in Victoria have their own local bus systems. These usually operate from the main train station, or, where this doesn't exist, from the main long-distance coach terminal. If the town is large enough to warrant having a taxi fleet, taxis will be found here as well. Local buses are usually timed to meet train departures and arrivals. Unfortunately, because of the lack of passengers, there may be only one or two departures each day, and services may be nonexistent on weekends.

For more on local transport, see the Getting Around sections of the destination chapters of this book.

TRAIN

Victoria's internal rail network, operated by **V/Line** (☎ 13 61 96; www.vline.com.au), is limited to a handful of services to major regional

TRANSPORT

centres around Victoria. However, one of the state government's election commitments was to improve the regional train network, introducing high-speed trains and returning some long-lost train services to country Victoria. In mid-2004, trains began operating to Bairnsdale and Ararat, and at the time of writing the government was promising to restore services to Mildura and South Gippsland as soon as track and signal upgrades were completed.

In Melbourne, long-distance trains operate out of the redeveloped **Southern Cross Station** (☎ 9619 2389). Extensive building and renovations have meant that services have been shuffled around, so give yourself plenty of time to buy your ticket and find the correct platform. Melbourne's local Met services operate from Flinders Street Station, but a V/Line ticket is valid for service between the two. **Viclink** (www.viclink.com.au) can help with timetables, fares and general information. Most services do not require a reservation, although you will need one if you're travelling on an interstate train (see p411).

One-way economy fares are quoted throughout this book; 1st-class fares are around 30% more than economy fares, and return fares are double the one-way fare. For the extra 30%, you'll travel with a little more space and comfort than you will in economy.

There are various special deals on return fares, most of which give a discount of about 30%. Off-Peak Saver fares are available for travel on weekdays between Melbourne and a wide range of destinations including Bendigo, Bairnsdale, Geelong, Warrnambool and Ballarat. Hours of travel are restricted to off-peak times (no arrivals in Melbourne before 9.30am, and no departures from Melbourne between 4pm and 6pm).

Major routes with economy fares (one way) from Melbourne include the following:

Destination	Adult/Child Fare ($)
Ararat	65/32
Bairnsdale	82/41
Ballarat	33/17
Castlemaine	36/18
Echuca	65/32
Geelong	20/10
Swan Hill	104/52
Warrnambool	82/41

Health Dr David Millar

Australia is a remarkably healthy country in which to travel. Tropical diseases, such as malaria and yellow fever, are unknown, and diseases of insanitation, such as cholera and typhoid, are unheard of. Thanks to Australia's isolation and quarantine standards, even some animal diseases, such as rabies and foot-and-mouth disease, have yet to be recorded.

Few travellers to Victoria will experience anything worse than an upset stomach or a bad hangover, and if you do fall ill the standard of hospitals and health care is high.

BEFORE YOU GO

Since most vaccines don't produce immunity until at least two weeks after they're given, visit a physician four to eight weeks before departure. Ask your doctor for an International Certificate of Vaccination (otherwise known as 'the yellow booklet'), which will list all the vaccinations you've received. This is mandatory for countries that require proof of yellow fever vaccination upon entry (sometimes required in Australia, see right), but it's a good idea to carry a record of all your vaccinations wherever you travel.

Bring medications in their original, clearly labelled, containers. A signed and dated letter from your physician describing your medical conditions and medications, including generic names, is also a good idea. If carrying syringes or needles, be sure to have a physician's letter documenting their medical necessity.

INSURANCE

Health insurance is essential for all travellers. While health care in Australia is of a high standard and is not overly expensive by international standards, considerable costs can build up and repatriation is extremely expensive. Make sure your existing health insurance will cover you – if not, consider getting extra insurance. Find out in advance if your insurance plan will make payments directly to providers or reimburse you later for overseas health expenditures. (In Australia, as in many countries, doctors expect payment at the time of consultation. Make sure you get an itemised receipt detailing the service and keep contact details for the health provider. See p420 for details of health care in Victoria.)

RECOMMENDED VACCINATIONS

Proof of yellow fever vaccination is required only from travellers entering Australia within six days of having stayed overnight or longer in a yellow fever–infected country. For a full list of these countries visit the website of the **World Health Organization** (www.who.int).

If you're *really* worried about health when travelling, there are a few vaccinations you could consider for Australia: diphtheria, tetanus, measles, mumps, rubella, chickenpox and polio, as well as hepatitis B. Most travellers wouldn't bother with those for Australia, but when you're planning your travel is a great time to ensure that all routine vaccination cover is complete.

MEDICAL CHECKLIST

For those who are extra vigilant about health while travelling, or intend to spend time in remote areas:

- antibiotics
- antidiarrhoeal drugs (eg loperamide)
- acetaminophen/paracetamol or aspirin
- anti-inflammatory drugs (eg ibuprofen)
- antihistamines (for hay fever and allergic reactions)
- antibacterial ointment for cuts and abrasions

- steroid cream or cortisone (for poison ivy and other allergic rashes)
- bandages, gauze, gauze rolls
- adhesive or paper tape
- scissors, safety pins, tweezers
- thermometer
- pocketknife
- DEET-containing insect repellent for the skin
- permethrin-containing insect spray for clothing, tents and bed nets
- sun block
- oral rehydration salts
- iodine tablets or water filter (for water purification)

INTERNET RESOURCES

There is a wealth of travel health advice to be found on the Internet. For further information, the **Lonely Planet website** (www.lonely planet.com) is a good place to start. The **World Health Organization** (www.who.int/ith/) publishes a superb book called *International Travel and Health*, which is revised annually and is available online at no cost. Another website of general interest is **MD Travel Health** (www.md travelhealth.com), which provides complete travel health recommendations for every country, and is updated daily.

FURTHER READING

Lonely Planet's *Healthy Travel Australia, New Zealand & The Pacific* is a handy, pocket-sized guide packed with useful information, including pre-trip planning, emergency first aid, immunisation and disease information, and what to do if you get sick on the road. *Travel with Children* from Lonely Planet includes advice on travel health for younger children.

IN VICTORIA

AVAILABILITY & COST OF HEALTH CARE

Australia has an excellent health-care system. It's a mixture of privately run medical clinics and hospitals, alongside a system of public hospitals funded by the Australian government. The Medicare system covers Australian residents for some health-care costs (as well as citizens of New Zealand, the UK, the Netherlands, Sweden, Finland, Italy, Malta and Ireland). There are good specialised, public-health facilities for women and children in Melbourne.

Self-care

In some of Victoria's remote locations it is possible there'll be a significant delay in emergency services reaching you in the event of serious accident or illness. If you're heading into the wild, consider taking a wilderness first-aid course, such as those offered at the **Wilderness Medicine Institute** (www.wmi.net.au); take a comprehensive first-aid kit that is appropriate for the activities planned; and ensure that you have adequate means of communication. (Victoria has extensive mobile-phone coverage but additional radio communications is important for remote areas.)

Pharmaceutical Supplies

Over-the-counter medications are widely available at privately owned chemists throughout Australia. These include painkillers, antihistamines for allergies and skin-care products.

You may find that medications readily available over the counter in some countries are only available in Australia by prescription. These include the oral contraceptive pill, most medications for asthma and all antibiotics. If you take medication on a regular basis, bring an adequate supply and ensure you have details of the generic name as brand names may differ between countries.

INFECTIOUS DISEASES

Giardiasis Widespread in the waterways around Australia. Drinking untreated water from streams and lakes is not recommended. Water filters and boiling or treating water with iodine are effective in preventing the disease. Symptoms consist of intermittent bad-smelling diarrhoea, abdominal bloating and wind. Effective treatment is available (tinidazole or metronidazole).

Hepatitis C Still a growing problem among intravenous drug users. Blood transfusion services fully screen all blood before use.

HIV Rates in Australia have stabilised and levels are similar to other Western countries. Clean needles and syringes are widely available through all chemists.

Meningococcal disease Occurs worldwide and is a risk with prolonged, dormitory-style accommodation. A vaccine exists for some types of this disease, namely meningococcal A, C, Y and W.

Sexually transmitted diseases Occur at rates similar to most other Western countries. The most common symptoms are pain while passing urine and a discharge.

Infection can be present without symptoms, so medical screening after any unprotected sex with a new partner. Throughout the country, you'll find sexual-health clinics in all of the major hospitals. Always use a condom with any new sexual partner. Condoms are readily available in chemists and from vending machines in many public places, including toilets.

ENVIRONMENTAL HAZARDS
Animal Bites & Stings
FLIES & MOSQUITOES
For four to six months of the year you'll have to cope with those two banes of the Australian outdoors: the fly and the mosquito ('mozzie'). Flies aren't too bad in the city but they start getting out of hand in the country, and the farther out you go the more numerous and persistent they seem to be. A March fly looks like a bigger, uglier version of the common fly – its bite is painful for an instant, but the aftermath is much like a mosquito bite. Widely available repellents, such as Aerogard and Rid, may also help to deter the little bastards, but don't count on it.

Mozzies are a problem in summer. Try to keep your arms and legs covered as soon as the sun goes down and make liberal use of insect repellent.

SNAKES
Australian snakes have a fearful reputation that is justified in terms of the potency of their venom, but unjustified in terms of the actual risk to travellers and locals. Snakes are usually quite timid in nature, and in most instances will move away if disturbed. They only have small fangs, making it easy to prevent bites to the lower limbs (where 80% of bites occur) by wearing protective clothing (such as gaiters, boots, socks and long trousers) around the ankles when bushwalking. Snakes are quite common in country Victoria. If you see one, leave it alone.

In all confirmed or suspected bites, preventing the spread of toxic venom can be achieved by applying pressure to the wound and immobilising the area with a splint or sling before seeking medical attention. Firmly wrap an elastic bandage (you can improvise with a T-shirt) around the entire limb, but not so tight as to cut off the circulation. Along with immobilisation, this is a life-saving first-aid measure. Don't use a tourniquet, and *don't* (despite what you might have seen on *Tarzan*) try to suck out the poison!

LET 'EM STARVE

Various hungry biteys can be a source of irritation, although in Victoria you won't contract any diseases from them. Protection from mosquitoes, march flies, ticks and leeches can be achieved by:

- Wearing loose-fitting, long-sleeved clothing.
- Applying 30% DEET repellent on all exposed skin and repeating every three to four hours.
- In the case of mozzies, the default technique is to share a room with someone who is tastier to them than you are!

SPIDERS
Australia has a number of poisonous spiders. Victoria's most dangerous spider is the redback. It has a very painful, sometimes lethal, bite. Bites cause increasing pain at the site followed by profuse sweating and generalised symptoms (including muscular weakness, sweating at the site of the bite, nausea). First aid includes application of ice or cold packs to the bite, then transfer to hospital.

White-tailed spider bites may cause an ulcer that is very slow and difficult to heal. Clean the wound thoroughly and seek medical assistance.

TICKS & LEECHES
The common bush-tick (found in the forest and scrub country all along the eastern coast of Australia) can be dangerous if left lodged in the skin, as the toxin excreted by the tick can cause partial paralysis and, in theory, even death. Check your body for lumps every night if you're walking in tick-infested areas. The tick should be removed by dousing it with methylated spirits or kerosene and levering it out, but make sure you remove it intact. After a walk in the bush, remember to check children and dogs for ticks.

Leeches are common, and while they will suck your blood, they are not dangerous and are easily removed by the application of salt or heat.

Heat Illness
Very hot weather can be experienced in Victoria during the summer months. When arriving from a temperate or cold climate,

A BIT OF PERSPECTIVE

There's approximately one shark-attack fatality per year in Australia. Blue-ringed octopus deaths are even rarer – only two in the last century. You're still over 100 times more likely to *drown* than be killed by one of these nasties.

On land, snakes kill one or two people per year (about the same as bee stings, or less than a thousandth of those killed on the roads). There hasn't been a recorded death from tick bite for over 50 years, nor from spider bites in the last 20 years.

remember that it takes two weeks for acclimatisation to occur. Before the body is acclimatised an excessive amount of salt is lost in perspiration, so increasing the salt in your diet is essential.

Heat exhaustion occurs when fluid intake does not keep up with fluid loss. Symptoms include dizziness, fainting, fatigue, nausea or vomiting. On observation the skin is usually pale, cool and clammy. Treatment consists of rest in a cool, shady place and fluid replacement with water or diluted sports drinks.

Heatstroke is a severe form of heat illness that occurs after fluid depletion or extreme heat challenge from heavy exercise. This is a true medical emergency, with heating of the brain leading to disorientation, hallucinations and seizures. Prevention is by maintaining an adequate fluid intake, especially during physical exertion, to ensure the continued passage of clear and copious urine.

Hypothermia

Hypothermia is a significant risk to those engaging in outdoor pursuits, like bushwalking, especially during the winter months in Victoria. Despite the absence of high mountain ranges, strong winds produce a high chill factor that can result in hypothermia even in moderately cool temperatures. Early signs include the inability to perform fine movements (such as doing up buttons), shiv-

ering and a bad case of the 'umbles' (fumbles, mumbles, grumbles, stumbles). The key elements of treatment include moving out of the cold, changing out of any wet clothing into dry clothes with wind- and water-proof layers, adding insulation and providing fuel (water and carbohydrate) to allow shivering, which builds the internal temperature. In severe hypothermia, shivering actually stops – this is a medical emergency requiring rapid evacuation in addition to the above measures.

Sunburn & Skin Cancer

Australia has one of the highest rates of skin cancer in the world. Monitor your exposure to direct sunlight closely. UV exposure is greatest between 10am and 4pm, so avoid skin exposure during these times. Always use 30+ sunscreen, apply 30 minutes before going into the sun and reapply regularly to minimise damage.

Surf Beaches & Drowning

Victoria has exceptional surf, particularly along the Great Ocean Rd, Shipwreck Coast and at Philip Island. Beaches vary enormously in their underwater conditions: the slope offshore can result in changeable and often powerful surf. Check with local surf-lifesaving organisations, and be aware of your own expertise and limitations before entering the water. See also rips information on p397.

Water-Borne Illness

Tap water is universally safe in the region. Increasing numbers of streams and rivers and lakes, however, are being contaminated by bugs that cause diarrhoea, making water purification essential in those areas. The simplest way for you to purify water is to boil it thoroughly. Also consider purchasing a water filter. Chlorine tablets will kill many pathogens, but not some parasites like giardia and amoebic cysts. Iodine is more effective in purifying water and is available in tablet form; follow the directions carefully.

Glossary

ace – super, excellent
arvo – afternoon
ATM – Automated Teller Machine, public cash dispenser operated by banks
Aussie rules – Australian rules football

barbie – barbecue (BBQ)
bathers – swimming costume
battler – struggler, someone who tries hard
beaut, beauty – great, fantastic
biffo – blow or punch
bikies – motorcyclists
billabong – waterhole in dried-up riverbed
billy – tin container used to boil water in the bush
bloke – man
blowies, blow flies – large flies
bludger – lazy person, one who refuses to work
blue – argument or fight ('have a blue')
boogie board – bodyboard, half-sized surfboard
boomerang – a curved, flat, wooden instrument used by Aborigines for hunting
booze bus – police van used for random breath-testing for alcohol
brumby – wild horse
Buckley's – no chance at all
bug – germ, not insect
bull bar – outsized front bumper on car or truck, the ultimate barrier against animals on the road, also *roo bar*
bush, the – country, anywhere away from the city
bushrangers – Australia's equivalent of the outlaws of the American Wild West (some goodies, some baddies), Ned Kelly is Australia's most famous.
BYO – bring your own (generally, alcohol)

camp oven – large cast-iron pot with lid, used for cooking in an open fire
cask – wine box (a great Australian invention)
catch ya later – goodbye, see you later
chook – chicken
chuck a U-ey – make a U-turn, turn a car around within a road
cobber – archaic version of *mate*
cooee – long, loud call used in the *bush* to attract attention
counter meal – pub meal
crack the shits – lose one's temper
crook – ill or substandard
cut lunch – sandwiches

dag – dirty lump of wool at back end of a sheep; also an affectionate term for a socially inept person

daggy – untidy; uncool
damper – bush loaf made from flour and water
dead set – true
didgeridoo – wind instrument made from a hollow piece of wood
dill – idiot
dingo – indigenous wild dog
dinky-di – the real thing
dob in – to inform on someone
doof doof – loud, thumping music (as from car speakers)
Dreamtime – complex concept that forms the basis of Aboriginal spirituality, incorporating the creation of the world and the spiritual energies operating around us
drongo – worthless or stupid person
dunny – outdoor lavatory

eftpos – Electronic Funds Transfer at Point of Sale; allows you to make retail purchases with a debit card.
esky – large insulated box for keeping food and drinks cold

fair dinkum – honest, genuine
flake – shark meat, often used in fish and chips
fossick – hunt for gold or semiprecious stones

galah – noisy parrot, thus noisy idiot
g'day – good day, traditional Australian greeting
grog – general term for alcoholic drinks
grazier – large-scale sheep or cattle farmer
grouse – very good

homestead – residence of a station owner or manager
hoon – idiot, hooligan

icy pole – frozen lollipop, ice lolly
iffy – dodgy, questionable
indie – independent music

joey – young kangaroo or wallaby

kick the bucket – to die
knackered – broken, tired
knock – to criticise, deride
Koories – Aboriginal people of southeastern Australia

lamington – square of sponge cake covered in chocolate icing and coconut
larrikin – hooligan, mischievous youth
lemon – faulty product, a dud
little ripper – extremely good thing

lollies – sweets; candy
loo – toilet

main – a meal's main course
mallee – low, shrubby, multi-stemmed eucalypt
March fly – horsefly; gadfly
mate – general term of familiarity, whether you know the person or not
mia-mia – bark lean-to
milk bar – small shop selling milk and other basic provisions
mobile phone – cell phone
Mod Oz – modern Australian cuisine influenced by a wide range of foreign cuisines
mozzies – mosquitoes
muster – to round up livestock

no-hoper – hopeless case
no worries – no problems, that's OK

ocker – uncultivated or boorish Australian
offsider – assistant, partner
outback – remote part of the bush
Oz – Australia

pavlova – traditional Australian meringue, fruit and cream dessert; named after the Russian ballerina Anna Pavlova
perve – to gaze with lust
pissed – drunk
pissed off – annoyed
plonk – cheap wine
pokies – poker machines
pot – 285ml beer glass
potato cake – fried potato snack from a fish-and-chip shop; 'scallop' in some other states
prang – collision; small car accident

RACV – Royal Automobile Club of Victoria
ratbag – friendly term of abuse
rego – registration (as in 'car rego')
rip – a strong ocean current or undertow
roo bar – outsize front bumper, also *bull bar*
ropable – very bad-tempered or angry

salvo – member of the Salvation Army
sanger – sandwich
sealed road – bitumen road

she'll be right – no problems, *no worries*
shoot through – to leave in a hurry
shout – buy a round of drinks (as in 'it's your shout')
smoothie – thick milkshake with added fruit, ice cream, yoghurt etc
snag – sausage
sparrow's fart – dawn
squatter – pioneer farmer who occupied land as a tenant of the government
station – large sheep or cattle farm
stickybeak – nosy person
stolen generations – Aboriginal and Torres Strait Islander children forcibly removed from their families during the government's policy of assimilation
stoush – fist fight; brawl (also verbal)
stubby – 375ml bottle of beer
swag – canvas-covered bed roll used in the outback; a large amount (as in 'a swag of tourists')

ta – thanks
take the piss – deliberately tell someone an untruth, often as social sport
thongs – flip-flops
tinny – 375ml can of beer
togs – swimming costume; also *bathers*
too right! – absolutely!
trucky – truck driver
true blue – the real thing
tucker – food
two-pot screamer – person unable to hold their drink
two-up – traditional heads-or-tails coin-gambling game

unsealed road – dirt road
ute – utility, pick-up truck

wag – to skip school or work
walkabout – lengthy walk away from it all
warrung – Aboriginal word for 'language'
Wathaurong – Koories of Geelong and the Bellarine Peninsula area
woomera – device used by Aborigines to aid the throwing of spears

yabby, yabbie – small freshwater crayfish
yakka – work
yobbo – uncouth, aggressive person
yonks – a long time

Behind the Scenes

THIS BOOK

The 1st and 2nd editions of *Victoria* were researched and written by Mark Armstrong. The 3rd edition was updated by Jon Murray, Mark Armstrong, Michelle Bennett, Joyce Connolly and Richard Nebeský. The 4th edition was updated by Chris Rowthorn, Kate Daly and Alex Landragin, with the Wineries of Victoria special section contributed by Campbell Mattinson. This 5th edition is proudly brought to you by the Vic Chix: Susie Ashworth (coordinating author), Jocelyn Harewood (Central West, Northwest, North to the Murray), Cathy Lanigan (South & Far East), Lisa Mitchell (Southwest), Sally O'Brien (Melbourne), Miriam Raphael (High Country) and Nina Rousseau (Around Melbourne). Weighing in on the y-chromosome side, Australia's leading environmental scientist Tim Flannery wrote the Environment chapter, wine guru extraordinaire Campbell Mattinson wrote the Victorian Wineries chapter and Dr David Millar wrote the Health chapter.

Other contributors include David Burnett for the Bush Doof (p193) and The Ascent of Natimuk (p274) boxed texts. For her work on the Culture and Food & Drink chapters Susie Ashworth is indebted to Simone Egger and Matthew Evans.

THANKS from the Authors

Susie Ashworth Thanks to my co-authors Jocelyn Harewood, Cathy Lanigan, Lisa Mitchell, Sally O'Brien, Miriam Raphael and Nina Rousseau for their enthusiasm and excellent work on this project. I'm grateful to all the readers who sent in their recommendations and every friendly, helpful Victorian who generously offered information, advice and tips. Thanks to Errol Hunt and Marg Toohey for giving me the job in the first place, and being so supportive during the project. As always, kudos must go to the production team at Lonely Planet, particularly Maryanne Netto and Kusnandar. Finally, thanks to Gordon for keeping me sane.

Jocelyn Harewood Heaps of thanks to Errol and Marg at Lonely Planet for sending this backpacking grandmother out on the road again. And (almost) thank you to an ex-premier who left us with a network of extraordinarily good visitors centres, staffed by wonderful folk, too many to mention – thanks so much for your advice and friendly service. The people of country Victoria are fantastic. I especially remember good times at Echuca Gardens YHA, Daylesford's Lake House and Dimboola's Riverside Host Farm, and activities with Hangin' Out and the Horseriding Centre in the Grampians. To the great chefs of the region: your food was brilliant. Finally thanks to my travelling companions, Peregrine Sellick, Anne Calvert, Carole Annesley and Caryn Pentecost, for adding to the fun.

Cathy Lanigan Thanks to Parks Victoria staff, particularly Graeme Baxter, Andrew Schulze, and Peter Kershaw for nitty-gritty details on national parks; Rhonda James at East Gippsland Shire Council for information on local transport innovations; Andrea Hall, Jenny Doran, Eva Schain, Kirstie Pearce, Barb Young, Jack Travis, Deb Morgan, Hilary Rigg, Jenny Hurley, Pauline Crunden, Rachel Hughes and

THE LONELY PLANET STORY

The story begins with a classic travel adventure: Tony and Maureen Wheeler's 1972 journey across Europe and Asia to Australia. There was no useful information about the overland trail then, so Tony and Maureen published the first Lonely Planet guidebook to meet a growing need.

From a kitchen table, Lonely Planet has grown to become the largest independent travel publisher in the world, with offices in Melbourne (Australia), Oakland (USA) and London (UK). Today Lonely Planet guidebooks cover the globe. There is an ever-growing list of books and information in a variety of media. Some things haven't changed. The main aim is still to make it possible for adventurous travellers to get out there – to explore and better understand the world.

At Lonely Planet we believe travellers can make a positive contribution to the countries they visit – if they respect their host communities and spend their money wisely. Every year 5% of company profit is donated to charities around the world.

Helen Wilson for Gippsland eating recommendations; Noel and Fiona Maud in South Gippsland for local recommendations and inspiration; and a huge thanks to my partner John for doing all the driving, helping with the maps and providing constant support, and big, big thanks to Zoe for researching all of Gippsland's playgrounds.

Lisa Mitchell For their local expertise, heaped thanks to Pete and Sandy, Richard McVeigh at Aireys Inlet, Gary and Wendy at Forrest, and Rex Brown at Apollo Bay. Thank you visitors centre staff who moved mountains of information my way: especially Elizabeth Wohlfarth at Lorne, Lisa and Kelly at Apollo Bay, Julie Stanley at Geelong, and Karleigh & Sally at Portland. Thanks Parks Victoria, especially ranger Marcel Hoog Antink at Portland for walks advice. A debt of hospitality to Damian and Carli at Lorne; to dedicated wildlife carer Annie Fraser at Peterborough, a debt of sleep! To countless canines for being overjoyed at the sight of this stranger – 'woof!'. And, thank you Abby, my winged chariot.

Sally O'Brien Many thanks to all my friends who accompanied me on research jaunts for this book – the more the merrier. Thanks also to Marg Toohey, Susie Ashworth, Corrie Waddell and Errol Hunt at Lonely Planet, plus Adrienne Costanzo for editing and Kusnandar for the maps.

Miriam Raphael Thanks to all the helpful people in the impressive visitors centres around northeast Victoria. Dad was, as usual, a wonderful and reliable editor. Is, Laurs and Lisa B were great and constant company during the write up. Cheers to Marg Toohey, Corrie Waddell (and the new mapping key system!) and all the 'Chicks Do Vic' team.

Nina Rousseau As always, Luc McKenna – for being Luc. Onya tiger to my helpful research buddy and old-time mate Jo Argent. George Dunford and Susannah Farfor for crucial talk-you-down-off-the-ledge phone calls. Susie Ashworth and all the other Vic Chix. Errol and Marg for CE'ing. Many thanks to Parks Victoria and the super-helpful staff at the tourist information centres that are dotted around Melbourne. Cheers!

CREDITS

Commissioning Editors: Marg Toohey, Errol Hunt
Coordinating Editors: Maryanne Netto, Emma Koch
Coordinating Cartographer: Kusnandar
Coordinating Layout Designer: Jacqui Saunders
Managing Cartographer: Corie Waddell

Assisting Editors: Meg Worby, Kate Evans, Adrienne Costanzo, David Andrew, Monique Choy, Kristin Odijk, Suzannah Shwer, Trent Holden
Assisting Cartographer: Tony Fankhauser, Valentina Kremenchutskaya
Assisting Layout Designer: Kaitlin Beckett
Cover Designer: Gerilyn Attebery
Project Manager: Ray Thomson, Chris Love

Thanks to Darren O'Connell, Sally Darmody, Adriana Mammarella, Lachlan Ross, Simon Tillema, Will Gourlay, Brendan Dempsey, Nick Wood, Fiona Siseman, Nicole Hansen, Karen Emmerson, Rebecca Lalor, Daniel Fennessy.

THANKS from Lonely Planet

Many thanks to the travellers who used the last edition and wrote to us with helpful hints, useful advice and interesting anecdotes:

A Daniel Aeberli, Julie Alexander, Bernhard Andrea, **B** Sabine Basista, Jacinta Boyle, Mark Brooks, Ian Buxton, **C** Anthony Cairns, Marie Cappuccio, Sam Carter, Jeni Charter, Julie Comey, Elaina Conneely, Katherine Cooper, Emily Corkhill, **D** Margaret Devlin, **E** Sandra Eastern, Roger Paul Edmonds, Pierre Eric, Kathleen Evans, Linda L Evans, **F** Bos Family, Charles Fellowes, Cynthia Fenton, Jamie Foxley, Emily Friedman, **G** Eveline Gebhardt, Dave Gerrish, Linda Giddy, Rakesh Goel, **H** Robyn Hall, Justine Halls, Janine Harrison,

Bels Hillard, Matthias Hils, Robin Hingley, Anthony Hobson, Geoff & Carol Hodgson, Calvin Holbrook, Caroline Hurd, **I** Anna Illner, Markus Imhof, Stephen Ireland, **K** Katherine Kelly, Ellen Knuepfer, Deborah Koch, Silke Korbl, **L** James Lamb, Varry Lavin, Alexandra Lawrence, Anna Lehman, Mun Yi Leong, Alan Lewis, Wolfgang Liebelt, **M** Corinne MacKenzie, Sarah Matheson, Michaela Matross, Najida Matthews, Kimberly Merris, Robert Metzger, Lynn Molleson, Roger Mueller, Jennifer Mundy-Nordin, **N** Kate Nielsen, Aleem Nisar, **O** Aidan Oleary, Martin Olinger, Sharon Oliva, Kim Oostveen, **P** Birte Peters, Maureen Pierre, Wiebke Poppinga, Rick Pratley, Lynne Preston, **R** Yvonne Raateland, Jeremy Rawlins, Abe Remmo, Dan Richards, Domi Rossi, Grace Rowland, **S** Robert Schmeer, Maren Schrock, Andrew Sharpe, Arend Sijpestein, Adian Staeubli, Johannes Stoffels, Bill & Ann Stoughton, Roy Streeter, Darren Sugrue, Natalie Surrey, **T** Matty Taylor, Martin D Thomas, Tineke Timmer, Gareth Trickey, Poul Tvermoes, **V** Hans van Boeckel, Kim van den Anker, Guido van Garsse, **W** Adrian Warren, Anthony Warren, Nicholas Waters, John Watts, Juliet West, Leslie White, Joan Wilkinson, Eoin Wrenn, **Z** Rene Zangger, Marc Zangwill

ACKNOWLEDGEMENTS

Many thanks to the following for the use of their content:

Melbourne Train Network Map © 2005 Metlink.

ACKNOWLEDGEMENTS

Index

000 Map pages
000 Location of colour photographs

MAP LEGEND

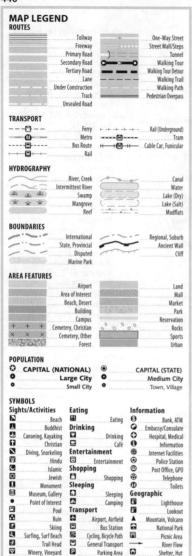

ROUTES

	Tollway		One-Way Street
	Freeway		Street Mall/Steps
	Primary Road		Tunnel
	Secondary Road		Walking Tour
	Tertiary Road		Walking Tour Detour
	Lane		Walking Trail
	Under Construction		Walking Path
	Track		Pedestrian Overpass
	Unsealed Road		

TRANSPORT

	Ferry		Rail (Underground)
	Metro		Tram
	Bus Route		Cable Car, Funicular
	Rail		

HYDROGRAPHY

	River, Creek		Canal
	Intermittent River		Water
	Swamp		Lake (Dry)
	Mangrove		Lake (Salt)
	Reef		Mudflats

BOUNDARIES

	International		Regional, Suburb
	State, Provincial		Ancient Wall
	Disputed		Cliff
	Marine Park		

AREA FEATURES

	Airport		Land
	Area of Interest		Mall
	Beach, Desert		Market
	Building		Park
	Campus		Reservation
	Cemetery, Christian		Rocks
	Cemetery, Other		Sports
	Forest		Urban

POPULATION

◉ CAPITAL (NATIONAL)		⊙ CAPITAL (STATE)	
● **Large City**		● Medium City
● Small City		○ Town, Village

SYMBOLS

Sights/Activities
- Beach
- Buddhist
- Canoeing, Kayaking
- Christian
- Diving, Snorkeling
- Hindu
- Islamic
- Jewish
- Monument
- Museum, Gallery
- Point of Interest
- Pool
- Ruin
- Skiing
- Surfing, Surf Beach
- Trail Head
- Winery, Vineyard
- Zoo, Bird Sanctuary

Eating
- Eating

Drinking
- Drinking
- Café

Entertainment
- Entertainment

Shopping
- Shopping

Sleeping
- Sleeping
- Camping

Transport
- Airport, Airfield
- Bus Station
- Cycling, Bicycle Path
- General Transport
- Parking Area
- Taxi Rank

Information
- Bank, ATM
- Embassy/Consulate
- Hospital, Medical
- Information
- Internet Facilities
- Police Station
- Post Office, GPO
- Telephone
- Toilets

Geographic
- Lighthouse
- Lookout
- Mountain, Volcano
- National Park
- Picnic Area
- River Flow
- Shelter, Hut
- Waterfall

LONELY PLANET OFFICES

Australia
Head Office
Locked Bag 1, Footscray, Victoria 3011
☎ 03 8379 8000, fax 03 8379 8111
talk2us@lonelyplanet.com.au

USA
150 Linden St, Oakland, CA 94607
☎ 510 893 8555, toll free 800 275 8555
fax 510 893 8572, info@lonelyplanet.com

UK
72-82 Rosebery Ave,
Clerkenwell, London EC1R 4RW
☎ 020 7841 9000, fax 020 7841 9001
go@lonelyplanet.co.uk

Published by Lonely Planet Publications Pty Ltd

ABN 36 005 607 983

5th Edition – Sep 2005

First Published – Aug 1993

© Lonely Planet 2005

© photographers as indicated 2005

Cover photographs by Lonely Planet Images: A patriot amongst many of the Brighton Beach Bathing Boxes, John Banagan (front); Cycling along the Burnley bike path in Melbourne, Phil M Weymouth (back). Many of the images in this guide are available for licensing from Lonely Planet Images: www.lonelyplanetimages.com

Although the authors and Lonely Planet have taken all reasonable care in preparing this book, we make no warranty about the accuracy or completeness of its content and, to the maximum extent permitted, disclaim all liability arising from its use.